W9-DDD-467

Islands of the Commonweath Caribbean
a regional study

Federal Research Division
Library of Congress
Edited by Sandra W. Meditz
and Dennis M. Hanratty
Research Completed
November 1987

On the cover: Fishermen drawing in their nets

*F
2131
I85
1989*

First Edition, First Printing, 1989.

Copyright ©1989 United States Government as represented by the Secretary of the Army. All rights reserved.

Library of Congress Cataloging-in-Publication Data

Islands of the Commonwealth Caribbean: A Regional Study.

(Area handbook series) (DA Pam.; 550–33)
"Research completed September 1987."
Bibliography: pp. 671–726.
Includes index.
Supt. of Docs. no.: D 101.22:55–33
1. West Indies, British. I. Meditz, Sandra W., 1950–
II. Hanratty, Dennis M., 1950–   III. Library of Congress.
Federal Research Division. IV. Series. V. Series: DA Pam.; 550–33.

F2131.I85   1989   972.9   88–600483

Headquarters, Department of the Army
DA Pam 550-33

39448

For sale by the Superintendent of Documents, U.S. Government Printing Office
Washington, D.C. 20402

Foreword

This volume is one in a continuing series of books now being prepared by the Federal Research Division of the Library of Congress under the Country Studies—Area Handbook Program. The last page of this book lists the other published studies.

Most books in the series deal with a particular foreign country, describing and analyzing its political, economic, social, and national security systems and institutions, and examining the interrelationships of those systems and the ways they are shaped by cultural factors. Each study is written by a multidisciplinary team of social scientists. The authors seek to provide a basic understanding of the observed society, striving for a dynamic rather than a static portrayal. Particular attention is devoted to the people who make up the society, their origins, dominant beliefs and values, their common interests and the issues on which they are divided, the nature and extent of their involvement with national institutions, and their attitudes toward each other and toward their social system and political order.

The books represent the analysis of the authors and should not be construed as an expression of an official United States government position, policy, or decision. The authors have sought to adhere to accepted standards of scholarly objectivity. Corrections, additions, and suggestions for changes from readers will be welcomed for use in future editions.

Louis R. Mortimer
Acting Chief
Federal Research Division
Library of Congress
Washington, D.C. 20540

Acknowledgments

The authors wish to acknowledge the contributions of Irving Kaplan, Howard I. Blutstein, Kathryn Therese Johnston, and David S. McMorris, who wrote the 1976 edition of the *Area Handbook for Jamaica,* and Jan Knippers Black, Howard I. Blutstein, Kathryn Therese Johnston, and David S. McMorris, who wrote the 1976 edition of the *Area Handbook for Trinidad and Tobago.* Their work provided a useful guide in organizing portions of chapters 2 and 3 of the present volume.

The authors are grateful to individuals in various agencies of the United States government and international and private institutions who gave of their time, research materials, and special knowledge to provide information and perspective. The staffs of various Commonwealth Caribbean embassies, the Inter-American Development Bank, and the World Bank provided materials that were unavailable from other sources. Stephen F. Clarke, senior legal specialist at the American-British Law Division, Library of Congress, offered insights on the structure and functions of the Eastern Caribbean court system. None of these individuals is in any way responsible for the work of the authors, however.

The authors also wish to thank those who contributed directly to the preparation of the manuscript. These include Richard F. Nyrop, who reviewed all drafts and served as liaison with the sponsoring agency; Martha E. Hopkins, who edited portions of the manuscript and managed its production; Barbara Auerbach, Vincent Ercolano, and Marilyn L. Majeska, who also edited portions of the manuscript; Donna G. Bruce, Barbara Edgerton, Janie L. Gilchrist, Monica Shimmin, and Izella Watson, who did the word processing; Andrea T. Merrill, who performed the final prepublication editorial review; Malinda B. Neale of the Printing and Processing Section, Library of Congress, who phototypeset the manuscript under the supervision of Peggy Pixley; and Mary Bodnar of Communicators Connections, who compiled the index.

David P. Cabitto, Sandra K. Cotugno, and Kimberly A. Lord provided invaluable graphics support. Kimberly A. Lord also designed the cover and illustrations for the title page of each chapter. Harriett R. Blood and the firm of Greenhorne and O'Mara prepared the maps, which were reviewed by Susan Lender. Various individuals, libraries, and public agencies generously provided photographs.

Finally, the authors would like to thank several individuals who provided research support. Joan C. Barch, Susan Lender,

Timothy L. Merrill, and Marjorie F. Thomas wrote the geography sections in chapters 2 through 6. Timothy L. Merrill also supplied the authors with data on telecommunications and transportation. Glennon J. Harrison assisted in the development of an outline for the book and performed initial research on Jamaica's economy and society.

Contents

Chapter 3. Trinidad and Tobago 161
Beatrice Berle Meyerson, Daniel J. Seyler,
and John F. Hornbeck

viii

List of Figures

Preface

This study is an attempt to treat in a compact and objective manner the dominant social, political, economic, and military aspects of the contemporary islands of the Commonwealth Caribbean. Sources of information included scholarly books, journals, and monographs; official reports of governments and international organizations; numerous periodicals; and interviews with individuals having special competence in Caribbean affairs. Chapter bibliographies appear at the end of the book; brief comments on sources recommended for further reading appear at the end of each chapter or country section. Measurements are given in the metric system; a conversion table is provided to assist readers unfamiliar with metric measurements (see table 1, Appendix A). A glossary is also included.

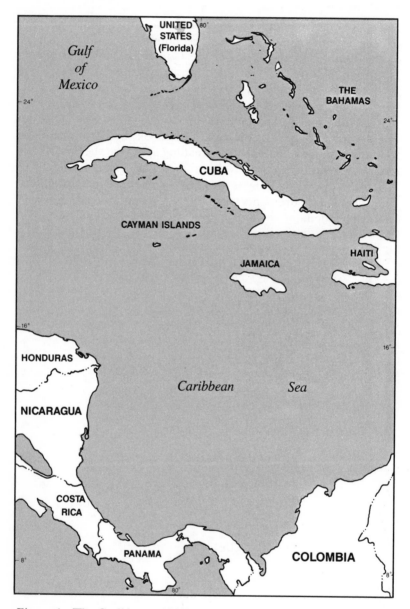

Figure 1. The Caribbean, 1987

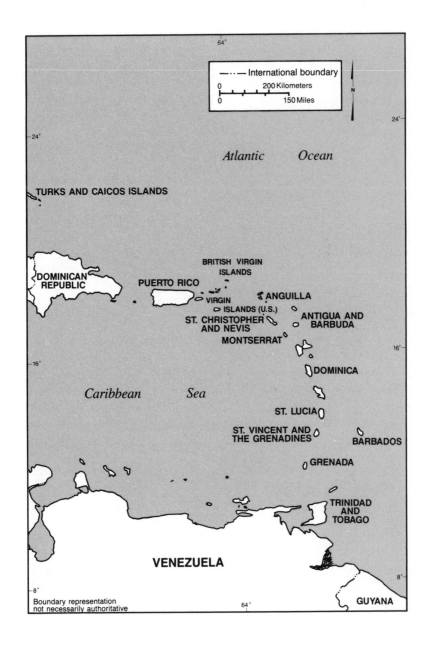

Atlantic Ocean

International boundary

0 200 Kilometers
0 150 Miles

N

TURKS AND CAICOS ISLANDS

BRITISH VIRGIN
ISLANDS

DOMINICAN
REPUBLIC

PUERTO RICO

ANGUILLA

VIRGIN
ISLANDS (U.S.)

ST. CHRISTOPHER
AND NEVIS

ANTIGUA AND
BARBUDA

MONTSERRAT

DOMINICA

Caribbean Sea

ST. LUCIA

ST. VINCENT AND
THE GRENADINES

BARBADOS

GRENADA

TRINIDAD
AND
TOBAGO

VENEZUELA

Boundary representation
not necessarily authoritative

GUYANA

Introduction

THE COMMONWEALTH CARIBBEAN is the term applied to the English-speaking islands in the Carribbean and the mainland nations of Belize (formerly British Honduras) and Guyana (formerly British Guiana) that once constituted the Caribbean portion of the British Empire. This volume examines only the islands of the Commonwealth Caribbean, which are Jamaica, Trinidad and Tobago, the Windward Islands (Dominica, St. Lucia, St. Vincent and the Grenadines, and Grenada), Barbados, the Leeward Islands (Antigua and Barbuda, St. Christopher [hereafter, St. Kitts] and Nevis, the British Virgin Islands, Anguilla, and Montserrat), and the so-called Northern Islands (the Bahamas, the Cayman Islands, and the Turks and Caicos Islands).

To the casual observer, these islands might appear to be too disparate to allow for a common discussion. Consider, for instance, the differences in population, size, income, ethnic composition, and political status among the various islands. Anguilla's 7,000 residents live on an island totaling 91 square kilometers, whereas Jamaica has a population of 2.3 million and a territory of nearly 11,000 square kilometers. The per capita gross domestic product (GDP—see Glossary) of the Cayman Islands is nearly fourteen times as large as that of St. Vincent and the Grenadines. Trinidad and Tobago's population is evenly divided between blacks and East Indians, a pattern quite different from that on the other islands, on which blacks constitute an overwhelming majority. Although most of the islands are independent nations, five (the British Virgin Islands, Anguilla, Montserrat, the Cayman Islands, and the Turks and Caicos Islands) remain British dependencies.

These and other differences, however, should not obscure the extensive ties that bind the islands of the Commonwealth Caribbean. For instance, the islands' populations clearly regard themselves as distinct from their Latin American neighbors and identify more closely with the British Commonwealth of Nations than with Latin America (see Appendix B). All of the Commonwealth Caribbean islands except Grenada supported Britain's actions during the 1982 South Atlantic War in the Falkland/Malvinas Islands, in sharp contrast to the strong Latin American defense of the Argentine position.

This perceived distinctiveness emerged from the islands' shared historical experiences. Their transformation during the seventeenth century from a tobacco- to a sugar-based economy permanently changed life on the islands, as a plantation society employing African slave labor replaced the previous society of small landholders (see The Sugar Revolutions and Slavery, ch. 1). By the early nineteenth century, blacks constituted at least 80 percent of the population in all but one of the British Caribbean islands. The exception was Trinidad, which had begun bringing in large numbers of slaves only in the 1780s and 1790s. When the British abolished slavery in the Caribbean in the 1830s, Trinidadian planters imported indentured labor from India to work the sugarcane fields. Despite their numerical minority, whites continued to control political and economic affairs throughout the islands. Indeed, the all-white House of Assembly in Jamaica abolished itself in 1865 rather than share power with blacks. This abrogation of local assemblies and establishment of crown colony government (see Glossary) was the norm in the British Caribbean in the late 1800s and impeded the development of political parties and organizations.

Demands for political reform quickened after World War I with the appearance of a nascent middle class and the rise of trade unions. In the mid-1930s, the islands became engulfed by riots spawned by the region's difficult economic conditions (see Labor Organizations, ch. 1). The riots demonstrated the bankruptcy of the old sugar plantation system and sounded the death knell for colonial government. Beginning in the 1940s, the British allowed increasing levels of self-government and encouraged the emergence of moderate black political leaders. As a prelude to political independence for the region, the British established a federation in 1958 consisting of ten island groupings. The West Indies Federation succumbed, however, to the parochial concerns of the two largest members—Jamaica and Trinidad and Tobago—both of which declared independence in 1962. Between 1966 and 1983, eight additional independent nations were carved out of the British Caribbean.

These ten island nations are located in a strategically significant area. Merchant or naval shipping from United States ports in the Gulf of Mexico—including resupply of North Atlantic Treaty Organization forces in wartime—cross narrow Caribbean passages that constitute "choke points." The Caribbean Basin also links United States naval forces operating in the North Atlantic and South Atlantic areas and provides an important source of many raw materials imported by the United States (see Current Strategic Considerations, ch. 7).

Throughout the first half of the twentieth century, the United States asserted its interest in the Caribbean by frequently intervening in the affairs of the Hispanic islands. It did not involve itself, however, in the British colonies, a difference that may explain the relatively harmonious state of relations between the United States and the Commonwealth Caribbean islands when compared with the often contentious tone evident in United States-Latin American interactions. During World War II, and especially after 1960, the United States began to assume Britain's security and defense responsibilities for the Commonwealth Caribbean. Nonetheless, Britain continued to provide police training and remained an important trading partner with the region.

The political systems of the Commonwealth Caribbean nations paradoxically are both stable and fragile. All have inherited strong democratic traditions and parliamentary systems of government formed on the Westminster model. Political succession generally has been handled peacefully and democratically. For example, Barbados' Parliament deftly coped with the deaths in office of prime ministers J.M.G.M. "Tom" Adams in 1985 and Errol Barrow in 1987. At the same time, however, the multi-island character of many of these nations makes them particularly susceptible to fragmentation. The British had hoped to lessen the vulnerability of the smaller islands by making them part of larger, more viable states. This policy often was resented deeply by the unions' smaller partners, who charged that the larger islands were neglecting them. The most contentious case involved one of the former members of the West Indies Federation, St. Kitts-Nevis-Anguilla. In 1967 Anguillans evicted the Kittitian police force from the island and shortly thereafter declared independence. Despite the landing of British troops on the island two years later, Anguilla continued to resist union with St. Kitts and Nevis. Ultimately, the British bowed to Anguillan sentiments and administered the island as a separate dependency. Separatist attitudes also predominated in Nevis; the situation there was resolved, however, by granting Nevisians extensive local autonomy and a guaranteed constitutional right of secession.

The fragility of these systems also has been underscored in the 1980s by a reliance on violence for political ends. Grenada, Dominica, and St. Vincent and the Grenadines offered the most dramatic examples (see Regional Security Threats, 1970–81, ch. 7). Over a four-year span, Grenada experienced the overthrow of a democratically elected but corrupt administration, the establishment of the self-styled People's Revolutionary Government (PRG), the bloody collapse of the PRG and its replacement by the hard-line Revolutionary Military Council, and the intervention of United States troops and defense and police forces from six Commonwealth Caribbean nations (Jamaica, Barbados, Antigua and Barbuda, Dominica,

St. Lucia, and St. Vincent and the Grenadines). In 1981 the Dominican government foiled a coup attempt involving a former prime minister, the country's defense force, the Ku Klux Klan, neo-Nazis, mercenaries, and underworld elements from the United States. Several months later, members of the then-disbanded defense force attacked Dominica's police headquarters and prison in an effort to free the coup participants. In 1979 Rastafarians (see Glossary) seized the airport, police station, and revenue office on Union Island in the Grenadines.

Most of the island governments were quite unprepared to deal with political violence; indeed, only five—Antigua and Barbuda, the Bahamas, Barbados, Jamaica, and Trinidad and Tobago— have defense forces, the largest of which has only a little over 2,000 members. In response, the governments of Antigua and Barbuda, Barbados, Dominica, St. Lucia, and St. Vincent and the Grenadines signed a regional security accord that allowed for the coordination of defense efforts and the establishment of paramilitary units drawn from the islands' police forces. Nonetheless, Commonwealth Caribbean leaders generally opposed creating a regional army and contended that such a force might eventually threaten democracy in the region (see A Regional Security System; Controversial Security Issues, ch. 7).

Drug trafficking represents an additional threat to the islands' political systems. The Caribbean has become increasingly important as a transit point for the transshipment of narcotics from Latin America to the United States. Narcotics traffickers have offered payoffs to Caribbean officials to ensure safe passage of their product through the region. Numerous examples abound of officials prepared to enter into such arrangements. In 1985 a Miami jury convicted Chief Minister Norman Saunders of the Turks and Caicos Islands of traveling to the United States to engage in narcotics transactions. A year later, a Trinidadian and Tobagonian government report implicated cabinet members, customs officials, policemen, and bank executives in a conspiracy to ship cocaine to the United States. Bahamian prime minister Lynden O. Pindling frequently has been accused of personally profiting from drug transactions, charges that he vehemently denied. The most recent accusation came in January 1988, when a prosecution witness in the Jacksonville, Florida, trial of Colombian cocaine trafficker Carlos Lehder Rivas claimed that Lehder paid Pindling US$88,000 per month to protect the Colombian's drug operations.

Yet the greatest challenges facing the Commonwealth Caribbean in the 1980s were not political but economic. The once-dominant sugar industry was beset by inefficient production, falling yields, a steady erosion of world prices, and a substantial reduction in United States import quotas. The unemployment level on most of the islands hovered at around 20 percent, a figure that would have been much higher were it not for continued Caribbean emigration to Britain, the United States, and Canada. Ironically, however, because the islands' education systems failed to train workers for a technologically complex economy, many skilled and professional positions went unfilled. In addition, the islands were incapable of producing most capital goods required for economic growth and development; imports of such goods helped generate balance of payments deficits and increasing levels of external indebtedness.

In the early 1980s, regional leaders hoped that President Ronald Reagan's administration's Caribbean Basin Initiative (CBI) would produce a substantial rise in exports to the United States, thus alleviating economic problems (see Appendix D). The most important part of the CBI—the Caribbean Basin Economic Recovery Act (CBERA) of 1983—allowed eligible Caribbean nations duty-free access to the United States for most exports until 1995. The CBERA, however, excluded some of the region's most important exports, such as textiles, apparel, footwear, and sugar. Although nontraditional exports from the Caribbean to the United States increased during the first five years of the CBI, Caribbean governments expressed disappointment with the program's overall results. Legislation introduced in the United States Congress in 1987 called for an extension of the CBI until 2007, an expansion of products included under the duty-free access provision, and a restoration of sugar quotas to 1984 levels. Although the status of the bill remained uncertain in mid-1988, few analysts anticipated changes in sugar import quotas.

Despite the generally troubling economic picture, the tourist sector demonstrated considerable vitality in the 1980s. Commonwealth Caribbean nations successfully marketed the region's beauty, climate, and beaches to a receptive North American and West European audience. As a result, many of the nations achieved dramatic increases in tourist arrivals and net earnings from tourism. For example, the number of foreign visitors to the Bahamas climbed from 1.7 million in 1982 to 3 million in 1986. The British Virgin Islands recorded 161,625 visitors in 1984, an increase of 91,338 as compared with 1976. Jamaica doubled its earnings over the 1980–86 period to stand at US$437 million in 1986. At the same time, however, the sector became quite susceptible to occasional slumps in the United States economy. Two months after the October 1987 stock market crash on Wall Street, tourist arrivals in Jamaica declined by 10 percent compared with the previous year.

In an effort to minimize their overall economic vulnerability, the independent nations of the Commonwealth Caribbean and the British crown colony of Montserrat established the Caribbean Community and Common Market (Caricom—see Appendix C) in 1973. Caricom had a number of goals, the most important of which were economic integration through the creation of a regional common market, diversification and specialization of production, and functional cooperation.

The organization's greatest success was in the area of functional cooperation; by the late 1980s, almost two dozen regional institutions had been created, including the University of the West Indies, the Caribbean Development Bank, the Caribbean Meteorological Council, the West Indies Shipping Corporation (WISCO), and the Caribbean Marketing Enterprise. Not all members of Caricom felt that they shared equitably in the services provided by these institutions, however. In 1987, for example, Dominica, St. Vincent and the Grenadines, and Belize withdrew from WISCO, claiming that the corporation had provided them with few benefits.

Despite success in functional cooperation, Caricom has an uneven track record in achieving economic integration and diversification and specialization. Although members registered substantial increases in intraregional trade during the 1973–81 period, much duplication of production occurred. Over the next five years, intraregional trade declined by more than 50 percent, the result in part of the adoption of protectionist measures by the region's largest consumer, Trinidad and Tobago. In 1987 the cause of regional integration was revived somewhat by Trinidad and Tobago's decision to repeal the provisions in question and by the Caricom members' joint pledge to remove all barriers to intraregional trade by the end of the third quarter of 1988. Even if this commitment is honored, however, depressed demand in the region will inhibit exports.

The most extensive level of cooperation has occurred among seven small islands and island groupings of the Eastern Caribbean (see Glossary). The seven—Antigua and Barbuda, Dominica, Grenada, Montserrat, St. Kitts and Nevis, St. Lucia, and St. Vincent and the Grenadines—have a long history of integration that includes a common market, shared currency, and joint supreme court. In 1981 they formed the Organisation of Eastern Caribbean States (OECS—see Glossary) as a Caricom associate institution to provide for enhanced economic, foreign policy, and defense cooperation. In May 1987 OECS leaders announced an agreement in principle to form one nation and called for referenda to be held on each island to approve or reject the proposed union. The original plan actually envisaged two separate votes: the first, scheduled for mid-1988, to determine whether unification was desired, and a subsequent ballot the following year to specify the kind of government of the new state. If approved, the union would be established in late 1989 or early 1990.

The fate of the proposed OECS political union remained uncertain as of May 1988. Although Antigua and Barbuda's prime minister Vere Cornwall Bird, Sr., announced his opposition to the plan in July 1987, the other six heads of government continued to support unification. Nonetheless, these leaders resisted demands from ten opposition parties to provide specific details of the proposed venture prior to the first vote. This resistance perhaps stemmed from the leaders' perception that most islanders favored unification in some form; indeed, even the opposition parties— under the banner of the Standing Committee of Popular Democratic Parties of the Eastern Caribbean (SCOPE)—felt compelled to endorse the idea of union. Still, SCOPE and others raised many issues that needed to be resolved. How much political authority would the six states retain under an OECS government? Would the states be granted equal representation in one of the houses of an OECS parliament? Would civil service employees be subject to transfer anywhere in the new state? Would a uniform wage structure be enacted for these employees? Would Nevisians continue to have local autonomy and a right of secession? Would Montserratians support independence? Thus, a positive vote in the first referenda might lead to contentious debates in the Eastern Caribbean in 1989.

Dynamic political activity was also in evidence in early 1988 in the Turks and Caicos Islands and Trinidad and Tobago. In March 1988 the People's Democratic Movement (PDM) crushed the Progressive National Party (PNP) in parliamentary elections in the Turks and Caicos, winning eleven of thirteen seats; PDM leader Oswald Skippings became the islands' chief minister. The elections were the first held in the Turks and Caicos since the British imposed direct British rule on the territory in July 1986 (see British Dependencies: The Cayman Islands and the Turks and Caicos Islands, Government and Politics, ch. 6). That action was taken after a Royal Commission of Inquiry found the chief minister and PNP head, Nathaniel "Bops" Francis, guilty of unconstitutional behavior and ministerial malpractices. Interestingly, the commission also determined that then-PDM deputy leader Skippings was unfit for public office.

The continued decline in 1987 of the economy in Trinidad and Tobago placed considerable strains on the ruling National Alliance for Reconstruction (NAR). Against a backdrop of sharp reductions in the GDP and in public expenditures, Prime Minister A.N.R. Robinson openly feuded with the former leaders of the East Indian-based United Labour Front, one of four political parties that had merged to create the NAR—the others being the Democratic Action Congress (DAC), the Organization for National Reconstruction (ONR), and Tapia House (see Political Dynamics, ch. 3). In November 1987 Robinson fired the minister of works, John Humphrey, for criticizing the government's economic performance. In response, Humphrey accused the prime minister of failing to consult with cabinet members. In January 1988, external affairs minister and the NAR deputy leader Basdeo Panday, public utilities minister Kelvin Ramnath, and junior finance minister Trevor Sudama participated in a meeting of over 100 NAR dissidents seeking Robinson's ouster; the prime minister dismissed the three from his cabinet the following month. Although each side accused the other of trying to divide the nation between blacks and East Indians, neither called for the breakup of NAR. All of the sacked ministers remained as NAR members of the House of Representatives; Panday also resumed his duties as president of the All Trinidad Sugar Estates and Factory Workers Trade Union.

Thus, the Commonwealth Caribbean islands offer a study in contrast, and sometimes conflict, within their individual boundaries and among themselves. A region gifted by abundant natural beauty and a pleasant climate, it looks to North America to generate increasing tourist dollars. Yet the islands also seek to maintain their independence from North American and West European dominance. Beset by internal bickering, the region nevertheless has seen economic interdependency blossom among some of its parts. Although distinct from Latin America, it suffers from some of the same ills, including the infiltration of the drug trade into its politics. It is a region that could be on the brink of true cooperation or on the path of further disunity.

May 26, 1988

*　　*　　*

Significant developments occurred in a number of Commonwealth Caribbean islands in the months following completion of research and writing of this book. Jamaica experienced a devastating hurricane and also held a general election that resulted in a change in government. Voters also cast their ballots in general elections in three other island groupings: Anguilla, Antigua and Barbuda, and St. Kitts and Nevis. Finally, Trinidad and Tobago was beset by continued economic problems and a fragmentation of its ruling party.

On September 12, 1988, Hurricane Gilbert roared through Jamaica with winds gusting at up to 280 kilometers per hour, thus qualifying it as the strongest storm ever recorded in the Western Hemisphere. The hurricane, described by Prime Minister Edward Seaga as the worst disaster in Jamaica's modern history, resulted in the deaths of over 30 people and the displacement of 20 percent of the population. Analysts estimated damage to the economy at US$1.3 billion. Agriculture was particularly hard hit; for example, the hurricane destroyed virtually all of the country's banana plantations.

As the nation grappled with the impact of Hurricane Gilbert, Jamaica's most famous politicians—Seaga and Michael Manley—prepared to face the voters in the first contested general election since 1980. Both Seaga and Manley carried heavy baggage into the electoral campaign. Although credited with attracting foreign aid and investment and strengthening tourism, Seaga was also attacked for slashing government spending on education, health, and housing. Many analysts contended that the quality of life for Jamaica's poor majority had declined during Seaga's eight years in office. In addition, polls indicated that Jamaicans generally viewed Seaga as an aloof leader. Manley, in turn, had to defend his own controversial record of leadership. As prime minister during the 1970s, Manley abrogated agreements with international aluminum companies, feuded with the International Monetary Fund (IMF—see Glossary), promoted a "new international economic order," and developed close relations with Cuba (see Role of Government; Foreign Relations, ch. 2). Critics asserted that the election of Manley would chill Jamaica's strong relations with the United States.

Responding to these criticisms, Manley sought during the campaign to present himself as a moderate leader who had learned much from the celebrated battles of the 1970s. Manley stressed the importance of close relations with the United States, pledged cooperation with foreign investors and the Jamaican business community, and promised to continue payments on the nation's estimated US$4-billion debt. By the close of the campaign, Manley had assuaged fears that he was too radical to lead Jamaica into the 1990s. On February 9, 1989, Manley's People's National Party scored a landslide victory, claiming almost 57 percent of the popular vote and 44 of the 60 seats in the House of Representatives. After assuming the prime ministership, Manley indicated that he would give top priority to an expansion of education and social services.

However, with almost half of all foreign exchange earnings committed to debt servicing, many analysts contended that Jamaica lacked the resources to fund an ambitious social agenda.

In contrast to Jamaica, incumbents won elections in Anguilla, Antigua and Barbuda, and St. Kitts and Nevis. Emile Gumbs retained his post as Anguilla's chief minister, although he needed the support of an independent candidate. Gumbs's Anguilla National Alliance captured three of the seven seats in the House of Assembly elections of February 27, 1989. The Anguilla United Party won two seats and the Anguilla Democratic Party, one. Gumbs's control of the government was assured, however, by the election of independent candidate Osbourne Fleming to the remaining House seat. Fleming, who served as finance and education minister in the previous government, again supported Gumbs's bid for the chief ministership. On March 9, 1989, voters in Antigua and Barbuda gave an overwhelming victory to Prime Minister Bird and his Antigua Labour Party (ALP). The ALP captured fifteen of the sixteen House of Representatives seats contested in Antigua; the remaining seat went to the United National Democratic Party. The Barbuda People's Movement claimed the seventeenth House seat, which is reserved for the residents of Barbuda. On March 21, 1989, Prime Minister Kennedy Simmonds led his People's Action Movement (PAM) to victory in the St. Kitts and Nevis National Assembly elections. PAM won six of the eight seats contested in St. Kitts, the remainder going to the Labour Party. PAM's coalition partner, the Nevis Reformation Party, claimed two of the three Assembly seats from Nevis. A new party, Concerned Citizens Movement, won the other Nevis seat.

Although general elections in Trinidad and Tobago were not expected until late 1991, the nation's economic woes helped erode support for the Robinson government. In July 1988, the Central Bank of Trinidad and Tobago announced the exhaustion of its international reserves—a stunning development for a nation whose reserves totalled US$3.3 billion in 1981. Faced with the need to finance an estimated US$1.8-billion foreign debt, Robinson submitted a request to the IMF in November 1988 for a 14-month Standby Arrangement totaling US$547 million. In exchange for assistance, Robinson pledged to reduce public spending from 7 percent to 4 percent of GDP, to trim the size of the public sector workforce by 15 percent over the next 2 years, to seek a delay in a court-ordered cost of living allowance (COLA), to enact a total liberalization of imports by 1990, and to eliminate price controls on all products except those deemed critical to low-income residents.

One month after the January 1989 IMF approval of the Standby Arrangement, Robinson received legislative support for a 10-percent pay cut for public employees and a 2-year suspension of the COLA payments.

The economic crisis proved too large a stumbling block for continued unity within the NAR. In September 1988, the NAR National Council expelled Panday, Ramnath, and Sudama from the party after the three established their own movement—the Caucus of Love, Unity, and Brotherhood (more commonly known as Club '88)—and persisted in their criticisms of government policies. Following the expulsions, Tapia House withdrew from the NAR, leaving the ruling party with only the former members of the DAC and the ONR. In early 1989, Panday announced that Club '88 supporters would meet on April 30, 1989, to create a new political party, the United National Congress. Trinidadians and Tobagonians anticipated a bitter political struggle over the next two years.

April 10, 1989   Dennis M. Hanratty

Chapter 1. Regional Overview

Arawak carving of a dog's head from a conch shell

THE COMMONWEALTH CARIBBEAN ISLANDS have a distinctive history. Permanently influenced by the experiences of colonialism and slavery, the Caribbean has produced a collection of societies that are markedly different in population composition from those in any other region of the world.

Lying on the sparsely settled periphery of an irregularly populated continent, the region was discovered by Christopher Columbus in 1492. Thereafter, it became the springboard for the European invasion and domination of the Americas, a transformation that historian D.W. Meinig has aptly described as the "radical reshaping of America." Beginning with the Spanish and Portuguese and continuing with the arrival more than a century later of other Europeans, the indigenous peoples of the Americas experienced a series of upheavals. The European intrusion abruptly interrupted the pattern of their historical development and linked them inextricably with the world beyond the Atlantic Ocean. It also severely altered their physical environment, introducing both new foods and new epidemic diseases. As a result, the native Indian populations rapidly declined and virtually disappeared from the Caribbean, although they bequeathed to the region a distinct cultural heritage that is still seen and felt.

During the sixteenth century, the Caribbean region was significant to the Spanish Empire. In the seventeenth century, the English, Dutch, and French established colonies. By the eighteenth century, the region contained colonies that were vitally important for all of the European powers because the colonies generated great wealth from the production and sale of sugar and other tropical staples.

The early English colonies, peopled and controlled by white settlers, were initially microcosms of English society, in which small yeomen farmed economies based mainly on tobacco and cotton. A major transformation occurred, however, with the establishment of the sugar plantation system. To meet the system's enormous manpower requirements, vast numbers of black African slaves were imported throughout the eighteenth century, thereby reshaping the region's demographic, social, and cultural profile. Although the white populations maintained their social and political preeminence, they became a numerical minority in all of the islands. Following the abolition of slavery in the 1830s, the colonies turned to imported indentured labor from India, China, and the East Indies, further diversifying the region's culture and society. The result of all these immigrations is a remarkable cultural heterogeneity in contemporary Caribbean society.

The abolition of slavery was also a watershed in Caribbean history in that it initiated the long, slow process of enfranchisement and political control by the nonwhite majorities in the islands. The early colonies enjoyed a relatively great amount of autonomy through the operations of their local representative assemblies. Later, however, to ease administration and to facilitate control of increasingly assertive colonial representative bodies, the British adopted a system of direct administration known as crown colony government (see Glossary), in which British-appointed governors wielded nearly autocratic power. The history of the colonies from then until 1962, when the first colonies became independent, is marked by the rise of popular movements and labor organizations and the emergence of a generation of politicians who assumed positions of leadership when the colonial system in the British Caribbean eventually was dismantled.

Despite shared historical and cultural experiences and geographic, demographic, and economic similarities, the Caribbean islands of the former British Empire remain diverse, and attempts at political federation and economic integration both prior to and following independence have foundered. Thus, the region today is characterized by a proliferation of ministates, all with strong democratic traditions and political systems cast in the Westminster parliamentary mold, but all also with forceful individual identities and interests.

Geographic Setting

The Commonwealth Caribbean islands make up a large subcomponent of the hundreds of islands in the Caribbean Sea, forming a wide arc between Florida in the north and Venezuela in the south, as well as a barrier between the Caribbean Sea and the Atlantic Ocean (see fig. 1). Varying considerably in size, the islands, which are the isolated upper parts of a submerged chain of volcanic mountains, are scattered over thousands of square kilometers of sea. The entire region lies well within the northern tropics.

The three principal geological formations found throughout the Caribbean are igneous and metamorphic rocks, limestone hills or karst, and coastal, sedimentary plains of varying depths, resulting in three prevailing kinds of topography, found either separately or in combination. The first consists of high (over 1,200 meters), rugged, sharply dissected mountains—such as the Blue Mountains in eastern Jamaica, the Morne Diablotin in central Dominica,

Mount Soufrière in St. Vincent, and the Northern Range in Trinidad—covered with dense, evergreen rain forests and cut by swiftly flowing rivers. The second kind of topography consists of very hilly countryside, such as the high plateau of central Jamaica, or the terrain on the islands of Antigua and Barbados. There, the hills seldom rise above 600 meters and are more gently sloped than the high mountains, but karst areas are still rugged. The third kind of topography consists of the coastal plains skirting the hills and mountains; their greatest extensions are usually on the southern or western sides of the mountains. Active volcanoes exist in Dominica, St. Vincent, and St. Lucia, and there are crater lakes formed by older activity in Grenada. All the islands have rugged coastlines with innumerable inlets fringed by white or dark sands (depending on the rock substratum) of varying texture. The beaches of Negril in Jamaica and Grand Anse in Grenada have fine-textured white sands that extend for nearly eleven kilometers each.

The Caribbean climate is tropical, moderated to a certain extent by the prevailing northeast trade winds. Individual climatic conditions are strongly dependent on elevation. At sea level there is little variation in temperature, regardless of the time of the day or the season of the year. Temperatures range between 24°C and 32°C. In Kingston, Jamaica, the mean temperature is 26°C, whereas in Mandeville, at a little over 600 meters high in the Carpenters Mountains of Manchester Parish, temperatures have been recorded as low as 10°C. Daylight hours tend to be shorter during summer and slightly longer during winter than in the higher latitudes. Rather than the four seasons, the conventional division is between the long rainy season from May through October and the dry season, corresponding to winter in the Northern Hemisphere.

Even during the rainy period, however, the precipitation range fluctuates greatly. Windward sides of islands with mountains receive a great deal of rain, whereas leeward sides can have very dry conditions. Flat islands receive slightly less rainfall, but the pattern is more consistent. For example, the Blue Mountains of eastern Jamaica record around 558 centimeters of rainfall per year, whereas Kingston, on the southeastern coast, receives only 399 centimeters. Bridgetown, the capital of Barbados, has an average annual rainfall of 127 centimeters, whereas Bathsheba on the central east coast receives 254 centimeters—despite the fact that Bathsheba is only about 27 kilometers away by road. Recording stations in the Northern Range in Trinidad measure some 302 centimeters of rainfall per year, while at Piarco International Airport on the Caroni Plain the measurement is only 140 centimeters. Most of the rainfall occurs in short heavy outbursts during daylight hours. In Jamaica about

80 percent of the rainfall occurs during the day. The period of heaviest rainfall usually occurs after the sun has passed directly overhead, which in the Caribbean islands would be sometime around the middle of May and again in early August. The rainy season also coincides with the disastrous summer hurricane season, although Barbados, too far east, and Trinidad and Tobago, too far south, seldom experience hurricanes.

Hurricanes are a constant feature of most of the Caribbean, and have a "season" of their own lasting from June to November. Hurricanes develop over the ocean, usually in the Eastern Caribbean (see Glossary) during the summer months when the sea surface temperature is high (over 27°C) and the air pressure falls below 950 millibars. These conditions create an "eye" about 20 kilometers wide, around which a steep pressure gradient forms that generates wind speeds of 110 to 280 kilometers per hour. The diameter of hurricanes can extend as far as 500 to 800 kilometers and produce extremely heavy rainfalls as well as considerable destruction of property. The recent history of the Caribbean echoes with the names of destructive hurricanes: Janet (1955), Donna (1960), Hattie (1961), Flora (1963), Beulah (1967), Celia and Dorothy (1970), Eloise (1975), David (1979), and Allen (1980).

The natural resources of the Commonwealth Caribbean islands are extremely limited. Jamaica has extensive deposits of bauxite (see Glossary), some of which is mined and processed locally into alumina (see Glossary); the United States is the largest market for the bauxite and alumina. In addition, Jamaica has large quantities of gypsum. Trinidad and Tobago has petroleum, pitch, and natural gas. Small, noncommercially viable deposits of manganese, lead, copper, and zinc are found throughout most of the islands. Nevertheless, most of the territories possess nothing more valuable than beautiful beaches, marvelously variegated seas, and a pleasant climate conducive to the promotion of international tourism.

Industrialization varies from territory to territory, but agriculture is generally declining on all the islands. The sugar industry, once the mainstay of the Caribbean economies, has faltered. Although the labor force employed in sugar production (and in agriculture in general) still forms the major sector of the employed labor force in Barbados and Jamaica, the contribution that sugar makes to the gross domestic product (GDP—see Glossary) has steadily dropped. Barbados has kept its sugar industry going, but it has steadily reduced dependence on sugar exports and diversified its economy. For example, in 1946 Barbados had 52 sugar factories producing nearly 100,000 tons of sugar and employing more than 25,000 persons during the season. Although production had increased by 1980, the number of factories had declined to 8, and the number employed was slightly less than 9,000. Furthermore, the proportion of GDP contributed by sugar and sugar products had declined from 37.8 percent to 10.9 percent over the same period.

Since the 1950s, light manufacturing, mining, and processing of foods and other commodities have been used to bolster employment and increase the local economies. Although these sectors have been important contributors to the GDP of the individual states, in no case does this contribution exceed 20 percent of the total. Moreover, industrialization has provided neither sufficient jobs nor sufficient wealth for the state to offset the decline in agricultural production and labor absorption.

The Commonwealth Caribbean islands, like the rest of the region (except Cuba), find themselves in a difficult trading situation with the United States. On the one hand, the United States accounts for between 20 and 50 percent of all imports and exports in the region. On the other hand, the Commonwealth Caribbean states account for less than 1 percent of all United States imports and exports and less than 5 percent of the more than US$38 billion of overseas private investment in the Western Hemisphere. But the interest in the Commonwealth Caribbean islands cannot be measured in economic terms only. The Caribbean is clearly within the United States sphere of interest for political and strategic considerations that defy economic valuation.

Historical and Cultural Setting
The Pre-European Population

Before the arrival of Christopher Columbus in 1492, most of the Caribbean was peopled by three groups of inhabitants: the Ciboney (or Guanahuatebey), the Arawaks (or Tainos), and the Caribs. The cultural distinctions among the three groups are not great; the single greatest differentiating factor appears to be their respective dates of arrival in the region. The Ciboney seem to have arrived first and were found in parts of Cuba and the Bahamas. They also seem to have had the most elementary forms of social organization. The most numerous groups were the Arawaks, who resided in most of the Greater Antilles—Cuba, Jamaica, Hispaniola (the island containing Haiti and the Dominican Republic), and Puerto Rico. The Lesser Antilles was the home of the Caribs. Barbados and a number of smaller islands were not permanently inhabited.

Estimates of the size of the pre-Hispanic population of the Americas vary considerably. Both Columbus and Father Bartolomé de Las Casas (who wrote the first history of the Spanish conquest and treatment of the Indians) produced estimates that appear to defy credibility. Las Casas thought the population of the Caribbean might have been in the vicinity of several million, and by virtue of his having lived in both Hispaniola and Cuba where he held *encomiendas,* or the right to tribute from the Indians, he is as close as we get to an eye-witness account. Las Casas had a penchant for hyperbole, and it is doubtful that he could have produced reliable estimates for areas where he did not travel.

Nevertheless, some more recent scholars have tended to agree with Las Casas, estimating as many as 4 million inhabitants for the island of Hispaniola alone in 1492. Although the dispute continues, a consensus seems to be developing for far lower figures than previously accepted.

An indigenous population of less than a million for all of the Caribbean would still be a relatively dense population, given the technology and resources of the region in the late fifteenth century. Probably one-half of these inhabitants would have been on the large island of Hispaniola, about 50,000 in Cuba, and far fewer than that in Jamaica. Puerto Rico, Dominica, St. Lucia, St. Vincent, and Trinidad all had fairly concentrated, if not large, populations.

The pre-European populations of the territories that later formed the Commonwealth Caribbean belonged to the groups designated as Caribs and Arawaks. Both were tropical forest people, who probably originated in the vast expanse of forests of the northern regions of South America and were related linguistically and ethnically to such present-day tropical forest peoples as the Chibcha, the Warao, the Yanomamo, the Caracas, the Caquetío, and the Jirajara—in short, the peoples found anywhere from Panama to Brazil.

The Arawaks lived in theocratic kingdoms and had a hierarchically arranged pantheon of gods, called *zemis,* and village chiefs, or caciques. The *zemis* were represented by icons of wood, stone, bones, and human remains. Arawaks believed that being in the good graces of their *zemis* protected them from disease, hurricanes, or disaster in war. They therefore served cassava (manioc) bread as well as beverages and tobacco to their *zemis* as propitiatory offerings.

The size of the community and the number of *zemis* he owned were directly related to the chief's importance. Chiefs lived in rectangular huts called *bohios,* while the other members of the community lived in round thatched huts called *caneyes.* The construction

A carbet *(local social gathering place)*
on a Carib reserve, northeastern Dominica
Courtesy Jonathan French

of both kinds of buildings was the same: wooden frames, topped by straw, with earthen floor, and scant interior furnishing. But the buildings were strong enough to resist hurricanes.

From the European perspective, the wealth of the indigenous Indians was modest indeed. While Columbus and his successors sought gold and other trading commodities of value on the European market, the native Antilleans were not interested in trade and used gold only ornamentally. Their personal possessions consisted of wooden stools with four legs and carved backs, hammocks made of cotton cloth or string for sleeping, clay and wooden bowls for mixing and serving food, calabashes or gourds for drinking water and bailing out boats, and their most prized possessions, large dugout canoes for transportation, fishing, and water sports. One such canoe found in Jamaica could transport about seventy-five persons.

The Indians painted their bodies in bright colors, and some wore small ornaments of gold and shells in their noses, around their necks, or hanging from their ears. Body painting was also employed to intimidate opponents in warfare.

Arawak villagers produced about two crops per year of manioc, maize, potatoes, peanuts, peppers, beans, and arrowroot. Cultivation was by the slash-and-burn method common throughout

Middle America, and the cultivated area was abandoned after the harvest. The Indians worked the soil with sticks, called *coas,* and built earthen mounds in which they planted their crops. They may also have used fertilizers of ash, composted material, and feces to boost productivity. There is even evidence of simple irrigation in parts of southwestern Hispaniola.

Hunting and fishing were major activities. Arawaks hunted ducks, geese, parrots, iguanas, small rodents, and giant tree sloths. Parrots and a species of mute dog were domesticated. Most fishing, done by hand along the coast and in rivers, was for mollusks, lobsters, and turtles. Bigger fish were caught with baskets, spears, hooks, and nets. In some cases, fish were caught by attaching the hooks of sharpened sticks to remoras, small sucking fish that fastened themselves to larger sea creatures, such as sharks and turtles.

Food was prepared by baking on stones or barbecuing over an open fire, using peppers, herbs, and spices lavishly to both flavor and preserve the food. In some places, beer was brewed from maize. The descriptions of the first Europeans indicated that the food supply was sufficient and that in general the inhabitants were well fed—until the increased demand of the new immigrants and the dislocation created by their imported animals created famine.

The Caribs of the Lesser Antilles were a highly mobile group; they possessed canoes similar to those of the Arawaks, but they employed them for more warlike pursuits. Their social organization appeared to be simpler than that of the Arawaks. They had no elaborate ceremonial courts like those of the Arawaks, but their small, wooden, frame houses surrounding a central fireplace might have served as ceremonial centers. Many of their cultural artifacts—especially those recovered in Trinidad—resemble those of the Arawaks. This might be explained in part by the Carib practice of capturing Arawak women as brides, who then could have socialized the children along Arawak lines.

The social and political organization of Carib society reflected both their military inclination and their mobile status. Villages were small, often consisting of members of an extended family. The leader of the village, most often the head of the family, supervised the food-gathering activities, principally fishing, done by the men, and the cultivation activities, done by the women. In addition, the leader settled internal disputes and led raids against neighboring groups. The purpose of these raids was to obtain wives for the younger males of the village.

Warfare was an important activity for Carib males, and before the arrival of the Spanish they had a justified reputation as the most feared warriors of the Caribbean. Using bows, poisoned arrows, javelins, and clubs, the Caribs attacked in long canoes, capturing Arawak women and, according to Arawak informants, ritualistically cooking and eating some of the male captives. There are, however, no records of Caribs eating humans after the advent of the Europeans, thus casting doubts on the Arawak tales.

When the Spanish arrived in the Caribbean at the end of the fifteenth century, the Caribs and Arawaks, like all other frontier peoples, were undergoing mutual adaptations. The generally more peaceful Arawaks were becoming more adept at fighting; and, away from the contested frontier, the Caribs, such as those in Trinidad, were spending more time on agriculture than warfare.

The Caribs and the Arawaks were progressively wiped out by the aftereffects of the conquest, the peaceful Arawaks suffering the greater catastrophe. The concentrated populations on Hispaniola, Cuba, Puerto Rico, and Jamaica declined rapidly, victims of enslavement, social dislocation, and epidemics of diseases brought by the Europeans and the African slaves. The smaller, more scattered populations of the Eastern Caribbean survived much better. In the seventeenth century, the Caribs resisted European settlements on Dominica, St. Lucia, and St. Vincent, destroying the first English colony on St. Lucia in 1605 and thwarting the second attempt in 1638, thus delaying the effective occupation of Dominica and St. Vincent until the middle of the eighteenth century. Some Caribs resisted assimilation or acculturation by the Europeans, and a few of their descendants still live on a reservation in Dominica. Both the Caribs and the Arawaks left indelible influences on the language, diet, and way of life of the twentieth-century people who live in the region. Caribbean food crops, such as peanuts, cashew nuts, potatoes, tomatoes, pineapples, pumpkins, manioc, and maize, have spread around the world. The Indians' habit of smoking tobacco has become widespread, and tobacco has become an important commercial commodity. Arawak and Carib words have permeated the languages of the region, words such as agouti, avocado, barbecue, *bohio,* buccaneer, *calpulli* (an urban zone), *caney,* cannibal, canoe, cassava, cay, *conuco* (a cultivated area), *guagua* (a bus or truck), *guajiro* (a peasant), guava, hammock, hurricane, iguana, maize, manatee, and *zemi.*

The Impact of the Conquest

The Europeans who invaded and conquered the Caribbean destroyed the internally cohesive world of the native peoples and subordinated the region and the peoples to the events of a wider world in which their fortunes were linked with those of Africa, Europe, and the Americas. The Caribbean peoples were devastated

11

by new epidemic diseases, such as measles, smallpox, malaria, and dysentery, introduced by the Europeans and the Africans imported as slaves. Their social and political organizations were restructured in the name of Christianity. Their simple lives were regimented by slavery and the demands of profit-oriented, commerce-minded Europeans. Above all, they were slowly inundated culturally and demographically by the stream of new immigrants in the years immediately after the conquest.

The European Settlements

European settlements in the Caribbean began with Christopher Columbus. Carrying an elaborate feudal commission that made him perpetual governor of all lands discovered and gave him a percentage of all trade conducted, Columbus set sail in September 1492, determined to find a faster, shorter way than overland to China and Japan. He planned to set up a trading-post empire, modeled after the successful Portuguese venture along the West African coast. His aim was to establish direct commercial relations with the producers of spices and other luxuries of the fabled East, thereby cutting out the Arab middlemen who had monopolized trade since capturing Constantinople in 1453. He also planned to link up with the lost Christians of Abyssinia, who were reputed to have large quantities of gold—a commodity in great demand in Europe. Finally, as a good Christian, Columbus wanted to spread Christianity to new peoples. Columbus, of course, did not find the East. Nevertheless, he called the peoples he met "Indians" and, because he had sailed west, referred to the region he found as the "West Indies."

However, dreams of a trading-post empire collapsed in the face of the realities of Caribbean life. The Indians, although initially hospitable in most cases, simply did not have gold and trade commodities for the European market.

In all, Columbus made four voyages of exploration between 1492 and 1502, failing to find great quantities of gold, Christians, or the courts of the fabled khans described by Marco Polo. After 1499 small amounts of gold were discovered on Hispaniola, but by that time local challenges to Columbus's governorship were mounting, and his demonstrated lack of administrative skills made matters worse. Even more disappointing, he returned to Spain in 1502 to find that his extensive feudal authority in the New World was rapidly being taken away by his monarchs.

Columbus inadvertently started a small settlement on the north coast of Hispaniola when his flagship, the *Santa María*, wrecked off the Môle St. Nicolas on his first voyage. When he returned a year

*Statue of Columbus,
Nassau, The Bahamas
Courtesy Inter-American
Development Bank*

COLUMBUS
1492

later, no trace of the settlement appeared—and the former welcome and hospitality of the Indians had changed to suspicion and fear.

The first proper European settlement in the Caribbean began when Nicolás de Ovando, a faithful soldier from western Spain, settled about 2,500 Spanish colonists in eastern Hispaniola in 1502. Unlike Columbus's earlier settlements, this group was an organized cross section of Spanish society brought with the intention of developing the West Indies economically and expanding Spanish political, religious, and administrative influence. In its religious and military motivation, it continued the *reconquista* (reconquest), which had expelled the Moors from Granada and the rest of southern Spain.

From this base in Santo Domingo, as the new colony was called, the Spanish quickly fanned out throughout the Caribbean and onto the mainland. Jamaica was settled in 1509 and Trinidad the following year. By 1511 Spanish explorers had established themselves as far as Florida. However, in the Eastern Caribbean, the Caribs resisted the penetration of the Europeans until well into the seventeenth century and succumbed only in the eighteenth century.

After the Spanish conquest of Mexico in 1519 and the subsequent discovery of gold there, interest in working the gold deposits of the islands decreased. Moreover, by that time the Indian population of the Caribbean had dwindled considerably, creating a

13

scarcity of workers for the mines and pearl fisheries. In 1518 the first African slaves, called ladinos because they had lived in Spain and spoke the Castilian language, were introduced to the Caribbean to help mitigate the labor shortage.

The Spanish administrative structure that prevailed for the 131 years of Spanish monopoly in the Caribbean was simple. At the imperial level were two central agencies, the House of Trade, which licensed all ships sailing to or returning from the West Indies and supervised commerce, and the Council of the Indies, which attended to imperial legislation. At the local level in the Caribbean were the governors, appointed by the monarchs of Castile, who supervised local municipal councils. The governors were regulated by *audiencias* (appellate courts). A parallel structure regulated the religious organizations. Despite the theoretical hierarchy and clear divisions of authority, in practice each agency reported directly to the monarch. As set out in the original instructions to Ovando in 1502, the Spanish New World was to be orthodox and unified under the Roman Catholic religion and Castilian and Spanish in culture and nationality. Moors, Jews, recent converts to Roman Catholicism, Protestants, and Gypsies were legally excluded from sailing to the West Indies, although this exclusiveness could not be maintained and was frequently violated.

By the early seventeenth century, Spain's European enemies, no longer disunited and internally weak, were beginning to breach the perimeters of Spain's American empire. The French and the English established trading forts along the St. Lawrence and Hudson rivers in North America. These were followed by permanent settlements in Virginia and Massachusetts.

Between 1595 and 1620, the English, French, and Dutch made many unsuccessful attempts to settle along the Guiana coastlands of South America. The Dutch finally prevailed and established one permanent colony along the Essequibo River in 1616 and another, in 1624, along the neighboring Berbice River. As in North America, the initial loss of life in the colonies was discouragingly high. In 1623 the English gave up in the Guianas and created a colony on St. Christopher (hereafter, St. Kitts) in the Leeward Islands; the French followed suit in 1624. At that time, St. Kitts was occupied only by Caribs. Because the Spanish were deeply involved in the Thirty Years' War (1618–48) in Europe, conditions were propitious for colonial exploits in what until then had been reluctantly conceded to be a Spanish domain.

In 1621 the Dutch began to move aggressively against Spanish territory in the Americas—including Brazil, temporarily under Spanish control between 1580 and 1640. They joined the English

14

in settling St. Croix in the Leeward Islands in 1625 and then seized the minuscule, unoccupied Leeward Islands of Sint Eustatius, Sint Maarten (part of the divided island of St. Martin/Sint Maarten), and Saba and also the island of Curaçao off the Venezuelan coast. The Dutch thereby expanded their former holdings in the Guianas, as well as those at Araya and Cumaná on the Venezuelan coast.

The English and the French also moved rapidly to take advantage of Spanish weakness in the Americas and overcommitment in Europe. In 1625 the English settled Barbados and tried an unsuccessful settlement on Tobago. They took possession of Nevis in 1628 and Antigua and Montserrat in 1632. They established a colony on St. Lucia in 1605, but it was destroyed by the Caribs; they tried again in 1638 to establish a colony but were again unsuccessful. The French, under the auspices of the French West Indian Company, chartered by Cardinal Richelieu in 1635, successfully settled Martinique and Guadeloupe, laying the base for later expansion to St. Barthélemy, St. Martin, Grenada, St. Lucia, and western Hispaniola, which was formally ceded by Spain in 1697 in the Treaty of Ryswick (signed between France and the alliance of Spain, the Netherlands, and England and ending the War of the Grand Alliance). Meanwhile, an expedition sent out by Oliver Cromwell under Admiral William Penn (the father of the founder of Pennsylvania) and General Robert Venables in 1655 seized Jamaica, the first territory captured from the Spanish. (Trinidad, the only other British colony taken from the Spanish, fell in 1797 and was ceded in 1802.) At that time, Jamaica had a population of about 3,000, equally divided between Spaniards and their slaves—the Indian population having been eliminated. Although Jamaica was a disappointing consolation for the failure to capture either of the major colonies of Hispaniola or Cuba, the island was retained in the Treaty of Madrid in 1670, thereby more than doubling the land area for potential British colonization in the Caribbean. By 1750 Jamaica was the most important of Britain's Caribbean colonies, having eclipsed Barbados in economic significance.

The first colonists in the Caribbean were trying to recreate their metropolitan European societies in the region. In this respect, the goals and the worldview of the early colonists in the Caribbean did not vary significantly from those of the colonists on the North American mainland. "The Caribbee planters," wrote the historian Richard S. Dunn, "began as peasant farmers not unlike the peasant farmers of Wigston Magna, Leicestershire, or Sudbury, Massachusetts. They cultivated the same staple crop—tobacco—as their cousins in Virginia and Maryland. They brought to the tropics the English common law, English political institutions, the English parish [local administrative unit], and the English church.'' These institutions survived for a very long time, but the social context in which they were introduced was altered by time and circumstances. Attempts to recreate microcosms of Europe were slowly abandoned in favor of a series of plantation societies using slave labor to produce large quantities of tropical staples for the European market. In the process of this transformation, complicated by war and trade, much was changed in the Caribbean.

The Colonial Period

The mid-seventeenth-century development of a sugar plantation society based on slave labor was an important watershed in Caribbean history. Introduced by the Dutch when they were expelled from Brazil in 1640, the sugar plantation system arrived at an opportune time for the fledgling non-Spanish colonists with their precarious economies. The English yeoman farming economy based mainly on cultivation of tobacco was facing a severe crisis. Caribbean tobacco could compete neither in quality nor in quantity with that produced in the mid-Atlantic colonies. Because tobacco farming had been the basis of the economy, its end threatened the economic viability of the islands. As a result, the colonies were losing population to the mainland. Economic salvation came from what has been called in historical literature the Caribbean ''sugar revolutions,'' a series of interrelated changes that altered the entire agriculture, demography, society, and culture of the Caribbean, thereby transforming the political and economic importance of the region.

In terms of agriculture, the islands changed from small farms producing cash crops of tobacco and cotton with the labor of a few servants and slaves—often indistinguishable—to large plantations requiring vast expanses of land and enormous capital outlays to create sugarcane fields and factories. Sugar, which had become increasingly popular on the European market throughout the seventeenth century, provided an efficacious balance between bulk and value—a relationship of great importance in the days of relatively small sailing ships and distant sea voyages. Hence, the conversion to sugar transformed the landholding pattern of the islands.

The case of Barbados illustrates the point. In 1640 this island of 430 square kilometers had about 10,000 settlers, predominantly white; 764 of them owned 4 or more hectares of land, and virtually every white was a landholder. By 1680, when the sugar revolutions were underway, the wealthiest 175 planters owned 54 percent of the land and an equal proportion of the servants and slaves. More important, Barbados had a population of about 38,000

Francis Stephen Cary etching with view of
Port Royal and Kingston Harbour, Jamaica, 1782
Courtesy Prints and Photographs Division, Library of Congress

African slaves and more than 2,000 English servants who owned no land. Fortunes, however, depended on access to land and slaves. For example, Thomas Rous, who arrived in Barbados in 1638, had a farm of 24 hectares in 1645. By 1680 the Rous family owned 3 sugar works, 266 hectares of land, and 310 slaves and were counted among the great planters of the island.

The Sugar Revolutions and Slavery

The sugar revolutions were both cause and consequence of the demographic revolution. Sugar production required a greater labor supply than was available through the importation of European servants and irregularly supplied African slaves. At first the Dutch supplied the slaves, as well as the credit, capital, technological expertise, and marketing arrangements. After the restoration of the English monarchy following the Commonwealth (1649–60), the king and other members of the royal family invested in the Company of Royal Adventurers, chartered in 1663, to pursue the lucrative African slave trade. That company was succeeded by the Royal Africa Company in 1672, but the supply still failed to meet the demand, and all kinds of private traders entered the transatlantic commerce.

Between 1518 and 1870, the transatlantic slave trade supplied the greatest proportion of the Caribbean population. As sugarcane

17

cultivation increased and spread from island to island—and to the neighboring mainland as well—more Africans were brought to replace those who had died under the rigorous demands of labor on the plantations, in the sugar factories, and in the mines. Acquiring and transporting Africans to the New World became a big and extremely lucrative business. From a modest trickle in the early sixteenth century, the trade increased to an annual import rate of about 2,000 in 1600, 13,000 in 1700, and 55,000 in 1810. Between 1811 and 1830, about 32,000 slaves per year were imported. As with all trade, the operation fluctuated widely, affected by regular market factors of supply and demand as well as by the irregular and often unexpected interruptions of international war.

The year 1810 marked the apogee of the system. About 60 percent of all the Africans who arrived as slaves in the New World came between 1700 and 1810, the period during which Jamaica, Barbados, and the Leeward Islands peaked as sugar producers. Antislavery societies sprang up in Britain and France, using the secular, rationalist arguments of the Enlightenment—the intellectual movement centered in France in the eighteenth century—to challenge the moral and legal basis for slavery. A significant moral victory was achieved when the British chief justice, Lord Mansfield, ruled in 1772 that slavery was illegal in Britain, thereby freeing about 15,000 slaves who had accompanied their masters there—and abruptly terminating the practice of black slaves' ostentatiously escorting their masters about the empire. In the British Parliament, antislavery voices grew stronger until eventually a bill to abolish the slave trade passed both houses in 1807. The British, being the major carriers of slaves and having abolished the trade themselves, energetically set about discouraging other states from continuing. The abolition of the slave trade was a blow from which the slave system in the Caribbean could not recover.

Sugar and slavery gave to the region a predominantly African population. Approximately 17 percent of the 10 million African slaves brought to the Americas came to the British Caribbean. Although the white populations maintained their superior social positions, they became a numerical minority in all the islands. In the early nineteenth century, whites constituted less than 5 percent of the total population of Jamaica, Grenada, Nevis, St. Vincent, and Tobago and less than 10 percent of the population of Anguilla, Montserrat, St. Kitts, St. Lucia, and the Virgin Islands. Only in the Bahamas, Barbados, and Trinidad was more than 10 percent of the total population white. By sharp contrast, Trinidad was the only colony in the British Caribbean to have less than 80 percent of its population enslaved.

This demographic revolution had important social consequences. Rather than being a relatively homogeneous ethnic group divided into categories based on economic criteria, Caribbean society had complex overlapping divisions of class and caste. The three basic divisions were free white persons, free nonwhite persons, and slaves.

Whites were divided along status lines based on wealth. In the British colonies these were called "principal whites" and "poor whites." In reality they formed three ranks. The upper subdivision of the principal whites, forming an elite, were families who owned slaves and successful plantations. Some of their names became important in the history of one or more of the islands, names such as Guy, Modyford, Drax, Sutton, Price, Bannington, Needham, Tharp, and Beckford in Jamaica; Drax, Hallet, Littleton, Codrington, and Middleton in Barbados; and Warner, Winthrop, Pinney, and Jeaffreson in the Leeward Islands. The lower subdivision of the principal whites consisted of merchants, officials, and such professionals as doctors and clergymen, who were just a shade below the big planters.

At the bottom of the white ranks came the so-called "poor whites," often given such pejorative names as "red legs" in Barbados or "walking buckras" in Jamaica. This group included small independent farmers, servants, day laborers, and all the service individuals from policemen to smiths, as well as the various hangers-on required by the curious "Deficiency Laws." These were laws designed to retain a minimum number of whites on each plantation to safeguard against slave revolts. A Jamaica law of 1703 stipulated that there must be one white person for each ten slaves up to the first twenty slaves and one for each twenty slaves thereafter as well as one white person for the first sixty head of cattle and one for each one hundred head after the first sixty head. The law was modified in 1720, raising the ratios and lowering the fines for noncompliance, but the planters seemed more prepared to pay the fines for noncompliance than to recruit and maintain white servants, so the law degenerated into another simple revenue measure for the state. This was true throughout the British Caribbean islands during the eighteenth century.

Regardless of rank, skin color gave each person of European descent a privileged position within plantation society. The importance of race and color was a significant variation from the norms of typical European society and accentuated the divergence between the society "at home" and that overseas.

Each slave society in the colonies had an intermediate group, called the "free persons of color," an ambiguous position. Governor Francis Seaforth of Barbados colorfully expressed this dilemma in 1802: "There is, however, a third description of people from whom I am more suspicious of evil than from either the whites or the slaves: these are the Black and Coloured people who are not slaves, and yet whom I cannot bring myself to call free. I think *unappropriated people* would be a more proper denomination for them, for though not the property of other individuals they do not enjoy the shadow of any civil right." This group originated in the miscegenation of European masters and their African slaves. By the nineteenth century, the group could be divided into blacks who had gained their freedom or were the descendants of slaves, and the mixed, or mulatto, descendants of the associations between Europeans and non-Europeans. By the time of Britain's abolition of slavery in the 1830s, the heterogeneous free nonwhite population represented about 10 percent of the population of Jamaica, 12 percent of the population of Barbados, and about 20 percent of the population of Trinidad. A number of these free nonwhites had been free for generations, if not centuries, and had carved a niche in the local societies as successful merchants, planters, professionals, and slave owners.

Throughout the British Caribbean the free nonwhites manifested a number of common traits. They were predominantly female, largely urban, and clearly differentiated from the slaves both by law and by custom. Although adult females outnumbered males, the free nonwhite population tended to be the most sexually balanced overall and was the only group that consistently reproduced itself in the British colonies during the era of the slave trade. Moreover, with the exception of Trinidad, where, as Bridget Brereton indicates, just as many free nonwhites lived in the rural parishes as in the towns of Port-of-Spain, San Fernando, and St. Joseph, the free nonwhites were strongly urban. After 1809 about 61 percent of all the free nonwhites in Barbados lived in the parish of St. Michael in the capital city, Bridgetown. More free nonwhites lived in Kingston, Jamaica, than in all the other parishes combined.

The free nonwhite population faced competition from both ends of the spectrum. At the lower end of the economic scale they had to compete with jobbing slaves, who were often working arduously to get enough money to purchase their freedom and so join the free group. At the upper end they competed with the artisan, commercial, and semiskilled service sector of the lower orders of whites. The whites often used their political power—or in some cases their access to political power in Britain—to circumscribe the free nonwhites as much as possible. Throughout the Caribbean it was common to find laws distinguishing comportment, dress, and residence; denying nonwhites the right to practice certain professions; or

"Sunday Morning in Town," Port-of-Spain, Trinidad
Courtesy Prints and Photographs Division, Library of Congress

limiting the material legacy of individual free nonwhites. But at the time of the abolition of slavery, nonwhites were aggressively challenging the political hegemony of the whites, and their successes were very important in the subsequent development of British Caribbean society.

The Post-Emancipation Societies

The second great watershed in Caribbean history resulted from the abolition of slavery in the nineteenth century. In the British Caribbean this came between 1834, when a law was passed by the British Parliament to abolish slavery throughout the empire, and 1838, when the apprenticeship system collapsed prematurely. The apprenticeship system was designed to ease the transition from slavery to freedom by forcing the ex-slaves to remain on their plantations for a period of six years. Its main purpose was to prevent the immediate large-scale abandonment of estates by the workers, although, with cruel irony, it was the masters and not the slaves who were awarded compensation for the loss of their "property." The system proved too cumbersome to administer and was prematurely terminated in 1838.

Abolition of slavery was difficult for the colonies, which had to adjust to having a majority of new citizens who could not be denied the civil rights already grudgingly extended to the few. Extending

21

those civil rights, then as now, was neither easily nor gracefully achieved because the political systems had existed for centuries as the narrow instruments of the small, white, landed elite—largely absentee—whose members were threatened by the removal of their special trade preferences. Above all, there were economic difficulties. Sugar prices were falling, and West Indian producers were facing severe competition not only from other producers in the British Empire (such as India, South Africa, and Australia) and non-imperial cane sugar producers (such as Cuba and Brazil) but also from beet sugar producers in Europe and the United States. Falling prices coincided with rising labor costs, complicated by the urgent need to regard the ex-slaves as wage laborers able and willing to bargain for their pay.

To mitigate labor difficulties, the local assemblies were encouraged to import nominally free laborers from India, China, and Africa under contracts of indenture. Apart from the condition that they had a legally defined term of service and were guaranteed a set wage, the Asian indentured laborers were treated like the African slaves they partially replaced in the fields and factories. Between 1838 and 1917, nearly 500,000 East Indians (from British India) came to work on the British West Indian sugar plantations, the majority going to the new sugar producers with fertile lands. Trinidad imported 145,000; Jamaica, 21,500; Grenada, 2,570; St. Vincent, 1,820; and St. Lucia, 1,550. Between 1853 and 1879, British Guiana imported more than 14,000 Chinese workers, a few of them going to some of the other colonies. Between 1841 and 1867, about 32,000 indentured Africans arrived in the British West Indies, the greater number going to Jamaica and British Guiana. Because the families of important British politicians, such as Prime Minister William Ewart Gladstone, owned sugar estates in British Guiana, that colony, directly administered by the crown, assumed great importance in the Caribbean.

Indentured labor did not resolve the problems of the plantations and the local governments in the Caribbean during the nineteenth century, but it enabled the sugar plantations to weather the difficulties of the transition from slave labor. The new immigrants further pluralized the culture, the economy, and the society. The East Indians introduced rice and boosted the local production of cacao (the bean from which cocoa is derived) and ground provisions (tubers, fruits, and vegetables). Although some East Indians eventually converted to Christianity and intermarried with other ethnic groups, the majority remained faithful to their original Hindu and Muslim beliefs, adding temples and mosques to the religious architecture of the territories. The Chinese moved into local commerce, and, by the beginning of the twentieth century, the corner Chinese grocery store and the Chinese restaurant had become commonplace in all the colonies.

Emancipation of the slaves provided the catalyst for the rise of an energetic, dynamic peasantry throughout the Caribbean. A large proportion of the ex-slaves settled in free villages, often forming cooperatives to buy bankrupt or abandoned sugar estates. Where they lacked the capital, they simply squatted on vacant lands and continued the cultivation of many of the food crops that the planters and the colonial government had exported during the days of slavery.

The villages, although largely independent, provided a potential labor pool that could be attracted to the plantations. The growth of these free villages immediately after the emancipation of the slaves was astonishing. In Jamaica black freeholders increased from 2,014 in 1838 to more than 7,800 in 1840 and more than 50,000 in 1859. In Barbados, where land was scarcer and prices higher, freeholders having fewer than 2 hectares each increased from 1,110 in 1844 to 3,537 in 1859. In St. Vincent about 8,209 persons built their own homes and purchased and brought under cultivation over 5,000 hectares between 1838 and 1857. In Antigua 67 free villages with 5,187 houses and 15,644 inhabitants were established between 1833 and 1858. The free villages produced new crops, such as coconuts, rice, bananas, arrowroot, honey, and beeswax, as well as the familiar plantation crops of sugarcane, tobacco, coffee, cacao, limes, and ground provisions.

Political Traditions

The political traditions of the Commonwealth Caribbean islands reflect the diverse ways in which they were brought into the British Empire and administered, as well as the dominant political views in London at the time of their incorporation. Some of these traditions can still be observed in the operation of contemporary politics in the region. Three patterns emerged: one for colonies settled or acquired before the eighteenth century; another for colonies taken during the Seven Years' War (1756–63) and ceded by France in 1763; and a third for colonies conquered in the late eighteenth and early nineteenth centuries and ceded by France in the early nineteenth century.

The first group—Barbados, the Bahamas, the Leeward Islands, and Jamaica—developed during the early attempts to found colonies. Like the mainland North American colonies (and Bermuda), these territories had representative assemblies based on the bicameral system of the mother country. Each colony had a governor who represented the monarch, an appointed upper house, and an elected lower house. The electoral franchise, however, was extremely restricted, being vested in a few wealthy male property holders. Power was divided between the governor, who executed the laws, and the assembly, which made them. However, the assembly retained the right to pass all money bills—including the pay for the governor—and so used this right to obstruct legislation or simply to control new officials.

These older colonies also had an effective system of local government based on parish vestries. The vestries were elected annually by the freeholders and met frequently to levy local revenues for the maintenance of the poor, the support of the clergy, the construction of roads, and other local business, such as the licensing of teachers.

A second pattern of local government developed in Dominica, Grenada, St. Vincent, the Grenadines, and Tobago. All were ceded by France to Britain under the Treaty of Paris of 1763, although France succeeded in temporarily recapturing them in the late 1770s or early 1780s. Like the older British territories in the Caribbean, these "ceded islands" also had assemblies. However, the small size of the free landholding population in these islands vitiated the functions of the assemblies and precluded development of a viable system of local government such as had developed in Jamaica and Barbados.

The British governed the last Caribbean possessions ceded by the French—Trinidad and St. Lucia—in a radically different manner from the two patterns just discussed. Employing a system known as crown colony government (see Glossary), the British ruled directly through appointed officials rather than elected representatives. Royal governors were vested with virtually autocratic powers. At the same time, the British retained the previous Spanish, French, and Dutch forms of government, gradually altering them through time. No sustained attempt was made to foster local government in these newer colonies, although the leading cities—Port-of-Spain in Trinidad and Castries in St. Lucia—had municipal councils. Perhaps as a result, a strong grass-roots democracy failed to develop early in the latter territories.

The British decision to administer Trinidad and St. Lucia as crown colonies resulted from a number of complex factors. First, the British, cognizant of the difficulty that they had had with the various local planters' assemblies, were not anxious to create legislative bodies on two more islands. Beyond that, the acquisition of Trinidad presented the British with several new challenges. First, the free nonwhite population on the island outnumbered the white residents. The British were unwilling to extend voting rights to a nonwhite majority but also felt that free nonwhites would not accept an electoral system only open to whites. Second, French and Spanish planters on the island outnumbered those from Britain. Even if a way could be found to restrict the vote to whites, "foreigners" would dominate the assembly. Finally, with the British abolition of the slave trade in 1808, the British wanted to prevent illegal arrivals of new slaves into Trinidad. Enforcement of the new law could be handled more easily through direct control.

Colonial acquisition and administration were not neatly and easily accomplished. Tobago changed imperial masters more than a dozen times before finally being reacquired by Britain in 1802. It experienced many forms of administration before being confirmed as a ward of Trinidad in 1898. The Bahamas, irregularly colonized by the British beginning in 1649, had a representative assembly in 1728 but eventually settled into a dull routine as a minor crown colony until the granting of complete internal self-government in January 1964. The Cayman Islands, erratically settled by the British, were administered by the Bahamas until 1848. After a short period of legislative government (1848–63), they reverted to the administration of Jamaica until 1962, when they became a crown colony. In 1871 the British grouped St. Kitts, Nevis, Barbuda, Anguilla, Antigua, Montserrat, the British Virgin Islands, and Dominica into the Leeward Islands Federation. Throughout the nineteenth century, the British attempted to govern St. Lucia, St. Vincent, the Grenadines, Grenada, and Barbados under a single Windward Islands administration. Although this entity nominally existed until 1958, it was largely ineffective.

Emancipation of the slaves placed great strains on the representation system. Designed originally for colonies of British settlers, the assemblies no longer represented the majority of citizens but merely a small minority of the oligarchy. Sometimes these oligarchies were too small to provide the necessary administrative apparatus, which explains the shifting nature of colonial government in some of the smaller islands and the constant quest of the British government to reduce administrative costs. The power of the purse, once astutely wielded by the planter class, declined along with the value of the export economy, denying to the assemblies their former intimidating power over governors. The British government had always been uneasy about the colonial representative assemblies, especially given the increasing number of non-Europeans in the population. In Jamaica, just before the collapse of the system in 1865, the assembly had 49 members representing 28 constituencies elected by 1,457 voters. Only 1,903 registered voters existed in a population of 400,000—nearly half of whom were adult males.

In Jamaica the Morant Bay Rebellion of October 1865 brought about the end of the old representative assemblies. The "rebellion" was really a protest of rural black peasants in the southeastern parish of St. Thomas. The conflict had unmistakable racial and religious overtones, pitting George William Gordon and Paul Bogle, who were black Baptists, against the *custos* (senior vestryman), a German immigrant named Baron Maximilian von Ketelholdt; the rector of the established church, the Reverend S.H. Cooke; and the governor of the island, Edward John Eyre, a hostile incompetent with limited intelligence but long service in minor colonial posts. The original demonstrators were protesting what they believed to be unjust arrests at the courthouse in Morant Bay when, failing to obey an order to disperse, they were fired on by the militia, and seven protesters were killed. The crowd then rioted, burning the courthouse and killing fourteen vestrymen, one of whom was black. Bogle and Gordon, arrested in Kingston, were tried by court-martial in Morant Bay and hanged. (In 1965 the Jamaican government—an independent and representative entity—declared the two to be its first "national heroes.") Altogether, Governor Eyre ordered nearly 500 peasants executed, 600 brutally flogged, and 1,000 houses burned by the troops and by the Maroons, descendants of former runaway slaves with whom the government had a legal treaty. In December 1865 the House of Assembly abolished itself, making way for crown colony government. The act was the final gesture of the old planter oligarchy, symbolizing that it did not wish to share political power in a democratic way with the new groups.

Crown colony rule was soon established in other colonies. In the constitutional reorganization of the late nineteenth century, only Barbados managed to retain its representative assembly. Jamaica and the Windward Islands joined Trinidad as colonies fully administered by the crown, while the Leeward Islands experimented with a federal system. With periodic adjustments, crown colony government endured until the middle of the twentieth century. Despite its paternalistic rhetoric, and many practical reforms in the social, educational, and economic arenas, it retarded political development in the West Indies by consistently denying the legitimacy of political organizations while elevating the opinions of selected individuals. By so doing, it narrowed rather than broadened the social base of political power.

The limited political opportunities offered by service in the various municipal councils and parish vestries emphasized the inadequacies of the system of appointed councils in which social considerations overrode merit as the primary basis for selection. Appointed members had no political constituency—the basis on which they were chosen—and therefore no responsibility to the majority of the people. Because there were no elected assemblies to represent the islands' interests, opposition to the crown colony system of government came more often from the local level alone.

Social and Economic Developments, 1800–1960

Education

Before the middle of the nineteenth century, there were three systems of education throughout the British Caribbean. These consisted of education abroad on private initiative; education in the islands in exclusive schools designed for local whites lacking the resources for a foreign education; and education for the academically able free nonwhites.

The wealthy planters generally sent their children abroad, mainly to Britain, but a surprisingly large number went to study in British North America. As early as 1720, Judah Morris, a Jew born in Jamaica, was a lecturer in Hebrew at Harvard College. Alexander Hamilton, born in Nevis in 1755, attended King's College (present-day Columbia University), where his political tracts attracted the attention of George Washington. Other students attended such colleges as the College of William and Mary in Virginia and the College of Philadelphia.

Less wealthy whites attended local schools founded by charitable bequests in the eighteenth century. Such schools included Codrington College and Harrison College in Barbados and Wolmer's, Rusea's, Beckford and Smith's, and Manning's schools in Jamaica.

Slaves and their offspring were given little more than religious instruction. Indeed, in 1797 a law in Barbados made it illegal to teach reading and writing to slaves. In the early nineteenth century, the endowment from the Mico Trust—originally established in 1670 to redeem Christian slaves in the Barbary States of North Africa—opened a series of schools for blacks and free nonwhite pupils throughout the Caribbean and three teacher-training colleges—Mico in Antigua and Jamaica and Codrington in Barbados.

After 1870 there was a minirevolution in public education throughout the Caribbean. This coincided with the establishment of free compulsory public elementary education in Britain and in individual states of the United States. A system of free public primary education and limited secondary education became generally available in every territory, and an organized system of teacher training and examinations was established.

Nevertheless, the main thrust of public education in the nineteenth and early twentieth centuries did not come from the local government but rather from the religious community. Competing Protestant groups—the Anglicans, the Baptists, the Moravians, the Wesleyans, and the Presbyterians—and the Jesuits operated a vast system of elementary and secondary schools. At the end of the nineteenth century, the churches monopolized elementary education in Jamaica and Barbados and ran a majority of the primary schools in Trinidad, Grenada, and Antigua. The most outstanding secondary schools—St. George's College, Kingston College, Jamaica College, Calabar High School, and York Castle High School in Jamaica; Harrison College, Codrington College, Lodge School, and Queen's College in Barbados; and Queen's College, St. Mary's College, and Naparima College in Trinidad and Tobago—as well as the principal grammar schools in the Bahamas, Antigua, St. Kitts, and Grenada owe their origins to the religious denominations. Each territory had a board of education, which supervised both government and religious schools. Government assistance slowly increased until by the middle of the twentieth century the state eventually gained control over all forms of education. Although far from perfect—most colonies still spent more on prisons than on schools—public education fired the ambitions of the urban poor.

Based on the British system—even to the use of British textbooks and examinations—the colonial Caribbean education system was never modified to local circumstances. Nevertheless, it created a cadre of leaders throughout the region whose strong sense of local identity and acute knowledge of British political institutions served the region well in the twentieth century.

Precursors of Independence

Education produced two groups in the British West Indies. The first identified closely with the British system—especially with the Fabian Society of radical thinkers within the British Labour Party—and sought political reforms through conventional parliamentary channels. The most ardent representatives of this group were individuals in the local legislatures, such as Sandy Cox and J.A.G. Smith in Jamaica, T. Albert Marryshow in Grenada, and Andrew Arthur Cipriani in Trinidad and Tobago. Although they did not depend on the masses for political support (because the masses did not yet have the vote), they knew how to draw the masses into political action. They joined the municipal and parish

Barbadian schoolgirls
Courtesy Barbados Board of Tourism

councils in urging a reduction in the privileges of the old planter classes and greater local representation in local affairs. They also advocated legal recognition of the fledgling trade union movement in the Caribbean.

The second group, inspired by the idea of a spiritual return to Africa, was more populist and more independent than the first group. From this group came individuals such as John J. Thomas (an articulate socio-linguist), Claude MacKay, H.S. Williams (founder of the Pan-African Association in London in 1897), George Padmore (the gray eminence of Ghanaian leader Kwame Nkrumah), Richard B. Moore, W.A. Domingo, and Marcus Mosiah Garvey, founder of the United Negro Improvement Association in Jamaica (1914) and Harlem (1916). Thomas, Williams, and Padmore came from Trinidad; MacKay, Garvey, and Domingo, from Jamaica; and Moore, from Barbados.

In addition to these organizers, there were a number of individuals from all the colonies who had served abroad in World War I in the West India Regiment of the British Army. Some of these individuals were of African birth. After the war they were given land and pensions in several West Indian territories, where they formed the nucleus of an early pan-Caribbean movement. Their war experiences left them critical of the British government and British society, and they tended to agitate for political reforms to bring self-government to the Caribbean colonies.

29

The political agitation of these groups laid the groundwork for the generation of politicians who later helped dismantle colonialism in the British Caribbean: Norman W. Manley and William Alexander Bustamante in Jamaica; Robert Bradshaw in St. Kitts and Nevis; Vere Cornwall Bird, Sr., in Antigua and Barbuda; Eric Matthew Gairy in Grenada; Grantley Adams in Barbados; and Tubal Uriah Butler, Albert Gomes, and Eric Williams in Trinidad and Tobago.

The political agitation that periodically enveloped the British Caribbean had roots in its dismal economic situation. The colonial government had placed its faith in sugar and large plantations, but sugar was not doing well economically. Increased productivity in Jamaica, Barbados, and Trinidad could not mask the problems of unstable prices and difficult marketing conditions. Unemployment was rife. Wages on sugar estates were one-quarter to one-half of those paid on Cuban sugar estates during the same period. Many of the smaller islands had abandoned sugar production altogether. Not surprisingly, large numbers of West Indians emigrated for economic reasons to Venezuela, Panama, Costa Rica, Nicaragua, Guatemala, Cuba, Mexico, and the United States. When economic opportunities abroad ended with the Great Depression, the discontent of the returning migrants and frustrated laborers erupted into violence throughout the region in the late 1930s.

Political Independence

Changes in the Social Base of Political Power

Although the riots of the late 1930s brought swift political changes, the conditions that precipitated the explosion had been building slowly for more than half a century. The long period of direct and modified crown colony government after the Morant Bay disturbances produced two political patterns throughout the British Caribbean. The first, to which allusion has already been made, was based on strong executive power in the hands of a governor. Whereas this undoubtedly made administration easier for governors, it had negative effects on the social basis of political power and political development. As Carl Campbell so eloquently put it, "[Crown colony government] sought constantly to increase the area of government and decrease the area of politics." He was, of course, describing the situation in Trinidad in the middle of the nineteenth century, but his portrayal would have been apt for any British colony at the beginning of the twentieth century. Colonial governors were not inhibited by the threat of vetoes of their decisions by the legislatures nor by the kind of obstructionism that had characterized the legislatures before 1865. Colonial governors were responsible only to the secretary of state for the colonies in London. By appointing to the legislature members whose views were compatible with the goals of empire, the governors reduced the range of experience and advice available to them. They were not interested in local opinion and local advice. If they had been, they would not have stifled public opinion by consistently discouraging political organizations and insisting that only individuals could express their views.

Not surprisingly, the dominant views of the local governments were those of the planter classes, especially the older, more established planter classes. Nevertheless, by the end of the nineteenth century, the planter class not only was divided but also was being challenged by the popular classes. This challenge created a series of recurring political crises among the governors, the legislatures, and the Colonial Office in London, leading to some modest reforms in the system in the early twentieth century.

After emancipation, dissolution of the old caste structure of the Caribbean slave society, which was based on the confusing divisions of race, occupation, and status, gave rise to a new, more complex class society. Class divisions within the declining castes generated new groups and produced new tensions. For example, the planter class, which had never been homogeneous, became even more variegated.

In the nineteenth century, a new petit bourgeois class emerged, consisting of merchants, successful estate owners without the ancestry and traditions of the older landed class, members of the professions, and an expanding managerial sector. This class was far more heterogeneous than the class it was gradually displacing in economic and political affairs. In Jamaica a very large number of Jews were given the franchise and participated actively in politics. Remarkably, Jews obtained equality in Jamaica and sat in the House of Assembly long before they secured such privileges in Britain. In Barbados a small number of free nonwhites and Jews moved up, but the resilience of the planter aristocracy inhibited the opening of opportunities found elsewhere. In Trinidad the white elites included those of English, French, Scottish, and Spanish descent, and the religious division along Catholic and Protestant lines was as great as along political and social lines. Although governors might prefer the older planter families, especially those of English ancestry, the new reality was inescapable, and gradually the appointments to high political office reflected the social arrival of these new individuals. They tended to be politically conservative, but theirs was a less rigid conservatism than had prevailed for centuries in the Caribbean.

31

Although the small, predominantly planter and merchant elites retained political control until the 1940s, increasing social and political democratization of the Caribbean societies occurred. This democratization derived from four sources: economic diversification, which opened up economic opportunities; the expanded education system, which produced a new professional class; the dynamic expansion of organized religion; and the rise of labor unions. Although not of equal weight, all these forces contributed to the formation of the strong tradition of democratic government that has characterized the British Caribbean during the twentieth century.

Between 1880 and 1937, expanded economic opportunities helped create a new, broader based middle class throughout the British Caribbean. Much of this middle class was non-European—formerly from the free nonwhite community of the days of slavery, reinforced by the East Indians and other new immigrant groups of the late nineteenth century. Thus, the black and colored middle class in the Caribbean has antecedents going as far back as the white class. The nonwhite middle class expanded significantly during the post-slavery period.

The lower ranks of the civil service had always provided an opening for nonwhite talent because in a typical colony not enough Europeans could be found to fill all vacancies. On some of the more populated islands, such as Jamaica, nonwhites from these islands could staff all low-level civil service slots. However, other islands, such as Trinidad, had labor shortages, thus requiring them to staff their civil service with nonwhites from other parts of the British Caribbean. For example, the police force of Trinidad was composed mainly of immigrants from Barbados, although the senior officers were always European. Bridget Brereton points out that in 1892 only 47 of 506 policemen in Trinidad were local (7.8 percent), compared with 292 from Barbados (57.7 percent) and 137 from the other islands (27 percent).

New exports, such as rice, bananas, limes, cacao, nutmeg, and arrowroot, provided the means for a few people to join the middle economic classes and for their offspring to rise even higher. Rice cultivation, although primarily a peasant activity in Trinidad, also helped propel a number of its black, East Indian, and Chinese producers into the ranks of the middle class. Wealth, of course, was not enough to endow middle-class status, but it often facilitated the upward social mobility of the sons of peasants, who with the requisite education could aspire to middle-class status.

Education was the great social elevator of the British Caribbean masses. Beginning in the middle of the nineteenth century, public education expanded rapidly. A primary-level education that was combined with some knowledge of Spanish was useful in commercial concerns because most of the British Caribbean states conducted much of their commerce with neighboring Spanish-speaking countries. A secondary-level education was helpful in getting into the lower ranks of the bureaucracy and essential for entering the professions. A system of scholarships enabled lower class children with ability to move into secondary schools and into the professions. The number was never large, but the stream was constant, and the competition for scholarships was fierce. Studying for these scholarships was more than an individual effort—it was a family enterprise. Moreover, by the early decades of the twentieth century, this process of academic selection and rigorous preparation for the British examinations—uniform for both British and local students—was controlled by predominantly black schoolteachers, the foundation of the emerging "certificated masses."

As Guyanese political activist and historian Walter Rodney wrote, "The rise of the middle class can only be effectively chronicled and analyzed in relationship to the schools . . . The position of headmaster of a primary school must be viewed as constituting the cornerstone of the black and brown middle class." Eric Williams, a distinguished product of the system, wrote, "If there was a difference between the English public school and its Trinidadian imitation, it was this, that the Trinidad school provided a more thorough preparation for the university than the average English school, partly because the students stayed to the age of twenty rather than eighteen and took a higher examination, partly also because it was not even the cream of the crop, but the top individual from Trinidad who found himself competing with a large number of English students of varying ability." The fact that village primary-school headmasters were also lay preachers and intellectual and quasi-legal arbiters of the community increased their importance both socially and politically.

The churches became important in molding the intellect and the political sophistication of the masses beginning in the nineteenth century. In the 1980s, churches continued to play an important role in the Caribbean. Even more interesting, the churches have managed to be both politically revolutionary and conservative, avant-garde and reactionary, depending both on the issues involved and on the denomination.

Whereas the mainstream churches—mainly Anglican and Roman Catholic—accompanied the expansion of imperialism with the expressed desire of converting "the heathens," their close identity with the established order was a severe handicap to their

33

effective incorporation of the lower orders of society. They were especially ineffective with the Hindus and Muslims from India. As a result, what early religious conversion took place was most effectively accomplished by the so-called nonconformist groups— Baptists, Methodists, Moravians, Presbyterians, and Quakers. These essentially evangelical sects originated in the metropolitan countries and had a mass, or working-class, urban clientele in mind. Their strongest converts were among the poorer classes. In the Caribbean they were faced with a rather anomalous situation: the hostility or indifference of the planters and the established churches and no real working class as in metropolitan countries. They had either to work among the slaves and free nonwhites or to change their clientele. They chose the former course and so came into direct conflict with the local elites. Nonconformist missionaries, white and nonwhite, were some of the unsung heroes in the struggle for the disintegration of the Caribbean slave systems.

The nonconformist churches enjoyed phenomenal success among the nonwhites until the late nineteenth century, but they paid a price. Their practice and their preaching became syncretized with the rival Afro-Caribbean religions, such as Kumina and Myal. When social practice blocked the upward mobility of nonwhite members within the hierarchy of the churches, they flocked to form their own congregations, much as occurred in the United States. Some of these congregations moved into a succession of charismatic religions beginning with the rise of Pocomania in the 1880s, Bedwardism in the early twentieth century, and Rastafarianism (see Glossary) in the 1930s. All of these religions espoused trances, public confessions, dreams, spirit possession, and exotic dancing. The churches provided experience in mass mobilization and grass-roots organization. More important, they provided the psychological support for the black masses and gave them comfort and a self-confidence rare among those of their color, class, and condition. Politicians such as Marcus Garvey successfully tapped this popular religious tradition for support.

Labor Organizations

Political experience emerged directly from the difficult growth of labor organizations throughout the Caribbean. Trade unionization derived from the plethora of mutual aid and benevolent societies that existed from the period of slavery among the Afro-Caribbean population. Not having the vote or a representative in power, the lower classes used these societies for their mutual social and economic assistance. To obtain political leverage, the working and employed classes had only two recourses: the general strike and the riot.

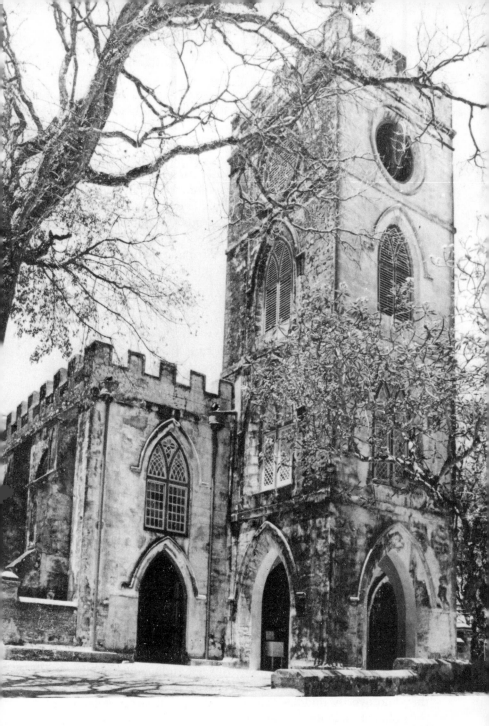

St. John's Parish Church, Barbados, established 1649
Courtesy Barbados Board of Tourism

From time to time some of these strikes were widespread enough to bring the plight of the masses to the attention of the Colonial Office and forced significant changes in the constitutional order. Such was the case with the so-called Water Riots of Trinidad in 1903, which began as middle-class dissatisfaction over the colonial government's attempt to install water meters and reduce waste. The municipal Ratepayers Association, a solidly middle-class organization, appealed to the working and unemployed classes of the city of Port-of-Spain. An excited mob assembled outside the Legislative Council building, resulting in an altercation in which sixteen people were killed and forty-three injured by reckless police shooting, and the Legislative Council building was burned to the ground. After the usual official inquiry, the Colonial Office gradually agreed to the insistent demands of a number of middle- and working-class organizations for the restoration of an elected city council, which was put in place between 1914 and 1918.

Another such riot occurred in Demerara, British Guiana, in 1905. Starting as a localized dispute over wages by some stevedores in Georgetown, it quickly spread to sugarcane field-workers, factory workers, domestics, bakers, and porters, engulfing an ever widening area beyond the city limits. The causes of the disturbance were essentially economic, and the workers—as opposed to their middle-class sympathizers—lacked any organizational structure. Nevertheless, the governor of the colony called out the military forces to put down the disturbances, causing seven deaths and a score of serious injuries. Although the riots failed to achieve their economic goals, for a few days they brought together a great number of the middle and lower classes. The coincidence of these riots throughout the British Caribbean created an impression in Britain that the political administration of the colonies required greater attention— an impression reinforced with each commission report issued thereafter.

Between 1880 and 1920, the British Caribbean witnessed a proliferation of organizations, despite the authorities' marked coolness to them. A number represented middle-class workers, such as teachers, banana growers, coconut growers, cacao farmers, sugarcane farmers, rice farmers, lime growers, and arrowroot growers. Sometimes, as in the case of the Ratepayers Association in Trinidad, they had overtly middle-class political aspirations: a widening of the political franchise to allow more of their members access to political office. However, more and more workers were forming unions and agitating for improvements in their wages and working conditions. Furthermore, as in the case of the 1905 riots, the two sets of organizations (middle-class and working-class) worked in concert—although the martyrs to the cause were singularly from the working and unemployed classes. One reason that the two sets of organizations could work together was their common belief that political reform of the unjust and anachronistic colonial administrative system was the major element needed to achieve their divergent goals. They realized that historically the governors had worked with a small and unrepresentative segment of the old planter class serving their narrow economic ends. To the middle classes and the workers—and to a certain extent the masses of urban unemployed—social and economic justice would be possible only if they secured control of the political machinery, and there were only two ways to gain that control: through persuasion or through force.

To a great degree, this conviction still exists among the populations of the Caribbean. It was given further authenticity when the British Labour Party, especially the Fabian wing of the party, expressed sympathy with this view. But the Fabians did more. They actively sought to guide these fledgling political associations along a path of "responsible reform," thereby hoping to avert revolutionary changes. After World War I, the Fabians grew more influential—as did the British Labour Party—in British politics. The experience of both the Boer War and World War I strengthened the anti-imperialists within Britain and weakened Britain's faith in its ability to rule far-flung colonies of diverse peoples. There was even less enthusiasm for colonial domination when the administrative costs exceeded the economic returns. The result of this ambivalence about empire was a sincere attempt to rule constitutionally and openly. British critics of colonial rule expressed their opinions freely, and even the government reports produced annually on each colony detailed shortcomings of bureaucrats and policies. Nevertheless, talking about West Indian problems was not the same as doing something about them, and by the 1930s, it was clear that British colonial policy was intellectually bankrupt.

Throughout the 1920s and the 1930s, British labor unions had sought to guide and encourage the formation of West Indian affiliates. As a result, unionization was common throughout the region, and many of the unions were formally or informally affiliated with the British Trades Union Congress. However, Fabian tutelage and reformist policies appeared to have failed when workers broke out in spontaneous demonstrations throughout the region, beginning in St. Kitts in 1935 and culminating with Jamaica (and British Guiana) in 1938. A hastily dispatched royal commission, dominated by Fabians and chaired by Lord Moyne (hence called the Moyne Commission), toured the region and reported on the dismal conditions, making strong recommendations for significant political reform. The Moyne Commission noted as causes of the riots increased politicization of workers in the region, deriving from the war experiences of West Indian soldiers, the spread of elementary education, and the influence of industrial labor unrest in the United States. After the riots, the reforms sought by the union of the middle classes and the workers were formalized. In 1940 the British Parliament passed the Colonial Development Welfare Act, the first foreign assistance program legislated specifically for the islands. The British government also extended the franchise to all adults over the age of twenty-one and set about building the apparatus for modified self-government with greater local participation.

Jamaica held its first general election under universal adult suffrage in 1944, and the other territories followed soon thereafter. The alliance of professionals and labor leaders easily captured the state apparatus from the old combination of planters and bureaucrats. Thus, in most colonies a very close bond developed between the political parties and the workers' unions. In Jamaica the Jamaica Labour Party drew its basic support from the Bustamante Industrial Trade Unions. Its rival, the People's National Party, was at first affiliated with the Trades Union Congress; after the purge of the radicals from the party in 1952, the party created the National Workers Union—the popular base that catapulted Michael Manley to political eminence in 1972 (see Historical Setting, ch. 2).

In Barbados the Barbados Labour Party depended in the early days on the mass base of the members of the Barbados Workers Union. Likewise, labor unions formed the catalyst for the successful political parties of Vere Bird, Sr., in Antigua and Barbuda, Robert Bradshaw in St. Kitts and Nevis, and Eric Gairy in Grenada. The notable exception was Eric Williams in Trinidad and Tobago. His People's National Movement, established in 1956, succeeded despite a constant struggle against a sharply divided collection of strong unions (see Historical Setting, ch. 3).

Beginning after World War II and lasting until the late 1960s, a sort of honeymoon existed between the political parties and the labor unions. Expanding domestic economies allowed substantial concessions of benefits to workers, whose real wages increased significantly as unionization flourished.

The West Indies Federation, 1958–62

As part of Britain's decision to push modified self-government, the British authorities encouraged an experiment in confederation. The idea had been discussed in the Colonial Office since the late nineteenth century, but it was brought to new life with a regional conference held at Montego Bay, Jamaica, in 1947. The British were interested in administrative efficiency and centralization. The West Indians talked about political independence. At the conference, a compromise was worked out. The West Indian Meteorological Service (the forerunner of the Caribbean Meteorological Council) and the University of the West Indies, as a College of London University, were set up, and plans were made for the creation of a political federation that would unite the various territories and eventually culminate in the political independence of the region. These new regional organizations joined others already in existence, such as the Caribbean Union of Teachers, established in 1935; the Associated Chambers of Commerce, organized in 1917; and the Caribbean Labour Congress, inaugurated in 1945.

The West Indies Federation was established on January 3, 1958, and consisted of ten island territories: Jamaica, Trinidad and Tobago, Barbados, Grenada, St. Kitts-Nevis-Anguilla, Antigua and Barbuda, St. Lucia, St. Vincent and the Grenadines, Dominica, and Montserrat. The federation began inauspiciously, however, when the leading politicians in Jamaica (Prime Minister Norman Manley and Alexander Bustamante) and in Trinidad and Tobago (Eric Williams) refused to participate in the federal elections. A federative assembly election was held on the ten island territories in 1958. Manley, Williams, and Bustamante did not seek election as assembly members, although the political parties of Manley and Williams did participate in the election. Bustamante was opposed to the idea of federation. Doomed from the start by lukewarm popular support, the federation quickly foundered on the islands' uncompromisingly parochial interests, especially those of the principal participants, Trinidad and Tobago and Jamaica. The former would not accept unrestricted freedom of movement; the latter would not accept a binding customs union. On September 19, 1961, some 54 percent of the Jamaican electorate voted to end their participation. It was the lowest popular vote in any Jamaican election, but the government accepted the decision and initiated the plans to request complete independence for the state. Attempts by Trinidad and Tobago and Barbados to salvage the federation after the withdrawal of Jamaica failed. Trinidad and Tobago thereupon voted to withdraw from the federation, which was formally dissolved in 1962.

In 1962 Jamaica and Trinidad and Tobago became the first British Caribbean countries to achieve independence. Barbados gained its independence in 1966; the Bahamas in 1973; Grenada in 1974; Dominica in 1978; St. Lucia and St. Vincent and the Grenadines in 1979; Antigua and Barbuda in 1981; and St. Kitts and Nevis in 1983. In late 1987, Montserrat, the British Virgin Islands, the Cayman Islands, and the Turks and Caicos Islands remained crown colonies with limited internal self-government. Anguilla, having broken away from St. Kitts and Nevis in 1967, became an associated state (see Glossary) of Britain in 1976. The proliferation of ministates in the British Caribbean will most likely continue. The five remaining British dependencies may yet seek independence. Moreover, it is not inconceivable that one or more multiple-island states, such as St. Kitts and Nevis, St. Vincent and the Grenadines, or even Trinidad and Tobago, might split into separate entities.

Political Systems

Despite generally similar political traditions throughout the region, there are marked differences among the political systems in the various countries. For example, in the Bahamas, Jamaica, and Barbados, a strong two-party political system has developed, and the performance of third parties has been dismal in elections. Trinidad and Tobago has a multiparty system, which, between 1956 and 1986, was dominated by the People's National Movement, first under the leadership of Eric Williams (party leader, 1956–81) and then under George Chambers (party leader, 1981–86). Furthermore, in Trinidad and Tobago, ethnic politics constitutes a significant part of the political equation, as Hindu and Muslim East Indians compete and form coalitions with black Trinidadians and Tobagonians (see Political Dynamics, ch. 3).

In the smaller islands, a number of factors have coincided to make dual-party, democratic politics a difficult achievement. In some cases the populations are simply too small to provide the critical mass of diversity and anonymity. Family and kin relations make secret balloting and privacy elusive. The associations and cooperative organizations that were so important in Jamaica, Barbados, and Trinidad and Tobago did not exist in the smaller societies. As a result, political stability and coherence of the kind found in the larger countries have been difficult to achieve in smaller countries. For example, between 1979 and 1983, the government of Grenada was taken over by a band of self-avowed Marxists led by Maurice Bishop. The People's Revolutionary Government, as it called itself, tried to create a new kind of politics in the British Caribbean—namely, a populist government ruling without the benefit of elections (see Grenada, Government and Politics, ch. 4). The experiment, which went against a long, strong tradition of elections in the Commonwealth Caribbean, ended abruptly in confusion as a result of the military intervention by troops from other

Caribbean states and the United States in October 1983 (see Current Strategic Considerations, ch. 7).

Social and Cultural Characteristics

With the exception of Trinidad and Tobago, where East Indians and Africans are nearly equal in number, the Caribbean states have predominantly African-derived populations. Race, ethnicity, class, and color, however, do not constitute the mutually reinforcing cleavages found elsewhere. No regional political or social organization is based exclusively on race, class, or color. Overt forms of segregation and discrimination do not exist, and crude political appeals to race and color have not been successful. Nevertheless, color consciousness permeates the societies, and various forms of more subtle social discrimination against non-Christians and East Indians, for example, have persisted.

Despite the common official language, common institutions, and common historical experience, each island and state has a distinct set of characteristics. For example, the local inflection of the English spoken in Jamaica varies significantly from that spoken in Barbados or Trinidad and Tobago.

In a region where a constant racial and cultural mixing over centuries has resulted in extreme heterogeneity, any ethnic ideal clashes with the observed reality of everyday life. Nevertheless, ideals exist, often based on European models, and are at variance with the expressed rhetoric of the political majority, which tries to emphasize the African cultural heritage. At all levels of Caribbean societies, tensions exist between state policies and ideals on the one hand and individual beliefs, family, and kin on the other hand. These tensions are exacerbated by the fragile political structures and even more delicate economic foundations on which a viable, cohesive nationalism must be forged among the Commonwealth Caribbean peoples. The most urgent challenges for the new political leaders lie in satisfying the constantly rising expectations amid the reality of constantly shrinking resources.

Perhaps as a result of its heterogeneity, the area is extremely dynamic culturally. There has been a veritable explosion of local talent since World War II. Poets and novelists of international renown include Samuel Selvon, V.S. Naipaul, and Earl Lovelace from Trinidad; Derek Walcott from St. Lucia; George Lamming from Barbados; and Mervyn Morris, Vic Reid, John Hearne, Andrew Salkey, and Roger Mais from Jamaica. In painting and sculpture, the late Edna Manley of Jamaica was universally recognized. Commonwealth Caribbean music in the form of the calypso, reggae, *ska*, and steelband orchestra has captivated listeners around

41

the world. Like the people themselves, art forms in the Caribbean demonstrate an eclectic variety combining elements of European, African, Asian, and indigenous American traditions.

*   *   *

General regional historical background on the islands of the Commonwealth Caribbean may be obtained from Franklin W. Knight's *The Caribbean: The Genesis of a Fragmented Nationalism;* Eric Williams's *From Columbus to Castro;* John H. Parry and Philip M. Sherlock's *A Short History of the West Indies;* and Gordon K. Lewis's *The Growth of the Modern West Indies.* Much useful information also is available in *Baedeker's Caribbean, Including Bermuda, 1987,* as well as in *The Caribbean: Survival, Struggle and Sovereignty.* Individual political histories can be found in Michael Craton's *A History of the Bahamas;* George E. Eaton's *Alexander Bustamante and Modern Jamaica;* Norman Washington Manley's *Norman Washington Manley and the New Jamaica;* Trevor Munroe's *The Politics of Constitutional Decolonization;* George I. Brizan's *Grenada, Island of Conflict;* W. Richard Jacobs and Ian Jacobs's *Grenada: Route to Revolution;* David Lewis's *Reform and Revolution in Grenada, 1950–1981;* and Bridget Brereton's *A History of Modern Trinidad, 1783–1962.* Economic information is available in the annual reports published by the Inter-American Development Bank for the member states, i.e., the Bahamas, Barbados, Jamaica, and Trinidad and Tobago; J.R. Mandle's *Patterns of Caribbean Development;* Ransford W. Palmer's *Problems of Development in Beautiful Countries* and *Caribbean Dependence on the United States Economy;* Anthony Payne and Paul Sutton's *Dependency under Challenge;* and Clive Y. Thomas's *Plantations, Peasants, and State.* Migration information is treated in Robert A. Pastor's *Migration and Development in the Caribbean.* Information about relations with the United States is given in Lester D. Langley's *The United States and the Caribbean in the Twentieth Century.* (For further information and complete citations, see Bibliography.)

Chapter 2. Jamaica

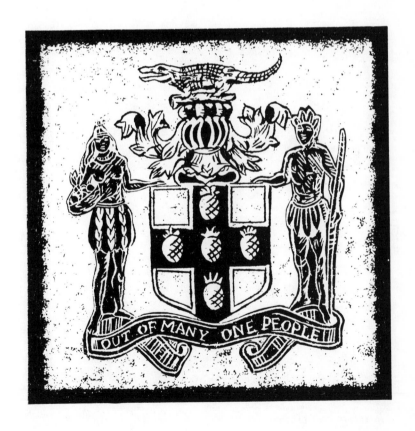

Jamaican coat of arms

Jamaica

Official Name .... Jamaica

Term for Citizens .... Jamaican(s)

Capital .... Kingston

Political Status .... Independent, 1962

Form of Government .... Parliamentary democracy
and constitutional monarchy

Geography
Size .... 10,911 sq. km.
Topography .. Narrow coastal plain; mountainous interior;
limestone plateau covering two-thirds of the country
Climate .. Upland tropical on windward side of mountains,
semiarid on leeward side

Population
Total estimated in 1986 2,304,000
Annual growth rate (in percentage) in 1986 .... 0.9
Life expectancy at birth in 1985 73
Adult literacy rate (in percentage) in late 1970s 85
Language .... English; some patois
Ethnic groups ... Black (76 percent), mulatto (15 percent),
black-East Indian or black-Chinese (4 percent),
East Indian (2 percent), Chinese (1 percent);
remainder white, of European or Middle Eastern descent
Religion .... Protestant (75 percent), Roman Catholic
(8 percent), Rastafarian (5 percent);
remainder Muslim, Jewish, or spiritualist

Economy
Currency; exchange rate .... Jamaican dollar(J$);
J$5.50 = US$1.00
Gross domestic product (GDP) in 1985 .... US$1.7 billion
Per capita GDP in 1985 .... US$940
Distribution of GDP (in percentage) in 1985
Public administration 19
Manufacturing 16
Distributive trade 15

45

Financial services and real estate 12
Agriculture 9
Financial institutions 7
Transportation and communications 7
Mining 5
Construction 5
Electricity and water 1
Other 4

National Security
Armed forces personnel 1,780
Paramilitary personnel 0
Police 5,601

BEFORE THE SPANIARDS occupied Jamaica in the early sixteenth century, the island was inhabited by the Arawak Indians, who called it Xaymaca, meaning "land of springs" or "land of wood and water." Lying on the trade routes between the Old World and the New World, Jamaica served variously for centuries as a way station for Spanish galleons, a market for slaves and goods from many countries, and a prize for the Spaniards, the British, buccaneers, and entrepreneurs. By far the largest of the English-speaking islands in size and population, independent Jamaica has played a leading role within the Commonwealth Caribbean and has been active in international organizations.

Jamaica's story is one of independence that began in the seventeenth century with the Maroons, runaway slaves who resisted the British colonizers by carrying out hit-and-run attacks from the interior. Their 7,000 descendants in the Cockpit Country have symbolized the fervent, sometimes belligerent, love of freedom that is ingrained in the Jamaican people as a result of both their British tutelage and their history of slavery. Independence came quietly, however, without a revolutionary struggle, apparently reflecting the lasting imprint of the British parliamentary legacy on Jamaican society.

Despite its people's respect for the rule of law and the British Westminster system of government, Jamaica's first twenty-five years as an independent state were marked by significant increases in criminal violence and political polarization. The extremely violent 1980 electoral campaign and the boycott by the opposition party of the 1983 local elections strained the island's two-party political system. In 1987 Jamaica was still bitterly divided, both politically and socially. This trend seemed to belie the motto beneath the Jamaican coat of arms, reading "Out of Many, One People." Both kinds of violence on the island—political and criminal—have been attributed among other things to Jamaican cultural and societal traits, the socioeconomic structure of Jamaican politics, worsening economic conditions, narcotics trafficking, and inadequate law enforcement.

Notwithstanding the periodic outbursts of violence around elections and the one-party legislative situation, the nation's well-institutionalized political system remained generally intact during the first quarter-century of independence. Jamaicans have cherished their inherited parliamentary system of government, whose roots extend back to the seventeenth century. Despite the divergent ideologies and intense antipathy of the two principal political parties, they have recognized their common stake in the stability of political life. Jamaica has no history of coups, assassinations of national leaders, or racial confrontation. The two main parties have alternated in power every ten years, and neither has ever retained power beyond its constitutionally mandated term of office. It was widely expected that a changeover would result from the elections constitutionally required in early 1989.

Historical Setting

From May 5, 1494, when Christopher Columbus first set foot on what he described as "the fairest isle that eyes have beheld," to its emergence as an independent state on August 6, 1962, Jamaica passed through three main periods. First, it served for nearly 150 years as a Spanish-held way station for galleons en route to and from the Spanish Main (the mainland of Spanish America). Second, from the mid-1600s until the abolition of slavery in 1834, it was a sugar-producing, slave-worked plantation society. Thereafter, it was a largely agricultural, British colony peopled mainly by black peasants and workers.

The Spanish adventurer Juan de Esquivel settled the island in 1509, calling it Santiago, the name given it by Columbus. In the period of Spanish dominance from 1509 to 1655, the Spaniards exploited the island's precious metals and eradicated the Arawaks, who succumbed to imported diseases and harsh slavery (see The Pre-European Population, ch. 1). An English naval force sent by Oliver Cromwell attacked the island in 1655, forcing the small group of Spanish defenders to capitulate in May of that year (see The European Settlements, ch. 1). Within 3 years, the English had occupied the island, whose population was only about 3,000 (equally divided between the Spaniards and their slaves), but it took them many years to bring the rebellious slaves under their control.

Cromwell increased the island's white population by sending indentured servants and prisoners captured in battles with the Irish and Scots, as well as some common criminals. This practice was continued under Charles II, and the white population was also augmented by immigrants from other Caribbean islands and from the North American mainland, as well as by the English buccaneers. But tropical diseases kept the number of whites well under 10,000 until about 1740.

Although the slave population in the 1670s and 1680s never exceeded about 9,500, by the end of the seventeenth century imports of slaves increased the black population to at least five times the number of whites. Thereafter, Jamaica's blacks did not increase significantly in number until well into the eighteenth century, in part because the slave ships coming from the west coast of Africa preferred to unload at the islands of the Eastern Caribbean (see Glossary). At the beginning of the eighteenth century, the number of slaves in Jamaica did not exceed 45,000, but by 1800 it had increased to over 300,000.

Beginning with the Stuart monarchy's appointment of a civil governor to Jamaica in 1661, political patterns were established that lasted well into the twentieth century. The second governor, Lord Windsor, brought with him in 1662 a proclamation from the king giving Jamaica's nonslave populace the rights of English citizens, including the right to make their own laws. Although he spent only ten weeks in Jamaica, Lord Windsor laid the foundations of a governing system that was to last for two centuries: a crown-appointed governor, an appointed advisory council that doubled as the upper house of the legislature, and a locally elected—but highly unrepresentative—House of Assembly.

England gained formal possession of Jamaica from Spain in 1670 through the Treaty of Madrid. Removing the pressing need for constant defense against Spanish attack, this change served as an incentive to planting. For years, however, the planter-dominated House of Assembly was in continual conflict with the various governors and the Stuart kings; there were also contentious factions within the assembly itself. For much of the 1670s and 1680s, Charles II and James II and the assembly feuded over such matters as the purchase of slaves from ships not run by the royal English trading company. The last Stuart governor, the duke of Albemarle, who was more interested in treasure hunting than in planting, turned the planter oligarchy out of office. After the duke's death in 1688, the planters, who had fled Jamaica to London, succeeded in lobbying James II to order a return to the pre-Albemarle political arrangement, and the revolution that brought William III and Mary to the throne in 1689 confirmed the local control of Jamaican planters belonging to the assembly. This settlement also improved the supply of slaves and resulted in greater protection, including military support, for the planters against foreign competition. This was of particular importance during the Anglo-French War in the Caribbean from 1689 to 1713.

Early in the eighteenth century, the Maroons took a heavy toll on the British troops and local militia sent against them in the interior; their rebellion ended, however, with the signing of peace agreements in 1738. The sugar monoculture and slave-worked plantation society characterized Jamaica throughout the eighteenth century. After the abolition of the slave trade in 1808 and slavery itself in 1834, however, the island's sugar- and slave-based economy faltered (see The Post-Emancipation Societies, ch. 1). The period after 1834 initially was marked by conflict between the plantocracy and elements in the Colonial Office over the extent to which individual freedom should be coupled with political participation for blacks. In 1840 the House of Assembly changed the voting qualifications in a way that enabled a majority of blacks and people of mixed race to vote. But neither the change in the political system nor the abolition of slavery changed the planters' chief interest, which lay in the continued profitability of their estates, and they continued to dominate the elitist assembly. Nevertheless, at the end of the eighteenth century and in the early years of the nineteenth century, the crown began to allow some Jamaicans—mostly local merchants, urban professionals, and artisans—into the appointed council.

In 1846 Jamaican planters, still reeling from the loss of slave labor, suffered a crushing blow when Britain passed the Sugar Duties Act, eliminating Jamaica's traditionally favored status as its primary supplier of sugar. The House of Assembly stumbled from one crisis to another until the collapse of the sugar trade, when racial and religious tensions came to a head during the Morant Bay Rebellion of 1865 (see Political Traditions, ch. 1). Although suppressed ruthlessly, the severe rioting so alarmed the planters that the two-centuries-old House of Assembly voted to abolish itself and asked for the establishment of direct British rule.

In 1866 the new crown colony government (see Glossary) consisted of the Legislative Council, which replaced the House of Assembly, and the executive Privy Council, but the Colonial Office exercised effective power through a presiding British governor. The Legislative Council included a few handpicked prominent Jamaicans for the sake of appearance only. In the late nineteenth century, Britain modified crown colony rule on the island and, after 1884, gradually reintroduced representation and limited self-rule. Britain also reformed the colony's legal structure along the lines of English common law and county courts and established a constabulary force.

The smooth working of the crown colony system was dependent on a good understanding and an identity of interests between the governing officials, who were British, and most of the nonofficial, appointed members of the Legislative Council, who were Jamaicans. The elected members of this body were in a permanent minority and without any influence or administrative power. The unstated alliance—based on shared color, attitudes, and interest—

between the British officials and the Jamaican upper class was reinforced in London, where the West India Committee lobbied for Jamaican interests. Jamaica's white or near-white propertied class continued to hold the dominant position in every respect; the vast majority of the black population remained poor and unenfranchised.

Marcus Mosiah Garvey, a black activist and labor leader, founded one of Jamaica's first political parties in 1929 and a workers association in the early 1930s. The so-called Rastafarian Brethren (commonly called the Rastafarians—see Glossary), which in 1935 hailed Ethiopia's emperor Haile Selassie as God incarnate, owed its origins to the cultivation of self-confidence and black pride promoted by Garvey and his black nationalist movement. Garvey, a controversial figure, had been the target of a four-year investigation by the United States government. He was convicted of mail fraud in 1923 and had served most of a five-year term in an Atlanta penitentiary when he was deported to Jamaica in 1927. Garvey left the colony in 1935 to live in Britain, where he died heavily in debt five years later. He was proclaimed Jamaica's first national hero in the 1960s after Edward Seaga, then a government minister, arranged the return of his remains to Jamaica. In 1987 Jamaica petitioned the United States Congress to pardon Garvey on the basis that the federal charges brought against him were unsubstantiated and unjust.

Dissatisfaction with crown colony rule reached its peak during the period between the world wars, as demands for responsible self-government grew. A growing mulatto middle class with increasingly impressive education, ability, and even property identified with British social and political standards. Nevertheless, Jamaicans, including whites, began to feel offended by a perceived British indifference to their economic difficulties and political opinions. They also resented British monopoly of high positions and the many limitations on their own mobility in the colonial civil service, especially if they were of mixed race.

The rise of nationalism, as distinct from island identification or desire for self-determination, is generally dated to the 1938 labor riots that affected both Jamaica and the islands of the Eastern Caribbean. William Alexander Bustamante, a moneylender in the capital city of Kingston who had formed the Jamaica Trade Workers and Tradesmen Union (JTWTU) three years earlier, captured the imagination of the black masses with his messianic personality, even though he himself was light-skinned, affluent, and aristocratic (see Growth and Structure of the Economy, this ch.). Bustamante emerged from the 1938 strikes and other disturbances as a populist leader and the principal spokesperson for the militant urban working class, and in that year, using the JTWTU as a stepping stone, he founded the Bustamante Industrial Trade Unions (BITU), which inaugurated Jamaica's workers movement.

A distant cousin of Bustamante's, Norman W. Manley, concluded as a result of the 1938 riots that the real basis for national unity in Jamaica lay in the masses. Unlike the union-oriented Bustamante, however, Manley was more interested in access to control over state power and political rights for the masses. On September 18, 1938, he inaugurated the People's National Party (PNP), which had begun as a nationalist movement supported by the mixed-race middle class and the liberal sector of the business community with leaders who were highly educated members of the upper-middle class. The 1938 riots spurred the PNP to unionize labor, although it would be several years before the PNP formed major labor unions. The party concentrated its earliest efforts on establishing a network both in urban areas and in banana-growing rural parishes, later working on building support among small farmers and in areas of bauxite mining.

The PNP adopted a socialist ideology in 1940 and later joined the Socialist International, allying itself formally with the social democratic parties of Western Europe. Guided by socialist principles, Manley was nonetheless not a doctrinaire socialist. The ideology of the PNP during the 1940s was similar to that of the British Labour Party concerning state control of the factors of production, equality of opportunity, and a welfare state. A left-wing element in the PNP, however, held more orthodox Marxist views and worked for the internationalization of the trade union movement through the Caribbean Labour Congress, inaugurated in 1945. In those formative years of Jamaican political and union activity, relations between Manley and Bustamante were cordial. Manley defended Bustamante in court against charges brought by the British for his labor activism in the 1938 riots and looked after the BITU during Bustamante's imprisonment.

Bustamante had political ambitions of his own, however. In 1942, while still incarcerated, he founded a political party to rival the PNP, called the Jamaica Labour Party (JLP). The new party, whose leaders were of a lower class than those of the PNP, was supported by conservative businessmen and 60,000 dues-paying BITU members, who encompassed dock and sugar plantation workers and other unskilled urban laborers. On his release in 1943, Bustamante began building up the JLP. Meanwhile, several PNP leaders organized the leftist-oriented Trade Union Congress (TUC). Thus, from an early stage in modern Jamaica, unionized labor was an integral part of organized political life.

For the next quarter-century, Bustamante and Manley competed for center stage in Jamaican political affairs, the former espousing the cause of the "barefoot man" and the latter the cause of "democratic socialism," a loosely defined political and economic theory aimed at achieving a classless system of government. Jamaica's two founding fathers projected quite different popular images. Bustamante, lacking even a high school diploma, was an autocratic, charismatic, and highly adept politician; Manley was an athletic, Oxford-trained lawyer, Rhodes scholar, humanist, and liberal intellectual. Although considerably more reserved than Bustamante, Manley was well liked and widely respected. He was also a visionary nationalist who became the driving force behind the crown colony's quest for independence.

Following the 1935–38 disturbances in the West Indies, London sent the Moyne Commission to study conditions in the British Caribbean territories. Its findings led in the early 1940s to better wages and a new constitution in Jamaica (see Labor Organizations, ch. 1). Issued on November 20, 1944, the new constitution modified the crown colony system and inaugurated limited self-government based on the Westminster model and universal adult suffrage. It also embodied the island's principles of ministerial responsibility and the rule of law. Elections were held in 1944, but only 31 percent of the population participated. The JLP—helped by its promises to create jobs, its practice of dispensing public funds in pro-JLP parishes, and the PNP's relatively radical platform—won an 18-percent majority of the votes over the PNP, as well as 22 seats in the newly created 32-member House of Representatives. Five percent of the vote went to the PNP, and another 5 percent went to short-lived parties. In 1945 Bustamante took office as Jamaica's first chief minister (the preindependence title for head of government).

Under the new constitution, the British governor—assisted by the six-member Privy Council and ten-member Executive Council—remained responsible solely to the crown. The Legislative Council became the upper house, or Senate, of the bicameral Parliament. Members of the House of Representatives were elected by adult suffrage from single-member electoral districts called constituencies. Despite these changes, ultimate power remained concentrated in the hands of the governor and other high officials.

After World War II, Jamaica began a relatively long transition to full political independence. Jamaicans preferred British culture over United States culture, but they had a love-hate relationship with the British and resented British domination, racism, and the dictatorial Colonial Office. Britain gradually granted the colony more self-government under periodic constitutional changes. Jamaica's political patterns and governmental structure were shaped during two decades of what was called "constitutional decolonization," the period between 1944 and independence in 1962.

Having seen how little popular appeal the PNP's 1944 campaign position had, the party shifted toward the center in 1949 and remained there until 1974. The PNP actually won a 0.8-percent majority of the votes over the JLP in the 1949 election, although the JLP won a majority of the seats in the House of Representatives. In the 1950s, the PNP and JLP became increasingly similar in their sociological composition and ideological outlook. During the cold war years, socialism became an explosive domestic issue. The JLP exploited it among property owners and churchgoers, attracting more middle-class support. As a result, PNP leaders diluted their socialist rhetoric, and in 1952 the PNP moderated its image by expelling four prominent leftists who had controlled the TUC. The PNP then formed the more conservative National Workers Union (NWU). Henceforth, PNP socialism meant little more than national planning within a framework of private property and foreign capital. The PNP retained, however, a basic commitment to socialist precepts, such as public control of resources and a more equitable distribution of income. Manley's PNP came to power for the first time after winning the 1955 elections with an 11-percent majority over the JLP and 50.5 percent of the popular vote.

Amendments to the constitution that took effect in May 1953 reconstituted the Executive Council and provided for eight ministers to be selected from among members of the House of Representatives. The first ministries were subsequently established. These amendments also enlarged the limited powers of the House of Representatives and made elected members of the governor's Executive Council responsible to the Jamaican Parliament. Manley, elected chief minister, accelerated the process of decolonization during his able stewardship beginning in January 1955. Further progress toward self-government was achieved under constitutional amendments in 1955 and 1956.

Assured by British declarations that independence would be granted to a collective West Indian state rather than to individual colonies, Manley supported Jamaica's joining nine other British territories in the West Indies Federation, established on January 3, 1958 (see The West Indies Federation, 1958–62, ch. 1). Manley became Jamaica's first premier after the PNP again won a decisive victory in the general election in July 1959, securing thirty of forty-five seats in the House of Representatives.

Membership in the federation remained an issue in Jamaican politics. Bustamante, reversing his previously supportive position on the issue, warned of the financial implications of membership—Jamaica was responsible for a disproportionately large share (43 percent) of the federation's financing—and an inequity in Jamaica's proportional representation in the federation's House of Assembly. Manley's PNP favored staying in the federation, but he agreed to hold a referendum in September 1961 to decide on the issue. When 54 percent of the electorate voted to withdraw, Jamaica left the federation, which dissolved in 1962 after Trinidad and Tobago also pulled out. Manley believed that the rejection of his profederation policy in the 1961 referendum called for a renewed mandate from the electorate, but the JLP won the election of early 1962 by a fraction. Bustamante assumed the premiership that April, and Manley spent his remaining few years in politics as leader of the opposition.

Jamaica received its independence on August 6, 1962. The new nation retained, however, its membership in the Commonwealth of Nations and adopted a Westminster-style parliamentary system (see Appendix B). Bustamante, at age seventy-eight, became the new nation's first prime minister and also assumed responsibility for the new ministries of defense and foreign affairs. Jamaicans welcomed independence, but they had already spent their nationalistic passion over the emotional issue of federation. The general feeling was that independence would not make much difference in their lives.

Geography

Jamaica lies 145 kilometers south of Cuba and 160 kilometers west of Haiti (see fig. 1). Its capital city, Kingston, is about 920 kilometers southeast of Miami. At its greatest extent, Jamaica is 235 kilometers long, and it varies between 35 and 82 kilometers wide. Having an area of 10,911 square kilometers, Jamaica is the largest island of the Commonwealth Caribbean and the third largest of the Greater Antilles, after Cuba and Hispaniola (the island containing Haiti and the Dominican Republic). Jamaican territory also includes a number of cays (see Glossary). A cluster of cays is above, with the Pedro Banks, an area of shallow seas lying southwest of Jamaica that extend generally east to west for over 160 kilometers. To the southeast of Jamaica lie the Morant Cays, fifty-one kilometers from Morant Point, the easternmost point of Jamaica.

Jamaica and the other islands of the Antilles evolved from an arc of ancient volcanoes that rose from the sea billions of years ago. During periods of submersion, thick layers of limestone were laid down over the old igneous and metamorphic rock. In many places, the limestone is thousands of feet thick. The country can be divided into three landform regions: the eastern mountains, the central valleys and plateaus, and the coastal plains (see fig. 2).

The highest area is that of the Blue Mountains. These eastern mountains are formed by a central ridge of metamorphic rock running northwest to southeast from which many long spurs jut to the north and south. For a distance of over 3 kilometers, the crest of the ridge exceeds 1,800 meters. The highest point is Blue Mountain Peak at 2,256 meters. The Blue Mountains rise to these elevations from the coastal plain in the space of about sixteen kilometers, thus producing one of the steepest general gradients in the world. In this part of the country, the old metamorphic rock reveals itself through the surrounding limestone.

To the north of the Blue Mountains lies the strongly tilted limestone plateau forming the John Crow Mountains. This range rises to elevations of over 1,000 meters. To the west, in the central part of the country, are two high rolling plateaus: the Dry Harbour Mountains to the north and the Manchester Plateau to the south. Between the two, the land is rugged, and the limestone layers are broken by the older rocks. Streams that rise in the region flow outward and sink soon after reaching the limestone layers.

The limestone plateau covers two-thirds of the country, so that karst formations dominate the island. Karst is formed by the erosion of limestone in solution. Sinkholes, caves and caverns, disappearing streams, hummocky hills, and terra rosa (residual red) soils in the valleys are distinguishing features of a karst landscape; all these are present in Jamaica. To the west of the mountains is the rugged terrain of the Cockpit Country, one of the world's most dramatic examples of karst topography.

The Cockpit Country is pockmarked with steep-sided hollows as much as fifteen meters deep and separated by conical hills and ridges. This area of the country was once known as the "Land of Look Behind," because Spanish horsemen venturing into this region of hostile runaway slaves were said to have ridden two to a mount, one rider facing to the rear to keep a precautionary watch. Where the ridges between sinkholes in the plateau area have dissolved, flat-bottomed basins or valleys have been formed that are filled with terra rosa soils, some of the most productive on the island. The largest basin is the Vale of Clarendon, eighty kilometers long and thirty-two kilometers wide. Queen of Spain's Valley,

Nassau Valley, and Cave Valley were formed by the same process.

The coastline of Jamaica is one of many contrasts. The northeastern shore is severely eroded by the ocean. There are many small inlets in the rugged coastline but no coastal plain of any extent. A narrow strip of plains along the northern coast offers calm seas and white sand beaches. Behind the beaches is a flat raised plain of uplifted coral reef.

The southern coast has small stretches of plains lined by black sand beaches. These are backed by cliffs of limestone where the plateaus end. In many stretches with no coastal plain, the cliffs drop 300 meters straight to the sea. In the southwest, broad plains stretch inland for a number of kilometers. The Black River courses seventy kilometers through the largest of these plains. The swamplands of the Great Morass and the Upper Morass fill much of the plains. The western coastline contains the island's finest beaches, stretching for more than six kilometers along a sandbar at Negril.

Two kinds of climate are found on Jamaica. An upland tropical climate prevails on the windward side of the mountains, whereas a semiarid climate predominates on the leeward side. Warm trade winds from the east and northeast bring rainfall throughout the year. The rainfall is heaviest from May to October and peaks in those two months. The average rainfall is 196 centimeters per year. Rainfall is greatest in the mountain areas facing the north and east. Where the higher elevations of the John Crow Mountains and the Blue Mountains catch the rain from the moisture-laden winds, rainfall exceeds 508 centimeters per year. Since the southwestern half of the island lies in the rain shadow of the mountains, it has a semiarid climate and receives less than 762 millimeters of rainfall annually.

Temperatures are fairly constant throughout the year, averaging 25°C to 30°C in the lowlands and 15°C to 22°C at higher elevations. Temperatures may dip to below 10°C at the peaks of the Blue Mountains. The island receives, in addition to the northeast trade winds, refreshing onshore breezes during the day and cooling offshore breezes at night. These are known on Jamaica as the "Doctor Breeze" and the "Undertaker's Breeze," respectively.

Jamaica lies at the edge of the hurricane track; as a result, the island usually experiences only indirect storm damage. Hurricanes occasionally score direct hits on the islands, however. In 1980, for example, Hurricane Allen destroyed nearly all of Jamaica's banana crop.

Although most of Jamaica's native vegetation has been stripped in order to make room for cultivation, some areas have been left

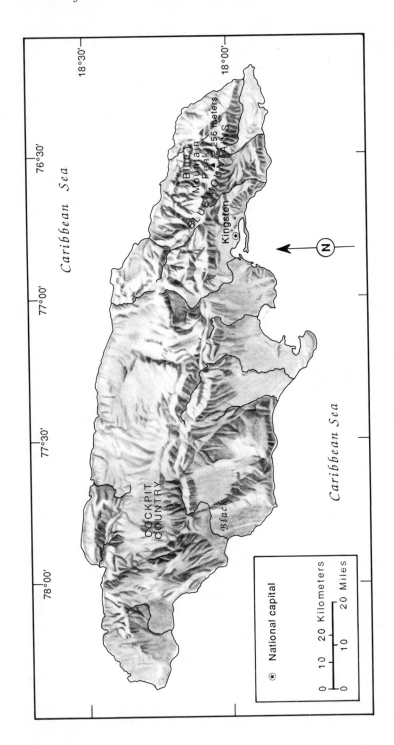

Figure 2. Jamaica. Topography and Drainage

virtually undisturbed since the time of Columbus. Indigenous vegetation can be found along the northern coast from Rio Bueno to Discovery Bay, in the highest parts of the Blue Mountains, and in the heart of the Cockpit Country.

Population

In 1986 Jamaica had an estimated population of 2,304,000 persons, making it the most populous of the English-speaking Caribbean islands. The most recent census, in June 1982, recorded a total population of 2,095,858 persons, an increase of 13.4 percent over the 1970 census count of 1,848,508. Between 1970 and 1982, Jamaica's average annual rate of population growth was 1.1 percent, a relatively low rate in comparison with other developing countries. In 1986 the rate of population growth had dropped further, to 0.9 percent. Jamaica's low rate of population growth reflected gradually declining birth rates and high levels of emigration, the country's most striking demographic features. Nevertheless, significant reductions in mortality rates, resulting from better health care and sanitation, also affected the overall population growth rate, tending to raise it.

Jamaica's annual rate of population growth has been relatively stable since the end of World War I. Between 1881 and 1921, emigration and disease caused the rate of population growth to fall to very low levels. Some 156,000 Jamaicans emigrated during this period, 35 percent of the country's natural increase. Between 1911 and 1921, the rate of growth was only 0.4 percent per year as workers left Jamaica for Costa Rican banana plantations, Cuban sugar estates, and the Panama Canal. The burgeoning industries of the United States and Canada also attracted many Jamaicans during this period. Thousands of Jamaicans, however, returned home when sugar prices fell because of the Great Depression. As a result, from 1921 to 1954 the rate of population growth rose, averaging 1.7 percent per year.

Increased emigration after World War II reduced the rate of population growth once again. Between 1954 and 1970, the rate of growth was only 1.4 percent because large numbers of Jamaicans moved to Britain, the United States, Canada, and elsewhere. This exodus continued unabated during the 1970s and early 1980s, when 276,200 men and women, over 10 percent of the total population, departed. A significant percentage of the emigrants were skilled workers, technicians, doctors, and managers, thus creating a huge drain on the human resources of Jamaican society. The world economic recession of the early 1980s reduced opportunities for migration as a number of countries tightened their immigration laws.

Nevertheless, by the mid-1980s, it was estimated that more than half of all Jamaicans lived outside the island.

In July 1983 the Jamaican Parliament adopted the National Population Policy, which was developed by the Population Policy Task Force under the auspices of the Ministry of Health. The objectives of the policy were to achieve a population not in excess of 3 million by the year 2000; to promote health and increase the life expectancy of the population; to create employment opportunities and reduce unemployment, underemployment, and emigration; to provide access to family-planning services for all Jamaicans and reduce the average number of children per family from four to two, thus achieving replacement fertility levels; to promote balanced rural, urban, and regional development to achieve an optimal spatial distribution of population; and to improve the satisfying of basic needs and the quality of life through improved housing, nutrition, education, and environmental conditions.

Family planning services have been visible, accessible, and active in Jamaica since the 1960s. The success of family planning reduced the country's birth rate by about 35 percent from 1965 to 1985. The Planning Institute of Jamaica, a government agency, estimated that the crude birth rate (the annual number of births per 1,000 population) was 24.3 per 1,000 in 1985. The fertility rate (the average number of children born to a woman during her lifetime) decreased from 5.5 in 1970 to 3.5 by 1983. The government perceived its population goal of 3 million or less by the year 2000 as feasible only if the yearly population growth rate did not exceed 1.6 percent and the replacement fertility rate were two children per woman.

The crude death rate (the annual number of deaths per 1,000 population) was quite low at 6 per 1,000 in 1985. By comparison, the United States had a crude death rate of 9 per 1,000 in the same year. Between 1965 and 1985, Jamaica's crude death rate declined by 44 percent, the result of significant levels of investment in health care delivery systems and improved sanitation facilities during the 1970s. In 1985 life expectancy at birth (the average number of years a newborn infant can expect to live under current mortality levels) was very high at seventy-three years. The infant mortality rate (the annual number of deaths of children younger than 1 year old per 1,000 births) was 20 per 1,000 births during the mid-1980s, and this rate was consistent with the average rate of 23 per 1,000 found in other English-speaking Caribbean islands.

Jamaica, like most of the other Commonwealth Caribbean islands, was densely populated. In 1986 its estimated population density was 209.6 persons per square kilometer. In terms of arable land, the population totaled nearly 1,000 persons per square kilometer, making it one of the most densely populated countries in the world. Since the 1960s, the population has become increasingly urban. In 1960 only 34 percent of the population lived in urban areas, but in the late 1980s more than 50 percent of the population was urban. Kingston and the heavily urbanized parishes of St. Andrew, St. James, and St. Catherine accounted for 48.3 percent of Jamaica's total population in 1983 (see fig. 3).

Jamaica is a country of young people. Roughly 40 percent of the population was under 15 years of age in the late 1980s. The fastest growing age-groups were those ten to thirty-four years of age and those seventy and over. Slower growth for middle-aged groups was generally explained by their greater tendency to emigrate. The 1982 census revealed that the group up to nine years of age was the only one not becoming larger; this suggested both that the country's population was aging and that family planning was working. The 1982 census also revealed that 51 percent of the population was female.

The country's national motto points to the various ethnic groups present on the island. Although a predominantly black nation of West African descent, Jamaica had significant minorities of East Indians, Chinese, Europeans, Syrians, Lebanese, and numerous mixtures thereof in the late 1980s. Approximately 95 percent of all Jamaicans were of partial or total African descent, including 76 percent black, 15 percent mulatto, and 4 percent either black-East Indian or black-Chinese. Nearly 2 percent of the population was East Indian, close to 1 percent Chinese, and the remainder white, of European or Middle Eastern descent. Although racial differences were not as important as class differences, the lightness of one's skin was still an issue, especially since minorities were generally members of the upper classes.

About 75 percent of Jamaica's population was Protestant, and 8 percent was Roman Catholic; various Muslim, Jewish, and spiritualist groups were also present. Rastafarians constituted roughly 5 percent of the population. Religious activities were popular, and religion played a fairly important role in society. The most striking religious trend occurring in Jamaica in the 1980s, as it was throughout the Americas, was the increasing number of charismatic or evangelical Christian groups.

Education

The education system was slow to reach most Jamaicans until the early 1970s. Even after the abolition of slavery, education remained uncommon; early efforts were conducted mostly by

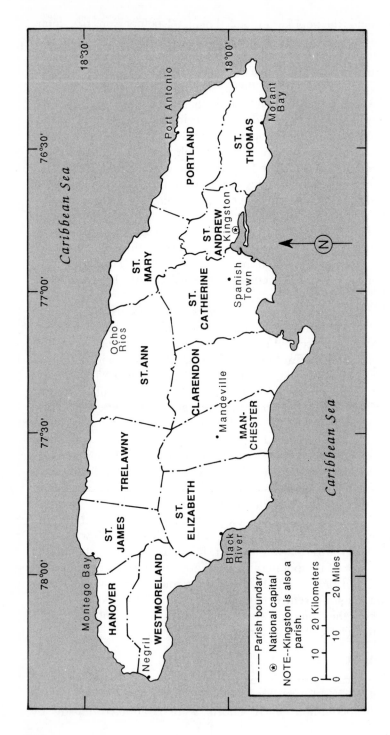

Figure 3. Jamaica. Administrative Divisions, 1987

Christian churches. In the late 1800s, some secondary schools created in Kingston served primarily the light-skinned elite. The limited availability of schools, especially beyond the primary level, and the elitist curriculum intensified class divisions in colonial society. A dual system of education, characterized by government-run primary schools and private secondary schools, effectively barred a large part of the population from attaining more than functional literacy. In addition, much of the content of formal education in Jamaica was largely irrelevant for students unable to attend universities in Britain. In 1943 less than 1 percent of blacks and only 9 percent of the mixed races attended secondary school.

The start of early self-government in 1944 finally cleared the way for increased funding for education. From the establishment of the Ministry of Education in 1953 to independence in 1962, a national education policy was developed that expanded the scope of education and redefined educational priorities. During the 1960s, the major goal of the government in the field of education was the construction of an adequate number of primary schools and fifty junior secondary schools (grades seven, eight, and nine). Until the 1970s, however, the education system continued to provide insufficient opportunities at the postprimary levels because many of the features inherited from the British education system remained.

The PNP government elected in 1972 initiated major changes in the education system. Qualitative and quantitative improvements in education were identified as the key elements of the new government's program during its first term in office (1972–76). The two most important aspects of the program were universally free secondary and college education and a campaign to eliminate illiteracy. Education reforms were intended to redress the social inequalities that the system of secondary education had formerly promoted and to create greater access for all Jamaicans to the preferred government and private sector jobs that typically required a secondary school diploma.

The reforms of secondary education had positive but limited effects. Greater access to education was the main accomplishment of the reform process, but limited funding may also have lowered the quality of education for the increased numbers of students attending secondary schools. Nevertheless, the introduction of universally free secondary education was a major step in removing the institutional barriers confronting poor Jamaicans who were otherwise unable to afford tuition.

After changes in its literacy policies in the early 1970s, the PNP government in 1974 formed the Jamaica Movement for the Advancement of Literacy, which administered adult education programs with the goal of involving 100,000 adults a year. Although in 1987 specific data were lacking, increases in the national literacy rates suggested the program was successful. Literacy rates increased from 16.3 percent in 1871 to 47.2 percent in 1911, 67.9 percent in 1943, and more than 85 percent by the late 1970s.

The education system in Jamaica was quite complex in the 1980s. The public school system was administered principally by the Ministry of Education and regional school boards. Four major levels (preprimary, primary, secondary, and higher education) were divided into a number of different kinds of schools. The preprimary level was made up of infant and basic schools (ages four to six); primary education was provided at primary and "all-age" schools (grades one through six). Secondary schools included "new" secondary schools, comprehensive schools, and technical high schools (grades seven through eleven), as well as trade and vocational institutes and high schools (grades seven through thirteen). The twelfth and thirteenth years of high school were preparatory for university matriculation. The government also administered a school for the handicapped in Kingston.

Although education was free in the public schools and school attendance was compulsory to the age of sixteen, costs for books, uniforms, lunch, and transportation deterred some families from sending their children to school. Public school enrollment ranged from 98 percent at the primary level to 58 percent at the secondary level in the early 1980s. Schools were generally crowded, averaging forty students per class.

There were also some 232 privately run schools in Jamaica, ranging from primary school to college. The total enrollment in private schools was 41,000, or less than 7 percent of total public school enrollment. Most private-school students were enrolled in university preparatory programs. Both public and private schools were characterized by numerous examinations that determined placement and advancement. This testing material was originally British, but by the 1980s the Caribbean Examinations Council was increasingly the author of such tests.

Several colleges and universities served a limited number of Jamaican students. These included the largest campus of the University of the West Indies (UWI); the College of Arts, Science, and Technology (CAST); the College of Agriculture; various teachers colleges and community colleges; and a cultural training center made up of separate schools of dance, drama, art, and music. Located at Mona in the Kingston metropolitan area, the UWI was the most prominent institution of higher learning on the island, offering degree programs in most major fields of study. As a regional

Campus of the University of the West Indies, Mona
Courtesy Inter-American Development Bank

university serving the needs of all the Commonwealth Caribbean islands, the UWI also maintained campuses in Trinidad and Tobago and Barbados. Approximately 5 percent of the Jamaican population participated in university studies, although some students pursued their academic training outside the Caribbean. In 1985 the government announced plans to begin reorganizing higher education, including the eventual merger of CAST and the College of Agriculture into a polytechnical institute or a university.

In the early 1980s, the government reoriented its development strategies for education, emphasizing basic education in grades one to nine and human resources training. The government's plan stressed rehabilitating and upgrading primary and basic education facilities, improving the quality and efficiency of basic education, implementing a full curriculum for grades seven to nine in all-age schools, and establishing an effective in-service training program for teachers. Problems in secondary education were also identified, such as the existence of a complicated, secondary-school system that produced graduates of varying quality and that wasted scarce financial resources.

The goal of developing the human resource potential of the population intended to provide educational opportunities for students to prepare them for the kinds of jobs available in Jamaica. According to Prime Minister Seaga, elected in 1980, a major policy in the area of primary education was to ensure that primary-school graduates achieved functional literacy. Secondary education was restructured to provide students with an education sufficient to meet the requirements of upper secondary school. The government reported in June 1986 that only 9,000 of 82,000 students in lower secondary schools were receiving an acceptable level of education.

At the postsecondary level, the most important initiative of the government was the Human Employment and Resource Training Program (HEART). Announced in 1982, HEART aimed at providing training and employment for unemployed youths finished with school. In 1983 roughly 4,160 persons began job training or entered continuing business education classes. In 1985 six specialized HEART academies provided training in agriculture; hotel, secretarial, and commercial services; postal and telegraph operations; industrial production; and cosmetology. Nearly 1,400 persons completed agricultural or construction trades programs administered by the Ministry of Agriculture and the Ministry of Youth and Community Development. The HEART program called for the eventual construction of 12 academies capable of training 500 youths at a time in various skills. The program's critics charged, however, that funds could be better spent on community colleges.

Education became increasingly politicized in the late 1980s, mostly as a result of the scarcity of resources. Spending on education declined to about 11 percent of government expenditures in the early 1980s, after peaking at nearly 20 percent of the 1973 budget. Issues of increased pay for teachers and renewed tuition expenses at the UWI threatened to make education a national political issue.

Health and Welfare

Most Jamaicans enjoyed a relatively high quality of life in the 1980s, in part the result of health services' having been a government priority for decades. The most distinguishing characteristic of the health care system was the dominant role of the public sector. As early as 1921, government expenditures on health-related activities reached 10 percent of the national budget. In 1966 Jamaica became one of the first countries in the world to establish a national health service. Preventive health services expanded rapidly in the 1970s as the government's real per capita spending on health services increased more than 30 percent. Health expenditures, however, were curtailed sharply in the wake of Jamaica's financial crisis in the early 1980s, resulting in the conversion of rural hospitals into health centers, large layoffs of personnel from the

Ministry of Health, and the reintroduction of hospital fees. In 1985 government health expenditures stood at 2.6 percent of the gross domestic product (GDP—see Glossary), down from 3.5 percent in 1980.

The Ministry of Health formulated, implemented, and administered the health policies of the government. The ministry was directly responsible for public hospitals, health centers, dispensaries, family planning, and public health services. In the early 1980s, the Ministry of Health provided inpatient and outpatient services in 22 general hospitals, 7 specialized hospitals (1 each for maternity, pediatrics, tuberculosis and cardiothoracic surgery, physical rehabilitation, mental disorders, terminal care, and leprosy), a teaching hospital at the UWI, and more than 150 health centers, clinics, and dispensaries. It was difficult to estimate the exact number of health facilities during the mid-1980s, as the ministry was being reorganized.

The country's major public hospitals were Kingston Public Hospital, the University Hospital in Mona, Cornwall Regional Hospital in Montego Bay, and Mandeville Hospital, all run by semiautonomous regional management boards. The total number of beds provided in public hospitals in 1985 was 5,700, roughly 10 percent below the 1980 number of 6,300. Compared with other Commonwealth Caribbean islands, Jamaica had a ratio of hospital beds to population that was relatively low. General surgery and general medicine accounted for nearly 44 percent of available hospital beds. In addition to public hospitals, there were 6 private hospitals with nearly 300 beds in the mid-1980s. Private hospitals were generally small, expensive, service oriented, and affiliated with religious organizations.

At the local level, each parish council employed a medical officer, public health nurses, public health inspectors, and district midwives, and three parishes had community health aides. Three forms of health centers existed. The first offered only a midwife and perhaps two community health aides. The second had a public health nurse and a public health inspector in addition to the midwife and the aides. The third included all the features of the first two as well as a nurse and a medical doctor, who generally referred patients to either other health centers or regional hospitals. Community health aides, positions deemphasized in the 1980s, served to educate the public on nutrition, infant care, family planning, and first aid. Public health nurses conducted clinics on pregnancy, gave vaccinations, and visited schools and homes. Public health inspectors examined the sanitation of food and made certain that slaughterhouses and food shops were clean; they were also responsible for mosquito control, the source of most tropical diseases.

Tropical diseases were greatly reduced in the postwar period through persistent immunization programs and mosquito control. Deaths from yellow fever, malaria, dengue fever, typhoid, pertussis, poliomyelitis, and other childhood diseases were virtually eliminated. No vaccinations were needed for most visitors to the island. Some of the most common diseases reported in 1985 were gastroenteritis (generally related to malnutrition), measles, venereal diseases (mostly gonorrhea), tuberculosis, hepatitis, leptospirosis (transmitted by animals), and a small number of nonlethal cases of malaria, typhoid, and dengue fever. As of mid-1987, there were 18 reported cases of acquired immune deficiency syndrome reported on the island, and 150 persons were reported to have been infected with the virus. The island also suffered from an unusually large number of cases of leprosy. Another serious health problem was mental disorder, especially schizophrenia. More than 50 percent of the island's hospital beds were located on the large grounds of Kingston's Bellevue Hospital. Although bed occupancy rates remained high in the late 1980s, little was being done to alleviate the hospital's growing understaffing problem.

In the mid-1980s, the Ministry of Health employed 5,500 people, but government cutbacks were expected to reduce that number. Although Jamaica housed a regional medical school, the number of doctors was insufficient to meet levels recommended by the Pan American Health Organization (PAHO). With fewer than 500 doctors, the island had a doctor-to-population ratio of only 1 to 5,240, whereas PAHO recommended a ratio of 1 to 910. As with professionals in general, many Jamaican doctors emigrated to earn higher salaries. The island was even more deficient in the number of dentists, who were not trained locally. Slightly more than 100 dentists were registered on the island, but many unlicensed dentists also practiced. The licensed dentist-to-population ratio was 1 to 20,000, far from the 1 to 2,857 ratio PAHO recommended. Dental assistants were trained locally through a dental auxiliary school at CAST. In 1985 Jamaica's nurse-to-population ratio of some 1 to 1,172 was also below the recommended PAHO level of 1 to 769, as was the 1 to 385 ratio of assistant nurses, compared with the recommended 1 to 274. Nevertheless, Jamaica's ratio of nurses still surpassed that in many Latin American and Caribbean countries.

Various professional and regulatory organizations on the island maintained standards, licensed physicians, and educated the public. These included the Medical Council of Jamaica, the Medical

Association of Jamaica, the Dental Health Council, the Nursing Council, the Nurses Association of Jamaica, the Jamaican Association for Mental Health, the Jamaican Red Cross Society, and the Pharmaceutical Society of Jamaica.

Since 1966 the government of Jamaica has offered a wide-ranging, contributory social security service at the national level called the National Insurance Scheme, operated by the Ministry of Social Security. Jamaica Blue Cross, an international, voluntary, nonprofit organization, offered a prepayment health plan and also served to set standards and control costs. Medical research was conducted at the central bacteriology laboratory in Kingston and at the University hospital in Mona. The Caribbean Food and Nutrition Institute, at the UWI, also served regional research purposes. A national blood bank was located in Kingston.

Economy

Jamaica is a middle-income, oil-importing country that attempted diverse economic development strategies during the 1970s and 1980s. Jamaica had the third largest GDP of the Commonwealth Caribbean, behind only Trinidad and Tobago, an oil exporter, and the Bahamas. The island's GDP for 1985 was US$1.7 billion, or US$940 per capita. The major sectors of the economy were bauxite (see Glossary) and alumina (see Glossary), tourism, manufacturing, and agriculture. Bauxite and alumina, in particular, set the pace of Jamaica's postwar economic growth through new investment and foreign exchange earnings. Bauxite production declined rapidly in Jamaica in the 1980s, however, because of the prolonged recession in the world aluminum industry, global oversupply, and the departure of multinational producers. Tourism declined in the 1970s but recovered between 1980 and 1986, thus becoming the second most important sector of the economy. Manufacturing, a quite diversified sector, underwent structural changes in the 1980s when production was refocused on exports rather than on the domestic market. Agriculture, the heart of the Jamaican economy for centuries, has been in relative decline since World War II.

The Jamaican economy enjoyed rapid growth rates during the 1950s and 1960s as the bauxite industry boomed. Real GDP growth averaged about 4.5 percent per year during these two decades. Economic growth was sporadic and weak from 1972 to 1986, however. Indeed, the Jamaican economy did not register two consecutive years of significant growth during that period. Between 1973 and 1980, the island experienced seven consecutive years of negative growth. The economic downturn in the 1970s, precipitated by the oil crisis of 1972–73, demonstrated the highly mobile nature of both labor and capital in Jamaica, as skilled labor and investment capital left the island. The democratic socialist government of Michael Manley from 1972 to 1980 was popularly blamed for the poor performance during the 1970s (see Political Dynamics, this ch.). Nevertheless, Manley's successor and conservative political opponent, Seaga, was also unable to turn the economy around during his first six years in office. The economy experienced sporadic and unsustained growth in the early 1980s. GDP declined by 4.5 percent in 1985 but rose again in 1986 by more than 2 percent. In the mid-1980s, the Jamaican economy was about where it was in 1980 in terms of real GDP. Negative growth in the 1980s was generally attributed to the acute decline in the world bauxite market.

Most Jamaicans enjoyed a relatively high quality of life when compared with their neighbors. For example, in the early 1980s, Jamaica's physical-quality-of-life index computed by the Overseas Development Council was higher than that of Mexico and Venezuela and equal to that of Trinidad and Tobago. Nevertheless, Jamaica still suffered from severe social problems resulting from the skewed distribution of the country's wealth, often said to be the legacy of colonialism and slavery. For example, in 1960 the top 20 percent of society received 61 percent of the national income; after independence income distribution continued to worsen. Land tenure was also highly inequitable. In 1961, the year before independence, 10 percent of the population owned 64 percent of the land; this pattern continued in the 1970s, despite the implementation of a land reform program. Less than 1 percent of the country's farms covered about 43 percent of the land in 1978. Jamaicans in urban areas had much more access to piped water, sanitary plumbing facilities, and high-quality health care than their rural counterparts. These disparities in income and service were believed to have widened even more as a result of the austere economic policies of the 1980s.

Jamaica was hardly immune from the structural economic problems affecting other developing countries in the era. Beginning in the mid-1970s, inflation was generally double digit, caused primarily by the increase in world oil prices, expansionary fiscal policies, and entrenched labor unions. Chronic unemployment and recession coexisted with high inflation during the 1970s, causing stagflation. Unemployment averaged roughly 25 percent during the 1975–85 period, affecting women and urban youth the most. The country also faced rapid urbanization as economic opportunities in rural areas deteriorated. In 1960 about 34 percent of the island's population was considered urban, but by 1982 that figure had risen to about 48 percent as opportunities in rural areas declined. Like other countries in the Western Hemisphere, Jamaica quickly compiled a large external debt in the 1970s and 1980s; by the end of 1986, it amounted to US$3.5 billion, one of the highest per capita debts in the world.

In the 1980s, Jamaica's economy was generally defined as free enterprise, although major sectors were government controlled. The PNP governments in the 1970s were the most active in increasing state ownership. Although some private companies were purchased, the more usual pattern was to create joint public-private enterprises or to increase government regulation of the private sector, especially of foreign multinationals. In the 1970s, state ownership was largely financed by a levy on bauxite production, introduced in 1974, and by deficit spending.

In 1980 Seaga was elected on a platform of denationalization and deregulation of the economy. In his first six years in office, however, Seaga achieved mixed results. Denationalization did occur in tourism and agriculture, but the role of government actually increased in oil refining and bauxite production after several large firms unexpectedly left the island. As of early 1987, the structural adjustment (see Glossary) of the economy was nearly completed, and increased government divestments were forecast.

Jamaica's economy was rather open. Trade as a percentage of GDP was estimated to be over 50 percent in the 1970s, a percentage believed to be increasing in the 1980s. As part of structural adjustment policies to further open up the economy, the Jamaican dollar was devalued several times in the early 1980s. Although imports fell as a result, the country's overall trade deficit actually increased as prices collapsed for its major primary product exports, bauxite and sugar. The country's trade deficit rose to over US$500 million during 1985. The island's direction of trade changed; a greater share went to the United States and less to the Caribbean Community and Common Market (Caricom), particularly to Jamaica's major trading partner in the community, Trinidad and Tobago (see Appendix C).

Growth and Structure of the Economy

The first European settlers, the Spanish, were primarily interested in extracting precious metals and did not develop or otherwise transform Jamaica. In 1655 the English settled the island and began the slow process of creating an agricultural economy based on slave labor in support of England's Industrial Revolution. During the seventeenth century, the basic patterns and social system of the sugar plantation economy were established in Jamaica (see The

71

Sugar Revolutions and Slavery, ch. 1). Large estates owned by absentee planters were managed by local agents. The slave population increased rapidly during the last quarter of the seventeenth century, and by the end of the century slaves outnumbered white Europeans by at least five to one. Because conditions were extremely harsh under the slave regime and the mortality rate for slaves was high, the slave population expanded through the slave trade from West Africa rather than through natural increase.

During most of the eighteenth century, a single-crop economy based on sugar production for export flourished. In the last quarter of the century, however, the Jamaican sugar economy declined as famines, hurricanes, colonial wars, and wars of independence disrupted trade. By the 1820s, Jamaican sugar had become less competitive with that from high-volume producers such as Cuba, and production subsequently declined. By 1882 sugar output was less than half the level achieved in 1828. A major reason for the decline was the British Parliament's 1807 abolition of the slave trade, under which the transportation of slaves to Jamaica after March 1, 1808, was forbidden; the abolition of the slave trade was followed by the abolition of slavery in 1834 and full emancipation within four years (see The Post-Emancipation Societies, ch. 1). Unable to convert the ex-slaves into a sharecropping tenant class similar to the one established in the post-Civil War South of the United States, planters became increasingly dependent on wage labor and began recruiting workers abroad, primarily from India, China, and Sierra Leone. Many of the former slaves settled in peasant or small farm communities in the interior of the island, the "yam belt," where they engaged in subsistence and some cash-crop farming.

The second half of the nineteenth century was a period of severe economic decline for Jamaica. Low crop prices, droughts, and disease led to serious social unrest, culminating in the Morant Bay Rebellion of 1865 (see Political Traditions, ch. 1). However, renewed British administration after the 1865 rebellion, in the form of crown colony status, resulted in some social and economic progress as well as investment in the physical infrastructure. Agricultural development was the centerpiece of restored British rule in Jamaica. In 1868 the first large-scale irrigation project was launched. In 1895 the Jamaica Agricultural Society was founded to promote more scientific and profitable methods of farming. Also in the 1890s, the Crown Lands Settlement Scheme was introduced, a land reform program of sorts, which allowed small farmers to purchase two hectares or more of land on favorable terms.

Between 1865 and 1930, the character of landholding in Jamaica changed substantially, as sugar declined in importance. As many former plantations went bankrupt, some land was sold to Jamaican peasants under the Crown Lands Settlement Scheme, whereas other cane fields were consolidated by dominant British producers, most notably by the British firm Tate and Lyle. Although the concentration of land and wealth in Jamaica was not as drastic as in the Spanish-speaking Caribbean, by the 1920s the typical sugar plantation on the island had increased to an average of 266 hectares. But, as noted, small-scale agriculture in Jamaica survived the consolidation of land by sugar growers. The number of smallholdings in fact tripled between 1865 and 1930, thus retaining a large portion of the population as peasantry. Most of the expansion in smallholdings took place before 1910, farms averaging between two and twenty hectares.

The rise of the banana trade during the second half of the nineteenth century also changed production and trade patterns on the island. Bananas were first exported in 1867, and banana farming grew rapidly thereafter. By 1890 bananas had replaced sugar as Jamaica's principal export. Production rose from 5 million stems (32 percent of exports) in 1897 to an average of 20 million stems a year in the 1920s and 1930s, or over half of domestic exports. As with sugar, the presence of United States companies, like the well-known United Fruit Company in Jamaica, was a driving force behind renewed agricultural exports. The British also became more interested in Jamaican bananas than in the country's sugar. Expansion of banana production, however, was hampered by serious labor shortages. The rise of the banana economy took place amidst a general exodus of up to 11,000 Jamaicans a year (see Population, this ch.).

The Great Depression caused sugar prices to slump in 1929 and led to the return of many Jamaicans. Economic stagnation, discontent with unemployment, low wages, high prices, and poor living conditions caused social unrest in the 1930s. Uprisings in Jamaica began on the Frome Sugar Estate in the western parish of Westmoreland and quickly spread east to Kingston. Jamaica, in particular, set the pace for the region in its demands for British economic development assistance.

Because of disturbances in Jamaica and the rest of the region, the British in 1938 appointed the Moyne Commission (see Labor Organizations, ch. 1). The resulting Colonial Development Welfare Act of 1940 provided for the expenditure of approximately £1 million a year for twenty years on coordinated development in the British West Indies. Concrete actions, however, were not implemented to deal with Jamaica's massive structural problems.

The expanding relationship that Jamaica entered into with the United States during World War II produced a momentum for change that could not be turned back by the end of the war (see Political Dynamics, this ch.). Familiarity with the early economic progress achieved in Puerto Rico under Operation Bootstrap, renewed emigration to the United States, the lasting impressions of Marcus Garvey, and the publication of the Moyne Commission report led to important modifications in the Jamaican political process and demands for economic development. As was the case throughout the Commonwealth Caribbean in the mid- to late 1930s, social upheaval in Jamaica paved the way for the emergence of strong trade unions and nascent political parties. These changes set the stage for early modernization in the 1940s and 1950s and for limited self-rule, introduced in 1944.

Patterns of Development

An extensive period of postwar growth transformed Jamaica into an increasingly industrial society. This pattern was accelerated with the export of bauxite beginning in the 1950s. The economic structure shifted from a dependence on agriculture that in 1950 accounted for 30.8 percent of GDP to an agricultural contribution of 12.9 percent in 1960 and 6.7 percent in 1970. During the same period, the contribution to GDP of mining increased from less than 1 percent in 1950 to 9.3 percent in 1960 and 12.6 percent in 1970. Manufacturing expanded from 11.3 percent in 1950 to 12.8 percent in 1960 and 15.7 percent in 1970.

Seven consecutive years of negative economic growth were registered from 1973 to 1980 as several external and internal factors changed postwar patterns of economic development. The most important factor was the supply-side shock of quadrupled oil prices. Jamaica was particularly vulnerable in that its economy was relatively oil intensive for a developing country, primarily because the bauxite industry's technology predated the energy crisis. As a result of the crisis, Jamaica's oil import bill increased 172 percent between 1973 and 1974. The economy was simultaneously hurt by the plateau experienced in foreign investment in the bauxite sector in the early 1970s, as the major multinational companies were then operating on the island. Also, both internal and external factors affected the tourist industry. Internal politics, some violence, and the PNP's defiant Third World stance scared away some tourists. PNP politicians, however, blamed the fall in tourist arrivals primarily on biased press coverage in North America and United States attempts at "destabilization."

PNP policies also contributed to negative growth. Unlike other governments in the Caribbean, the PNP in Jamaica was proposing very expansionary fiscal policies during a period of both serious inflation and recession. Government expenditures on badly needed social programs expanded much more rapidly than government revenues, creating chronic budget deficits that increasingly were financed by external loans. By 1980 external debt was as high as 82 percent of GDP, and debt service was over 20 percent of exports. Government budget deficits went from a level equal to 6 percent of GDP in 1974 to a level of 18 percent of GDP in 1980. Chronic deficits were coupled with restrictive import controls, unrealistic exchange rates, and tight monetary policies; the result was a sharp drop in investment and a decline of 18 percent in GDP from 1973 to 1980. The deteriorating economic situation and increasing political violence generated serious capital flight and emigration of skilled labor, thereby creating further long-run obstacles to future growth and development.

Although growth did occur in the 1980s, it was sporadic and unsustained. Real GDP growth was 4 percent in 1981, 0 percent in 1982, 1.8 percent in 1983, 0.4 percent in 1984, negative 4.5 percent in 1985, and an estimated 2 percent in 1986. Despite some growth in the first half of the decade, 1985 GDP was still below 1981 levels in real terms. Furthermore, economic growth did not keep pace with population growth; as a result, per capita GDP, in constant terms, declined 7.5 percent from 1981 to 1985. Observers estimated that real per capita GDP in the mid-1980s was close to preindependence levels. Modest annual growth was expected in the late 1980s.

The economy went through a structural adjustment process with the help of unprecedented funding from the World Bank (see Glossary), the International Monetary Fund (IMF—see Glossary), and the United States Agency for International Development. The adjustment process integrated the local economy more fully with the international economy by reducing tariffs, promoting nontraditional exports, increasing the role of the private sector, and devaluing the Jamaican dollar (J$). Nonetheless, recession in the world economy and the depressed prices for traditional exports prevented significant net increases in foreign investment or exports. Although there was substantial growth in nontraditional exports, such growth was unable to offset the large fallout in traditional exports and production. Unemployment, the greatest social problem, remained stagnant at 25 percent in the mid-1980s.

75

Role of Government

The government's first attempts to intervene in the economy occurred during the early stages of self-government in the form of national, macroeconomic planning that stated only the broadest of economic objectives. The first such government plan was the Ten-Year Plan of Development issued in 1947 and revised in 1951. Industrialization, however, was eventually spurred on more by industrial incentive legislation than by macroeconomic planning.

Legislation during the first two decades after World War II changed the pace of industrialization and the structure of the economy. Generous fiscal incentives—such as tax holidays, accelerated depreciation rates, duty-free importation of raw materials, tariff protection, and subsidized factory space—served to emphasize industry and services over agriculture, particularly manufacturing, mining, and tourism. The manufacturing sector grew as a result of important government acts, such as the Pioneer Industries Law of 1949, the Industrial Incentives Law of 1956, and the Export Industries Law of 1956. Investment in the bauxite and alumina sector was encouraged by the Bauxite and Alumina Act of 1950. The Hotel Aid Law of 1944 provided a similar catalyst to investment in the tourism sector.

During the first decade of independence, government policies generally continued the efforts of the 1950s to lure investment in mining, manufacturing, tourism, and, by the 1960s, banking and insurance. A large number of foreign corporations, mostly from the United States, were established in Jamaica as a result of the "industrialization by invitation" strategy that was based on the Puerto Rican growth model of development.

Government involvement in the economy increased significantly from 1972 to 1980, establishing one of the largest public sectors in the Caribbean. In 1974 Prime Minister Michael Manley declared his government socialist and announced its intention of controlling the "commanding heights of the economy." Although the economy was nominally socialist, its production patterns during the 1970s were actually mixed. Private enterprise dominated in nearly every sector, and the "right to private property" was maintained. Internationally, the government led the call for a New International Economic Order in the world's economic system.

Manley's first term as prime minister (1972–76) was much more populist and nationalist in orientation than his second term. Manley advocated a "third path" development strategy that viewed Jamaica as a nonaligned, independent member of the Third World. This approach rejected both the Puerto Rican and the Cuban models of development and sought to reverse democratically the inequitable distribution of wealth in Jamaica. Policies included the creation of rural health programs, food subsidies, literacy campaigns, free secondary and higher education, a national minimum wage, equal pay for women, sugar cooperatives, and rent and price controls.

Beginning in 1973, the Manley government carried out a small agrarian reform program, Project Land Lease, that sought to alleviate high unemployment by introducing job creation programs and redistributing concentrated landholdings. The reform process included the creation of agricultural cooperatives, including the formation of the Sugar Workers Cooperative Council, an important actor in the country's political economy. Seeking to reduce dependency on foreign investment, the government also nationalized with compensation all of the foreign-owned utility companies (electricity, telephone, and public transportation companies). The government also purchased sugar factories and the foreign-owned Barclays Bank. The new role of government in the economy was financed through deficit spending and a greatly increased levy on bauxite production; the latter move quickly brought the Manley government into conflict with the United States and Canadian aluminum companies.

The bauxite conflict involved Jamaica's abrogation of its agreements with international aluminum companies in 1974. The dispute resulted from Jamaica's decision to impose a new 7.5-percent bauxite levy in order to gain greater national benefits from the industry and offset the increased cost of imported oil. This measure had the broad, and perhaps overwhelming, support of nearly all sectors of Jamaican society. From January 1974 to March 1975, the bauxite levy provided close to J$200 million, increasing bauxite revenues sevenfold in the first fiscal year of the tax (see table 2, Appendix A). The new bauxite levy was the most important and dramatic example of expanded government involvement in the economy.

The Manley government also began negotiating with the aluminum companies over acquisition of a significant equity position in their Jamaican operations (albeit a smaller share than that sought in bauxite production). Between 1974 and 1978, Jamaica and the international companies concluded agreements that gave Jamaica a 51-percent stake in both Kaiser's and Reynolds's local operations, a 6-percent share of Alcoa's, and a 7-percent share of Alcan's. Revere Aluminum and the government could not agree on a price, resulting in Revere's withdrawal from Jamaica. The government also purchased much agricultural land surrounding the bauxite mines. Throughout the proceedings, the government was able to acquire the companies' landholdings at book value.

An important element of Jamaica's bauxite policy during the 1970s was the formation of the eleven-member International Bauxite Association (IBA). Modeled on the Organization of Petroleum Exporting Countries (OPEC), by 1976 the IBA controlled about 70 percent of world bauxite production and 90 percent of world bauxite trade from its Kingston headquarters. The greater availability of bauxite compared with oil, however, and the reluctance of other key members of the IBA to impose taxes equivalent to those of Jamaica reduced the IBA's effectiveness.

Although extremely popular among most social classes in Jamaica, Manley's bauxite levy produced mixed results. In the short run, the policy provided significant revenues for the government's social programs and generated scarce foreign exchange earnings for Jamaica's businessmen; it alienated the foreign companies, however, and encouraged them to develop new resources in Brazil, Australia, and Guinea during the 1970s and 1980s. A long-term decline in new investment in Jamaican bauxite caused a fall in the country's share of world output.

Manley's second term (1976–80) was characterized by protracted attempts to come to terms with the IMF for economic support. As the economy gradually deteriorated and as international reserves dwindled during Manley's first term, the government had been forced to approach the IMF for assistance with balance of payments support. Strapped with an ailing economy, the Jamaican government agreed to an IMF stabilization program a few months before the 1976 election. The IMF agreed to make a loan to Jamaica if the government undertook a large currency devaluation, instituted a wage freeze, and made a greater effort to balance the budget. After the election, however, Manley rejected the IMF recommendations, citing the harsh measures demanded by the fund in return for balance of payments support and arguing that the IMF conditionalities constituted interference in the internal affairs of the country.

The government then produced an austerity plan, the Emergency Production Plan of 1977, that emphasized self-reliance and agricultural development. The plan included provisions for establishing a two-tier exchange system and devaluing the Jamaican dollar. Although the plan did not conform to IMF demands, it laid the groundwork for an eventual reconciliation between Manley and the IMF. In May 1977, IMF negotiators arrived in Jamaica to arrange a two-year Standby Agreement that was to provide Jamaica with a much-needed US$75 million. The IMF suspended the

Standby Agreement in December, however, because Jamaica had failed to meet one of the targets monitored by the IMF on a quarterly basis.

In January 1978, the IMF was once again invited to Jamaica to negotiate a three-year Extended Fund Facility (EFF) in the amount of US$240 million. In order to qualify for the EFF, Jamaica devalued its two-tiered currency by 13.6 percent (basic rate) and by 5.2 percent (special rate). Under the terms of a rigid May 1978 agreement, the government reunified and devalued its currency, agreed to place the currency on a crawling-peg system of regular devaluations during the next year, imposed new taxes on consumer goods, reduced government expenditures, increased charges for government services, lifted price controls, guaranteed profits for private firms, set a ceiling on wage increases, and limited the activities of several state-owned corporations.

The IMF program exacerbated political and social tensions. Although Jamaica generally followed the terms of the agreement, inflation soared, real wages fell, foreign reserves collapsed, and the trade deficit rose, all of which were expected as part of the short-term adjustment to stabilization policies. The decline in living standards caused by the agreement increased unrest, violence, and opposition protests.

Because Jamaica had complied with its policies, the IMF increased its lending to Jamaica in June 1979. The new limits for the EFF were set at US$428 million to cover the costs of severe floods and the increased price of oil, which skyrocketed again during 1979. Despite the new funding, relations between Jamaica and the IMF soured in late 1979 as the economy continued to perform poorly even though the island followed the fund's basic guidelines. Jamaica continued to negotiate with the IMF until March 1980, when Manley broke off negotiations and outlined a new, non-IMF path to economic recovery. In the subsequent election of October 1980, the PNP carried only 41 percent of the vote, an apparent repudiation of Manley's policies of initially seeking IMF support and later imposing severe austerity measures on the population.

The election of Seaga in October 1980 marked the beginning of the second major shift in economic policy since independence. Seaga's JLP was quick to put virtually all of the blame on Manley for the steep economic decline of the previous decade. The Seaga government, a close ally of the newly elected administration of United States president Ronald Reagan, also favored a supply-side approach to economic management. Provided with unprecedented external financing from multilateral and bilateral lending agencies, the Seaga government embarked on a structural adjustment program under the specific guidelines of the IMF and the World Bank.

The Seaga government changed the general outlook of the Jamaican government by the structural adjustment of the economy, stressing private sector initiative and market mechanisms. Determined to reverse the export bias of the manufacturing industry, the government refocused exports on "third country markets" (other than the domestic or Caricom markets), particularly the United States, using foreign exchange export incentives to increase trade. This strategy coincided with the duty-free importation of goods destined to the United States market covered under the Caribbean Basin Initiative (CBI—see Appendix D).

Basing its policies on comparative advantage studies, in the early 1980s the government announced seven priority subsectors where investment and production would be emphasized and foreign exchange would be focused: clothing and sewn products, footwear and leather products, construction materials, food and agroindustry, automotive products, furniture, electronics, and electrical products. Primary emphasis was placed on light or value-added manufacturing that used Jamaica's comparative advantage of cheap labor through sharing production with United States or Asian companies. The new industrial push also entailed a variety of physical infrastructure improvements and projects. For example, the government used World Bank loans to build factory space in export-free zones in Kingston, Montego Bay, and later in Spanish Town, where the bulk of the new export-oriented industries operated. New clothing factories were generally referred to as 807 program (see Glossary) factories, named after the corresponding Tariff Schedules of the United States number that allowed these exports preferential access. Light manufacturing factories were the busiest, and clothing and other sewn products in particular enjoyed the most rapid growth of all priority subsectors.

Structural adjustment policies were also aimed at reducing state ownership in directly productive enterprises, such as hotels, which were divested. Although the JLP government sought similar policies of divestment in oil refining and bauxite mining, the abrupt decisions of large foreign companies to leave Jamaica limited Seaga's flexibility. For example, when the Exxon Corporation decided to sell its Jamaican refinery, the Seaga government felt obliged to buy it so the country could refine oil locally and continue a small reexport program. A similar situation arose in the early to mid-1980s, when most of the major bauxite companies on the island decided to close operations or leave Jamaica, despite the government's proforeign investment stance. In the case of the closing and sale of the

Alpart plant in Clarendon, the government once again bought the enterprise in order to maintain a necessary level of production and exports. In 1987 a new round of divestment of state enterprises was announced, including the National Commercial Bank and branches of the national media. The government decided to retain ownership in utilities, however.

Beyond the outright buying and selling of private enterprises, the structural adjustment also entailed promoting investment, finding new markets for nontraditional products, and improving financing for exporters. The attempt to achieve these economic goals led to important organizational changes in government agencies, most notably the establishment of the Jamaican National Investment Promotion (JNIP). The JNIP's task was to lure more foreign investment to Jamaica while promoting the island's newly developed exports through offices in the Caribbean, North America, Western Europe, and Asia. The high-profile offices were established to act as a one-stop shop for foreign investors, who were often dismayed by Jamaican bureaucracy. Although the JNIP was able to solicit new investment during the 1980s, these gains could not replace the aggregate investment losses represented by the departure of major oil and mining companies.

The government also sought to improve available financing for exporters. In 1981 the government established the Export Development Fund to troubleshoot export problems and strengthen the budget and promotional role of the Jamaica National Export Corporation. In 1986 the government disbanded the Jamaica Export Credit Insurance Company and replaced it with the more sophisticated Jamaican Export-Import Bank, which was expected to give more effective support to exporters.

Privatization was the government's focus in agriculture as well. Several large foreign companies were invited to the island to manage previously government-run activities, especially in the sugar industry. In addition, a special, high-profile government agency, Agro-21, established as part of the prime minister's office, was created in 1983 to develop new agricultural products and to modernize farming methods. Like the JNIP, Agro-21 had mixed success; some subsectors, such as floral exports and inland fisheries, flourished, whereas Agro-21's largest endeavor, the Spring Plains Project, had not proved successful as of 1987.

The Seaga government also pursued more orthodox fiscal and monetary policies in attempts to retain access to external financing under structural adjustment lending. On the fiscal side, the government attempted to reduce budget deficits primarily through public sector layoffs and divestment of enterprises and secondarily through ad hoc sales taxes and a comprehensive tax reform. Further policies included the elimination of food subsidies and other price controls, increased public school fees and a reestablishment of university tuition, and a gradual reduction in quantitative restrictions on imports. Monetary policy was characterized by a tight control of the money supply. Although emphasis was placed on savings to stir investment, local investment was hindered by relatively high interest rates. Despite orthodox policies, deficits remained relatively large until 1986, when national accounts began to improve.

The Seaga government's structural adjustment and economic reform measures were only partially successful by the end of 1986. On the positive side, the virtual completion of the structural adjustment process had increased confidence in the economy. Decreased oil prices and some improvement in the bauxite sector spurred the economy to grow once again in 1986. At the same time, however, it was evident that there would be no easy recovery from the deep recession of the early 1980s. In the late 1980s, debt, unemployment, and unequal distribution of wealth continued to be major economic problems facing Jamaica. As had happened with Manley's policies, Seaga's economic policies were offset by adverse trends in the international economy, especially commodity prices. Seaga also discovered that the opposition political forces and the country's economic legacy represented major constraints on establishing those policies. Neither Manley nor Seaga succeeded in transforming the economic structures of Jamaica to the extent proposed in their rhetoric. Finally, Seaga, too, came into some conflict with the IMF over both the pace and the nature of economic conditionalities as the political tide turned against the JLP in 1986. Although most pressures abated after a January 1987 IMF agreement, the JLP softened its strict orthodoxy of the early 1980s and focused economic policies on the electoral challenge ahead.

National Income and Public Finance

The greatest contributor to national income in 1985 was public administration, accounting for 19 percent of GDP, followed by manufacturing at 16 percent, distributive trade at 15 percent, financial services and real estate at 12 percent, agriculture at 9 percent, and various other goods and services, including tourism, for the balance (see fig. 4). The decline of agriculture and the rise of industry and services marked the Jamaican economy in the 1980s. A large underground economy also persisted. Many self-employed peddlers, locally referred to as "higglers," worked in the large redistributive trade that often fell outside the formal economy and

therefore were not taxed or recorded in official data. Some higglers received merchandise through illicit imports, thus circumvent-
ing official import regulations. More important, there was a large
underground economy based on marijuana growing and trafficking. Some analysts estimated that the underground economy was
equivalent to over half of the official economy.

The fiscal year in Jamaica extends from April 1 through March 31.
As required by the Constitution, the minister of finance and planning submits the annual budget to the House of Representatives,
the final authority on the budget, before the end of the preceding
fiscal year. Budgeted expenditures are divided into a capital account
and a current account. For decades, the surpluses on the current
account were not adequate to finance the envisioned capital expenditures, such as physical and social infrastructure, creating structural budget deficits.

Beginning in the early 1970s, expansionary fiscal policies created
deficits in both current and capital accounts, financed by internal
and external borrowing. Although the fiscal deficit as a percentage of GDP rose from 5 percent in 1972 to 20 percent by 1979,
it had decreased to under 12 percent by 1985 and to under 2 percent by 1986. Total government expenditures in 1985 amounted
to US$823 million, whereas revenues reached only US$583 million, resulting in an overall deficit of US$240 million, or 11.6 per-
cent of GDP. Budget deficits in the 1970s and 1980s were
increasingly financed by external borrowing. Fueled by extensive
foreign borrowing and relatively high interest rates, the national
internal debt rose from 9 percent of GDP in 1972 to 45 percent
in 1979 and exceeded 58 percent of GDP in 1985. By the early
1980s, the economy had spiraled into serious indebtedness, causing total debt servicing to account for 43.6 percent of total government expenditures in 1985. The crisis appeared likely to continue,
as over 65 percent of the debt servicing bill was destined for interest payments alone.

Expenditures

Total government expenditures in 1985 were estimated to have
reached US$823 million, or nearly 50 percent of GDP at current
prices. If debt servicing was excluded from expenditures, they
equaled only 22.5 percent of GDP. Current account expenditures
totaled US$591 million, or 72 percent of total government expen-
ditures; thus, a rather high percentage of the Jamaican budget was
dedicated to current expenditures. The capital account in 1985
amounted to US$232 million, or 28 percent of total expenditures.
More expansionary and politically oriented budgets in the late 1980s

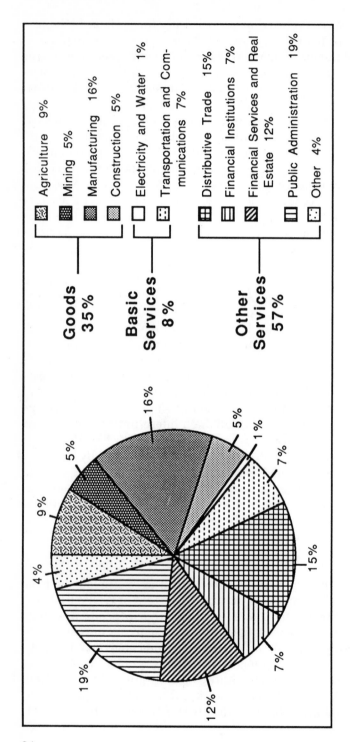

Goods 35%
- Agriculture 9%
- Mining 5%
- Manufacturing 16%
- Construction 5%

Basic Services 8%
- Electricity and Water 1%
- Transportation and Communications 7%

Other Services 57%
- Distributive Trade 15%
- Financial Institutions 7%
- Financial Services and Real Estate 12%
- Public Administration 19%
- Other 4%

Source: Based on information from Jamaica, National Planning Agency, *Economic and Social Survey of Jamaica, 1985*, Kingston, Jamaica, 1986, 1.9.

Figure 4. Jamaica. Distribution of Gross Domestic Product by Sector, 1985

were expected to increase the capital account's share of the budget to over 30 percent.

The government's current and capital accounts were divided into general services, social and community services, economic services, and miscellaneous services. Over 61 percent of current account expenditures were devoted to general services; two-thirds of that total were interest payments, followed by payments for administrative services, police, defense, justice, and prisons. Social and community services (comprising education, health, social security, housing, and water) represented 29.7 percent of current account expenditures, and economic services made up 6.5 percent. The remaining 2.4 percent consisted of miscellaneous services, all of which were grants to local government.

The distribution of capital expenditures changed markedly in the 1980s as compared with previous decades, primarily as a result of the increasingly unmanageable national debt. Fifty percent of all capital expenditures in 1985 fell under general services, of which over 90 percent went to repay the principal of the public debt and other fiscal services. Economic services accounted for 39 percent of capital expenditures. The largest share of economic services was destined for industry and commerce, followed by agriculture, roads, transportation and communications, and natural resource development. Eleven percent of capital expenditures were devoted to social and community services, primarily for school facilities, health centers, water systems, and housing. This pattern of expenditure was in sharp contrast to the situation in the 1960s and 1970s, when lower debt repayment had allowed the Jamaican government to emphasize the development of physical infrastructure.

Revenues

Total revenue in 1985 was US$583 million. The figure was US$240 million short of the expected expenditure, thus creating a budget deficit equal to 29 percent of the total budget and 11.6 percent of GDP. In 1985 about 84 percent of total revenues came from tax revenues, comprising mainly income tax, consumption duties, and stamp duties. In contrast to previous policy, budget deficits were commonly being financed through external financing. In 1985 over 90 percent of the funds used to pay for the budget deficit came from external financing, an unusually high percentage. The United States provided 39 percent of external loans, followed by France, Britain, the Netherlands, Japan, and the Federal Republic of Germany (West Germany). Multilateral lending agencies also financed a significant portion of revenue shortfalls.

In the mid-1980s, the Seaga government enacted a comprehensive tax reform package in which it sought to simplify the reporting system, reduce the number of taxpayers, lessen tax evasion, and lower marginal rates; all of these problems were thought to discourage private sector initiative. The key feature of the revised system, effective January 1, 1986, was complete tax relief for the first US$1,500 of annual income for all taxpayers, which was expected to relieve 150,000 citizens of paying taxes. After the tax-free income level, all were taxed at a flat rate of 33.3 percent; in addition, interest on savings was taxed for the first time. Corporate taxes were also cut to less than 33.3 percent during the second phase of the reform program from a typical top rate of 45 percent. The early results of the reform indicated that annual tax revenues would increase as a result of better collection. Other ad hoc taxes that were proposed to increase government revenues in the mid-1980s frequently caused heated political debate. Most controversial were new taxes for license plates and a proposed annual tax on satellite dishes.

Labor Force and Industrial Relations

The labor force in 1985 consisted of some 1,042,000 persons, or less than half of all Jamaicans. The level of employment stood at 787,700, or about 75 percent of the labor force, allowing for an official unemployment rate of 25 percent. Sixty-one percent of the registered labor force was male. Almost 15 percent of the work force was regarded as part time, defined as those working fewer than thirty-three hours per week; of that total, 60 percent were women. According to the Statistical Institute of Jamaica, the most numerous category of employed persons fell under the title of "own account workers," or self-employed persons, representing nearly 44 percent of the total work force. They were followed by blue-collar workers (25 percent), white-collar workers (18 percent), and service workers (13 percent).

As in other Commonwealth Caribbean nations, unemployment continued to be a pressing economic, social, and political issue. Throughout the first six years of the 1980s, unemployment remained at or above 25 percent despite emigration. Women under 25 years of age made up over 65 percent of those without work, whereas men over 25 experienced only a 9.7-percent unemployment rate. Whereas in United States unemployment statistics only job seekers are considered as members of the labor force, Commonwealth Caribbean countries include nonseekers as part of the labor force as well. If only job seekers had been included in the 1985 unemployment figures, the unemployment rate would have been 13 percent. Because of the prevalence of underemployment and disguised unemployment, however, many economists feel that the Caribbean method provides the most accurate measurement.

Organized labor has played a central role in both the economic and the political development of Jamaica since the earliest days of self-government. By 1985 there were over fifty active trade unions on the island dominated by two large unions, the BITU and the NWU (see Historical Setting, this ch.). The BITU, the predecessor of the Jamaica Labour Party, was established in 1938 and consisted of over 100,000 workers in the 1980s. The NWU, closely affiliated with the PNP, was established in 1952 and reached a membership as high as 170,000 in the mid-1970s. In 1985 over 30 percent of the labor force was unionized, the overwhelming majority belonging to the BITU or the NWU.

Throughout the first half of the 1980s, Jamaica averaged roughly 600 industrial disputes a year, including 80 to 90 annual work stoppages. Unlike the labor disputes of the 1970s, which were characterized by greater wage demands in manufacturing and in mining, strikes in the 1980s were most often over public sector layoffs. Work stoppages numbered 83 in 1985, a fairly typical number, causing the loss of 110,457 man-days. Labor strikes and disputes also occurred as a result of violations of various labor acts, such as the Minimum Wage Act, the Holiday with Pay Act, and the Act of Women Employment. Industrial disputes were generally administered through the Industrial Disputes Tribunal (IDT) of the Ministry of Labour. IDT decisions were binding with the exception of an appeal to the Supreme Court.

Industry

Mining

In spite of its relative decline, during the 1980s mining remained the most important sector of the economy in terms of foreign exchange earnings. Bauxite was by far the most dominant mineral and subsector in the economy. The mining of bauxite had generated over 50 percent of export earnings since the 1960s. Nevertheless, bauxite production was declining, and output in 1985 amounted to 5.7 million tons, less than half of the 1980 level (see table 3, Appendix A). As bauxite exports declined and receipts from tourism increased in the 1980s, it seemed possible that tourism might replace bauxite as the greatest foreign exchange earner.

Although a large foreign exchange earner, bauxite production represented only 5 percent of GDP in 1985 and employed under 1 percent of the labor force. The very capital-intensive nature of the industry made it a controversial subsector because of the high rates of unemployment on the island. Likewise, the large presence of North American aluminum companies extracting the ore was also a prominent issue.

Bauxite was first produced commercially in Jamaica in 1952 by Reynolds Metals. In only six years, Jamaica became the largest producer of bauxite in the world and retained this position until 1971, when it was surpassed by Australia. In the late 1980s, Jamaica ranked third in worldwide production behind Australia and Guinea and accounted for roughly 13 percent of world output of bauxite and 7 percent of alumina. During the first half of the 1980s, Jamaican bauxite production declined drastically as half of the six North American companies in Jamaica ceased production or left the island completely and as world prices for bauxite entered a prolonged depression because of oversupply. The departure of foreign companies encouraged the government to buy into the bauxite industry, and by 1986 the government-run Clarendon Aluminum Plant was the most successful producer on the island.

Jamaica's bauxite reserves are large, exceeding 1.5 billion tons. At the present rate of extraction, reserves could last another 150 years. Jamaica's bauxite is not extremely alumina pure; one ton of Jamaican bauxite contains only about 0.4 ton of alumina. The island's bauxite is easily extracted because of its close proximity to the surface.

Although generally beneficial for the economy, Jamaica's bauxite industry must import large amounts of caustic soda and heavy machinery to mine and export the ore, making the industry highly import intensive. Likewise, the mining of the ore has raised environmental concerns over bauxite by-products discharged in highly visible red lakes.

Jamaica also has significant reserves of several other commercially viable minerals, including limestone, gypsum, silica, and marble (see fig. 5). Limestone covers about 80 percent of the island, making the total estimated reserves of 50 billion tons virtually inexhaustible. Certain limestone reserves are of very high quality. Nevertheless, limestone production has been rather small and extremely dependent on external market forces. Although 83,000 tons of limestone were exported in 1984, none were exported in 1985; estimates for 1986 were placed at close to 100,000 tons.

Gypsum, mined in eastern Jamaica since 1949, was the second most important mineral in the 1980s. Reserves of at least 80-percent purity amounted to over 4 million tons out of total reserves exceeding 40 million tons. Some gypsum was used in the local manufacturing of tiles and cement, but over 90 percent of the mineral and its derivative, anhydrite, were exported unprocessed to the United States and Latin America. Jamaica normally produced roughly 180,000 tons of gypsum a year.

Manufacturing

For a small developing country, Jamaica had quite diversified manufacturing. Sugar, condensed milk, rum, edible oils, carpets, cigarettes, and shoes were some of the more basic manufactured goods. Production also included heavier industrial goods, such as sulfuric acid, detergents, fertilizers, gasoline, petroleum, batteries, and steel. The manufacturing sector accounted for 15.7 percent of GDP in 1985 and employed 127,000 workers, or 12 percent of the labor force.

During the 1980s, the manufacturing sector underwent its first major changes since independence, reflecting the government's structural adjustment policies, which emphasized labor-intensive, export-oriented light manufacturing. As a result, a growing percentage of manufactured goods, particularly nontraditional items, were produced solely for export. Clothing and sewn products, mineral fuels, and miscellaneous manufactured goods experienced the fastest growth rate.

The manufacturing sector was historically linked to agricultural processing until World War II, when general shortages encouraged import substitution industrialization (see Glossary) in such areas as clothing and footwear. From 1950 to 1968, the sector's growth outpaced all other sectors of the economy, expanding an average 7.6 percent annually from 1950 to 1963 and over 10 percent annually from 1963 to 1968. The growth of domestic industries also relied on generous government import protection in the form of quantitative restrictions beginning in the 1960s and an overvalued exchange rate starting in the 1970s. Chemicals, cement, furniture, and metal products were the most important subsectors to emerge as a result of the import substitution policies.

Two general kinds of manufacturing firms operated in Jamaica after World War II. The first kind was generally foreign owned, capital intensive, and export oriented, usually operating under the Export Industries Law. Some of these firms, however, were labor intensive and commonly called "screwdriver" industries because only a small percentage of the value added was performed in Jamaica. The second kind of firm was typically locally owned, generously protected, and domestically oriented. Many of these manufacturers were quite inefficient but did serve to integrate certain subsectors of the national economy.

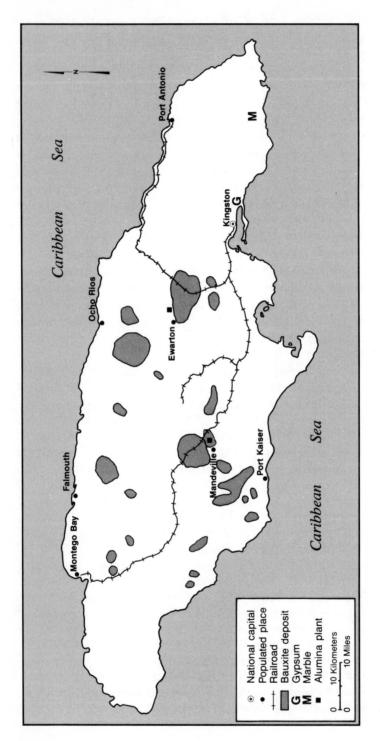

Figure 5. Jamaica. Mining and Related Activities, 1987

In an attempt to reduce previous price distortions, the manufacturing sector undertook structural adjustment reforms from 1982 to 1985. The adjustment measures included numerous currency devaluations, unification of the two-tier exchange rate, relaxation of import licensing, reductions in quantitative restrictions, encouragement of foreign investment, and export promotion to third-country or hard-currency markets. During the structural adjustment process, many less efficient producers reduced output or closed altogether. Factory closings were particularly common in 1982. Declines in investment and output were most frequent in the metal, chemical, and clothing subsectors. In 1985 traditional manufacturing's output was 30 percent less than 1984 levels. At the same time, however, investment in new export-oriented industries increased quickly, helping to keep the sector afloat.

The Seaga government defined seven "priority subsectors" in the early 1980s, emphasizing them in terms of investment, factory space, and financing. Of all the priority subsectors, only the clothing subsector and agro-industrial products had achieved any real success by 1987. In 1985 clothing and processed food exports increased 15 percent and 11 percent, respectively, over 1984 levels. Clothing factories in particular skyrocketed, totaling 148 companies by 1986; 56 new 807 program firms were established from 1981 to 1986. Although roughly 50 percent of these new firms were small and employed fewer than 50 people, 6 companies had over 500 workers. The great majority of production in these priority subsectors was destined for third-country markets, primarily the United States. Third-country markets' share of exports rose from 47 percent to 74 percent between 1983 and 1985. Simultaneously, manufactured exports to Caricom countries decreased by 50 percent.

Regarded as the engine of growth under the structural adjustment policies, manufacturing received renewed government attention in the 1980s. Several government-sponsored agencies or activities were introduced or reorganized to provide technical assistance, financing, export promotion, and marketing assistance. New efforts to improve technical assistance to exporting manufacturers were offered by both the JNIP and the Jamaican Industrial Development Corporation (JIDC). In 1985 the Technical Assistance Fund for Exporters was created to provide further aid in new product development. Institutional support for financing exports was available from the National Development Bank, the Trafalgar Development Bank, the Export Development Fund, and the Jamaican Export-Import Bank, all newly organized or reorganized.

Export promotion and marketing assistance were provided by the Jamaica National Export Corporation and the JNIP.

Construction

In the early 1980s, the construction industry had yet to recover from the short- and long-term decline experienced during the 1970s. Construction had increased during the initial expansion of the bauxite and tourist industries because both required a great deal of physical infrastructure. Construction stagnated in the 1970s, however, because of aggregate declines in investment, downturns in tourism, and the peak in bauxite mining. By the 1980s, the most common construction activities were new factory space, tourist hotels, and residential housing.

Construction recovered in 1982 and 1983, but real production declined in 1984 and 1985 by 5 percent and 14 percent, respectively. Construction's share of GDP dropped from 6.1 percent in 1982 to 5.4 percent in 1985. Total output in 1985 equaled US$171 million; virtually all activity was dedicated to the local market. Only 745 housing starts and 1,867 completions were registered in 1985, down sharply from 1984 levels of 3,114 starts and 3,132 completions. Private sector construction operations decreased by over 50 percent in 1985 alone. A 29-percent increase in Ministry of Construction expenditures helped to stabilize the sector's downturn; the JIDC's national factory-building program was important in this regard.

Many of the materials used in the construction industry were produced locally, although imports of iron, steel, and wood remained significant. Cement production reached 240,000 tons in the mid-1980s. All cement was produced at the Caribbean Cement Plant in Kingston; government shares in the plant were sold to a Norwegian company in 1987. Steel, produced by the Caribbean Steel Company and BRC, Ltd., stood at 18,300 tons by the mid-1980s. The Jamaica Mortgage Bank and the National Housing Trust were the key financial institutions in the construction sector.

Energy

Jamaica has no known oil reserves; as a consequence, the island was about 90-percent dependent on imported oil for energy generation in the late 1980s. Most of Jamaica's oil imports came from Mexico, Venezuela, Trinidad and Tobago, and the Netherlands Antilles. Over 30 percent of imported petroleum imports were destined for the oil-intensive alumina subsector. Oil resources and imports were managed by the state-owned Petroleum Corporation of Jamaica (PCJ). In 1985 the PCJ accounted for 73 percent of the imported petroleum; private bauxite companies directly imported the other 27 percent. Total oil consumption averaged nearly 13 million barrels a year in the 1980s.

The island's only oil refinery, located in Kingston, had a refining capacity of 36,000 barrels per day. Formerly owned by Exxon, the refinery was purchased by the government of Jamaica in 1982 for US$55 million. Subsequent to the sale of the refinery to the government, PetroJam, a subsidiary of the PCJ, managed the plant's operations. The Kingston refinery was considered strategically important to Jamaica because of the country's great dependence on foreign oil and the highly oil-intense nature of the economy. For example, the per capita energy consumption of Jamaica in the early 1980s exceeded that of Brazil and the Republic of Korea (South Korea), mostly as a result of the bauxite industry.

Ethanol, an octane enhancer, was produced for export for the first time in 1985. The first ethanol plant was established in the early 1980s by Tropicana, a subsidiary of a California-based firm. Representing an investment of about US$23 million, the plant was easily the largest investment that had entered Jamaica (or the Caribbean) under the CBI by 1987. Even though the plant had not completed a full year of production in 1985, output still reached approximately 75 million liters of anhydrous ethanol. The ethanol was exported solely to the United States market. In addition, in 1987 the Jamaican government arranged with Belize to process ethanol from sugarcane there.

Demand for electricity grew with the country's aggregate growth. In the mid-1980s, roughly 90 percent of all energy generated was based on petroleum. Hydroelectric power and bagasse (sugarcane residue) fuels made up most of the balance of energy generation. Government energy policy in the 1970s focused on increasing rural access to electricity. Before 1975 only about 10 percent of rural areas had electricity. In 1975 the government of Jamaica, in conjunction with the Inter-American Development Bank, launched the Rural Electrification Program, which improved rural access to electricity. By 1987 general access to electricity was greater than in most developing countries, about 54 percent, and access in urban areas reached close to 100 percent.

Power outages were very common until the mid-1980s, when the sector was upgraded and expanded as part of physical infrastructure improvements in the new industrial strategy. The island's installed capacity increased from 680 megawatts in 1980 to over 700 megawatts by 1983. Government electric policy, implemented by the Ministry of Public Utilities and Transport, focused on efficiency, conservation, and alternative energy sources in the 1980s. Work on developing alternative energy sources focused on hydroelectric power and peat, coal, bagasse, and other fuels.

In 1983 approximately 70 percent of total electricity was generated by the government-owned Jamaica Public Service Company; the remaining 30 percent was produced by private industry in alumina, sugar, and cement factories. Electricity was produced primarily by steam plants (83 percent), although hydroelectric systems (11 percent) and gas/diesel plants (6 percent) were increasingly being used. At least 60 percent of electricity was consumed in the major urban areas of Kingston and Montego Bay. Total commercial energy consumption was equivalent to 11.2 million barrels of oil in 1985. The electrical transmission system included 864 kilometers of 138-kilovolt and 69-kilovolt lines in addition to some 8,000 kilometers of primary distribution lines at a voltage of 24 kilovolts and below. Oil prices and electricity rates became political issues in the 1980s, as oil prices remained above market prices and electricity rates increased very sharply.

Services

Tourism

Tourism was one of the brightest spots of the economy in the 1980s as, depending on bauxite output in a given year, it became the first or second leading foreign exchange earner. Net earnings from tourism nearly doubled in the first six years of the decade, reaching US$437 million in 1986. Tourist arrivals increased 53 percent over the five-year period from 1981 to 1985. Hotel occupancy rates rose from 41.5 percent in 1981 to the 70-percent range in 1986 and early 1987.

Jamaica's appeal to tourists came from its scenic beauty, warm climate, and white sand beaches, as well as the warmth of its people. The island's proximity to the large North American tourist market was another advantage. An expensive government advertisement campaign, beckoning North American tourists to ''come back to Jamaica,'' as well as more cruise ship stopovers spurred tourist development in the early 1980s. Jamaica ranked second only to the Bahamas as the preferred vacation location for North American tourists in the Caribbean. Direct employment in tourist hotels increased from 9,527 in 1980 to 13,619 in 1985. Although this employment represented only a small percentage of the total work force, the industry indirectly created numerous service jobs in restaurants, transportation, entertainment, and handicrafts.

Tourism began in Jamaica in the 1890s, when the United Fruit Company, seeking to use the excess capacity of its ships, encouraged cruises to Jamaica. The construction of tourist hotels on the island soon followed. Tourism, however, did not flourish until after World War II, when accelerated depreciation allowances for investment in that sector helped to triple the number of hotels from 1945 to 1970. Further hotel incentive legislation in 1968 continued to transform the industry, eventually strengthening the role of larger hotels. After a twenty-year period of growth, tourism slumped in the mid-1970s for a variety of reasons, ranging from radical domestic policies to negative press coverage abroad. In the 1980s, the tourist market was recaptured, and it expanded more quickly than the rest of the economy. North American tourists were believed to be traveling more often to the Caribbean as a result of growing terrorism in Western Europe. In addition, Jamaica became particularly attractive as numerous devaluations of the Jamaican dollar made the United States dollar more valuable. The number of West European tourists was also expected to increase in the 1980s, following the decline in value of the United States dollar, to which the Jamaican currency was pegged.

Jamaica recorded 846,716 visitor arrivals in 1985. Stopover visitors numbered 571,713, and cruise ship passengers totaled 261,508. Some 13,495 servicemen also visited the island, many of whom were United States soldiers from the naval base in Guantanamo Bay, Cuba. Ninety percent of all tourists in Jamaica originated in North America, about 75 percent coming from the United States. West Europeans and Latin Americans made up the remaining 10 percent. Canadians and West Europeans tended to stay longer than United States visitors, whose average stay was roughly one week. Although Jamaican citizens received discounted hotel rates, costs remained too high for most Jamaicans.

Jamaican tourism was quite diversified, ranging from campgrounds in the Blue Mountains, to small beach houses in Negril, to large tourist hotels in Montego Bay and Ocho Rios. The country's room capacity exceeded 11,000 rooms, served by over 700 hotels and various other guest houses. Most large hotels were foreign owned, whereas the majority of smaller hotels were locally owned. In the 1980s, the government divested itself of numerous hotels that it had purchased in the 1970s.

Since 1956 the tourist industry has been regulated by the Jamaican Tourist Board (JTB), which greeted tourists, provided courtesy police, trained workers, set standards, and promoted Jamaican tourism both at home and abroad. One of the largest problems that the JTB faced in the 1980s was the continued harassment of tourists. Most harassment stemmed from frequent peddling of goods to tourists, at times incessantly; this peddling most likely reflected the high unemployment rates. Tourists were also approached to purchase drugs, primarily marijuana, colloquially called "ganja."

Another issue for the JTB and tourist industry in the 1980s was whether or not to allow casino gambling, which would probably attract tourists. Largely as a result of strong church lobbying, casino gambling legislation had never been enacted, and it remained doubtful that it ever would be.

Although most Jamaicans were favorable toward tourism, certain sectors of society frowned on it for its perceived negative moral influences. Others doubted its contributions to the economy, given both the large percentage of imported goods used in the industry and the prominent role of foreigners.

Banking, Financial Services, and Currency

In the 1980s, Jamaica had a well-established financial system that was expanding. Since 1962 the number of financial institutions had more than doubled to over forty, including the country's central bank, development banks, commercial banks, trust companies, merchant banks, building societies, insurance companies, people's cooperative banks, finance houses, and credit unions. The government's economic policies in the 1980s favored greater use of monetary factors to influence the economy and tighter credit policies than previously used so as to restrain inflation.

The Bank of Jamaica was established in 1960 as the country's central bank. It was formed to replace the Currency Board, whose lack of authority to control the money supply had prevented the use of monetary policies. The bank issued currency, regulated the banking system, set minimum reserve ratios, adjusted liquid reserve ratios, established discount rates, and generally controlled credit. As part of the government's economic policies in the 1980s, the bank pursued a restrictive credit policy to lower aggregate demand in the economy. The tight credit policy was accomplished through higher reserve and liquidity ratios, which in 1985 required commercial banks to retain 50 percent of their assets in a liquid form. Likewise, the prime lending rate was maintained at high levels, reaching 23 percent in December 1985. Another monetary policy of the bank was the devaluation of the Jamaican dollar to adjust the real rate of exchange to more realistic levels. The bank devalued the Jamaican dollar numerous times in the 1980s, lowering the exchange rate several times over its value in the 1970s. These policies were designed to help reduce the balance of payments deficit by making exports more competitive.

Tourist vendor,
Runaway Bay
Courtesy Cortez Austin, Jr.

Market day,
Brownstown
Courtesy Cortez Austin, Jr.

As a result of the historical reluctance of many commercial banks to make medium- to long-term loans, several government banks were created to finance economic development. The most important such government-sponsored bank was the National Development Bank. Other government banks supplying credit to specific sectors of the economy included the Jamaica Mortgage Bank, the Agriculture Credit Bank, the JIDC, the Small Business Loan Board, and the Workers Savings and Loan Bank. These banks generally offered favorable interest rates and some technical assistance where appropriate.

There were eight commercial banks in Jamaica in 1985, all of which were originally or remained foreign owned. The British Barclays Bank was the first commercial bank on the island, established in 1836 to finance the sugar industry. It was followed by three large Canadian banks, which eventually came under local ownership and were renamed the Bank of Nova Scotia Jamaica, the Royal Bank of Jamaica, and the Bank of Commerce Jamaica. In the 1960s, United States banks such as Citibank and Chase Manhattan Bank also entered the island. Barclays Bank, later named the National Commercial Bank, was bought by the government in the 1970s; the government returned the bank to private hands in 1987, however. In 1985 about 63 percent of all private sector assets in major financial institutions were found in the commercial banks. Throughout the 1980s, commercial banks made three to four times more loans to the private sector than to the public sector. Loans were distributed approximately as follows: 25 percent to manufacturing; 20 percent to construction and land development; 16 percent to agriculture; 12 percent to transportation, storage, and communications; and the balance to various other sectors.

Life insurance companies, building societies, trust companies, and merchant banks were other prominent financial institutions in Jamaica. Their share of private sector assets ranked 19 percent, 7.4 percent, 7 percent, and 4 percent, respectively. In 1985 there were over twenty insurance companies in Jamaica, most of which held assets in large foreign firms. Insurance companies played an important role in building savings for investment in the economy. Building societies, all locally owned, were less numerous than insurance companies and generally attracted smaller savings to finance mortgages. Trust companies lent to commercial banks, provided trustee services, and held time deposits. Merchant banks functioned to underwrite securities, finance external trade, and offer managerial advice to industry. Several new merchant banks were established in the 1980s, including the Falcon Fund and the Jamaican Export-Import Bank.

The Jamaican Stock Exchange, the oldest in the Caribbean, was established in 1969 under the direction of the Bank of Jamaica. Only a small percentage of the country's capital assets were traded on the original exchange, as most companies were either foreign-owned or purely family-run businesses. The number of shares traded grew rapidly in the mid-1980s; these included the shares of some new publicly owned companies. As of early 1987, only thirty-nine companies were listed on the exchange. The exchange's performance in 1985 quadrupled the performance of 1984. In 1985 about 37.6 million shares were traded for US$21.3 million, compared with 9.7 million shares for US$7 million in the preceding year. From 1981 to 1986, the exchange's composite index increased 129 percent, standing at 1,499.87 by the end of 1986. A major cause of the rise was the increasing number of companies that issued public equity shares, rather than relying on commercial banks, to raise capital.

The Jamaican dollar became legal tender when it superseded the Jamaican pound in 1969. Because of tourism, United States, Canadian, and British currencies also circulated, and illegal black markets were common. Many of the tourist hotels listed prices only in United States dollars because of the greater stability of that currency. Also seen in circulation was the Eastern Caribbean dollar, the joint currency used by members of the Organisation of Eastern Caribbean States (OECS—see Glossary) and pegged to the United States dollar at EC$2.70 equals US$1.00. The value of the Jamaican dollar was tied to the British pound sterling until 1973, when it became pegged to the United States dollar. In the process, the Jamaican dollar moved from being the strongest currency in the Commonwealth Caribbean to being one of the weakest. After experiments with various kinds of exchange rates in the 1970s, exchange rates were unified in November 1983. Beginning in 1984, foreign exchange was allocated through a twice-weekly foreign exchange auction system.

Transportation and Communications

Jamaica's physical infrastructure developed primarily in response to the demands of the sugar and bauxite industries. The country's geography, especially its mountainous terrain, directly affected both the development of a transport network and the integration of the economy. Because of the central corridor of mountains, the island's roads were generally divided between north and south, winding along the various ports on the island's coast. As late as the 1880s, it was still cheaper to send goods within Jamaica by sea rather than by land because of the mountains. Eventually, north-south roads were constructed, passing through the scenic heights of the rising interior. Although north-south roads improved islandwide transportation considerably, even in the 1980s a 198-kilometer drive from Montego Bay to Kingston required about 4 hours, compared with an air passage of only 20 minutes.

Jamaica contained over 12,360 kilometers of roads in the mid-1980s; of that total, nearly 40 percent were paved. Roads were originally built on the paths of least resistance, along the coastlines, rivers, and mountains. As such, winding, narrow, and mountainous roadways were common. Road maintenance presented a nagging political and economic problem, as the tropical sun and seasonal rains quickly made the roads deteriorate, making potholes common.

In 1985 there were over 70,400 certified vehicles on the road, of which 60 percent were automobiles, 33 percent trucks or buses, and 7 percent motorcycles. Many vehicles, especially in rural areas, operated unlicensed. Taxis, numerous in most major towns, were cheap and generally offered unmetered rates, frequently negotiated by the driver and passenger.

Bus service was most extensive in Kingston, where in 1985 the buses carried more than 247 million passengers. The government divested itself of bus service ownership to ten franchises in Kingston during the 1980s; this move was widely perceived to have greatly improved efficiency. Nevertheless, private bus companies were criticized for pirating routes, not completing less popular routes, disregarding passenger comfort by overcrowding, and showing reluctance to transport lower fare passengers, such as children and the handicapped. Almost all rural buses and many urban buses were minibuses or minivans. In rural areas, passengers on minibuses entered and exited anywhere along a given route. Buses were typically overcrowded and in need of some repair. In addition, private charter buses were operated for the tourist industry.

Jamaica has the oldest colonial railroad in the world. Established in 1843 by the Jamaican Railway Company, the rail system was subsequently expanded, improved, and eventually sold to the government. The rail system covered 340 kilometers of tracks by the 1980s. The principal route was from Montego Bay to Kingston, passing through the heart of rural Jamaica. In the 1950s and 1960s, bauxite companies built small, unconnected rail lines to their major ports at Discovery Bay, Ocho Rios, Port Antonio, Rocky Point, and Port Kaiser. The rail system was run by the government-owned Jamaica Railway Corporation, which generally operated at a loss in the 1980s.

Even though it is a small country, extensive airfields existed in Jamaica. These included two international airports—the

Norman W. Manley International Airport at Kingston and the Donald Sangster Airport at Montego Bay—and scores of small airfields, both publicly and privately owned. Some small airfields were paved with asphalt or concrete, but most were grass airstrips. In the 1980s, the government was constantly closing clandestine airstrips used in marijuana trafficking, although these were frequently reopened illegally (see Narcotics Crime, this ch.).

Jamaica's vibrant tourist industry accounted for most of the 2.4 million passenger movements recorded in 1985, ranking it seventh in the world for air traffic to and from the United States. Thirty-five thousand aircraft movements were recorded at the Norman W. Manley International Airport compared with 24,300 at the Donald Sangster Airport; the latter, however, received more passengers. Trans Jamaica Airlines and various other private carriers serviced intraisland flights. The government-owned airline, Air Jamaica, was well established and profitable and operated a fleet of Boeing 727 jets servicing ten international routes. Major Caribbean, West European, and North American airlines made stops in Jamaica.

Numerous ports were found around the island; Kingston, the central shipping facility, possessed one of the ten largest natural harbors in the world. The port of Kingston covered over sixteen kilometers of usable waterfront, comprising eleven commercial wharves, deep-water loading facilities, a container terminal, and other modern infrastructure. Virtually all the country's imports entered through Kingston; less than 10 percent of exports left from the port, however. Exports were often shipped from first-class ports such as Falmouth, Port Antonio, Port Morant, Portland Bight, and Savanna-la-Mar as well as second-class ports in Ocho Rios, Montego Bay, Discovery Bay, St. Ann's Bay, Black River, and others. Some ports concentrated on only one or two exports, depending on the region. Over 2,100 ships and vessels made port calls to Jamaica during 1985, representing scores of shipping lines. Jamaica was also affiliated with the regional West Indies Shipping Corporation (see Appendix C). Only two rivers, the Rio Grande and the Black River, were deep and long enough to be viable transport routes. A major goal of sea transport in the 1980s was upgrading port facilities to accommodate growing cruise ship arrivals.

The government-owned Jamaica Telephone Company operated a fully automatic telephone network that included over 143,000 telephones in 1985. Sixty-three percent of all telephones were located in businesses, and 37 percent in residences. Telephone failures were common, and in 1985 over 60,000 consumers were awaiting telephone service. Submarine cables to the United States,

Panama, the Bahamas, and the Cayman Islands provided direct service with those countries or territories. An International Telecommunications Satellite Corporation (INTELSAT) Standard A earth station provided international telephone service, controlled by the government-owned Jamintel. Jamintel, formerly owned by Cable and Wireless, also provided telegraph, telex, and other major telecommunications services. Over 300 telegraph offices were located throughout the island. Mail service was available from over 300 post offices, nearly 500 postal agencies, and several subagencies. Mail service was slow, and former "Royal Mail" trucks were still in operation.

Jamaica's mass media included one television station, two major radio stations, and two daily newspapers. Television was operated by the government-run Jamaica Broadcasting Corporation (JBC), whose programming was often the source of derisive newspaper editorials. The government announced in 1987 that it would privatize the public media, and many Jamaicans were in favor of a nongovernmental television station. Because of the poor television service, wealthier Jamaicans bought satellite dishes.

The country's other major radio station was Radio Jamaica (RJR), which was independent but nevertheless received some government financing. Most listeners tuned into the RJR station on the AM dial, aired twenty-four-hours a day via four regional transmitters. Other small radio stations were also in operation during the 1980s. Radio programs were frequently educational and developmental. Some 750,000 radios were in use islandwide during the 1980s.

The major daily newspaper circulated in Jamaica was the *Daily Gleaner*, an independent newspaper founded by Jewish immigrants in 1834. The daily circulation of the *Daily Gleaner* was 45,000; on Sundays it was 95,000. Although formally independent, the *Daily Gleaner* was generally perceived as conservative and pro-JLP. The other newspaper was the afternoon tabloid, the *Star*.

Agriculture

The decline in agriculture's share of both GDP and the labor force continued in the 1980s. From 1980 to 1985, agriculture as a share of GDP dropped from 8.3 percent to 5.7 percent. Likewise, the percentage of the labor force in agriculture decreased from over 30 percent in the 1970s to 24 percent by 1985. Agriculture's inability to keep pace with other sectors of the economy or population growth forced an increase in food imports. As a result of these trends, Jamaica's total food import bill increased elevenfold from 1960 to 1980. These patterns were likely to persist because fewer younger people were entering farming. For example, in 1985 an estimated 50 percent of the agricultural labor force was over 50 years of age, and 30 percent was over 60 years of age. In the 1980s, government policies sought to revive declining production of traditional export crops and to introduce and promote nontraditional export crops through the commercialization and modernization of the sector.

Land Tenure and Use

Jamaica's total land area covers over 1 million hectares, 25 percent of which were under cultivation in the 1980s. In 1985 about 145,000 hectares, mostly in the coastal plains, were determined to be highly fertile, and 350,000 hectares were suitable for cultivation, but with various limitations. Some 160,000 hectares of agricultural land remained idle or underused. Twenty-four percent of the total land area, some 262,000 hectares, was covered with natural forest of commercial value. By the mid-1980s, Jamaica had roughly 155,000 farms, down considerably from the 1978–79 agriculture census total of 179,700. Most farms were small; over 90 percent of all farms had 4 hectares or fewer. Farms having more than 20 hectares contained 43 percent of total cultivated land, however. According to the agriculture census of 1978–79, the average farm measured 3 hectares, and the island's largest farms, those 200 hectares and over, averaged 784 hectares. Sugarcane still covered over 25 percent of all agricultural land in use, followed by bananas, root crops, coconuts, citrus, and pimento.

Historically, land tenure in Jamaica has been rather inequitable. Most concentration of land in the post-World War II period resulted from urban migration and the purchases of very large tracts of land by incoming bauxite companies. The most important land reform programs in the postwar period were the 1966 Land Development and Utilization Act (also known as the Idle Land Law) and Project Land Lease, introduced in 1973. The 1966 act allowed the government to encourage either the productive use, the sale, or the lease of some 40,000 hectares identified for the program. Project Land Lease attempted a more integrated rural development approach, providing small farmers with land, technical advice, inputs such as fertilizer, and access to credit. The plan helped more than 23,000 farmers cultivate 18,000 hectares. It is estimated that 14 percent of idle land was redistributed through Project Land Lease. Redistribution was still perceived by some as slow, inadequate, and containing marginally arable land, however; still others saw it as highly uneconomical and partisan in political terms. In the 1970s, unrealistically high expectations over land reform, as

103

well as economic frustration, caused some sporadic land seizures and squatting, which found little government support. Redistribution of land in the 1970s emphasized cooperative ownership, a decision that sharply increased the number of cooperatives on the island and made members an important political force.

Government policies toward land tenure and land use shifted in the 1980s in favor of privatization, commercialization, and modernization of agriculture. Sugar cooperatives were dismantled, some government holdings were divested, and foreign investment was sought to update farming methods and help develop new product lines, or "nontraditional exports." Agro-21, established in 1983 to spearhead the new agriculture policies, held the ambitious objective of putting 80,000 hectares of idle land into the hands of the private sector in four years. The program relied heavily on international consultants and foreign investment; for example, the most prominent Agro-21 project, the Spring Plains Project, used Israeli technology. Although success was mixed, the program was responsible for growth in the production and export of nontraditional crops, such as winter vegetables, flowers, and Jamaican specialty crops, such as ginger, papaya, and akee.

Traditional farming methods, including slash-and-burn methods, still dominated on most small farms. The mountainous island suffered from serious erosion problems, the result of farming on overly steep hillsides in the interior. Such farming has caused long-term damage to the country's topsoil, lowering soil productivity up to one-third according to some estimates. Most small farmers tended to grow a diversity of crops along with one main crop. Few peasants were solely subsistence farmers, as the great majority traded a part of their produce and participated in the exchange economy.

In the 1980s, the use of such agricultural inputs as machinery, fertilizers, irrigated water, and technical assistance was slowly growing. Most small farmers still used hand tools, especially the machete, instead of more expensive power tools. A large percentage of the machinery was found on medium-sized to large farms, but farms of up to two hectares used a surprisingly large amount of machinery for the size of the plots. According to data from the United Nations Food and Agriculture Organization, the number of tractors in use on the island increased by 5.6 percent from 1971 to 1980, averaging 11 in use per 1,000 hectares of arable land in 1983; despite the improvement, this ratio was relatively low.

Fertilizers, pesticides, and irrigated water were likewise used in moderate amounts. Chemical fertilizers were not widely used, and animal manure and mulch were more commonly used by small

Rural life in
Grant's Mountain
Courtesy Cortez Austin, Jr.

farmers. The use of chemical fertilizers declined by 4.8 percent in the 1970s after an increase of some 7.2 percent in the 1960s. Declining use of fertilizers continued in the 1980s. Fertilizer use was most prevalent for large export crops such as sugarcane, bananas, and citrus. Pesticides were even less common than fertilizers and were used mostly for sugarcane. Irrigated water covered 12 percent of arable land in 1983, up from an 8-percent level in 1965.

Most agricultural research was carried out by the Ministry of Agriculture, but various farmer associations, such as the Coffee Industry Board and the Coconut Industry Board, provided research, as did the UWI at Mona. The Saturday edition of the *Daily Gleaner* provided farmers with valuable information on planting, harvesting, and new techniques. Agricultural extension workers were also active in Jamaica, including Ministry of Agriculture officials, crop associations, and agents of both local and foreign development organizations. The most important national farmer's organization was the Jamaica Agricultural Society, to which most farmers belonged.

Access to credit had increased since the integrated rural development plans of Project Land Lease in the 1970s, and augmenting credit to farmers continued to be an important government policy in the 1980s. The most customary sources of credit included the People's Cooperative Bank, the Agriculture Credit Board, the Agriculture Credit Bank, the Jamaican Agricultural Development Foundation, and commercial banks. High interest rates in Jamaica throughout the 1980s prevented most small farmers from obtaining commercial bank loans. Nonetheless, the growth of private commercialized farming doubled the number of outstanding agricultural loans from commercial banks between 1980 and 1985. Multilateral and bilateral development agencies supported a number of projects in 1987 designed to improve export crops, rural parish markets, fumigation, certification, and overseas marketing.

Crops

Jamaica's monoculture sugar economy became diversified after emancipation, when former slaves planted a wide variety of food and some cash crops. Agricultural produce was quite varied in the 1980s and included export crops, domestic crops, mixed crops, and nontraditional export crops, comprising both new crops and those traditionally grown but not previously exported.

Sugar has been the dominant crop in Jamaica for centuries, except for the fifty-year period from 1890 to 1940. Even in the late 1980s, sugarcane fields covered over 25 percent of the total area under cultivation and employed about 18 percent of the total work force, although the demand for labor was seasonal. Sugar production (including rum) accounted for nearly 50 percent of agricultural export earnings in the early 1980s. Nevertheless, sugar production declined sharply from 1965, when 60,000 hectares of cane fields produced 515,000 tons, to 1984, when 40,000 hectares produced only 193,000 tons. Many factors contributed to the decline of sugar, such as world price declines, falling yields, declining quality, labor unrest, and factory inefficiency. Farms over 200 hectares held the overwhelming share of the land under cane, usually on the fertile coastal plains. Jamaica's history as a slave-based, sugar plantation society marked sugarcane, and cane cutting in particular, with a strong social stigma.

Jamaica enjoyed two preferential markets for its sugar in the mid-1980s in the European Economic Community (EEC) through the Lomé Convention (see Glossary) and in the United States market via the United States sugar quota. In the 1980s, Jamaica was allocated 1.1 percent of the sugar imported into the United States from the world market. Although the United States sugar quota for Jamaican sugar dropped rapidly from 1984 to 1986, from 30,000 tons to 17,000 tons, Jamaica's own dwindling production prevented it from meeting the quota level in 1984. In 1985 the island actually imported several thousand tons of refined sugar for the domestic market. Meanwhile, the EEC remained a stable market.

Bananas were the only food crop in Jamaica to have surpassed sugar in export revenues. After the peak years of the early twentieth century, however, banana production and exports were cyclical and generally in decline. During the 1970s, production decreased rapidly from 136,000 tons in 1970 to 33,000 tons in 1980. Although major efforts were made by the government and farmers, the production decline continued in the 1980s; the figure for 1984 totaled only 11,100 tons, one of the worst of the century. Several factors accounted for ebbing production, including slow technological advance, diseases, shortage of inputs, natural disaster, and transportation bottlenecks. In contrast to sugar, bananas were typically produced by small farmers. Most farms that grew bananas grew other crops as well. Banana exports were destined for Britain, where Jamaica had preferential access for up to 150,000 tons of its bananas against non-Commonwealth nations.

Citrus products, which included oranges, sweet oranges, tangerines, grapefruits, and various hybrids, were usually grown on small farms. The large interior town of Mandeville was the hub of the industry. Citrus output was stable in the first half of the 1980s and reached 754,000 boxes in 1985. Citrus fruits enjoyed a large domestic market for direct consumption and processing. Many farmers picked their own produce to sell directly to consumers. Government policies in the 1980s sought to expand larger scale production and emphasized fruit processing for juices, concentrates, preserves, or canned fruit.

Coffee, cultivated since the early 1720s, remained an important export crop for small and large farmers in the 1980s. All coffee growing was regulated by a central organization, the Coffee Industry Board. Two varieties of coffee grew in Jamaica. Lowland coffee was generally grown on small farms and accounted for about 80 percent of output in the early 1980s. Blue Mountain coffee represented 20 percent of output but was steadily gaining a larger share of production. The number of hectares with Blue Mountain coffee doubled in the first 5 years of the 1980s to over 2,000 hectares, but the cultivated area of Lowland coffee remained constant. New coffee farms were generally medium to large in size. Jamaican coffee enjoyed exceptional prices relative to world prices. The price of Lowland coffee averaged two to three times the world price, whereas the highly aromatic Blue Mountain coffee received four to five times the world price. Some 1,000 tons of coffee were exported in 1984. Almost all of Jamaica's Blue Mountain coffee was sold to the Japanese, who were willing to pay top prices.

Jamaica produced a number of other traditional export crops such as cocoa (derived from the cacao plant), tobacco, coconuts, pimento, and ginger. Jamaican cacao plants were relatively free of disease and pests. Most cacao was cultivated on small farms on hillsides as a mixed crop. Although world cocoa prices were cyclical, Jamaica tended to receive a premium price for its cocoa. Some 51 tobacco farms produced 269,000 kilograms of tobacco in 1985 for both the domestic and the export market. The tobacco industry was undergoing a process of deregulation. Coconuts were recovering from a lethal yellowing disease that killed 88 percent of the Jamaican variety. New varieties were being grown to continue to produce coconut derivatives such as soaps and oils from copra. The production of pimento, from which allspice is derived, remained stable and was also deregulated. The island's ginger was of high quality and found easy market access abroad, as well as being sold locally for use in nonalcoholic ginger beer, chocolate, and national dishes.

Numerous domestic crops, both fruits and vegetables, were also grown. Tubers, the most important staple crop, included yams, sweet potatoes, cassava, and dasheens. Popular vegetables included calaloo (a kind of greens), sweet and hot peppers, tomatoes, cucumbers, corn, and pumpkins. Abundant fruits such as plantains, avocados, mangoes, pineapples, soursop, breadfruit, akee, and

Street market, Port Antonio
Courtesy Inter-American Development Bank

melons were also grown. Legumes were common, especially gungo peas, red peas (Jamaicans call beans peas), and peanuts. Jamaica was relatively self-sufficient in vegetable production.

Livestock, Fishing, and Forestry

Livestock were healthy, diversified, and relatively numerous in the late 1980s. Self-sufficiency was close to 100 percent for pork, 80 percent for beef, and 60 percent for poultry. Agro-21's 1983 plan called for self-sufficiency in beef to be reached nationwide, a goal generally perceived as feasible. Nevertheless, livestock production declined in the mid-1980s, largely as a result of increased feed costs brought on by numerous devaluations of the Jamaican dollar. Virtually all of the poultry produced were chickens, of which there were nearly 6 million on the island. Most chicken farms were small, but a few large producers were influential. Poultry production was dependent on price changes relative to the price of other meats. An increase in the price of chicken in the late 1980s forecast lowered output. Besides chicken, the most common farm animals in Jamaica were goats, totaling more than 295,000, raised for both their milk and their meat. Pigs were common on small farms. Swine disease rates were low compared with other Caribbean islands.

109

Two large dairy farms produced 80 percent of domestic milk, although 60 percent of dairy cattle were owned by small farmers. During 1984 two formerly government-owned dairies were closed as part of the government's divestment policies; the closings further hindered output. As a result of climate and resources, Jamaicans also consumed a large quantity of imported powdered milk. In 1985 the country remained dependent on imported dairy products to meet 84 percent of local demand.

Other livestock included mules, donkeys, and horses, all of which were used primarily for transport. The agricultural census also reported nearly 7,000 sheep and almost 24,000 rabbits. An increasingly popular activity was beekeeping for the commercial production of honey.

One of the most important obstacles that faced the government in the 1980s was the high price of imported feeds. To overcome this problem, agricultural policies stressed import substitution, such as increased corn production and experimentation with nontraditional feeds, including sugarcane tops, fish waste, and other agricultural by-products.

Fish was consumed in large quantities in Jamaica, exceeding domestic production. Dried saltfish, historically imported from Canada in exchange for Jamaican rum, still entered the country, but supply was irregular by the late 1980s. The island also imported more than 50,000 kilograms of shrimp, codfish, sardines, mackerel, and herring in 1985. Fish production dropped markedly from 18,500 tons in 1980 to 6,000 tons in 1984 as a result of the high cost of equipment, but production rebounded in 1985, reaching 9,550 tons. From 1983 to 1985, pond area grew by 55 percent in an attempt to increase freshwater production for local markets and shrimp production for the export market. Improved marketing, which would require a switch of preference in consumer taste from saltwater fish to freshwater fish, remained an obstacle to the success of inland fish farming. Fish ponds were one of several priority subsectors of the Agro-21 plan.

Natural forests, defined as land with at least 20 percent tree cover, represented 24 percent of total land. Government forestry preserves were large. Policies sought self-sufficiency in general-purpose timber, with a target of an additional 1,700 hectares of forest and production of 40,000 cubic meters of sawlogs a year. In the late 1980s, however, self-sufficiency was still far away. The long-term development of mostly hardwoods, pines, and other species was planned to support the furniture, craft, and construction industries. Small sawmills were common but generally undersupplied.

External Sector

External Trade

Trade has always played a major role in Jamaica's economic activity; indeed, the island is one of the most trade-dependent countries in the world. Trade as a percentage of GDP was over 50 percent in the 1970s, a figure that increased in the 1980s as the economy opened further to international trade. Although trade allowed Jamaica to import productive resources and consumer goods, chronic trade deficits generated a long-term drain on government finances. During the first twenty-five years of independence, Jamaica ran a trade surplus in only three years: 1963, 1977, and 1978. Trade deficits reached unprecedented levels, in excess of US$500 million, by the mid-1980s. Jamaican exports generally suffered in the 1980s because of unfavorable prices for traditional exports such as bauxite and sugar. Newly developed nontraditional exports experienced rapid growth, but their small volume improved the negative trade balance only marginally.

Total imports in 1985 were valued at over US$1.1 billion. Imports were divided as follows: fuels (37 percent), machinery and transport equipment (17 percent), food (15 percent), manufactured goods (15 percent), chemicals (11 percent), and the balance in various other categories. The United States was the major supplier of goods and services to Jamaica, accounting for approximately 40 percent of imports in the mid-1980s. Other major suppliers were Britain, Canada, Venezuela, the Netherlands Antilles, and Caricom. Imports fluctuated throughout the 1980s. The relative price of oil was an influential factor in determining the total import bill and the origin of imports. The Seaga government sought to reduce imports in the 1980s as part of an overall strategy to reduce aggregate demand in the economy. Although the government devalued the Jamaican dollar several times over its 1970s value in an effort to discourage imports, the dismantling of import controls, licensing, and quantitative restrictions actually increased imports, at least in the short run. Import liberalization policies were scheduled to continue into the late 1980s.

Exports were generally broken down into three categories in Jamaica: traditional exports, reexports, and nontraditional exports. Traditional exports included bauxite, alumina, gypsum, sugar, bananas, citrus, coffee, cocoa, pimento, and rum. Reexports were goods shipped to Jamaica and then reexported for a profit, usually transshipments. Nontraditional exports were all remaining exports. In the 1980s, the major exports remained alumina, bauxite, and sugar. Total exports averaged US$650 million from 1983 to 1985, or roughly half of imports. The substantial trade gap between exports and imports created large annual trade deficits. In fact, the 1985 trade deficit equaled over a third of total trade. Despite a downturn in the bauxite market worldwide, the bauxite sector still accounted for over half of export earnings. Nontraditional exports made up a quarter of total exports in the 1980s, a share that was steadily increasing. Contributing most to the expansion of nontraditional exports were clothing manufacturing, nontraditional agriculture, and mineral fuels and lubricants. The principal markets for exports were generally the same countries from which imports were obtained. As Jamaicans sought to break into new markets with nontraditional goods and services, the United States share of Jamaican exports increased from 35 percent in 1982 to over 40 percent by mid-decade.

In the mid-1980s, Jamaica enjoyed wide access to foreign markets for its exports. As a former European colony, it participated in the Lomé Convention, which provided guaranteed access levels for certain products, often at favorable prices. Jamaican exports to the United States entered under various preferential agreements, including the United States Generalized System of Preferences, the CBI, and the 807 program. Canada also introduced a trade initiative in 1986 called Caribcan, which provided preferential access to its market similar to that of the CBI. Access to the Caricom market, the traditional market for Jamaica's manufactured goods, declined in the 1980s; recession, devaluation, and other exchange rate and import licensing policies in Jamaica and Trinidad and Tobago, the two principal members of the community, caused a steady decline in regional trade. Although various bilateral and multilateral accords had been signed and the political support for Caricom existed, increased trade was not a reality in the late 1980s. As a result of its foreign exchange shortage, Jamaica was increasingly involved in countertrade or barter deals that circumvented currency exchanges. The most prominent agreement of that kind allowed Jamaica to export bauxite to the Soviet Union in exchange for Lada automobiles.

Balance of Payments and Debt

Jamaica has displayed a negative balance in its current account each year since 1963, primarily the result of large trade deficits. Capital account surpluses were generally not large enough to offset current account deficits, thus producing overall negative balances of payments. In the 1970s and 1980s, balance of payments shortfalls were financed increasingly through very large capital inflows in the form of concessional loans from multilateral and bilateral lending agencies. The IMF was the largest source of balance of payments support.

In the 1980s, the greatest source of payment deficits appeared in the merchandise trade portion of the current account (see table 4, Appendix A). As trade was liberalized and export prices depressed, unprecedented trade deficits appeared during the first five years of the 1980s. The terms of trade for Jamaica quickly declined. A serious decline in bauxite exports caused the greatest damage to the merchandise trade deficit and the economy as a whole. By contrast, Jamaica's service balance progressively became positive. Increased tourist receipts steadily bolstered invisible exports despite the drain made on the service account by the considerable amount of investment income, or profits, repatriated abroad. Net transfers were generally positive, as funds received from regional and international organizations were greater than contributions. Surpluses on the capital account in the 1980s were generally the result of official capital flows, in the form of balance of payments support, rather than private investment capital. Although new foreign capital was invested in Jamaica, significant foreign investment left the island, especially in 1983. As a result, official capital movements accounted for over 90 percent of the surplus on the capital account in the first five years of the 1980s. Net international reserves, with the exception of those in 1984, continued to decline in the first half of the decade after a previous decline from 1974 to 1979.

Jamaica's rapidly growing debt dated back to the oil price increases and expansionary fiscal policies of the 1970s. The balance of payments crisis experienced in the mid-1970s, however, was only the start of a spiraling debt crisis. From 1980 to 1986, Jamaica's total debt doubled, making the island one of the most indebted countries in the world on a per capita basis. Jamaica's debt peaked in the mid-1980s at US$3.5 billion and was not expected to exceed that level into the 1990s. Seaga's 1987 debt rescheduling negotiations with the IMF and the Paris Club (see Glossary) resulted in generous grace periods and at least a short-term easing of the crisis. Nonetheless, Jamaica's debt loomed large and unmanageable; by 1983 the total debt surpassed 150 percent of GDP. As noted previously, debt servicing accounted for over 40 percent of government spending by 1985. Similarly, debt servicing as a proportion of exports reached levels higher than those in virtually any Latin American or Caribbean nation.

Jamaica's strategy for managing its indebtedness primarily involved rescheduling and export-led growth (see Glossary). Although the rescheduling goal was generally achieved by the late 1980s, the export-led growth strategy, as outlined in the structural adjustment policies, had not been successful. Exports showed little dynamism in the 1980s, suffering from unfavorable terms of trade. Modest growth in nontraditional exports, at least by 1987, was unlikely to reduce significantly the huge national debt. In May 1987, Jamaica initiated another strategy of selling government equity shares in tourism and manufacturing for the private purchase of a portion of the country's foreign debt. "Debt-to-equity swaps," as they are called, were not perceived to relieve a significant percentage of the debt, however. No definitive strategies to overcome the debt crisis had been devised by the late 1980s.

Foreign Assistance

Jamaica received unprecedented levels of foreign assistance in the 1980s; the primary lenders were the IMF, the World Bank, and the United States Agency for International Development (AID). Most analysts perceived the generous aid as support for the Seaga government's more orthodox economic policies, which favored market forces, trade liberalization, foreign investment, and the structural adjustment of the economy. The island's relations with the IMF provided badly needed balance of payments support and stimulated renewed investor confidence in the island. With the signing of a US$650 million loan in April 1981, Jamaica became the number-one per capita recipient of IMF lending in the world. The government signed three more agreements with the fund through 1987 on relatively favorable terms. IMF lending, however, entailed economic policy conditionalities and austerity measures. Jamaica also received generous funding from the World Bank, ranking as the number-one per capita recipient in 1982. As in the case of IMF funding, the structural adjustment loans of the World Bank included economic policy reform conditions that Jamaica was to meet prior to obtaining further disbursements.

United States bilateral assistance to Jamaica after 1981 was also unprecedented. From 1981 to 1985, Jamaica ranked as the second or third per capita recipient of AID funding, or around the tenth in absolute terms. In 1981 and 1982 alone, Jamaica received more assistance from the United States than it did during the entire period since World War II. It was estimated that the United States would provide Jamaica with US$1 billion during the 1980s. Most funding went to balance of payments support. By the mid-1980s, funds were typically transferred in the form of grants rather than concessional loans. AID's assistance to Jamaica generally went to strengthen the policies of the IMF and the World Bank; the three organizations often operated together.

Finally, Jamaica also received generous funding from traditional multilateral donors such as the Inter-American Development Bank and the United Nations Development Programme. Canada, West European countries, and Japan provided bilateral assistance at the government level. In addition, numerous nonprofit development organizations, particularly from the United States, operated throughout Jamaica.

The abundant outside assistance that Jamaica received from international donors in the 1980s was directly related to the major economic policy reforms that the government pursued. Foreign assistance not only framed the country's economic reforms but also served to insulate the island from international recession and the regional debt crisis, at least temporarily. As these adjustment policies neared completion in 1987, the government's stance toward reform softened, and economic policies became increasingly sensitive to the political consequences of years of austerity.

Government and Politics

The Governmental System

Jamaica is a constitutional monarchy and a parliamentary democracy based on the Westminster model, with a functional two-party system. Under this democratic system of government, the prime minister and his cabinet are responsible to the legislature, and universal suffrage exists for citizens over the age of eighteen. The clauses of the 1962 Constitution, which consists of 138 articles in 10 chapters, may be amended by majorities of two-thirds in both houses of Parliament or, if the upper house, the Senate, does not concur, with the approval of a special majority of the electorate voting in referendum.

Jamaica's Constitution entitles anyone born on the island to Jamaican citizenship, which may be revoked if that person becomes a citizen of another country. Children and spouses of Jamaicans also may claim citizenship even if born outside of Jamaica. Chapter 3 of the Constitution grants all persons residing in Jamaica fundamental individual rights and freedoms, such as life, liberty, security of person, ownership of property, and protection from arbitrary arrest or detention. The Constitution also guarantees freedom of conscience and expression, including freedom of speech and press; peaceful assembly and association, including the right to join a trade union; freedom of movement and residence within the country and of foreign travel, emigration, and repatriation; and due process of law, including protection against double jeopardy or retroactive punishment.

The Constitution forbids inhumane treatment and racial, sexual, or political discrimination. Jamaican women are accorded full equality, and the 1975 Employment Act guarantees them equal pay for the same work. The legal status of women was reflected in the substantial number of women in influential positions in the civil service and government in the 1980s. The Supreme Court is given original jurisdiction over matters concerning civil rights, and cases arising from them are promised a fair hearing within a reasonable time. Individual rights and freedoms are explicitly subject to respect for the rights of others and the public interest in matters of defense, order, health, and morality.

Although an independent member of the British Commonwealth of Nations since 1962, Jamaica has retained the British monarch as its chief of state (see Appendix B). Executive power is vested nominally in the queen but exercised by the governor general, whom the queen appoints on the recommendation of the prime minister. The governor general, who has the right to be kept informed on any aspect of the conduct of government, wields the prerogatives of judicial pardon, performs the ceremonial duties of head of state, makes appointments to public offices, formally assents to bills before they can become law, and summons and adjourns Parliament. In most matters, the governor general acts only on the advice of the prime minister, but occasionally the governor general acts on the advice of both the prime minister and the leader of the opposition or on the advice of the Privy Council, whose six members are appointed by the governor general after consultation with the prime minister. At least two members of the Privy Council must be persons holding or having held public office. The Privy Council also advises the governor general on exercising the prerogative to grant appeals for mercy in cases involving the death penalty. Its decisions can be appealed to the Judicial Committee of the Privy Council in London, which is the final resort.

The cabinet, which is responsible to the House of Representatives, is the "principal instrument of policy." Directed by the prime minister, it usually has had from thirteen to fifteen members heading ministries staffed chiefly by the civil service. During the 1980s, the three most important portfolios have been those of finance and planning, national security, and foreign affairs. The Constitution stipulates that "not less than two nor more than four of the Ministers shall be persons who are members of the Senate."

As a result of the cabinet reorganization of October 1986, ministries were as follows: agriculture; construction; education; finance and planning; foreign affairs and industry; health; justice; labor; local government; mining, energy, and tourism; national security;

public service; public utilities and transport; social security and consumer affairs; and youth and community development. Ministries were often separated or combined. For example, the Ministry of National Security was combined with the Ministry of Justice in 1974 but separated again in October 1986 as a result of cabinet changes announced by Prime Minister Seaga.

Ministers, especially the prime minister, may hold more than one portfolio, and they may also supervise statutory boards set up to augment the usual departments. Ministers may be assisted by parliamentary secretaries. A cabinet member may lose his or her position or be forced to resign as a result of losing either his or her seat in Parliament or the confidence of the prime minister. A minister's power and prestige depend on party standing and loyalty, as well as individual ability.

The prime minister is the most important member of the cabinet and the acknowledged leader of the majority party. The governor general selects as prime minister the party leader favored by the majority of House members. The prime minister selects the other cabinet members from Parliament, directs the arrangement and conduct of cabinet business, and acts as the government's chief spokesperson at home and abroad. Control over foreign policy has remained firmly in the hands of the prime minister. The prime minister may be removed by resigning or otherwise ceasing to be a member of the House of Representatives or by being given a vote of no confidence by a majority of House members.

Under Jamaica's two-party system, the leader of the opposition is an institutionalized position, receiving a higher rate of remuneration than ordinary members of Parliament and exercising consultative functions, especially on appointments to public offices. The opposition leader is appointed by the governor general and is either the one who is "best able to command the support of the majority of those who do not support the government" or the leader of the largest single group in opposition. The opposition leader is expected to challenge the government and provide an ever-ready alternative for Parliament and the public. The institutionalized role of the opposition leader and Jamaica's democratic tradition give the opposition considerable freedom to criticize the government.

Modeled after the British Parliament, Jamaica's Parliament is the country's supreme legislative body. In addition to an elected House of Representatives and an appointed Senate, the Jamaican Parliament consists of a ceremonial head, who is the queen or her representative, and the governor general. The latter appoints the twenty-one members of the Senate: thirteen on the prime minister's advice and eight on the opposition leader's advice. The sixty House members (formerly fifty-three) are elected by universal adult suffrage for five years in elections held in each of the country's sixty constituencies. The Constitution requires that the prime minister call a general election no later than five years after the first sitting of the previous Parliament. To qualify for appointment to the Senate or for election to the House, a person must be a citizen of Jamaica or another Commonwealth country, be age twenty-one or over, and ordinarily have resided in Jamaica for the immediately preceding twelve months.

In addition to submitting bills, the Senate reviews legislation submitted by the House and may delay legislative bills for seven months and money bills for one month. The Senate delay may be overridden if a majority in the House passes such bills three times in succession. For a constitutional amendment to pass Parliament, however, Senate concurrence is essential. As in many other Commonwealth countries, the existence of an upper house (Senate) permits useful participation in public affairs to those who might not wish to run for election; it also encourages the political patronage by the major political parties. The cabinet, which is the executive branch of government responsible to Parliament, must include two to four senators; others may be appointed as parliamentary secretaries to assist cabinet members.

The House of Representatives initiates all funding bills, but other bills may be introduced in either house. Bills designed to implement government policy usually are introduced by a cabinet minister. The House regulates its own procedures and chooses its own officers, including the speaker, who acts as a nonpartisan chairman of proceedings and enjoys considerable prestige. Although Parliament, and particularly its House of Representatives, has a number of standing committees, these have relatively little investigative power; they also have not provided a locus for checking the executive, a task undertaken by the parliamentary opposition.

The conduct of parliamentary business requires the presence of quorums: eight in the Senate and sixteen in the House. Absenteeism, a longstanding problem, often has been criticized publicly. A majority of those present and voting usually make the decisions. Parliamentary sessions must not be held more than six months apart. Elections must take place every five years, but the terms of members of Parliament may be extended twice, each time for one year, in case of war or national emergency. Although the legislature traditionally has enjoyed a high position, effective legislative powers are concentrated in the cabinet.

Members of Parliament are immune from arrest and protected against lawsuits arising from their duties. Each house may exempt members from vacating their seats over conflict of interest matters. Members, however, may be disqualified for insanity, bankruptcy, allegiance to a foreign power, holdings in firms contracting with the government, holding other public office, or conviction for corrupt electoral practices.

The prime minister may call elections earlier than the law requires if his or her government loses the confidence of the House of Representatives or if he or she feels the need to call for a public mandate on an important issue. Thus, the incumbent government holds the initiative, although the Constitution attempts to safeguard the impartiality of the actual process. Elections are supervised by a senior civil servant as chief electoral officer, a staff consisting of a returning officer in each constituency, election clerks, and a polling clerk at each polling station. Votes are counted in the presence of the candidates or their agents to minimize charges of fraud. A returning officer may cast a vote to decide a tie. Constituencies are demarcated by a six-member standing parliamentary committee, but alterations favoring the party in power are not unknown. Security forces vote in advance of election day so that they can be deployed across the island on that date.

Each constituency elects one candidate, and the winner requires only a simple majority. Thus, the number of seats won by a party may not reflect accurately the number of votes cast for it, and the disparity in seats won by the two parties is usually higher than the variance between the total votes. Candidates, most of them sponsored by the JLP or the PNP, are nominated twenty-three days before an election. The central committees of these two parties select those who will receive the party tickets and the constituencies from which they will run. Each nomination must be accompanied by a deposit, which is forfeited if the candidate receives fewer than one-eighth of the votes cast. Campaign expenses are limited by law, and influencing voters unduly is prohibited. Loopholes exist, however, and have been used.

Although the Constitution is explicitly declared to be supreme, it may be subject to judicial review, as may laws inconsistent with its provisions. A Parliament in which the ruling party has a comfortable majority may amend the charter relatively easily in accordance with the traditional doctrine of parliamentary sovereignty. The content and concepts of Jamaican law are basically the same as those of Britain. Nevertheless, the Jamaican Parliament occasionally has questioned the relevance of British decisions; statutes enacted by the Jamaican legislative body increasingly have taken into consideration local conditions.

Despite Jamaica's well-developed judicial system, it and the police force were widely criticized in the mid-1980s because of dramatic increases in political and criminal violence. Many believed that the judicial system had deteriorated and that the authority and dignity of the courts had diminished. Critics noted that many of the new judges and lawyers were not as well educated as in the past and lacked self-confidence. Since the early 1970s, only graduates of the three-year West Indies Faculty of Law or the two-year graduate School of Legal Education have been permitted to practice law in Jamaica, whereas previously most Jamaican lawyers received their legal training in Britain. In February 1986, Carl Stone, Jamaica's leading political scientist, criticized what he referred to as the criminal justice system's corrupt practice of bribing juries and rendering corrupt judgments in favor of those who have political or economic power.

Despite antiquated laws and overcrowded jails, Jamaicans generally have respected the rule of law and the system of justice inherited from the British. The principle of habeas corpus, which is rooted in English common law, is stated explicitly in Jamaican statutes enacted either before or since independence. It is also respected by the courts and the police. Bail may be granted on a discretionary basis. The courts operate at three broad levels: the Court of Appeal; the Supreme Court; and the nineteen resident magistrate's courts. Other judicial bodies are the coroner's courts, traffic courts, petty sessions courts, juvenile courts, revenue courts, family courts, and Gun Court (see National Security, this ch.). Justices of the peace, who are local notables without legal training, preside over petty sessions courts.

The eight-member Court of Appeal is at the apex of the court hierarchy in Jamaica. This court is headed by a president, who is appointed by the governor general on the recommendation of the prime minister after consultation with the leader of the opposition. It is also staffed by a chief justice and six other judges appointed by the governor general on the advice of the prime minister and the opposition leader. It sits in two divisions in Kingston throughout the year. A person who is dissatisfied with the decision of another court, except the petty sessions courts, may appeal to this court. Article 110 of the Constitution provides that decisions of the Court of Appeal can be taken on appeal to the Judicial Committee of the Privy Council in London in grave civil or criminal cases, in matters deemed of great public importance, or in situations as decided by the Jamaican Parliament or the Court of Appeal itself. The Judicial Committee of the Privy Council in London is given final jurisdiction on interpretation of the Constitution.

The Supreme Court is headed by a chief justice, who is appointed in the same manner as the president of the Court of Appeal. It is also staffed by five other judges, a senior puisne judge, and other judicial officials. The Supreme Court has unlimited jurisdiction in civil and criminal cases and can dispense summary justice without jury in certain criminal cases. It sits in Kingston for the trying of civil cases; for criminal cases, it serves as a circuit court in the capital town of each parish.

The resident magistrate's courts, which include the petty sessions courts, deal with minor infractions but may also indict an individual for a serious offense, which would then be adjudicated in a circuit court. Kingston has four resident magistrate's courts. St. Andrew has three, and the other parishes have one each. Circuit court judges exercise broad discretion in imposing sentences for serious violations of law.

Constitutional provisions relating to the appointment and tenure of members of the higher judiciary provide safeguards for their independence from government. Appointments are made by the governor general in consultation with the prime minister, the leader of the opposition, and the Judicial Service Commission. Judges are almost always appointed from within the judicial department of the civil service.

The career civil service is largely responsible for administering governmental policy; as in Britain, it is organized into six categories: administrative, professional, technical, executive, clerical, and manual. The Constitution details the conditions of service, including pensions. Seniority and performance in competitive examinations are taken into consideration for promotion. The civil service is presumed to be nonpartisan in discharging its duties. Separate public commissions, appointed on the recommendation of the prime minister and opposition leader, are responsible for the employees of the career civil service, including the judicial branch, police, local government employees, and public school teachers. The Ministry of Finance and Planning also has supervisory authority over personnel management.

Under Seaga's Staff Adjustment Programme, employment in public administration was reduced sharply during the 1984–86 period from an estimated 120,000 employees in 1984 to 79,900 by late 1986. Jamaica's relatively large public sector in 1984 included 36,486 members of the civil service; 16,613 employees in local government service; and about 5,600 members of the Jamaica Constabulary Force (JCF), the service primarily responsible for internal security. Although the nation inherited a well-trained civil service from the British, by 1980 observers were describing it as heavily overstaffed and highly inefficient.

Before Jamaica achieved internal autonomy, senior civil servants were generally British, enjoyed high prestige, and wielded considerable power. Policies and administrative decisions were decided mostly in Whitehall or Jamaica House (the governor's residence). This situation changed when political authority passed into the hands of popularly elected Jamaicans, with whose nationalist goals civil servants were not necessarily in sympathy. The status and power of the senior civil servants have declined since then. The more capable civil servants were lured away by foreign or private companies offering attractive working conditions and substantially higher wages. Consequently, economic and political development was hindered by shortages of skilled personnel at the higher management levels. Jamaican leaders frequently have bypassed the career civil service and the ministries by creating statutory boards or corporations and appointing their supporters to high positions in these entities. Career diplomats are chosen by competitive examination, and career civil servants may move between the foreign service and the senior civil service.

At the local level, the nation, a unitary state, is divided into fourteen administrative parishes. The parishes of Kingston and St. Andrew are amalgamated as the Kingston and St. Andrew Corporation. A parish council, which exercises limited self-government, is elected in each parish by universal adult suffrage at times other than those at which general elections are held. The 278 parish councillors were voluntary workers whose allowances only covered attendance at council meetings. Although established to provide the basic amenities for local populations, the parish councils became increasingly dependent on financial assistance from the central government because of insufficient revenues from local taxes, fees, and licenses. Government indifference sometimes has frustrated local initiatives directed toward feasible projects, regardless of the party in power. Because wealthier individuals tended to monopolize parish council positions, relations of this local elite with the poorer masses were based more on authoritarian paternalism than on cooperation.

Central government financial assistance has diminished the autonomy of local governments and reinforced habits of subservience acquired in the colonial period. The general trend since 1944 has been toward the centralization of political power away from the parishes to the capital. Stone, who is also Jamaica's leading pollster and a professor of political sociology at the UWI, documented this trend in his frequent and respected Stone Polls, sponsored and published, beginning in 1976, by the independent but generally pro-JLP *Daily Gleaner* newspaper. A decrease in voter turnout for local elections since 1944 was symptomatic of this trend. By the 1980s, politics had become highly centralized, and political issues focused on the national rather than the local level. A September 1984 Stone Poll revealed that only 58 percent of registered voters were likely to vote in any forthcoming local government elections. Many voters felt that local government had become useless.

Political Dynamics

Jamaica's two-party system, which had its roots in the rivalry between William Alexander Bustamante and Norman W. Manley, resembles traditional North American patterns (see Historical Setting, this ch.). Both parties—the JLP and PNP—were formed and operated by a relatively small number of men and with a high degree of British and intraparty cooperation. By the 1960s, politics had changed significantly from the time of the 1944 elections, when the country was predominantly rural and voting was based as much on local issues and personalities as on national affairs. The JLP and PNP, responding to sectional interest groups, appeared to move closer to each other and away from the basic concerns of the population, namely, employment opportunities. Their paths later diverged, but some similarities remained. Both parties operated as multiclass alliances, whose adherents cut across class and racial lines. Both represented frequently shifting group interests and sought a large independent vote. Moreover, in their attempt to appeal to all sectors of the population for votes and funds, both parties adopted somewhat similar policies. Differences in foreign policy, however, became more pronounced.

The two-party arrangement differed from the British and United States systems in two important respects. One is that Jamaica's elites, from which the island's leaders have emerged, are closely knit groups; four of the nation's first five prime ministers were related. The other difference is that party identification, not race or class, is the primary political frame of reference. Each party has a fiercely loyal, almost tribal, inner core defined by family ties and neighborhood. Antagonism to the other party is passionate and frequently violent.

Despite the intensity of party rivalry in Jamaica, Stone Poll surveys revealed the increasing importance of the "swing vote" (uncommitted voters) in determining electoral outcomes. At the time of independence, the swing vote was only 5 percent, but by 1985 the percentage of uncommitted voters had stabilized at 26. The growth of the swing vote was accompanied by a periodic pattern

123

of support for the two parties. For example, the percentage of voters not committed to either the JLP or the PNP rose from 15 percent in November 1976 to 40 percent by mid-1978. During the same period, PNP support declined from 40 to 28 percent, whereas that of the JLP fell from 37 to 32 percent. These declines were interpreted at the time as a loss of support for the two major parties. Nevertheless, by December 1979 the percentage of uncommitted voters had dropped back down to 16, whereas JLP support had climbed from 32 to 47 percent and PNP support from 28 to 37 percent. Although their political interest was seasonal, the uncommitted voters remained an integral part of the support for the two major parties.

Unlike much of Hispanic Latin America and many former colonies in Africa and Asia, Jamaica has enjoyed a tradition of political stability, notwithstanding the escalating political violence on the island during the 1974–80 period. The JLP and PNP alternated in power every ten years in the general elections held between 1955 and 1980. Turnout at the polls during the postwar period and the first 25 years of independence was consistently high, in contrast to the average 3-percent voting rate in the seven general legislative elections held between 1901 and 1934. Voter participation increased steadily from 65 percent of the electorate, or 495,000, in 1955 to 85 percent, or 736,000, in 1976.

A review of political dynamics in independent Jamaica can begin in 1965, when illness forced Prime Minister Bustamante, one of Jamaica's two founding fathers, to resign from politics. Donald Sangster took over as acting prime minister and later became prime minister as a result of the narrow JLP victory in the February 1967 elections. He died suddenly two months later, however, and Hugh Shearer, the BITU president, succeeded him on April 12. The Shearer government was known for its weak management, factionalism, and corruption.

After Norman Manley's death in 1969, the JLP and PNP evolved along increasingly divergent lines. Beginning in 1970, the JLP's identification with domestic and foreign business interests became increasingly evident. After Manley died, his son Michael, a Third World-oriented social democrat, succeeded him as PNP leader and began to revive the party's socialist heritage. Michael Manley, who had been educated at Jamaica College and the London School of Economics, worked as a journalist and trade unionist (1952–72). Eloquent, tall, and charismatic, he defeated Shearer impressively in the February 1972 election, winning 56 percent of the popular vote, which gave the PNP 36 of the 53 seats in the House of Representatives. Manley, who represented Central Kingston, won

Michael Manley,
prime minister, 1972–80
Courtesy Agency for
Public Information, Jamaica

Edward Seaga,
prime minister, 1980–
Courtesy Agency for
Public Information, Jamaica

support not only from the lower classes, including the Rastafarians, but also from members of the middle and business classes disenchanted with the Shearer government.

Michael Manley's PNP won the 1972 election on a Rastafarian-influenced swing vote of 8 percent. During the 1972 election campaign, Manley had tried to change his party's image by evoking the memory of Marcus Garvey, using symbols appealing to the Rastafarians, and by associating with their leader, Claudius Henry. Manley also had appeared in public with an ornamental "rod of correction" reputedly given him by Haile Selassie. Manley's informal dress and the PNP's imaginative use of two features of Rastafarian culture—creole dialect and reggae music—in the 1972 campaign were designed to dispel fears of elitism and woo the votes of those who had disparaged Norman Manley's facility with the English language.

During Michael Manley's terms as prime minister (1972–80), the PNP aligned itself with socialist and "anti-imperialist" forces throughout the world. Thus, for the first time, political divisions within Jamaica reflected the East-West conflict. Manley's PNP did not publicly announce its resurrected goal of "democratic socialism"

125

until the fall of 1974, on the occasion of a state visit to Jamaica by Tanzania's socialist president Julius K. Nyerere. In addition to redirecting the PNP along these lines, Manley began building a mass party, with emphasis on political mobilization.

Manley's populist policies gave impetus to a shift, begun with independence, of many more dark-skinned middle-class Jamaicans moving upward into political and social prominence, taking over political and civil service positions from the old white elite. Prior to independence, most top leaders had Anglo-European life-styles and disdained many aspects of Jamaican and West Indian culture. By the 1970s, most Jamaican leaders preferred life-styles that identified them more closely with local culture.

In 1974 Seaga succeeded Shearer as JLP leader and began playing an active role as leader of the opposition (1974–80). Seaga and Manley continued the traditional JLP–PNP leadership rivalry in the 1970s, but on a far more bitter and intense level than had Bustamante and Norman Manley. Born in Boston in 1930 of Jamaican parents of Syrian and Scottish origin, Seaga was educated at Wolmer's Boys School in Kingston and at Harvard University. He joined the JLP in the late 1950s and was appointed by Bustamante to the Senate in 1959. A social scientist with expertise in financial, cultural, and social development areas, Seaga also served as minister of development and social welfare (1962–67) and minister of finance and planning (1967–72). Contrasting sharply with the affable and oratorical Manley, Seaga often has been described as remote and technocratic, with a stiff, formal manner. Although he did not endear himself to the common man, Seaga earned a reputation as a highly disciplined, hard-working, and intellectual leader. Despite being white and wealthy, he represented Denham Town, one of the poorest and blackest constituencies of West Kingston, which regularly gave 95 percent of its vote to the JLP.

The December 1976 elections witnessed major realignments in class voting for the two parties, as well as unprecedented political violence and polarization on ideological and policy issues. The support of manual wage laborers and the unemployed resulted in another sweeping victory in the elections for the PNP; the party won 57 percent of the vote and 47 of the 60 seats in the House of Representatives. The PNP was also aided by the lowering of the voting age from twenty-one to eighteen. Despite losing a substantial number of votes among the upper-middle and upper classes as well as among white-collar employees, the PNP retained majority support among these sectors. Many Jamaicans did not share JLP concerns about the direction that the Manley government was taking. A Stone Poll found that 69 percent of the electorate at that time rejected the JLP view that the PNP was leading the nation toward communism. The JLP had depicted the rising number of Cubans in Jamaica, who included technical, economic, and medical personnel, as a national security threat. According to a Stone Poll, however, a 63-percent majority viewed the Cuban presence in Jamaica favorably, believing the Cubans to be providing technical and economic assistance.

During his second term in office, Manley, having broadened the PNP's electoral base by wooing a number of charismatic left-wing leaders, veered sharply leftward. One of his left-wing cabinet appointees, Donald K. Duncan, headed the new Ministry of National Mobilization and had responsibility for supervising the government's "people's programs" in worker participation in industry and in the "democratization" of education. Despite the efforts of Duncan and others, the PNP left wing never succeeded in radically transforming the polity or the economy.

The PNP's dominant position in politics in the 1970s was reinforced on March 8, 1977, when the party won 237 out of 269 municipal seats in local government elections, in which 58 percent of the electorate participated. By mid-term, however, internal PNP infighting between left-wingers and moderates had intensified, and JLP opposition had escalated. Support for the PNP declined considerably as the public became increasingly concerned over the PNP's alliance with the communist Workers Party of Jamaica (WPJ), as well as growing unemployment, crime and other violence, internal party divisions, mismanagement of the government, and the government's close ties to Cuba.

The JLP, which continued to enjoy strong support in the business community, remained more pragmatic and flexible in policy than the PNP. JLP business executives and technocrats emerged in the top party positions, replacing the old guard labor leaders. Endorsing a platform described simply as "nationalism," JLP leaders continued to stand in the ideological center of the political system. They advocated a pro-United States, pro-free enterprise, and anti-Cuban ideology.

The 1980 election campaign, Jamaica's most bitter and violent, was waged in the context of extreme scarcity of foreign exchange and consequent shortages of all kinds of goods. Two central issues in the campaign were the state of the economy, including the Manley government's relations with the IMF, and the JLP's charges that the Manley government had lost the people's confidence because of its close relations with Cuba (see Role of Government, this ch.). Seaga alleged in particular that the security forces were being subjected to "communist infiltration" and that young *brigadistas* (construction brigade members) who had received vocational training in Cuba were subjected to political indoctrination. By 1980 the majority of Jamaicans regarded the PNP government as incapable of managing the economy or maintaining order in the society. Even the security forces joined the opposition to the government.

In the October 30, 1980, elections, the PNP was unable to withstand the alliance of the private sector, church, security forces, media, intelligentsia, workers, and unemployed. The electorate gave Seaga's JLP a landslide victory; the opposition party won 59 percent of the vote and 51 of 60 seats in the House of Representatives. Despite the electoral violence, the election, in which a record 86 percent of the voters turned out, was considered one of the fairest and most important in the nation's history. Other than some incidents of fraud and box tampering, the number of contested votes was relatively low. Stone has noted that the election was also the first in which a party had won a majority of the parish vote in all parishes.

After taking office as prime minister, Seaga, who also assumed the finance portfolio, redirected the island's economy along free-enterprise lines, emphasizing the role of the private sector and continuing to encourage foreign investment. As the governing party, the JLP under Seaga was described by Stone as "conservative reformist." It continued to receive substantial support from the 100,000-member BITU, and JLP policies were subject to strong labor influence. Nevertheless, the party has not been able to take BITU support for granted, and the BITU had been known to act independently.

In the early 1980s, Manley's opposition PNP, described by Stone as "radical reformist," tried to moderate its political image. Stone Polls conducted in early 1981 showed that over 70 percent of the electorate was critical of the PNP's links with local communists. The PNP subsequently broke with the WPJ in a move supported by 71 percent of the electorate. As leader of the opposition in the 1980s, Manley has been the country's most popular party leader. His personality as an emotional nationalist and socialist idealist has contrasted sharply with Seaga's. Manley also has continued to represent Central Kingston, a middle-class district, and serve as the NWU leader.

In late November 1983, Prime Minister Seaga responded to a PNP leader's call for his resignation as finance minister by announcing the holding of early elections on December 15, 1983. Having achieved a significant increase in popularity because of Jamaica's participation in the United States-Caribbean operation in Grenada in late October, an action that a Stone Poll indicated was supported by 56 percent of the electorate, Seaga was confident of winning the snap elections. The PNP, unable to nominate candidates within the four days allowed, boycotted the elections, arguing that the government had broken a promise to update the voters' register and to implement antifraud measures. The PNP claimed that up to 100,000 eligible voters were disenfranchised. As a result of the PNP's boycott, the JLP had token opposition in only six of the sixty parliamentary constituencies. By winning those races, the JLP completed its control of the House of Representatives, occupying all sixty seats. The PNP's decision not to contest the election also made the prime minister responsible for selecting the eight non-governmental opposition members of the Senate. When the government chose non-PNP individuals with independent views, Jamaica found itself with an unprecedented one-party Parliament and without an official leader of the opposition. Ironically, a Stone Poll found that had it not boycotted the election, the PNP would have won the December 1983 elections with 54 percent of the vote and a 10-percent margin over the JLP.

Although the holding of the snap elections was a constitutional prerogative of the prime minister, it marked a departure from Jamaica's traditional consensus politics and weakened the Seaga government's public standing. A 59- to 38-percent majority disapproved of the holding of early elections using the old voters' register. At the same time, according to a December 1983 Stone Poll, the public was generally divided over the PNP's boycott; 47 percent disapproved of it, and 46 percent approved of it. By a margin of 70 to 30 percent, Jamaicans favored calling new elections when the voters' list was ready. The PNP campaigned unsuccessfully during 1985 for a general election to be held by October. The party reasoned that this date would mark the end of the five-year mandate that the electorate had given the JLP in 1980. Opinion polls throughout 1985 showed that the PNP enjoyed a considerable lead over the governing JLP. Nevertheless, the JLP held all sixty seats in the House until early 1986, when two members defected.

Municipal elections, scheduled originally for June 1984 but postponed twice, were held on July 29, 1986. Disputes over a reduction in the number of parish council seats and a redrawing of local constituency boundaries caused the delay. In what was the first real contest between the two main parties since 1980, the opposition PNP defeated the JLP soundly, taking 57 percent of the vote and obtaining control of 11 of the 13 municipalities in which polling had taken place. An estimated 60 percent of the 970,000 eligible voters cast ballots. The JLP's heavy defeat in the local elections was blamed largely on Seaga's austere economic policies and deteriorating social and economic conditions. Buoyed by the victory, Manley appealed, again unsuccessfully, for an early general election; it was not expected to be held, however, before late 1988.

At a JLP retreat held on October 12, 1986, Seaga announced his decision to resign as prime minister in August 1987 and not to seek re-election as leader of the JLP because of "personal considerations" and unhappiness with the progress of his economic recovery program. Seaga revoked his decision, however, at a JLP meeting on November 5, 1986, after JLP members of Parliament and parish councillors voted unanimously not to accept it. Critics expressed skepticism over the strength of support for Seaga and noted that he had used the resignation ploy twice before to rally support successfully: in the early 1970s in a bid to challenge Shearer for the JLP leadership and in 1979 as JLP leader.

Seaga's declining electoral prospects were again reflected in a January 1987 Stone Poll. About 63 percent of those polled said conditions had worsened since 1980 when the PNP had left office, and 56 percent felt that Manley could run the country better than Seaga; the poll gave Seaga only a 45-percent positive rating. Another Stone Poll conducted nationwide in June 1987 found that the JLP had picked up 2 percentage points, but still trailed the PNP by 15. In August 1987, Seaga became the target of serious criticism as a result of his creation of a commercially run tourist attraction in Ocho Rios called the Gardens of Cariñosa, which was also open to the public for an admissions fee. The PNP and several columnists questioned the propriety of public officials being involved in private investments while still holding office. Although Manley was clearly Jamaica's most popular political leader and favored next prime minister in late 1987, health problems, including major intestinal surgery the previous April, had cast a shadow on his long-term political prospects.

As of 1987, Jamaica's two-party system had not been conducive to the emergence of a third parliamentary party. During the nation's first twenty-five years of independence, twenty-seven minor political parties had tried to take over that role but had become defunct within a year. There is no constitutional impediment, however, to third-party representatives or even independents becoming recognized as "the opposition," provided they can win the second largest bloc of seats in Parliament. Jamaicans generally were satisfied with the two-party system. A February 1985 Stone Poll indicated that a 78-percent majority saw no need for a new political party. Only 11 percent supported the idea of forming a new party.

The communist WPJ, having functioned as Jamaica's officially recognized third party since the late 1970s, has set a longevity record. Founded by Trevor Munroe, its secretary general, on December 17, 1978, the WPJ (formerly known as the Workers Liberation League) adopted a pro-Moscow, avowedly Marxist-Leninist orientation. It advocated a "nonalignment" policy for Jamaica that Munroe defined as distancing the country from the United States and Britain. Munroe, who had earned a doctorate at Oxford University, where he was a Rhodes scholar, had held the position of senior lecturer in government at the UWI. According to a March 1985 Stone Poll, the WPJ had increased its popular support from 3 to 4 percent, but 58 percent of Jamaicans were still hostile to the party. The WPJ failed to elect a single councillor islandwide in the July 1986 local elections; its best showing in any of the parishes was 7 percent. The WPJ's relations with Cuba were strained in the mid-1980s because of WPJ criticism of Cuba's perceived failure to back the regime of Bernard Coard and Hudson Austin in Grenada that overthrew and assassinated Prime Minister Maurice Bishop. The Communist Party of Cuba and the WPJ repaired relations, however, and Munroe attended the Third Congress of the Communist Party of Cuba in Havana in early February 1986.

A United States resident, James Chrisholm, founded another third party of quite different orientation, the Jamaican-American Party (JAP), on April 5, 1986. Advocating a United States statehood platform, the JAP nominated six candidates in the July 29, 1986, local elections. Less than 1 percent of Jamaicans questioned in a May 1986 Stone Poll indicated they would vote for the JAP, although 41 percent had heard about it.

JLP and PNP leadership relations during the Seaga administrations have been characterized by clashing viewpoints on a wide range of domestic and foreign policy issues. Stone noted in 1985 that on every politically sensitive issue, ranging from security and police matters to government economic policies and political issues, JLP and PNP opinions were separated by a huge gap and deep mutual distrust. Somewhat contradictorily, however, Stone Polls found that during the 1970s and 1980s the public gradually became less inclined to vote according to partisan loyalties. According to a May 1986 Stone Poll, political opinions appeared to be converging at the center, and PNP and JLP supporters were agreeing more than disagreeing on many sensitive political issues. For example, according to the poll 85 percent of the PNP and 65 percent of the

JLP opposed United States statehood, whereas in a poll taken in the early 1980s 32 percent of the PNP and 57 percent of the JLP favored it. Nevertheless, the JLP and PNP continued to disagree on many issues.

Manley's views on foreign affairs in the 1980s continued to reflect his left-of-center, Third World orientation and therefore clashed frequently with those held by Seaga. Manley maintained close relations with Fidel Castro, whom he visited periodically in Havana for private talks. The PNP declared its intention to renew Jamaican-Cuban relations, broken by Seaga in 1981, if it should win the elections that were expected to be held in 1989 (see Foreign Relations, this ch.). Manley and the PNP also were critical of the alleged militarization of the Commonwealth Caribbean and United States military activities in the region. The PNP opposed Jamaica's participation in the joint United States-Caribbean military operation in Grenada in October 1983, as well as participation in regional military maneuvers with the United States.

With the principal exceptions of South Africa and the events in Grenada, the Jamaican electorate generally has evinced little interest in foreign policy issues since independence. The level of public and parliamentary information or discussion on international problems has been low. Public commentaries on foreign policy issues were limited to views expressed by the urban elite and intellectuals in the *Daily Gleaner* and on radio talk shows. Stone Polls revealed, however, that international issues had begun to have a greater impact on domestic politics in the late 1970s; Grenada was a particularly divisive issue in 1979–83. The assassination of Maurice Bishop in Grenada and the subsequent multinational military intervention in October 1983 had a major impact on Jamaican domestic politics. PNP supporters favored the Bishop regime, whereas JLP adherents were strongly critical of it. According to a December 1983 Stone Poll, 86 percent of the JLP was in favor of the intervention, and 60 percent of the PNP was opposed.

Although Jamaica has traditionally had a free press and an absence of censorship, the government was not without considerable influence over news media such as the Jamaica Broadcasting Corporation (JBC) and the independent Radio Jamaica (RJR). The PNP has accused the Seaga government of using the RJR and JBC in a partisan manner. Similar charges were made by the JLP when the JBC and other media, except for the *Daily Gleaner*, were controlled by Manley's government in the 1970s. During the 1980 election campaign, the JBC waged a vitriolic propaganda campaign against the United States. Since the mid-1970s, both national radio stations have broadcast popular "phone-in" programs that have increasingly politicized the mass media. On October 8, 1984, the Seaga government made the Jampress News Agency, which had been suspended since 1980, its official news outlet. Jampress replaced the news-gathering function of the Jamaica Information Service, which was restructured and remained a full department of government under the Ministry of Public Service.

Marijuana eradication was another sensitive political issue, especially insofar as the appearance of foreign pressure was concerned. There was widespread and bitter resentment against the antimarijuana drive. Traffickers in Jamaica, known as "Robin Hoods," had cultivated selected local loyalties by supplying funds for school construction and road improvements. Whereas 66 percent of Jamaicans expressed support for the policy of marijuana eradication in a 1979 Stone Poll, a January 1987 poll found that opinion had swung against the government's antidrug policies. Forty-seven percent of the population rejected the policies because they prevented many rural people from earning money during hard economic times. The 46 percent of the public who supported the government's actions felt that drugs were destroying the youth, corrupting the country, and fueling crime and other violence. Opinion was divided along party lines; 70 percent of JLP supporters were for marijuana eradication, and 57 percent of PNP supporters were against it.

Several religious groups or cults, primarily the Rastafarians, traditionally have used marijuana (called "ganja" in Jamaica) as a sacramental drug. Cultivated clandestinely in mountainous areas, ganja is rolled into huge flute-shaped cigarettes called spliffs and smoked. In other popular uses, ganja leaves are baked into small cakes, brewed for tea, soaked in rum, drunk with roots as an aphrodisiac, used as a poultice to reduce pain and swelling, or used popularly as a cold remedy.

Both the JLP and the PNP were widely believed in the 1980s to have received campaign contributions from narcotics traffickers. A January 1987 Stone Poll revealed that 68 percent of those polled felt that both parties received drug money. Seaga noted on November 31, 1986, that marijuana barons were fast becoming deeply involved in Jamaica's political situation. Two years earlier, on October 1, 1984, Seaga reported that the security forces had discovered a plot by narcotics traffickers to assassinate him; no suspects were named, however, and no arrests were made.

Foreign Relations

Relations with the United States, Britain, and Canada

Close ties with the United States, Britain, and Canada traditionally have been of prime importance and have existed at the political, commercial, and personal levels. After World War II, the three nations all provided economic assistance to Jamaica through international organizations, private investment, and encouragement of the idea of West Indian federation. By the 1950s, the United States and Canada had replaced the once dominant British trade role. On August 7, 1962, the day after independence, Prime Minister Bustamante described Jamaica as pro-Western, Christian, and anticommunist, and he announced ''the irrevocable decision that Jamaica stands with the West and the United States.''

Independent Jamaica adopted Western models for internal development and external perspective. Jamaican leaders, recognizing the strong United States disapproval of Soviet influence in Cuba and British Guiana (present-day Guyana), rejected the Soviet alternative. As British influence in Jamaica eroded rapidly following independence, the United States began paying closer attention to political events on the island. Beginning with the seizure of power in Cuba by Fidel Castro, Jamaica's proximity to both Cuba and the United States raised Jamaica's profile in American foreign policy circles. Growing United States economic interest in Jamaica paralleled the former's increasing political interest. Jamaica sided frequently with the United States in its United Nations (UN) voting on cold war issues during the first few years of independence. The nation became visibly less pro-West in its UN voting beginning in 1965–66, however. Jamaica moved out of the United States orbit for the first time when it abstained on the 1971 vote to admit China into the UN. According to a survey by academic researchers, favorable attitudes toward Jamaica's alignment with Western nations declined from 71 percent in 1962 to 36 percent in 1974.

Nevertheless, during his visit to the United States in 1970, Prime Minister Shearer declared that his party, the JLP, had reoriented its foreign relations priority away from Britain to the United States. Relations between Jamaica and the United States, Canada, and Britain remained generally friendly. Tensions arose occasionally, however, over the dominance of foreign firms in the Jamaican economy in the 1970s, continuing colonial patterns of trade, racial antagonism, emigration of well-educated Jamaicans to the United

States, and the nation's ambivalent attitude toward the United States as a global power.

Jamaica's foreign policy orientation shifted again under Michael Manley, who decided that Jamaicans, in order to solve their economic problems, needed to break out of their traditional reliance on the United States and the Commonwealth of Nations. Jamaican-United States relations were strained after the Manley government established diplomatic relations with Cuba in late 1972, at a time when a majority of the Organization of American States (OAS) had voted against such recognition. In July 1973, the Manley government declared the United States ambassador, who was a political appointee, persona non grata; the ambassador had claimed before a congressional committee that he had made a "deal" with Manley, promising United States support of Manley's candidacy in the 1972 elections in exchange for his promise not to nationalize the bauxite industry. Also contributing to strained relations were the Manley government's imposition in mid-1974 of a production levy on companies producing bauxite in Jamaica and its move to acquire 51-percent control of the industry; however, subsequent negotiations largely overcame these issues (see Role of Government, this ch.). In the late 1970s, Jamaican-United States relations were aggravated further by Manley's anti-United States rhetoric in Third World forums, his government's close relations with Cuba, his staunch support for Cuban interventionism in Africa, and his defense of the placement of Soviet combat troops in Cuban bases.

After becoming prime minister in 1980, Seaga reversed Jamaica's pro-Cuban, Third World-oriented foreign policy and began close, cooperative relations with the United States administration of President Ronald Reagan. Seaga was the first foreign leader to visit Reagan following Reagan's inauguration in January 1981. A Stone Poll conducted that month indicated that 85 percent of the Jamaican electorate supported Seaga's close ties to Reagan. That year United States aid to Jamaica increased fivefold; it averaged more than US$125 million a year during the 1981–86 period but was cut by 40 percent in 1987 (see External Sector, this ch.). The Reagan administration made Jamaica the fulcrum of its Caribbean Basin Initiative (CBI), a program that Seaga helped to inspire (see Appendix D). Seaga met periodically with Reagan and other senior United States government officials during 1980–87, and in April 1982 Reagan became the first United States president to visit Jamaica. In addition to its pro-CBI stance, Jamaica adopted pro-United States positions on Grenada and relations with Cuba (see Economy, this ch.). The Seaga government favored a return to principles of détente in hopes of ensuring the security of small states,

135

and it firmly supported nuclear weapons reductions with adequate verification. The Seaga government has disagreed strongly with the United States, however, on two issues in particular: South Africa and the Law of the Sea Treaty. Jamaica, for example, disputed territorial water boundaries recognized by the United States.

Jamaica's international horizons remained limited mainly to the United States, Canada, and Britain, except during the 1970s, when Manley's government maintained close relations with the Soviet Union and Cuba. Although twenty-seven countries had missions in Kingston in 1985, Jamaica maintained a minimal diplomatic presence in foreign capitals. Even its most important missions abroad—in London, Washington, Ottawa, and at the UN—were kept small. Jamaican ambassadors usually were accredited concurrently to several countries.

Relations with Communist Countries

Jamaica had no formal relations with any communist state until Manley's government opened ties with the Soviet Union, Cuba, and China in 1972. The Manley government later developed diplomatic ties with Eastern European countries. In addition to his ideological sympathies with the socialist world, Manley sought new relationships of trade, technical assistance, loans, and direct aid from communist countries. He made his first visit to the Soviet Union in April 1979. While there, he signed a long-term agreement for Jamaican aluminum exports, as well as joint accords on sea navigation and fisheries. In addition, Moscow granted Jamaica a long-term loan to finance the purchase of Soviet goods. Manley also signed trade agreements with Hungary and Yugoslavia and established diplomatic and commercial relations with Bulgaria, Czechoslovakia, Poland, Romania, and the German Democratic Republic (East Germany).

Manley's government developed particularly close relations with Cuba during the late 1970s. Manley visited Cuba in July 1975 and sent a PNP delegation to the First Congress of the Communist Party of Cuba in Havana that December. Cuban president Fidel Castro reciprocated Manley's visit by going to Jamaica in October 1977. Numerous Jamaicans, including members of the Manley government, were sent to Cuba for ideological indoctrination and paramilitary training as members of *brigadista* groups. According to the United States Department of State, by 1980 nearly 500 Cubans were working in Jamaica.

Having made Jamaica's relations with Cuba a major issue during the 1980 election campaign, Seaga, in his first official act as prime minister, terminated the *brigadista* program with Cuba in January 1981. He also expelled most of the Cubans, including Ambassador Armando Ulises Estrada, identified by the Department of State as a Cuban intelligence operative. Although the Seaga government stopped short of severing diplomatic ties with Cuba at that time and allowed a few Cuban embassy officials to remain, it broke diplomatic relations with Cuba on October 29, 1981, in an unprecedented move of major significance in Jamaica's foreign relations. Havana's refusal to extradite three Jamaicans wanted on murder and other charges served as an apparent pretext. In a speech to Parliament on November 1, 1983, Seaga announced the expulsion of a Cuban journalist and four Soviet diplomats, whom he identified as operatives of the KGB, for espionage and conspiracy to murder a protocol officer at the Jamaican Ministry of Foreign Affairs and Industry. Jamaican-Cuban relations have remained severed under Seaga's government.

The Seaga government has maintained correct but limited relations, mainly of an economic nature, with other communist governments, mostly with the Soviet Union, Yugoslavia, and China. The Soviet Union and the Democratic People's Republic of Korea (North Korea) have maintained embassies in Kingston. Under Seaga, Jamaica has not had any military relations with communist countries.

Relations with Latin American and Caribbean Countries

Jamaica joined the OAS in 1969 in an effort to overcome the tradition of mutual indifference between the English-speaking Caribbean and the Hispanic countries. Jamaica and Mexico were the only countries to speak out in OAS meetings in the early 1970s in favor of normalization of relations with Cuba. In addition, Jamaica made a number of exchanges and agreements with Hispanic countries in the 1970s, particularly with Mexico and Venezuela; it also established a shipping line with seven Latin American countries. Jamaica was one of the signatories to the treaty establishing the Latin American Economic System in 1975 and has been an active member of the Inter-American Development Bank. Jamaica supported Panama in the Panama Canal dispute with the United States in the 1970s, and in 1986 the Seaga government sought and received assistance from Puerto Rico, with which it signed a trade agreement. Jamaica's closest non-English-speaking neighbors in the Greater Antilles—Cuba, Haiti, and the Dominican Republic—were not a significant factor in its foreign policy, with the exception of Cuba during the Manley administrations (1972–80). Jamaica did, however, play a key role in negotiating the exit of President-for-Life Jean-Claude Duvalier from Haiti in late 1986.

The Seaga government's position on the Central American crisis has been that it can best be resolved on the basis of peace initiatives introduced by the Contadora Group, which initially consisted of Panama, Mexico, Colombia, and Venezuela, whose representatives first met on the Panamanian island of Contadora in January 1983 to address the problems of Central America. Jamaican relations with Nicaragua were not nearly as controversial as those with Cuba. Jamaica's deputy prime minister and minister of foreign affairs and industry received the first ambassador of Nicaragua to Jamaica on September 19, 1984. Seaga's government has been concerned, however, about the authoritarian nature of the Sandinista regime.

Jamaica has been an active member of the Commonwealth of Nations. It hosted a conference of the Commonwealth Parliamentary Association in 1964 and became the first Caribbean country to host a Meeting of Heads of Government of the Commonwealth in 1975. Jamaica's relations with other Commonwealth Caribbean members have been determined more by the nation's incorporation in the British West Indies than by geography. Jamaica has preferred to cooperate more with these members than with its closer Hispanic neighbors; the Manley government's close relations with Cuba in the 1970s were an exception. An advocate of regional economic integration with the other English-speaking Caribbean countries, Jamaica in 1968 joined the Caribbean Free Trade Association (Carifta). On July 4, 1973, Carifta was replaced with Caricom, formed by Jamaica, Trinidad and Tobago, Barbados, and Guyana. Jamaica also joined several institutions associated with Caricom, including the Caribbean Development Bank, Caribbean Examinations Council, Caribbean Marketing Enterprise, Caribbean Meteorological Council, Council of Legal Education, and Regional Shipping Council.

Jamaica's diplomatic ties with the Commonwealth Caribbean increased during Seaga's administration. For example, having supported the right of the Belizean people to self-determination and independence, Jamaica welcomed Belize's independence, which was granted on September 21, 1981. The Seaga government declared its solidarity with Belize in the event of an armed attack against it and opened diplomatic relations with Belize in late October 1984. Jamaica also developed closer ties to the Eastern Caribbean microstates. Jamaican-Trinidadian ties, which had long been relatively close, increased. In return for a visit to Jamaica by Prime Minister George Chambers in November 1985, Seaga visited Trinidad and Tobago on March 1–4, 1986.

Jamaica was not close to all of the Commonwealth Caribbean members, however. Jamaica's relations with the Cayman Islands were poor. The islands were close when they were ruled (along with the Turks and Caicos Islands) under the same protectorate from the mid-nineteenth century to 1962. They drifted apart, however, after Jamaica received independence. As Jamaica suffered financial hardships as an independent state, the Cayman Islands prospered as a tax haven and banking center. In 1985 Jamaica reportedly had a negative image in the Cayman Islands because of Jamaican higglers, marijiuana, and marriages of convenience entered into by Jamaicans seeking residency status in the Cayman Islands.

Although Jamaica avoided any formal political or military integration with the other Commonwealth Caribbean islands, it actively sought regional cooperation in these areas in the 1980s. At a meeting of regional prime ministers and other high government officials held in Kingston in January 1986, Seaga fulfilled a long-held dream by forming a conservative regional organization called the Caribbean Democratic Union (CDU) to provide a forum for exchange of views on political matters of a regional and international nature. A regional affiliate of the International Democratic Union, the CDU included the ruling centrist parties of seven other Caribbean countries: Belize, Dominica, Grenada, St. Christopher and Nevis, St. Lucia, St. Vincent and the Grenadines, and Montserrat. The prime minister of Bermuda attended the inaugural meeting as an observer. Seaga, who was elected CDU chairman, described the organization as an attempt to revive a regional political alliance similar to the West Indies Federation of 1958–62.

Other Third World Relations

After independence Jamaica's foreign policy increasingly emphasized the nation's connection with Africa and issues such as colonialism, racism, and South Africa's apartheid system. These concerns reflected the African ethnic origin of about three-fourths of Jamaica's population. In recognition of the cultural importance of the Rastafarians, who actually constituted less than 5 percent of the Jamaican population, the government of Prime Minister Shearer hosted a state visit by Ethiopia's Haile Selassi on April 2, 1966. Jamaica opened low-level diplomatic relations with black African states in 1968 but established an embassy only in Ethiopia. Shearer and Manley, the leader of the opposition, made extended tours of Africa in 1969, including visits to Addis Ababa. In the early 1970s, Jamaica opened resident missions in Algeria and Nigeria.

Jamaica's UN voting in the 1960s reflected its pro-African stances on four issues: Southern Rhodesia (present-day Zimbabwe), Namibia, African territories under Portuguese administration, and apartheid in South Africa. Since independence Jamaica's voting record on these issues has closely followed that of other Commonwealth Caribbean and other nonwhite states. Until 1973 Jamaica gave only verbal and moral support to the antiapartheid and anticolonial causes. That year, however, Prime Minister Manley visited several African countries on his way to the Nonaligned Movement summit conference in Algiers and pledged material support for guerrillas seeking to overthrow the white-dominated regime in Southern Rhodesia. In 1976 Jamaica signed the International Convention on the Suppression and Punishment of the Crime of Apartheid. The Seaga government continued to support UN resolutions and actions against apartheid and for the independence of Namibia, rejecting the view that Namibia's independence must be conditioned on the withdrawal of Cuban troops from Angola.

Jamaica, which had become a full member of the Nonaligned Movement by the time of the Belgrade Conference in 1968, began playing a prominent role in that organization after Manley became prime minister in 1972. Saying he was trying to find a "third way" between capitalism and communism, Manley emphasized nationalism and railed against what he called United States imperialism. He headed a high-level Jamaican delegation to the Nonaligned Movement conference in Algiers in 1973, traveling to the meeting by airplane with Fidel Castro. In addition to its leading role in establishing the International Bauxite Association (IBA) in early 1974, Jamaica was involved in the international negotiations that led to the signing of the Lomé Convention in early 1975. A Jamaican delegation also played a key coordinating role in promoting a New International Economic Order at the 1976 United Nations Conference on Trade and Development.

Seaga's government continued the nation's nonaligned status on key political and economic issues before the UN. Jamaica generally continued to vote with the positions of the Nonaligned Movement. For example, in 1986 Foreign Minister Shearer advocated a comprehensive settlement of the problem in the Middle East and the right of the Palestinian peoples to a homeland. He also called for Israel to pull back to its 1967 borders but, at the same time, stressed the right of the Jewish state to exist. The Seaga government advocated the UN as the best forum for negotiating a solution to the conflict in the Middle East. Although Seaga expanded his nation's relations with Third World countries in the 1980s, he lowered its profile as an advocate of Nonaligned Movement causes.

In addition to participating in the UN, Jamaica has participated actively in international institutions such as the World Bank, IMF, General Agreement on Tariffs and Trade, EEC, IBA, INTELSAT, and the International Seabed Authority, which made Kingston its headquarters.

National Security

During its long history as a British colony, Jamaica looked to London for its defense and security needs. Unlike many Hispanic countries of Latin America, including nearby Cuba and the Dominican Republic, Jamaica remained immune from foreign military intervention while under British protection. Jamaica reciprocated by supporting Britain's war efforts. As a member of the British West Indies, Jamaica participated in World War I by sending over 10,000 men to the front.

After World War II broke out, the United States became the recognized protector of the British West Indies, acquiring a ninety-nine-year lease for base rights in Jamaica and other islands under the Lend-Lease Agreement (also called the Bases-for-Destroyers Agreement) of 1941 (see The Strategic Setting, ch. 7). Jamaica also became a part of North Atlantic defense preparations, hosting United States naval and air bases. Many volunteers from Jamaica joined the various services, particularly the Royal Air Force. The Jamaica Contingent of the First Battalion of the West India Regiment went overseas in May 1944. When the war ended, the United States deactivated its bases in Jamaica, and Britain reassumed responsibility for Jamaica's defense and foreign affairs until independence. On August 7, 1962, the day after independence, Bustamante announced that the United States was free to establish a military base in Jamaica without any obligation to provide aid in return, but the offer was declined. Nevertheless, as the Castro regime consolidated its power in Cuba during the 1960s and the Soviet military presence in the region expanded, Jamaica's importance to United States national security interests grew.

Jamaica experienced no direct military threat during its first twenty-five years as an independent state; in the early 1980s, however, it had to deal with indirect threats to its national security interests posed by Cuban activities in Jamaica and by the events in Grenada. The Seaga government handled the issue of the Cuban presence in Jamaica by expelling the Cubans and breaking diplomatic relations in 1981 (see Relations with Communist Countries, this ch.). Seaga's concerns about Grenada's undemocratic practices in the 1979–83 period and its close ties to Cuba and the Soviet Union also prompted his government to take a more active regional

141

security role. Jamaica did not, however, sign the 1982 memorandum that established the Regional Security System (RSS) in the Eastern Caribbean (see A Regional Security System, ch. 7). When Maurice Bishop was overthrown and assassinated by the short-lived Coard-Austin regime in October 1983, the Seaga government's concern turned to alarm. Jamaica joined several members of the Organisation of Eastern Caribbean States in an appeal for United States military intervention in Grenada to restore order and democracy and then participated in a joint United States-Caribbean military operation in Grenada (see Current Strategic Considerations, ch. 7). Jamaica, whose population favored the joint military action by a 56-percent majority, also provided the largest Caribbean contingent (250 troops) to the peacekeeping force in Grenada from late October 1983 to June 1985. The Seaga government continued actively to support security cooperation among the Commonwealth Caribbean islands by having Jamaican troops participate in regional military exercises, such as Operation "Exotic Palm" in September 1985. In addition, Jamaica cooperated with the United States and RSS member states on regional security matters by holding joint military and narcotics interdiction exercises and by offering some training and technical assistance to the Eastern Caribbean.

The Public Security Forces

Jamaica has endorsed measures to ensure security of the Western Hemisphere but has not participated in any formal defense agreements. Despite its proximity to Cuba, Jamaica has not felt a need to maintain a large defense force, perhaps because it has always had powerful protectors. Even with the support of the police, the armed forces would be totally inadequate to resist foreign military aggression, especially from Cuba. Like the other English-speaking island nations in the Caribbean, Jamaica would have to rely on the assistance of a powerful ally in the event of outside military aggression. The nation's combined forces also would be inadequate to control a significant internal disturbance. Jamaica has not been threatened by military or mercenary invasion or internal insurgencies, however, in part because of its powerful allies but also because of its traditional political stability and its relative isolation from mainland countries and the more vulnerable Eastern Caribbean microstates.

In 1987 the Ministry of National Security (which had included the justice portfolio during 1974–86) remained responsible for maintaining the internal and external security of the island, but it no longer administered justice. This ministry oversaw the Jamaica

Defence Force (JDF), Jamaica Constabulary Force (JCF), and correctional programs and institutions. The Ministry of National Security's 1986 budget allocation was approximately US$69 million for current expenses and US$6.5 million for capital expenses, accounting for 5.9 percent of the central government's budget. In 1984 US$38 million of the ministry's budget was allocated to the JCF. The JDF budget declined in the 1980s for budgetary reasons; it was approximately US$20 million in 1986, as compared with US$25.4 million in 1985 and US$38.9 million in 1984.

Although traditionally apolitical, both the JDF and the JCF were subject to governmental policy directives. Their commanders—the JCF commissioner and the JDF chief of staff, respectively—were responsible for managing their respective forces on a day-to-day basis. JCF and JDF commanders explained in December 1986 that the minister of national security could make suggestions or recommendations to either force and that the JDF or JCF high commands could consider them as they saw fit.

The Armed Forces

In late 1987, Jamaica's combined armed forces, the JDF, consisted of a ground force supported by small air and coastal patrol contingents. Although not strictly an army, the JDF is referred to as such in common parlance. Its mission was to defend the country against aggression and to support the JCF, as required, in maintaining essential services and in protecting the civil population in the event of a disaster. The JDF also was responsible for coastal surveillance and air-sea rescue operations. In addition, the JDF has supported antidrug operations; since early 1982, JDF Eradication Units have helped to destroy marijuana crops and illegal air strips. Since the defense portfolio was dropped in the 1970s, the JDF has been under the minister of national security. As in the other Commonwealth Caribbean islands, the prime minister is the de facto head of the defense forces.

The predominant element in the JDF is the Jamaica Regiment, whose origins go back to the West India Regiment that was founded in 1798 and used by the British in the American Revolution and various colonial campaigns in West Africa, as well as during World War I. The regiment, reconstituted as the New West India Regiment, formed the core of the defense force of the short-lived West Indies Federation in 1958–62. After the federation disintegrated, the First Battalion and Third Battalion of the regiment became the First Battalion and Third Battalion of the Jamaica Regiment. The Second Battalion was incorporated by Trinidad and Tobago in its new national forces. In 1962 the Jamaica Local Forces (JLF) was formed as one of the conditions under which Jamaica was granted independence. The JLF soon evolved into the JDF, but the First Battalion and Third Battalion of the JDF retained their historical designations.

In the mid-1980s, the JDF's predominant ground force element consisted of the First Battalion and a support and service battalion. The First Battalion included an air wing and coast guard, as well as a headquarters unit at Up Park Camp in Kingston, an engineering unit, and other support units. Detachments were stationed at the JDF camp in a facility first established by the British in the mid-nineteenth century at Newcastle, high in the Blue Mountains, and in outstations located in various parts of the island. The Third Battalion, consisting of part-time volunteers, constituted the ground force reserve, called the Jamaica National Reserve (JNR). Commanded by a lieutenant colonel, the JNR, which had 1,030 members in 1986, consisted of a ground force supported by air and coastal patrol elements organized into an infantry battalion.

Once the sole operational element of the former Ministry of Defence, the JDF, together with the police, was placed under the Ministry of National Security and Justice in 1974. The prime minister commanded the JDF through a major general. In 1986 the JDF had a complement of 1,780 officers and personnel. In addition, a civilian staff of about 360 included functional and administrative personnel.

By 1986 JDF ground force equipment was almost exclusively of British origin and included the SLR rifle, Sterling submachine gun, general-purpose machine gun, and twelve 81mm mortars. The army also had a small number of Ferret scout cars, supplemented by fifteen Cadillac-Gage V-150 Commando wheeled armored personnel carriers received from the United States.

The JDF's Air Wing, which was formed in July 1963, was headquartered at Up Park Camp and had a base at Montego Bay. Expanded and trained successively by British Army Air Corps and Canadian Air Force personnel, the Air Wing had a strength of 250 officers and personnel in 1986. It was equipped for ground force liaison, search and rescue, police cooperation, survey, and transport missions. In 1986 its inventory included predominantly United States-made aircraft but also some Canadian, British, and French models: five Bell 206A, three Bell 212, and two Aerospatiale Alouette II light helicopters; two of the Britten-Norman Islander light transports of the short-take-off-and-landing type; one each of DHC-6 Beech KingAir 90 and Beech Duke DHC-6 light transport models; and four Cessnas, including two 185s and two light transports: the 210 and 337. The aircraft were well adapted for use in areas of the hilly interior of the country, where there were few landing fields.

The JDF's coastal patrol element, the Coast Guard, was established at independence. In 1986 it had a complement of about 150 active personnel, including 18 officers and 115 petty officers and personnel under the command of an officer with the rank of lieutenant commander. It had an additional sixteen personnel in its reserve and thirty in other ranks. Equipped with predominantly United States-made equipment, the Coast Guard modernized its three 60-ton patrol vessels in 1972–73 and augmented them in 1974 with the 103-ton multipurpose transport patrol vessel H.M.J.S *Fort Charles*. The Coast Guard operated from its base at Port Royal in cooperation with the harbormasters and the harbor patrol of the JCF. A Coast Guard unit was responsible for maritime antismuggling operations. The JDF's Coast Guard was too small, however, to patrol adequately the island's 1,022-kilometer-long coastline.

Following independence, Jamaica retained a British training mission for the three JDF components; all JDF officers were trained in Britain. Canada later took over Air Wing training functions. All Coast Guard officers received training at the Royal Naval College in Dartmouth, England. The United States Navy also has provided training assistance for Coast Guard officers and other ranks. After a four-year lapse (mid-1980 to 1984), the British Army and JDF resumed their program of reciprocal defense exercises in June 1984. In addition, a group of 140 JDF soldiers was flown to Dover, England, for a month of training. Jamaica signed a new military training agreement with Canada in 1985, replacing the one in effect since 1965. Over 250 JDF candidates were trained in Canada during the 1965–85 period.

The United States began providing some military assistance to Jamaica's small defense force after Jamaica requested training and equipment assistance in 1963. Jamaica's military aid allocation, however, was zero in the last year of the Manley government in 1980, partially because of the government's close ties to Cuba. The United States resumed military assistance to Jamaica after Seaga took office, and in 1986 assistance totaled US$8.3 million, mostly for enhancing the JDF's narcotics interdiction and marijuana eradication capabilities. Jamaica was scheduled to receive a total of US$6.3 million in United States military assistance in 1988, including US$300,000 in International Military Education and Training funds. Under the Seaga government, the JDF had received heavy equipment, including jeeps, trucks, and patrol boats from the United States.

145

Jamaica's military recruitment was entirely voluntary. Young men between the ages of eighteen and twenty-four who had left school at the secondary and postsecondary levels were required to register for two years of public service work as members of the National Youth Service. This service could be performed in the JDF, an all-volunteer force, and prospective registrants were encouraged to consider service in the JDF with an eye toward making it a career. JDF personnel were eligible for retirement under the Government Pensions Scheme.

The Jamaica Combined Cadet Force (JCCF) was a uniformed training contingent founded in 1943. Funds provided by the prime minister's office covered expenses for training, uniforms, equipment, travel and subsistence, and pay of salaried personnel. JCCF operations were expanded substantially in 1972, and in 1973 the organization consisted of some 2,000 officers and cadets in 33 postprimary school units in all parts of the island, together with an independent unit and a small headquarters unit at Up Park Camp. Its mission was to provide youths with training, discipline, good citizenship, and leadership. Although not a part of the JDF, the JCCF provided a substantial reservoir of young men who had undergone some military training.

Apart from its training assignments, the JDF was active principally in support of the larger JCF. A mobile reserve unit, the JDF was called on when a local police detachment was too small to deal with an incident such as an unauthorized strike or a riot. It also furnished manpower for patrols during civil unrest, search-and-rescue missions, and searches for firearms or marijuana. The Air Wing gave mobility to ground detachments, and the Coast Guard acted in cooperation with harbormasters and the police harbor patrol.

The Police

The major police force is the Jamaica Constabulary Force (JCF), which was established in 1867 shortly after the institution of crown colony government. Generally viewed as poorly trained, underpaid, and overburdened, the JCF generated the country's most persistent human rights concerns in the 1980s. Police auxiliary reserve units included the 1,500-member Island Special Constabulary Force (ISCF), which assisted the JCF in large operations; the 1,700-member Special District Constables, who served as local police in smaller localities when called on to assist the JCF or ISCF; the Police Mobile Reserve Division (PMRD), whose duties included controlling or suppressing civil disturbances, providing security for parades and rallies, and conducting raids related to marijuana and the

Firearms Act; the Parish Special Constables, who served in the regular force on special occasions; and the Authorized Persons, who had limited police powers. Larger cities had municipal police forces, but their functions were restricted to enforcing municipal regulations and guarding municipal property. A senior superintendent of police headed the JCF's narcotics unit, which has been the lead agency for combating drug trafficking since 1974.

The JCF was reorganized in 1984. At that time, the Police Staff College was created to provide higher training and education. The school was located at Fort Charles near Port Royal at the end of the Palisades Peninsula. New recruits, called cadets, were required to take written, oral, and medical tests before being admitted to the school. They received an eighteen-week basic course in police law, self-defense, first aid, and drill. Usually, they were sent to a rural post for ten months of on-the-job training and returned to the school for a six-week senior recruit course before becoming constables. More advanced training was provided for constables, corporals, and sergeants in such areas as pathology, sociology, and political science. Completion of the advanced courses was required before being considered for promotion to a higher rank. Some officers and personnel received advanced training in other countries.

In 1986 the JCF had an authorized strength of 6,317 and an actual strength of 5,601, which was 3.9 percent below that of 1985. This figure represented a ratio of police to population of about 1 to 400. Despite an attrition rate in 1986 of 6.1 percent, the recruitment rate was 7.5 percent below that of 1985. The continuing decline in the number of recruits was attributed largely to attempts by the JCF high command to attract a higher level of recruits by raising educational and mental aptitude criteria. In 1985 only 181 of 5,418 applicants were accepted for training. Applicants had to meet height, age, and literacy requirements, as well as produce a certificate of character from a magistrate or person of similar standing and pass a medical examination. Constables were enrolled for five years and spent the first six months in a probationary capacity. Reasons for the JCF's failure to attract qualified individuals included relatively low salaries, the high levels of risk facing the police, and significant reductions in the size of the police cadet corps, a major supplier of recruits in previous years.

In late 1987, the JCF comprised four branches: administration, services, security, and special operations. Each was commanded by an assistant commissioner, with the exception of the Security Branch, which was headed by a deputy commissioner. In addition to providing physical security to visiting dignitaries, the Special Operations Branch was responsible for the Criminal

Investigation Department; the Police Marine Division (in charge of harbor patrol), located in Newport; and the PMRD, which was quartered at Harman Barracks and made up of the Mounted Troops, the Patrol Section, the Traffic Department (including the Radio Patrol Division), and the Women's Police. Under a December 1984 reorganization, the Special Operations Branch also was tasked to combat hard-core criminal groups and individuals who target the security forces.

The JCF's Security Branch handled immigration and passport services. The Police Marine Division's harbor police operated in Kingston Harbour and a few other seaports, enforcing harbor regulations and carrying out rescues, as well as fighting crime on the waterfront. Customs Protective Officers checked the documents of goods going in or out of the customs areas at Kingston Harbour, called Western Terminals, and at the two international airports.

Under the Suppression of Crime (Special Provisions) Act, in effect since 1974, the JDF was authorized to conduct joint operations with the JCF in order to maintain the peace. The act permitted the JDF to cordon off any area on the island while police conducted house-to-house searches within those areas without warrants. Police forces relied on the act extensively, and detention of suspects ''reasonably'' suspected of having committed a crime occurred regularly without a warrant, particularly in poor neighborhoods. Almost all detainees were released eventually without being charged.

Until the 1970s, the police generally had a good reputation and were supported by the mass media and the middle and upper classes. The rural peasant and urban lower classes, however, generally mistrusted the police. Public esteem for police morality was lowered in the 1970s by increased newspaper reportage of allegations of police improprieties and brutality. An Americas Watch report documented an average of 217 police killings a year from 1979 to 1986, representing one-half of the country's total killings. The Jamaica Council of Human Rights reported that police killed 289 persons in 1984. Adverse public opinion resulting from charges of human rights abuses by the police prompted Seaga to reshuffle his cabinet on October 17, 1986. In the process, Winston Spaulding was dropped as minister of national security and justice, and the ministry was reorganized to eliminate the justice portfolio. The public also increasingly questioned police competence as a result of the growing number of unsolved crimes in the country, particularly those involving members of political parties.

The Penal System

To combat an increase in crime, judges began imposing stiffer prison sentences and an average of twelve death sentences annually. Penal administration also was improved in the mid-1970s. The JCF, JDF, and other elements in the legal and penal systems were placed under the Ministry of National Security and Justice, which had been formed in 1974. Although the justice and national security portfolios had been separated in October 1986, the Ministry of National Security retained responsibility for Jamaica's prisons, Probation Department, and reform schools through its Department of Correctional Services. The latter department also operated a training school for prison guards, called wardens, in methods of supervision and correctional control of prison inmates and their rehabilitation.

Prison conditions also posed a problem in Jamaica. The parliamentary ombudsman reported in 1986 that prison conditions had deteriorated further since 1984, when he had released a study detailing the deplorable facilities and degrading conditions. Overcrowding, unsanitary conditions, inadequate food, and limited medical care for inmates were the principal problems in the nation's two maximum security prisons and in its many police stations, where conditions were generally the worst.

In 1986 Jamaica had eight correctional centers: the General Penitentiary, St. Catherine District Prison, South Camp Rehabilitation Centre (also known as the Gun Court prison), Fort Augusta Prison, Tamarind Farm Prison, New Broughton Prison, Richmond Farm Prison, and St. Jago Women's Centre. In 1986 these prisons had a total inmate population of 3,452 (rated capacity: 2,861). Female admissions increased by 129, a 10-percent increase over the 1985 figure. Approximately 32 percent (954) of the 1985 total were incarcerated for major offenses such as murder, robbery, and felonious wounding and the rest for minor offenses such as larceny. Over 70 percent of those imprisoned were under the age of 30 whereas 47 percent were 24 years or younger. The average age-group for females ranged from thirty to thirty-nine, whereas males averaged twenty to twenty-four.

The country's principal maximum security prison, the General Penitentiary, was located in downtown Kingston near the harbor. Designed for 800 inmates, it had long been overcrowded and was scheduled for eventual replacement by a newer building. In 1986 it held 1,601 prisoners, including habitual male adult offenders serving long sentences. The St. Catherine District Prison, another maximum security institution for habitual male offenders serving short sentences, held 1,056 prisoners in 1986. The facility served as the site of death row, where condemned persons awaited execution. Projects for improving the General Penitentiary and other correctional centers were undertaken in 1985, and others were being planned.

The South Camp Rehabilitation Centre housed 320 prisoners in 1986. Open to public view, the steel-meshed, gun-turreted facility was located in central Kingston. Fort Augusta Prison, located in a fortress built in 1970 to guard Kingston Harbour, was used as a minimum security facility; it held 105 inmates in 1986. Selected persons who had responded favorably to liberal treatment were transferred there from the General Penitentiary to finish their sentences. Tamarind Farm Prison held 134 first offenders and some selected recidivists serving short sentences. Richmond Farm Prison was a maximum security prison housing first offenders serving long-term sentences; its inmate population in 1986 was 119. New Broughton Prison and St. Jago Women's Centre had 12 and 104 prisoners, respectively, in 1986. Adults held in remand were placed either in police lockups distributed nationwide or in the adult remand centers administered by the Department of Correctional Services. The number of persons admitted to the adult remand centers in 1985 declined by 3 to 1,274.

In order to reduce the rate of recidivism, the Legal Reform Division drafted the Criminal Records (Rehabilitation of Offenders) Bill and the Corrections Act, which was enacted on December 2, 1985. Under this act, the label ''prisoner'' was changed to ''inmate,'' ''prison officer'' to ''correctional officer,'' and ''prison'' to ''adult correctional centre.'' The act also established gainful employment programs for inmates, prerelease and halfway houses for the rehabilitation and social integration of inmates, and provisions governing the standards and inspection of correctional institutions. In addition, it permitted temporary absences of inmates from correctional institutions for specified periods.

Young persons under the age of seventeen charged with committing offenses were generally, but not always, tried before a juvenile court. While awaiting trial, which could occur up to three months after the charge, they were detained in ''places of safety'' where they received classroom and vocational training. Places of safety may be operated by the government or charitable and religious institutions or hospitals. If found guilty by the court, juveniles could be placed on probation or sentenced either to reform schools, called juvenile correctional centers (approved schools), or to a children's home. Juveniles receiving custodial sentences were committed to four special rehabilitation institutions. Boys went to Hilltop (maximum security) in St. Ann Parish or Rio Cobre Community School (open) in St. Catherine Parish, and girls went to Armadale (open) in St. Ann Parish or Lower Esher (open) in St. Mary Parish. In 1985 these facilities, with a combined capacity of 318 (218 boys and 100 girls), held 230. The only juvenile remand center, the St. Andrew Remand Center for Boys, was located in Stony Hill, St. Andrew Parish, where thirty-five were held in remand in 1985.

Most of the work of the Probation Department consisted of juvenile cases. Generally, in at least one-third of all juvenile court cases the offender was placed on probation. Probably less than 20 percent of the adults sentenced every year were placed on probation. Each parish had a Parish Probation Committee to oversee the work of individual probation officers, who were assigned to every court in the country.

Incidence of Crime

Jamaican national security concerns under the Seaga government have focused on countering three growing threats: crimes involving firearms, gunrunning, and narcotics production and trafficking. Although violent crime had become a major social problem, none of these phenomena appeared to pose a major threat to Jamaica's national security in 1987. The government was mainly concerned about the adverse impact that violent crime against tourists could have on the tourism industry, on which the island was dependent economically.

The number of reported crimes, especially crimes of violence involving firearms, began growing during the 1960s and escalated sharply in the early 1970s. According to the Planning Institute of Jamaica, however, in 1986 the number of reported crimes decreased for the first time in several years, going from 53,066 in 1985 to 49,511 in 1986. Although violent crimes against individuals declined from 21,123 in 1985 to 19,301 in 1986, reported murders increased slightly, going from 434 in 1985 to 449 in 1986. Shootings declined in 1986 by about 100; there were 1,050 reported cases during the year. The largest single cause of murders in 1986 (46 percent) was domestic disputes. Other murders in 1986 were perpetrated under circumstances that included the following: 18.7 percent in association with other crimes such as robberies; 10.9 percent in revenge or reprisals (as compared with 6.9 percent in 1985); and 3.8 percent in drug-related activities (as compared with 2.3 percent in 1985).

Violent confrontations between police and crime suspects were frequent, and criminals often possessed firearms. Breaches of the

Firearm Act continued to increase in the early 1980s, from 842 reported cases in 1982 to 1,312 in 1985; incidents declined to 1,258 in 1986. Security forces recovered more than 2,700 firearms, including 126 M-16 and 7 M-14 assault rifles, in 1977–84.

In the 1980s, violent crime continued to be most intense in the St. Andrew-Kingston District, which usually accounted for about half of all reported cases. In general, law enforcement agencies did not adequately control crime. Beginning in the late 1970s, mob killings or lynching of thieves increased, especially in rural areas. There were 226 cases reported in 1982; prosecution of vigilantes was rare.

Much of the increased crime, particularly petty theft and pilferage, was attributed to poverty and unemployment. Gasoline price rises in January 1985 led to riots that left ten dead and fifteen wounded. Although Seaga dismissed the protests as the work of extremists, 53 percent of Jamaicans and 66 percent of Kingston residents who were polled sympathized with the rioters. Violent crimes against tourists on the north coast increased dramatically during the 1986–87 tourist seasons; most of these incidents involved armed robberies.

An increasing number of crimes, including major offenses such as breaking and entering, larceny, and felonious wounding, were being committed by juveniles under the age of seventeen. The number of juveniles brought before the courts in 1985 increased by 9 percent to 2,599. Those in need of care or protection (1,004) comprised the largest group brought before the courts, whereas those charged with wounding and assault (571) and larceny (516) comprised the other categories. Some juveniles were tried in regular courts rather than in juvenile courts.

Political Violence

Although the political system has enjoyed a tradition of stability, a darker side of politics—endemic violence—intruded increasingly on the public consciousness after the mid-1970s. Violence has characterized Jamaican politics since the slavery era and has surfaced at times of protest or repression. Almost every general or municipal election since independence has been preceded and followed by gang warfare, street outbreaks, and occasional assassinations.

The first use of guns in Jamaican politics reportedly took place in Seaga's West Kingston constituency in the months before the 1967 election between Seaga and PNP politician Dudley Thompson. The political tension heightened after Walter Rodney, a Guyanese university professor and Black Power movement (see Glossary) advocate, was banned from Jamaica in October 1968. The government of Prime Minister Shearer suppressed the riots that ensued.

The level of political violence escalated dramatically in the 1976 election campaign, in which 162 persons were killed. The political disorder and rising crime caused the Manley government to declare a state of emergency, which remained in effect until June 1977. Some observers blamed the JLP for the sharply increased political violence in the late 1970s, but others attributed it to PNP militants linked to Cuba. More likely, extremist elements of the three parties—PNP, JLP, and WPJ—bore some responsibility for the increase. These parties are all known to have employed and armed thugs and criminals at election time. In 1979–80 Armando Ulises Estrada, Cuba's ambassador to Jamaica, aided an extreme left PNP faction in smuggling an estimated 600 M–16 assault rifles into Jamaica from Cuba. Some of these automatic weapons originated from former United States stockpiles in Vietnam; others may have been obtained from black-market sources by JLP extremists. Their use during the nine-month 1980 election campaign escalated the level of violence in Jamaican politics. Rampant electoral violence during that period left 745 persons dead, including one member of Parliament.

In contrast with 1980, the 1983 and 1986 elections were generally peaceful. Whereas political and gang feuds had accounted for 19 percent of all murders in 1984, this percentage declined to 12.2 in 1986. At the inauguration of the new Parliament in January 1984, however, Manley led about 7,000 PNP supporters in demonstrations against Seaga's snap elections, resulting in 4 persons killed and 160 arrested. A municipal election code of conduct between the JLP and PNP minimized violence in the local elections of July 29, 1986. Nevertheless, there were some reports of beatings of electoral clerks, the seizure of polling stations by armed men, harassment of voters, and a mob killing.

By raising popular expectations and not fulfilling them, Jamaica's political parties and governmental leaders were partly responsible for the alienation and protest that surfaced in violence. Until Manley's tenure at Jamaica House in the 1970s, each party in power had followed cautious policies designed to maintain the status quo, so as not to lose domestic or foreign sources of funds. In addition, on several occasions governments formed by each party attempted to use repression to control violence, thereby setting up a chain reaction. The legal system was not effective in dealing with politically motivated violence because suspects, victims, and witnesses remained silent and because police were reluctant to get involved in political disputes. In the interests of security, governments resorted to armed police, martial law, or emergency powers, practices that sometimes resulted in violent protests.

The nation's political violence derives from the socioeconomic structure of Jamaican politics, that is, social stratification along racial and economic class lines. Increasing political, social, and economic polarization in Jamaica has contributed to both political and criminal violence. According to Stone, it is rooted in what he has called "bullyism," or a propensity to resort to violence, that is deeply ingrained in Jamaican culture. For example, since the 1960s armed gangs have "ruled" some ghetto areas of Kingston, using violence and intimidation against anyone suspected of sympathizing with a rival party. These and other gangs, consisting of hardened criminals and numbering up to 3,000 members, have been blamed by observers for much of the street and electoral violence in Kingston since the late 1960s. Some groups believed or were led to believe that their sectional interests, such as race identity, would not be served by either of the two political parties and that violent expression of demands was an alternate form of participation in the national political process. Violence also erupted occasionally as a result of trade union rivalries, which were underscored by the affiliation of the major unions with political parties.

No known armed terrorist or guerrilla group was active in Jamaica in the late 1980s, but there had been occasional subversive incidents on the island in the 1980s, and several armed groups had been linked to such activities. The Seaga government tied several subversive and criminal activities in Jamaica to Cuban-trained extremists. In a speech to Parliament in 1984, for example, Spaulding, then minister of national security and justice, blamed the violence against policemen on the Hot Steppers Gang. The minister described gang members as "specially trained and highly motivated persons who constitute a special threat to Jamaica's security," and he linked the group to drug trafficking and Cuba, which, he alleged, provided guerrilla training for gang members. Spaulding also charged that the gang had political links with people in the top echelons of the WPJ, as well as with PNP activists. Security forces dispersed the gang from its camps in the Wareika Hills in 1984. Nevertheless, in 1985–87 there were several armed attacks by unidentified groups against police stations, from which weapons were stolen. The Seaga government blamed the WPJ for several bank robberies.

As of late 1987, Jamaica had not been subjected to any significant acts of international terrorism. Nevertheless, the country has expressed concern about the potential threat of terrorism and has subscribed to the principal international antiterrorism conventions.

154

In a UN speech in October 1986, Foreign Minister Shearer called for a strengthened international law against hostage taking, as well as consideration of a UN convention on the suppression of international terrorism. The Suppression of Crime (Special Provisions) Act empowers the government to combat terrorism. At the request of the Seaga government, the House of Representatives has extended this act at six-month intervals.

Narcotics Crime

According to the *New York Times,* reporting on information from a United States and British law enforcement conference held in Miami in July 1987, a widespread Jamaican criminal organization consisting of about twenty gangs of illegal aliens was operating in fifteen metropolitan areas in the United States and trafficking in firearms and drugs between Florida and Jamaica. A United States government official described the gangs as the fastest growing and most violent of the criminal groups operating in the United States. Between 400 and 500 homicides in the United States in the previous two years were attributed to these self-described "posses." Seaga government officials have stated publicly that many of the guns in Jamaica were flown in by narcotics traffickers from Florida and other Gulf Coast locations and landed on illegal airstrips or deserted roads.

Marijuana production in Jamaica, especially western Jamaica, has increased dramatically since the mid-1960s, even though production of the drug has been illegal since 1913. As the major illicit drug activity on the island, cannabis cultivation has been of particular concern to the Seaga government. By the mid-1980s, an estimated 20 percent or less of the marijuana produced in Jamaica was consumed locally; the rest was smuggled to other countries. Jamaica was supplying an estimated 10 to 15 percent of the total amount of marijuana smuggled into the United States each year. Marijuana traffickers included members of every ethnic group in Jamaica, as well as "United States citizens," according to the minister of public utilities and transport. Moreover, the minister reported in late 1984 that more than 50 percent of the people involved in marijuana also were involved in cocaine. Jamaica was rapidly becoming a major cocaine transshipment point for Latin American suppliers to the North American market.

The Jamaican government has been firmly committed to reducing marijuana cultivation. In 1972 a special JCF narcotics squad began combating the increasing use and illegal export of drugs. After three police members were killed and mutilated by marijuana growers in December 1983, the government began cracking down harder on cultivators by stepping up eradication and confiscation efforts. Although limited by a lack of equipment and other resources, the thirty-three-member squad and JDF Eradication Units carried out many successful operations against marijuana traffickers in the mid-1980s. The security forces also have attempted to damage illegal air strips with explosives (twenty-three damaged in 1986), but in many cases the traffickers quickly rebuilt them.

In the mid-1980s, the United States urged Jamaica to undertake large-scale eradication using slash-and-burn methods and chemical weed killers, but these proposals met with growing resistance in a country where marijuana is referred to as "the poor man's friend." In May 1985, the Jamaican government asked for increased United States assistance in combating drug production and in assisting farmers to introduce alternative high-yield crops. Seaga also announced in December 1986 that the country would begin herbicidal backpack spraying in order to avoid jeopardizing United States economic aid to Jamaica. The 1986 eradication figure of 2,756 hectares was a record, but that year smugglers exported twice as much marijuana to the United States as normal. In the mid-1980s, the United States increased aid to Jamaica's narcotics interdiction and eradication programs, earmarking more than US$2.6 million in 1986 for this purpose, as compared with US$45,000 in 1985.

The narcotics squad has cooperated with United States law enforcement officers. Jamaican authorities have alerted United States authorities about vessels and small aircraft suspected of carrying narcotics directly from Jamaica or in transit from Latin American countries. The United States Coast Guard has stopped and searched those carriers whenever possible. Commercial airlines flying between the United States and Jamaica incurred millions of dollars in fines in the 1985–87 period as a result of substantial quantities of marijuana being discovered aboard their aircraft.

In 1986 a total of 4,123 persons, including 736 foreigners (608 Americans, 78 Canadians, and 50 Britons) were arrested for various breaches under Jamaica's Dangerous Drugs Act. Measures used by the security forces to reduce the extent of trafficking included roadblocks, surveillance of air and sea craft, and use of trained dogs at international airports and sea terminals.

The Criminal Justice System

Jamaica's legal system, including much of the substantive and procedural criminal law, derives from Britain's legal code. The relevant statutes are those in force at the time of independence, including a number enacted by the British Parliament in London and those subsequently enacted by the Jamaican Parliament. As in all countries with roots in the English system, a body of case law governs the interpretation and application of statutes; some issues may be resolved by common law.

The Jamaican Penal Code and the Prevention of Crime Law of 1963 established minimum penalties for certain crimes. Minor crimes are prosecuted in the courts of petty session, headed by justices of the peace, who are also called lay magistrates. The resident magistrate's courts and the Supreme Court hear both civil and criminal cases (see Government and Politics, this ch.). The more serious criminal cases usually are tried in the circuit courts of the Supreme Court. All circuit court trials are jury trials; the jury is composed of seven persons except for homicide cases, which require twelve jurors. A majority of jurors may render verdicts, except in capital cases in which unanimity is required. The resident magistrate's courts, petty sessions courts, and the Gun Court hold trials without juries. Most trials, with the exception of the Gun Court, are open to the public.

The Gun Court was established on April 2, 1974, as a combination court and prison to combat the increase in violent crimes involving firearms. It operates as an extension of the Supreme Court and deals with crimes involving guns. The Gun Court Act allowed detention and prosecution of subjects and authorized a single resident magistrate's court to issue prison sentences to those convicted of illegal possession of firearms or ammunition. In July 1975, the Privy Council in London ruled that the Gun Court Act was constitutional. The Privy Council held, however, that mandatory sentences of indefinite detention with hard labor could not legally be imposed by the resident magistrate presiding over the Gun Court. The 1983 Gun Court Amendment Act enabled the resident magistrate's courts in all parishes except Kingston, St. Andrew, and St. Catherine to decide whether a particular charge would be dealt with in a resident magistrate's court or should be referred to the Gun Court.

If the conviction occurs in a resident magistrate's court, the accused party may often obtain bail while his case is being appealed. If the conviction is in either a circuit court or the Gun Court, there is no bail during appeal proceedings, except under certain special considerations. Appeals to the Privy Council in London can take up to a year. No bail is permitted in Gun Court cases even before conviction; all persons convicted receive an indeterminate jail sentence of up to life, and release is given only when these cases are reviewed by the Privy Council. The 1983 Gun Court Amendment Act eliminated the previously mandatory sentence of life

157

imprisonment. It also removed to juvenile courts the hundreds of cases involving youths under the age of fourteen, who had been given life prison sentences before its enactment; many were paroled. In addition, the Gun Court Amendment Act allowed resident magistrates greater leeway to set trial dates, grant bail, etc., and gave magistrates outside the Kingston area discretion in referring noncapital offense cases to the Gun Court. The number of new gun cases filed in 1986 rose by 30 percent to 536.

The Suppression of Crime (Special Provisions) Act limits the period a person can be detained before being charged formally with a crime to "a reasonable time." The detainee must be brought before a court "without delay," or within twenty-four hours. The Department of State's 1986 report on human rights noted, however, that Jamaicans detained under the act were often held for two weeks or longer without being brought before a judicial officer. Individuals charged with a criminal offense may have access to legal representation.

Before independence the attorney general was in charge of prosecutions, but his court functions were dropped when he was made chief legal adviser of the government. Since then the official responsible for criminal prosecutions has been the director of public prosecutions, whose office may bring all legal proceedings except a court-martial against anyone in any court, take over criminal proceedings initiated by another authority, or terminate legal proceedings at any stage.

The Jamaican Penal Code provides for capital punishment, which was made applicable again in 1982, after a period in which executions were suspended while a parliamentary committee considered whether or not the death penalty should be abolished. Jamaica resorted to executions more frequently than did other Commonwealth Caribbean countries. In the late 1960s, about twelve executions were carried out annually. Between August 1980 and February 1987, fifty-four convicted murderers were executed, including fourteen in 1986. An extensive appeals system exists, however, and condemned persons may appeal to the governor general, the Jamaican Privy Council, and the Privy Council in London.

Amnesty International has criticized Jamaican policy on capital punishment, claiming that it contravenes the International Covenant on Civil and Political Rights, ratified by Jamaica in 1975. In early 1987, there were 170 prisoners in Jamaica who remained under sentence of death. Two Jamaicans who had been facing the death sentence for more than eight years won a further stay of execution in April 1987 after the UN Committee on Human Rights in Geneva ruled that a final appeal was admissible. As a result, the Jamaican government was required to show that the delays in judicial process were not a denial of the prisoners' rights under the 1966 International Covenant on Civil and Political Rights.

Strict laws exist against the use of marijuana. As of 1987, possession led to a minimum jail sentence of eighteen months. Jamaica's Dangerous Drugs Act of April 15, 1948, provides penalties for various offenses related to producing, using, and trafficking in drugs. Minor marijuana cases are dealt with by resident magistrate's courts, whereas serious offenses are adjudicated in a circuit court following indictment by the lower court. Circuit court judges have considerable judicial discretion regarding sentences.

The Act to Amend the Dangerous Drugs Act was adopted in March 1987. It gave jurisdiction to the resident magistrate's courts over offenses pertaining to cocaine and other hard drugs. It also increased the maximum penalties that may be imposed under the act by a circuit court, or on summary conviction in a resident magistrate's court. In the case of marijuana, it provided for the imposition by the courts of minimum fines based on the weight of the marijuana in the convicted person's possession. Under the amendment, a person convicted on a marijuana import or export offense by a circuit court may be sentenced to a fine of not less than US$500 for each 28 grams or to imprisonment not exceeding 25 years, or both. On conviction before a resident magistrate's court, a person is liable for a fine of not less than US$300 per 28 grams and a maximum of 3 years' imprisonment, or both. Convictions in a circuit court of cultivating, selling, or transporting marijuana may result in a fine of no less than US$200 per 28 grams and up to 25 years' imprisonment, or both. A fine of no less than US$100 per 28 grams or imprisonment up to 5 years may be imposed for a conviction by a circuit court on a marijuana possession offense. There are slightly lower penalties for conviction in a resident magistrate's court.

The Civil Aviation (Control of Aerodromes and Airstrips) Regulations of November 1984 provided for increases in penalties for offenses related to illegal or unauthorized operation of aircraft, including confiscation of the aircraft. The act was amended in December 1984 to provide for additional restrictions against illegal air activity associated with narcotics trafficking. Under the act, penalties for landing and taking off in aircraft at locations other than licensed airfields included a fine of up to US$100,000 or three times the value of the aircraft and its engine, accessories, and equipment, whichever is greater, or up to five years in prison. The same penalty applied to constructing an unlicensed airfield or preparing land for use as an airstrip. In order to facilitate United States efforts to prosecute narcotics conspiracies, the Treaty on Extradition was signed at Kingston on June 14, 1983.

* * *

Clinton V. Black's *The Story of Jamaica* and Samuel J. Hurwitz's *Jamaica: A Historical Portrait* offer helpful overviews of Jamaica's history. A valuable description of the education system can be found in Millicent Whyte's *A Short History of Education in Jamaica*. The debate over the experience of the Jamaican economy in the postwar era has been quite prolific. Some of the better arguments include Owen Jefferson's *The Post-War Economic Development of Jamaica*, Norman Girvan's *Foreign Capital and Underdevelopment in Jamaica*, and various books and articles from the Caribbean's best-known economist, W. Arthur Lewis. Mahmood Ali Ayub's *Made in Jamaica* is rich in its analysis of not only the growth in manufacturing but also the use of industrial incentives and the dilemmas of import substitution policies. Michael Kaufman's analysis of the Manley experiment in *Jamaica under Manley* is well documented and insightful. Robert E. Looney's *The Jamaican Economy in the 1980s* offers an objective and quantitative analysis of the Jamaican economy. The most comprehensive statistical and analytical publication is the annual *Economic and Social Survey of Jamaica,* published by the government's National Planning Agency. The best data available in Jamaica are located at the Statistical Institute of Jamaica, and the best analytical works can be found at the Institute of Social and Economic Research on the campus of the University of the West Indies in Mona, and through the institute's journal, *Social and Economic Studies.*

Relatively few up-to-date books on Jamaica's governmental system, politics, foreign relations, and military and police forces are available. A useful and informative primer is John D. Forbes's *Jamaica: Managing Political and Economic Change.* For serious students of Jamaican politics, Carl Stone's *Democracy and Clientelism in Jamaica* is essential reading. His numerous articles in academic journals and in the *Daily Gleaner,* as well as his frequent polls, provide useful insights on Jamaican politics. Other useful articles include Anthony Payne's "Jamaica and Cuba, 1959–86: A Caribbean Pas de Deux" and "From Michael with Love: The Nature of Socialism in Jamaica;" Carlene J. Edie's "Domestic Politics and External Relations in Jamaica under Michael Manley, 1972–1980;" and Michael Massing's "The Jamaica Experiment." (For further information and complete citations, see Bibliography.)

Chapter 3. Trinidad and Tobago

Steel drum musicians

Trinidad and Tobago

Official Name .... Trinidad and Tobago

Term for Citizens .... Trinidadians(s), Tobagonian(s)

Capital .... Port-of-Spain

Political Status .... Independent, 1962

Form of Government .... Parliamentary democracy
and republic

Geography
Size .... 5,128 sq. km.
Topography .... Mountains and plains
Climate .... Maritime tropical, high humidity

Population
Total estimated in 1986 1,199,000
Annual growth rate (in percentage) in 1986 .... 2.0
Life expectancy at birth in 1986 .... 68.9
Adult literacy rate (in percentage) in 1984 95
Language .... English
Ethnic groups .... Black (40 percent), East Indian
(40 percent); remainder several other groups
Religion .... Roman Catholic (33 percent), Hindu
(25 percent), Anglican (15 percent),
Muslim (6 percent); remainder other Protestant
denominations and African sects

Economy
Currency; exchange rate .... Trinidad and Tobago
dollar (TT$); TT$3.60 = US$1.00
Gross domestic product (GDP) in 1985 .... US$7.7 billion
Per capita GDP in 1985 .... US$6,000
Distribution of GDP (in percentage) in 1985
Petroleum 24
Public administration 15
Construction 11
Transportation and communications 10
Financial services and real estate 10
Distributive trade 9

163

Manufacturing 7
Agriculture 3
Electricity and water 2
Other 9

National Security
Armed forces personnel 2,130
Paramilitary personnel 0
Police 3,000

TRINIDAD AND TOBAGO, an oil-rich nation, is nearer to mainland South America than any of the other Commonwealth Caribbean island countries. It has had one of the highest per capita incomes in the Caribbean and is a producer of oil, steel, and petrochemicals. Most of its population is descended from African slaves and East Indian indentured laborers, and the two-island nation has a rich and varied culture within which different races have lived together in relative harmony.

Trinidad and Tobago became independent in 1962, one of the first states of the Commonwealth Caribbean to do so. Transition to independence was quite smooth. The People's National Movement (PNM), a mainly black, middle-class party with Eric Williams as its leader, came to power in 1956, led the country into independence, and remained in office for thirty years. Trinidad and Tobago's independent history has been a relatively peaceful continuum, broken only in 1970 by Black Power movement (see Glossary) riots that threatened the government. There have been regular, free, contested elections every five years, and there have been no coups—or attempted coups—since independence. After Williams's death in 1981, the PNM continued to rule until 1986. That year the National Alliance for Reconstruction (NAR), a recently formed coalition party led by A.N.R. Robinson, won the election by a large majority. The NAR differed from the PNM in that it included many East Indians among both leaders and members. In 1987 the NAR's greatest challenge was the revitalization of an economy depressed by the fall in world oil prices.

Historical Setting

Colonial Heritage

Spain received the island of Trinidad as part of the fief of Christopher Columbus and controlled the island for nearly 300 years (see The European Settlements, ch. 1). The Spaniards subdued and enslaved the native Caribs and Arawaks but until the late 1700s paid little attention to Trinidad as other ventures were more profitable. As a result, Trinidad's population was only 2,763 in 1783. Amerindians composed 74 percent of that total (2,032). Although African slaves were first imported in 1517, they constituted only 11 percent of the population (310) in 1783. Indeed, the slave total was barely larger than the 295 free nonwhites who had emigrated from other islands. The remaining 126 Trinidadians were white.

In an effort to make Trinidad more profitable, the Spanish opened the island to immigration in 1776 and allowed Roman Catholic planters from other Eastern Caribbean islands to establish sugar plantations. Because French Catholic planters on the islands that had been granted to Britain after the Seven Years' War (1756–63) were subject to religious and political discrimination, they were attracted by Spanish promises of land grants and tax concessions in Trinidad. In seeking immigrants, Trinidad linked landownership to the ownership of slaves; the more slaves, the more land. Land grants were also given to free nonwhite immigrants, and all landed immigrants were offered citizenship rights after five years. As a result of this new policy, thousands of French planters and their slaves emigrated to the island in the 1780s and 1790s. By 1797 the demographic structure of the island had changed completely. The population had expanded dramatically to 17,718, about 56 percent of whom were slaves. There were also 4,476 free nonwhites and 2,151 whites. The Amerindian community declined by 50 percent from the level achieved 14 years earlier and represented only 6 percent of the total population. As of 1797, there were hundreds of sugar, coffee, and cotton plantations producing for export (see Growth and Structure of the Economy, this ch.).

The British, who were at war with Spain and France, conquered Trinidad in 1797 during the Caribbean unrest that followed the French Revolution. Trinidad was formally ceded to Britain in 1802. After debating how to govern the new island, the British finally decided on crown colony (see Glossary) rule under a governor (see Political Traditions, ch. 1). As this was occurring, investors and colonists expanded the sugar plantations to take advantage of high sugar prices. During the first five years of British rule, the number of sugar estates increased markedly. The British census of 1803 counted 28,000 people, a tenfold increase in 20 years; of these, there were 20,464 slaves, 5,275 free nonwhites, and 2,261 whites. About half of the free people and most of the slaves spoke French, and the rest of the population was divided between Spanish and English speakers. The Amerindian population continued to decline, with several hundred members scattered in rural settlements.

A decade after slavery was abolished in 1834, the British government gave permission for the colonies to import indentured labor from India to work on the plantations. Throughout the remainder of the century, Trinidad's population growth came primarily from East Indian laborers. By 1871 there were 27,425 East Indians, approximately 22 percent of the population of Trinidad and Tobago; by 1911 that figure had grown to 110,911, or about 33 percent of all residents of the islands. Small numbers of Chinese, Portuguese, and other groups also immigrated, contributing to the multiracial character of the islands.

Tobago, Robinson Crusoe's island, changed hands twenty-two times between 1626 and 1814, as various European countries tried to secure possession of its safe anchorages. Its population in 1791 was 15,102, about 94 percent of whom were slaves. The British finally acquired Tobago permanently in 1814, after several previous attempts to conquer the island. The British continued to govern through a local assembly that they had installed during an earlier conquest of Tobago in 1763. Under this arrangement, political control rested with a number of British civil servants and the assembly, elected by a tiny electorate and supported by the sugar plantations.

By the late nineteenth century, Trinidad and Tobago were no longer profitable colonies because sugar was being produced more cheaply elsewhere. In 1889 the British government united Trinidad and Tobago in an effort to economize on government expenses and to solve the economic problems of the islands. In 1898 Tobago became a ward of Trinidad, thereby losing its local assembly, which was not reinstated until 1980. Subsequently, Britain ruled Trinidad and Tobago as a crown colony until 1956. Between 1889 and 1924, the government of Trinidad and Tobago included, in addition to its governor, a wholly appointed Legislative Council. The first step toward self-government was taken in 1925 when there were limited elections to the Legislative Council and to the governor's Executive Council.

As noted, the populations of both Trinidad and Tobago owe their main origins to massive eighteenth- and nineteenth-century importations of African slaves and East Indian indentured servants who were needed to work on the sugar plantations. When the sugar industry declined, unemployment became widespread. In the early twentieth century, oil replaced sugar as the major export; oil is a capital-intensive industry, however, and it did not solve the problem of unemployment in Trinidad and Tobago.

The labor movement began to assume importance after World War I, spurred by the return of Trinidadians who had fought with the British armed forces. The most important of these was Captain Andrew Arthur Cipriani, a white man of Corsican descent, who had served as commander of the West India Regiment. Cipriani resented the fact that the West India Regiment was not allowed to fight for the British Empire but instead was sent to Egypt, where its forces served as labor battalions. Upon his return to Trinidad, Cipriani organized the masses, giving them national pride and teaching them to oppose colonialism. He revitalized the Trinidad

Workingman's Association, which was renamed the Trinidad Labour Party (TLP) in 1934; by 1936 the TLP had 125,000 members. Because Cipriani was white, he was able to transcend the black-East Indian racial dichotomy and became known as "the champion of the barefoot man." In the first elections held for the Legislative Council, Cipriani was elected in 1925 and remained a member until his death in 1945. He was also elected mayor of Port-of-Spain eight times. In these two offices, Cipriani struggled against racial discrimination and fought for constitutional reform, universal suffrage, and better rights for workers.

During the 1930s, Trinidad and Tobago suffered severely from the effects of the worldwide depression. Living standards deteriorated as workers were laid off from the plantations. The situation was aggravated by unjust labor practices. Wages on the sugar estates and in the oil fields were kept low while shareholder dividends in London rose. Workers moved away from Cipriani's moderate policies, and the labor movement became radicalized. Between 1934 and 1937, there were strikes and riots on the sugar plantations and in the oil fields throughout the Caribbean. Tubal Uriah Butler, a black Grenadian who had been expelled from the TLP for extremism, emerged as the leader of the black oil workers, who were the best paid and most politicized laborers on the island. Butler called for racial unity among black workers and organized strikes, heading a highly personalized party that was known as the "Butler Party." Although the British labeled Butler as a "fanatical Negro" during the 1930s, Trinidad and Tobago has since recognized him as a man who sensitized the common man to the evils of colonialism. The strikes in Trinidad and Tobago in the 1930s included many incidents of racial violence, culminating in twelve deaths and over fifty injuries in 1937.

The British responded by deploying marines from Barbados and appointing two successive commissions from London to investigate the causes of the riots in Trinidad and Tobago and elsewhere in the Caribbean. Both commissions noted the low wages and poor working conditions throughout the region. The second commission, chaired by Lord Moyne, which completed its report in 1940, was very critical of the British colonial system in the Caribbean and recommended housing construction, agricultural diversification, more representative government for the islands, and promotion of a middle class in preparation for eventual self-government (see Labor Organizations, ch. 1). Although the Moyne Commission's findings were not made public until after World War II, some of its recommendations were put into effect under the Colonial Development Welfare Act of 1940.

View of Maracas Bay, Trinidad
Courtesy Trinidad and Tobago Tourist Board

The British government had encouraged the formation of trade unions in the belief that labor organization would prevent labor unrest. After the islandwide strikes of 1937, Butler succeeded Cipriani as the leader of the Trinidadian labor movement. Butler's associate, Adrian Cola Rienzi, an East Indian, organized both oil workers under the Oilfield Workers Trade Union (OWTU) and the sugar workers under the All Trinidad Sugar Estates and Factory Workers Trade Union (ATSE/FWTU). Railroad and construction workers were organized under the Federated Workers Trade Union (FWTU), and a number of smaller unions were also formed.

Following a recommendation of the Moyne Commission, government was made more representative. Constitutional reform in 1925 had provided for six elected members on the twenty-five-member Legislative Council, but franchise restrictions limited voters in the 1925 election to 6 percent of the population. In April 1941, the number of unofficial elected members on the Legislative Council and the governor's Executive Council was increased, giving the elected members a majority. Some of these elected members were included on official committees and the governor's Executive Council, although the governor retained ultimate authority and veto power.

Trinidad and Tobago had been profoundly changed by World War II. For the first time since British annexation, the islands were widely exposed to another foreign influence. The 1941 Lend-Lease Agreement (also called the Bases-for-Destroyers Agreement) between the United States and Britain included ninety-nine-year leases of the deepwater harbor at Chaguaramas to the United States Navy and of Waller Field in central Trinidad to the United States Army (see Historical Background, ch. 7). Many United States and Canadian personnel were brought in to work at these bases, and thousands of Trinidadian workers were employed at the bases for higher wages under better conditions than ever before (see Patterns of Development, this ch.). As a result, by the end of World War II many Trinidadians had become used to a higher standard of living and wanted to keep it.

Although the election in 1946 was the first under universal adult suffrage, less than half of the registered voters cast ballots. The trade unions did not consolidate into a cohesive political entity. The labor vote fragmented, as blacks and East Indians divided and as racial slurs became a common part of campaign rhetoric. Butler, who had been detained throughout the war, was released from jail and campaigned for the Legislative Council, but he was defeated by Albert Gomes, a trade unionist of Portuguese descent. The labor movement was unable to gain a majority because no leader could command the widespread support of both the blacks and the East Indians, a pattern that continued throughout the ensuing forty years. The middle class—comprising primarily blacks and a smaller number of East Indians—came to dominate the political scene in the crucial elections that led to independence and has dominated it into the late 1980s.

The Road to Independence

Self-government was gradually increased between 1946 and 1961. The elections of those years served as dress rehearsals for independence. From 1946 to 1955, East Indians were the best organized group in Trinidad and Tobago. Comprising only 35 percent of the population in 1946, East Indians united under the leadership of Bhadese S. Maraj and won almost half of the elected seats in the Legislative Council that year. They used their votes to finally secure the legal right to marry and bury their dead according to Hindu and Muslim rites. Since their arrival in Trinidad more than a century earlier, many East Indians had been classified as illegitimate because no unregistered marriage was considered legal for inheritance purposes (see Population, this ch.).

Political parties remained fragmented in the 1950 elections, often united, as one historian has put it, by nothing more than a "common passion for the spoils of office." One hundred forty-one candidates contested the eighteen elected seats; the single largest bloc of seats on the Legislative Council, eight out of twenty-six, was captured by an alliance between the "Butler party" and East Indian leaders. The British and the non-East Indians disliked the idea of having Butler and his supporters come to power. After the 1950 elections, none of Butler's party was chosen to sit on the Executive Council, the result being that Gomes practically ran the government. Within the restrictions of his semiautonomous government, Gomes tried to function as a mediator between capital and labor and to placate both Britain and Trinidad and Tobago. He had limited success, however, and constitutional reform was postponed until 1955, with elections scheduled for the following year.

The election of 1956 was a watershed in the political history of Trinidad and Tobago because it determined the course of the country for the next thirty years. Gomes was defeated, and a new party, the PNM, captured power and held it until 1986. PNM founder and leader Eric Williams dominated the political scene from 1956 until his death in 1981.

Williams was a native Trinidadian who had spent almost twenty years abroad in Britain and the United States. Although his family was poor, Williams had received a very good education by winning scholarships and had earned a First Class Oxford degree. Williams's academic prowess set the standard for all Trinidadian and Tobagonian political leaders through the late 1980s. While at Oxford, Williams was subjected to a number of racial slights, and he also suffered racial discrimination when he worked for the Anglo-American Caribbean Commission in Washington from 1948 to 1955, an organization created in 1942 to coordinate nonmilitary aspects of Caribbean policy. This discrimination profoundly and permanently affected Williams's outlook on life and his politics. He was a man who knew himself to be the intellectual equal of educated people in Oxford, London, and Washington, and he felt that he had not been accepted as such. Returning to Trinidad in 1948 as deputy chairman of the Caribbean Research Council of the Caribbean Commission, Williams involved himself in cultural, educational, and semipolitical activities and became well known. In 1956 he decided to enter politics and to forge a political party, the PNM. The PNM was created by middle-class professionals who were mainly but not exclusively black. Its main support came from the black community, although Williams was also able to attract some whites and East Indians. Williams gained a public constituency and a loyal party following by giving lectures in Woodford Square, the main square in Port-of-Spain. His lectures on Caribbean history were attended by thousands, and Williams dubbed his interaction with the crowd the "University of Woodford Square." There, Williams forged a bond with the people that remained even after his death twenty-five years later. Trinidadians and Tobagonians were proud to have an international scholar in their midst. Williams gave them a sense of national pride and confidence that no other leader was able to match. His charisma and leadership made it possible for the new party to be independent from existing political organizations and from trade unions. PNM leaders envisioned a broad national party that would include both capitalists and laborers; as such, the PNM rejected socialism and welcomed foreign capital investment.

In 1956 the PNM captured a slim majority of the elected seats on the Legislative Council, receiving 39.8 percent of the vote. Butler's party and the TLP split the other elected seats. The British governor, who controlled five appointed seats and two ex officio seats, filled all of these with men acceptable to the PNM, thus giving the party a majority of two-thirds of the seats on the Legislative Council. Because the British were hoping to form a Caribbean federation or, as a second choice, to launch viable independent countries, it was in their interest to support Williams, a charismatic black leader who had founded a strong political party, who had international education and experience, and who believed in private domestic and foreign investment. Between 1956 and 1962, Williams consolidated his political base and resolved two very important issues: federation and the presence of United States bases on Trinidad.

The British created the West Indies Federation in 1958 (see The West Indies Federation, 1958–62, ch. 1). During the next four years, ten island nations, including Trinidad and Tobago, struggled without success to make the federation into a government. The two largest nations, Trinidad and Tobago and Jamaica, had opposing viewpoints; the former advocated a strong federal government, whereas the latter preferred a weak one. Trinidad and Tobago, with its higher revenues, preferred representation according to financial contribution, but Jamaica, with its larger population, wanted representation on the basis of population. After Jamaica decided in September 1961 not to remain in the federation, Trinidad and Tobago also decided to withdraw, not wishing to be tied to eight small, poor islands for which it would be financially responsible.

Despite British assistance and Williams's compelling personality, the PNM did not come to rule Trinidad and Tobago without a struggle. A number of groups united to oppose the PNM in the federal elections of 1958 under the banner of the Democratic Labour

172

Party (DLP). Once again the campaign became racially polarized as the DLP attracted the East Indians and others who were left out of the PNM. East Indians felt that their cultural identity might be lost if they did not stick together. They deplored marriages between East Indians and blacks because they considered blacks to have an inferior culture; East Indians were less hostile to marriage with whites. Blacks also looked with disfavor on intermarriage with East Indians. In addition, the East Indian middle class, which had developed since the 1930s, seemed a threat to the black professionals who were just coming to power. The PNM increased its share of the vote in the 1958 election from 39.8 percent in 1956 to 48 percent; under the winner-take-all rule, however, the DLP won 6 out of the 10 contested seats, as most of its victories came in regions where the East Indians had an absolute majority.

The PNM profited from the British policy of granting increasing self-government to Trinidad and Tobago. Cabinet government was introduced in 1959; the governor no longer presided over the Executive Council, the Executive Council and chief minister were renamed cabinet and premier (the preindependence title for prime minister), and the premier had the right to appoint and dismiss ministers. Mindful of their slim majority in the 1958 election, leaders of the PNM determined to take whatever steps were necessary to win the 1961 elections and be the party to lead Trinidad and Tobago into independence. The PNM decided to use the issue of the withdrawal of the United States from the Chaguaramas naval base to unify the country and solidify its political base. In party rallies in 1959 and 1960, Williams pledged that the flag of Trinidad and Tobago would soon fly over Chaguaramas and also declared independence from Britain and from the 1941 Lend-Lease Agreement. Declaring that Trinidad and Tobago would not exchange British colonialism for the United States variety, Williams rallied the country to oust the United States from Chaguaramas and to support the PNM.

When British prime minister Harold Macmillan came to Port-of-Spain in June 1960, he told the government that he would open negotiations between the United States and Trinidad and Tobago over Chaguaramas and that Trinidad and Tobago would be an independent participant. Once Williams had won the right for Trinidad and Tobago to sit as an equal with the United States and Britain, he cooled his anti-imperialist rhetoric. The December 1960 settlement gave the United States base rights until 1977 and granted Trinidad and Tobago US$30 million in United States Agency for International Development assistance money for road construction and education. The United States closed the naval base at Chaguaramas in 1967 (see Historical Background, ch. 7).

The December 1961 election, which took place after Trinidad and Tobago had received full internal self-government within the West Indies Federation, was characterized by the use of racial appeals by both parties. The main constitutional issue was the drawing of electoral boundaries. Pro-PNM supporters broke up DLP meetings with stone throwing; the government declared a state of emergency in areas where East Indians were a majority and called out 3,000 police. The PNM used its government leadership to good advantage. Responding to labor unrest, Williams gave all government workers a raise during the summer of 1961. He also moved politically to the right, purging some left-wing supporters who had been prominent in the Chaguaramas fight. The PNM profited from the fact that the DLP was not a unified party. Its leader, Maraj, had been ill, and younger East Indians felt that his lack of education was a liability when contrasted with Williams. During the DLP political infighting, the new generation of East Indian professionals chose R.N. Capildeo, a high-caste Hindu, to head the DLP. Although Capildeo was highly educated, a Ph.D. and a fully qualified barrister, he lacked Williams's ability to appeal to the masses. Eighty-eight percent of the voters turned out for the December 1961 election; in a vote that largely followed ethnic lines, Williams and the PNM won with 57 percent. Reflecting the ethnic split, Williams filled the twelve cabinet slots with eight blacks, two whites, and two East Indians—one Christian and one Muslim. Appointees for the newly created Senate followed similar lines. As Trinidad and Tobago faced independence, the black middle class was firmly in power.

Geography

Trinidad and Tobago are the southernmost islands of the Lesser Antilles, located close to the South American continental shelf (see fig. 1). Trinidad lies 11 kilometers off the northeast coast of Venezuela and 130 kilometers south of the Grenadines. It is 60 kilometers long and 80 kilometers at its maximum breadth and comprises an area of 4,828 square kilometers. Trinidad appears rectangular in shape with three projecting peninsular corners. Tobago is located thirty kilometers northeast of Trinidad, from which it is separated by a channel thirty-seven kilometers wide. The island is 42 kilometers long and 13 kilometers wide, with a total area of 300 square kilometers. Tobago is cigar-shaped in appearance and has a northeast-southwest alignment.

Geologically, the islands are not part of the Antillean arc. Rather, Trinidad was once part of the South American mainland, and Tobago is part of a sunken mountain chain related to the continent. The islands are now separated from the continent of South America by the Gulf of Paria; a nineteen-kilometer-wide northern passage—Dragon's Mouths; and a fourteen-kilometer-wide southern passage—Serpent's Mouth (see fig. 6).

Trinidad is traversed by three distinct mountain ranges that are a continuation of the Venezuelan coastal cordillera. The Northern Range, an outlier of the Andes Mountains of Venezuela, consists of rugged hills that parallel the coast. This range rises into two peaks. The highest, El Cerro del Aripo, is 940 meters high; the other, El Tucuche, reaches 936 meters. The Central Range extends diagonally across the island and is a low-lying range with swampy areas rising to rolling hills; its maximum elevation is 325 meters. The Caroni Plain, composed of alluvial sediment, extends southward, separating the Northern Range and Central Range. The Southern Range consists of a broken line of hills with a maximum elevation of 305 meters.

There are numerous rivers and streams on the island of Trinidad; the most significant are the Ortoire River, fifty kilometers long, which extends eastward into the Atlantic, and the forty-kilometer-long Caroni River, reaching westward into the Gulf of Paria. Most of the soils of Trinidad are fertile, with the exception of the sandy and unstable terrain found in the southern part of the island.

Tobago is mountainous and dominated by the Main Ridge, which is 29 kilometers long with elevations up to 640 meters. There are deep, fertile valleys running north and south of the Main Ridge. The southwestern tip of the island has a coral platform. Although Tobago is volcanic in origin, there are no active volcanoes. Forestation covers 43 percent of the island. There are numerous rivers and streams, but flooding and erosion are less severe than in Trinidad. The coastline is indented with numerous bays, beaches, and narrow coastal plains.

Tobago has several small satellite islands. The largest of these, Little Tobago, is starfish shaped, hilly, and consists of 120 hectares of impenetrable vegetation.

Trinidad and Tobago, well within the tropics, both enjoy a generally pleasant maritime tropical climate influenced by the northeast trade winds. In Trinidad the annual mean temperature is 26°C, and the average maximum temperature is 33°C. The humidity is high, particularly during the rainy season, when it averages 85 to 87 percent. The island receives an average of 211 centimeters of rainfall per year, usually concentrated in the months of June through

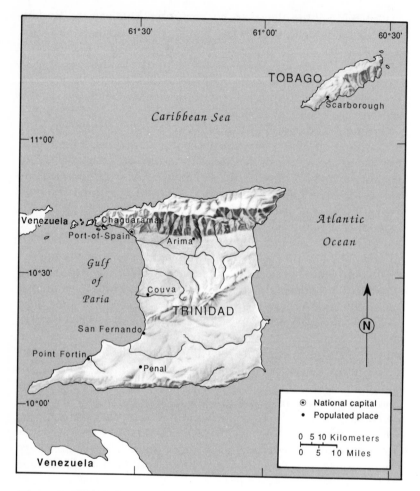

Figure 6. Trinidad and Tobago, 1987

December, when brief, intense showers frequently occur. Precipitation is highest in the Northern Range, which may receive as much
as 381 centimeters. During the dry season, drought plagues the
island's central interior. Tobago's climate is similar to Trinidad's
but slightly cooler. Its rainy season extends from June to December; the annual rainfall is 250 centimeters. The islands lie outside
the hurricane belt; despite this, Hurricane Flora damaged Tobago
in 1963, and Tropical Storm Alma hit Trinidad in 1974, causing
damage before obtaining full strength.

Because it was once part of South America, Trinidad has an assortment of tropical vegetation and wildlife considerably more varied

176

than that of most West Indian islands. Tobago has a generally similar but less varied assortment.

Population

In the 1980s, Trinidad and Tobago was ethnically diverse and was experiencing a renewed period of relatively rapid population growth. According to the 1980 national census, Trinidad and Tobago's population was 1,079,791; of that total, 96 percent lived on the island of Trinidad, predominantly on the west coast. Interim estimates by the national government in 1985 and 1986 placed the population at 1,176,000 and 1,199,000, respectively. Average annual population growth in the 1980s, adjusted for migration, was 1.5 percent; it was 1.6 percent in 1985 and 2 percent in 1986. Population density in 1986 was estimated at 234 people per square kilometer.

Trinidad and Tobago's population in the 1980s illustrated the society's diverse cultural influences acquired during the colonial period and included descendants of emigrants from Europe, Africa, Asia, and the Middle East. Population growth in the late eighteenth and nineteenth centuries was the result of colonial powers importing unskilled labor to work the plantations. This was initially accomplished with African slaves, who were later replaced by indentured servants from India (and to a lesser extent China) following emancipation.

Trinidad and Tobago was also a leading destination of intraregional migration. From 1870 until 1910, an estimated 65,000 workers migrated to Trinidad and Tobago from British possessions in the Windward Islands and in other regions, contributing to approximately one-third of total population growth. Immigration to Trinidad and Tobago decreased in the twentieth century because of the discontinuation of indentured servitude and the expansion of other regional economies; as a result, population growth slowed during the first third of the century.

After 1930 mortality rates were drastically reduced by improved health and sanitation facilities. This caused the annual population growth rate to surge to an average of nearly 3 percent until 1960, a level that was for the first time considered detrimental to social development. The first privately run health clinic was established in the late 1950s, and initial efforts to enact a comprehensive family planning program were enormously successful at reducing population growth. By 1967 a nationally funded family planning program had been organized under the Ministry of Health, and the National Population Council coordinated both private and public clinics. By the late 1970s, about 95 percent of the female population

177

was aware of contraceptive alternatives, and average annual population growth was reduced to slightly above 1 percent. As contraception became commonly accepted, family size shrank from an average of six children in the 1950s to fewer than three in the early 1980s.

The dominant ethnic groups in the 1980s were those of African (referred to as blacks) and Indian (known as East Indians) descent; the 1980 census revealed that nearly 80 percent of the population was almost evenly split between the two groups. Only 1 percent of the population was classified as white, and the pure Chinese element represented no more than 0.5 percent of the population; the remainder comprised mixed racial and ethnic elements, including small numbers of Portuguese, Syrians, and Lebanese.

Blacks by and large have adopted the European way of life. Although East Indians considered themselves culturally superior, blacks maintained a slightly privileged position in society because of their earlier arrival. Status within this group was determined by the shade of one's skin. The lightest-toned blacks traditionally were associated with the elite members of the social hierarchy.

Although East Indians represented the largest nonblack element in contemporary society, they were still accorded an inferior status and maintained their own social and religious customs. In the 1980s, East Indians made some strides at becoming more influential members of society, including accession to ministerial positions in government. Nevertheless, complete interaction with blacks still had not occurred.

Ethnic and cultural characteristics remained complicated components of society in the 1980s. Although a stratified social structure was passed on from the British, the society was not defined strictly along class lines. Numerous studies have demonstrated that Trinidadians have consistently differentiated themselves and their place in society based on their ethnic affiliation. To the extent that well-defined economic class distinctions may be made, there was a distinct lack of cohesion within each class. Although the major ethnic groups were represented in all classes of society, an informal ranking was also common within each class. Generally, blacks attained a preferred position at all levels within the stratified class framework, which led to a disunity in class structure. For example, it was observed that the protests of 1970, which were designed to force change throughout society, were unable to unify black and East Indian elements. In fact, the failure of the Black Power movement, as it became known, to effect more sweeping reforms was attributed in part to an inability to mobilize other segments of the population (see Political Dynamics, this ch.). Although there has

Mosque, St. Joseph, Trinidad
Courtesy Trinidad and Tobago Tourist Board

been little overt racial disharmony, social stratification remained as much a cultural phenomenon as a socioeconomic one.

Religious distinctions in society paralleled the diverse cultural influences. According to the 1980 census, 33 percent of the population considered themselves Roman Catholics, including a large portion of the black population. Early Spanish and French influences were the principal reasons for the preponderance of Catholic worship. The East Indian population contained both Hindus and Muslims, who represented 25 percent and 6 percent of the total population, respectively. The British influence was also noticeably present, with 15 percent of the population claiming membership in the Anglican Church. Other religious affiliations included the Baptist, Methodist, and Pentecostal churches and also non-Christian sects, such as Rada and Shango.

By the mid-1980s, the national government had identified three disturbing demographic trends: excessive population growth, regional migration imbalances, and a gradual shift in the population toward urban centers. High fertility rates, which were curtailed in the 1970s, appeared to be a problem again in the mid-1980s. The increased number of births indicated that an annual population growth rate of between 1.5 and 2 percent was again a long-term possibility. Some researchers have theorized that fears that one of the two principal ethnic groups would attain numerical

179

superiority over the other prodded both to procreate at higher levels. The detrimental effects of high birth rates motivated the government to redouble its birth control efforts through existing programs, primarily by increasing public awareness of the burden of excessively large families on both individuals and society.

Government concerns were also directed at mitigating the effects of regional migration imbalances. Immigration of unskilled workers had been a problem for decades. The 1980 census estimated that 17,000 foreign persons had entered Trinidad and Tobago since 1970, mostly from neighboring Caribbean countries. Furthermore, the United Nations suggested that this number might be as much as 50 percent short of the real total because of misleading reporting. Emigration of skilled workers has also been a problem. Although the government actively supported emigration of unskilled workers, it had not developed a policy to entice educated and trained personnel to remain on the island. The so-called "brain drain" was addressed through pleas to nationalism, particularly to those who completed training and education with government subsidies. This migration imbalance was considered a significant factor contributing to welfare and unemployment problems.

By the mid-1980s, Trinidad and Tobago had become an urbanized society with approximately one-half of the population living in or near cities; this number was expected to grow to 65 percent by the year 2000. Urban areas had expanded beyond the ability of local governments to provide essential services to all; in addition, overcrowding was already taxing the limits of existing physical infrastructure. The development of new, smaller urban groups centered on untapped oil fields was a popular policy alternative. The construction of so-called "petro-poles" was seen as a means of alleviating urban stress as well as a necessary condition for further development of the economy.

Education

Until the twentieth century, education in Trinidad and Tobago was designed primarily to prepare the elite for study abroad and the eventual assumption of political and economic leadership roles in the society. With the exception of a few missionary schools, slaves were discouraged from attaining even minimal literacy skills. Educational opportunities did not expand greatly following emancipation; the first teacher-training program was not begun until 1852, and the first public secondary institution did not open its doors until 1925.

The public school program, which was modeled after the British system, took form in the twentieth century and eventually opened up avenues for upward mobility to all elements of society. The East Indian population, because of its lower socioeconomic status, was the last segment of society to benefit from education, but it eventually became known as one of the most academically motivated groups on the islands.

In addition to government-sponsored schools, private denominational institutions were created to pass on cultural and religious instruction, as well as traditional academic knowledge and skills. Public financial assistance to Roman Catholic, Presbyterian, Muslim, and Hindu institutions eventually evolved into the modern education system of the 1980s, which incorporated schools that were both publicly and privately administered.

Under the authority of the Ministry of Education, the school system in the late 1980s consisted primarily of government and publicly assisted denominational schools. The former were administered and financed under public supervision, whereas the latter were privately controlled by religious groups, yet financed with public funds. Both maintained a similar curriculum and were free to all students who could pass the admission tests. Approximately 27 percent of all primary students attended government schools; the rest were enrolled in denominational programs, most of which were Roman Catholic.

Formal primary education commenced at age six, although many parents elected to send younger children to readily available kindergarten programs for one or two years prior to entering the school system; education was compulsory through age eleven. In the 1982–83 school year, virtually all school-age children were enrolled in one of the 467 primary institutions. At that time, there were approximately 7,500 teachers, who instructed nearly 167,000 primary students, providing a student to teacher ratio of 23 to 1.

Successful completion of primary school, as determined by a national examination, permitted students to pursue instruction at the secondary level; those who did not pass were allowed to continue primary education for an additional two years, enter a private secondary institution, or leave the school system. Junior secondary education was also available at government and assisted schools, of which there were a total of twenty-three in 1983. Total enrollment was approximately 39,000 pupils with a teaching staff of 1,400. The program consisted of three years of study in general academic subjects. Virtually all those who finished were advanced to the senior comprehensive program, which afforded an additional four years of more specialized academic or vocational instruction. There were

181

18 such schools in 1983, employing roughly 1,600 teachers and instructing approximately 22,000 students.

Numerous options were available during the secondary-school years in the late 1980s. In addition to academic programs, students could enter five-year technical education or teacher-training programs at the Point Fortin Vocational Center, John S. Donaldson Technical Institute, San Fernando Technical Institute, or one of the five teacher-training colleges. Instruction was offered in mechanical repair, clerical skills, construction, and education. The Eastern Caribbean Institute of Agriculture operated a two-year program that graduated approximately fifty students each year. Students who completed the full seven years of secondary academic training were eligible for further instruction at the university level.

The St. Augustine Campus of the University of the West Indies was the only local institution of higher education in Trinidad and Tobago in the 1980s. It offered both graduate and undergraduate programs in liberal arts, agriculture, science, engineering, and law. Total enrollment, including foreigners, was between 2,000 and 3,000 in the mid-1980s.

Although education was looked upon as a way of achieving upward mobility and was generally admired in Trinidadian society in the 1980s, the education system achieved only partial success in meeting the needs of society. Despite increases in the national literacy level from 74 percent in 1946 to 95 percent in 1984 and expanded efforts to develop both academic and vocational programs, employment statistics suggested that significant gaps still existed in the 1980s between formal education and the needs of a developing society.

In the mid-1980s, some observers contended that vacillating employment figures were the result of simultaneous surpluses and shortages in the work force. Although additional statistical evidence was needed to determine detailed manpower trends, it was clear that the unemployment rate of unskilled workers had gone above 25 percent, while many skilled and professional positions could not be properly filled. This situation was attributed to a deficient education system (particularly the lack of vocational training), the emigration of trained personnel, and unrealistic expectations of unskilled job seekers. These observers also noted that the highest unemployment rate was among those who had attained between one and six years of education. Members of this group refused to take menial jobs held by less educated segments of the population, yet they were unqualified to fill positions requiring specific knowledge or skills.

Increased training of teachers, greater skills instruction for those students considered unlikely to complete the junior secondary programs, and realignment of expectations of both students and workers were thought to be critical improvements. Without these changes the education system would be unable to affect employment patterns and assist with national development.

Health and Welfare

Based on standard health care indicators, Trinidad and Tobago's medical system continued to improve in the 1980s. The mortality rate had been reduced from 18.9 per 1,000 inhabitants in 1930 to 7 in 1980. The infant mortality rate for the same year was 19.7 per 1,000 live births, reduced from 34.4 in 1970. Life expectancy at birth in 1986 averaged 68.9 years.

Morbidity indicators also improved but were nevertheless below expectations. In 1983 only 60 percent of children one year of age and younger had been immunized against measles, poliomyelitis, diphtheria, pertussis, and tetanus. The implication of the deficient inoculation programs was evident in the 4.7 percent of total deaths resulting from infectious and parasitic diseases; this was significantly higher than on other English-speaking Caribbean islands.

Despite the fact that 95 percent of the population had access to potable water in 1984 and 100 percent was serviced by sanitary waste disposal, communicable diseases were still a problem. In 1983 dengue fever was endemic, venereal diseases were rampant, and tuberculosis was still a minor threat. As of 1986, there were 134 confirmed cases of acquired immune deficiency syndrome in Trinidad and Tobago, 93 resulting in death.

Drug addiction and noncommunicable diseases were becoming increasingly prevalent in the late 1980s. A 1987 government report named alcoholism as the most serious drug abuse problem and also pointed to a noticeable rise in the use of marijuana and cocaine. Abuse of other drugs, however, had not yet become a serious problem. Drug abuse in general, and alcoholism in particular, was considered a significant contributor to the relatively high incidence of motor vehicle fatalities and the increasing suicide rate. Cancer, hypertension, and heart disease were the most common noncommunicable health problems.

The government redirected its national health strategy in the 1980s to reflect the Pan American Health Organization's emphasis on primary health care. The principal goal was to provide basic health care to all communities, utilizing a decentralized, public education format, and giving maternal and child health care priority status.

183

In the 1980s, the overall public health program was the responsibility of the Ministry of Health, Welfare, and Status of Women. It was divided into four divisions responsible for community services, environmental health, institutional health care, and epidemiology. Community services oversaw the primary (curative and preventative), secondary (hospitalization), and tertiary (specialized and long-term) community health service program. At the local level, each county had a medical officer responsible for the health care system, particularly primary health care.

Primary health care revolved around the 102 health centers located throughout the country. They provided outpatient services on a daily basis, which included the rotation of medical specialists. Public health nurses were also available to make house calls and visit schools. The health centers were the primary vehicles for extending the immunization programs. Secondary health care was available at eight district hospitals, as well as two large government hospitals in Port-of-Spain and San Fernando.

Tertiary health care was available only in Port-of-Spain. The main facility was the Mount Hope Medical Complex, which housed a 340-bed general-purpose hospital, 200-bed pediatric facility, and 110-bed maternity hospital. Other specialized facilities included the St. Ann's Hospital for psychiatric care, Caura Hospital for cardiology and pathology services, and St. James Infirmary for geriatric, oncological, and physical therapeutic care.

The total number of public hospital beds in 1986 was approximately 4,900; there were 15 private health institutions that provided an additional 300 beds. Private sector health services concentrated primarily on ambulatory care; some publicly employed physicians maintained separate private practices, however. In 1984 Trinidad and Tobago had 1,213 doctors, or a ratio of 10.6 per 10,000 inhabitants. At the same time, there were 104 dentists and 3,346 nurses, or ratios of 0.9 and 29.6 per 10,000 inhabitants, respectively.

In spite of noted improvements in health care delivery, serious deficiencies were still evident in the late 1980s. The ratio of population to health centers was twice as large as desired, requiring a long-term commitment to the construction of additional facilities. There was also a lack of critical medicines and trained medical personnel, particularly technicians. Physical facilities and equipment also required attention, as did the lack of dental care nationwide.

The National Insurance Scheme acted as the equivalent of a social security system in the late 1980s. Welfare disbursements went to public assistance programs, food stamps, and retirement pensions and played a small role in health care by providing compensation for injuries and diseases acquired on the job.

Economy

In the 1980s, Trinidad and Tobago was an upper-middle-income, oil-exporting country that was highly dependent on the world price of oil for its economic growth. The nation displayed the largest gross domestic product (GDP—see Glossary) of the Commonwealth Caribbean, one of the highest per capita GDPs among the nations of the Western Hemisphere, and one of the highest standards of living in the developing world. The country's GDP in 1985 stood at roughly US$7.7 billion at current prices, or about US$6,000 per capita.

The major sectors of the economy were petroleum and petrochemicals, construction, services, and agriculture. Petroleum had fueled the economy since the early twentieth century and in 1985 still represented roughly 24 percent of GDP and 80 percent of exports. Oil reserves at the current rate of extraction were expected to last approximately ten years, but the islands enjoyed large reserves of natural gas. New petrochemical plants, utilizing the country's natural gas resources, came on-stream in the early 1980s and included ammonia, urea, and methanol. These large industrial projects were located at the newly built Point Lisas industrial park, which, along with the park's new iron and steel plant, provided Trinidad and Tobago with an industrial base that was unmatched throughout the Caribbean. Construction, the major employer in the economy and often considered the bellwether of general economic activity, expanded rapidly during the oil boom of the 1970s but contracted greatly in the 1980s. Services, such as financial services and utilities, also had expanded rapidly since the 1970s and played a major role in the economy; by contrast, tourism was rather undeveloped when compared with other Caribbean islands. The agricultural sector was suffering from a long-run decline, but growth in domestic agriculture in the 1980s helped to revive that shrinking sector, albeit only partially.

In the postwar era, the economy experienced two great boom decades, both of which were followed by decades of slow or negative growth. Real GDP growth averaged 8 percent in the 1950s as the economy diversified into manufacturing and construction through the use of import substitution industrialization (see Glossary) strategies. Growth in import substitution manufacturing and the economy as a whole waned in the late 1960s, exacerbating the social unrest at the end of the decade. The quadrupling of oil prices in 1973 revived the economy and created a 9.6-percent real annual growth rate from 1974 to 1979. Trinidadians and Tobagonians, nicknamed the "Arabs of the Caribbean," were known throughout the region in the 1970s for the carnival of consumption that they participated in with their instant oil wealth. The downturn in oil prices in 1982, however, plummeted the economy into a deep depression in 1983 from which the country had not emerged by 1987. Negative growth peaked in 1984, when the economy contracted by nearly 11 percent.

Even with cyclical growth, the citizens benefited from a quality of life that surpassed that of not only most other Caribbean islands but of other Western Hemisphere oil exporters such as Mexico and Venezuela as well. The country also enjoyed a literacy rate higher than Italy's, a per capita energy consumption rate that exceeded Britain's, a per capita newspaper circulation above that in several Western European countries, an income distribution comparable to that of the United States, and an access to electricity and potable water that was better than most developing countries. Nevertheless, the country also suffered problems associated with more developed societies, including pollution, obsessive consumption, entrenched labor disputes, and growing drug abuse. As in other Caribbean countries, chronic unemployment, which had climbed to 17 percent by 1987, was the major social problem. In addition, East Indians and women lacked the same economic opportunities as white or black males; these disparities were narrowing, however.

Unlike other Caribbean nations, Trinidad and Tobago benefited immensely from the energy crisis of the 1970s. The oil boom of the 1970s flooded the national treasury, cut the unemployment rate in half, created large balance of payments surpluses, and stimulated the economy at large. Nonetheless, it also devastated the agriculture sector, which declined 25 percent because of the resulting shortages of laborers, who migrated to west coast cities for higher wages. Although the boom was reversed in the early 1980s, Trinidad and Tobago's accumulated wealth permitted it to weather the impact of the international recession better than most developing countries and avoid the debt crisis that confronted its neighbors. Although some charges of government waste and corruption were voiced during the 1970s and 1980s, sufficient discipline in public finance prevailed to allow the country to elude the fiscal crisis that confronted other oil-exporting, developing nations such as Mexico, Venezuela, and Nigeria.

In the late 1980s, Trinidad and Tobago displayed a mixed economy that allowed for a level of government involvement second only to that in Cuba among the countries of the Western Hemisphere. The large role in the economy of subsidies, transfers, and joint ventures between the government and the private sector created an intertwining of the public and private sectors that often blurred distinctions between them. During the 1970s, the government purchased a share in over fifty major companies in banking, insurance, agriculture, utilities, and manufacturing. As a consequence, the government also became the largest single employer in the country. Although Trinidad and Tobago was a country where capitalism generally flourished, free enterprise, especially the foreign sector, was highly regulated by the government.

Trinidad and Tobago was a very open economy, dependent on the export of oil to purchase large amounts of imported food, consumer goods, and capital goods. Oil represented approximately 80 percent of exports, whereas food accounted for as much as 20 percent of imports in the late 1980s. Trinidad and Tobago was the most important exporter of oil to the United States from the Caribbean Basin. The country supplied nearly 50 percent of that region's oil exports to the United States, as well as 18 percent of the region's total exports to that same market. Unlike virtually every other Caribbean country, Trinidad and Tobago generally enjoyed yearly trade and balance of payments surpluses. The country depended on the United States for roughly 50 percent of its trade, but the islands also maintained important trade relations with the European Economic Community (EEC) and the Caribbean Community and Common Market (Caricom—see Appendix C). Once a donor nation that aided its poorer Caribbean neighbors, Trinidad and Tobago in the late 1980s was increasingly in need of external financing to weather its economic adjustment period.

Growth and Structure of the Economy

Trinidad was neglected by Spanish mercantilists until the late 1700s because it was perceived to be poorly endowed. In 1776 Spanish authorities finally allowed French planters from other Eastern Caribbean islands to enter Trinidad, stimulating the subsequent expansion of a sugar plantation economy based on slave labor (see Colonial Heritage, this ch.). After the creation of the first sugar plantation in 1787, agriculture expanded so rapidly that a decade later there were 159 sugar plantations, 130 coffee estates, 60 cacao (the bean from which cocoa is derived) estates, and 103 cotton estates. The rapid success of the French planters attracted the interest of the British, who captured the island in 1797.

In the early 1800s, Trinidad's agricultural economy was based on highly productive cane fields and on coffee, cacao, and other export crops. Trinidad's average sugar plantation (over 240 hectares) was larger than that in other Commonwealth Caribbean islands. Unlike smaller islands, such as St. Christopher and Antigua, Trinidad was less dependent on sugar for its labor and exports,

187

as other export crops held relatively important economic roles. Agricultural estates were worked by slaves imported from West Africa until 1807, when the British abolished the slave trade. After complete emancipation in 1838, freed blacks played a decreasing role in agriculture because of the annual importation of about 2,000 indentured East Indians, more than in any other Caribbean island. At a time when other English-speaking islands were suffering declines in sugar production, Trinidad's quadrupled from 1828 to 1895, mostly as a result of the imported East Indian labor force. Although sugar wages were low, wages of Trinidadian sugar workers in the 1800s already surpassed those of their Caribbean counterparts.

Tobago, officially linked to Trinidad in 1889, was traditionally neglected by both the Spanish and the British in economic terms. Nevertheless, Tobago was one of the top sugar producers in the West Indies in the early 1800s. Tobago's agricultural production was characterized by the French *métayer* system, a form of sharecropping, imported with French planters from St. Lucia. As late as 1839, the island registered an annual trade surplus as large as 20,000 British pounds sterling. As its sugar industry declined in the late 1800s, however, it received less and less attention from the British, preventing significant infrastructural development. Economic neglect continued for decades, so that by 1946 Tobago was the most underpopulated island in the British Caribbean.

Trinidad and Tobago entered the twentieth century with the fortuitous discovery of oil in 1907. The discovery changed Trinidad's patterns of economic development and further differentiated it from other English-speaking islands in the Caribbean. Exports of oil left the island for the first time in 1909, but production did not drastically increase until the British Royal Navy converted to oil during the following decade. During World War I, Trinidad and Tobago became the major source of oil for the navy. As oil output skyrocketed from 125,000 barrels a year in 1910 to over 2 million barrels by 1920, so did the number of foreign oil companies competing for control of the precious resource. The oil boom during the second decade of the 1900s was not experienced in the rest of the economy, however, which was depressed.

As the decade came to a close, two events changed Trinidad's economic future. The termination of East Indian indentureship in 1917 created greater economic demands from the agricultural labor force, whose wages had hardly increased over a century. The other major event was the return of Trinidadian soldiers from World War I who served in the West India Regiment. Exposed to greater personal freedoms and workers' rights, as well as prejudice, these veterans were at the forefront in organizing for greater economic benefits for labor from foreign sugar and oil companies.

The first visible signs of Trinidad's growing labor movement appeared in the aftermath of the riots of 1919 when Cipriani assumed the clear leadership of the movement. The Cipriani-led labor movement in the 1920s fought for a minimum wage, eight-hour day, child labor laws, compulsory education, heavier taxation of foreign oil companies, and general social reform. A moderate, Cipriani tempered the burgeoning labor movement under British colonial rule until the early 1930s, when the labor movement was radicalized by the advent of the Great Depression.

The economic hardship of the depression resulted in fewer jobs, poor health conditions, low wages, and growing resentment of foreign ownership in the oil and sugar industries. The decline in sugar that accompanied the depression, severe droughts, and disease of the cacao crops drastically increased rural unemployment in the early 1930s. The downturn in sugar, in particular, led to the consolidation of the landholdings of the dominant British firm, Tate and Lyle, which continued to pay its London stockholders handsome dividends. Decreased economic opportunities in the countryside sparked widespread demonstrations in the sugar belt by 1934. Meanwhile, health conditions remained poor, as many Trinidadians suffered from malaria, ancylostomiasis, tuberculosis, and yellow fever. As unemployment remained high, wages were kept low—only US$0.72 a day for an unskilled oil worker and US$0.35 a day for an unskilled sugar worker in 1937. Large profit remittance continued in the oil industry as well as in the sugar industry, causing growing worker resentment of foreign ownership; this resentment culminated in the riots of 1937.

Butler emerged from the islandwide strikes of 1937 as the undisputed successor to Cipriani as the leader of the Trinidadian labor movement. Butler, more radical and uncompromising than Cipriani, continued to forge a strong trade union movement in Trinidad and Tobago. Rienzi, Butler's associate, was another rising labor leader who came to lead the powerful OWTU and later presided over the FWTU, an umbrella labor organization. The labor movement in the 1930s was also marked by the growing participation of East Indians, most notably through the ATSE/FWTU. Although by 1940 Trinidad and Tobago had extensive and relatively responsible trade unions, it was not until 1943 that they possessed the procedural framework to negotiate industrial disputes effectively with the British. Nonetheless, Trinidad and Tobago generally enjoyed strong negotiating power with the British because of the colony's vital oil resources.

Patterns of Development

World War II profoundly transformed the economy and society of Trinidad and Tobago. As in World War I, World War II produced an oil boom as the nation fueled the Allied forces' war efforts, causing oil to replace sugar as the most important sector in the economy. A more profound social and economic transformation, however, resulted from the new military presence of the United States in Chaguaramas, Trinidad, as an outcome of the 1941 Lend-Lease Agreement between the United States and Britain (see The Road to Independence, this ch.; Historical Background, ch. 7). The building of a United States base in Trinidad created a strong upswing in construction activity, directly employing approximately 30,000 workers, or between 15 and 20 percent of the labor force. The United States presence had many spin-offs, both economic and social. The Americans, having no colonial relationship with the Trinidadians, generally saw them as their equal and were willing to pay them relatively high wages. Real wages rose, employment improved, ports were upgraded, and the economy was stimulated by greater consumption from high wages. Higher urban wages, however, accelerated rural-urban migration, causing a shortage of agricultural labor as sugar employment dropped from 30,000 in 1939 to 18,000 in 1943. The Americans' fewer class prejudices also helped dispel myths of white supremacy as they, too, performed manual labor and consumed their earnings alongside Trinidadians. The United States presence also caused a greater penetration of American culture and consumption habits, which unrealistically increased the economic expectations of many Trinidadians.

The diminished world trade resulting from the war changed the production patterns in Trinidad and Tobago. Decreased markets for traditional agricultural exports and declining food imports caused total land under food production to more than double during the war. Although high urban wages resulting from the United States presence were a drain on the rural labor supply, food production actually increased as output shifted from export agriculture to domestic agriculture. Domestic agriculture was also bolstered by guaranteed prices for farmers, price controls, and government "back to the land" slogans. The fall in imports had a similar effect on Trinidad's small manufacturing sector, which previously was limited to the processing of export crops. Shortages in consumer goods during the war stimulated the import substitution of those products most easily produced domestically, such as edible oils, fats, matches, some textiles, and other consumer necessities.

Oil refinery, Trinidad
Courtesy Inter-American Development Bank

In the 1950s, the economy of Trinidad and Tobago experienced a postwar boom unprecedented on both islands. Real GDP increased an average of 8.5 percent annually from 1951 to 1961; in the second half of the period, from 1956 to 1961, growth averaged 10 percent annually. In spite of rapid population growth during this period, real per capita income increased 15 percent. The evolving structure of the economy was characterized by the rise of industry and services and the decline of agriculture. Oil, construction, and manufacturing emerged as dominant industrial sectors. In 1956 a United States oil company, Texaco, entered Trinidad and Tobago and consolidated several holdings of other companies. Oil production jumped from under 60,000 barrels per day (bpd) prior to 1950 to 80,000 bpd toward the end of the decade. In addition, the price of oil continued to rise, allowing for increased oil earnings and growing government revenues. Early self-government in the 1950s launched extensive infrastructure projects, causing construction to more than double in over ten years. Manufacturing's output, encouraged by generous fiscal incentives since 1950, also increased rapidly, although its share of GDP rose only slightly from 11 to 13 percent. In terms of services, the banking industry enjoyed the fastest growth in the whole economy, and tourism was stimulated by new fiscal incentives as well. Agriculture, by contrast, decreased as public finance favored industry. During the 1950s, agriculture's share of total output dropped from 17 to 12 percent. Domestic agriculture, emphasized during World War II, shrank after the war and was the main reason for the sector's decline. Export agriculture, although faced with serious challenges, such as continued cacao diseases and changes in British agreements on sugar, was generally able to maintain production levels.

In the early 1960s, Trinidad and Tobago's tremendous growth spurt slowed, and the economy entered a ten-year period of sluggish growth. By the 1960s, the islands' labor force was highly unionized and urbanized, many belonging to the middle class, a situation unknown in most developing countries. As economic growth slowed, increased demands were voiced for adequate housing, better labor rights, more jobs, improved living and working conditions, more equitable distribution of wealth, and national ownership of resources. Despite these demands, the socioeconomic problems present in Trinidad and Tobago were hardly as acute as in other Caribbean countries; nonetheless, such issues as negative attitudes toward foreign ownership tended to dominate. The key sectors of the economy—oil, sugar, and banking—were dominated by multinational corporations. Growing resentment over foreign control of national resources intensified as the economy deteriorated in the late 1960s. The high unemployment rate of 15 percent tended to increase the number of industrial disputes and fortify union militancy. These events, culminating in the Black Power movement of 1970, set the stage for increased nationalization of resources during the 1970s.

In late 1973 world oil prices quadrupled and rescued Trinidad and Tobago from the decaying economic and political trend of the late 1960s and early 1970s. During the rest of the decade, the economy experienced rapid growth and was drastically transformed. In the 1970s, the country enjoyed its second major economic boom in only thirty years. At a time when many of the world's economies entered a deep recession, Trinidad and Tobago's economy experienced real annual growth of 9.6 percent from 1974 to 1979. Unemployment declined to a low of 8 percent by 1980. Government revenues from oil increased from a level equal to 20 percent of GDP in the early 1970s to 41 percent by 1980, fueling 65 percent of government revenues by the end of the decade. Escalating government revenues heartened Prime Minister Williams to remark that "money is no problem," epitomizing the nation's feel of instant wealth. Money was indeed no problem; the government spent more than US$120 million to purchase shares of over fifty major companies in the country, including majority or minority ownership in oil, gas, aviation, agriculture, utilities, and banking.

Major new government investments, such as the multibillion-dollar industrial park at Point Lisas, low-cost housing projects, and expanded utility services, caused the construction industry to soar. Free-flowing petrodollars spawned strong consumption that, in turn, stimulated local manufacturing to grow at an annual pace of 9 percent. In contrast, agriculture was severely neglected and shrank by 25 percent during the oil boom. The decline in agriculture was symbolized by the 1984 sugar harvest, the country's worst in forty-five years. Increased consumption and declining agricultural production made the economy much more import intensive as higher oil prices temporarily footed the import bill.

The sharp fallout in oil prices in the early 1980s forced Prime Minister George Chambers in 1983 to state bluntly that "the fête is over." From 1983 to 1986, the economy experienced strong negative growth: negative 2.6 percent in 1983, negative 10.8 percent in 1984, negative 6.5 percent in 1985, and negative 5.1 percent in 1986; continued negative growth was estimated in 1987. The islands' international reserves, which soared from a low US$34 million in 1973 to US$3.3 billion in 1981, had declined to under US$500 million by 1985. As a result of deteriorating economic conditions, the Trinidad and Tobago dollar was devalued by 50 percent in December 1985. Worth double the United States dollar in the 1970s, the Trinidad and Tobago dollar was valued at less than a third of the United States dollar by the mid-1980s. The unemployment rate crept as high as 17 percent by 1987. As the economy continued in a deep recession in the late 1980s, there was growing evidence of increased underground economic activity linked to cocaine trafficking (see National Security, this ch.).

Role of Government

Government involvement in the economy increased rapidly with early self-government in 1950. Spurred by the economic decision making of Gomes, the young government embarked on an "industrialization by invitation" strategy in an attempt to emphasize manufacturing (see The Road to Independence, this ch.). The strategy was a natural outgrowth of the success of import substitution manufacturing that had occurred during World War II. The most significant pieces of legislation that changed the government's stance on the economy were the Aid to Pioneer Industries Ordinance and the Income Tax Reform Ordinance to Benefit Industry, both enacted in 1950. These measures provided wide-ranging fiscal concessions for infant industries. Similar measures were also developed for tourism. Fiscal incentives permitted new investment to benefit from accelerated depreciation allowances, duty-free importation of machinery and raw materials, and provisions for the repatriation of profits. These fiscal measures marked the first time Trinidad and Tobago sought foreign capital outside of Britain. In 1962 drastically increased tariffs complemented the fiscal incentives designed to encourage manufacturing and to protect it from outside competition. Although tourism did not receive the attention accorded to manufacturing, there was renewed interest in Tobago, the island traditionally neglected by Port-of-Spain officials.

These policies, bolstered by an expanding world economy, proved a general success as the unprecedented growth of the 1950s included the establishment of over 100 pioneer industries by the mid-1960s. These comprised basic manufacturing, such as bricks, beer, textiles, glass, cement, paints, and chemicals. Although incentive legislation helped expand output in manufacturing, many expectations for the sector were not met. Manufacturing's share of GDP did rise, but the sector never obtained the dominance it held in Jamaica. Employment expectations were also not met as foreign investment brought industries that were more capital intensive than anticipated. In general, there were few economic linkages forged between the oil and manufacturing sectors in the 1960s. The employment absorption of new manufacturing generally went unseen as Trinidadian society experienced its fastest population growth rate ever, increasing over 50 percent from 1940 to 1960.

The government's industrial push in the postwar era also included heavy investments in the islands' physical, social, and organizational infrastructure. To meet growing commercial and residential demands, the country's water, electricity, communication, and transportation systems were expanded. Likewise, self-government emphasized the need for improved social services such as medical and educational facilities. Beginning in 1958, the government issued the first in a series of five-year plans. The last five-year plan (1974–78) was never completed, as expectations of continued oil wealth apparently precluded the need for further plans.

The role of the government in the economy increased drastically during the 1970s. The move toward increased government involvement in the economy was the direct result of the Black Power movement of 1970 and the long-term consequence of decades of trade union criticism of foreign ownership. Some foreign firms were nationalized with compensation; the government typically acquired only a 51-percent equity share of these companies. Other firms were simply localized in ownership via the purchase of a majority of shares by private Trinidadian citizens. In 1971 the government bought a 51-percent share of the Caroni Sugar Company, which controlled over 90 percent of sugar activity in the country. The banking industry underwent a nationalization and localization process in 1972. In that year the government purchased a 51-percent share of the Royal Bank of Canada, subsequently renamed the Royal Bank of Trinidad and Tobago. Meanwhile, Barclays Bank (renamed the Republic Bank), the Bank of Nova Scotia, and numerous insurance companies were localized in ownership. Although the government's prominent entrance into the economy predated the oil boom, increased government revenues from oil accelerated the process. Between 1968 and 1974, the government entered the oil industry in force, purchasing the oil holdings of the British Petroleum Company and Shell Corporation and integrating them into the newly established Trinidad and Tobago Oil Company (Trintoc). In the same year, Texaco's gas stations were localized islandwide. By the late 1970s, the government had become the largest employer in the country.

Petrodollar revenues expanded the state's range of activities in the economy from nationalization and localization to the introduction of widespread subsidies and large-scale public works programs, the creation of numerous state-owned enterprises, and the implementation of huge industrial projects. Like other oil economies, Trinidad and Tobago suffered from the "Dutch disease," the process by which oil-wealthy nations tend to subsidize non-oil sectors of the economy. During the 1970s, subsidies and transfers represented the greatest share of current government costs, moving from 25 percent of government expenditure in 1977 to 36 percent by 1980. Subsidies alone more than tripled during this period. For example, subsidies on gasoline allowed prices to remain the same throughout the decade, when market prices more than quadrupled. Although subsidies were primarily redistributive in their intent, they also handsomely benefited the private sector, whose inputs such as water and electricity were also supported. Ambitious public works programs, developed to alleviate unemployment, employed some 50,000 citizens but were largely inefficient and unclear in their objectives.

The multibillion-dollar industrial park at Point Lisas, more than any other single activity, symbolized the thorough role of government involvement. The park was constructed, in part, with revenues from the so-called Special Funds for Long-Term Development, consisting of over forty different funds. Cost overruns were so prevalent during the construction of the park that no final cost was ever obtained. The park sought to use the country's oil and natural gas reserves for a well-integrated petrochemical industry, alongside heavy industries like steel. Most of the site's plants came on-stream in the early to mid-1980s, including steel, urea, ammonia, cement, and methanol plants and an oil refinery. Although these plants were still young in the 1980s, concerns existed that some of these projects could turn into white elephants. Also considered, but not constructed as of the late 1980s, were an alumina (see Glossary) smelter (Trinidad is a bauxite [see Glossary] transshipment site) and a plant to process liquefied natural gas.

The government's attitudes toward its role in the economy remained unchanged in the 1980s. Despite minor policy differences, both Prime Minister Chambers (1981–86) and subsequently Prime Minister Robinson (1986–) continued to perceive an extensive role for the state in the country's mixed economy. One significant change enacted by the Chambers government was to reduce the number of bids offered to foreign contractors for large industrial projects. After a Ministry of External Affairs report concluded that these foreign firms had financially exploited the arrangements and hurt local competitors, the process was changed to favor locals.

Chambers, however, confronted much more devastating economic difficulties as a result of the deep recession brought on by the sharp fall in oil prices in 1982. Decreased oil production lowered government revenues, a sizable portion of which were derived from the petroleum industry. Growing fiscal deficits prompted the Chambers government to pursue unpopular domestic policies, such as decreased subsidies, increased utility rates, an increased tax base, and, most important, deep reductions in capital expenditures, thereby eliminating most funds for economic development. To stabilize the country's deteriorating balance of payments position, the government opted for equally unpopular trade policies. These measures included a new import licensing system and a dual exchange rate, both of which drew the ire of other Caricom nations. To help smooth the adjustment period, the Chambers government invited William Demas, a well-known Trinidadian economist and president of the Caribbean Development Bank, to write a broad ''Imperatives of Adjustment Plan'' to help stabilize the country's accounts and work toward a recovery.

A recovery, however, never materialized under Chambers, and the Robinson government was faced with the same task of reversing the recession, reducing budget deficits, and stabilizing the balance of payments, but with fewer resources. In 1987 the Robinson government proposed few policies that diverged widely from those of Chambers. A major goal of the Robinson government, however, was to improve relations with Caricom trading partners, which had soured because of Trinidad and Tobago's protectionist policies in the early to mid-1980s. The unification of the country's exchange rate in January 1987, followed by the removal of a

12-percent import duty for most Caricom countries in July, did help to revive regional integration. On the budgetary side, Robinson continued to reduce capital expenditures; unlike Chambers, however, he attempted deep cuts in current expenditures, most notably the cost of living allowances of civil servants. That proposal was withdrawn, however, after a storm of protest. Nonetheless, the issue was important in that it symbolized the difficulty the Robinson government might face in seeking economic concessions after a decade of great wealth. In his 1987 budget speech, Robinson warned of the possible divestment of some state-run enterprises, thus earning his government an early reputation as pro-business. In the late 1980s, the NAR government's main economic objectives remained economic recovery and diversification; nonetheless, the new government cautioned that its economic program would require ten years to be completely effective.

National Income and Public Finance

Trinidad and Tobago's GDP in 1985 totaled US$7.7 billion at current prices, a figure that had declined in real terms every year since the country's peak performance of 1982. In 1985 the petroleum industry continued to dominate the country's production, contributing 24 percent of national output. This was followed by public administration (15 percent), construction (11 percent), financial services and real estate (10 percent), transportation and communications (10 percent), distributive trade (9 percent), other services (9 percent), manufacturing (7 percent), agriculture (3 percent), and electricity and water (2 percent) (see fig. 7). The most prominent changes in the structure of the economy occurred in the petroleum and construction sectors, which had contributed as much as 36 and 14 percent, respectively, to national output during the first five years of the decade. The largest sectoral increases occurred in government, up 7 percentage points, and other services, up over 3 percent.

The fiscal year in Trinidad and Tobago in the late 1980s was the same as the calendar year. The budget was listed by ministries and various government agencies, often broken down by subunits. There were both current and capital accounts, but capital expenditures were not listed in detail.

The national accounts of Trinidad and Tobago were affected greatly by the oil boom of the 1970s and then by the subsequent decline in the 1980s. Because of the increase in oil prices, government revenues tripled in 1974 and expanded rapidly thereafter until they peaked in 1982. Expenditures also expanded rapidly, but less rapidly than revenues, creating budget surpluses every year except for a slight deficit in 1979. Over half of government oil revenues

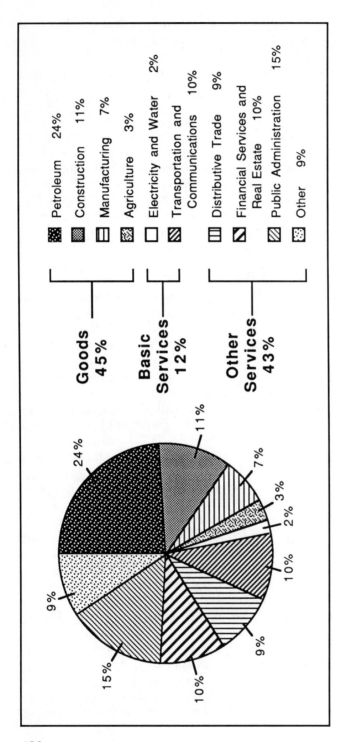

Goods
45%

Basic
Services
12%

Other
Services
43%

■ Petroleum   24%
■ Construction   11%
⊞ Manufacturing   7%
▨ Agriculture   3%
□ Electricity and Water   2%
▨ Transportation and
    Communications   10%

⊟ Distributive Trade   9%
▨ Financial Services and
    Real Estate   10%
▨ Public Administration   15%
▨ Other   9%

Source: Based on information from Central Bank of Trinidad and Tobago, *Annual Report, 1985.* Port-of-Spain, Trinidad and Tobago, 1986, 68.

Figure 7. Trinidad and Tobago. Gross Domestic Product by Sector, 1985

went into the Special Funds for Long-Term Development. In contrast to the 1970s, budget deficits occurred every year in the 1980s, beginning in 1982. A record budget deficit of approximately US$766 million was recorded in 1986. Budget deficits in the 1980s were financed primarily by borrowing from the Central Bank with minimal external lending. In addition, revenue shortfalls were financed by transfers from the Special Funds for Long-Term Development, which generated roughly US$3 billion during the 1970s. These funds, however, were depleted by the mid-1980s from project and deficit spending. Reductions in expenditures in the mid-1980s were attained almost exclusively by deep cuts in capital expenditures. In the late 1980s, the Robinson government planned to curtail current account spending, make state enterprises more accountable, and possibly divest certain government entities. Robinson chose to avoid what he termed the ''debt trap and dependence on the IMF'' (International Monetary Fund—see Glossary) in favor of belt tightening, reducing expenditures, and increasing revenues through higher taxation.

The public sector investment program that had evolved in the 1970s involved a budgetary process that caused concern in the following decade. As the state took on a greater role in the economy with its oil windfalls, there was less discipline in the establishment of cost restraints for large investment projects, making many capital outlays open ended in terms of expected final costs. In 1987, however, the Robinson government called for the review of the organization and structure of each state enterprise and announced that there would be an in-depth study of the viability of state enterprises. Likewise, Robinson announced that state-owned corporations would need to improve their internal financing and auditing procedures. As part of a plan of capital restructuring, Robinson noted in his 1987 budget speech that most current expenditures that continued to go to these enterprises would be transferred to the capital account.

Expenditures

Total government expenditures in 1985 reached approximately US$3.2 billion, US$380 million more than revenues. Government expenditures peaked in 1982 after a decade of rapid growth that was paid for by increased revenues from oil. As oil revenues increased, so did the government's role in the economy, causing government spending as a percentage of GDP to increase from 20 percent in the early 1970s, to 35 percent by 1980, to approximately 40 percent by 1985.

Current expenditures in 1985 totaled US$2.5 billion, or 78 percent of total expenditures. Current expenditures experienced an average annual increase of 40 percent from 1973 to 1976, decreased slightly in 1977, and then expanded 32 percent annually from 1978 to 1981. Expenditures grew more slowly than revenues, however, generating annual surpluses on the current account from 1974 to 1979 that averaged 18 percent of GDP. The fastest growing portion of current expenditures in the 1970s was subsidies and transfers, which tripled from 1977 to 1980, increasing from 5.4 percent of total expenditures to 12 percent in that same period. Ninety percent of subsidies went to agricultural production, food, and cement. Although total expenditures decreased after 1982, current expenditures decreased only slightly, peaking once again in 1986.

The current account in 1985 was broken down into five functional categories: general services, community services, social services, economic services, and unallocated expenditures. The largest share of current expenditures, 44 percent, went to social services, comprising health, education, welfare, and housing. General services trailed social services with 21 percent, including fiscal services, economic regulation, defense, justice, and police. Unallocated expenditures followed with 17 percent, generally for public debt servicing and payments to local government. Economic services accounted for 11 percent, primarily toward agriculture, energy, and transportation. Community services accounted for the balance of 7 percent, the majority going to roads.

The distribution of current account expenditures in 1985 was typical of the trends in the decade. In terms of economic classification, 1985 current expenditures were divided as follows: 45 percent to subsidies and transfers, 42 percent to wages and salaries, 8 percent to goods and services, and 5 percent to interest payments. Salary increases for civil servants often accounted for a large percentage of increases on the account in a given year. Interest payments' share of current expenditures was lower than in other Commonwealth Caribbean countries because of the economy's manageable debt. The minor cutbacks made to current account expenditures in the 1980s went primarily to reduce transfers and subsidies.

Capital expenditures totaled US$683 million, or roughly 21 percent of total expenditures in 1985. Public sector capital investment during the 1970s grew rapidly, accounting for nearly 70 percent of total investment. From 1972 to 1980, capital expenditures grew 46 percent annually, faster than even current expenditures. The growth in capital investment by the government increased the account's share of GDP from 6 percent in the early 1970s to 18 percent by 1980. During the 1970s, a large percentage of capital expenditures went to purchase numerous state-run enterprises, large industrial and infrastructure projects, and lending to public sector entities. Capital expenditures peaked in 1982 and then declined by 55 percent from 1982 to 1985. These cutbacks drastically changed capital expenditures' share of total government expenditures from the peak in 1982 of 47.7 percent to a low of 21.5 percent by 1985. In 1985 over one-third of capital expenditures were destined for state enterprises. Most of the remaining capital outlays went to housing, schools, agriculture, public utilities, and transportation.

Revenues

Government revenues in 1985 stood at US$2.8 billion, causing a budget deficit of some US$380 million. Revenues tripled in 1974 as the price of oil soared, causing total revenues to rise from roughly US$245 million in 1973 to over US$700 million in 1974. Between 1970 and 1986, total government revenues as a share of GDP doubled to 40 percent of GDP. Oil tax receipts dominated, contributing 65 percent of total government revenues by 1980. Taxes on the oil sector included corporate taxes, royalties, unemployment levies, excise duties, and others. Government revenues declined substantially after 1982, however, as a result of the fall in oil prices. By 1985 oil-sector tax revenues accounted for only 39 percent of total current revenue; nonetheless, Trinidad and Tobago continued to have one of the highest corporate taxes in the region.

Although the oil sector was the most visibly taxed part of the economy, approximately 60 percent of revenues in 1985 came from taxes from the non-oil sector, primarily individual income taxes, sales taxes, and import duties. Non-tax revenues accounted for less than 1 percent of total revenues. Plans to increase government revenues in the late 1980s included increases in taxation of individuals and corporations, taxes on oil and airplane tickets, and a 5-percent increase in the purchase tax. The new government in 1987 was also studying the possibility of tax reform or major simplifications of the tax system.

Labor Force and Industrial Relations

The labor force in 1985 consisted of 463,900 persons, or about 39 percent of the total population. Men outnumbered women almost two to one in the registered work force, although women dominated the informal service sector, where they were not recorded. Nearly half of the work force, 49 percent, were classified under "other services," which included many self-employed or own-account workers. Construction was the largest employer of productive labor (18 percent), followed by manufacturing (15 percent), agriculture (11 percent), and transportation and communications (7 percent).

Unemployment remained Trinidad and Tobago's principal economic and social problem in the late 1980s. Unemployment worsened steadily throughout the decade from a low of 8 to 9 percent in the early 1980s to a high of 17 percent in 1987. Trinidad and Tobago used a different method to calculate its unemployment rate from that used by the United States, however, in an attempt to compensate for the high levels of underemployment and disguised unemployment (see Labor Force and Industrial Relations, ch. 2). Women and urban youth faced higher levels of unemployment. In 1985 youths 15 to 19 years of age suffered a 39-percent unemployment rate, whereas those 20 to 24 years of age experienced a 28-percent unemployment rate. The capital-intensive structure of the economy meant that efforts to alleviate high unemployment would require a structural or long-term approach.

Organized labor has played a central role in the country's political economy since the 1920s. Strikes were curtailed somewhat after Prime Minister Williams enacted the controversial Industrial Stabilization Act of 1965, which granted the government the authority to resolve disputes with the Industrial Court. In contrast to most other Commonwealth Caribbean nations, trade unions in Trinidad and Tobago did not directly affiliate with political parties. Nonetheless, unions strongly influenced major issues, such as the policy of nationalization of the major sectors of the economy in the 1970s. Approximately 40 percent of the labor force was unionized and was represented by more than 100 official trade unions. The OWTU, comprising some 16,000 members, was the most prominent union and was frequently at the forefront of labor's demands for national control over production. Three-quarters of all organized labor were members of ten other major trade unions, including the important ATSE/FWTU. Most of the country's labor organizations were affiliated with the main labor umbrella organization, the Trinidad and Tobago Labour Congress, or the more radical offshoot, the Council of Progressive Trade Unions.

The power of trade unions declined in the 1980s as the recession provided labor with less for which to negotiate. Union demands had continued to grow in the 1970s, even after one of their long-time goals, the nationalization of the major industries, had been met. Trade unions were responsible for large gains in real wages during the 1970s, but as these advances eventually outstripped output, productivity declined. Labor disputes decreased in numbers by the 1980s after the relative labor turbulence of the 1970s. For example, in 1981 industrial disputes involving 2,588 workers accounted for the loss of only 51,389 workdays, compared with 36,974 employees losing 777,389 workdays in 1975. As with real wages in general, minimum wage rates declined during the mid- to late 1980s.

Industry

Trinidad and Tobago possessed an industrial base that was un-matched in the Caribbean in the late 1980s and, for a country of about 1.2 million people, perhaps in the world. As new heavy in-dustries came on-stream in the early 1980s, Trinidad and Tobago was a producer of oil, asphalt, natural gas, ammonia and urea fer-tilizers, methanol, iron, and steel. Petrochemicals based on natural gas became the center of the industrial strategy envisioned in the 1970s to diversify away from oil and export agriculture. In 1985 the petroleum sector accounted for 24 percent of GDP and nearly 70 percent of export earnings, and it affected most major sectors of the economy. The country also contained a large construction sector. Large industrial projects, asphalt roads, and government housing projects were responsible for the sector's prominence for decades, frequently making it a barometer of the economy's general health. The manufacturing sector was relatively small compared with the rest of the economy. Manufacturing, historically linked to agricultural processing, was very modern by the 1980s and com-prised the assembly of automobiles, televisions, and refrigerators and the production of steel. Light manufacturing was less signifi-cant, as Trinidad and Tobago tended to import many smaller con-sumer items.

Petroleum and Asphalt

Petroleum and its derivatives have been the major sector of the economy since World War II, achieving its greatest importance during the boom of the 1970s, when it accounted for as much as 40 percent of GDP and more than 90 percent of export earnings. Oil output peaked in 1978 with the production of 84 million bar-rels. Output then declined from 1979 to 1983 but rebounded to 64 million barrels by 1985. Although the earliest oil fields were lo-cated on the southwestern peninsula of Trinidad, significant reserves were later tapped off the island's southeastern coast and off Point Fortin in the Gulf of Paria. Since 1974, however, there have been no major oil discoveries, causing a slow decline in the country's ratio of reserves to production. Although proven reserves were es-timated to last fewer than ten years at the 1987 rate of extraction, decreased production and anticipated new oil finds were expected

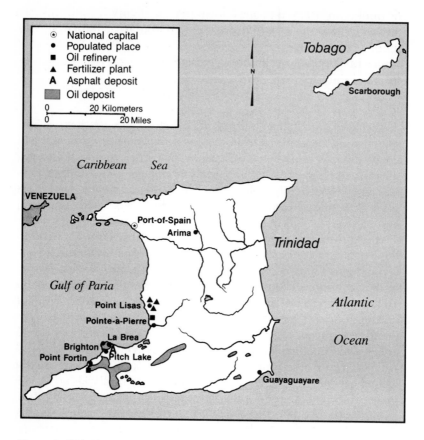

Figure 8. Trinidad and Tobago. Oil Production and Related Activities, 1987

to allow the country to produce into the twenty-first century. Proven oil reserves stood at 540 million barrels in 1987. It was estimated that over three-quarters of Trinidad and Tobago's crude oil reserves had already been found. Over 60 percent of reserves were located offshore. In 1985 approximately 77 percent of oil produced was drilled offshore. In the late 1980s, Trinidad and Tobago was not a member of the Organization of Petroleum Exporting Countries.

The first exploratory wells were drilled in Trinidad near Pitch Lake at La Brea during the 1850s and 1860s, making them some of the earliest wells in the world (see fig. 8). Commercially viable production did not flow from the wells, however, until 1909 (see Growth and Structure of the Economy, this ch.). The young oil industry suffered from many industrial hazards, making injury rather common, which helped create strong oil worker unions.

Production expanded again during World War II and thereafter until it peaked toward the close of the oil boom in 1978. The output of oil was revived briefly in the mid-1980s because of a reduction in some production taxes, but dwindling reserves and low oil prices continued to restrict output (see table 5, Appendix A).

Oil production was historically controlled by large foreign companies, such as Shell, British Petroleum, Texaco, and Amoco, the latter also known as the Standard Oil Company of Indiana. By the late 1980s, however, the government had purchased all foreign operations except Amoco. In 1985 the government completed the purchase of the remaining operations of Texaco as well as the residual 49-percent share of a small Texan company, Tesoro, from a previous joint venture with the government. Nonetheless, even with the new government purchases, Amoco still produced over 50 percent of the country's oil, possessed most of the newer and more productive oil fields, and controlled over 70 percent of the natural gas reserves. As oil reserves and production continued to decline in the late 1980s, the government once again was considering inviting foreign oil companies to assist with the exploration and drilling of less accessible oil.

Amoco did not refine any of its oil locally, as both of the island's refineries, at Pointe-à-Pierre and at Point Fortin, were government owned. The Pointe-à-Pierre refinery, with a capacity of 220,000 bpd, was traditionally the main facility. Point Fortin's share of refining, however, climbed to 30 percent in 1985 because of the installation of a pipeline connecting the two refineries to improve efficiency. Total refinery capacity was 310,000 bpd. For decades crude oil was imported by Trinidad and Tobago from Saudi Arabia, Venezuela, Iran, Indonesia, Nigeria, and Ecuador and then refined and reexported. Refinery activity, however, was reduced more than 50 percent in the first half of the 1980s; after 1983 refining of the imported oil ceased altogether as a result of the depressed world oil market. The percentage of domestically refined crude diminished as well. By the late 1980s, only 20 percent of refinery capacity was in regular use, making operations very inefficient and entailing large financial losses by the government.

In addition to its oil reserves, Pitch Lake at La Brea contained the world's largest source of natural asphalt. The lake, considered by some to be one of the wonders of the world, had been producing asphalt for decades. Asphalt production continued its slow decline in the 1980s, however. In 1985 only 21,400 tons of asphalt were produced, in contrast to the figure of 128,300 tons achieved in 1970. Although most asphalt was exported, it was also used domestically for paving roads and in the construction industry.

Roughly 80 percent of asphalt output took the form of dried asphalt, whereas the remainder was asphalt cement.

Natural Gas

In the late 1980s, Trinidad and Tobago had proven reserves totaling approximately 481 billion cubic meters of natural gas, as well as a further 566 billion cubic meters that were likely to be recovered. Trinidad and Tobago contained about 0.3 percent of world gas reserves and contributed about 0.2 percent of world gas production. A large percentage of Trinidad and Tobago's gas was not associated with oil production and was located in separate fields off both the southeastern and the northern coasts. Although gas deposits were discovered in the 1940s, significant production did not get underway until the 1950s, when natural gas was needed to supply the small Federations Chemical (Fedchem) fertilizer plant. From 1973 to 1986, proven reserves of natural gas more than doubled during oil explorations off the country's southeastern shores. These discoveries encouraged the natural gas-based development strategy that evolved in the 1970s. The production of natural gas nearly doubled in the 1970s and expanded rapidly in the 1980s to meet the growing demand of the petrochemical industries that were coming on-stream. Gas production reached a record 7.6 billion cubic meters in 1985. The efficiency of production also increased, reaching a utilization rate of 78 percent by 1985. Amoco possessed approximately 72 percent of natural gas reserves and produced over 80 percent of the gas in 1985. Whereas oil fueled the country's economy throughout the twentieth century, the nation was expecting the same from natural gas and related industries into the twenty-first century.

By the 1980s, natural gas was becoming increasingly integrated into the national economy. Natural gas feedstock was the most important input to the anhydrous ammonia, urea, and methanol plants that commenced operations at the Point Lisas industrial park in the early to mid-1980s (see Role of Government, this ch.). Natural gas also fueled over 70 percent of the country's generators of electricity, powered the new mill of the Iron and Steel Company of Trinidad and Tobago (Iscott), and was piped into Port-of-Spain residences. New gas pipelines along Trinidad's southern and western coasts were a decisive factor in the country's greater utilization of its gas resources during the 1980s. The steady supply of natural gas to the Point Lisas industrial park became essential to efficient operations, as demonstrated by the production problems that resulted from supply shortages in 1982. The National Gas Company (NGC) was the prime purchaser and distributor of natural gas. The NGC allocated over 60 percent of all gas to fertilizer production during the mid-1980s. The methanol plant, the steel mill, and oil companies in general consumed most of the balance of gas production. The NGC sold the gas at a wide range of prices, which included generous subsidies to the infant petrochemical industries.

Petrochemicals

In the late 1980s, Trinidad and Tobago became the world's second leading exporter of fertilizers behind only the Soviet Union. Three fertilizer plants constructed during the late 1970s and early 1980s nearly tripled fertilizer production between 1980 and 1985. Two of these plants, Trinidad Nitrogen Company (Tringen) and Fertilizers of Trinidad and Tobago (Fertrin), produced liquefied anhydrous ammonia, whereas the third plant processed granular urea. Fertilizer production reached 1.6 million tons by 1985, of which over 90 percent were exported. In 1985 about 82 percent of all fertilizers were anhydrous ammonia, and 18 percent were urea. Although fertilizer exports were on the rise, declining prices as a result of market oversupply actually reduced export revenues. In the late 1980s, the government was also considering projects to process and export liquefied natural gas and ethanol (an octane enhancer derived from sugarcane).

The Tringen and Fertrin ammonia plants were both government joint ventures that provided the government with a 51-percent equity share in each plant. The minority share of the Tringen plant was owned by the conglomerate W.R. Grace, whose subsidiary, Fedchem, operated the 800,000-square-meter fertilizer complex inside Point Lisas. The profitable Tringen plant expanded its capacity in the late 1980s. By 1988 its original capacity was expected to more than double to 900,000 tons of ammonia per year. Fertrin, a joint venture between Amoco and the government, did not come on-stream until the early 1980s, with a two-unit plant of 2,000-tons-per-day capacity. Although large cost overruns occurred in the construction phase, ammonia production was expected to be profitable during the 1980s and 1990s as long as fertilizer prices stabilized.

The first full year of urea production occurred in 1985 at the fully government-owned plant at Point Lisas. The plant had a 580,000-ton capacity per year and produced 339,800 tons in 1985, or about 60 percent of capacity in its first full year. Capacity utilization was expected to increase by the end of the 1980s as the plant's exports entered large foreign markets, such as India and China. In the late 1980s, however, the EEC accused Trinidad and Tobago of dumping urea on the West European market and was considering taking action against the islands. Urea production accounted for roughly a fifth of total fertilizer production in the country. In 1987 Trintoc was also building a plant to produce urea and formaldehyde adhesives inside the Point Lisas complex. The future profitability of the recently opened plant was perceived to be dependent on world price changes and the government's ability to find markets.

Trinidad and Tobago's first methanol plant also experienced its first full year of operations in 1985. Approximately 358,200 tons of methanol were produced in 1985, and the plant averaged a 90-percent capacity utilization rate. Over 360,000 tons of methanol were exported in 1985, which included stocks from the previous year. The government-owned methanol plant turned a profit in its first full year of operation; continued profitability was dependent on the expansion of the world methanol market. Doubts over the rate of expansion of methanol appeared in Trinidad and Tobago during 1986 when the construction of a second methanol plant, involving a joint venture between a British firm and the government, was canceled because of continued uncertainty about energy prices. All methanol was produced for the export market in the late 1980s, and it was estimated that in 1985 Trinidad and Tobago supplied approximately 18 percent of United States imports of methanol. As in the case of urea, however, the EEC was studying allegations that Trinidad and Tobago was dumping low-priced methanol on its regional market.

Iron and Steel

Iron and steel production was the core industry in the new heavy industry strategy of the 1970s and 1980s. Unfortunately, the state-owned venture, Iscott, was the most unprofitable industry located at the Point Lisas complex. Although the modern plant was technically sound and well integrated into the energy resources and deep harbors of the complex, it faced serious marketing and management problems. Iscott's marketing problems were exacerbated in 1983 when five United States steel companies filed an anti-dumping suit against it. The government's deep involvement at Point Lisas in general, especially its provision of cheap inputs to iron and steel production, made for a difficult defense against claims that the government subsidized the steel industry. After paying countervailing and antidumping duties for several years, in 1987 Trinidad and Tobago signed a voluntary export restraint agreement with the United States to limit iron and steel exports to 73,000 tons per year for a three-year period. Management problems, particularly in the steel mill's melt shop, caused steel production to fall for the first time in 1984 and 1985. Declining production and large financial losses persuaded the government to hire two West European firms to manage Iscott's operations under a two-year contract. Production did increase in 1986, signaling the early success of the outside management contract.

Iscott's modern facilities at Point Lisas included two direct reduction plants with a combined capacity of 900,000 tons a year. The US$500 million plant used imported iron ore from Brazil in processing its steel. Iron and steel production reached 522,900 tons in 1985, marking the second year of declining production and the first year of a fall in exports. Exports reached 143,200 tons in 1985, only 27 percent of production, but exports were expected to expand again in the late 1980s. Output included direct reduced iron, steel billets, and wire rods. Direct reduced iron accounted for 42 percent of the subsector's output, the greatest share of iron and steel production, and 45 percent of exports. Production of steel billets represented 33 percent of the subsector's output, followed by wire rods with 20 percent. Over three-fourths of all wire rods were exported, whereas under 10 percent of steel billets were exported in the first half of the 1980s. A large portion of iron and steel was used domestically because of Iscott's marketing difficulty.

Manufacturing

Although the manufacturing sector remained relatively small in the 1980s, it spanned a wide range of activities from sugar processing to automobile assembly. In 1985 manufacturing output reached approximately US$542 million, or 7 percent of GDP. Light manufacturing in particular experienced sharp declines of over 10 percent annually during the mid-1980s; nonetheless, the sector as a whole was growing by the late 1980s because of the inclusion of petrochemical and steel production in manufacturing data.

Historically, manufacturing was an insignificant sector in the economy, dwarfed by agriculture and oil. In the postwar era, however, import substitution industrialization development strategies provided generous fiscal incentives toward new investment in manufacturing. The Aid to Pioneer Industries Ordinance of 1950 provided accelerated depreciation allowances and duty-free importation of machinery and raw materials, which was instrumental in attracting foreign investment to Trinidad and Tobago. Likewise, the establishment of the Industrial Development Corporation (IDC) in 1959 served to expand the sector's role in the economy. By the 1960s, producers of manufactured goods were protected through increased tariffs as well. These measures encouraged the establishment of over 100 new manufacturing operations by the mid-1960s. Increasingly, the sector moved beyond agricultural processing and easily substituted goods toward the assembly of consumer durables, such as televisions, refrigerators, and automobiles. By the 1980s, most locally manufactured goods remained protected through quantitative import restrictions.

The structure of manufacturing in the 1980s was that of a highly protected, inward-looking industry that produced mostly for the domestic and Caricom markets. Exports of manufactured goods in the early 1980s, before petrochemicals and steel manufacturing were in full force, accounted for as little as 2 percent of domestic exports. Since the manufacturing industry tended to emphasize mixing, bottling, and assembly, the value added of the final product was generally low. As such, these activities often did little to link various sectors of the domestic economy. Price controls were also used by the government to reduce the power of a few local producers, who faced minimal competition as a consequence of import controls. The implementation of a heavy industry strategy changed manufacturing by the late 1980s. Although light manufacturing declined with the economy's general contraction in the mid-1980s, it was believed that Trinidad and Tobago was consuming more locally produced goods because it could not afford the import splurge of the 1970s.

The manufacturing sector was broken down into six principal subsectors: assembly, chemicals and nonmetallic products, food processing, beverages and tobacco, printing, and wood products. Discussion of manufacturing generally excluded oil and sugar, which if included would have accounted for 45 percent of manufacturing in 1985. Assembly was the most important subsector, contributing more than a quarter of manufacturing's output. Assembly included radios, televisions, refrigerators, gas stoves, vehicles, batteries, tires, and boat building. Less than 1 percent of assembly manufacturing was exported. The second most important subsector was chemicals and nonmetallic products, contributing 19 percent of the sector's output and consisting of petrochemicals, paints, pharmaceuticals, bricks, cement, and glass. This subsector grew rapidly in the 1980s with the development of petrochemicals and new cement factory capacity. Food processing, such as edible oils, feeds, meat, baked goods, and dairy products, was the third most important subsector, accounting for 16 percent of manufacturing. Trinidad and Tobago continued to produce its world-famous flavoring, Angostura Bitters. Beverages and tobacco, textiles, printing, wood products, and miscellaneous manufacturing followed in importance, all contributing between 5 and 10 percent of total manufacturing.

Construction

During the mid-1980s, construction activity declined sharply as the major public sector investment programs of the 1970s and early 1980s were completed and as tight monetary conditions reduced the availability of credit. From 1983 to 1985, the construction industry's output fell some 21 percent annually, reducing its share of GDP from 15 percent in 1982 to 11 percent in 1985. Total output in 1985 equaled US$792 million. Most construction activity in the late 1980s was limited to minor road building, housing and factories, and some hotel construction. Although the Robinson government in the late 1980s was proposing that the construction sector be the catalyst of new economic activity, it remained unlikely that the industry would regain the prominence it held in the 1970s. The sharp decline in construction, the major employer of the economy, was expected to exacerbate the worsening unemployment rate.

In the late 1980s, Trinidad and Tobago was becoming less dependent on imports in the construction industry as increased steel and cement capacity was attained. The low quality of locally produced cement also encouraged the introduction of higher grade cements in the 1980s. Housing projects were also becoming more sophisticated, including self-help schemes, after improper design and construction had made government housing projects unpopular in previous years.

Services

Banking, Financial Services, and Currency

Financial institutions expanded rapidly as a result of the oil-based liquidity that the financial system experienced in the 1970s. This was especially true of nonbanking intermediaries, such as finance houses, which underwent the fastest growth. In the late 1980s, the islands' financial network included the Central Bank, various government development organizations, commercial banks, finance companies, mortgage and trust companies, insurance companies, a stock exchange, and other business services. Although legislation granted the Central Bank generous control over the financial system, bank intervention was generally restrained. Increasing regulation over nonbanking financial institutions was instituted in the mid-1980s, however, as several poorly managed finance companies collapsed and were subsequently rescued by the Central Bank. The sector as a whole contracted after the country's assets peaked in 1982. Government policies generally favored tight monetary policies to restrain inflation and help stabilize national and international accounts during the post-boom adjustment period.

The Central Bank was established in 1964 and was authorized to issue currency, regulate credit, buy and sell securities and discount notes, and underwrite government loans. Although the Central Bank contained about 30 percent of the nation's assets in 1985, its share was declining as international reserves were being depleted. The government also owned and managed numerous development finance institutions, most notably the IDC, the Agricultural Development Bank (ADB), and the Mortgage Finance Company (MFC). These organizations controlled about 4 percent of national finances. The IDC, established in 1959, was the most important development finance organization and was one of the top lenders to industry. The portfolio of IDC lending generally reflected government industrialization strategies and also contained purely government projects. The ADB was the most important lender to agriculture, especially to the livestock subsector. Although the MFC was the key lender to the construction industry, in 1985 the government created the Home Mortgage Bank to serve as a major institution in the construction industry.

The country had 8 commercial banks with 117 branches, almost all of which were controlled by Trinidadian and Tobagonian nationals as prescribed by law. The process of localization of the islands' banks began in the 1970s, which eventually placed a large share of Canadian and British banks in the hands of nationals. The islands' largest bank was the Republic Bank, formerly the British Barclays Bank. Commercial banks contained 56 percent of the nation's assets in 1985. Twenty-seven percent of commercial bank loans went to individuals, primarily for automobiles, followed by government, particularly public bodies, with 15 percent, manufacturing 13 percent, distributive trade 12 percent, construction 8 percent, and the balance to various other services and productive activities. Interest rates for deposits and loans averaged 8 and 12 percent, respectively, in the mid-1980s, roughly comparable with industrial nations and low compared with most developing countries. Reserve ratios were freely utilized to control the money supply and credit; in 1985 the cash reserve ratio was 17 percent, and the liquidity reserve ratio reached upwards of 22 percent. In 1986 the government introduced the Deposit Insurance Fund, which protected and insured savings up to about US$14,000.

Nonbanking financial institutions, encompassing finance houses, trust and mortgage companies, insurance companies, and other business services, have proliferated since the 1970s. These institutions contained over 10 percent of the country's assets in 1985, trailing the commercial banks and the Central Bank. In the mid-1980s, there were twenty-two finance companies with some seventy-six branches. After the 1984 collapse of International Trust and the faltering of other nonbanking institutions because of cash flow problems, the Central Bank increased regulation of these services. As of December 1985, there were fifty-nine insurance companies registered on the islands, although some of these were also faltering. There were eight trust and mortgage finance companies, devoted mostly to real estate. Unlike other Commonwealth Caribbean countries, financial services in Trinidad and Tobago were operated predominantly by citizens of that nation, and laws specified strict limitations on the extent of the participation of foreigners.

Trinidad and Tobago also operated a small stock exchange, which was established in 1981. In 1985 nearly 50 million shares of stocks were sold, involving over 11,000 transactions at a market value of US$62 million. The exchange's composite index was declining in the 1980s because of the falling value of most stocks and discouraging economic indicators. The exchange was limited by extensive government involvement in the economy and the large number of family-run businesses, which limited the number of companies whose shares were publicly traded. In addition, few firms sought the sale of stocks as a viable way to raise capital, instead opting for commercial bank loans.

In 1964 the Trinidad and Tobago dollar replaced the British West Indian dollar as the national currency. Eastern Caribbean dollars—the common currency of members of the Organisation of Eastern Caribbean States (OECS—see Glossary) and pegged to the United States dollar at EC$2.70 equals US$1.00—and other currencies also circulated. From 1972 to 1976, the Trinidad and Tobago dollar was floated against the British pound sterling; after 1976, however, the Trinidad and Tobago dollar was pegged to the United States dollar. The first major depreciation of the Trinidad and Tobago dollar since June 1976 occurred in December 1985, when the country's currency was devalued 50 percent against the United States dollar. As a result of the devaluation, the exchange rate moved from US$1.00 to TT$2.40 to US$1.00 to TT$3.60. This reduced international reserves but was expected to increase export competitiveness. Government foreign exchange controls existed, particularly for foreign travel by nationals.

Tourism

The tourism sector played a rather minor role in the economy of Trinidad and Tobago compared with other Commonwealth

Caribbean islands. In the mid-1980s, tourism represented only 3 percent of GDP, slightly above the 1960 level of 2 percent but below the 1970 level of 4 percent. Annual foreign exchange earnings derived from tourism averaged about US$200 million during the mid-1980s, making the sector the third largest earner behind oil and overseas investment. As the most southern and eastern of the Caribbean islands, Trinidad and Tobago did not enjoy the close proximity to the large North American tourist market of other Commonwealth Caribbean nations such as the Bahamas and Jamaica. Nonetheless, tourists were attracted to Trinidad and Tobago to enjoy its world-famous carnival, steelband and calypso music, Hindu and Muslim festivals, and the unspoiled natural beauty of Tobago. Government policies have historically sought to limit and control tourist activity through prohibiting private beaches, casino gambling, and land sales to foreigners (although the latter was available through long-term leases). Substantial tourist growth was realized in the 1960s as a result of fiscal incentives offered under the Hotel Development Act of 1963. The advent of the oil boom in the 1970s diverted attention away from tourism as a source of foreign exchange revenues; as a result, by the mid-1980s no major hotel construction projects had occurred in nearly a decade. By the late 1980s, however, the government looked to tourism as a way to diversify away from a dependence on oil-based export revenues and as a stimulus to domestic agriculture and employment.

Trinidad and Tobago recorded 187,090 tourist arrivals in 1985, a number that was rather typical for the first half of the decade. In addition, over 6,000 cruise ship visitors were registered, which was well below the 28,000 level of 1981. Over half of all tourists were classified as private holiday tourists; this category consisted primarily of expatriate Trinidadians who stayed at private residences while visiting the country. Roughly 20 percent of all arrivals were for business purposes, and only about 10 percent were vacationing hotel tourists. North Americans comprised about 45 percent of tourist arrivals, of which the United States share was over 30 percent. Tourists from the Commonwealth Caribbean represented 35 percent of total arrivals, followed by West Europeans and South Americans. Trinidadians also frequented Tobago in large numbers, creating a rather large domestic tourist subsector. Some 45,000 Trinidadians traveled to neighboring Tobago during 1985. Hotel occupancy rates in the mid-1980s averaged 55 percent, below the industry's estimated break-even point of 60 percent.

The lack of physical infrastructure for the tourist industry was the main obstacle to further development of the sector. The country

Steel band preparing for music festival
Courtesy Trinidad and Tobago Tourist Board

contained only about 2,000 hotel rooms and 300 guest rooms, or about one-fifth of the number of rooms in Jamaica. Tobago, much more dependent on tourism than Trinidad, possessed only 600 rooms and also suffered from water distribution problems. Although government plans called for 3,000 first-class hotel rooms to be operative by 1990, some observers doubted that this goal could be achieved. The lack of adequate airports also hindered tourism. Both of the country's major airports needed some upgrading and expansion to handle the growth of tourism envisioned by the government. The Piarco International Airport, located twenty-six kilometers east of Port-of-Spain, was the nation's principal facility. As of 1987, the government had not yet implemented longstanding plans for the complete expansion and renovation of Piarco. These plans included five-star hotels, longer and emergency runways, aircraft maintenance facilities, a bonded industrial park, and a cargo warehouse, all with the objective of making Piarco the air transportation hub of the Eastern Caribbean and northern South America. Crown Point Airport, located on Tobago, was the nation's other major airport. Although it received upgrading in the 1980s, these limited provisions were not expected to allow it to accommodate greatly increased international traffic. For example, in 1987 Tobago received only one direct flight a week from Miami.

Ports represented another tourist infrastructure problem. One of the reasons for the sharp decline in cruise ship arrivals in the early 1980s was the congested conditions at the Port-of-Spain docks. This problem was expected to be partially relieved in 1988 with the completion of the deepening of the inner harbor of Tobago's major port, Scarborough, allowing the smaller island to receive large cruise ships. Tobago's infrastructure for tourism was expected to expand in general after 1987 as a consequence of the 1986 election of a native Tobagonian as prime minister.

As with the rest of the economy, government involvement in the tourist industry was quite widespread. The most prominent example of government's role in tourism was its ownership of the British West Indian Airways (BWIA). BWIA, the oldest airline in the Caribbean, not only served Trinidad and Tobago but also was a principal carrier for other Eastern Caribbean islands. Despite its important role in the country's tourist industry, BWIA and the government's Tourist Board pursued only limited promotional activities overseas, especially in Western Europe; this was perceived to have hindered the performance of the sector. The government also owned or had an equity share in many of the islands' hotels. Since 1960 the government's Trinidad and Tobago Hotel and Catering School has trained workers for the tourist industry. In addition, the government operated the Hotel Management Company, offering various inn services to smaller lodging operations on a contract basis.

Transportation, Communications, and Electricity

As a result of Trinidad and Tobago's rapid economic growth, the islands' physical infrastructure generally lagged behind other sectors of the economy, causing various bottlenecks or failures in the country's transportation, communications, and electrical systems. For example, Trinidad and Tobago's road system tended to be concentrated along the industrial ports of Trinidad's west coast. The country's road system was constrained by three corridors of mountains (see Geography, this ch.). Most major roads in Trinidad were north-south. In the late 1980s, only two large east-west roads were in place, making travel through the center of the country more difficult. On Tobago, one major loop road existed from Scarborough to Roxborough to Plymouth, with one major offshoot to the Crown Point Airport on the southwestern tip of the island. The two islands contained more than 8,000 kilometers of roads, of which roughly half were paved with locally produced asphalt. Approximately 4,000 kilometers of roads were not paved, of which three-quarters were of unimproved earth and one-quarter of improved earth. Poor road conditions in the country, especially during the rainy season, contributed to the islands' high accident rate. In the late 1970s and early 1980s, the country averaged over 5,000 accidents annually, and 1984 marked the first time in more than 10 years that the rate had dropped. Similarly, narrow, winding streets and the extremely high number of automobiles made Port-of-Spain infamous for its traffic jams.

Unlike most developing countries where public transportation systems dominate, the private automobile was the most typical means of transportation in Trinidad and Tobago. There were some 180,000 registered automobiles on the islands in the late 1980s, and some 8,000 new automobiles were being sold annually. It was estimated that Trinidad and Tobago possessed one of the highest numbers of automobiles per capita in the Western Hemisphere, a result of the local assembly of over 15,000 automobiles annually, destined for the domestic market. In addition, cheap, subsidized gasoline made motoring relatively inexpensive for many Trinidadians. As noted, however, the country's infrastructure did not expand as fast as automobile sales, and inadequate parking facilities, poor road conditions, and old narrow bridges all contributed to general congestion and the high accident rate. There was a public bus service operated by the Public Transport Service Corporation, but mass transportation services were generally deficient. Nevertheless, bus services were expanding rapidly in the 1980s, and the number of passengers doubled in the first half of the decade. Route taxis or minibuses, visible throughout the Caribbean, were generally available. Since 1968 there has been no major railroad, but a small loop of railroad operated for agricultural purposes in San Fernando.

An essential part of the economy's oil- and gas-based development strategy was the transportation of those resources via pipelines. In the mid-1980s, Trinidad possessed over 1,000 kilometers of pipeline for crude oil and 19 kilometers of pipeline for refined petroleum products. There also existed more than 900 kilometers of gas pipelines, construction of which occurred in conjunction with the development of gas-based petrochemicals at the Point Lisas complex.

In the late 1980s, Trinidad and Tobago had a total of six airfields, five of which were usable and three of which had permanent surfaced runways. Piarco International Airport's 3,600-meter runway could accommodate the largest of commercial aircraft in the 1980s and was a busy airport because of the great number of North American and South American flights that connected via the airport. A new passenger terminal and a 2,700-meter runway were being built in the late 1980s at Crown Point Airport in an

217

effort to upgrade that airport to international status. Trinidad and Tobago in the late 1980s maintained some fourteen major transportation aircraft. Several major West European, North American, and South American airlines operated regular flights to Trinidad, and many other carriers transited the island. Tobago was expected to be the site of more regular routes as the island's airport gained international status. Caricargo, a joint venture between the governments of Trinidad and Tobago and Barbados, offered air freight services from Piarco International Airport.

There were seven major ports on Trinidad and one on Tobago. The central shipping location for the nation was Port-of-Spain. Port-of-Spain's modern facilities included advanced handling equipment, extensive warehousing, ancillary sheds, refrigeration areas, bunkering, and freshwater facilities. The port contained only eight berths in the late 1980s, however, and congestion was common because of the high number of ships bunkering in Port-of-Spain en route to North America or South America. Port development was an ongoing activity. Other major ports were specific-use facilities and included Point Lisas, Pointe-à-Pierre, Chaguaramas, Point Fortin, Brighton, Tembladora, and Scarborough. Point Lisas specialized in fertilizers, chemicals, petrochemicals, and sugar. Pointe-à-Pierre and Chaguaramas were ports of entry, and the latter also served as a timber and bauxite transshipment site. Point Fortin handled primarily oceangoing oil tankers, Brighton served the asphalt industry, and Tembladora was a privately owned port used as a transshipment point for Guyanese and Surinamese bauxite. Numerous shipping companies made port calls to the country, and Trinidad and Tobago was a member of the regional West Indies Shipping Corporation (WISCO—see Appendix C).

Trinidad and Tobago contained a rather sophisticated communications system. In the late 1980s, the 2 islands had 90,000 installed telephones, or about 7 phones per 100 people, a ratio higher than Jamaica's but much lower than the rate in the Bahamas or Barbados. Domestic telephone services were operated by the state-owned Telephone Company of Trinidad and Tobago. Periodic breaks in local telephone service were not uncommon. Trinidad and Tobago External Telecommunications Company (Textel), a joint venture between the government and the British firm Cable and Wireless, provided excellent international service, including direct dialing via tropospheric links and an Atlantic Ocean satellite station. Telegram and telex services were also offered through Textel.

The country's mass media included one television station servicing five channels, two major radio stations operating four channels, and numerous daily newspapers and weeklies. The government-run Trinidad and Tobago Television Company offered over seventy hours of weekly viewing, including many locally produced programs. Television was popular, and television sets were common, numbering over 300,000 in the late 1980s. The government's National Broadcasting Service was the most important station, operating on both 610 AM and 100 FM and reaching an estimated 650,000 listeners. Other major stations included Radio Trinidad, operated by a subsidiary of the British firm Rediffusion, and Radio 95 FM, both of which were broadcast over parts of the Windward Islands and Leeward Islands as well. Two smaller radio stations also broadcast. There were an estimated 350,000 radios in Trinidad and Tobago in the late 1980s.

The country's high literacy rate allowed the printed media to hold an important role in the dissemination of information. Trinidad and Tobago had the highest per capita consumption of newsprint in the Caribbean. The country's 4 major newspapers enjoyed a daily circulation of 240,000. The *Trinidad Guardian* and the *Trinidad and Tobago Express* were responsible for two-thirds of that total. Established in 1917, the *Trinidad Guardian* was the oldest newspaper on the two islands and played an influential role throughout the twentieth century. Although officially independent, the newspaper was often branded as pro-colonial, ''white,'' and status quo during the ascendancy of Eric Williams and the independence movement. The *Trinidad and Tobago Express,* established in 1967, came to usurp some of the readership of the *Trinidad Guardian;* in the late 1980s, each paper enjoyed a circulation of 80,000. The country's 2 afternoon newspapers were the *Evening News* and the *Sun,* each with a circulation of 40,000; they were owned by the *Trinidad Guardian* and the *Trinidad and Tobago Express,* respectively. Several weekly newspapers, such as the *Bomb,* circulated as well.

Trinidad and Tobago surpassed Britain in per capita consumption of total energy, and in 1985 its per capita installed capacity and consumption of electricity was the highest in Latin America and the Caribbean. As of 1986, installed capacity stood at 1.17 million kilowatts; 2.72 billion kilowatts were produced in that same year, or 2,260 kilowatts per capita. Virtually all electricity was powered via three stations on Trinidad. Over 70 percent of electricity was provided by natural gas turbines, and the remainder was powered by steam. Trinidad and Tobago was one of only three countries in the Western Hemisphere with no hydroelectricity or hydroelectric potential. The electric system was interconnected through power stations between Port-of-Spain and Penal by one 132-kilovolt and three 66-kilovolt transmission lines, as well as through a small central substation. A standby diesel plant was located on Tobago. Tobago was linked electrically to Trinidad by two forty-one-kilometer submarine cables of thirty-three kilowatts. In 1977 the system was expanded by the installation of an eighty-eight-megawatt power plant at the Point Lisas industrial park.

Access to electricity was very good and was estimated to be over 90 percent. Electricity was produced and distributed primarily by the government's Trinidad and Tobago Electricity Commission (T&TEC). The T&TEC operated at a financial loss because of the high operating expenses that resulted from the country's excess installed capacity. For example, in 1985 the country utilized only 42 percent of its installed capacity. Private companies produced less than 5 percent of total electricity generated in the 1980s. According to government data, industry consumed nearly one-half of all electricity, followed by home use with nearly 30 percent, commercial use with 10 percent, and the balance for street lighting and other purposes.

Agriculture

Agricultural output in Trinidad and Tobago during the 1970s and 1980s was inversely related to the performance of the oil sector: depressed during the oil boom, stimulated during oil's decline. Increasing wage costs, shortages of labor, and oil wealth all directly affected agricultural output. The trend was most pronounced in the 1970s, when the sharp increase in the price of oil exports discouraged traditional agricultural exports and encouraged the importation of food crops previously produced locally. As the oil industry's boom attracted more Trinidadians to urban areas, the rural labor force declined nearly 50 percent, representing only 10 percent of the total work force by 1980. Meanwhile, agriculture's share of GDP dropped from slightly over 6 percent in 1970 to just above 2 percent in 1980. Sugar, the most important crop, typified the decline, as its output fell nearly 50 percent during the 1970s. Other major export crops also suffered drastic declines from 1970 to 1980, including cacao (61 percent), coffee (15 percent), citrus fruit (75 percent), and copra (56 percent). Although agriculture rebounded in the mid- to late 1980s, it was far from approaching its status prior to the oil boom. Output in 1985 stood at about US$365 million, or 3 percent of GDP, well below the 1970s level in constant dollars. Nonetheless, the agricultural sector in the 1980s did experience the fastest growth among all sectors in the recessed economy. Growth in agricultural output in the 1980s was led by the strong performance of domestic agriculture, especially small-scale family gardening.

Land Tenure and Use

Trinidad and Tobago's total land area covers 513,000 hectares, of which less than one-third was arable. Approximately 11,000 hectares, or only 2 percent of total area, were devoted to pasture, the lowest percentage in Latin America or the Caribbean. By contrast, approximately 45 percent of total land was forest or woodland, making timber abundant. Although Trinidad's three corridors of mountains place the greatest restriction on agricultural activity, the plains between the ranges were generally fertile. Only about 13 percent of the arable land was irrigated, but there were numerous streams and small rivers. Flooding was common during the rainy season.

According to the most recent agricultural census from the early 1970s, there were over 35,000 farms on Trinidad and Tobago, occupying nearly 130,000 hectares. The average farm had 6 hectares, but the 40 largest farms were extremely large, all over 400 hectares. Landholdings were usually of two kinds. Small farms were numerous, used traditional methods, and produced mostly food crops for the domestic market. Larger farms were generally more capital and input intensive and produced cash crops for export. Land distribution on the islands was not believed to be as skewed as in other Commonwealth Caribbean islands; in 1987 current data were unavailable, however. The relative abundance of land and the large availability of state lands did not make land reform or landownership a prominent issue. In fact, the opposite was true; Trinidad and Tobago had difficulty retaining citizens in rural areas to work the land.

Agricultural inputs such as machinery, fertilizers, and technical assistance were generally available but were mostly utilized for export crops. Although agriculture was increasingly mechanized, it was still relatively labor intensive. According to the United Nations (UN) Food and Agriculture Organization, Trinidad and Tobago had only 2,500 tractors in use in 1983, or only 8 tractors per 1,000 hectares. This made Trinidad and Tobago less machinery intensive than Jamaica. In spite of being one of the leading producers and exporters of fertilizers in the world, Trinidad and Tobago's fertilizer use in the 1980s was still below 1970 levels. In 1983 approximately forty-nine kilograms per hectare of fertilizer were used compared with sixty-five kilograms in 1970 and forty-five kilograms in 1975. Although the Ministry of Agriculture, Lands, and Food Production provided some technical assistance in the rehabilitation of various aging and diseased tree crops, these programs were generally unsuccessful, and yields continued to decline. In 1982 a successful citrus rehabilitation program was

introduced, however, which helped expand citrus output in the mid-
to late 1980s.

Government agricultural policies did not focus on technical assistance per se but instead utilized pricing policies, such as subsidies, price controls, and guaranteed earnings for agriculture
producers. Subsidies, the most rapidly expanding portion of government expenditure in the 1970s, were directed almost entirely at
agriculture, especially sugar and livestock. Because of the small
number of producers, however, price controls were also introduced
to keep prices at fair levels and to help subsidize poorer consumers.
As a result of the dwindling production of export crops, the government also instituted guaranteed prices for agricultural output that
could be sold to the government via the Central Marketing Agency.
Agricultural research took place at the regional Caribbean Agricultural Research and Development Institute. Although credit for
farmers was available from numerous sources, the most influential lender was the government's ADB.

Crops

Sugar continued to be the most important cash crop despite the
overwhelming structural problems that the sugar industry faced.
As late as the 1880s, there existed over 300 independent sugar plantations on Trinidad; a century later, however, the industry was
completely dominated by one state-run firm, Caroni Sugar Company. The government bought a 51-percent share of Caroni from
the near monopoly of Tate and Lyle in 1971; within five years,
the enterprise was fully government owned. By the mid-1980s,
Caroni merged with the government's joint-venture Orange Grove,
making Caroni almost a complete monopoly.

Although the sugar industry hit a forty-five-year low in 1984,
output did recover somewhat in the late 1980s. Nonetheless, the
industry continued to face several major obstacles to long-run success. As the standard of living for Trinidadians increased in the
1970s, real wages of sugar workers rose faster than output, causing productivity to decline. Falling yields per hectare in the cane
fields also exacerbated dwindling productivity. Additional problems
included seasonal labor shortages, factory equipment problems, and
numerous unplanned cane fires. In spite of government efforts to
revive the industry, production costs of Trinidadian sugar in the
1980s were estimated to be three times greater than market prices
and well above the EEC's price offered through preferential agreements. Inefficiencies and low world sugar prices caused a large
annual drain on government finances that paid for the shortfall.
The option of reducing or eliminating sugar production was a very

difficult one because of its long history on the islands and its role as a major source of employment for a country with chronically high unemployment rates.

In the 1980s, sugarcane continued to occupy under a third of land in use (fewer than 20,000 hectares). The sugar subsector employed approximately 20,000 workers, or slightly less than half of all the agricultural labor force. Most cane was grown on the central plains, primarily by East Indians. In 1985 about 65 percent of all sugar was harvested on large estates; the number of small farmers was declining because fewer young people were entering the cane fields. The sugar harvest in 1984, one of the worst ever, yielded 70,000 tons, or only about one-third of the harvest of 1970. Sugar production rose to over 80,000 tons in 1985, and in the late 1980s the government was aiming for 100,000-ton sugar harvests. Nonetheless, major increases beyond the 100,000-ton mark were unlikely without even larger government losses. Eighty percent of the country's sugar was exported in 1985 compared with 60 percent five years earlier. Beginning in 1984, the government also began a program to process imported raw sugar.

Reduced market access to its major preferential export markets, Britain and the United States, was another major problem facing the sugar industry in the 1980s. Trinidad and Tobago's sugar quota with the EEC was reduced at the 1985 Lomé Convention (see Glossary) from 69,000 tons to 47,300 tons as a result of its inability to fill the previous quota. As production rebounded after mid-decade, however, Trinidad and Tobago was allocated a portion of the quota commitments of some African countries to export to the EEC. Trinidad and Tobago gained even less access to the United States market because of cutbacks in the United States International Sugar Agreement (ISA). Trinidad and Tobago's ISA quota dropped to only 6,504 tons by 1987, a 60-percent reduction from 1984. This reduction was expected to cause the loss of millions of dollars to the sugar industry in Trinidad and Tobago. Because of these unfavorable market conditions, Caroni was diversifying away from sugar in the late 1980s into rice production and livestock.

Cocoa, derived from the cacao plant, was the other major crop in Trinidad and Tobago. From the late 1880s until the 1930s, cocoa was the most important crop on both islands, and in the late 1980s it remained the leading crop on Tobago. In fact, Trinidad and Tobago was once the second leading producer of cocoa in the world. Brought by the Spanish in the 1700s, cocoa still occupied more agricultural land than sugar in the 1980s, although it was frequently cultivated with bananas and coffee. Over half the cacao farms were small, but large estates accounted for over 80 percent of output. Trinidad and Tobago's cocoa crop was ravaged for decades by successive diseases. The government formulated numerous rehabilitation schemes for the industry, the most recent one in 1980, but they were generally unable to meet their goals, and production continued to fall. The 1980 program was no exception, as production declined beginning in 1982. For example, in 1985 cocoa output was 1.3 million kilograms, or under 50 percent of the 1981 output. Falling yields were another major problem the industry faced as average yields declined from 275 kilograms per hectare in the 1930s to under 100 kilograms per hectare in the 1980s. Virtually all cocoa was exported. The Cocoa and Coffee Industry Board, a central regulatory agency, handled all export functions. Despite the state of depressed international cocoa prices in the 1980s, Trinidad and Tobago continued to receive premium prices for its high-quality cocoa.

The other major export crops were all tree crops: coffee, citrus fruits, and coconuts. Coffee production expanded after 1930 in response to the decline in cocoa output. Production of Trinidad and Tobago's major variety, robusta, however, declined by more than 50 percent from the late 1960s to the mid-1980s. Exports also dropped sharply, demonstrating the lack of success of a 1970–71 rehabilitation plan undertaken by the government. Output was so low in 1984 that no coffee was exported. Nevertheless, coffee production did rebound strongly in 1985, reaching 2.1 million kilograms, 35 percent of which was exported. The expansion of citrus crops, especially oranges, grapefruits, and limes, also coincided with the decline of cocoa in the 1930s. Output of citrus products peaked in the mid-1950s and later decreased drastically to a low of 4.7 million kilograms in 1982, or about 20 times below peak output. During the early 1980s, citrus exports fell to an insignificant 2 percent of total production. A rehabilitation program was successfully introduced in 1982 that greatly expanded production in the mid-1980s to over 6 million kilograms. Although the citrus industry was affected by viruses, old trees, and high wages, new plantings, renewed supplies of labor, and favorable weather in the late 1980s all spurred renewed growth in citrus crops.

Coconut, and its main derivative, copra, was another major export crop and was the second most important crop in Tobago. Like other export crops, output of coconuts declined in the 1970s, making the island no longer self-sufficient in oils. All coconuts went to the local processing industry for soaps and oils. Copra output in 1985 exceeded 4,000 tons.

The fastest growing subsector in agriculture in the 1980s was domestic agriculture, consisting mainly of vegetables, rice, tubers, and livestock. The revival of domestic agriculture was the consequence of falling oil prices, balance of payments constraints, the return of labor to the land, and growing experimentation with larger scale farming for domestic agriculture. In the late 1980s, Trinidad and Tobago was approaching self-sufficiency in green vegetables, which were typically grown on small garden plots. Rice, a staple food, was an expanding domestic crop but was still imported in large quantities. Such vegetables as yams, sweet potatoes, dasheens, and eddoes (a tuber) were also produced, mostly for direct consumption, and were also expected to increase as long as the oil sector was recessed.

Livestock, Fishing, and Forestry

Livestock activity was not as developed as other areas of agriculture. Although livestock was targeted for generous subsidies and government programs, only the poultry and pork industries were very developed. The country's beef and dairy industries in particular were lacking. Pork was consumed in large quantities, and except for a few specialty items such as ham and bacon, the country was self-sufficient in pork. Beef production was very low; less than one-third of the estimated 30,000 head of cattle were dedicated to beef production. Most beef was imported from New Zealand and Australia. Water buffalo were also present, however, generally tended by rural East Indians. In the late 1980s, farmers were experimenting with a cattle-buffalo hybrid appropriately called a "buffalypso." Dairy production was inadequate, and the islands were about 90-percent dependent on imported milk, handled almost exclusively by Trinidad Food Products, a subsidiary of Nestlé. In fact, Trinidad and Tobago had the smallest percentage of its farmland used as pastures in all of Latin America and the Caribbean.

The fishing potential of Trinidad and Tobago continued to be underutilized in the 1980s despite numerous generous government subsidies instituted to promote the industry. Fish was an important part of the national diet, especially among Tobagonians. Catches of fish, including kingfish, grouper, redfish, snapper, shrimp, and tuna, totaled about 3 million kilograms per year in the first half of the 1980s. There were over sixty fishing beaches on Trinidad and Tobago, but only a few had adequate facilities to exploit the coast's potential. Most deep-sea trawling activity occurred in the Gulf of Paria, which continued to spark territorial water disputes with Venezuela. Although an important mutual fishing agreement was signed between Venezuela and Trinidad and

Fishermen at work on a beach in Tobago
Courtesy Cortez Austin, Jr.

227

Tobago in 1985, there remained signs that disagreements persisted (see Foreign Relations, this ch.). Although inland fisheries were expanding rapidly in the 1980s, they were still only small in scale and were a government-run activity. Despite strong institutional support for the industry in general, such as from the National Fisheries Company, the Fisheries Development Fund, and the Caribbean Fisheries Training Institute, inefficient methods still prevailed, preventing fishermen from meeting local demand.

The forestry industry was small considering that about 45 percent of the islands were forested. There existed sixty-two small sawmills that fed the local furniture industry and a match factory. Wood was also used for firewood and charcoal, and many exotic woods were exported in small quantities. Production in the 1980s exceeded 5 million board meters annually. Large tracts of forestland were owned by the government and have been held as preserves since the 1700s. Because Trinidad and Tobago was geologically tied to South America, there existed a rich variety of woods, sixty species of which were commercially lumbered. Nonetheless, the islands were not self-sufficient in wood products and relied on imports to meet local demand. Some reforestation programs were implemented in the 1980s to prevent creeping erosion.

External Sector

External Trade

Trinidad and Tobago was very dependent on trade; export revenues from oil represented the major source of dynamism in the economy. More than any other factor, fluctuations in the world price of oil determined the country's annual trade performance during the 1970s and 1980s. The quadrupling of oil prices in 1973 provided Trinidad and Tobago with extremely favorable terms of trade; this pattern was reversed in 1982, when oil prices declined. Export prices also affected the country's productive base, as increased oil revenues encouraged the greater importation of goods and services that were previously produced locally, especially in agriculture. Between 1960 and 1980, Trinidad and Tobago's food import bill at current prices increased ninefold. Unlike other Commonwealth Caribbean countries, Trinidad and Tobago frequently attained annual trade surpluses because of its oil resources, a position that was also achieved when oil prices were depressed, as was the case in 1984 and 1985. In 1982 and 1983, however, unprecedented trade deficits were recorded.

Total imports in 1985 were valued at US$1.4 billion, well below the peak import level of US$2.4 billion in 1982. Imports were reduced in the mid-1980s through revised exchange controls that sought to stabilize the country's balance of payments, a goal that was generally achieved through large reductions in consumption items. In 1985 machinery and transport equipment comprised 30 percent of imports, followed by food at 20 percent, manufactured goods at 20 percent, chemicals at 10 percent, and the balance in various other categories. The country's level of food imports was high even for a Caribbean country. The absence of oil as a major import category further differentiated Trinidad and Tobago from its Caribbean neighbors. The structure of imports changed drastically in 1983, when the processing of imported crude oil was discontinued, which had accounted for as much as 30 percent of total imports. In 1985 the United States provided 39 percent of the country's imports, trailed by Britain (10 percent), Japan (10 percent), Canada (8 percent), Caricom (6 percent), and other West European and Latin American and Caribbean countries. Major changes in the origin of the country's imports also resulted from the termination of the oil-processing program. In 1981 about 26 percent of all imports had come from Saudi Arabia; after the discontinuation of the program, the Saudi share of total imports dropped to 0.1 percent. These events in turn directly affected the share of total imports from the United States, which increased from 26 to 42 percent over the same time period.

In the 1980s, Trinidad and Tobago sought to stabilize its balance of payments by reducing the flood of imports that had become customary during the previous decade. Unable to sustain that level of imports after 1982, the Chambers government introduced a new system of import licensing and a two-tier exchange rate that hindered the flow of Caricom goods. Jamaica was most affected by these maneuvers. In an effort to improve bilateral trade relations, the two governments signed the Port-of-Spain Accord in 1985. Trade did improve somewhat as a result and was expected to expand further with the unification of the two-tier exchange system in 1987. Nevertheless, in the late 1980s imports continued to be restrained by a restrictive import quota system—dubbed the "negative list"—that completely protected hundreds of locally manufactured goods.

Exports totaled US$2.1 billion in 1985, or about 20 percent below the country's peak export performance of 1981. A marginal increase in exports and a significant reduction in imports produced a trade surplus in 1985 of US$750 million. Petroleum products continued to dominate export revenues, accounting for 79 percent of exports in 1985. Other major export categories included chemicals (13 percent), machinery (3 percent), and manufacturing (2 percent). The price of oil was the most important determinant of the structure of Trinidad and Tobago's exports. As the price of oil declined in the 1980s, so did oil's share of exports. Oil fell from 93 percent of exports in 1980, to 83 percent in 1983, and to 79 percent by mid-decade. The other major change in the structure of exports in the 1980s was the increased share for chemicals. As the new petrochemical plants opened in the early 1980s, chemicals rose from 3 percent of total exports in 1980 to 13 percent by 1985. The overwhelming share (63 percent in 1985) of the country's exports went to the United States market. Exports were also shipped to the EEC (13 percent), Caricom (11 percent), and various other countries, particularly developing countries. Inside Caricom, most exports went to Guyana, Barbados, and Jamaica.

Trinidad and Tobago benefited from wide access to foreign markets, often under numerous preferential agreements. As a former British colony, it enjoyed special access to Britain's markets through the Commonwealth of Nations (see Appendix B) and access to the EEC under the provisions of the Lomé Convention. Exports to the United States entered under three preferential programs: the Generalized System of Preferences, the Caribbean Basin Initiative (CBI—see Appendix D), and the 807 program (see Glossary), which was named after its corresponding Tariff Schedules of the United States number. Nonetheless, Trinidad and Tobago benefited little from the CBI's trade provisions. Despite providing 18 percent of the region's exports, the nation contributed only 3 percent of CBI exports and less than 1 percent of 807 program exports. Trinidad and Tobago gained preferential access to Canada's market through Caribcan, a 1986 Canadian trade initiative similar in scope to the CBI. Although total trade within Caricom was in decline in the 1980s as a result of the international recession, Trinidad and Tobago continued to enjoy a trade surplus with the region.

The drive for increased exports was bolstered in 1984 by the creation of the Export Development Fund, which was designed to improve marketing and finance for local exporters and to diversify into light manufacturing and nontraditional items destined for hard currency markets. Export competitiveness was also expected to increase as a result of the devaluation of the Trinidad and Tobago dollar in December 1985.

Balance of Payments and Debt

Unlike other Caribbean countries, Trinidad and Tobago's balance of payments was generally favorable because of its strong, oil-based export performance and its ability to attract foreign investment in the oil and petrochemical subsectors. Prior to the oil boom, net international reserves were generally adequate to avoid large external loans, although current account surpluses were rare.

When energy prices soared in the 1970s, international reserves did the same, climbing from US$34 million in 1973 to US$3.3 billion by 1981. Reserves fell, however, during the 1980s to under US$500 million by mid-decade. The position of reserves was expected to worsen further as a result of the currency devaluation of December 1985 and continued current account deficits. In 1985 the overall balance of payments was in a deficit position of approximately US$300 million and was financed primarily by the country's international reserves. Although the deep recession of the early 1980s depleted most of the country's oil windfalls of the previous decade, it appeared that those accumulated reserves were sufficient for Trinidad and Tobago to avoid the debt crisis confronting most of the Western Hemisphere.

The nation's current account expanded rapidly in the 1970s, moving from a deficit of US$25 million in 1973 to a surplus of US$282 million a year later. Large surpluses on the current account were registered until 1982, when a deficit once again appeared and remained into the late 1980s. Surpluses on the current account averaged 18 percent of GDP during the 1974–79 period and allowed for the liberal importation of goods and services. These surpluses also augmented international reserves, which covered more than twenty months of imports by the early 1980s. The downturn in oil prices in 1982 reversed this trend and generated an unprecedented current account deficit of US$969 million in 1983. These deficits were increasingly reduced later in the decade, making the current account deficit only US$205 million by 1985. The reduction in the account's deficit was achieved primarily through a sharp decrease in imports, thus substantially improving the merchandise trade portion of the current account. Nonetheless, the account remained in a deficit position because of large deficits in the service account, especially in terms of foreign travel, the repatriation of profits, and interest payments. The deficit on the service portion of the current account reached an unprecedented level of US$732 million in 1984. Since 1981, receipts from the country's tourism industry were less than the expenses of the foreign travel of Trinidadians, thus weakening the service portion of the current account. More stringent foreign exchange controls in regard to foreign travel by Trinidadians were instituted in the mid-1980s to restrict that drain.

Net movements on the country's capital account were almost always positive, allowing for some shortfalls in the current account. Surpluses on the capital account peaked in 1982, largely as a result of greater direct foreign investment associated with the ambitious industrial projects of the late 1970s and early 1980s. As the economy contracted in the mid-1980s, direct foreign investment declined; by 1985 a debit for investment arose, indicating a net disinvestment in that year. External borrowing was not a major factor on the capital account until the mid- to late 1980s, when more lending was sought to help stabilize the country's balance of payments.

Trinidad and Tobago's debt was significant but manageable in the late 1980s. In 1985 the country's total external debt reached US$1.2 billion. Seventy-eight percent of the county's debt was with private commercial banks, followed by a 19-percent bilateral debt share. Only 3 percent of the country's debt was with multilateral lending agencies such as the IMF, the World Bank (see Glossary), and the Inter-American Development Bank (IDB). During the 1970s and 1980s, Trinidad and Tobago was not involved in any major transactions with the IMF, a rarity among developing countries in the Americas. Nearly 90 percent of the country's debt was classified as long term, with only US$149 million of outstanding short-term debt registered in 1985. As of 1987, Trinidad and Tobago had never rescheduled its external debt. In 1985 principal payments were slightly over US$100 million, and interest payments were US$80 million. As a percentage of GDP, the nation's total debt reached an all-time high in 1985 of approximately 17 percent. Debt servicing payments as a percentage of exports reached more than 15 percent by 1985. Both percentages were well below the respective Latin American and Caribbean averages of 44 and 26 percent. Nonetheless, Trinidad and Tobago's excellent credit rating, industrial base, international reserve position, and oil resources gave it considerable advantages in debt servicing compared with other developing countries.

Foreign Assistance

As an upper-middle-income country, Trinidad and Tobago received only minimal foreign assistance from bilateral and multilateral agencies and obtained most of its external funds from commercial banks. The country received only small amounts of bilateral aid from the United States via regional economic assistance programs. Likewise, its high income precluded it from receiving funds from the World Bank's "soft loan" window, the International Development Association. In fact, no major multilateral institution undertook a major, sustained, mission to Trinidad and Tobago during the 1970s or the first half of the 1980s. As a consequence of Trinidad and Tobago's growing financial difficulties in the late 1980s, however, some multilateral agencies were considering funding for the nation.

Older and newer housing areas, Port-of-Spain
Courtesy Inter-American Development Bank

233

The country actually became an important donor nation during the energy crisis of the 1970s, when other Caribbean countries experienced difficult adjustments in their balance of payments. In 1987 Caricom nations, primarily Jamaica and Guyana, still owed Trinidad and Tobago in excess of US$200 million from earlier lending. Beyond direct, concessional loans to other Caribbean nations, Trinidad and Tobago also played an important role in providing cheap oil sales, generous contributions to Caricom institutions, and a boost to regional trade in the 1970s because of its rising import demand.

Government and Politics

The Governmental System

Trinidad and Tobago in the late 1980s was a bicameral parliamentary democracy based on the Westminster model. The Constitution, which took effect at the time of independence in 1962, was revised in 1976 to provide for an elected president to serve as head of state and commander in chief, a function filled earlier by a governor general appointed by the British monarch. Under the Constitution, Trinidad and Tobago remains a member of the Commonwealth of Nations.

Since independence, Parliament has been the major ruling body in Trinidad and Tobago. The Constitution provides for a bicameral legislature consisting of a Senate and a House of Representatives. The executive consists of the president and the cabinet, headed by the prime minister. The president is elected by the Senate and House of Representatives to serve a five-year term as head of state and commander in chief of the armed forces. He also has the authority to grant pardons under constitutional provisions. The president must be a citizen of Trinidad and Tobago, at least thirty-five years old, and a resident of the country for the preceding ten years. In case of incapacity, the president is succeeded by the president of the Senate, and then by the speaker of the House of Representatives.

The leader of the majority party or majority coalition in the House of Representatives is named prime minister. The prime minister is by far the most powerful figure in the government and is responsible for running the government. The prime minister chooses cabinet ministers from Parliament, who are then appointed by the president, and he can change ministers and ministries at will.

Bills may be introduced in either house, with the exception of money bills, which must be introduced in the House of Representatives. Bills passed by the House of Representatives and the Senate, and signed by the president, become law. The president must call Parliament into session at least once a year and may dissolve Parliament at any time. No Parliament may sit for more than five years; in case of a vote of no confidence, Parliament must be dissolved in seven days. After dissolution, a general election of the House of Representatives must be held within three months. Elections are by secret ballot, and citizens over the age of eighteen are eligible to vote. From independence through 1986, Parliament was never dissolved in less than four years, nor had there been a vote of no confidence.

The Senate is an unelected body; all thirty-one members are appointed by the president. Sixteen senators are appointed after consultation with the prime minister, six on the advice of the leader of the opposition, and nine from among outstanding leaders who must be citizens of Trinidad and Tobago and at least twenty-five years old. A Senate quorum is ten, and all senators are required to leave office upon dissolution of Parliament.

The House of Representatives consists of thirty-six members and has a quorum of twelve. Its number equals the constituencies in the nation, plus the speaker of the House, if the speaker is not already a member of the House. Two of the thirty-six constituencies must be in Tobago. Representatives must be citizens over the age of eighteen who have been residents of Trinidad and Tobago for at least two years. As is the case with senators, representatives must vacate their seats upon dissolution of Parliament. Members of Parliament are protected from prosecution for ''words spoken in Parliament.''

The Constitution provides for an ombudsman to be appointed by the president after consultation with the prime minister and the leader of the opposition. The ombudsman serves for a five-year term and may be reappointed. He investigates government acts that do not come under the jurisdiction of the courts, after a complaint of injustice has been filed.

In the late 1980s, government continued to be the largest employer. Although government employment traditionally has been considered a privilege, that perception has changed somewhat as salaries in the public sector have failed to keep up with those in the private sector. Since political administrators are expected to be in positions to influence policy, the Constitution authorizes independent public service commissions that are empowered to appoint, promote, transfer, and discipline personnel in the public career. These commissions are intended to protect career officers from political pressure. The public service commissions oversee the appointment of permanent secretaries, as well as judicial, teaching, and police service personnel. A public service commission review board was established in 1966 to receive appeals on disciplinary action taken by the public service commissions.

Public service workers have been categorized as administrative, professional, executive, technical, clerical, and manual. Each division has required an appropriate university, professional, or technical degree or general certificate of education (similar to a high school certificate), although personnel could also be hired in a temporary capacity pending completion of the required degree. The hiring process has included entry exams and an interview process. Although public servants have been allowed to join political parties, they have been barred from appearing on a political platform or campaigning openly for candidates.

The legal and judicial system is based on English common law and practice, and its powers derive from the Constitution. The Supreme Court consists of the High Court of Justice and the Court of Appeal. Other courts include courts of summary jurisdiction and petty civil courts. According to the Constitution, the High Court of Justice consists of the chief justice, who serves ex officio, and a prescribed number of other judges. The judges have equal power, authority, and jurisdiction. There is vested in the High Court the same original jurisdiction as is vested in, or exercised by, the High Court of Justice in Britain under the provisions of the Supreme Court of Judicature (Consolidation Act of 1925 [U.K.]).

The Court of Appeal consists of the chief justice, who serves as president, and a prescribed number of justices of appeal. The Court of Appeal is a superior court of record and, unless specified by Parliament, has all the powers of such a court. The Constitution provides that appeals from the Court of Appeal may be made to the Judicial Committee of the Privy Council in London under certain circumstances. In 1987 Prime Minister Robinson proposed replacing the Privy Council in London with a Caribbean Court of Appeal. This idea was discussed at the 1987 Caricom summit and endorsed by a number of other Caribbean politicians and jurists and by the British, whose taxpayers support all the costs for the London Privy Council; as of late 1987, however, no action had been taken.

The chief justice is appointed by the president, after consultation with the prime minister and the leader of the opposition. The other judges of the Supreme Court are also appointed by the president, acting on the advice of the Judicial and Legal Service Commission.

Political Dynamics

Between independence in 1962 and 1986, politics in Trinidad and Tobago was inseparable from the story of Williams and the party he founded, the PNM. Even after his death in 1981, Williams's legacy helped win another five-year term for the PNM. As the first leader in a newly independent country, Williams set many precedents and came to be seen as the father of the country. Williams's legitimacy derived from his education, his charisma, his speaking ability, and his personal identification with the lower class blacks in Trinidad. He also was an astute politician who did not hesitate to be ruthless if maintaining his power and leadership depended on it. As time went on, power within the PNM became increasingly centralized and Williams less tolerant of dissent. In spite of his high-handed way of dealing with PNM members who disagreed with him during his twenty-five years as prime minister, Williams left Trinidad and Tobago with a functioning democratic political system, including a free press and a healthy opposition whose leaders had been trained in PNM ranks. Throughout Williams's tenure as prime minister, there were numerous strikes and labor disputes. Labor leaders formed various coalitions and parties, but none of these was sufficiently powerful to gain control of the government.

Postindependence PNM rule can be divided into four phases: 1962–69, a period of consolidation and economic hardship; 1970–73, a time of economic and political troubles that included the Black Power riots; 1974–81, a period of prosperity and increased government centralization; and 1981–86, the period after Williams's death when George Chambers was prime minister.

On December 15, 1986, the National Alliance for Reconstruction (NAR), under the leadership of A.N.R. Robinson, won the election by a landslide. The NAR captured thirty-three out of the thirty-six House seats, including that of Prime Minister Chambers and his two deputies.

Consolidation and Economic Hardship, 1962–69

At the time of independence, politics in Trinidad and Tobago was conducted by the middle class; both the PNM and the DLP were nationalistic, largely pro-capitalist parties that were controlled by the middle class and supported by the working class. Earlier, more radical labor movements had been defeated or sidelined. Race was an important component of party loyalty, and the dominant PNM drew its support largely from black voters. Blacks controlled most PNM leadership positions; Williams's cabinet in 1961 had only two East Indians—Winston Mahabir, a Christian, and Kamaluddin Mohammed, a Muslim. East Indians generally supported the DLP.

After his election in 1961, Williams reached an understanding with R.N. Capildeo, the Hindu DLP leader, under which the DLP was consulted in some national decisions and DLP members were sent abroad on diplomatic missions. Capildeo was allowed a special leave of absence from Parliament to spend the greater part of the year in London. Although the understanding appeared, on the surface, to be a magnanimous gesture on Williams's part, it was a skillful political move because it left the opposition party without a leader in Trinidad and Tobago. Capildeo's high-handed absentee management alienated many within the DLP, especially blacks. In 1964 many non-East Indians defected from the DLP and founded the Liberal Party of Trinidad, reducing the DLP representation in the House from ten to seven.

Serious problems in the Trinidadian economy between 1962 and 1965 caused by the falling prices of its main exports generated strikes in the sugar and oil industries, and the black-dominated Oilfield Workers Trade Union (OWTU) became increasingly radicalized. The new leader of the OWTU, George Weekes, charged that the PNM had sold out to big business. Despite an increasing sense of dissatisfaction with the PNM, the DLP was unable to capitalize on this opportunity to assume the role of champion of the working class because of intraparty squabbles and black loyalty to the PNM. Instead, the DLP provided crucial support to a PNM bill in March 1965 curbing strikes and lockouts. As the 1966 elections approached, the DLP continued to fragment, whereas the PNM closed ranks and campaigned hard. The PNM won 24 of the 36 seats in the House of Representatives and received 52 percent of the vote. The other 12 seats were won by the DLP with 34 percent of the vote. Several new smaller parties, such as the Liberal Party of Trinidad, failed to win any seats. In response, Capildeo claimed that the election was rigged because of the use of voting machines, and he pledged that the DLP would not contest any elections if voting machines were used. This strategy only succeeded in further reducing DLP influence, because many PNM candidates ran unopposed in the 1968 municipal elections and Capildeo himself was defeated. The PNM was able to increase its seats significantly on a very low turnout, but observers believed that this represented disillusionment rather than endorsement on the part of the voters.

Since there was little political opposition, the PNM was able to concentrate on economic matters. The population was expanding, but the oil industry needed fewer workers because of retrenchment and automation, so unemployment had increased, reaching about 15 to 17 percent by 1967. In response to the many strikes in 1967 and 1968, the government announced a development plan that attempted to increase employment. It also increased its participation in the economy by buying out the British Petroleum Company (see Role of Government, this ch.). Government companies were inefficient, and the PNM did not solve the economic problems but in the process of trying became more rigid and bureaucratic.

Political Unrest and Economic Troubles, 1970–73

Although the PNM dominated the national bureaucracy and the civil service, by 1970 its popularity among the electorate was considerably lower than it had been at the time of independence. Election turnouts were lower, and election procedures increasingly were questioned. The poorest segments of the population, which were also East Indian, were largely left out of the government and the growth process. The PNM became quite centralized as Williams made most decisions by himself. By April 1970, he had not held a press conference in five years and was poorly prepared to respond to the challenge of the Black Power movement that spread across the Caribbean.

The Black Power movement was introduced into Trinidad and Tobago in 1970 by the National Joint Action Committee (NJAC), a party that sought fundamental changes in Trinidadian and Tobagonian society. The NJAC charged that the root cause of the nation's 14-percent general unemployment was white dominance. According to the NJAC, foreign and local white capitalists owned the country and oppressed blacks, defined by the NJAC as Trinidadians and Tobagonians of African and East Indian descent. In fact, a 1970 survey had found that 86 percent of business leaders were white. The NJAC maintained that Williams had white Anglo-Saxon values and decried his leadership. A major political crisis began on February 26, 1970, when the NJAC joined the Students Guild at the UWI in a march of 250 students in Port-of-Spain. The march was organized to protest the trial in Canada of Trinidadian students accused of occupying a computer center there. The government's arrest of nine marchers generated solidarity marches that over the next few months attracted increasing numbers of people and nearly toppled the government. After 20,000 marched in San Juan, the NJAC attempted to gain the support of the East Indians by asking the largely black marchers to cut cane for a day to show solidarity for East Indian sugar workers. East Indian leaders opposed this, and a forty-five-kilometer march from Port-of-Spain to Couva was substituted. Significantly, fewer than 100 of the 5,000 to 10,000 people who took part in that march were East Indians.

Williams tried to defuse the Black Power movement by supporting it and by paying the fines of the Trinidadian students in Canada, but the marches continued and attracted additional supporters, reaching their peak during April 1970. Thirty percent of the population of Tobago took part in solidarity marches on April 4 and 5, and more than 30,000 marched in a funeral procession on April 9 for an NJAC supporter shot by police. After several strikes the following week, the deputy prime minister, A.N.R. Robinson, a Tobagonian who was also minister of external affairs, resigned from the cabinet. In an attempt to preempt a general strike and march on the capital, Williams declared a state of emergency on April 21. Some of the officers and men in the Trinidad and Tobago Defence Force seized control of the barracks at Teteron, however, thus depriving the government of arms; Williams was then forced to make hasty purchases of arms from the United States and Venezuela. Once rearmed, the 2,500-member Defence Force remained loyal to the government and was supported by the citizens. The crisis passed after the trade unions called off several scheduled strikes.

As a consequence of the 1970 uprising, Williams became increasingly disillusioned. His government moved farther to the right, introducing several measures to curtail individual freedom. Although a bill proposing very stringent state control over public meetings and freedom of speech was defeated, several other bills passed regulating public freedom, broadening police search powers, and requiring licenses for firearms. Concern about these measures led to the drafting and adoption of a new constitution in 1976.

There was general discontent with the government by the time of the 1971 elections, but the PNM again benefited from disunity in the opposition camp. An opposition alliance collapsed following the withdrawal of Robinson and his new party, the Action Committee of Democratic Citizens. The opposition's subsequent decision to boycott the election enabled the PNM to capture all thirty-six seats in the House of Representatives.

Despite its electoral victory, Williams's government reached a low point in 1973. The PNM was in power because of a majority boycott rather than a majority election. Strikes were frequent, the government treasury was nearly bankrupt, and there was concern that the government would not be able to pay its employees. Williams became so disillusioned by strikes that at the PNM convention in 1973 he resigned as prime minister and left the convention. Karl Hudson-Phillips was elected to succeed him, overwhelmingly defeating East Indian Kamaluddin Mohammed; Williams returned later in 1973, however, reassumed leadership, and forced Hudson-Phillips to leave the party.

Prosperity and Government Centralization, 1974–81

The Arab oil embargo was a boon to the Williams government. The oil price increases that followed it created a prosperity that made the government of Trinidad and Tobago not only solvent but financially comfortable. Concerns about the PNM were muted because of the healthy economy, and since the opposition did not come forward with a better alternative, voters continued to endorse Williams. As GDP rose, however, various segments of society fought for larger slices of the pie. Strikes, which had been frequent in the lean years of 1972 and 1973, continued. During the spring of 1975, an estimated 45,000 people were involved in strikes.

The 1976 election again illustrated the difficulty of developing a political movement in Trinidad and Tobago that appealed to working-class people of both African and East Indian origin. The black-dominated OWTU joined the East Indian-dominated All Trinidad Sugar Estates and Factory Workers Trade Union (ATSE/FWTU), the Trinidadian Islandwide Cane Farmers' Union, and left-of-center intellectuals to form a new political party, the United Labour Front (ULF). A Trinidadian political scientist has called the ULF "a political banyan tree" that provided shelter for many ideologically incompatible elements involved in the protest movements of the 1960s and 1970s. Envisioning itself as the representative of the working class, the ULF called for land reform, nationalization of multinational firms, and worker participation in management. Nonetheless, the ULF was unable to overcome ethnic suspicions. Working-class blacks feared that East Indians would control any ULF-led government. The ULF was also hurt by the perception that the party was communist. Williams exploited this view, promising to preserve individual landownership and capitalism; as a result, the PNM captured twenty-four of the thirty-six House seats in 1976. The ULF's ten seats came primarily from former DLP seats with constituencies in East Indian working-class areas.

Two remaining House seats, both in Tobago, were captured by the Democratic Action Congress (DAC). The DAC was founded by Robinson, the PNM minister of external affairs who had resigned during the 1970 Black Power riots. A Tobagonian-based party, the DAC promised to lobby for some regional autonomy for Tobago and specifically called for the reinstatement of its legislative body. Once in Parliament, the DAC members proposed the Tobago

House of Assembly Bill, which passed in 1980. This measure gave some self-government to Tobago in the form of a fifteen-member elected House of Assembly, although Port-of-Spain still retained a number of controls. In the first election for Tobago's House of Assembly in 1980, the DAC won two-thirds of the seats.

Subsequent to the 1976 election, Williams continued to gather more power into his own hands, so that even the smallest decisions came to be referred to him. He created the National Advisory Council (NAC), which was a think tank made up entirely of individuals selected by, and responsible to, Williams. The NAC did the planning for the national bureaucracy and also masterminded the increasing government participation in the economy. Because of the oil windfall, per capita income increased and unemployment declined. The state used the additional revenue to increase educational expenditures and to attempt to restructure the economy. State spending increased dramatically as over fifty government-owned companies were created. Subsequently, the Williams administration was accused of corruption; high officials were alleged to have taken bribes in connection with purchases of Lockheed airplanes for the national airline BWIA and Sikorsky helicopters for the Ministry of National Security and in awarding contracts for a racing complex. In the PNM convention of September 1980, Williams attributed the erosion of popular support to the trade unions and to ''enemies within.'' A poll conducted in January and February 1981 indicated widespread suspicion that the PNM cabinet was engaged in a cover-up of corrupt practices. Fifty percent of those polled, including both blacks and East Indians, felt that Williams should resign.

In March 1981, as the nation prepared for as yet unannounced elections, Williams died. Although members of the cabinet knew that Williams had been sick, his death was an unexpected shock to the rest of the nation. Contrary to dire predictions, Williams's death did not cause political disarray in Trinidad. Despite Williams's own disillusionment with his role as leader and his increasing centralization of power, he and the nation's British heritage had forged a firm democratic tradition in Trinidad and Tobago. A few months after his death, democratic elections took place on schedule, reelecting the PNM once again.

The Post-Williams Era, 1981–86

After Williams's death, the PNM appointed Chambers to succeed him as prime minister and as party leader in the 1981 elections. Chambers had entered PNM politics in 1966 and had served the government as head of several ministries in succeeding years.

One of the main factors in Chambers's selection was that, as a black Trinidadian, he was more acceptable as prime minister than two more senior East Indian PNM ministers, Kamaluddin Mohammed and Errol Mahabir, both of whom remained in Chambers's cabinet.

The 1981 election marked the appearance of a new political party, the Organization for National Reconstruction (ONR). The ONR, led by former PNM prime minister Hudson-Phillips, attacked government inefficiency and called for a rollback of "massive state capitalism." The party attempted to appeal to a cross section of voters, including black and East Indian workers as well as all groups in the middle class. In addition, three opposition parties—the ULF, the DAC, and Tapia House (a reformist party of intellectuals and the middle class)—attempted to form an electoral coalition appropriately termed the Alliance. The coalition fragmented over ethnic divisions, however.

Chambers campaigned on the PNM party record, pointing with pride to twenty-five years of accomplishments in education, housing, and culture and to the prosperous economy. Although only 30 percent of the registered voters voted for the PNM, the party once again won, getting over half the vote and taking two seats from the ULF to win a total of twenty-six out of the thirty-six seats in the House of Representatives. The ULF lost ground, receiving only 15 percent of the vote and retaining only eight of its ten seats; the DAC kept its two Tobagonian seats. Because of the winner-take-all rule, neither the ONR nor the Alliance won any seats despite the fact that the ONR received nearly a quarter of the popular vote. Observers attributed the PNM victory in 1981 to healthy economic conditions, poor organization by the opposition, and a fear of unknown and untried parties.

Chambers's five-year rule as prime minister was plagued by economic and political problems (see Role of Government, this ch.). He had ridden in on a wave of prosperity but was defeated five years later by an economic downturn. Oil prices fell in 1982 and 1983, and the oil industry, faced with lower revenues, forced concessions from the OWTU. Oil layoffs increased unemployment, and the 1982 sugar crop was below target level, compounding the problem. The government ran a deficit in 1982 for the first time in many years. During the oil boom, the PNM government had subsidized many consumer items, especially food and transport. Chambers reduced these subsidies, resulting in significant increases in food and transport prices.

Chambers changed many controversial government-to-government arrangements under which Williams had invited foreign governments to engage in development projects using their own companies. The foreign contractors had had frequent cost over-runs and had angered local producers by sometimes refusing to work with local materials and local personnel. Chambers was also faced with the aircraft purchase and racetrack complex corruption scandals involving officials of Williams's government.

Hoping to reduce imports, the government instituted a system of import licensing in November 1983. This caused much criticism from other Caricom members because Trinidad and Tobago absorbed half of the intraregional trade (see External Sector, this ch.). Despite these efforts, foreign reserves continued to dwindle.

By the time of the 1983 municipal elections, PNM support had seriously eroded. With an eye on the elections, Chambers raised the salaries of 52,000 public workers, thereby increasing government expenditure by 76 percent. Despite this action, the ONR and the Alliance joined forces to win a total of 66 of the 120 municipal seats, the first opposition victory since 1958. The PNM also lost disastrously in the 1984 elections for the Tobago House of Assembly. That contest, which became a personal clash between Robinson and Chambers, resulted in the DAC's winning eleven out of fifteen seats.

The PNM was under heavy criticism by the time parliamentary elections were called for December 15, 1986. The opposition coalesced in the NAR, formed earlier in the year. The four parties comprising the NAR included the three that had formed the Alliance in 1981—the ULF, the DAC, and Tapia House—and the ONR. These four included a wide spectrum of Trinidadian political views: the ULF, headed by Basdeo Panday, president of the ATSE/FWTU, represented the indigenous working class and was mainly East Indian and left of center; Robinson's DAC primarily represented Tobagonian interests; Tapia House was a small intellectual party under the leadership of Lloyd Best; and the ONR, led by Hudson-Phillips, was largely middle class and right of center. Robinson was chosen head of the NAR, and Hudson-Phillips and Panday became deputy leaders.

Campaigning under the slogan "one love," the NAR issued a broad appeal to all ethnic groups. Robinson cited details of government corruption that the PNM was not able to dispel. Surprisingly, in response to a question at a political rally about corruption, a PNM candidate replied, "we are all thieves." Robinson promised to name an Integrity Commission, as provided by the Constitution, and to create a Register of Gifts to keep track of gifts to cabinet ministers. He also outlined a massive campaign to improve employment and promised to publish a report on drugs that had been suppressed by the government (see National Security, this ch.). Deputy leader Panday said that a NAR government would concentrate on divestment of some state enterprises.

The 1986 election was remarkable, for both voter participation and results. In the highest voter turnout (63 percent) in twenty years, the NAR captured 67 percent of the vote and won a stunning 33 out of the 36 seats in the House of Representatives. Most of the NAR seats were won by large margins, even in districts where the PNM candidates were cabinet ministers. Chambers was swept out of office with the tide. Despite losing almost all of its seats, the PNM, according to subsequent analysis of the election, retained almost half the votes of the black community. Although middle- and upper-middle-class blacks voted for the NAR, less affluent blacks stayed loyal to the PNM. Much of the NAR strength came from East Indian votes. Patrick Manning, one the three representatives who had survived the 1986 elections, was chosen to head the PNM.

The Robinson Government

Robinson was sworn in as prime minister on December 17, 1986. He had been involved in Trinidadian politics since 1958, when he was first elected as a representative from Tobago. Robinson had served the PNM as finance minister from 1961 to 1967 and as minister of external affairs from 1967 to 1970, when he resigned from the party. He returned to Tobago to head a local party that later became the DAC; when the DAC joined the NAR in 1986, he was elected leader of the new party.

Robinson reorganized the cabinet, creating a number of new ministries. In April 1987 the ministries were those for education; energy; external affairs, international marketing, and tourism; finance and economy, which Robinson kept for himself, designating two additional ministers to serve with him; food production, marine exploitation, and forestry; health, welfare, and status of women; industry, commerce, and enterprise; labour, employment, and manpower resources; national security; planning and reconstruction; works, resettlement, and infrastructure; and youth, culture, and creative affairs. He named Selwyn Richardson as attorney general, a post Richardson had formerly held under the PNM. Deputy leader Panday resigned his post as head of the ATSE/ FWTU to become minister of external affairs, international marketing, and tourism.

The Robinson government was immediately faced with serious economic problems. On taking office, Robinson found that financial affairs were much worse than had been apparent. In April 1987, in his report to the nation Robinson painted a grim picture of an empty treasury with little relief in sight. The 1986 deficit was US$2.8 billion rather than the US$1 billion claimed by the previous government. Because the deficit had been covered by borrowing from the Central Bank, there were few financial reserves left. Reserves, which had been US$3.3 billion in 1981, dropped to less than US$400 million by the end of 1986. Oil prices fell, aggravating the situation, and the state-owned oil companies expected to lose money in 1987. Robinson promised to conduct a more open government than the PNM and proposed a number of construction projects to stimulate economic growth. He also attempted to cut costs by withdrawing the cost-of-living allowance in the public sector, causing a storm of union protests (see Role of Government, this ch.).

Since independence Trinidad and Tobago had never had a change in party administration, and it experienced transition problems when the NAR took over in December 1986. Questions arose as to whether the public service commissions could be fair and nonpartisan since they were a product of thirty years of PNM government. The commissions and the civil service were scrutinized to ensure that their members would serve an NAR government as loyally as the former PNM government, to which they owed their jobs. Provisions for retraining were made, and new guidelines on discipline were established. When President Ellis Clarke, the first president of Trinidad and Tobago, came to the end of his five-year term, Parliament elected Noor Mohammed Hassanali, a Muslim and a former judge. Immediately prior to the end of his term in March 1987, Clarke made two appointments to public service commissions that angered Robinson, the latter claiming he had not been ''consulted'' as provided in the Constitution. Robinson caused a storm of protest by proposing a constitutional amendment to clarify the legality of appointments made by an outgoing president. The proposed constitutional amendment was later withdrawn because of the intense criticism, and a commission was appointed to review the Constitution for possible changes.

In an effort to deal with government corruption, the Robinson administration published a formerly unpublished drug report that detailed an increase in cocaine activity made possible by corruption in the Trinidad and Tobago Police Service (see National Security, this ch.).

By the time of its party convention in July 1987, the NAR was struggling with the responsibilities of trying to solve large national problems with few resources; as a result, there were strains within the four-party coalition as well as strikes by various unions. Local government elections called for September 14, 1987, were the first referendum on the Robinson government. The NAR held together and scored some gains, winning two of the four municipalities previously controlled by the PNM and retaining six of seven county councils. It failed, however, to capture the important Port-of-Spain municipality from the PNM, giving both the NAR and the PNM reason to feel confident about the future.

Foreign Relations

Since achieving self-governing status in 1956, Trinidad and Tobago has followed a nationalistic and independent course in its foreign policy, and it has taken an active role in international and regional organizations, such as the UN and the Organization of American States (OAS). Trinidad and Tobago has made a point of insisting on its autonomy from United States foreign policy and its right to maintain relations with communist countries, especially Cuba. It has been an advocate of close Caribbean cooperation, as long as this did not adversely affect the domestic economy. Trinidad and Tobago was a founding member of the Caribbean Free Trade Association (Carifta) and is also an important member of its successor organization, Caricom, which was established in 1973.

Prior to independence in 1962, Williams took several positions that emphasized the islands' sovereignty and their right to make their own decisions. He fought for, and achieved, the right to sit as a sovereign member with the United States and Britain at the 1960 conference that decided the fate of the United States base at Chaguaramas (see The Road to Independence, this ch.). Prompted by economic considerations, Williams also made the decision to pull out of the West Indies Federation in 1962, thereby giving it the coup de grace. Both of these decisions illustrate fundamental policies of autonomy and zealous concern for a standard of living that is much higher than that of the other Commonwealth Caribbean islands. Implementation of both these policies was made much easier by substantial oil revenues and the stability of the government.

Since independence, Trinidad and Tobago has associated itself with, and participated in, many international organizations. Upon independence, it became a member of the Commonwealth of Nations, and later that year it was admitted to the UN. In March 1967, Trinidad and Tobago became the first Commonwealth Caribbean member of the OAS, and the following June it signed the Inter-American Treaty of Reciprocal Assistance (Rio Treaty) of 1947, thus becoming a part of the inter-American regional security mechanism under the framework of the UN Charter. In these organizations it has traditionally followed a policy of nonalignment and respect for sovereignty of states, a policy that in the late 1980s the Robinson government made a point of endorsing.

Trinidad and Tobago has taken an independent stance in the UN. In the fortieth UN General Assembly in 1985–86, only 17.8 percent of Trinidad and Tobago's votes supported United States positions. It opposed the trade embargo against Nicaragua and took opposing sides on other issues important to the United States.

Trinidad and Tobago has also demonstrated its independence from United States foreign policy initiatives in the OAS. In 1972 Trinidad and Tobago, Barbados, Jamaica, and Guyana defied the United States and the OAS and established diplomatic relations with Cuba. After the OAS lifted sanctions against Cuba in 1975, Williams visited Cuba and also visited the Soviet Union, Hungary, Romania, and China. He was not, however, impressed with Cuba and, in the 1976 campaign, used examples from Cuba to demonstrate the superiority of capitalism. Trinidad and Tobago has been ambivalent about closer ties with Cuba, maintaining correct diplomatic relations but not encouraging Cuban initiatives.

Although Trinidad and Tobago denounced the 1983 coup against Grenadian leader Maurice Bishop and imposed sanctions against the Revolutionary Military Council, it opposed the subsequent United States-Caribbean intervention in that country (see Grenada, Foreign Relations, ch. 4). Prime Minister Chambers condemned the use of force as a "first resort," arguing that a nonmilitary solution should have been pursued. Chambers was angered that he had not been consulted before the operation, as he was serving as Caricom chairman at the time. The government took the position that the Grenada crisis was a Caribbean affair and, as such, was the sole responsibility of the people and governments of the Caribbean. Chambers and his external affairs minister, Basil Ince, felt that the United States-Caribbean intervention set a dangerous precedent for invasions of other states in the Caribbean. Nevertheless, the government expressed willingness for Trinidad and Tobago to be part of a peacekeeping force.

Public opinion in Trinidad and Tobago did not necessarily endorse the government's position on Grenada. A poll taken by an independent research group in Trinidad and Tobago showed that 63 percent felt that force was the only alternative. A majority (56 percent) thought that Trinidad and Tobago should have "joined the invasion;" 61 percent maintained that the decision by a majority of Caricom states to "invite" United States intervention was "justified."

Trinidad and Tobago's Grenada policy affected its relations with some of its Commonwealth Caribbean neighbors. Following the coup against Bishop, Trinidad and Tobago deployed soldiers along its northern and southern coasts to prevent illegal landings by refugees from Grenada and put extra restrictions on Grenadian immigration. Relations with Barbados were also strained, as the two countries argued about whether or not the Trinidadian ambassador in Barbados had been fully informed of the plans to send a task force to the Caribbean.

Although nationalistic and independent, Trinidad and Tobago has maintained a strong attachment to Britain. In April 1982, Trinidad and Tobago joined Chile, Colombia, and the United States in abstaining from voting on an OAS resolution recognizing Argentine sovereignty over the Falkland/Malvinas Islands. The following month it joined the same three countries in abstaining from a resolution that condemned the British military operation and called on the United States to halt its aid to Britain.

Trinidad and Tobago also demonstrated its respect for the British in its Constitution by retaining the Judicial Committee of the Privy Council in London as the highest court of appeal. Polls taken just before the Constitution went into effect showed that many citizens felt that resort to the Privy Council in London would achieve a more just solution than that found in courts in Trinidad and Tobago. The poll also revealed that 52 percent of those answering agreed with the statement that "Trinidad and Tobago would have been better off if it had not become independent." Only 18 percent disagreed.

Policy in Trinidad and Tobago has favored Caribbean economic cooperation as long as that cooperation did not threaten the nation's standard of living. After Jamaica's withdrawal from the West Indies Federation in 1961, Trinidad and Tobago followed suit the following year because it did not want to be responsible for eight small, much poorer islands. Half of all Trinidadians interviewed in a 1976 poll agreed with the statement that "Trinidad and Tobago should go its own way and not worry about the Caribbean." Nonetheless, Trinidad and Tobago was generous to its Caribbean neighbors during the oil-rich years. Assistance from Trinidad and Tobago totaled nearly US$300 million and included issuance of grants to the CDB, establishment of an aid council to provide loans to other countries, and creation of an oil, asphalt, and fertilizer facility to help its Caricom partners pay for the increased cost of imports. In the 1980s, however, oil prices fell, and the Chambers government instituted a system of import licensing and dual exchange rates that severely restricted Trinidad and Tobago's importation of goods from Caricom. By 1986 intraregional trade accounted for only a little over 5 percent of total imports.

Shortly after his December 1986 electoral victory, Robinson promised that the NAR government would increase intraregional trade. Robinson signaled his desire for closer relationships with the Caribbean by inviting all the Caricom leaders to a ceremonial opening of Parliament in January 1987. Six Caribbean leaders accepted the invitation, among them Prime Minister Errol Barrow of Barbados, who met with Robinson in April to discuss fishing rights and to sign an agreement on Caribbean air service. Robinson also offered to host the Caricom conference in May 1988. By mid-1987 the Trinidad and Tobago government had removed the 12-percent import duty for 8 of the other 11 Caricom countries.

Trinidad and Tobago's relations with Venezuela in the late 1980s were cordial but surprisingly distant, considering the physical proximity of the two countries. President Jaime Lusinchi of Venezuela visited Trinidad and Tobago in September 1986 at Prime Minister Chambers's invitation, the first Venezuelan president ever to visit the islands while in office. Disputes over fishing rights were addressed in a 1985 fishing agreement, signed at the time of Lusinchi's visit, along with a number of other agreements on industrial and technical collaboration. At the same time, Spanish-language courses were arranged for members of the Trinidad and Tobago Defence Force coast guard. By 1987, however, the NAR government was criticizing the fishing agreement as detrimental to Trinidad and Tobago's interests. On a number of occasions, Venezuelan guards detained fishing boats from Trinidad and Tobago and seized the cargo. Both countries hoped to remedy this problem by organizing joint patrols of disputed areas.

Trinidad and Tobago has strongly opposed apartheid in South Africa. This has been a tenet of foreign policy with grass-roots appeal, expressed in 1986 in a popular calypso chorus that chanted "Botha, you need a kick in the bottom."

National Security

The national security forces of Trinidad and Tobago in late 1987 included the Trinidad and Tobago Defence Force and the Trinidad and Tobago Police Service, both of which were under the Ministry of National Security. The Defence Force consisted of approximately 2,130 personnel distributed among the army, the coast guard, and the air force; the Police Service included about 3,000 members, divided among the police and the fire and ambulance services.

Recruitment was voluntary, and many of the officers had been trained in Britain. In 1986 the army, the ground forces arm of the Defence Force, had 1,500 personnel organized into one infantry battalion, one reserve battalion, and one support battalion. The army had no heavy equipment or armored vehicles, and its rifles and machine guns were all of British origin. The coast guard, which was the naval arm of the Defence Force, had about 580 personnel and 13 patrol craft in 1986. The larger naval vessels included two 200-ton Swedish patrol vessels and four 100-ton Swedish Vosper patrol craft. The air force became a separate branch of the Defence Force in 1977; by 1986 it had about fifty personnel, one Cessna 402, and six helicopters, operating from bases at Piarco International Airport and Crown Point Airport.

Newspaper articles in 1986 and 1987 indicated that equipment in the armed forces was deteriorating and poorly maintained. Very few of the 150 vehicles in the Defence Force were believed to be operational in early 1987. In late 1986, four coast guard vessels were said to be inoperable, and three of the five customs and excise launches were reported to be down, with repairs delayed indefinitely because of lack of funds. At the same time, there were reports of large-scale arms smuggling into Trinidad and Tobago from Grenada, Barbados, Venezuela, Colombia, and the United States. A group of highly sophisticated "special operations" weapons—including the Israeli Uzi, the Soviet AK–47, the 9mm semiautomatic and automatic Beretta—and even sniper rifles with an infrared lens were being sold in Trinidad and Tobago. Most households had a gun, and there was a ready market for small arms, but the final destination of the sophisticated weapons was not known.

Although the Police Service has existed since colonial times, it was not until 1943 that a local man was appointed a commissioned police officer from the ranks. In the mid-1980s, the Police Service was divided between the police and the fire and ambulance services. In 1986 the police had eight divisions—seven on Trinidad and one on Tobago. Branches included a riot control unit (called the Police Mobile Force), units for highway control and crime investigation, and a court and process unit, which was responsible for preparing court cases up to committal proceedings. Although most police personnel were trained at the Police Training School, trainee constables were occasionally sent to Britain for additional training.

Approximately 14,000 serious crimes were reported to the police in 1985, a rise of 43 percent since 1976; nonetheless, prosecutions for these crimes only rose by 700 to 2,856, and convictions fell to 550, a drop of 531. There were ninety-nine reports of murder and twelve of manslaughter in 1985, compared with sixty-eight and fourteen for the same crimes in 1976. The only convictions obtained for any of the crimes just mentioned were four murder convictions in 1976. Despite a nearly fivefold increase in prison expenditures from 1976 to 1985, the daily average number of prisoners only grew from 1,048 in 1976 to 1,110 in 1985. The number of individuals committed to prison did expand to 4,231 in 1985, an increase of 81 percent over 1976.

Drug trafficking presented serious national security problems in 1987. In April 1984, the Chambers government appointed a commission to examine the drug problem. Two years later, the commission produced the Scott Drug Report, which was suppressed by Chambers and not released until the NAR took over the government in 1987. The Scott Drug Report described an explosive increase in the use of cocaine, attributing it to Trinidad and Tobago's location on the trade route between the producers in Peru, Bolivia, and Colombia and the main market in the United States. It implicated five cabinet officials in the PNM government, as well as customs officials, bank executives, and many policemen, some of whom held senior posts. Police Commissioner Randolph Burroughs, who had been tried and acquitted in 1986 on murder and drug-related charges, resigned a few days after the Scott Drug Report was published.

Promising a national crusade against drugs, Robinson suspended fifty-three police officers, four magistrates, and a customs official and asked for stronger legislation permitting confiscation of property acquired with drug profits. He named Louis Rodriguez, a former member of the commission that prepared the Scott Drug Report, as police commissioner. Rodriguez had been working with authorities at the airport to strengthen security at Piarco International Airport, cited by the Scott Drug Report as one of the main ports of entry for cocaine. A special police task force, set up by Robinson to deal with drug trafficking, was reported to have destroyed millions of marijuana plants throughout Trinidad and Tobago and conducted dozens of raids against cocaine dealers.

*   *   *

Bridget Brereton's *A History of Modern Trinidad, 1783–1962* gives a comprehensive discussion of events in Trinidad and Tobago until independence and is particularly useful on the rise of the PNM. Eric Williams's many books and speeches, especially his autobiography *Inward Hunger,* are invaluable in showing the thinking of the man who was the most important influence on independent Trinidad and Tobago. Jack Harewood's *The Population of Trinidad and Tobago* and *Female Fertility and Family Planning in Trinidad and*

Tobago provide a good understanding of population trends. Information on health care is available in the Pan American Health Organization's *Health Conditions in the Americas, 1981-1984.* Supporting statistical evidence for health, education, and welfare may be found in Trinidad and Tobago's *Annual Statistical Digest* and *Report on Education Statistics.* Book-length studies on the economy of Trinidad and Tobago are few. Most research on the country appears in various academic journals. Likewise, there are few well-centralized sources of data on the economy, causing statistical variations. The best statistical and analytical annual publications on the economy are the government's Central Statistical Office's *Review of the Economy* and the Central Bank's *Annual Report.* Selwyn Ryan's many studies of politics and the electorate in Trinidad and Tobago give insight into events as seen contemporaneously. Paul Sutton's "Black Power in Trinidad and Tobago: The Crisis of 1970" describes the crisis from start to finish, and Scott B. MacDonald's *Trinidad and Tobago* is one of the few sources that covers the whole postindependence period. (For further information and complete citations, see Bibliography.)

Chapter 4. The Windward Islands and Barbados

Preparing bananas for export

THE WINDWARD ISLANDS consist of Dominica, St. Lucia, St. Vincent and the Grenadines, and Grenada. The name *Windward* dates back to the 1700s, to the time when English ships bound for Jamaica followed the trade-wind passage, stopping at islands along the way. The islands constitute a north-south chain in the southern section of the Lesser Antilles and share a volcanic rock formation. The Windward Islands nations also have highly similar political and economic systems. Despite these parallels, the Windwards are much more heterogeneous than other Commonwealth Caribbean island groupings. These differences prevented the establishment in the nineteenth and early twentieth centuries of a federation along the lines found in the Leeward Islands.

A French legacy distinguishes the Windward Islands from their Commonwealth Caribbean neighbors. The French established permanent settlements on Dominica, St. Lucia, St. Vincent, and Grenada in the 1600s and controlled them until the islands were seized by the British in the 1760s. Even after the British takeover, France continued to compete with Britain for authority over the Windwards, regaining control over St. Lucia, for example, on several occasions. France did not relinquish its claim to St. Lucia until 1815.

The islands varied widely in the degree to which they subsequently assimilated British culture and mores. The most extensive acculturation occurred in St. Vincent, where the population easily adopted the English language and Protestantism. In Grenada, on the other hand, the majority of the residents remained Roman Catholics even though English became the sole language of the island. Dominica and St. Lucia offered the greatest resistance to British influence. In the late 1980s, a French creole language or patois was still in use by much of the rural population of both islands. Dominicans and St. Lucians were also overwhelmingly Roman Catholic.

The British made numerous, largely unsuccessful, efforts to administer the Windward Islands as a single entity. In 1764 the British established the Southern Caribbee Islands and grouped together the colonies of Grenada, the Grenadines, St. Vincent, Dominica, and Tobago. Within two decades, however, the government collapsed as each colony except the Grenadines won the right to have its own governor and assembly. In 1833 Barbados, Grenada, St. Vincent, and Tobago were incorporated into the Windward Island

Government with headquarters in Barbados. St. Lucia was absorbed into this government in 1838. In actuality, however, lieutenant governors and assemblies on each of the islands exercised considerable autonomy.

Yet another British effort aimed at unifying the Windward Islands occurred in the last quarter of the nineteenth century. In 1875 the governor of Barbados attempted to implement a British directive calling for a Windward Islands confederation. Fearing a loss of political and financial autonomy, Barbadian planters successfully defeated the measure. Although the Barbadian action dealt a severe blow to the confederation effort, the British established in 1885 the office of governor and commander in chief of the Windward Islands of Grenada, St. Vincent, St. Lucia, and Tobago. Four years later, Tobago withdrew from this government to form a union with Trinidad. Dominica, a reluctant member of the Leeward Islands Federation since 1871, rejoined the Windwards in 1940. Although the Windwards structure lasted until 1956, it had only limited authority. Its members were absorbed in 1958 in the ill-fated West Indies Federation and became independent nations between 1974 and 1979 (see The West Indies Federation, 1958–62, ch. 1).

The nations of the Windward Islands generally share common political and economic patterns. St. Lucia, St. Vincent and the Grenadines, and Grenada are formally constitutional monarchies with a parliamentary system of government based on the West-minister model. Each has a bicameral legislature consisting of an elected House and non-elective Senate. The prime minister is the leader of the party that secures a majority of House seats. Dominica's political system differs from those of its neighbors in two important ways. First of all, Dominica is a republic with a president as head of state and prime minister as head of government. In addition, House and Senate members form part of a unicameral body, called the House of Assembly. Agriculture is the leading component of the gross domestic product for each of the islands. In the case of Grenada, however, tourism replaced agriculture as the primary earner of foreign exchange by the mid-1980s. All of the Windwards have high levels of unemployment and emigration.

In the late 1980s, following a tumultuous decade, national security remained an important consideration for the leaders of the Windward Islands. The overthrow in 1979 of the Grenadian government and its replacement by the People's Revolutionary Government (PRG), the temporary seizure the same year of Union Island in the Grenadines, the attempted coup in 1981 in Dominica, and the assassination in 1983 of PRG leader Maurice Bishop shocked the Windwards population. These events led to the creation of paramilitary Special Service Units within each of the national police organizations. At the same time, however, leaders generally continued to oppose the establishment of a regional army, fearing that such an institution could endanger democracy.

Despite its nineteenth-century ties to the Windward Islands, Barbados differs from its neighbors in several ways. Barbados lies east of the Windwards and is characterized by lowlands, plains, and rolling hills rather than the mountainous terrain of the Windwards. The island also followed a distinct historical path. Barbados is regarded as the most British nation in the Commonwealth Caribbean, a reflection undoubtedly of the uncontested control exercised by the British from 1625 until the granting of independence in 1966. Barbados also managed to maintain a representative assembly throughout the colonial period. In contrast, Dominica, St. Lucia, St. Vincent and the Grenadines, and Grenada adopted crown colony government (see Glossary) at varying periods during the nineteenth century (see Political Traditions, ch. 1). Barbados' economic base also differs from that of most of the Windwards nations; tourism replaced agriculture as the primary foreign exchange earner by the 1970s. Barbados is also distinguished from its neighbors by the maintenance of a standing army. Barbados' political structure, however, is identical to that found in St. Lucia, St. Vincent and the Grenadines, and Grenada.

Dominica

Official Name . . . . Commonwealth of Dominica

Term for Citizens . . . . Dominican(s)

Capital . . . . Roseau

Political Status . . . . Independent, 1978

Form of Government . . . . Parliamentary democracy
and republic

Geography
Size . . . . 750 sq. km.
Topography . . . . . . Mountainous, covered by multilayered
rain forest and swift-flowing highland streams
Climate . . . . Tropical, wet

Population
Total estimated in 1985 77,900
Annual growth rate (in percentage) in 1982–85 . . . . 1.4
Life expectancy at birth in 1984 . . . . 76.7
Adult literacy rate (in percentage) in 1981 94
Language . . . . English; some patois
Ethnic groups . . . . Primarily black; some Carib
Religion . . . . Roman Catholic (83 percent);
remainder other Christian donominations or no religion

Economy
Currency; exchange rate . . . . Eastern Caribbean dollar
(EC$); EC$2.70 = US$1.00
Gross domestic product (GDP) in 1986 . . . US$90.2 million
Per capita GDP in 1986 . . . . US$1,047
Distribution of GDP (in percentage) in 1986
Government and other services 61.8
Agriculture 29.4
Manufacturing 8.8

National Security
Armed forces personnel 0
Paramilitary personnel 80
Police 310

Dominica

Dominica is the most mountainous island in the Caribbean. The land rises in places straight from the sea, towering to high peaks. This rugged landscape is softened somewhat by the luxuriant forests that coat the hills and give the island its distinctive verdant beauty.

After nearly 3,000 years of human habitation, Dominica, known to many as "the Nature Island of the Caribbean," is one of the few places where untouched primary tropical forests can still be found. More than in most islands, this rugged terrain has guided the course of Dominica's history. The steep mountains and deep valleys provided the early Carib Indians with a natural fortress against European colonizers, making Dominica one of the last islands to be fully colonized. These same features later provided a safe haven for escaped slaves. Since then, the struggle between man and mountain has significantly affected the direction and pace of Dominica's development by determining the location and cost of roads, farms, and buildings.

The island's first settlers were the Arawaks, an Indian people from the Orinoco region of South America, who arrived in Dominica and the neighboring islands of Martinique and Guadeloupe about 1000 B.C. (see The Pre-European Population, ch. 1). These first known settlers lived peacefully until they were almost completely decimated by the more aggressive Carib Indians, who arrived in Dominica in A.D. 900. In the late 1980s, there were no known living descendants of the Arawaks in Dominica, but the Carib population numbered about 1,500 and lived in a 1,500-hectare reserve near the island's northeast coast. Actually, only a few dozen Caribs were pure blooded. Tribal rules allowed Carib men to marry women of other races, a right not extended, however, to Carib women.

Some 593 years after the Caribs settled in Dominica, Christopher Columbus first sighted the island on his second voyage to the New World. Unaware that the Caribs had already named the island Waitukubuli ("Tall is her body"), Columbus renamed it Dominica, after the Spanish word for Sunday, the day of his arrival, November 3, 1493.

For the next 200 years, no European power was able to conquer Dominica. The determined and often violent resistance of the island's Carib inhabitants was a major deterrent to colonization. As the Spanish Empire grew in the 1500s, Dominica became increasingly important, but only as a point for collecting wood and water. The island's resources were abundant, but attacking Caribs put the mariners at great risk. Only in the year 1627, when the French standard was raised, did a European power claim the island as an occupied possession. Fifty years later, following repeated hostilities between the French and English over the island's ownership, a treaty was signed between the two countries declaring Dominica a neutral territory to "be inhabited by the savages to who [sic] it has been left."

Long years of battle against French and English settlers and diseases contracted from these adversaries took their toll on a once defiant people until the Carib population was reduced drastically from a high of 5,000 in the year 1647 to just 400 in 1730. At this point, permanent settlers from Europe and other island colonies began to move into Dominica in increasing numbers.

French settlers were the first to establish themselves on Dominica, extracting timber and commencing small-scale farming. As more land was cleared, the French met labor needs by bringing in African slaves, who were already in the other West Indian colonies. In addition to working the plantation fields, these slaves were permitted to establish provision gardens and to raise small stock. Much of this produce was sold at Sunday markets, where slaves from neighboring plantations gathered to socialize and trade. Many slaves saved the income from these sales and used it to buy their freedom from the estate owners. This practice led to the early establishment of a group of free black inhabitants known as *affranchis*, many of whom later owned small estates and slaves. This unique mix of slave plantations owned by Europeans and Africans, existing alongside small garden plots and farms cultivated by escaped slaves, freed slaves, and Carib Indians, charted a markedly different colonial course for Dominica compared with that of the sugar colonies of Barbados and Jamaica. In these other islands, classic slave plantation structures became entrenched around large-scale sugar cultivation, which delayed the emergence of the system of small-scale, peasant farming that still characterizes Dominica's agriculture.

The evolution of this mixed agricultural sector was interrupted between 1756 and 1763 by the Seven Years' War between Britain and France. After several battles, the British finally occupied Dominica in 1761, and two years later, in the Treaty of Paris, the French ceded the island to Britain.

Under this new European power, several changes occurred that greatly affected Dominica's future. Although the British initially attempted to unite Dominica in a common colonial government along with several other Windward islands, by 1771 Dominica had

View of Roseau, 1837
Courtesy Prints and Photographs Division, Library of Congress

its own two-chamber legislature: a popularly elected House of Assembly and a Council, the members of which were appointed by the governor. Nonetheless, the British placed two significant limitations on popular participation. First, free blacks were completely excluded from the electoral process. In addition, government officials had to take an oath in which they repudiated basic tenets of the Roman Catholic faith. This helped create a system of government that effectively excluded large numbers of French planters from political participation.

Another significant development of this period that still affects landownership patterns in Dominica was the distribution and sale of large tracts of land to British citizens resident in Britain. A land tenure system of absentee ownership rapidly became entrenched, and speculation by the owners kept good agricultural land out of production.

Beginning with the 1770s and continuing for the next sixty years, events throughout the world caused rapid and major changes in the island's colonial status. The 1776 declaration of war by the North American colonies against Britain disrupted a thriving trade that had developed between the colonies and Dominica in wood, rum, horses, cattle, and other items. In 1778 France took advantage of British difficulties in North America to reclaim several British colonies in the West Indies, including Dominica; however, only

265

a few years later, control of Dominica returned to the British through terms of the Treaty of Versailles of 1783. Finally, the Abolition of Slavery Act was passed in the British Parliament in 1833 and became law in Dominica on August 1, 1834.

In 1831 the House of Assembly enacted the Brown Privilege Bill, which allowed propertied free blacks to vote and to seek political office. The following year, three blacks were elected to the House of Assembly. By 1838 the House of Assembly had a black majority. Dominica thus became the only British Caribbean colony in the nineteenth century to have a black-controlled legislature.

Over the next thirty years, black legislators led by Charles Gordon Falconer promoted social welfare measures and were bitterly opposed by those allied with the British absentee owners. In an effort to weaken black control of the legislature, whites formed the Dominican Association for the Reform of Abuses in the Administration of Public Affairs and promoted the merger of the House of Assembly and the Council. In 1863, a year after regaining control of the House of Assembly, a white majority dissolved that body and the Council and established the Legislative Assembly, consisting of nineteen elected members and nine appointees. Further limitations on representative government came in 1865, when membership in the Legislative Assembly was divided evenly between elected and appointed officials. In 1898 the last blow to the representative system occurred when the British established crown colony government (see Glossary).

Determined to demonstrate that crown colony rule was more efficient than the previous approach, the British attempted to address Dominica's social and infrastructure needs. Roads were built through the mountainous interior; agriculture was supported with research, extension services, and training; and agro-industry was begun with the processing of lime juice for export to Britain. By the start of World War I, sufficient goodwill toward Britain had been re-established to encourage locals to volunteer for service in the British Army.

The event that singlehandedly thrust Dominica into the modern era was the publication of the Moyne Commission report in 1940. The commission itself had been formed in response to riots that erupted throughout the British West Indies in the late 1930s. The report exposed the primitive conditions of the colonies and called for a comprehensive economic development program (see Labor Organizations, ch. 1). During the next twenty years, Dominica experienced what many of that generation refer to as "the good old days," when British aid, trade, and investment boosted local living standards, created jobs, trained public servants, and provided education and health facilities.

The expectations of workers and farmers rose with the advent of roads, radios, and newspapers. In the 1950s, demands for better work conditions, higher farm prices, and more land for farming began a period of popular social and political activism that led to the formation of trade unions and political parties representing the interests of workers and small farmers on the one hand and business interests on the other hand. The 1961 election of a government led by Edward Oliver Leblanc, a small farmer and agricultural extension worker, marked an important turning point in Dominica's history. Leblanc was the first person without links to the city-based ruling elite to ascend to government leadership in Dominica.

The political platform of his Dominica Labour Party (DLP) was very simple: "it was time for the little man to begin enjoying the fruits of his labour." Leblanc had first come to prominence as a member of the Federal Party, which represented Dominica in the short-lived West Indies Federation, and subsequently led the DLP to electoral victories in 1965 and 1970 (see The West Indies Federation, 1958–62, ch. 1). In 1967 he negotiated associated statehood (see Glossary) with Britain, a constitutional status essentially one step removed from political independence, which made the Dominica government responsible for all aspects of state except external affairs and defense. Although Leblanc resigned as premier (the pre-independence title for head of government) in 1974, the DLP, under Patrick John, won the next general election in 1975 and led Dominica to political independence in 1978.

Geography

Geographically, Dominica is distinctive in many ways. The country has one of the most rugged landscapes in the Caribbean, covered by a largely unexploited, multilayered rain forest. It is also among the earth's most rain-drenched lands, and the water runoff forms cascading rivers and natural pools. The island, home to rare species of wildlife, is considered by many as a beautiful, unspoiled tropical preserve. According to a popular West Indian belief, Dominica is the only New World territory that Columbus would still recognize.

Dominica is the largest and most northerly of the British Windward Islands (see fig. 1). The island faces the Atlantic Ocean to the east and the Caribbean Sea to the west. Its nearest neighbors are the French islands of Guadeloupe, some forty-eight kilometers north, and Martinique, about forty kilometers south.

267

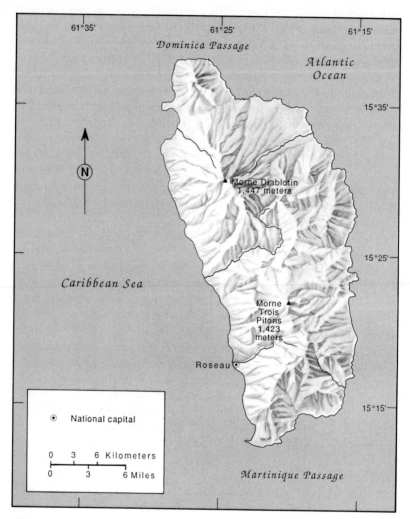

Figure 9. Dominica, 1987

Oblong-shaped and slightly smaller than New York City, Dominica is 750 square kilometers in area, 47 kilometers in length, and
29 kilometers in width. Roseau, the nation's capital and major port,
is favorably situated on the sheltered, southwestern coast (see fig. 9).
    Geologically, Dominica is part of the rugged Lesser Antilles vol-
canic arc. The country's central spine, a northwest-southeast axis
of steep volcanic slopes and deep gorges, generally varies in elevation from 300 meters to 1,400 meters above sea level. Several east-
west trending mountain spurs extend to the narrow coastal plain,

which is studded with sea cliffs and has level stretches no wider than 2,000 meters. The highest peak is Morne Diablotin, at 1,447 meters; Morne Trois Pitons, with an elevation of 1,423 meters, lies farther south and is the site of the national park.

Dominica's rugged surface is marked by its volcanic past. Rock formations are mainly volcanic andesite and rhyolite, with fallen boulders and sharp-edged protrusions peppering slope bases. The light- to dark-hued clayey and sandy soils, derived from the rocks and decomposed vegetation, are generally fertile and porous. Only a few interior valleys and coastal strips are flat enough for soil accumulations of consequence, however. Although scores of mostly mild seismic shocks were recorded in 1986, volcanic eruptions ceased thousands of years ago. Sulfuric springs and steam vents, largely concentrated in the central and southern parts of the island, remain active, however. One of the largest springs, Boiling Lake, is located in the national park.

Dominica is water rich with swift-flowing highland streams, which cascade into deep gorges and form natural pools and crater lakes. The streams are not navigable, but many are sources of hydroelectric power. Trafalgar Falls, located near the national park, is one of the most spectacular sites on the island. The principal rivers flowing westward into the Caribbean are the Layou and the Roseau, and the major one emptying eastward into the Atlantic is the Toulaman. The largest crater lake, called Boeri, is located in the national park.

Dominica has a tropical, wet climate with characteristically warm temperatures and heavy rainfall. Excessive heat and humidity are tempered somewhat by a steady flow of the northeast trade winds, which periodically develop into hurricanes. The steep interior slopes also alter temperatures and winds. Temperature ranges are slight. Average daytime temperatures generally vary from 26°C in January to 32°C in June. Diurnal ranges are usually no greater than 3°C in most places, but temperatures dipping to 13°C on the highest peaks are not uncommon.

Most of the island's ample supply of water is brought by the trade winds. Although amounts vary with the location, rain is possible throughout the year; the greatest monthly totals are recorded from June through October. Average yearly rainfall along the windward east coast frequently exceeds 500 centimeters, and exposed mountainsides receive up to 900 centimeters, among the highest accumulations in the world. Totals on the leeward west coast, however, are only about 180 centimeters per year. Humidity is closely tied to rainfall patterns, the highest values occurring on windward slopes and the lowest in sheltered areas. Relative humidity readings between 70 percent and 90 percent have been recorded in Roseau.

Hurricanes and severe winds, most likely to occur during the wettest months, occasionally are devastating. The most recent hurricanes of note were David and Frederick in August 1979 and Allen in August 1980. The 1979 hurricanes caused over 40 deaths, 2,500 injuries, and extensive destruction of housing and crops. Many agricultural commodities were destroyed during the 1980 storm, and about 25 percent of the banana crop was demolished by strong winds in 1984.

Population

The 1981 census recorded a population of 73,795, a 6-percent increase over the figure registered in 1970. Mid-1987 estimates placed the total at 77,900, and the annual growth rate at 1.4 percent in the 1982–85 period. Crude birth rates per 1,000 population increased from 22 in 1980 to 24.3 in 1983 but decreased to 21.3 in 1984. Crude death rates per 1,000 population increased slightly from 4.7 in 1980 to 5.5 in 1983 and 1984. The rate of natural increase, which was a low 1.3 percent in 1980 following a large out-migration after Hurricane David, showed a slight increase to 1.8 percent in 1981 and 1982 and 1.9 percent in 1983 but dropped back to 1.6 percent in 1984. The migration rate per 1,000 population fluctuated from net increases of 5.5 in 1980 and 25.7 in 1982, to a negative 13.3 in 1983, and a net increase of 5.9 in 1984. Life expectancy at birth was 76.7 years in 1984.

Comparisons between the 1970 and 1981 censuses suggested an increasingly older Dominican population. The number of islanders under age 15 declined from 49 to 40 percent; by contrast, the 15- to 64-year age-group increased from 45 to 53 percent. Those 65 years of age and over increased from 6 to 7 percent. The Pan American Health Organization (PAHO) projected that these trends would continue through at least the early 1990s.

Settlement patterns in Dominica have been affected by the island's physical features. In the 1980s, the population was dispersed into fifty or more villages, towns, and hamlets, most of them along the coast. Despite this general pattern, almost 36 percent of the population in 1981 resided in the parish of St. George, where the capital city of Roseau is located.

Although black descendants of African slaves comprised the overwhelming majority of the population in the 1980s, Dominica's ethnic, racial, and cultural composition also reflected Carib, French, and British influences. This diverse historical legacy was expressed in many ways. It could be seen in Carib art; Roman Catholicism and the French language; British law, politics, education, language, and trade links; and a predominantly black population, work force, electorate, and leadership.

In the 1981 census, approximately 92 percent of the population identified itself as Christian. Of this group, Roman Catholics comprised 83 percent; Methodists, 5.3 percent; Seventh-Day Adventists, 3.5 percent; Pentecostals, 3.2 percent; Baptists, 2.6 percent; Anglicans, 0.9 percent; members of the Church of God, 0.8 percent; and Jehovah's Witnesses, 0.7 percent. The remaining 8 percent of the population was divided between those who adhered to a variety of minor denominations and those who claimed no religion. The Christian makeup of the island was not surprising, given the history of colonization first by France and later by Britain. Both countries were as intent on converting the Caribs and African slaves to Christianity as they were on conquering the island for their respective monarchs.

Education

Churches have played a significant role in Dominica through the establishment of institutions for formal and informal education. The influence of the church began with the arrival of the colonizers, and the institution played an important role in subduing the Caribs and Westernizing the African slaves. Direct involvement in formal education by the churches began in the 1800s, when the Roman Catholic and Methodist churches, which had already established congregations in various parts of the islands, became involved in providing primary education. Secondary education began in the 1850s, when nuns of the Roseau Convent started classes for a limited number of girls in the city. The Dominica Grammar School for boys was established by the government in 1893, and in 1932 the Roman Catholic St. Mary's Academy opened its doors to Roman Catholic boys. Soon after, the Methodists started a secondary school for girls.

Until the 1960s, the difficulty of access by road and the continuing concentration of most services in the capital prevented all but a select few students living in the city from attending secondary school. It was only when roads and schools were constructed throughout the island that formal education became available to the resident rural population. This period of the 1960s also saw the emergence of a public education system, especially on the primary level. In the mid-1980s, all but two of the nation's sixty-six primary schools were operated by the government. Dominica's six secondary schools were equally divided between government and religious institutions. Enrollment figures for 1984 indicated that 17,456 students

271

attended primary schools and that 3,443 went to secondary schools. Beyond the secondary level, Dominica had a two-year technical college that in 1984 enrolled 120 students.

An islandwide network of day care centers and preschools— operated by a Roman Catholic women's organization called the Social League—served children up to the age of five. Since the mid-1970s, the preschool program has benefited from training and financial support provided by the government and international agencies.

Children attended the primary-school system between the ages of five and fifteen. By age fifteen, they were usually in third form (equivalent to eighth grade in the United States) and prepared to enter secondary school. Four of the secondary schools accepted students at the age of twelve on the basis of their performance on the Common Entrance Examination administered by the Ministry of Education and Sports. In the period from 1979 to 1984, only 28 percent of the 11,346 students who took this examination passed. A great deal of controversy surrounded the Common Entrance Examination, which was viewed by many educators as an inadequate assessment of a student's potential to perform at the secondary-school level. Critics also suggested that the test was too limited in scope to assess capacity for training other than that provided by the traditional secondary-school curriculum.

Secondary school continued up to fifth form (the equivalent of tenth grade). Most students ended their formal education at this point; few continued private studies in preparation for the Advanced Level Examination to qualify them for university entry at the sophomore level. Technical training was available at the Government Technical College, which conducted courses in such areas as electrical engineering, mechanics, woodwork and carpentry, and agriculture, as well as a parallel program in the academic subjects taught at the secondary schools.

Campuses of the University of the West Indies (UWI) are located on the islands of Trinidad, Barbados, and Jamaica. Nevertheless, the prohibitive cost of study at the UWI (approximately US$6,000 per year) meant that in the absence of a scholarship, loan, or independent family income, many capable students from Dominica were unable to continue their education. In 1980 the UWI Extra-Mural Department introduced a local program that enabled high school students and working adults to study for and take the Advanced Level Examination. Those attaining passing grades were able to take courses in Dominica equivalent to the first year of university education. This program has allowed students to cut one full year out of their overseas university costs. Since 1970,

272

Roman Catholic church in rural Dominica
Courtesy Jonathan French

loans also have been available at competitive interest rates (9 to 10 percent) from the local Development Bank for overseas study; repayment does not commence until after the course of studies is completed.

In the late 1980s, there were no laws requiring children to attend school, and it was not uncommon for school-age children to work full- or part-time. Education has, however, been the channel through which many have advanced themselves materially and socially. Dominica has a better than 94-percent literacy rate, and peers, family, and community have pressured young people to attend school and to do well. The pressure for formal education, however, has unfortunately depreciated the value of farming as a career.

Health and Welfare

Dominican health statistics in the 1980s suggested a number of challenges confronting medical personnel on the island. Typhoid was a concern, with 207 cases reported during the period 1979 to 1984. Deaths from cancer increased from 55 in 1980 to 70 in 1984, and deaths from cardiovascular diseases increased from 58 to 117 over the same period. At least 70 percent of all deaths occurring in women over age 45 during the early 1980s were attributed to cardiovascular disease. A survey of school-age children in the early

273

1980s indicated that 38 percent suffered from gastroenteritis. Infant mortality rates were on the rise in the early 1980s. After steadily declining in the 1970s, the rate increased from 10.2 per 1,000 live births in 1981 to 23.9 in 1984. PAHO researchers cautioned, however, that the increase could actually be the result of an improvement in Dominica's health information system as well as a statistical aberration resulting from the small number of infant deaths. Child mortality as a whole had declined from the levels recorded in the late 1970s and was stable at 0.4 per 1,000 live births in 1984. As of 1986, there were no reported cases in Dominica of acquired immune deficiency syndrome. Many of the medical problems on the island could be attributed to deficiencies in environmental health. Twenty-one percent of the estimated 16,000 houses in Dominica had access to drinking water; another 43 percent had access to piped water at a distance of less than 100 meters; the remainder (approximately 36 percent, or 5,760 houses) had no acceptable and convenient access to water supplies. Nineteen percent of the population had access to regular solid waste collection services. Only the two major urban centers, Roseau and Portsmouth, had central sewage systems; they lacked treatment facilities, however, and instead disposed of raw sewage in the nearby sea.

Water pollution was a serious problem in Dominica in the 1980s. Large amounts of liquid and solid wastes from an oil and soap factory, a paint factory, rum distilleries, citrus processing, bay oil distilleries, and banana packaging were being dumped untreated into rivers, streams, and the sea. Health hazards also accompanied banana cultivation, particularly through the use of agrochemicals. In the 1980s, the herbicide paraquat, banned by the United States Environmental Protection Agency as a carcinogenic substance, was widely used throughout Dominica's banana industry without the benefit of protective clothing. It was quite common to see village children carrying fresh water to their homes in bright yellow plastic bottles labeled PARAQUAT.

In an effort to address these clinical and environmental concerns, in 1982 Dominica unveiled a five-year national health plan with an emphasis on decentralization of administration and delivery of health care. At the base of the plan was the primary health care unit, designed to serve a minimum population of 600 within an 8-kilometer radius. The primary health care approach included home visitation by multidisciplinary teams of nurses, extension agents, and public health workers; education sessions at the village and family levels; radio programs; use of posters; and

Woman and child on Carib reserve, northeastern Dominica
Courtesy Jonathan French

mobilization of community groups around public sanitation, the environment, nutrition, and health. Four or five health care units were supported by a health center, where more comprehensive services were available. The Princess Margaret Hospital in Roseau served as the nation's secondary referral facility and offered inpatient services in medicine, general surgery, pediatrics, obstetrics, gynecology, and psychiatry. One hundred and forty beds were available for general care and another forty for psychiatry. Limited inpatient care was available in the sixteen-bed Marigot Hospital and the thirty-six-bed Portsmouth Hospital. Limited medical care and long-term nursing care were offered at the ninety-bed Central Geriatric Institution.

Although a comprehensive assessment of the national health plan had not been conducted by the mid-1980s, there were some encouraging signs. In 1984 about 88 percent of pregnant women received prenatal care, and approximately 42 percent were attended to by the sixteenth week of pregnancy. Child health care services covered 100 percent of children and included immunization, nutrition, education and counseling, and growth monitoring. In 1984 immunization levels for diphtheria, pertussis, tetanus, poliomyelitis, measles, and tuberculosis were above 90 percent.

Economy

Macroeconomic Overview

Dominica's gross domestic product (GDP—see Glossary) totaled US$90.2 million in 1986. This figure represented a 4-percent increase over the previous year and was a substantial improvement over the 1.9-percent growth recorded in 1985. The GDP advance in 1986 was led by a 10.8-percent gain in agricultural production. Per capita GDP averaged US$1,047 in 1986.

The government made substantial progress in the 1980s in controlling inflation. In 1980 the consumer price index increased by 30.5 percent over the previous year. This increase resulted from shortages following the hurricanes, high wage settlements, and the effects of the second round of oil price increases on the international economy. The index dropped sharply to 13.3 percent in 1981 and then to 4.4 percent in 1982; by 1985 the rate of inflation was barely 2.1 percent. Favorable international trends, especially the easing of the rate of increase in import prices, and increases in domestic foodstuffs were primarily responsible for the improvement. The consumer price index increased slightly by 3 percent in 1986. Substantial increases in prices for clothing, footwear, meat, fish, and dairy products were largely mitigated by lower fuel prices.

According to the 1981 census, Dominica had an economically active population of 25,000; 18.5 percent of this population was unemployed. Unemployment was particularly high among the 15- to 19- and 20- to 24-year age-groups, with rates of 55.7 and 23.8 percent, respectively. The two sectors contributing most to employment remained agriculture and government. Between 1978 and 1981, the number of workers employed by government decreased marginally from 5,751 to 5,433, or from 32.4 percent of the work force to 31.9 percent. The decrease was more significant in agriculture, which employed 4,517 workers in 1978 and 3,294 in 1981, a shift from 25.5 percent of the work force to 19.3 percent. During that same period, however, the number of farmers increased from 11,000 to 14,000. This possibly indicated that more agricultural workers became full-time farmers in response to land distribution programs, improved farm credit, and stable banana prices in the late 1970s. Dominican wage rates compared unfavorably with the general levels found elsewhere in the Commonwealth Caribbean. In 1984 the minimum wage for a 40-hour week was raised to US$27.55.

Banking and Finance

Dominica was a member of the Caribbean Development Bank (CDB) and the Eastern Caribbean Central Bank (ECCB). The CDB provided financial facilities for infrastructure and development program activities either bilaterally or as a cofinancing partner with the World Bank (see Glossary), the United States Agency for International Development, and other international agencies. The ECCB acted as a common central bank for the members of the Organisation of Eastern Caribbean States (OECS—see Glossary). Dominica and the six other members of the OECS also have shared a common currency, the Eastern Caribbean dollar, since July 1976. The exchange rate has remained fixed at EC$2.70 per US$1.00.

The institutional arrangements of a shared common currency mean that decisions about exchange rates cannot be made by any one member nation. Given the differing production profiles of the OECS countries, the various national economic policy imperatives do not necessarily coincide either in objective, direction, or timing. When coupled with the difficulty of decision making within a regional institution, the arrangements concerning the CDB and the ECCB are major constraints on the effective use of the exchange rate as a tool of national economic policy. In Dominica's case, the constraints have led to the use of wage policy as an alternate tool of macroeconomic policy, a situation that can be domestically unpopular and can limit the ability of the government to direct economic growth. Throughout 1986 Dominica was able to mitigate the effect of a fixed exchange rate because of the strength of the British pound sterling, the currency in which most foreign exchange earnings were earned.

Role of Government

In the 1980s, the Dominican government attempted to strengthen public finances, develop productive capital infrastructure, and diversify agricultural production. On two occasions, the government entered into an extended arrangement with the International Monetary Fund (IMF—see Glossary) to accomplish these goals. Although the nation's stated development policy called upon the private sector to be the engine of economic growth, the government's involvement in key sectors of the economy remained strong.

Dominica entered into an Extended Fund Facility program with the IMF for the period 1982 to 1984. Under the program, the government reorganized public finances, eliminating subsidies to unproductive state enterprises, and expanded government revenues through increased consumption taxes. Expenditure controls were also introduced; the hallmark of this effort was the decision to restrict salary increases of public employees to a level below the anticipated rate of inflation. This decision appeared to influence the rate of increase of private sector wage settlements.

In 1987 the Dominican government signed a three-year structural adjustment program (see Glossary) with the World Bank. The
adjustment program was expected to encourage policies and programs that would increase GDP through investment by the private sector. In preparing this favorable investment environment,
the government developed a package of incentives for private investment that included the removal of export taxes as well as the
foreign exchange levy, the termination of price controls on 40 percent of controlled items, and a substantial reduction in corporate
taxes for eligible manufacturing firms. To stimulate diversified
agricultural production, the government removed price controls
on imported livestock products and took steps to revitalize export
market development for fruit and vegetable crops. At the public
sector level, procedures for investment promotion were streamlined
and located in one agency, the Industrial Development Corporation. Each ministry received technical assistance in project design,
planning, and management of public sector projects. The Economic
Development Unit, the government's central planning body, was
staffed with a multidisciplinary pool of technical experts. In addition, wages in the public sector were no longer to be raised automatically each year; wage negotiation guidelines were drawn up
that were expected to help keep increases in the public wage bill
to 3 percent per year.

In support of these policy reforms, the International Development Association of the World Bank made available US$3.1 mil-
lion in credit as a structural adjustment loan. In addition, the CDB
was to provide US$2 million in parallel financing.

The IMF program of structural adjustment was entered into
largely because of the failure of the private sector to lead the way
in economic development. As a result, the government was playing a greater role in direct investment and commerce than originally had been intended. In the late 1980s, the government owned
and operated a citrus-processing plant, lime-producing estates, and
an export-import company and remained directly involved in communications, transportation, electricity, and commercial banking.

Communications on Dominica were fair. A subsidiary of an international company operated a fully automatic telephone system
with about 4,600 sets. New radio-relay links to Martinique and
Guadeloupe provided high-quality international service. The
government-owned Dominica Broadcasting Corporation operated
a radio station on 595 kilohertz. Radio Caribbean, with studios
on St. Lucia, had a small relay on 1210 kilohertz, and the Gospel
Broadcasting Corporation had facilities on 1060 kilohertz.

The transportation network on Dominica was not well developed. The island had about 370 kilometers of paved roads and 380 kilometers of gravel roads. Road conditions were often poor, however, and many areas of the interior and northwest could not be reached by vehicle. A new small airport outside Roseau was completed in the mid-1980s, and an older, larger international airport was located near Melville Hall on the northeast coast. The island had no railroads. Several streams were navigable by canoe, but none had economic significance. Roseau and Portsmouth were the only ports.

Sectoral Performance

In 1986 the leading sectors of the economy, as measured by percentage of GDP, included agriculture (29.4 percent), government services (21 percent), and manufacturing (8.8 percent). Agriculture remained the primary productive sector of the economy in the 1980s, accounting for more than half of all export revenue. Dominica's agriculture was characterized by the estate-peasant dichotomy in evidence at the time of the abolition of slavery in 1834. The large estates continued to be located near the coast on the deep river valley soils, whereas most small farms were located in the interior on steep, highly erodible soils. This simultaneous existence of small and large farms led to an imbalance in the distribution of land resources, which remained a major constraint on the island's economic development. In spite of land settlement programs (notably at the Geneva, Melville Hall, and Castle Bruce estates), in the mid-1980s just over 30 percent of the farmland was owned and occupied by 3 percent of the farming population.

The banana industry was the most important component of the agricultural sector. The industry was devastated by the hurricanes of 1979 and 1980, when production dropped from 48,244 tons in 1978 to 13,716 tons in 1980. In the early and mid-1980s, production was also hurt by the depreciation of the British pound, the currency of payment for bananas, against the United States dollar. The situation of the industry improved markedly, however, in the late 1980s. Production totaled 56,274 tons in 1986, a 43-percent increase over the previous year. Quality also increased in 1986 as the industry achieved its goal of packing all bananas in the fields, thus reducing spoilage. Finally, the strengthening of the British pound resulted in farmers receiving the highest prices in the history of the industry. The fragility of these high prices was quite evident, but because there were no firm markets for other island crops, increasing the dependency of the economy on bananas appeared to be the only alternative.

Coconuts and citrus fruits (grapefruits, limes, and oranges) were also important agricultural products. Copra was an increasingly significant element of agriculture-based manufacturing. Grapefruit production expanded from 6,803 tons in 1985 to an estimated 9,683 tons in 1986, a 42.3-percent increase.

In the 1980s, Dominica's manufacturing sector increasingly focused on enclave industry (see Glossary) and the processing of agricultural products. Enclave industries were designed to increase export earnings and provide employment. In the early 1980s, the government established two industrial estates and expanded factory facilities by over 16,500 square meters. Agricultural processing industries included the production of laundry and toilet soaps from local copra and of imported chemicals and tallow.

Unlike what was true typically in the Commonwealth Caribbean, tourism was a relatively insignificant component of the Dominican economy. The comparative absence of white sand beaches and tourist infrastructure greatly hindered the industry's development. Nonetheless, the island's rugged beauty provided considerable opportunities for expansion of tourism through the development of a marketing strategy emphasizing mountain climbing, camping, and the like.

Foreign Trade and Balance of Payments

Dominican exports totaled US$42.3 million in 1986, a 48.9-percent increase over the previous year. This improvement resulted primarily from substantially higher production of and prices for bananas; indeed, bananas accounted for 57.3 percent of exports in 1986. In contrast, laundry and toilet soaps declined from 25.2 percent of exports in 1985 to 17 percent in 1986. Britain and the United States absorbed most of Dominica's exports in 1986.

Imports—primarily machinery and equipment, foodstuffs, manufactured goods, and cement—amounted to US$55.7 million in 1986, a mere US$400,000 increase over the previous year. This minuscule growth in imports, coupled with the increase in exports, resulted in a reduction of Dominica's trade deficit from US$26.9 million in 1985 to US$13.4 million in 1986. The United States and Britain supplied most of Dominica's imports in 1986.

In 1986 Dominica recorded increases in both foreign debt and debt service payments as compared with the previous year. The external debt grew from US$40.4 million in 1985 to US$45.5 million in 1986; debt service payments expanded over the same period from US$4.2 million to US$4.7 million. On the positive side, the debt service ratio as a percentage of merchandise exports declined from 14.8 percent in 1985 to 11.1 percent in 1986.

Scenes on Carib reserve, northeastern Dominica
Courtesy Jonathan French

Government and Politics

The Governmental System

Under the republican Constitution adopted at independence on November 3, 1978, the president is head of state and is elected by the House of Assembly, the nation's unicameral parliament, to a five-year term following nomination by the prime minister in consultation with the leader of the opposition. In the exercise of most of his executive functions, the president must follow the recommendations of the Cabinet of Ministers. The prime minister is the head of government and in that capacity is the chairman of the Cabinet of Ministers. Ministers are chosen by the prime minister from a group composed of the elected members of the House of Assembly and senators appointed by the prime minister.

The House of Assembly is composed of twenty-one elected representatives and nine senators, five appointed by the prime minister and four appointed by the opposition leader. Whatever member commands the support of the majority of the elected members in the House of Assembly is named prime minister. The person commanding the majority of the rest of the House becomes opposition leader. (The pre-independence legislature was also known as the House of Assembly.) The movement of the ceremonial mace to the lower position on its stand in the House chamber indicates that the House is sitting in committee, usually to discuss details of a bill before returning to a plenary session for a vote. Decisions are by simple majority vote, except on selected matters, such as constitutional amendments and the declaration of a state of emergency, when a two-thirds majority is required.

The Constitution allows for any citizen of the country, eighteen years of age and over, who is literate and not bankrupt, to organize and take part in political activity. The Constitution does not recognize political parties, nor is their formation required for participating in elections. Candidates may, therefore, run for election either associated with a party or as independents.

Supporting this government structure is a civil service of about 2,500 persons. In the past, jobs in the civil service were much sought after because of the employment security and status that they offered. Because of the expansion of the commercial private sector and nongovernmental organizations since the early 1970s, more attractive conditions of work in the private sector, including salaries, training, and travel, have encouraged a shift of top- and middle-level professionals away from the public sector. In the late 1980s, major adjustments in the size and structure of the civil service were anticipated as part of the government's program of structural adjustment. These changes were expected to result in a streamlined, performance-oriented civil service in which productivity and merit, not longevity of service, would be rewarded.

Dominica has a multilevel judicial system commencing with the Magistrate's Court, which is the first level of recourse for violators of the country's laws. The government-employed magistrate makes decisions at this level without the benefit of a jury. At the next level, a judge, assisted by a jury, presides over civil and criminal cases. Jurors are selected from the list of registered voters and, unless excused by the court, are obliged to serve when called. Appeals may be made to the Eastern Caribbean States Supreme Court, which consists of the Court of Appeal and the High Court. A panel of judges is appointed to hear appeals, and these sittings take place on the island. The court of last resort for Dominicans is the Judicial Committee of the Privy Council in London, where decisions of the Eastern Caribbean States Supreme Court may be reviewed for final ruling.

The Office of the Director of Public Prosecution is a government department located in the Ministry of Legal Affairs; it is headed by the attorney general. The lawyers in this office conduct the prosecution of cases on behalf of the state. There are no legal aid organizations, and citizens are expected to utilize lawyers in private practice as defense attorneys.

Political Dynamics

The 1961 election victory of the DLP under the leadership of Leblanc ushered in a period in Dominica's history when workers and farmers united in one political movement. This alliance of town and country challenged the descendants of landowners and businessmen residing in the capital and began the vigorous involvement in politics of large numbers of poor, uneducated persons.

At the community level, those who had exercised authority through control of land, shops, credit, and transportation and were associated with the defeated Dominica United People's Party were challenged by small farmers and laborers. At the national level, it was made abundantly clear that the "little people" had acquired political power guaranteed by universal adult suffrage and the presence of a political institution (the DLP) through which to act.

In 1968 the Leblanc government responded to incipient signs of social unrest by pushing a bill through the House of Assembly to curb press criticism of government officials. This act shook the moral imperative of the new social order and resulted in the formation of the Dominican Freedom Party (DFP) under the leadership of Mary Eugenia Charles. Yet despite this act, the DLP's popularity among rural Dominicans enabled it to score an easy victory over the Roseau-based DFP in the 1970 general elections.

In 1974, however, the combined pressures of high unemployment among the island's youth and increasingly aggressive activity by trade unions and opposition political parties led to the resignation of Leblanc as premier and DLP leader and his replacement by deputy premier Patrick John. The new premier capitalized on public concerns over criminal activity by Rastafarians (see Glossary)—called Dreads in Dominica—to gain legislative support for the Prohibited and Unlawful Societies and Associations Act. The so-called Dread Act forbade criminal or civil proceedings against any person who killed or injured a member of an unlawful society or association. John's image as a strong supporter of law and order served the DLP well in the 1975 elections and enabled it to capture sixteen of the twenty-one elective House seats.

Fresh from his election victory, John resorted to a high-handed use of the security forces, and he also proposed punitive legislation aimed again at curbing press freedoms. Following a successful strike by the civil service union in 1977 for increased wages, John attempted to solve the increasing economic problems by signing investment deals with persons later discovered to have very questionable business records. One such deal with a United States businessman involved the creation of a free-trade zone comprising about one-quarter of the island's most productive agricultural land. The deal was scuttled after street demonstrations throughout the island in 1979.

In 1978 the backbone of the economy, the banana industry, was hit by a severe disease that wiped out 30 percent of the cultivated acreage. An inquiry laid the blame on poor management by industry officials known to have very strong ties with the government and the DLP. This led to vigorous demonstrations against the government, inspired this time by the farmers who traditionally had constituted the bulk of the party's supporters. This threat to the power base of the party apparently pushed the John administration to take drastic measures. Bills designed to muzzle trade unions and the press were introduced in the House early in 1979.

Following weeks of public meetings all over the island by opposition forces, some 10,000 demonstrators, including rural and urban dwellers, gathered outside the House on May 29, 1979, the day on which the bills were due to be debated and passed. What began as a peaceful demonstration was soon thrown into tragic confusion by the arrival of Defence Force personnel, who in the ensuing shooting killed one youth and injured several other persons.

This set the stage for Dominica's first recorded removal of an elected government from office by other than electoral means. The country was shut down by an alliance of farmers, workers, private businessmen, and members of opposition political parties and churches, grouped under the banner of the Committee for National Salvation. This situation prevailed for twenty-eight days until the resignation of members of government one by one eroded the constitutional majority required for the prime minister to stay in office. On June 21, John's former agriculture minister, James Oliver Seraphine, became prime minister, and an interim government was constituted from among the representatives of the organizations that had led the uprising.

The interim government, although constitutional, was seen by the major opposition party, the DFP, as transitional. Within weeks of the inauguration of the government, the DFP was calling for general elections. Many contenders emerged in the long and bitter electoral campaign that ensued. They included a faction of the DLP, the DFP, the Dominican Liberation Movement Alliance (DLMA—a left-wing party led by young activists and academics), and Seraphine's recently formed Dominica Democratic Labour Party. Accusations that the government had misappropriated relief funds received in the wake of Hurricane David and that it had sold Dominican passports to exiled Iranians seriously damaged the Seraphine campaign. In July 1980, the DFP, polling 52 percent of the votes, won 17 of the 21 elective parliamentary seats, and Mary Eugenia Charles became the Caribbean's first woman prime minister. The party soon began to make inroads into the traditional rural and working-class base of the DLP. This was accomplished in part by the active mobilization of youth into the party in the late 1970s and the formation of the Young Freedom Movement, which by the late 1980s was an aggressive, well-organized, and evidently well-funded organ of the party.

The DFP also benefited from its control over all electronic media and favorable support from the only newspaper published in the country, the weekly *New Chronicle*. Control over the radio station was particularly crucial because the station reached practically the entire population. Although it had criticized the John government for exercising control over a publicly owned medium such as the radio, the DFP exercised much the same kind of control. The party, for example, strictly controlled the news and granted the political opposition only limited access to the radio.

The July 1985 parliamentary election was the first to take place in Dominica since the United States-Caribbean military intervention in Grenada (see Current Strategic Considerations, ch. 7).

OECS chairwoman, Charles, who had emerged as one of the most visible defenders of the intervention, portrayed the election as a choice between democracy and communism (see Foreign Relations, this section). The prime minister charged that the DLP had become communist, and she accused opposition leaders of receiving funds from Cuba, the Democratic People's Republic of Korea (North Korea), and Libya. In an effort to create a new image, the DLP combined with the Dominica Democratic Labour Party and the DLMA to form the Labour Party of Dominica (LPD). Nonetheless, the DFP captured 59 percent of the vote and 15 of the 21 elective House seats.

Despite a slightly reduced majority, DFP support remained strong. Two years after the election, the LPD still suffered from the effects of bitter leadership squabbles and a loss of credibility of its leaders, particularly John. In 1981 John was arrested and accused of conspiring to overthrow the Charles government. A Dominican court acquitted the former prime minister the following year; the government, however, successfully appealed the decision to the Eastern Caribbean States Supreme Court, which ordered John to stand trial again. After the Judicial Committee of the Privy Council in London rejected John's appeal in October 1985, a Dominican court convicted John of treason and sentenced him to twelve years in prison.

Foreign Relations

In the 1980s, the Dominican government became one of the strongest supporters of United States policies in the Caribbean. Charles endorsed economic measures such as the Caribbean Basin Initiative (CBI—see Appendix D) and favored support for the private sector (see Economy, this section). The DFP government also promoted United States efforts to prevent the spread of communism in the Caribbean.

Ties between Dominica and the United States were solidified during the October 1983 crisis in Grenada. After the assassination of Grenadian leader Maurice Bishop, Charles convoked a meeting of the OECS to discuss the crisis. On October 21, the OECS decided to intervene in Grenada and invited friendly governments to provide military assistance. Charles then joined the prime ministers of Barbados and Jamaica in extending a formal invitation to the United States through special emissary Ambassador Frank McNeil. Charles joined President Ronald Reagan at the White House in the official announcement of the intervention and vigorously defended the action. Charles also addressed the Organization of American States and the United Nations, insisting on both occasions that the intervention was necessary to stop communism.

Dominica's special relationship with the United States consisted of material as well as philosophical elements. Charles successfully pleaded with United States officials for funds to expand Dominica's infrastructure. In the 1980s, the United States provided approximately US$10 million in grants to expand the East Dominica Electrification Program and rehabilitate the highway linking the capital to Dominica's international airport near Melville Hall.

Dominica had deep historical and cultural ties to Britain and was a member of the Commonwealth of Nations. Britain also provided economic assistance to the country and was the single largest recipient of Dominican exports. Despite these links, the intervention in Grenada strained relations between Dominica and the Commonwealth. Leaders of African nations attending the Meeting of Heads of Government of the Commonwealth in New Delhi in November 1983 charged that the intervention had violated the principle of nonintervention in the internal affairs of sovereign countries. Charles categorically rejected the African position and stated that the intervention was vital to the interests of the Commonwealth Caribbean. Charles also criticized British prime minister Margaret Thatcher for her initially hostile reaction to the Grenada intervention, accusing Thatcher of having turned her back on her friends.

The government also attempted to extend Dominica's international relations farther afield and strengthened diplomatic ties with both Taiwan and the Republic of Korea (South Korea). Taiwanese technicians have conducted an agricultural research program in Dominica, and although no trade has developed between the two nations, Taiwan has supplied regular infusions of aid for small projects in schools, sporting facilities, and health services.

Relations within the Caribbean Community and Common Market (Caricom—see Appendix C) have been difficult as evidenced by the virtual collapse of Caricom's Multilateral Clearing Facility, the creation of nontariff barriers between member states, the violation of rules of origin regulations (utilizing extraregional garments, for example), and major difficulties over foreign policy. Partly in response to these Caricom difficulties, Charles worked vigorously with the six other members of the OECS to strengthen that subregional grouping.

National Security

When crown colony rule ended in the mid-1950s, the police were the sole security and peacekeeping force in the country. Training was conducted in Barbados and Britain, and until the mid-1960s the chief of police was British. During the early years of the Leblanc government, the police functioned primarily as apolitical protectors of the peace. Nonetheless, with the intensification of social unrest in the early 1970s, the government perceived a serious threat to the security of the state. As a result, the Volunteer Defence Force was established in 1974. This group worked closely with the police and a unit of special constables to comb areas of the island suspected to be hideouts for the Dreads; several violent and fatal clashes ensued between the security forces and the youths. In November 1975, the full-time Defence Force was established by an act of the House of Assembly to replace the Volunteer Defence Force. As prime minister and minister of security, John assumed direct control over the activities of the Defence Force.

As the months went by, it became clear that John had personalized his relationship with, and control over, the Defence Force (he named himself colonel). He also chose to ignore the deteriorating economic situation of the country, instead surrounding himself with cronies from Roseau and resorting to a strategy of confrontation rather than consultation.

After independence on November 3, 1978, the growing arrogance of the prime minister was surpassed only by the sense of elitism that was increasingly associated with the style and actions of the members of the Defence Force. By that time, the main center of training had shifted away from Britain to Guyana, and a growing rift appeared between the Defence Force and the police, who continued to be well trained in Barbados and Britain. For the first time, Dominica was faced with the prospect of a highly politicized military force. It was well armed and well trained, and although it was paid for by the country's taxpayers, it was accountable to persons who were fast being discredited.

Following the removal of the John government in June 1979, the domestic situation remained tense because the Defence Force, widely assumed to favor the ousted regime, had not been disbanded. Further complicating the situation, the country's infrastructure and economy had been destroyed by hurricanes David and Frederick in 1979. Regionally, the New Jewel Movement had overthrown the government of Eric Matthew Gairy in Grenada by military coup on March 13, 1979, and the Anastasio Somoza regime had been defeated by the Sandinistas in Nicaragua. Into this situation came the DFP government on July 20, 1980, soon to be followed by the swearing in of Reagan as president of the United States and Edward Seaga as prime minister of Jamaica in January 1981.

A series of actions in 1981 shook the stability of the Dominican political system. In February, Dreads kidnapped and killed Edward

"Ted" Honychurch, a prominent Dominican and father of government press secretary Lennox Honychurch. In response, Charles
declared a state of emergency, and the House of Assembly enacted
the Prevention of Terrorism Act, which authorized searches without a warrant and temporary detention. In March, Charles announced the discovery of a plot to overthrow her government. The
plot involved Patrick John, the Defence Force, elements of the Ku
Klux Klan, neo-Nazi groups, United States and Canadian mercenaries, and underworld figures from the United States. The dis-
closure led to the arrest of John and several senior officers of the
Defence Force and resulted in the enactment in April of a
parliamentary measure disbanding the Defence Force. In December former Major Frederick Newton of the Defence Force led an
assault against Dominica's police headquarters and prison in an
unsuccessful attempt to free John from imprisonment. Newton was
convicted of murdering one of the policemen defending the headquarters and was executed in August 1986.

The need for internal security was forcefully established by these
dramatic events. Nonetheless, having disbanded the Defence Force,
Charles tried to avoid going back on her position that small countries like Dominica did not need more than a police force. Instead,
the government created an 80-member Special Service Unit (SSU)
within the Commonwealth of Dominica Police Force to supplement
the capabilities of the 310 regular police personnel. The members
of the unit were specially selected by the government and trained
and equipped by the United States. The SSU constituted Dominica's contingent of the Regional Security System (RSS). Although
criticized by the DLMA, these moves were welcomed by the population.

Government concerns over internal security continued into the
mid-1980s. In 1984 the House of Assembly enacted the Treason
Act and the State Security Act. The Treason Act mandated the
death penalty ''for any person who owes allegiance to the State
to form an intention to levy war against the State, or to overthrow
the Government by force of arms, if such intention is supported
by some overt act.'' In addition, the Treason Act denied bail to
anyone arrested under its provisions. The State Security Act stipulated prison sentences for those passing information to an enemy
or foreign power or harboring spies. Its most controversial clause
granted Dominicans the right to arrest—without a warrant—anyone
believed to be violating the State Security Act. The LPD strongly
criticized both measures as unconstitutional.

* * *

Lennox Honychurch's *The Dominica Story* offers an excellent historical overview of the island. Thomas Atwood's *History of the Island of Dominica* provides an account of the earliest recorded conditions in the colony, including graphic descriptions of the Caribs and the Arawaks, the flora and fauna, and the early colonial government. Extensive economic information can be found in the World Bank's *Dominica: Priorities and Prospects for Development.* Data on current political and social conditions in Dominica are available in several publications of the Institute of Social and Economic Research of the UWI and the CDB. (For further information and complete citations, see Bibliography.)

St. Lucia

Official Name . . . . St. Lucia

Term For Citizens . . . . St. Lucian(s)

Capital . . . . Castries

Political Status . . . . Independent, 1979

Form of Government . . . . Parliamentary democracy
and constitutional monarchy

Geography
Size . . . . 616 sq. km.
Topography . . . . Mountainous, rain forest in interior
Climate . . . . Tropical, wet

Population
Total estimated in 1986 140,000
Annual growth rate (in percentage) in 1986 . . . . 1.8
Life expectancy at birth in 1986 . . . . 72.5
Adult literacy rate (in percentage) in 1984 80
Language . . . . English; patois
Ethnic groups . . . . Black (90.5 percent), mulatto
(5.5 percent), East Indian (3.2 percent),
white (0.8 percent)
Religion . . . . Roman Catholic (85–90 percent);
remainder other religions

Economy
Currency; exchange rate . . . . Eastern Caribbean dollar
(EC$); EC$2.70 = US$1.00
Gross domestic product (GDP) in 1985 . . . US$146 million
Per capita GDP in 1985 . . . . US$1,071
Distribution of GDP (in percentage) in 1985
Government and other services 64
Agriculture 18
Manufacturing 10
Tourism 8

National Security
Armed forces personnel 0
Paramilitary personnel 80
Police 270

St. Lucia

St. Lucia is the second largest island of the British Lesser Antilles after Dominica. Located roughly in the center of the Windward Islands chain, it is nestled between Martinique to the north and St. Vincent and the Grenadines to the south. Castries, the capital city, is situated on the northwest coast and is known for its magnificent harbor. St. Lucia, said to be named for the patron saint of the day on which it was discovered, has an uncommon heritage of mixed cultural and historical influences, including Amerindian, European, and African.

St. Lucia was inhabited by the Carib Indians when sighted by the Spanish in the first decade of the sixteenth century (see The Pre-European Population, ch. 1). Many believe that Christopher Columbus viewed the island in 1502; however, the sighting is not accepted by all historians. St. Lucia remained uncolonized until the mid-seventeenth century. Earlier attempts by the English in 1605 and 1638 had met with disaster; would-be colonizers were either forced from the shores of the island or killed by its inhabitants. The first successful attempt at appeasing the Caribs followed the ceding of the island by the king of France to the French West Indian Company in 1642. Permanent French settlement occurred in 1660, after an armistice had been agreed to by the indigenous population.

St. Lucia, however, was not to enjoy a lengthy period of peace. Military conflicts among the Dutch, British, Spanish, and French, both on the European continent and in the colonies, resulted in St. Lucia's falling alternately under the control of France and Brittain fourteen different times in the eighteenth and early nineteenth centuries. During this period of constantly changing European alliances, both the British and the French sought control of St. Lucia for strategic purposes. The island's natural deep-water harbors afforded ready protection for military vessels and also served as an ideal location from which to monitor enemy military movements in the Caribbean.

The years surrounding the French Revolution were particularly violent ones in St. Lucia. Britain declared war on France following the French declaration of support for the American revolutionary effort in the late 1770s. The battle for control of St. Lucia continued intermittently throughout the rise and fall of the French Republic because possession of the sugar-producing islands of the Caribbean was considered essential for raising revenue to support the ongoing war in Europe. From 1793 until Napoleon's fall in

1815, St. Lucia was captured alternately by France and Britain no fewer than seven times. Although the French permanently ceded St. Lucia to the British in 1815, it was many years before the population, whose sympathies rested with the French, accepted British rule without internal conflict.

In contrast to all other British possessions in the Caribbean in the nineteenth century except for Trinidad, St. Lucia did not have a popularly elected local assembly (see Political Traditions, ch. 1). Instead, the British imposed crown colony government (see Glossary) on St. Lucia. The governor ruled the island in conjunction with an appointed Legislative Council. In the second half of the nineteenth century, the British extended crown colony government to all British Caribbean territories with the exception of Barbados.

The twentieth century saw St. Lucia's gradual transition to self-governance. Representative government was introduced in 1924, when a constitution was established; however, there was only incremental progress toward the development of a locally controlled political system for the next thirty-four years. In 1958 St. Lucia joined the short-lived West Indies Federation, which was dissolved by the British Parliament in 1962 (see The West Indies Federation, 1958–62, ch. 1).

Following the dissolution, St. Lucia immediately agreed to become an associated state (see Glossary) of Britain, which entailed a mutually sanctioned relationship that could be dissolved at any time by either party. St. Lucia was granted full control over its local government, and Britain retained responsibility for foreign affairs and national defense. This arrangement lasted until 1975, when members of the West Indies States Association chose to pursue independence at their discretion and convenience. Following three years of planning and deliberation, St. Lucia gained independence on February 22, 1979.

Geography

St. Lucia is one of many small land masses composing the insular group known as the Windward Islands (see fig. 1). Unlike large limestone areas such as Florida, Cuba, and the Yucatán Peninsula or the Bahamas, which is a small island group composed of coral and sand, St. Lucia is a typical Windward Islands formation of volcanic rock that came into existence long after much of the region had already been formed.

St. Lucia's physical features are strikingly beautiful. Dominated by high peaks and rain forests in the interior, the 616-square-kilometer island is known for the twin peaks of Gros Piton and Petit

Piton on the southwestern coast, its soft sandy beaches, and its magnificent natural harbors (see fig. 10). Mount Gimie, the highest peak, is located in the central mountain range and rises to 950 meters above sea level, a contrast that is also evident in the abrupt climatic transition from coastal to inland areas. The steep terrain also accentuates the many rivers that flow from central St. Lucia to the Caribbean. Fertile landholdings, which support banana farming, are scattered throughout the island.

St. Lucia has a tropical, humid climate moderated by northeast trade winds that allow for pleasant year-round conditions. Mean annual temperatures range from 26°C to 32°C at sea level and drop to an average of 13°C in the mountains. The abundant annual rainfall accumulates to approximately 200 centimeters. Most precipitation occurs during the June to December wet season. Hurricanes are the most severe climatic disturbance in this area and have been known to cause extensive damage. Although St. Lucia has historically been spared from serious hurricane destruction, Hurricane Allen decimated the agricultural sector and claimed nine lives in 1980.

Population

St. Lucia's population was estimated at 140,000 in 1986. It grew consistently at a relatively high annual rate of 1.8 percent in the 1980s. These figures would have been even higher had it not been for the steady emigration of adult workers in search of employment; nearly 2 percent of the population left the island each year.

St. Lucia had a population density of approximately 227 inhabitants per square kilometer in the late 1980s, almost evenly dispersed between urban and rural areas. This pattern was expected to change, however, because limited amounts of arable land caused residents to migrate to the cities and towns. The Pan American Health Organization (PAHO) estimated that there was a net annual internal migration to Castries of approximately 0.8 percent in 1984. This trend was expected to continue into the foreseeable future and to place the greatest burden on Castries and Vieux Fort.

St. Lucia's rapidly increasing population, caused by the country's young population and high fertility rate, placed an enormous stress on the society, which was already experiencing underemployment, a growing informal economic sector, and increased pressure on livable space in urban areas. Although emigration might ameliorate the population problem, observers in the 1980s believed that the government might have to develop a national birth control program similar to those in other Eastern Caribbean islands.

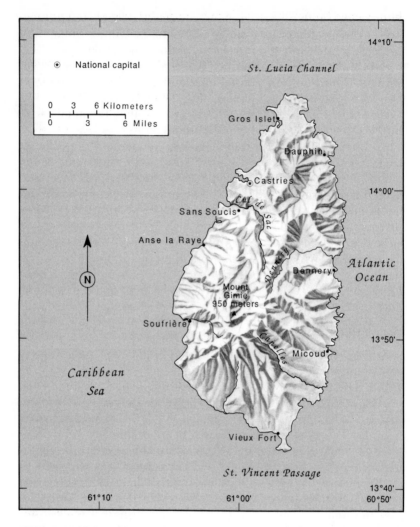

Figure 10. St. Lucia, 1987

Ethnically, St. Lucian society was homogeneous; 90.5 percent of the population was black. The balance of the population was mulatto (5.5 percent), East Indian (3.2 percent), or white (0.8 percent). The vast majority of St. Lucians were Roman Catholic; only 10 to 15 percent of the population practiced other religions. Nevertheless, St. Lucia was not as uniform a society as it appeared. Language remained a distinguishing characteristic and was the basis of social discrimination. The official language was English, and 80 percent of the population was considered literate in English.

However, a French creole language, or patois, was also commonly used, particularly in rural, interior portions of the country, and by lower socioeconomic groups throughout the country.

This linguistic dualism originated in the colonial period when St. Lucia was under the alternating stewardship of France and Britain. Linguistic influences at this time included those of the two European states, as well as the numerous African languages used by the slave population. The development of patois during the slavery period served two purposes. It facilitated communication between both the French and the slave population and among the various ethnolinguistic African groups, who often did not share a common language. Until St. Lucia became British, French and patois coexisted harmoniously and were used interchangeably by the middle and upper classes; the uneducated, however, particularly the slave population, communicated only in patois.

The British, as the dominant social, political, and economic group in the nineteenth and twentieth centuries, replaced French with English as the official language. English, however, lacked the common roots that French shared with patois, causing a clash of languages and cultures that previously had not existed. Although patois was replaced by English over time, it was still employed in some ceremonial functions. However, because patois continued to be associated with a sense of vulgarity and lack of culture and education, many St. Lucians hid their ability to communicate in it.

The effect of language on social status was still very pronounced. Those elements that did not speak English, comprising approximately 20 percent of the population, were excluded from the education system and hence unable to participate fully in political, economic, and social power sharing. The St. Lucian government recognized the problem and was attempting to incorporate this minority into the mainstream of society through language outreach programs. An improved infrastructure, especially an islandwide road network, was also bridging the gap between these two groups.

Observers believed that with time, English would be spoken by virtually the entire population, and as a result patois probably would become less influential even among the French descendants on the island. Nevertheless, it appeared unlikely that patois would disappear completely, given the fact that it was a symbol of cultural identity for many St. Lucians.

Education

The government of St. Lucia has made universal education a national priority. Although in the late 1980s a basic education still was not available to all members of society, government programs

297

had succeeded in bringing primary education to 80 percent of the population. Fulfilling all the educational requirements of the society, however, particularly the development of a work force capable of meeting the needs of a growing economy, remained an elusive goal.

Education in St. Lucia was free and compulsory from age five through age fifteen. In the 1980s, enrollment levels ran as high as 85 percent in the primary schools. Planning and operation of the school system were the responsibilities of the Ministry of Education and Culture. The ministry, which oversaw all primary, secondary, and postsecondary institutions, was considered professional and effective. The illiteracy rate remained high, at about 20 percent, and was a problem often attributed to the number of patois-speaking inhabitants who did not participate in the education system.

In 1985 the primary-school system included 82 schools, 35,000 students, and nearly 1,000 teachers, 35 percent of whom were considered trained. Although enrollment at the primary level was very high, many graduated without achieving basic skills in mathematics and English. A renewed effort at teaching English as a second language was developed at this level to hasten the assimilation of the patois-speaking population at an early age.

In 1985 there were eleven secondary schools in St. Lucia; six offered full secondary education programs, whereas the remainder provided a curriculum only through the junior secondary level. The schools were located in urban areas and provided education for approximately 3,100 students. As this number suggests, only one student in ten was able to continue education beyond the primary level. This situation had a profound impact on society, forcing some 2,000 to 3,000 new job seekers into the work force each year following completion of their primary education.

Postsecondary education was offered by four colleges and a regional technical training college for teachers operated under the auspices of the Commonwealth Fund for Technical Operations. St. Lucia's institutions of higher education included the Teacher's Training College, the Division of Technical Education and Management of the Sir Arthur Lewis Community College (formerly the Morne Fortune Technical College), the St. Lucia College of Agriculture, and the Sixth Form College. By late 1986, however, all postsecondary schools were being reorganized under the Sir Arthur Lewis Community College.

Although the number of teachers working in St. Lucia was growing and the upgrading of facilities continued at a steady pace, certain key problems still required attention. Space constraints prohibited the expansion of enrollments; advanced instruction for teachers was lacking, particularly at the primary level; and vocational programs needed to be added to the curriculum. In spite of the government's emphasis on educational development, the school system was not providing enough graduates at all levels to meet the societal needs of a developing country.

Health and Welfare

General health trends in St. Lucia improved noticeably in the 1980s. Life expectancy increased 4.5 percent from 1981 to 1986, the average for men and women rising to 72.5 years. The improvement in infant mortality rates was even more dramatic for the same time period. Infant deaths under 1 year of age fell from 25 per 1,000 live births to 17 per 1,000, representing a decline of 32 percent. The mortality rate for those over the age of 65 was reduced by 23 percent, and the overall mortality rate fell by 20 percent.

Indicators of morbidity were less well defined, but they suggested that strides had been made in eradicating the most common diseases. By 1984 a countrywide immunization program existed for six basic preventable diseases—diphtheria, pertussis, tetanus, poliomyelitis, tuberculosis, and measles—and other inoculation programs were being planned with the assistance of PAHO. The nutritional status of children under the age of five apparently also had improved, although definitive statistical evidence was lacking. Communicable diseases continued to be a major health problem, however, as evidenced by the increase in the incidence of venereal diseases. In 1986 PAHO reported three cases of acquired immune deficiency syndrome in St. Lucia.

Environmental health indicators were also encouraging. Approximately 75 percent of the population had basic sanitation facilities in 1985, and 85 percent of the population had access to piped water. Expansion of waste disposal facilities continued in 1985 and 1986, and government inspection of sewage treatment facilities, food-handling businesses, and schools brought corrective action in those areas.

The general improvement in the health situation was directly attributable to efforts by the government to enact a comprehensive health care system. A coordinated health care policy was developed with the assistance of the World Health Organization (WHO), PAHO, and numerous other organizations, including foundations and universities. Priority was given to primary health care delivery by a network of health clinics.

The health care system was directed by the Ministry of Health, which provided two basic kinds of health services free of charge:

preventive care and curative services. The former focused on prenatal, immunization, nutritional, and family planning programs, whereas the latter provided doctors and nurses to operate a network of health clinics. Government health services were offered throughout the country, which was divided into six health districts. The island had thirty-three health clinics, two district hospitals, two general hospitals, and one psychiatric hospital. The most complete facilities were located near Castries and Vieux Fort.

In an attempt to reach the entire population with some form of health care service, the Ministry of Health adopted a plan to train health care workers in various kinds of technical services to assist doctors and nurses with health care delivery. There were four kinds of health care representatives: community health aides, environmental health aides, family nurse practitioners, and community nutrition officers. As was evident in the structure of the health care system, the community health programs provided educational and preventive services, as well as actual hands-on health care. It was hoped that many health problems could be avoided by educating the population on nutrition, hygiene, and sanitation habits.

The success of St. Lucia's nutrition, immunization, health education, prenatal, and child health care programs was evident in the continued decline in morbidity and mortality rates, as well as the high population growth rate. Nevertheless, it was clear that a continued growth rate approaching 2 percent would place excessive constraints on the island's future health, employment opportunities, and quality of life. For these reasons, the Ministry of Health made reduction of fertility rates the health care priority of the late 1980s, targeting in particular the sexual behavior of adolescents.

In addition to health care programs, the government provided a social security system for workers who did not have a private pension plan. The National Insurance Scheme required workers to contribute a portion of their wages to be held for their retirement at age sixty-five, at which time they would receive regularly scheduled payments.

Economy

In the 1980s, St. Lucia's economy was similar to those of other small Eastern Caribbean islands. Its primary productive sectors were agriculture, tourism, and manufacturing, which provided 18 percent, 8 percent, and 10 percent of the gross domestic product (GDP—see Glossary), respectively, in 1985. Other significant contributors to aggregate economic output were government services (20 percent), wholesale and retail trade (14 percent), and transport and communications (10 percent). The national economy still

View of the twin peaks of
Gros Piton and Petit Piton
on the southwestern coast
Courtesy Michael Waddle

depended on the agricultural sector for most of its foreign exchange but had made gains in developing the manufacturing sector, as well as attracting a greater portion of the West Indies tourist trade. In sum, the economy performed well in the first half of the 1980s, a particularly impressive achievement considering that much of the island was devastated by Hurricane Allen in 1980.

The economy was open and highly dependent on foreign trade. It was, therefore, very susceptible to the international effects of the trade policies and economies of its two primary trading partners in the 1980s, the United States and Britain. Both countries were assisting the island with economic development.

In the 1980s, St. Lucia was implementing a long-term coordinated development program aimed at creating a diversified economic structure and gaining access to foreign markets. With extensive public sector investment, as well as private and public foreign assistance and investment, St. Lucia hoped to achieve sustained growth by expanding all of its primary economic sectors, particularly tourism and manufacturing.

Macroeconomic Overview

National economic production has experienced both structural change and growth since the 1960s. Traditionally dependent on agriculture, St. Lucia was dramatically transformed in the 1960s from a sugar-based economy to one dedicated to banana production.

301

This trend improved the economic situation of the small farmer because banana crops, unlike sugar, could be produced on small plots.

The economy experienced very little growth in 1980–81 because of hurricane damage and a disruptive political climate that temporarily hampered the country's ability to attract investment capital. Economic performance began to improve in 1982; within two years, real GDP had grown by 4.9 percent, a particularly impressive achievement because it was led by the agricultural sector with strong support from both tourism and construction. Manufacturing was the only sector not to share in economic growth, largely because of regional trade restrictions. This trend continued in 1985; manufacturing output as a percentage of GDP declined by 17 percent.

Employment was largely stimulated by the agricultural sector, which absorbed 40 percent of the work force in 1985. Manufacturing accounted for 8 percent, tourism 12 percent, construction 4 percent, and other services 36 percent. Government estimates of unemployment for 1986 ranged between 18 and 20 percent.

The structure of employment, however, was in the process of changing. Most arable land was already under production, restricting the agricultural sector from absorbing many of the 2,000 to 3,000 new job seekers who entered the employment market each year. Tourism and manufacturing were expected to absorb much of the future work force, but many of the unemployed would have to seek work elsewhere. The government planned to take an active role by promoting investment in manufacturing and tourism and adjusting the education system so that it would provide appropriately trained workers for these two sectors.

Employment patterns did not always exhibit a logical relationship to wages and prices in the mid-1980s. Although unemployment persisted in the 18- to 25-percent range, wages continued to climb, with no apparent relationship to productivity or inflation. The latter was below 2 percent in 1985. The World Bank (see Glossary) noted that wage increases would have to be curtailed if St. Lucia were to remain regionally competitive.

Price stability in St. Lucia has been affected primarily by inflationary trends in the United States and Britain. In the 1980s, St. Lucian trade was exceedingly dependent on the markets and prices of these two economies. The United States and Britain accounted for 50 percent of all St. Lucian imports and 73 percent of its exports in 1984. In addition, the purchasing power of the Eastern Caribbean dollar—the currency shared by members of the Organisation of Eastern Caribbean States (OECS—see Glossary) since July 1970 and pegged to the United States dollar at EC$2.70 equals

US$1.00—had been influenced by the performance of the United States dollar in world currency markets because they were tied so closely together. These influences, however, did not significantly raise the St. Lucian general price level in the mid-1980s.

Role of Government

The government of St. Lucia has been a leading force in the development of the national economy, in spite of its emphasis on private sector initiative. Government support of the private sector has materialized in two forms: direct government action by supporting public sector investment and indirect assistance through national economic policy tools.

In the late 1980s, public sector investment reflected the joint economic goals of the public and private sectors, emphasizing aggregate economic growth through diversification and export promotion. This was accomplished by soliciting external funds, primarily grants, and managing their investment with assistance from the World Bank, Caribbean Development Bank (CDB), United States Agency for International Development, and other government and multilateral development organizations.

Public investment funds reached all areas of the economy in 1984; 51 percent went to productive sectors (agriculture, tourism, and manufacturing), 33 percent to social sectors (housing, health, and education), and 16 percent to physical infrastructure (primarily secondary and feeder roads). Specific projects included providing factory space, developing a viable fisheries industry, diversifying small-farmer crop production, and upgrading road maintenance capabilities.

Improvements to communications and transportation were extensive in the 1980s. The fully automatic telephone system consisted of 9,500 instruments; international service was accomplished by radio relay to Martinique and St. Vincent and by tropospheric scatter to Barbados. The government-owned St. Lucia Broadcasting Corporation operated an AM transmitter in Castries on 660 kilohertz; a commercial station also broadcast on 840 kilohertz. The island had no television transmitters, although cable television was available in some localities. The *Crusader* and the *Voice of St. Lucia* were the two local newspapers.

Transportation infrastructure on the island was considered fair in the late 1980s. Although St. Lucia had approximately 500 kilometers of paved highways and another 260 kilometers of gravel roads, travel was usually slow because of the steep and winding terrain. The main road cut across the island south of Castries and circled the southern two-thirds of the island. A paved spur extended

303

from Castries to the northern tip. The northeast and interior portions of the island had almost no roads. The principal airport was Hewanorra International Airport (formerly Beane Field, built by the United States during World War II), located on the southern tip of the island near Vieux Fort; the airport's runway was extended in the 1980s to handle regularly scheduled international flights. Vigie Airport, an older airfield on the northern edge of the capital, was the site of a shuttle service to Hewanorra International Airport. Castries was the island's major port, although smaller vessels also put in at Vieux Fort. St. Lucia had no railroads or usable waterways.

Direct government support of economic development was coordinated by five organizations: the National Development Corporation, St. Lucian Development Bank, Agricultural Market Board, St. Lucian Tourist Board, and Banana Growers' Association. Working collectively, these associations provided the planning and administrative expertise to attract investment funds, ensure their appropriate use, and facilitate the marketing of final products both domestically and abroad.

By directing public funds to specific projects, the government also used fiscal policy to encourage economic growth. Government spending accounted for much of the infrastructural development, including improvements to roads and communications facilities, which had a beneficial impact on both tourism and agriculture. This strategy resulted in a national budget deficit, but it appeared that the deficit was accepted as necessary to accommodate national economic growth.

Although deficit spending is a common tool for encouraging economic development, the resultant fiscal problems have become a reality in St. Lucia, as in much of the developing world. Total deficit spending rose from 2.5 percent of GDP in 1982 to 6.5 percent in 1985, reflecting excessive investment in the public sector and poor performance in revenue collection. Increases in government salaries, financing of government projects, and interest payments on public debt were the largest expenditure items. Budget overruns were financed through short-term loans from commercial banks; foreign borrowing was restricted to loans from the CDB. St. Lucia's debt service ratio remained small at 4 percent of exports in 1985, but it was expected to increase in the future.

Continued deficit spending could pose major problems for St. Lucia. Observers in the mid-1980s suggested that the future burden of debt financing, even with a renewed high level of economic growth, could affect the economy adversely in the long run if an adjustment in government spending were not made. Given St.

Lucia's limited borrowing capacity and high domestic tax rates, the World Bank believed that restraint in future expenditures was the only logical fiscal option for achieving a balanced budget. A realignment of the budget was also being sought to provide more funds for capital expenditures as opposed to increases in public salaries. Capital budgets historically were overly dependent on foreign sources of revenue.

Fiscal constraints were also evident on the revenue side of the budget. Although the majority of current revenue came from domestic taxes, fully 31 percent was provided by foreign sources. Approximately 60 percent of this amount was grants from foreign countries and institutions, and the remaining 40 percent was borrowed from international and regional financial institutions, usually the CDB. This situation subjected St. Lucia's budget to the vicissitudes of foreign interests, a situation the government sought to minimize.

Sectoral Performance

Although St. Lucia's public and private services sectors contributed nearly one-half of GDP, the island's primary productive sectors were similar to other Windward Islands economies and included agriculture, manufacturing, and tourism. Agriculture, focused on export and food crops as well as on the production of raw materials for use in local manufacturing, continued to be a primary economic undertaking. In addition to providing needed consumable products, agriculture earned foreign exchange and provided employment opportunities for 40 percent of the population. Agriculture accounted for 67.5 percent of total exports in 1984.

The principal crops were bananas and coconuts. Bananas were grown on 6 percent of the total land area, or 70 percent of the arable land. They directly and indirectly supported approximately half of the island's population and constituted 83 percent of total agricultural exports in 1984. Most bananas were grown in small plots and supported a peasant farming system. Virtually all bananas were sold by the BGA to Britain's Geest Industries, which consistently procured most of the banana crop grown throughout the West Indies. Export volume varied greatly from year to year because of the crop's sensitivity to weather, pests, and disease.

Coconuts were the second most important crop and were sold mainly as copra. Because of the presence of the coconut mite, however, yields were minimal in the early 1980s. St. Lucia also grew various kinds of fruits and vegetables. These crops served the dual purpose of meeting some of the island's nutritional requirements and supporting the tourist trade.

In 1985 the government showed an interest in developing a fishing industry. St. Lucia had the potential to meet more of its domestic food needs, 20 percent of which was imported, by increasing the fish harvest. It lacked, however, the requisite boats and storage facilities outside the Castries area.

Although agricultural output had grown in the 1980s, certain areas still required improvement. Available agricultural credit could not match demand, and control of diseases and pests was still a problem. In spite of improvements in the physical infrastructure, continued feeder-road development was needed for quicker movement of produce to markets. Furthermore, a revamping of the land tenure code, based informally on French legal tradition, was essential to clarify ownership rights. Joint and multiple landownership based on family inheritance laws and the lack of authoritative titles obstructed the issuance of bank credit and often led to fragmented farm holdings.

Manufacturing was a growing sector of the economy in 1984, but it represented only 9.6 percent of GDP. Nevertheless, the diversity of manufacturing firms was large for a small economy and included paper and fabricated metal products, textiles, beer, furniture, industrial chemicals, and electronic components.

The government was attempting to develop manufacturing industries that supported other elements of the economy, stressing the use of local resources as much as possible. In addition, the government tried to ensure that the investment climate would be hospitable and protective of both domestic and foreign capital. Continued success of the manufacturing sector, however, would depend on St. Lucia's ability to obtain sufficient regional export markets for its goods.

St. Lucia has been successful in attracting manufacturing firms because of improvements made to the island's physical infrastructure in the 1980s. Roads, energy sources, and communications all progressed dramatically to the benefit of tourism and agriculture as well as of manufacturing. Investment incentives, such as tax holidays and generous profit repatriation laws, also encouraged the inflow of foreign capital. The largest single foreign investment project was a United States project, the Amerada Hess Company oil storage and transshipment terminal, where oil was held for shipping at a later date. In 1985 the project provided US$2 million in tax revenue for the public sector and also created employment opportunities for the private sector.

Future manufacturing growth was planned for the southern portion of the island. This region offered empty, flat tracts of land, proximity to the Hewanorra International Airport, and expanded

View of Soufrière
Courtesy Michael Waddle

port facilities at Vieux Fort. The development of the area was in keeping with the government's goals of diminishing congestion in the Castries area and expanding the country's manufacturing base.

Tourism's role as a major foreign exchange earner began only in the late 1970s. By 1984 total annual receipts from tourism reached US$42.4 million, more than double the amount generated seven years earlier. Continued growth was expected for the late 1980s. Although tourism's direct contribution to total GDP was only 7.3 percent in 1984, it also contributed indirectly to aggregate economic output by providing revenue to the wholesale and retail trade, banking, and transportation sectors.

Although there are many national tourist attractions in St. Lucia, growth in tourist receipts in the 1980s was the direct result of efforts by the national government to enact a national tourist development program. This included creating a tourist board, providing incentives to build and maintain hotels, and improving the physical infrastructure.

Regardless of the potential for a strong tourist trade, St. Lucia was still experiencing problems in the development of this industry. Coordinating government incentives and private sector investment was a complicated task, as was the containment of costs in a highly competitive regional market. St. Lucia was making strides in this area, but the World Bank noted that it still needed to improve its tourist position by making better use of local resources and by developing additional recreational alternatives.

Foreign Trade and Balance of Payments

With only a small domestic market at its disposal, in the 1980s St. Lucia's economy relied heavily on external trade. Primary merchandise exports were bananas, copra, fruits, vegetables, beer, paper products, and clothing; they accounted for 48.9 percent of total foreign exchange earnings from goods and services in 1984. Tourism and services contributed an additional 27.5 percent of foreign exchange earnings. St. Lucia's principal imports consisted of food, fuels, chemicals, manufactured goods, machinery, and transportation equipment, which accounted for 92.7 percent of total imports for 1984.

St. Lucia's largest export market was Britain, which purchased 57.6 percent of total goods and services sold abroad in 1984. Britain was followed by the Caribbean Community and Common Market (Caricom—see Appendix C) and the United States, which absorbed 23.7 percent and 16 percent, respectively, of St. Lucian exports. The United States provided the largest share of imports, supplying 36.7 percent of the total in 1984. Caricom and Britain provided 16.9 percent and 13.1 percent, respectively, of total imports.

St. Lucia's balance of payments position was not unusual for a developing country in the 1980s. It continually showed deficits in the merchandise trade (goods) and current account (goods and services) balances, with almost offsetting surpluses in the capital (foreign investment, loans, and grants) account. The figures reflected St. Lucia's negative trade balance, primarily the result of the need for expensive capital goods required for economic growth and development. The situation also was a consequence of the extensive number of grants provided to the island to bolster the finances needed to purchase those goods.

The current account had traditionally shown a deficit in the merchandise trade account and a surplus in the services account (tourism). Since 1977 the value of imports had been more than double that of exports because of a domestic demand for imported food, fuels, machinery, and manufactured goods. Tourism helped offset the trade imbalance, reducing the overall current account deficit.

St. Lucia's trading position was further weakened by regional trade barriers. Although Trinidad and Tobago accounted for 9 percent of regional imports in the form of fuels in 1985, that country simultaneously erected barriers against many of St. Lucia's exports.

Furthermore, restrictions on certain exports to the United States, such as textiles, also contributed to the negative trade balance. The capital account in the 1980s continued to show a surplus, principally because of project-related grants and direct private foreign investment. The 1984 balance, however, had declined by 40 percent since 1980 because of dwindling private direct investment, especially on the part of the Amerada Hess Company.

From 1982 to the late 1980s, the overall balance of payments deficit was relatively small, running near or less than US$1 million. Financing of the deficit was usually accomplished with loans from the Eastern Caribbean Central Bank (ECCB), the common central bank for members of the OECS, but International Monetary Fund (IMF—see Glossary) lending was significant in 1981 and 1982. Although the balance of payments deficit and debt financing were still manageable for St. Lucia, observers noted that any abrupt changes in the national economy could push lending above easily controlled levels. St. Lucia's ability to manage its balance of payments, minimize its foreign debt, develop its national economy, and attract foreign assistance will have a strong impact on the country's chances for avoiding the major economic problems experienced by other developing countries.

Government and Politics

Although St. Lucia is a country of many cultural influences, the island's political origins are distinctly British. Following the turmoil of intermittent French and British rule in the early colonial period, St. Lucia eventually assumed a fundamentally British political orientation. By the time independence was achieved in 1979, St. Lucia had abandoned most other political influences, with the exception of certain family and property laws inherited from the French.

The Governmental System

St. Lucia inherited a democratic political tradition, rooted in the legitimacy of constitutional rule and parliamentary governance. At independence, it adopted a Westminster-style parliamentary system, which provided a framework for the orderly transition of governments and established a tradition of minimal political upheaval, in spite of the existence of strong, conflicting political interests.

St. Lucia is governed by the 1979 Constitution, which went into effect at the time of independence. It guarantees citizens certain rights, including the right to life and personal property; protection from slavery, deprivation of property, arbitrary search, and discrimination; and freedom of expression, assembly, and movement.

Formally, St. Lucia is a constitutional monarchy; nominal executive authority rests with the British sovereign, who rules through his or her chief administrator, the governor general. The government operates as a parliamentary democracy, in which power is shared by the prime minister and a bicameral legislature.

The prime minister, although formally appointed by the governor general, rules as the leader of the majority party in Parliament. Other ministerial posts, as decreed by Parliament, are filled by the governor general on the advice of the prime minister. All ministers are members of Parliament.

Parliament comprises two chambers, the Senate and the House of Assembly. The Senate is composed of eleven members. All are appointed by the governor general, six on the advice of the prime minister, three on the advice of the leader of the opposition, and two at the sole discretion of the governor general. The House is elected by universal suffrage; each legally formed constituency is allowed one representative. In the late 1980s, there were seventeen representatives. A speaker and deputy speaker of the House are elected at the first meeting of Parliament. A leader of the opposition is appointed by the governor general to represent leadership for all parties other than the majority party.

Parliament is convened for a period of time not to exceed five years. It may be dissolved at the discretion of the governor general if the prime minister so advises under the laws of the Constitution or if a resolution of no confidence is passed by the House. Elections are to be held within three months of the dissolution of Parliament.

The primary duties of Parliament consist of making laws and amending the Constitution as necessary. The latter action requires a two-thirds vote of the House. Bills may be introduced into the House or Senate with the exception of money bills, which may originate only in the House of Assembly. A money bill includes any action regarding taxation or the spending or borrowing of public funds.

The Constitution also provides for two important commissions composed of parliamentary representatives, the Constituency Boundary Commission and the Electoral Commission. The former delineates boundaries in St. Lucia to be used to define electoral constituencies, of which there were seventeen in the late 1980s. Each constituency is represented by one member in the House. The Electoral Commission defines electoral procedures.

St. Lucia has sixteen parishes that form the basis of local govern-ment. Regional elections are held to select officials responsible for many of the local services, such as sanitation and maintenance of secondary roads.

St. Lucia's legal structure derives from English common law and is administered by an independent court system. There are dis-trict courts throughout the island. Appeals may be made to the Eastern Caribbean States Supreme Court, which is composed of the High Court and the Court of Appeal. The High Court tradi-tionally hears cases concerning basic rights and freedoms, as well as constitutional interpretations. A final appeal may be made to the Judicial Committee of the Privy Council in London. The prison system is managed by the Superintendent of Prisons under the Ministry of Social Affairs.

Political Dynamics

Political control of Parliament in the 1980s remained firmly in the hands of John G. M. Compton and the United Workers' Party (UWP). There were, however, two other political parties contending for parliamentary representation, the St. Lucia Labour Party (SLP) and the Progressive Labour Party (PLP), a relatively new party formed from a disaffected group of the SLP in 1982. The SLP was the only other party to have won control of Parliament since in-dependence.

The UWP, founded in 1964, held a majority in Parliament from 1964 until 1979 and again beginning in 1982. Compton has been the political leader since its inception and held the office of prime minister after 1982. The UWP was the most conservative of the three parties, but it had a long history of moderate economic and political policies that were widely supported by the island's voting constituency in the 1982 elections. These included support for so-cial development, such as improved education and health standards, and sound economic development founded on a capitalist-based economy stressing tourism and the expansion of the manufactur-ing sector with both foreign and domestic capital. Although sup-port for the UWP fell in the 1987 elections, it was not a clear refutation of the party's platform, but rather a general lack of response to the elections. Foreign policy goals of the UWP were directed primarily at continuing support for economic development by maintaining strong trade relationships and attracting grants for development projects. These foreign policy goals supported close ties with St. Lucia's traditional allies, the United States, Britain, and the Caricom countries.

311

The SLP, which dates back to 1950 and is the country's oldest existing political party, controlled Parliament from 1951 until 1964 and won the first postindependence election in July 1979. It has been the minority party, however, since 1982. The SLP's fundamental political and economic positions have been more liberal than those of the UWP. The SLP developed an electoral platform for 1987 that advocated closer relations with nonaligned countries and Cuba and suggested reevaluating St. Lucia's traditional support for the United States. Economically, the SLP promoted a stronger role for local entrepreneurs and capital in order to limit foreign investment as a controlling element of the economy. It proposed to accomplish its program by giving government a greater role in providing location and financing for the development of locally owned small businesses. Additionally, the SLP advocated diversifying the agricultural sector in order to meet local food needs through import substitution.

The radical PLP was created as a dissenting alternative during an SLP party leadership crisis in 1982. Headed by George Odlum, a former minister of foreign affairs and deputy political leader for the SLP, it has been the smallest parliamentary minority since its founding. The PLP took a very strong line against United States policies in the Caribbean, but it lacked a coordinated economic platform.

In the late 1980s, political interests also were upheld by trade unions. Unions represented about 20 percent of the work force and as a result were able to influence national politics and economics. Political parties had to consider the interests of union constituencies very carefully when developing a political agenda. In the past, general strikes had been employed to force changes in the prime minister's office, and they could be coordinated very quickly if an opposition consensus was found.

The largest unions, which had a combined membership of approximately 10,000 workers, were the Farmers' and Farm Workers' Union, National Workers' Union, St. Lucia Workers' Union, and Seamen and Waterfront Workers' Union. Other unions with some influence on St. Lucian politics were the St. Lucia Civil Servants' Association, St. Lucia Nurses' Association, St. Lucia Teachers' Union, and Vieux Fort General and Dock Workers' Union.

The dynamics of political interaction between trade unions and political parties was evident in the first two elections following independence. Labor played a key role in the election of SLP leader Allen Louisy in 1979; it also forced the party from office in 1982, however, largely because of its united stand against the divisive internal politics of the SLP leadership. A series of political moves

caused by feuding factions within the SLP actually led to the resignation of the party's prime minister in 1981 and brought to power
the attorney general, Winston Cenac. Because Cenac refused to
hold general elections as he promised, public outcry, led predominantly by labor groups, eventually turned into widespread protests
and a general strike. Cenac finally resigned in January 1982; he
was replaced by Michael Pilgrim, who essentially served as a
caretaker prime minister until the May 1982 general election.

Compton and the UWP ran a strong election campaign, espousing the return of economic growth, private investment, expanded
tourism, and diversification of the agricultural sector. Because of
the previous Parliament's inability to govern effectively and the
poor economic performance of the country in 1980–81 immediately following Hurricane Allen, the UWP captured a resounding
majority of fourteen seats and took firm control of government for
the next five years.

From 1982 until the next general election of April 6, 1987, St.
Lucia enjoyed relative economic success and continued political
stability. As the 1987 elections neared, preliminary reports by jour-
nalists and international observers speculated that the UWP would
be returned to power with another strong parliamentary majority. The 1987 elections, however, surprised all parties.

Although Compton remained prime minister, he did so with only
a single seat majority in Parliament. The UWP won only nine seats;
all others were captured by the SLP. A lack of substantive political issues, poor voter turnout, and a generally complacent attitude
among UWP supporters were considered the primary reasons for
the ruling party's loss of five seats in Parliament.

In an unprecedented move, Prime Minister Compton called for
new elections to be held on April 30, 1987. The prime minister
hoped to increase his majority position in Parliament by engen-
dering greater voter turnout for the second electoral contest.
Although the subsequent election produced a hotly contested seat
on the eastern side of the island, the voters returned the identical
candidates to office.

After Compton declared that he would accept the results, the
SLP's Cenac crossed over to the UWP in June 1987. The action
gave Compton a parliamentary majority of ten to seven. Cenac
was rewarded with the foreign minister's post, but he was formally
dismissed from the SLP. The election marked Compton's third
time as prime minister following the granting of independence in
February 1979. The Compton government, however, expected increasing opposition in its attempt to legislate the UWP platform
in the second half of the 1980s.

Foreign Relations

St. Lucia's foreign policy was firmly rooted in its historical association with Britain and culturally and economically linked to the goals of its Commonwealth Caribbean neighbors. The island's orientation was apparent in St. Lucia's close economic and political ties with Britain, as well as in its goal of a unified Caribbean based on strong support for Caricom.

St. Lucia's historical association with Britain dates back to the early nineteenth century and has significantly influenced the island's political and economic foreign policy. In addition to inheriting a British political system and attendant foreign policy outlook, St. Lucia continued to rely on Britain as its primary export market in the 1980s. These factors combined to instill a strong sense of cooperative spirit and sympathy for the foreign policies of Britain and other Commonwealth countries.

This shared outlook was particularly evident among the Caricom countries. Because they had experienced a fairly similar colonial heritage and also recognized the benefit of a unified position in dealing with larger states, Caricom's foreign policy predominantly represented the united foreign policies of individual members. This consensus was evident as early as 1975 with the presentation of a unified Caricom position at the first Lomé Convention (see Glossary), which established guidelines for improved trade relations between the European Economic Community and Third World countries. When St. Lucia became an active member of Caricom, it also linked its foreign policy goals, at least informally, with those of other Commonwealth Caribbean countries.

In spite of similarities in colonial heritage and external goals among many of the Caribbean islands, there were also elements of disunity in the region's foreign affairs. The lack of unity was most evident in the competitive nature of regional economic relations. The Caribbean economies were alike in that they all relied on exporting agricultural and light manufactured products, as well as attracting large numbers of tourists. Such similarities led to contention in foreign relations, as each country competed for the same foreign markets. The creation of Caricom in 1973 from earlier organizations responsible for regional integration was an attempt to recognize historical and geographical similarities, while also providing a forum for voicing regional disagreements. Caricom's attempts to achieve mutually beneficial foreign economic, political, and security goals have served to unite the area.

In the 1980s, St. Lucia's foreign policy, overall, was considered pragmatic and generally focused on meeting national goals within the framework of supporting regional and international alliances. It maintained formal relations with such politically diverse countries as Cuba and the United States and was a member of the Nonaligned Movement. St. Lucia had, however, adopted ardent national positions on important international issues. It was strongly opposed to the apartheid policies of South Africa and very supportive of arms control, as well as economic and security cooperation among the Caribbean states. Because of its political and security concerns, St. Lucia promoted regional cooperation and stability. The island, for example, supported the Regional Security System (RSS) and the deployment of United States and Caribbean forces to Grenada in 1983 (see A Regional Security System, ch. 7).

In the late 1980s, economic concerns were at the forefront of St. Lucian foreign affairs. Such concerns were evident in the Compton government's desire to promote free trade and to attract foreign investment. St. Lucia was a strong advocate of regional free trade, in part because trade barriers had contributed to its current account deficit. The island also supported a united Caricom position regarding extraregional trade; St. Lucia actively pursued a policy of attracting foreign capital as a way of promoting economic development. The government, for example, provided incentives to foreign private capital and attempted to attract financial assistance from regional and international development organizations.

St. Lucia's bilateral foreign relations were dominated by other Eastern Caribbean countries, the United States, and Britain. St. Lucia also maintained affiliations with the primary regional and international development organizations, including the CDB, World Bank, Organization of American States (OAS), IMF, WHO, and United Nations (UN). St. Lucia's development program welcomed a strong role for all of these groups.

St. Lucia was a signatory to major international and regional treaties. Obligations included mutual provisions regarding defense, extradition, investment guarantees, consular representation, telecommunications licensing, reciprocal protection of trademarks, and waivers of visa requirements with the United States and Britain. St. Lucia also adhered to responsibilities inherent in membership with the UN, OAS, and OECS.

The foreign policy apparatus exhibited a structural flexibility. Responsibility for formulation of foreign policy may be the sole duty of the prime minister or delegated to a subordinate parliamentarian. From 1982 until 1987, foreign policy was directed by Prime Minister Compton. As noted, he turned the portfolio over to Cenac after the second round of elections in April 1987. Compton took the action more to strengthen his parliamentary majority than because of a need to diminish his administrative responsibilities.

Foreign policy was conducted through the Ministry of Foreign Affairs, which had responsibility for operating embassies. Foreign economic affairs were also conducted by the National Development Corporation.

National Security

In the late 1980s, internal security in St. Lucia was directly related to regional security and foreign policy concerns. As a member of the OECS, St. Lucia had established police and paramilitary capabilities within the framework of the regional security plan developed by the newly independent Caribbean states. Like its Eastern Caribbean neighbors, St. Lucia had no means of guaranteeing national defense or internal security when independence was granted. The sovereign state of St. Lucia was literally incapable of ensuring its protection from either hostile external forces or violent internal political dissension. The creation of the OECS provided a forum for discussion of regional security in the Caribbean. The Defence and Security Committee of the OECS made initial suggestions on a collective regional approach to security matters, but no operating force was established. This discussion evolved into the RSS in October 1982. St. Lucia opposed original plans for an integrated regional army to be stationed in Barbados and instead favored a decentralized special forces approach to national and regional security.

The RSS program called for the eventual creation of Special Service Units (SSUs) within the respective national police organizations. Training and some basic matériel for this paramilitary program were provided by the United States and Britain; the former concentrated on miliary tactics, and the latter provided comprehensive training in police measures. The formation of the SSUs created the possibility for limited military response to hostilities within the framework of a police organization. RSS member states believed that such an organization would substitute for an armed force that it was thought would see little military use and might someday threaten the normal operation of national politics.

The Royal St. Lucia Police Force, the country's only armed force, was primarily responsible for enforcing the laws of the country rather than guaranteeing national defense. The Constitution calls for the commissioner of police to be appointed by the governor general based on the advice of the Public Service Commission. The commission may only make a recommendation subject to the approval of the prime minister. The Public Service Commission may also appoint police officials above the rank of inspector, whereas the commissioner of police makes all appointments below that level.

The police force grew marginally in the 1980s out of concern for regional defense responsibilities. In 1987 total strength stood at approximately 350 personnel; the development of an 80-member SSU program was an outward indication of the force's expanded role. The impetus for this growth came from heightened concern over regional stability, specifically the 1979 rise of a hostile regime in Grenada.

The RSS saw military action shortly after it was created. In October 1983, at the invitation of OECS countries, a combined United States and Caribbean security force landed troops in Grenada to counter the Marxist-Leninist government that came to power following the assassination of Prime Minister Maurice Bishop. The RSS, including a contingent from St. Lucia, constituted approximately 10 percent of the total force deployed to Grenada (see Current Strategic Considerations, ch. 7).

Training of the RSS by the United States and Britain accelerated after the Grenada intervention. The first postintervention group to graduate in early 1984 included troops from St. Lucia who were sent to Grenada as part of the Caribbean Peace Force. Training involved rudimentary military skills, including the use of automatic weapons, light machine guns, and grenade launchers. Later, combined forces training was conducted under the auspices of the United States and Britain; St. Lucia provided the site for the 1985 joint military exercise.

In 1986 the role of the RSS was once again reevaluated. An October 1986 meeting in St. Lucia of RSS ministers proved inconclusive on the issues of the mission and goals of the Caribbean armed forces. Although some states wanted to see an expanded RSS, St. Lucia supported only a limited military posture and maintained only a minimal paramilitary capability. In the late 1980s, it seemed likely that the development of an armed force in St. Lucia would continue to parallel developments in the RSS as a whole; it appeared unlikely, however, that the Royal St. Lucia Police Force would greatly expand its paramilitary force in either size or capabilities.

*   *   *

A comprehensive source on St. Lucia was not available as of late 1987. A discussion of St. Lucia's history and cultural background may be found in Philip M. Sherlock's *West Indian Nations: A New History,* John H. Parry and Sherlock's *A Short History of the West Indies,* and Carleen O'Loughlin's *Economic and Political Change in the Leeward and Windward Islands.* Data on population, health, and education are to be found in publications by the United States Agency for International Development, as well as the Pan American Health Organization's *Health Conditions in the Americas, 1981-1984* and the St. Lucia Ministry of Health's *Progress Report on Health Conditions.* A useful general reference on comparative Caribbean economics is the 1985 edition of the *Caribbean Economic Handbook* by Peter D. Fraser and Paul Hackett. Specific economic data may be drawn from the World Bank's country study *St. Lucia: Economic Performance and Prospects,* as well as from annual reports by the ECCB and the Caribbean Development Bank. St. Lucia's annual *Budget Address* also provides useful insights into the economy. Comprehensive political and foreign affairs analyses specifically dedicated to St. Lucia are sadly lacking. (For further information and complete citations, see Bibliography.)

St. Vincent and the Grenadines

Official Name .... St. Vincent and the Grenadines

Term for Citizens .... Vincentian(s)

Capital .... Kingstown

Political Status .... Independent, 1979

Form of Government .... Parliamentary democracy
and constitutional monarchy

Geography
Size .... 389 sq. km.
Topography .... Mountainous; windward side
gently sloping, leeward side rugged
Climate .... Tropical, wet

Population
Total estimated in 1985 110,000
Annual growth rate (in percentage) in 1973–83 .... 1.2
Life expectancy at birth in 1986 65
Adult literacy rate (in percentage) in 1986 82
Language .... English, some patois
Ethnic groups .... Black (65.5 percent), mulatto
(19 percent), East Indian (5.5 percent),
white (3.5 percent), Amerindian (2 percent),
other (4.5 percent)
Religion .... Anglican (47 percent), Methodist
(28 percent), Roman Catholic (13 percent);
remainder other Christian denominations,
Hindu, or Rastafarian

Economy
Currency; exchange rate .... Eastern Caribbean
dollar (EC$); EC$2.70 = US$1.00
Gross domestic product (GDP) in 1985 ... US$102 million
Per capita GDP in 1985 .... US$930
Distribution of GDP (in percentage) in 1985
Agriculture 17.7
Industry 15.4

Manufacturing 10.5
Tourism 2.0
Other 54.4

National Security
Armed forces personnel 0
Paramilitary personnel 80
Police 490

St. Vincent and the Grenadines

St. Vincent and the Grenadines, a West Indian island nation whose most conspicuous feature may well be its diminutive geographic and demographic size, was a stable, democratic state whose cultural, linguistic, and religious traditions had been influenced by constant political turnover in the first 300 years of its existence as a colonial territory.

Evidence suggests that the island of St. Vincent was discovered by Christopher Columbus in 1498, and legend fixes the date of discovery as January 22, St. Vincent's feast day. Columbus claimed the island for the Spanish monarchs; however, the strength of the native Carib presence prevented immediate colonization and retarded settlement by any European nation until the late seventeenth century (see The Pre-European Population, ch. 1). The British managed to settle the island by making treaties with the Caribs, but the French vied for control during the Seven Years' War (1756–63). St. Vincent was formally ceded to Britain by the Treaty of Paris in 1763 (see Political Traditions, ch. 1). France also lost most of the Grenadine Islands to Britain at the conclusion of the war.

During the next hundred years, the islands continued to change hands. Although the Caribs permitted St. Vincent to be divided between themselves and the British in 1773, the island was recaptured by the French in 1779. It was restored to Britain in 1783 by the Treaty of Versailles. Increasingly resentful of British sovereignty, the Caribs revolted and overran the island in 1795 with French assistance. The British subdued the Caribs by the following year and deported most of them to British Honduras (present-day Belize) in 1797. Some of the Grenadine Islands remained under French hegemony much longer, and they still retain a strong French cultural, architectural, and linguistic influence.

The islands sustained numerous sugar plantations in the nineteenth century. Africans were imported to work in the cane fields until slavery was abolished in 1834 (see The Post-Emancipation Societies, ch. 1). East Indians and Portuguese arrived soon afterward to alleviate the shortage of labor in the agricultural sector. When the world price of sugar fell in the mid-1800s, the islands suffered a depression that endured through the turn of the century. A hurricane in 1898 and a volcanic eruption in 1902 also hindered economic recovery for many years.

Although the British established a joint government of several Windward Islands colonies in 1764, St. Vincent withdrew from this union in 1776 and was granted the right to have its own

representative assembly. In 1877, however, the British imposed
crown colony government (see Glossary). From the mid-nineteenth
through the mid-twentieth century, the islands of St. Vincent and
the Grenadines were affiliated with other Windward Islands in
numerous associations ordained or encouraged by Britain, the last
of which was the West Indies Federation (see The West Indies Federation, 1958–62, ch. 1). As a result of political fragmentation
among the islands, each of the associations failed, and St. Vincent
and the Grenadine Islands reverted to colonial status under the
administration of the British crown. Many of the former West Indies
Federation states gained associated state (see Glossary) status in
1967; however, internal political differences delayed St. Vincent
and the Grenadines from acquiring associated statehood until October 27, 1969. Under the terms of this arrangement, which merged
St. Vincent and the northern Grenadine Islands into a single nation, St. Vincent and the Grenadines assumed complete responsibility over its internal affairs, whereas Britain retained control of
defense and foreign affairs. Exactly ten years later, after approval
by a two-thirds majority both in the islands' House of Assembly
and by plebiscite, the independent nation of St. Vincent and the
Grenadines was established.

Geography

St. Vincent and the Grenadines is located in the southern portion of the Lesser Antilles, islands formed from the peaks of a partially submerged chain of volcanic mountains (see fig. 1). The island
of St. Vincent lies 97 kilometers north of Grenada and 160 kilometers west of Barbados. The Grenadines are a chain of some 600
islets that stretch between St. Vincent and Grenada. The northern Grenadines belong to St. Vincent; the southern islands belong
to Grenada.

The total area of St. Vincent and its associated islands is 389
square kilometers, of which St. Vincent alone accounts for 345
square kilometers. The main island, which is approximately thirty-
two kilometers long and eighteen kilometers wide at its maximum
breadth, is roughly oval shaped and has a north-south alignment.

A nearly impenetrable ridge of volcanic mountains forms the
spine of St. Vincent and of each of the Grenadines (see fig. 11).
The highest peak is Mount Soufrière, which has an elevation of
1,234 meters. It is one of the two most active volcanoes in the
Antilles (the other is Mount Pelée in Martinique), and its eruptions, although sporadic, can be violent. In 1902 a major eruption
devastated the northern half of the island and killed 2,000 people.
The most recent eruptions occurred in 1971, 1974, and 1979.

Although all of these were also major eruptions, they were not as violent as the 1902 event, nor was there as great a loss of life. The summit region of Mount Soufrière includes several craters, one of which contains a fair-sized lake some 300 meters below the crater rim.

The island of St. Vincent is composed almost entirely of volcanic ash, other porous volcanic material, and lava. The windward side of the island slopes gently to the coast. The terrain there is undulating, with broad alluvial plains along the stream valleys. The leeward side has rugged, deeply dissected terrain. A number of fast-flowing streams that dry up before reaching the coast can be found at higher elevations. The soils on St. Vincent are extremely porous, and water seeps through them rapidly, leaving the surface very dry.

St. Vincent and the Grenadines enjoys a tropical climate. The northeast trade winds blow across the islands, releasing some of their moisture as they do so. The islands as a whole receive an average of 150 centimeters of rainfall per year; in the mountains, however, the average is 380 centimeters per year. Seventy percent of this precipitation falls during the rainy season from May to November. Temperatures average 28°C. Although the island group lies in the hurricane belt, it is not often subjected to massive damage. In recent history, hurricanes struck the island in 1956, 1967, and 1980. Tropical Storm Danielle did about US$9 million in damage to the banana crop in 1986.

Population

The population of St. Vincent and the Grenadines in mid-1985 was estimated to be 110,000; more than 70 percent of the inhabitants had been born since 1960. Statistics for 1985 cited the crude birth and death rates as 31.3 and 7.5 per 1,000, respectively. Although these rates suggested that the population would increase substantially, the high birth rate was mitigated by a sizable level of emigration. As a result of the emigration pattern, the annual rate of population growth for the period 1973–83 averaged only 1.2 percent. This outflow of islanders helped alleviate a serious unemployment problem, but it also deprived the island of its professional and most highly skilled workers.

In 1986 the prime minister stated that the potentially high rate of population growth was one of the greatest problems facing the country. Related to that issue was the large number of Vincentian children born to poor families. Many twentieth-century, lower class households were headed by single mothers, in part because of the migratory patterns of men who were forced to seek employment

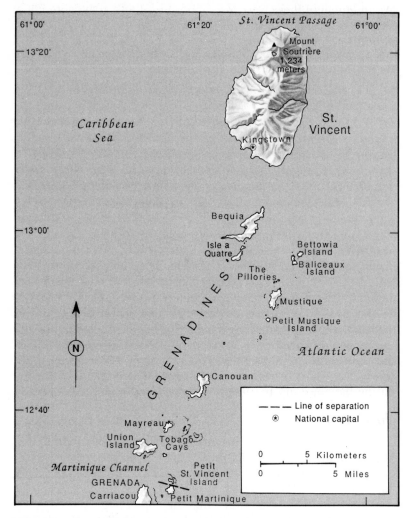

Figure 11. St. Vincent and the Grenadines, 1987

outside their towns of origin. Another contributing factor was the prevalence of consensual unions over more formal marriage arrangements in many lower class families. The unstable nature of these relationships rendered many children fatherless and poverty stricken. Recognition of the personal and national benefits of family planning increased after planned parenthood programs were commenced in the late 1960s, but many prospective parents continued to ignore or remained unaware of governmental attempts to control the size and spacing of their families. To contain the annual rate of population growth and reduce the many teenage pregnancies, the government inaugurated a controversial national family planning program in 1984 that strove to educate the population through schools, seminars, home visits, billboards, and the mass media. In the late 1980s, it remained to be seen whether the program would succeed in reducing the islands' population pressures.

Although Vincentian society in the late 1980s was characteristically multiracial, most islanders traced their ancestry from African slaves who were imported by Europeans to cultivate the sugar plantations. A majority (65.5 percent) was black, and a substantial minority (19 percent) was considered mulatto (of mixed white and black ancestry). East Indians, who had arrived to labor on the plantations after slavery was abolished, were the progenitors of 5.5 percent of the population. Whites, including many from Portugal's Madeira, constituted 3.5 percent. Two percent were Amerindian, and the remaining 4.5 percent had emigrated from North America, Latin America, and Asia.

Class lines roughly followed ethnic and racial delineations. The majority of the upper class was British in origin. The middle and working classes were made up of a sizable number of blacks, as well as East Indians and individuals of European descent. The majority below the poverty line was black.

The population distribution gave the country a decidedly rural slant. As of 1982, approximately 73.7 percent dwelled in the countryside, and 26.3 percent lived in urban areas, preponderantly in Kingstown. A majority of the nation's poor resided in relatively inaccessible areas of the main island or on the Grenadine Islands. Although rural to urban migration occurred, it was not a large problem because of the accompanying pattern of international emigration.

Linguistic and religious traditions stemmed primarily from the legacy left by two centuries of British rule over the country. Although French patois could be heard on some of the Grenadine Islands, the country's official language was English. The majority of people were Christian, and 47 percent of the church-going population attended the Church of England. Additional denominations represented included Methodist (28 percent) and Roman Catholic (13 percent). The remainder of the population were Seventh-Day Adventists, Baptists, or Hindus. A small, unorganized Rastafarian (see Glossary) sect also existed in the country; however, Rastafarianism was not a dominant factor in the society.

Education

The most striking characteristic of the education system was the absence of any compulsory attendance regulations. Faculties and facilities were inadequate, particularly outside the capital area, and students were generally required to purchase their own books and supplies. Consequently, although primary-school enrollment approached 90 percent, only a minority of children completed a twelve-year program. In 1986 the adult literacy rate (at the sixth grade level) was estimated to be 82 percent. To rectify these deficiencies, the government appropriated US$7.4 million for current expenditures on education, an increase of 10 percent over the previous year and the second largest portion of the budget for fiscal year (FY—see Glossary) 1986–87, and allocated US$630,000 for new educational facilities.

In the late 1980s, the government sponsored sixty-two seven-year primary schools. Secondary-school facilities were limited to six junior high schools, one public senior high school for girls, and one public coeducational secondary school. Eleven additional government-assisted secondary schools were directed by various religious organizations. At the university level, one teacher-training college and one technical college were located in St. Vincent. Most citizens who aspired to gain higher education were forced to go elsewhere, most often to the University of the West Indies or to institutions in Britain, Canada, or the United States.

Although the economic situation improved throughout the 1980s, the country's education system failed to prepare most students to fulfill their own or society's economic expectations. Because of the high number of islanders who did not complete high school and the time-consuming and costly nature of training for a professional career, the only employment that many Vincentians were able to secure upon entering the job market involved menial labor in the agricultural sector. As a consequence, a great number of jobs requiring more highly skilled professionals continued to be vacant.

Vincentian women were especially vulnerable to the constraints placed upon them by a poor education. Sex roles in the 1980s continued to be clearly defined along traditional lines; boys generally received a better education than girls because it was assumed that the latter would remain at home. This held true even though women officially constituted 38 percent of the labor force.

Health and Welfare

The infant mortality rate in St. Vincent and the Grenadines was one of the highest in the Caribbean at 46.8 per 1,000 live births. An underlying cause remained the large number of children born to teenage mothers. The child who reached five years of age, however, faced relatively few health-related problems. The health of the adult population was considered to be reasonably good; life expectancy at birth was about sixty-five years in 1986. Most insect-borne and communicable diseases were well under control, with the exception of yellow fever, which remained a problem in a few isolated areas. Three cases of acquired immune deficiency syndrome had been reported as of June 1986. The chief causes of death were parasitic diseases and diseases of the circulatory system. Gastroenteritis was also a common problem.

Diet and housing conditions were satisfactory for the upper and middle classes but inadequate for the rest of the population. The poorly balanced diet of the lower class was a major cause of the malnutrition of some children. Staples included rice, sweet potatoes, and fruit. Fish was readily available to most of the population, but certain other foodstuffs had to be imported and were thus out of reach of many poor Vincentians. Housing was in short supply for the lower class, especially for the country's large number of agricultural workers. The housing shortage, caused in part by the high birth rate among the increasingly young population, worsened after the 1980 Hurricane Allen, which destroyed many of the flimsier structures on the island and damaged some of the more substantially built homes.

The nation's failure to provide chlorinated water and adequate sanitation facilities for many of its citizens compounded residents' health problems, especially these related to gastroenteritis and parasitic diseases. Approximately three-quarters of the population had no access to potable water. The urban sewage system was operated in an inefficient manner, and pit latrines were still in use in some rural areas. Efforts were launched in the 1960s to provide adequate water supplies and sewage disposal systems, but as of the late 1980s they were only partially successful.

The nation spent more than US$3 million, approximately 3 percent of the gross domestic product (GDP—see Glossary), on health care in 1982. Medical centers were plentiful, but most only approached the size of a small health dispensary. There were four hospitals, two health centers, three specialist hospitals, and thirty-four medical clinics throughout the islands. The ratio of hospital beds to population was 1 to 1,695 in 1981. There were 368 medical personnel in the country in 1984, consisting of 24 physicians (only 5 of whom were native Vincentians), 1 dentist, 19 medical technicians, 290 nurses, and 34 community health aides. The ratio of physicians to population was 1 to 4,791 in 1981. Health services on the Grenadine Islands were characterized by a lack of well-trained health practitioners.

Following independence, the government played a more prominent role in legislating health and welfare issues. Beginning in 1970, the government sponsored a limited form of social security through the National Provident Fund, which provided retirement pensions, health insurance, and death benefits. This fund was scheduled to be converted into a full-scale National Insurance Programme in 1987. Some successful cooperative ventures existed at the grass-roots level. Called Friendly Societies, they were formed in the early twentieth century as self-help "insurance" groups to provide for members' medical needs and burial expenses in exchange for the payment of low annual dues. It appeared likely that these groups would continue to flourish until the government's new insurance program proved successful.

Economy

The economy of St. Vincent and the Grenadines, highly dependent upon agricultural exports, performed fairly well in the years following independence; the viability of some sectors of the economy remained questionable, however, and a large negative balance of payments was the young nation's greatest economic obstacle. Although these problems continued to exist in 1987, some economic difficulties were resolved after the emergence of a reform government following the 1984 national elections.

Macroeconomic Overview

The GDP totaled an estimated US$102 million in 1985, and per capita GDP approximated US$930, the lowest in the Eastern Caribbean. GDP grew at a high rate for the first six years of the 1980s, an average of 4.6 percent, but slowed to 2.5 percent in 1986 as a result of weather conditions affecting the agricultural sector. The inflation rate decreased from 12.7 percent in 1981 to 2.2 percent in 1986.

The labor force had averaged 40,000 since independence. Women comprised 38 percent of the official labor force; they probably comprised more than 50 percent if the informal sector of the economy was included in government figures. Unemployment was a pervasive problem, especially among workers between the ages of fifteen and twenty-five. According to 1986 estimates, more than one-third of the labor force was unemployed, a very high figure even for the Caribbean. The nation's employment capacity was severely strained because of the young labor force and the many students emerging from the education system before completing high school. Another serious problem was the rate of underemployment, which remained exceptionally high as a consequence of the country's dependence on seasonal agriculture.

Legislation guaranteeing a maximum work schedule and minimum daily wages for the labor force was in effect before independence. Young people were eligible for employment at fifteen years
of age, and a five-day work schedule of forty hours per week, as
well as a minimum of two weeks' annual vacation, was guaranteed by law. In 1987 daily minimum wage rates for men and women
continued to differ by more than 23 percent. Although men in the
industrial sector earned a minimum of US$5 per day, women em-
ployed in industry could be paid as little as US$3.85 for the same
period. Male agricultural workers received at least US$3.85 for
a day's work, whereas their female counterparts were entitled to
a daily minimum of only US$3. Lobbying efforts by a number of
women's groups and workers' unions sought to end the disparities; nevertheless, as of late 1987 the minimum wage regulations
remained unchanged.

Organized labor, which constituted approximately 10 percent
of the labor force, was not as vigorous in the Vincentian society
and economy as in other Eastern Caribbean nations. In 1987 five
labor unions existed in St. Vincent and the Grenadines for commercial and technical workers, public service employees, teachers,
national workers, and farmers. The Ministry of Housing, Labour,
and Community Development oversaw the reconciliation of disputes between workers and employers.

The poor infrastructure of the islands, especially outside Kingstown's immediate area, hindered economic possibilities for the nation's farmers and entrepreneurs. The more than 1,000 kilometers
of roadways varied greatly in terms of surface quality. Twenty-
seven percent were well-paved highways; 36 percent, rough-paved
or gravel roads; and 37 percent, barely passable tracks. The northern and interior mountainous parts of the island of St. Vincent
were inaccessible by highway. No railroad system or navigable inland waterways existed on any of the islands. A deep-water harbor, completed in 1964 at Kingstown, was the country's only port
capable of accommodating ocean-going vessels. As of 1984, an expansion project was underway to improve constraints at Kingstown
Harbour, such as congestion and inadequate handling facilities that
were limiting access to trade and cruise ships. St. Vincent and the
Grenadines was also the only Organisation of Eastern Caribbean
States (OECS—see Glossary) country to lack an airport capable
of accommodating international flights. Its principal airport, located three kilometers southeast of the capital at Arnos Vale, contained runways that ranged from 1,220 to 2,439 meters in length.
In addition, three landing strips for small aircraft existed in the
Grenadine Islands.

An improved digital telephone system costing more than US$7 million was installed in 1986, comprising 6,700 lines and capable of expanding to 20,000 lines. Although the system was linked to the Grenadine Islands, most telephones were located in Kingstown, which contributed toward the delay in developing the remainder of the country.

Because it lacked fossil fuel resources of its own, the nation had to import most fuels for energy consumption. The government-run St. Vincent Electricity Services, which in 1985 had the capacity to supply 6.7 megawatts of electricity to the country's two largest islands, operated on diesel fuel for 60 percent of its power. Most of the government's revenues from the sale of electricity were thus applied toward the purchase of more fuel. The remaining 40 percent of the electricity was generated through domestic hydroelectric power sources. To lessen the utility's dependence on highly priced imported fuel, the government in FY 1983–84 invested more than US$33 million in the Cumberland Hydroelectric Project, which featured the construction of three new hydroelectric power plants. The project promised to save the country approximately 34,500 barrels of fuel per year and more than US$1 million annually in foreign exchange.

Banking and Finance

The nation's largest financial institution was the state-run National Commercial Bank, and various branches of Canadian banks were prominent in Kingstown. The Eastern Caribbean dollar, the national currency shared with other OECS members since July 1976, was pegged to the United States dollar, and the exchange rate continued to be EC$2.70 to US$1.00 in 1987.

After Prime Minister James F. "Son" Mitchell took office in 1984, the country's budgetary figures went from a deficit of US$2.15 million in FY 1983–84 to a surplus of US$2.85 million in FY 1985–86. The turnaround was the result of more effective control over the central government's current expenditures and improved efficiency in tax collection. In 1984, once the country's accounts were balanced, the Mitchell government cut the unpopular personal income and business taxes introduced in 1983 to offset the budget deficit. The traditionally low percentage of the budget dedicated to the Grenadines was also a recurrent issue. It was estimated that before 1984 the Grenadines had received only about 1 percent per year of the country's total budget. During his election campaign that year, Mitchell promised to address the concerns of his Grenadines constituents regarding perceptions of continued economic neglect of those islands. As of late 1987, he had been somewhat successful with the limited resources at his disposal but had not been able to raise the money to do everything that was needed.

A budget of US$64.4 million for FY 1986–87 was presented by the prime minister in early 1986. Fifty-nine percent of the budget was allocated for current expenditures. The remainder funded the government's capital program, which included an unusually large percentage dedicated to the government's hydroelectric project and other capital improvements to the nation's physical infrastructure. The Ministry of Finance, Planning, and Development received the largest portion of spending, almost 14 percent. In early 1987, a reorganization of the nation's civil service was proposed by the prime minister, who recommended streamlining the large and cumbersome bureaucracy to eliminate waste and inefficiency.

Role of Government

The government was actively involved in the management of the economy through its ownership of many state-run enterprises and utilities and the influence it exerted over the various economic sectors and privately owned enterprises. When they elected him in 1984, voters expected that Mitchell, an agronomist by profession, would be able to resolve some of the economic problems faced by St. Vincent and the Grenadines in the early 1980s. Among the economic priorities that Mitchell enumerated during the campaign were the reduction of the national budget and trade deficits, a revision of the income tax code to promote private savings and investment, and the promotion of private sector export industries such as agricultural processing and manufacturing. The platform of Mitchell's New Democratic Party (NDP) also included government oversight of the management of the economy, the government's withdrawal from production, the construction and repair of tourist facilities, and the improvement of physical and social infrastructure on the islands. Upon becoming prime minister, Mitchell also assumed the office of minister of finance, planning, and development so that he could be more directly responsible for making and implementing economic policy. During his first three years in office, Mitchell reversed the central government's poor financial situation by increasing agricultural exports, streamlining state-owned enterprises, and improving control over the government's current expenditures; the performance of the industrial and tourist sectors of the economy was mixed, however, because of strong competition from neighboring islands and the country's poor infrastructure.

A year after he took office, Mitchell considered his major developmental achievement to be the government's nationalization of the 1,400-hectare Orange Hill Estates. The estates project was the centerpiece of the government's early proposals for land reform. Danish investors had purchased the land in 1985 from private owners for US$2 million and offered the land for resale to the Vincentian government for more than US$8.3 million. St. Vincent and the Grenadines subsequently nationalized the property and offered the Danish consortium a settlement of US$1.7 million as compensation for its loss. The government planned to make a cooperative from the old estate and distribute small plots for rent and subsequent purchase to the tenants already living and working there. Additional plans called for the establishment of a tourist complex with funds from international donors such as the European Economic Community and the Caribbean Development Bank. Despite this highly visible land reform effort, Mitchell repeatedly assured Vincentian large landowners that confiscation would not occur; rather, his government would purchase land only as it was offered for sale.

Sectoral Performance

Although agriculture's contribution to GDP dwindled considerably between 1961 and 1985 (from 40.3 percent to 17.7 percent), in the late 1980s agriculture remained the mainstay of the economy, as it had been from the late eighteenth century. The sector employed approximately 67 percent of all workers and earned 65 percent of the country's export revenue in 1985. Most of the country's land was not considered arable; only about 40 percent of its 389 square kilometers could be cultivated. Principal crops included bananas and arrowroot. Increasing emphasis was placed upon agricultural production for the export market.

After assuming leadership in 1984, Mitchell was successful in reversing some of the setbacks that agriculture traditionally had endured, such as a reliance upon a small number of crops and poor marketing strategies. Product diversification, improved advertising techniques, and a limited land reform program helped to strengthen the performance of the economy.

Although banana production was disrupted by a series of hurricanes and volcanic eruptions in the 1970s, in the late 1980s bananas continued to be the nation's primary cash crop and an especially lucrative export commodity for the nation's many small farmers. An exceptional yield of more than 40,640 tons was exported in 1985, contributing US$16 million to the nation's coffers; however, unfavorable weather conditions undercut the banana industry during the following two years. Tropical Storm Danielle in 1986 and a severe drought in 1987 reduced each year's crop by about one-half; the damage to banana production in 1986 contributed to a loss of export earnings in the amount of more than US$3 million. It also created widespread unemployment within the sector and also for boxing plant employees, truckers, and stevedores.

Through the late 1980s, St. Vincent and the Grenadines was the world's largest producer of arrowroot, a tuberous root whose starch is used in the production of baby food and computer paper. A consistent cash crop for the nation during the twentieth century, arrowroot trailed only bananas in importance from the 1970s through the following decade. Even the phenomenal growth of the computer industry, however, could not keep the demand for Vincentian arrowroot at a steadily high level. Competition from China and Brazil and marketing and finance problems besetting the agricultural sector as a whole led to a decline in the annual yield from about 813 tons in 1984 to an estimated 160 tons in 1987. The arrowroot industry had contracted a debt of almost US$3 million by 1987; the government planned to improve the economic viability of the sector by rescheduling the debt.

For a century and a half, sugar had been St. Vincent and the Grenadines' most important cash crop; in the mid-twentieth century, however, sugar production became a liability because of the fall of world commodity prices. Production declined in the 1960s and was terminated in the early 1970s. At the beginning of the 1980s, the government encouraged the return of the sugar industry to reduce unemployment and limit the amount of foreign exchange being spent for a crop that could be grown by the nation's own farmers. Nevertheless, cutbacks in United States sugar import quotas, continually depressed prices, and the growing use of high-fructose corn syrups made sugar a financially unsound investment for private growers and the government, and the last crop was harvested in 1986.

The livestock and fisheries industries were geared toward the domestic market. Local fish consumption was high because of the proximity to abundant fishing waters. The principal limitation hindering the export of livestock and fish was the lack of adequate refrigeration facilities.

Although light manufacturing was designed to be the key to industrial development, the country was a latecomer to this field. Consequently, industry constituted only a small fraction of the national economy in the late 1980s. Expanding by only 1 percent annually following independence, manufacturing employed 8 percent of the labor force and constituted 10.5 percent of GDP in 1985.

Because the economy was exceptionally small and yet linked to the OECS regional economic system, the country was inordinately dependent upon trade. For the most part, production was geared toward export, and agricultural processing had long been the primary national export industry. Other activities included clothing and textiles manufacturing, rum distillation, flour milling, cigarette and tobacco production, and yacht building. Among the most promising of domestic industries was the manufacture of concrete, flour, and furniture.

Following independence, the government strove to widen avenues for trade by providing incentives for foreign investment with liberal tax and currency exchange regulations. The government also financed the wide-ranging Development Corporation, which was designed to locate potential foreign investors for joint ventures in manufacturing and agriculture. Despite these efforts, manufacturing output remained rather sluggish in 1987. The economy continued to suffer from the absence of known natural resources, the small size of the domestic market, a poor local infrastructure, a shortage of factory space, high export transportation costs, intense regional competition, and the lack of a well-trained managerial and entrepreneurial cadre. In addition, the Development Corporation was considered to be overextended.

One industry that grew tremendously after the country's independence was the construction industry, which was oriented toward the domestic market. Private construction companies were few; employment opportunities in this field were excellent in 1987, however, because of the government's high capital expenditures for the development of the country's physical infrastructure.

In the late 1980s, the most promising long-term revenue enhancer for the economy, especially in the Grenadines, was a dynamic tourist industry. Tourists arrived principally from other Caribbean countries, North America, and Britain, and tourism's contribution to GDP remained a steady 2 percent in the 1980s. The beauty of the Grenadine Islands attracted many yachting enthusiasts, and some of the smaller islands functioned almost exclusively as resorts. The tourism industry profited from the 1983 crisis in neighboring Grenada; many cruise ships were diverted to St. Vincent and the Grenadines until the political turmoil was resolved. Despite a growing number of tourist arrivals each year, however, the potential for tourism was not as fully realized as in other Caribbean nations, primarily because of the lack of an international airport. A high incidence of foreign control over tourist facilities also contributed to a Vincentian loss of revenue. Mitchell encouraged citizens to invest in the tourist industry so that more earnings would remain in the country.

Foreign Trade and Balance of Payments

The nation's balance of payments improved during the 1980s as a result of the strong performance of agricultural exports, which stimulated a decline in the current account deficit from 23 percent of GDP in 1979 to under 10 percent in 1986. Nevertheless, a large negative trade balance continued to affect the nation. In 1985 the trade deficit was US$23.6 million. The country received US$61.5 million for its exports, composed primarily of agricultural products, and paid US$85.1 million for imports, such as food and beverages, machinery and equipment, and manufactured goods. In the late 1980s, principal trading partners remained other Caribbean Community and Common Market (Caricom—see Appendix C) member states, which were the recipients in 1983 of 57 percent of Vincentian exports and the sources of an estimated 32 percent of all imports. Of those states, Trinidad and Tobago dominated; 34 percent of Vincentian exports were shipped to that nation, and approximately 24 percent of Vincentian imports arrived from there. Britain received 32 percent of Vincentian exports and provided about 11 percent of its imports. The United States accounted for an estimated one-third of all imports into the country, and Canada provided about 6 percent of the same. The remaining percentages were exported to and imported from countries in Western Europe, Latin America, and Asia.

St. Vincent and the Grenadines received moderate amounts of aid in the years following independence. Canada granted aid and loans for many projects, and traditional donors, such as Britain, the United States, and some international organizations, also contributed funds toward the economic growth of the island.

Government and Politics

The Governmental System

The promulgation of the postindependence Constitution gave St. Vincent and the Grenadines a constitutional monarchy with an independent British-style parliamentary system of government. The Constitution in force in the late 1980s provides for the Parliament, which is composed of a thirteen-member elected House of Assembly, a six-member appointed Senate, and an elected attorney general. In 1986 a constitutional amendment was approved by the House to increase the number of seats in the House of

335

Assembly to fifteen. The country's head of state is the British monarch, who is represented in St. Vincent and the Grenadines by a governor general appointed for a five-year term. The governor general's duties include the appointment as prime minister of the member of the House who commands the support of the majority of the representatives. The governor general also appoints the senators, four on the advice of the prime minister and two on the advice of the leader of the opposition. In practice, the authority of the governor general is quite limited; he or she generally acts only with the approval of the government.

The nation's judicial system is built on the foundations of English common law. There are eleven courts in the country within three magisterial districts. Although the Constitution is the supreme law of the islands, it allows for continued association with the Eastern Caribbean States Supreme Court, which is known in St. Vincent and the Grenadines as the St. Vincent and Eastern Caribbean States Supreme Court. It consists of the Court of Appeal and the High Court. The court of last resort is the Judicial Committee of the Privy Council in London.

Prior to independence, natives of the British territories of St. Vincent and the Grenadine Islands held British citizenship. Following independence, all citizens continued to be considered British subjects under British law because of St. Vincent and the Grenadines' membership in the Commonwealth of Nations (see Appendix B). The Vincentian Constitution does not recognize dual citizenship, however. Every person born in St. Vincent and the Grenadines who was a British citizen prior to independence automatically became a Vincentian citizen on October 27, 1979. All persons born anywhere in the world to a Vincentian parent after that date were also granted citizenship.

Universal adult suffrage was first granted in 1951 for citizens twenty-one years of age. The new Constitution enfranchises citizens of eighteen years of age, and the minimum age for eligibility to hold office by election or appointment is twenty-one years.

The Constitution guarantees freedom of speech and of the press. The government-owned Radio St. Vincent and the Grenadines and the independent St. Vincent and the Grenadines Television remained relatively free from censorship and interference in the 1980s. Editorials in the *Vincentian,* the nation's independent weekly newspaper, routinely and openly criticized the nation's leaders. Because the major political parties published their own newspapers, the government refrained from pressuring the editorial staffs of the independent news organizations to print only the official government position.

Political Dynamics

Although the political system was among the most stable of Britain's former colonies, the country has perhaps the most colorful history of political parties in the Eastern Caribbean region. These parties, many of which had not yet been established prior to the nation's independence in 1979, enhanced the dynamic democratic traditions that, with very few exceptions, remained vibrant in St. Vincent and the Grenadines through the late 1980s.

The leadership of the various parties was extremely erratic; founders of one party frequently emerged as leaders of another party only a few years later. As of 1987, the most successful player of this game of political musical chairs was the man who became prime minister in 1984, James Mitchell. Mitchell initially won the Grenadines' parliamentary seat in 1966 as a member of the St. Vincent Labour Party (SVLP), which then became his principal opposition from 1984 through late 1987. He was reelected to Parliament in the 1972 elections despite personality differences that had led him to resign from the SVLP and run as an independent. Because Mitchell was able to form a coalition government with the People's Political Party (PPP), he served as premier, the preindependence equivalent of prime minister, until his government fell two years later. In the subsequent elections, Mitchell managed to retain his seat in the House of Assembly as an independent and continued as a member of Parliament through 1979. In a 1980 by-election, Mitchell was returned to the Grenadines seat in the House of Assembly as the leader of the five-year-old NDP, with which he continued to be affiliated through late 1987.

The first political party to gather mass support was the PPP. Founded in 1952 by Ebenezer Joshua, the party drew much of its large following from among trade union members. At the forefront of national policy making prior to independence, the pro-Western PPP won a majority of parliamentary seats in 1957, 1961, and 1966. The party began to lose its following soon afterward with the emergence of a more conservative middle class. The party suffered a total defeat in the 1979 elections, and Joshua relinquished leadership of the PPP in 1980. Although the party disbanded in late 1984, it regrouped in 1987 under a new name, the People's National Movement.

The SVLP, under the leadership of R. Milton Cato, dominated the country's political scene for almost two decades prior to 1984. Founded in 1955, the party owed much of its support to the black middle class. Cato's conservative platform advocated law and order,

337

a pro-Western foreign policy, and a mixed economy. Following victories in 1967 and 1974, the party won the country's first postindependence election in 1979. That triumph was attributed to an economy that had been strengthened under Cato's previous governments and his success in guiding the country to independence.

Expecting an easy sweep at the polls because of the splintered opposition, Cato called general elections in 1984 months before they were constitutionally required. The elections produced two surprising results: the largest voter turnout in Caribbean history (88.8 percent) and an NDP victory in nine of the thirteen seats. The SVLP was hindered by a number of issues in the 1984 election campaign. First, there was concern that Cato's advanced age and ill health would detract from his ability to govern effectively. The Cato government was also accused of gross mismanagement of government funds, resulting in a national deficit that could only be offset by a tax increase. Cato's attorney general had also lost popularity because he had refused to resign after involvement in a disputed land deal. Other problems included controversy surrounding 1981 legislation dealing with the prevention of subversion and strikes and resistance against the paramilitary Special Service Unit (SSU) set up by Cato in response to the 1983 events in Grenada (see National Security, this section). Cato retired from the party leadership soon after his election defeat.

The pro-Western NDP, founded by Mitchell in 1975, prevailed over the SVLP in the 1984 elections by a margin of 51 percent to 41 percent. As of 1987, the NDP's popularity rating remained high because of the belief that the prime minister was governing well with the limited resources at his disposal. Priorities on the NDP's agenda included the continued search for financial and technical assistance for the construction of an international airport and support for efforts to implement a nationwide family planning program. Mitchell, who was born on Bequia, the largest of the Grenadine Islands, also tried to upgrade services in the Grenadines to correct allegations that those islands traditionally were ignored by politicians once an election victory was assured.

Soon after the election, Mitchell's government succeeded in reducing the country's deficit and enforcing land reform without antagonizing landed Vincentians. Although many of his goals had not yet been met, Mitchell was given a vote of confidence during a 1987 by-election that followed the death of an NDP parliamentarian.

Another contender in the postindependence elections was a socialist coalition, the United People's Movement (UPM), formed in 1979 by Ralph Gonsalves. The UPM was an alliance of the left-wing Youlou United Liberation Movement, founded by Gonsalves in 1974; the leftist People's Democratic Movement (PDM), founded by Parnel Campbell; and Arwee, a rural party. By the time of the 1984 elections, the UPM's political prestige had been marred by numerous defections, including the PDM's departure in 1980 and Gonsalves's exit in 1982 to found a more moderate socialist political party, the Movement for National Unity. The UPM's aspirations to national leadership were also damaged by Vincentian revulsion to the violence that had consumed leftist forces in neighboring Grenada in 1983 (see Grenada, Government and Politics, this ch.).

Other active political parties in the late 1980s included the centrist Progressive Democratic Party, founded in 1981; the moderate Working People's Party, founded prior to the 1980 by-election; and the St. Vincent and the Grenadines National Movement, founded as a left-of-center response to the 1983 Grenada crisis.

Foreign Relations

As a result of its small physical and demographic size, historical ties to Britain, and geographic location, St. Vincent and the Grenadines traditionally conducted its foreign relations based upon alliances with other Eastern Caribbean states, Britain, and the United States. The country's foreign policy was administered by Britain until full independence was achieved in 1979. After independence, foreign policy was implemented by the prime minister through the Ministry of Foreign Affairs.

Mitchell made no fundamental changes in the overall foreign policy after taking office from Cato in 1984. His only modification of Cato's foreign policy, which reflected the pro-Western, conservative stance of his government, was a more outspoken articulation of Vincentian concerns regarding United States military assistance in the region.

Although Vincentians had not been especially alarmed by the coming to power of Maurice Bishop's Grenadian New Jewel Movement in 1979, domestic public opinion supported former Prime Minister Cato's decision to participate in the intervention. Mitchell, then the opposition leader, was actually one of the first Caribbean political leaders to call for a United States intervention in Grenada after the coup and Bishop's assassination in 1983. Mitchell pushed for the intervention in order to warn Cuba not to interfere in the politics of any other Eastern Caribbean nation. Mitchell was also a guiding force behind the three-party merger of moderates in Grenada under the banner of the New National Party prior to that country's elections in 1984. Mitchell was determined to promote moderate forces in Grenada because he believed that instability in Grenada could ultimately affect the durability of the Vincentian political establishment.

St. Vincent and the Grenadines' historical alliances with Britain, the United States, and Canada grew from common political and linguistic heritages and were strengthened further by the bilateral and multilateral economic aid granted by those countries. Although St. Vincent and the Grenadines maintained diplomatic relations with the Soviet Union and Cuba, the politically conservative Vincentian populace discouraged close relations with those communist states.

Foreign policy also focused strongly on mutual cooperation with island neighbors. As a result of its association with the West Indies Federation and its administration by Britain in conjunction with other English-speaking islands prior to the federation, St. Vincent and the Grenadines frequently manifested interests that overlapped with those of its neighbors. As in the case of the Grenada crisis, an occurrence on one island could have repercussions for the others; thus, any compromising of the physical security or economic well-being of one or more of the Commonwealth Caribbean nations was a catalyst for at least a limited Vincentian involvement in regional affairs.

No foreign envoys resided in St. Vincent and the Grenadines in late 1987. Diplomatic channels were maintained through missions in other Caribbean countries such as Barbados. St. Vincent and the Grenadines lacked the resources to maintain high-level diplomatic missions abroad. As of early 1987, the state maintained permanent diplomatic representation only in London, and both the United States and the United Nations (UN) ambassadorships were vacant.

A decade after independence, St. Vincent and the Grenadines was a member of Caricom and the OECS. The nation was formally admitted to the UN in 1980 and the Organization of American States in 1981 and gained full membership in the Commonwealth of Nations in 1985.

National Security

Although extremists and Black Power movement (see Glossary) partisans were active in St. Vincent and the Grenadines in the 1970s, and although terrorists assassinated the attorney general in 1973, there was comparatively little preoccupation with security-related issues until 1979. In that year, the prime minister of neighboring Grenada was overthrown and the Grenadines' Union Island temporarily fell to local insurgents. Following these incidents, the nation's vulnerability became increasingly apparent, and more emphasis was placed on security-related matters. Nevertheless, the civil defense capabilities of the Vincentian security forces remained very limited in the late 1980s. Like many of the other small island nations in the Caribbean, the country did not maintain a standing army. In case of external threat or insurgency from within, it relied upon the Regional Security System (RSS), of which it was a member (see A Regional Security System, ch. 7). Disturbances of a more limited nature were handled by a weaponless police force, under whose jurisdiction fell the armed paramilitary SSU and a small coast guard.

One of the most important issues debated in the late 1980s was the extent to which St. Vincent and the Grenadines should participate in the RSS. Mitchell, along with Barbadian prime minister Errol Barrow, prevented the upgrading of the 1982 Memorandum of Understanding into a treaty. During the 1984 elections, Mitchell campaigned against expensive defense commitments, stating numerous times that he opposed the establishment of a separate military institution. Mitchell also campaigned against what he termed the "excessive militarization" of the region because he feared that a strong military could endanger the democratic process in times of economic hardship. Although he recognized that the Eastern Caribbean states had to defend themselves, Mitchell believed that economic assistance would do more to secure the region than a military buildup. Ironically, St. Vincent and the Grenadines was one of only two countries in 1986 whose contribution to the RSS budget was not in arrears.

The internal security of the nation was the responsibility of the Royal St. Vincent and the Grenadines Police Force. Headquartered in Kingstown and headed by a commissioner, the force numbered about 490 members in the late 1980s. The organizational structure of the Police Force included the Criminal Investigation Department, the Fire Brigade, and branches for immigration, traffic, and transport. Although the Police Force had a good record with respect to human rights, there were four news media allegations between 1983 and 1987 of police brutality, two of them related, resulting in the deaths of detainees.

The most serious internal disturbance that the police were called upon to control was the uprising on Union Island in December 1979, which resulted when a group of young Rastafarians seized the local airport, police station, and revenue office. The perceived neglect of the small Grenadine island by the incumbent SVLP government was a factor in the Rastafarians' decision to take such drastic action. The situation was brought under control when the prime minister called upon Barbadian troops to keep order on St. Vincent while the Royal St. Vincent and the Grenadines Police Force was dispatched to Union Island to subdue the minirebellion (see Regional Security Threats, 1970–81, ch. 7).

Police Force members operated unarmed unless an emergency occurred, in which case they were provided with the equipment needed to resolve the situation. In response to the Grenada crisis in 1983, a Vincentian SSU was created in early 1984 under the auspices of the RSS to arm some of the police permanently. Functioning as a paramilitary unit, the SSU had eighty members, all under the direction of the local police commissioner. Under a United States security assistance program, the SSU received British and United States weapons and equipment.

The Police Force lauded Mitchell's election because of his reputation for anticorruption politics; Mitchell did not spare the institution, however, when he made changes in some of the nation's security policies. To ensure that the SSU would not become an elitist group unaccountable to civilians, Mitchell took the unit out of the official camouflage military uniform and returned it to the local police uniform. Because Mitchell had reservations regarding the military training that the SSU was receiving under the RSS, he declined to allow the unit to take part in the two paramilitary training maneuvers held in 1985 and 1986 involving United States, British, and Caribbean forces. Although Mitchell supported the intervention of United States soldiers during the Grenada crisis, in the late 1980s he was concerned about their training activities in the Eastern Caribbean. Recognizing that the nation would be unable to defend itself alone in case of serious threat and yet concerned about the inevitability of the United States presence, Mitchell sought to ensure that United States actions in the region were compatible with Vincentian and Eastern Caribbean interests.

Mitchell stressed the need for security-related alliances with other Eastern Caribbean countries, especially Barbados. Nevertheless, despite the continuing compatibility between the governments of St. Vincent and the Grenadines and Barbados, Mitchell remained wary of the high profile of Barbadian troops in the RSS. Throughout his first year as prime minister, Mitchell expressed misgivings about the alacrity with which former Barbadian prime minister J.M.G.M. "Tom" Adams had responded to two appeals for assistance from former Prime Minister Cato. In the first instance, as mentioned previously, Barbados sent troops to maintain order on St. Vincent while the native police force quelled the Union Island uprising; in the second, a Barbadian gunboat was dispatched to Vincentian waters ready to intervene during and immediately after the 1984 elections in case the Royal St. Vincent and the Grenadines Police Force was unable to ensure peace.

Also under the jurisdiction of the Police Force was the small Kingstown-based coast guard, which began operating in 1981. Its primary function was to participate in search-and-rescue missions, fisheries protection, smuggling prevention, and narcotics interdiction. As of 1984, the coast guard possessed one Singapore-built 22.9-meter patrol craft and two locally constructed 8.2-meter launches. One 15.3-meter Swiftship patrol craft reportedly was delivered to the country by the United States in 1986. The small number of vessels hindered the ability of the coast guard to police the vast expanses of the Grenadine Islands and surrounding territorial waters.

In 1987 St. Vincent and the Grenadines could boast of a relatively low crime rate. Theft of property and petty assault were the acts most often perpetrated, mostly in Kingstown. Although illegal, marijuana was readily available. The growing abuse of narcotics among all sectors of society had not escaped St. Vincent and the Grenadines.

Detention facilities were poor. Prisons were crowded, poorly funded, and understaffed, and rehabilitation centers were nonexistent. To reduce overcrowding, first-time offenders were given alternate sentences of fines and community service.

* * *

Solid studies relating to St. Vincent and the Grenadines are rare. Yearbooks, such as the 1986 edition of *The Europa Year Book* and *Political Handbook of the World, 1984–1985,* edited by Arthur S. Banks, comprise a substantial, if not always current, source of data. Geographical information may be garnered from the United States Agency for International Development's 1983 edition of *Countries of the Caribbean Community* and The Diagram Group's *Atlas of Central America and the Caribbean.* A guide to Vincentian economics is the 1986 edition of the Caribbean Development Bank's *Annual Report.* Articles by Gary Brana-Shute, Patrick Emmanuel, and Bernard Diederich in *Caribbean Review* provide useful information about the postindependence political scene, especially the numerous Vincentian political parties. *Caribbean Insight* contains articles on foreign relations and national security. (For further information and complete citations, see Bibliography.)

Grenada

Official name . . . . Grenada

Term for Citizens . . . . Grenadian(s)

Capital . . . . St. George's

Political Status . . . . Independent, 1974

Form of Government . . . . Parliamentary democracy
and constitutional monarchy

Geography
Size . . . . 433 sq. km.
Topography . . . . Mountainous
Climate . . . . Tropical, wet

Population
Total estimated in 1986 90,000
Annual growth rate (in percentage) in 1986 . . . . 0.3
Life expectancy at birth in 1984 66
Adult literacy rate (in percentage) in 1986 90
Language . . . . English
Ethnic groups . . . . Black (91 percent);
remainder East Indian or white
Religion . . . . Roman Catholic (65 percent),
Protestant (nearly 35 percent),
small Rastafarian sect

Economy
Currency; exchange rate . . . . Eastern Caribbean
dollar (EC$); EC$2.70 = US$1.00
Gross domestic product (GDP) in 1985 . . . US$105 million
Per capita GDP in 1985 . . . . US$1,135
Distribution of GDP (in percentage) in 1985
Government and other services 26.6
Agriculture 16.3
Wholesale and retail trade 15.5
Construction 7.5
Hotels and restaurants 6.4
Manufacturing 5.8
Other 21.9

National Security
Armed forces personnel 0
Paramilitary personnel 80
Police 520

Grenada

Although Grenada has much in common with the other small islands to its north, it has tended throughout its history to look to larger states in an effort to define its role in the world. Since its initial discovery by Christopher Columbus, Grenada has shared or sought associations of differing kinds with France, Britain, Trinidad and Tobago, Cuba (and, by extension, the Soviet Union), and the United States.

Spain's association with the island extended little beyond sighting it and giving it a name, inasmuch as the Spanish made no effort to establish a colony, perhaps because of the ferocity of the Caribs already in residence (see The Pre-European Population, ch. 1). Interestingly, the island's present name is not that given to it by Columbus. That name, which it bore but briefly, was *Concepción.* Assigned in 1498, it had given way by 1523 on maps and charts of the region to the Spanish variant of its current designation, *Granada.* Speculation has it that Spanish explorers, struck by the resemblance of Grenada's mountains to those of the Sierra Nevada in Spain, applied the familiar name of a great city to this strange place so far from home. Over the centuries, although control of the island passed from France to Britain (and briefly back to France again), the name endured with but the slightest of etymological alterations, changing from *Granada* to *La Grenade* to *Grenada.*

The French were the first to settle Grenada. Legend holds that in 1652 the last of the defending Caribs threw himself into the sea from a spot that was christened *le Morne des Sauteurs* and is known today as Leapers' Hill. Exploited first for indigo and later for sugar production, the island prospered and, like many others in the Caribbean, attracted the attention of the British. Taken by Admiral George Rodney in 1762, near the end of the Seven Years' War (1756–63) in Europe, Grenada reverted to French rule from 1779 to 1783, when it was restored to Britain by the Treaty of Versailles of 1783. The inhabitants' loyalties remained divided between the two European powers for many years, as illustrated by the Rebellion of 1795 (Fédon's Rebellion). In the course of this violent episode, a group of rebels under the command of the mulatto general Julien Fédon and inspired by the rhetoric of the French Revolution wreaked havoc on the island and its British settlers in an unsuccessful attempt to reunite with France.

From 1784 until its independence in 1974, Grenada remained a member of the British Empire, passing through various stages of colonial status and multiple associations with other regional states.

Early in the twentieth century, it produced one of the region's outstanding leaders, T. Albert Marryshow. His Representative Government Association, which inspired similar movements in other Windward Islands states and in Trinidad, did much to encourage the liberalization of British rule in the Caribbean.

It is ironic that the achievement in 1950 of universal adult suffrage, long a goal of Marryshow's, led directly to his displacement in Grenadian political life by a new figure, Eric Matthew Gairy. Whereas Marryshow had been a man of the middle class, Gairy and his Grenada United Labour Party (GULP) appealed to the lower class, the peasantry. Suddenly empowered by the vote, Gairy's supporters swept him to the leadership of the Legislative Council in 1951; he dominated the island's politics for almost three decades.

The most successful electoral challenge to Gairy between 1951 and 1979 was posed by Herbert Blaize's Grenada National Party (GNP) in 1962, mainly on the issue of union with Trinidad and Tobago (the "unitary state" proposal). Again reflecting the Grenadian penchant for looking outward for support and viability, the GNP campaigned on a platform urging acceptance of the Trinidadian offer of union. Although Blaize's party won the election, it subsequently lost a large measure of prestige and credibility when Trinidad failed to follow through on the proposal. The GNP's fall from grace paved the way for the return of Gairy, who has never tired of the role of political savior of his country.

In March 1979, Maurice Bishop and his followers in the New Jewel Movement (NJM) seized power in Grenada. Looking to Cuba and other Marxist-Leninist countries as its models, the NJM attempted to implement the first Marxist revolutionary state in the English-speaking Caribbean. The initial promises of this "revo"— as the revolution was dubbed—focused on the welfare of the people, for Bishop pledged to provide jobs, food, housing, and education. Free elections were also promised. The People's Revolutionary Government (PRG) established by the 1979 coup failed to live up to the expectations of the Grenadian people, however. Although representative government was promised, the constitution was suspended. In its place, the PRG brought forth a series of "people's laws," the most effective of which were those that curtailed individual freedoms and facilitated the detention of dissidents.

In the economic sphere, the PRG made only slow and halting progress toward socialism. Constrained by the need to attract high levels of foreign aid and frustrated by the intractable nature of the island's economic problems, the ideological fervor of some members of the NJM gave way to increased repression and intensified

conflict within the NJM Central Committee. This internal struggle, essentially a contest between the more pragmatic Bishop and
his doctrinaire deputy prime minister Bernard Coard, led directly
to the downfall of the PRG and the murder of Bishop and many
others on October 19, 1983. His death exposed the truth that the
hard-liners among the NJM had failed to recognize, namely, that
if the PRG had any claim to legitimacy at all, it was through the
charismatic authority of Bishop, who had remained generally popular in Grenada throughout the PRG period.

Bishop's murder set the stage for the October 25, 1983, military intervention by United States and Caribbean forces (see Current Strategic Considerations, ch. 7). After that date, Grenada
turned to the United States as its principal ally and benefactor.
Although the harsh repression of the PRG was a thing of the past,
Grenadians continued to face a number of thorny political and economic problems as they looked toward the future.

Geography

Grenada and its largely uninhabited outlying territories are the
most southerly of the Windward Islands (see fig. 1). The Grenadine Islands chain consists of some 600 islets; those south of the
Martinique Channel belong to Grenada, while those north of the
channel are part of the nation of St. Vincent and the Grenadines.
Located about 160 kilometers north of Venezuela, at approximately
12° north latitude and 61° west longitude, Grenada and its territories occupy a total area of 433 square kilometers. Grenada, known
as the Spice Isle because of its production of nutmeg and mace,
is the largest at 310 square kilometers, or about the size of Detroit.
The island is oval in shape and framed by a jagged southern coastline; its maximum width is thirty-four kilometers, and its maximum length is nineteen kilometers. St. George's, the capital and
the nation's most important harbor, is favorably situated near a
lagoon on the southwestern coast. Of all the islands belonging to
Grenada, only two are of consequence: Carriacou, with a population of a few thousand, and its neighbor Petit Martinique, roughly
40 kilometers northeast of Grenada and populated by some 700
inhabitants (see fig. 12).

Part of the volcanic chain in the Lesser Antilles arc, Grenada
and its possessions generally vary in elevation from under 300
meters to over 600 meters above sea level. Grenada is more rugged
and densely foliated than its outlying possessions, but other geographical conditions are more similar. Grenada's landmass rises
from a narrow, coastal plain in a generally north-south trending
axis of ridges and narrow valleys. Mount St. Catherine is the highest
peak at 840 meters.

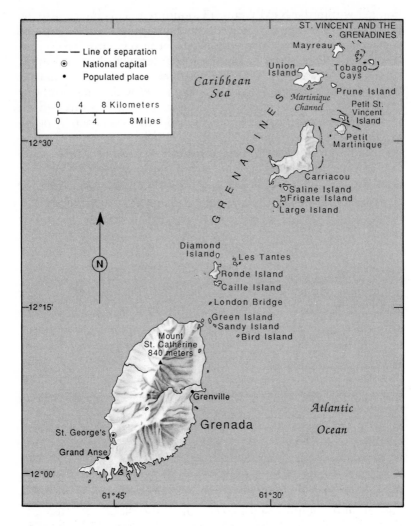

Figure 12. Grenada, 1987

Although many of the rocks and soils are of volcanic origin, the volcanic cones dotting Grenada are long dormant. Some of the drainage features on Grenada remain from its volcanic past. There are a few crater lakes, the largest of which is Grand Étang. The swift upper reaches of rivers, which occasionally overflow and cause flooding and landslides, generally cut deeply into the conic slopes. By contrast, many of the water courses in the lowlands tend to be sluggish and meandering.

The abundance of water is primarily caused by the tropical, wet climate. Yearly precipitation, largely generated by the warm and moisture-laden northeasterly trade winds, varies from more than 350 centimeters on the windward mountainsides to less than 150 centimeters in the lowlands. The greatest monthly totals are recorded throughout Grenada from June through November, the months when tropical storms and hurricanes are most likely to occur. Rainfall is less pronounced from December through May, when the equatorial low-pressure system moves south. Similarly, the highest humidities, usually close to 80 percent, are recorded during the rainy months, and values from 68 to 78 percent are registered during the drier period. Temperatures averaging 29°C are constant throughout the year, however, with slightly higher readings in the lowlands. Nevertheless, diurnal ranges within a 24-hour period are appreciable: between 26°C and 32°C during the day and between 19°C and 24°C at night.

Population

In 1985 the total population was estimated at 90,000, resulting in a population density of 300 people per square kilometer. Approximately 30 percent of the population lived in the capital city of St. George's; the balance was spread throughout the island in coastal towns and on inland farms. The population growth rate since 1970 has been near zero; some years have registered minor increases, whereas others have had offsetting decreases. In 1986 it was 0.3 percent. In spite of a relatively high crude birth rate, the population has remained relatively stable because of emigration.

Emigration was Grenada's most striking demographic feature in the late 1980s; the emigration pattern has been documented for nearly a hundred years. Throughout much of the nineteenth century, Grenada experienced a net migratory inflow to meet the shortage of labor. This trend was reversed, however, around 1890, when the labor market contracted. Shortly thereafter, Grenada experienced a net outflow of workers that eventually offset natural population growth. Grenada has long been considered overpopulated because of the economy's inability to absorb the growing labor force. This compelled many Grenadians to seek employment in foreign countries; most went to other islands in the Caribbean, Britain, the United States, and Canada.

In the late 1980s, the propensity for the work force to migrate was changing the structure of the population; emigration from Grenada not only neutralized the natural population growth rate but also skewed the age distribution. Because of the large numbers of working-age (fifteen to sixty-four) Grenadians continuing to leave the island, Grenada was slowly becoming a society with

351

a disproportionate number of very young and very old inhabitants.

These demographic trends were well entrenched by 1987 and were expected to persist into the twenty-first century, having significant ramifications for the economy. A high crude birth rate was thought likely to continue to exacerbate the unemployment problem unless expanded economic performance created new jobs or unless an effective national birth control program was implemented. The failure of these to materialize would perpetuate the need for much of the work force to migrate for generations to come.

Grenada had essentially one ethnic group. Approximately 91 percent of the population was black, descended from the African slaves brought to Grenada by the French and British to work on colonial plantations. East Indians and whites constituted the remaining 9 percent of the population. Virtually all traces of the Carib and Arawak Indians, the original inhabitants, were gone. The island's ethnic homogeneity has often been cited as the reason for the general lack of racial discord in the society. Although factions developed for political and economic reasons, the absence of racial prejudice minimized the social upheaval evident in societies with more distinct ethnic barriers. Social, political, and economic stratification based on color and education had existed from colonial times through the twentieth century, however. White and light-colored inhabitants, composing an elite minority of no more than 5 percent of the population, had long controlled the political and economic resources of the country. Nevertheless, diversification of the economy and political transformations since the rise and fall of the PRG had softened these distinctions (see Government and Politics, this section).

Religious affiliation was the product of Grenada's colonial heritage. Approximately 65 percent of the population was Roman Catholic, a lingering effect of periodic French domination. The remaining 35 percent primarily belonged to three Protestant denominations: Anglican, Methodist, and Presbyterian. There was also a small Rastafarian (see Glossary) sect.

Education

Grenada's education system was deficient in meeting the basic needs of the country in the 1980s. Although literacy was estimated at nearly 90 percent, much of the population was only marginally literate and had little hope of becoming proficient at reading.

In 1981, the last year for which statistics were available in 1987, education was free and compulsory from ages six to fourteen, and most students completed a primary education. There were 68 primary schools with a total enrollment of approximately 22,100 students; the majority did not continue on to a secondary-school program. The secondary-school program for the same year included 20 schools and 6,250 students. Students took a middle-level examination at age sixteen to determine their eligibility for the final two years of preparatory work for university entrance. Few, however, actually completed these two years.

Grenada had only three institutions beyond the secondary level for technical or academic training of its citizens: the Institute for Further Education, the Teacher Training College, and the Technical and Vocational Institute. The St. George's Medical School, although administered in Grenada, existed to serve foreign medical students, most of whom came from the United States.

Although Grenada maintained a basic educational infrastructure, it was not producing workers with the vocational and administrative skills required of a developing economy. Notably deficient was training in electricity, electronics, plumbing, welding, construction, and other technical skills. A World Bank (see Glossary) development project to upgrade vocational training to help meet Grenada's long-term vocational needs was being reviewed in the spring of 1987.

Education reform was a pillar of the development platform of the PRG. Beginning in 1979, Bishop initiated programs designed to reorganize the entire curriculum and move it away from the British model. The overall plan envisioned the development of a nationwide education system that would meet the vague goal of addressing the ''particular needs'' of the society. This goal, however, was never explicitly defined, and education reform never became the rousing success claimed by the PRG.

Although the PRG strove to retrain primary-school and secondary-school teachers, little was accomplished because of the burden placed on teachers, who were asked both to instruct students and to attend PRG seminars. In addition, many teachers eventually became alienated and dropped out of the programs because of the programs' strong political overtones.

Perhaps the PRG's most successful attempts at education reform were the volunteer programs designed to improve rural literacy levels and repair community schools. Observers have suggested that rural literacy did improve and that stronger community ties were forged because of the pride generated through rebuilding local schools with volunteer labor. The overall education reform program, however, was not considered successful. Nevertheless, the publicity generated by education reform did contribute to the PRG's popularity.

Developments in primary and secondary education since the fall of the PRG in October 1983 were similarly minimal. Data and analyses of the post-PRG education system were not readily available, but a return to the British school system model was effected in 1984.

Health and Welfare

Health care in Grenada compared favorably with that in other Eastern Caribbean islands in 1983, and mortality rates were actually lower than those of many neighboring countries. Grenada had an infant mortality rate of 21.2 per 1,000 live births, which was slightly below the average for the English-speaking Caribbean islands. The overall death rate was 7.3 per 1,000 inhabitants. In 1984 the average life expectancy at birth was sixty-six years.

Morbidity indicators for the same time period reflected mixed results. Immunization against diphtheria, pertussis, and tetanus reached 68 percent of the population; 78 percent had been inoculated against poliomyelitis. Inoculation against measles, however, was provided to only 7 percent of the targeted population, and other immunization programs, such as against typhoid fever, were not available. Approximately 85 percent of the inhabitants had access to potable water; infectious or parasitic diseases caused only 1 percent of reported deaths in 1983. Three cases of acquired immune deficiency syndrome were reported as of 1986.

Attempts to reduce morbidity levels in the mid-1980s included expanding immunization programs, increasing the number of health inspectors, and improving solid waste management. Only a small percentage of meat, food, and restaurants were inspected for sanitary conditions, and at least 35 percent of all solid waste went uncollected, causing high levels of rodent and fly infestation. Efforts were underway after 1983 to correct these deficiencies with assistance from the Pan American Health Organization, World Health Organization (WHO), United States Agency for International Development (AID), and Project HOPE.

Grenada's health care system was patterned after WHO's primary health care model. Its immediate goals were to provide essential health care to the entire population. Priority was given to maternal and child care, as well as the development of a dental program. Other efforts sought to expand the potable water base, improve disposal of solid waste, increase prevention of vector-borne and communicable diseases, initiate health awareness education programs, and improve the allocation of drugs and medication.

Implementation of the health care policy was conducted by the Ministry of Health. Operations were financed through the national government budget; only 3.4 percent of capital expenditures went to health care development in 1985. Grenada's health care infrastructure consisted of six hospitals and thirty-five outpatient clinics, including twenty-seven visiting stations, six health clinics, one maternity unit, and one outpost unit.

Foreign aid had been an essential component of the health care system for many years. Cuba provided a large amount of foreign assistance prior to the United States-Caribbean intervention. This effort peaked in 1983 with donations of approximately US$40 million in medical relief. The overall health care effort by the PRG, however, remained mediocre at best.

Project HOPE, under contract with AID, was the primary provider of assistance to the health care system of Grenada after 1983. Its goal was to provide immediate health care delivery and assist with planning technical and managerial development programs. This included providing doctors and nurses while simultaneously helping the Grenada government design a self-sufficient national medical program.

The success of AID-sponsored projects was critical if Grenada hoped to achieve its long-term health care goals. The government lacked the ability to organize a comprehensive national health care delivery system. Developing such a system required both administrative and clinical expertise, in addition to technically trained medical professionals. The successful completion of the AID-sponsored projects, however, could eventually provide Grenada with one of the best health care programs in the Eastern Caribbean.

A compulsory retirement plan was first instituted among urban workers by the PRG in the early 1980s and expanded to include agricultural workers under the Herbert Blaize administration after 1983. The National Insurance Scheme, administered by the Ministry of Social Security, was established to ensure that all workers would have income following their retirement after age sixty-five. It averaged approximately 20 percent of total transfer payments in 1984.

Economy

In the late 1980s, Grenada was in the midst of a lengthy economic transition following the downfall of the PRG government in October 1983. Although somewhat limited in choice by the country's economic resource base, the PRG and the parliamentary government of Blaize that followed opted for two distinct economic development strategies. The PRG's economic strategy was based on a centrally governed economy dependent on substantial Cuban assistance. The Blaize strategy was one that allowed market forces to regulate the economy, with financial assistance from the United States.

Bishop's PRG guided the economy into a phase aptly described as "foreign aid socialism," a form of socialism maintained by financial dependence on other socialist countries. Early PRG economic philosophy espoused a strong, diversified agricultural sector and government control of industry through cooperative management and nationalization. What actually developed was a program dependent on the construction industry for growth and on foreign grants for capitalization. Analyses following the removal of the PRG government suggested that the attempt at socialist transformation did not produce a revolution in economic development; there was no change in the distribution of income, and the standard of living actually declined slightly. This occurred because the PRG failed to develop a well-defined economic plan, managed economic enterprises poorly, and became overly concerned with political, rather than economic, priorities.

The Blaize government, by contrast, undertook a change in economic orientation emphasizing tourism and agriculture as the leading economic sectors. Private control of economic enterprises, attraction of both public and private foreign capital, and pursuit of a strong export trade were the fundamental elements of the development policy. This approach was in keeping with the economic realities of an island nation with natural resources limited to small amounts of arable land, natural tourist attractions, and an underutilized labor force. Because of this resource restriction, as well as limited domestic consumption, cultural and historical ties, and easy market penetration, Grenada's economy was naturally linked to the import markets of the United States, Britain, and the Caribbean Community and Common Market (Caricom—see Appendix C) countries.

Macroeconomic Overview

Aggregate economic production has increased steadily since 1983, a year in which there was an actual decline in gross domestic product (GDP—see Glossary) of 2.9 percent. GDP rose by 2 percent in 1984, 3.7 percent in 1985, and 4.3 percent in 1986. Continued growth in GDP between 4 and 5 percent is expected through 1990, provided the economy does not experience any major setbacks.

Many sectors of the economy contributed to the growth of GDP. In 1985 government services accounted for 26.6 percent of GDP, the largest share of aggregate output. Next came agriculture (16.3 percent), the wholesale and retail trade (15.5 percent), construction (7.5 percent), hotels and restaurants (6.4 percent), and manufacturing (5.8 percent).

Much of Grenada's new-found economic prosperity was attributed to the completion of the international airport at Point Salines in St. George's. In addition to boosting the construction sector, it provided an airport to support the expanding tourist and export trades. Manufacturing and agriculture, however, were also important. Preliminary figures for 1986 suggested that manufacturing actually grew for the first time since 1982, and higher prices for agricultural products more than offset slight declines in production. The rise in government services also contributed to GDP figures, registering an increase of 11.2 percent in 1985.

Government figures, although incomplete, indicated that there was a concomitant rise in employment with increased production; nearly 4,000 new jobs were created in 1986. Unemployment, however, remained high, averaging between 20 and 25 percent in 1985, but it was moving in a downward direction after peaking in 1984 at 28 percent. Government plans to reduce the public payroll by 1,500–1,800 personnel—announced in 1987 but not yet implemented in late 1987—would further exacerbate the unemployment problem. Agriculture was the largest employer, providing between 25 and 30 percent of all jobs.

The government was counting on the continuing structural adjustment (see Glossary) in employment to absorb newly displaced government workers, as well as many of the perpetually unemployed. Tourism and manufacturing were expected to take on larger portions of the work force. This adjustment actually began shortly after World War II as the number of workers employed by the agricultural sector began to decline. The manufacturing sector experienced uneven growth after World War II; however, in 1986 it showed signs of growth. Because of strong growth in tourism, the unemployment burden was partially alleviated in 1986. Although the structural change away from agriculture as the dominant employer was Grenada's best hope for development, it did not guarantee relief from chronic unemployment, which was the direct result of high birth rates and long-term overpopulation.

Inflation was the only macroeconomic indicator that improved throughout both the Bishop and the Blaize governments. The most dramatic downward movements in consumer prices occurred after 1984. Inflation as measured by the change in consumer prices remained the same for 1980–81, at 10.6 percent. The index fell in 1982, with prices rising only 6.9 percent; this dropped to 6.5 percent, 3.6 percent, and 1.8 percent for 1983, 1984, and 1985, respectively. The government of Grenada recorded an actual decline of 0.8 percent in the general price level for 1986.

Although the government took some credit for lower inflation rates, the decline in food and fuel prices in 1985 was largely responsible for the overall reduction in inflation. Although the government was in a position to select fiscal and monetary policies designed to minimize locally produced inflation, domestic prices were very dependent on world inflation and the international prices of Grenada's primary imports.

Banking and Finance

In 1987 Grenada, as a member of the Organisation of Eastern Caribbean States (OECS—see Glossary), was a member of the Eastern Caribbean Central Bank (ECCB), which was headquartered in St. Christopher (hereafter, St. Kitts) and Nevis. It was bound by the ECCB's general guidelines on money supply and bank regulation and used the Eastern Caribbean dollar, which was pegged to the United States dollar at a constant exchange rate of EC$2.70 equals US$1.00. This relationship had some unusual effects on Grenada's international transactions. Because Grenada's exports were sold to numerous nations, the strength of the United States dollar in relation to other foreign currencies affected the ease with which Grenadian exports were sold.

In the case of a strengthening dollar, the Eastern Caribbean dollar would also appreciate with respect to other world currencies. This would cause Grenadian exports to become more expensive in the world market, while imports would become less expensive and more competitive with domestically produced goods. The overall effect would be to reduce Grenada's terms of trade, negatively affecting its balance of payments position. The reverse situation would have the opposite effect, strengthening Grenadian exports abroad, which would discourage the purchase of imports and improve overall terms of trade and the balance of payments. This situation occurred in 1987 as a result of the depreciation of the United States dollar in world currency markets.

The financial needs of Grenada were served by numerous public and private institutions below the central bank level. In 1985 the commercial banking system included four financial institutions, two of which were controlled by the government. The system was a holdover from the PRG, which chose to absorb all but two commercial banks into the public sector. The Blaize government slowly returned financial intermediation (see Glossary) to the private sector and intended to solicit proposals in 1987 for the sale of the remaining two publicly controlled banks.

Credit was extended for development projects through the Caribbean Financial Services Corporation, which provided long-term funds to new businesses through AID, the Grenada Development Bank, and the Grenada Cooperative Bank. Foreign investors provided much of their own funds for capital-intensive investment. The government planned to establish a merchant bank in 1987 to facilitate lending to new small business ventures.

Role of Government

The Blaize government played only an advisory role in the economy, preferring a market-oriented system to the tightly controlled economy of the previous government. The government saw its role as one of overseeing the privatization of the economy and assisting national development through public sector investment, as well as through monetary and fiscal policies.

The government's principal role as overseer of public enterprises and manager of infrastructural development was coordinated through its program of public sector investment. The purpose of this program was to coordinate private sector and public sector development efforts to maximize the potential for national economic growth. This was accomplished by providing direct assistance to the productive sectors, while also supporting them with infrastructural development. In 1985 investment in the public sector focused on three major areas: the productive sectors of agriculture, tourism, and manufacturing; physical infrastructure, such as roads; and the social sectors, principally health and education. Seventy-four percent of the funds were placed in infrastructural projects, including roads, water and sewerage, communications, and energy. Agriculture commanded 12 percent of the funds invested in productive resources, and education, health, and housing received a combined total of 7 percent of public funds.

Major improvements to communication and transportation facilities were attributed to public sector investment. Domestic and international communication systems on Grenada were considered good in the mid-1980s. The Grenada Telephone Company served all parts of the island with a 5,600-instrument automatic telephone system. Radio-relay links to neighboring islands provided high-quality international telephone and telex service. St. George's had one government-owned AM radio station broadcasting on 535 kilohertz and one television station. The principal local newspaper, the *Grenadian Voice,* was independent and was published weekly.

Roads were the primary mode of local transportation. Grenada had approximately 900 kilometers of improved highways, 600 kilometers of which were paved. Of the two principal roads, one followed the coastline and the other bisected the island, connecting St. George's and Grenville. Municipal buses and taxis linked all areas of the island. There were two airports on the island: Point Salines International Airport in St. George's and the older Pearls Airport, located north of Grenville. Grenada had no railroads or inland waterways and was serviced by ports in Grenville and St. George's.

Future allocation of funds called for a greater emphasis on the productive and social sectors; total expenditures on infrastructure were to be reduced to approximately 47 percent of the public sector investment budget. Such allocation was expected to assist with Grenada's development over the long run, but allocation was vulnerable to regional and economic politics because it depended on the government's ability to attract sufficient foreign capital. Although financing of capital expenditures was to be accomplished using foreign funds on a matching basis, all financing of the 1985 budget came from external grants and loans.

The government's role as public enterprise manager diminished after 1986 because of its desire to see the private sector control as much of Grenada's economic assets as possible. Among the twenty-nine public sector enterprises existing in that year, only five were slated to remain either partially or totally controlled by the government. These included three utility companies that provided water, electricity, and telephone service.

The government's role in the economy also included the formulation of monetary and fiscal policies. In the case of monetary policy, however, the government was constrained by its reliance on the ECCB for controlling the money supply. This forced the government to rely heavily on fiscal policy to guide the economy.

Fiscal policy was a major government mechanism for encouraging economic development but became very controversial in 1987 with the introduction of the national budget. It provided for an entirely different tax structure in which a value-added tax (VAT—see Glossary) replaced virtually all other taxes, including personal income taxes, export duties, and consumption taxes. The primary purpose of the VAT was to raise funds to correct the budget imbalance, while simplifying attendant collection and oversight responsibilities. A reduction in inflation and increased domestic savings and investment were also expected to result from the new tax strategy.

These goals were to be achieved by encouraging individual production, while simultaneously discouraging immediate consumption in favor of increased personal savings. The elimination of the personal income tax would make more money available to wage earners and give them a greater incentive to work. Consumption would be penalized with a 20-percent VAT placed on all domestically produced goods. Many essential items, such as food, were

View of St. George's harbor
Courtesy Grenada Tourism Department

exempt from taxation. The resulting increase in personal savings would then provide a resource base for domestic investment, while also reducing aggregate demand and placing a check on inflation. In early 1987, the VAT did not appear to be succeeding. A large government deficit was projected because of a decline in aggregate tax revenue, and political repercussions were also apparent.

Opponents of the VAT argued that it penalized domestically produced items that faced regional or international competition. In some cases, such as Grenadian rum products, imported substitutes immediately became less expensive. Such a turnaround forced the government to make many concessions in the VAT, which reduced revenue needed for central government operations.

The VAT was created to correct the government's budget deficit that had persisted throughout the 1980s and had been financed by external grants. Nonetheless, it appeared that this problem would not be solved in 1987 because the VAT was not capable of generating sufficient revenue to cover government expenses. Alternative measures would have to be found, however, because continued reliance on foreign aid to solve fiscal shortfalls was not a long-term solution.

Sectoral Performance

Grenada's primary economic sectors competed directly with those of other Caribbean islands. Major productive contributors to GDP were tourism, agriculture, and manufacturing. Construction and government services also played an important role.

Agriculture has traditionally been the largest revenue producer; it accounted for 25 percent of GDP and 90 percent of total merchandise exports in 1984. The main crops were cocoa, bananas, nutmeg, and mace, all of which are tree crops and well suited for the steep terrain. In the mid-1980s, farmers also ventured into the cut flowers and fresh fruits markets to take advantage of increased regional demand for these items, particularly in Trinidad and Tobago and the United States.

Agricultural output actually fell in 1985 because of production problems with traditional crops. These problems attested to Grenada's inability to plan strategically. In this case, poor crop performance coincided with strong markets for Grenada's traditional exports. Many cocoa and banana plants had reached maturity in 1985 and required replanting, nutmeg was not effectively marketed, and the mace crop fell victim to poor harvest techniques that lowered production. These problems occurred at a time when the price of nutmeg had risen 150 percent because the only other world producer, Indonesia, was experiencing production problems. Had Grenada been able to react to these market conditions, the strong world market would have absorbed all of the country's banana and mace production, enabling it to improve its GDP and balance of payments position.

Government assistance and foreign aid were being directed to the agricultural sector to address these problems. Expectations for the late 1980s included sectoral growth approaching 5 percent, with banana production returning to previous high output levels and cocoa production coming on line after new plants reached reproductive age. Immediate earnings would come from the nontraditional crops.

After the overthrow of the revolutionary government in October 1983, tourism became the fastest growing sector of the economy. It accounted for 7 percent of GDP and 46 percent of foreign exchange earnings in 1985. It promised continued growth into the next decade.

Completion of the international airport at Point Salines in 1985 launched the expansion of the tourist trade. Grenada enticed major air carriers from Canada, the United States, and Western Europe to make direct flights to Point Salines; however, hotel capacity had not yet grown sufficiently to warrant a significant increase in tourist traffic in such a short period of time.

Tourist statistics varied among different sources, but all pointed to the growth trend in the 1980s. According to informed observers, stay-over visitors increased 34 percent in 1985, climbing to 39,000 tourists. Cruise ship passengers similarly increased in 1985 to over 90,000, almost three times the number who visited in 1984. Total receipts from tourism reached US$23.8 million in 1985.

Hotel capacity also expanded, but not quickly enough to meet demand. By 1986 total capacity ranged between 500 and 600 rooms, nearly double that available in 1983. An additional 900 rooms were planned for the end of 1988; analysts suggested that this was not a realistic completion date, however. The success of the tourist trade in 1987 remained limited only by the lack of hotel accommodations.

As of late 1987, manufacturing had not been a dynamic part of the Grenadian economy; output stagnated after 1981, accounting for only 5.8 percent of GDP in 1985. The structure and focus of this sector largely explained its inability to grow. It stressed production of locally used manufactured goods such as tobacco, food products, garments, and building materials. This emphasis encouraged the development of small, fragmented businesses that were unable to take advantage of economies of scale (see Glossary) and the export market. The garment industry was the only manufacturing business that also produced for export, and it accounted for only 3 percent of foreign exchange earnings in 1985. The government hoped to change this trend by enticing foreign investors with attractive investment and tax codes.

Shortages of skilled labor, managerial expertise, and proper industrial infrastructure hindered development of the manufacturing sector. For example, Grenada was unable to enter labor-intensive manufacturing markets, such as assembly of electronic components, as did many of its neighbors. In 1986 government programs were created to address Grenada's infrastructural needs, and foreign capital was being sought to finance start-up costs of local businesses.

Foreign Trade and Balance of Payments

Grenada's exports of goods and services grew rapidly after 1983. The primary foreign exchange earners were agricultural products and tourism, which together accounted for 85 percent of all goods and services sold to foreigners in 1985. Revenue from tourism was US$23.8 million, slightly higher than earnings from agriculture, which reached US$20.1 million; clothing and other exports amounted to US$1.8 million.

Leading agricultural exports were fresh fruits and cocoa, which accounted for 52 percent of total merchandise exports. Nutmeg, bananas, and mace followed, capturing a total of 40 percent of total goods exported. Textiles accounted for only 3 percent of merchandise sent abroad. Miscellaneous items composed the remaining 5 percent.

Grenada's chief export markets were Western Europe, Caricom, the United States, and Canada. Western Europe accounted for 52 percent of Grenada's exports in 1984, most of which went to Britain. Caribbean countries provided markets for approximately one-third of Grenada's exports; Trinidad and Tobago imported the most. The United States and Canada absorbed 6 percent and 2 percent, respectively.

Food consistently composed 25 to 30 percent of the island's imports from 1979 to 1983. Other significant items purchased abroad during this period were machinery (15 to 20 percent), fuel (10 to 15 percent), manufactured goods (10 percent), and other miscellaneous manufactures (10 percent).

The principal sources of imports were the Caricom countries, Britain, the United States, Canada, and, more recently, Japan. Caricom economies provided nearly one-third of Grenada's imports during the 1980s; oil from Trinidad and Tobago accounted for two-thirds of Caricom imports. Manufactured goods and machinery generally came from the United States and Britain, whereas Japan furnished many of Grenada's automobiles.

Imports of goods and services exceeded exports in 1985, causing a deficit in the current account of US$29.4 million. Historically, Grenada has had a nearly offsetting surplus in the capital account in the form of public borrowing or official foreign government grants.

Imports of goods and services increased in 1984 and 1985 because of greater demand for food, fuel, and manufactured goods, which contributed to the 1985 current account deficit. The United States provided over US$20 million in direct grants to Grenada in 1984 and 1985 to offset the deficit. This aid gave Grenada a positive overall balance of payments and allowed it to make substantial repayments to the International Monetary Fund (IMF—see Glossary) and the ECCB. Grenada still maintained a foreign debt of US$48 million in 1985, which represented 92 percent of exports. Debt service payments were US$8.3 million, or 16 percent of exports.

Informed observers expected Grenada's current account deficit to hover around US$30 million at least through 1990, in spite of the expectation that exports would more than double in this period. Plans called for Grenada to replace foreign grants with private investment to maintain a positive overall balance of payments, provided that tourism and agriculture continued to grow at anticipated levels.

Government and Politics

The Governmental System

Grenada has been an independent state within the Commonwealth of Nations since 1974 (see Appendix B). This status has been one of the few constants during Grenada's somewhat turbulent history since that date. Although the 1979–83 tenure of the PRG led by Bishop produced marked changes in the governmental system, the PRG chose not to break its formal ties with the Commonwealth.

The PRG did revoke the independence Constitution of 1973, preferring to rule by revolutionary decree (or "people's laws"). This action produced some legal complications, particularly in the case of the judiciary. After the United States-Caribbean military intervention of October 1983 that deposed the short-lived Revolutionary Military Council established by Bernard Coard and General Hudson Austin of the People's Revolutionary Army (PRA), the Constitution of 1973 was brought back into force by Governor General Paul Scoon (see Current Strategic Considerations, ch. 7). Some judicial provisions established under the PRG were retained, however, for the sake of continuity and for the facilitation of the transition to a more representative government.

The 1973 Constitution provides for a parliamentary system of government on the Westminster model. The theoretical head of state is the British monarch, whose authority is represented on the island by a governor general. When an elected Parliament is in place, the governor general has little real authority and limited official duties (a role similar to that of the monarch in the British government). The governor general is not altogether a figurehead, however, as demonstrated by the events of the 1983–84 period. Scoon assumed constitutional authority in October 1983; he subsequently appointed the Advisory Council (also known as the Interim Government) led by Nicholas Braithwaite, which guided Grenada until parliamentary elections could be held in December 1984.

Even when an elected Parliament is in place, the governor general retains a degree of latent constitutional authority. For example, it is the governor general who must dismiss members of Parliament (for nonattendance or criminal conviction, among other reasons), even though in practice this action is taken only at the urging of the prime minister or the leader of the opposition. The governor general also has the power to declare a state of emergency, a declaration that has the effect of dissolving Parliament.

Parliament is the major governmental institution in Grenada. It is a bicameral legislature, with a lower house referred to as the House of Representatives and an upper house known as the Senate. Representation in the House of Representatives is apportioned according to population. The leader of the party securing the majority of seats in Parliament is named prime minister by the governor general. The leader of the party winning the next largest bloc of seats is named leader of the opposition.

The position of senator is nonelective. The prime minister has the authority to recommend the appointment of seven senators of his own choosing, plus an additional three senators who are to be selected in consultation with "the organizations or interests which the Prime Minister considers the Senators should be elected to represent." These "organizations and interests," although not enumerated in the Constitution, traditionally encompass agricultural and business groups as well as trade unions. In addition to the ten senators nominated by the prime minister, the leader of the opposition is entitled to three nominations of his own. Thus, total membership of the Senate is thirteen.

According to the 1973 Constitution, Parliament "may make laws for the peace, order and good government of Grenada." Parliament has the power to amend the Constitution by a two-thirds vote of both houses. The Constitution also makes provision for amendment by referendum. The House of Representatives wields the power of the purse; so-called money bills (bills dealing with taxation, public debt, or grants of public funds) may only be introduced in that chamber. Nonmoney bills may be introduced in either chamber. Sessions of Parliament must be held at least once each year, with intervals of no more than six months between the end of the last sitting of one session and the beginning of the next.

The parliamentary system gives a great deal of power to the prime minister, who can control the workings of government through the authority granted the prime minister to call and dissolve sessions of Parliament. One complaint lodged against Prime Minister Blaize in the Grenadian press since 1985 has concerned his failure to call frequent parliamentary sessions. This tactic allows important governmental matters, e.g., the formulation of the budget, to be handled exclusively by the cabinet, thus limiting the input and oversight of Parliament.

The power of the prime minister rests further in the authority to name a cabinet of ministers who assume responsibility for the administration of the government in such areas as the prime minister may designate. The prime minister frequently assumes direct control over key portfolios or over ministries of particular

personal or political interest. For example, after his party's electoral victory in December 1984, Prime Minister Blaize took charge
of the ministries of home affairs, security, information, Carriacou
affairs (Blaize is a native of the island of Carriacou), finance and
trade, and industrial development and planning.

The Grenadian judiciary has been the branch of government
most affected by the political events of the post-1979 period. Prior
to the advent of the PRG, Grenada participated in the Eastern
Caribbean States Supreme Court along with Antigua and Barbuda,
Dominica, St. Kitts-Nevis-Anguilla, St. Lucia, and St. Vincent
and the Grenadines as provided for by the West Indies Act of 1967.
The Bishop government severed this association and set up the
Grenada Supreme Court and the Court of Appeal. Magistrate's
courts were retained by the PRG to exercise summary jurisdiction.

After the events of October 1983, the status of the courts set up
by the PRG came into question. The legality of their continued
operation was challenged specifically by defense attorneys for Coard,
Austin, and other defendants who were to stand trial for the October 19, 1983, murder of Bishop and others in Fort Rupert (the
name given to Fort George between 1979 and 1983 in honor of
Bishop's father) in St. George's. The Grenada Supreme Court and
the Court of Appeal considered several such challenges under its
civil jurisdiction, but it rejected them under the doctrine of ''state
necessity,'' thus permitting both the court and the trial to continue.
Meanwhile, the Blaize government formally applied in July 1986
for readmission to the Eastern Caribbean States Supreme Court.
Upon acceptance into this court system, the Grenada Supreme
Court and Court of Appeals will be abolished because cases involving both original jurisdiction and appeal can be submitted to
the regional court.

The civil service (or public service, as it is known in Grenada)
is professional and generally apolitical, although there have been
instances in Grenada's colonial history when an entrenched
bureaucracy has acted to frustrate the ambitions of a ruler, e.g.,
Eric Gairy's conflicts with the bureaucracy during his brief tenure
as the island's chief minister in 1961–62. The civil service still owes
much to its British colonial origins. Its relative autonomy, once
a product of isolation from the mother country, was legally reinforced by the Constitution of 1973. During the period of the Constitution's suspension by the PRG, the civil service was politicized
to some degree as the ruling NJM sought to solidify its control over
all aspects of Grenadian life. During the time the PRG was in
power, the civil service lost a great many experienced employees

to emigration. The loss reflected to some extent the traditionally high levels of outmigration; in the case of civil servants, however, the motivation was in many cases more political than economic, expressing the employees' unwillingness to cooperate or collaborate with the workings of the "revo."

The basic unit of the electoral system is the constituency. For the elections of 1984, the country was divided into several constituencies (some constituencies are grouped into parishes, a traditional designation deriving from the discontinued local government organization). In the December 1984 elections, fifty-two candidates competed for the fifteen seats in the House of Representatives. The total number of registered voters was 48,152; of these, 41,041 (or 85.2 percent) went to the polls, a reflection of the general enthusiasm for the return of electoral politics.

Political Dynamics

Politics in Grenada traditionally has been more concerned with personalities and class interests than with ideology. Political parties, even those that grow out of labor union movements, are usually dominated by charismatic leaders who can motivate their followers through strong emotional (or, in the case of Gairy, even mystical) appeal. The aspect of class interest has tended to devolve into lower versus middle-class aspirations, there being no political party or parties commonly identified with the interests of the upper class.

In this respect, as in many others, the PRG represented an aberration in Grenadian history. The "vanguard" of the revolution— the NJM—was a party whose membership was drawn from the urban middle class (mainly young professionals who saw their opportunities limited under the corrupt Gairy government). When the PRG assumed power in March 1979, it presented the novel impression of a middle-class junta that sought, at least rhetorically, to reach out to the poor (the workers and peasantry). This initial promise never bore fruit, however, as the PRG was unable to make lasting economic gains and eventually fell victim to ideological infighting between Leninists and pragmatists, an internal conflict that paved the way for external intervention.

The New National Party (NNP) scored a resounding electoral victory in December 1984, winning fourteen of the fifteen seats in the House of Representatives. The NNP was neither an established party nor a homogeneous one, but rather an amalgamation of three separate parties that, with some outside encouragement, ultimately joined forces to ward off the potential restoration to power of Gairy.

*New Jewel Movement photograph of a political meeting during
the regime of Maurice Bishop; background posters of Bishop,
Nicaraguan leader Daniel Ortega, and Cuban leader Fidel Castro
Courtesy United States Department of Defense*

The senior partner in the NNP was Blaize's Grenada National
Party (GNP). Established in 1956, the GNP has traditionally
represented the interests of the urban middle class, drawing the
majority of its support from St. George's. The GNP led the government in Grenada during the periods 1957–61 and 1962–67. These
two periods of GNP government represented the only interruptions in the domination of Grenadian politics by Gairy and GULP
between 1951 and 1979. In 1976 the GNP joined an opposition
coalition that included Bishop's NJM, but it played no part in the
PRG after the 1979 coup.

Another member of the NNP was the National Democratic Party
(NDP), established in February 1984 and led by George Brizan.
Formerly a member of the NJM, Brizan dissociated himself from
the group after it came to be dominated by Bishop, Coard, and
others who envisioned it as a Marxist-Leninist vanguard party.
Brizan's political leanings were said to be social democratic.

The third constituent of the NNP was the Grenada Democratic
Movement (GDM), founded in Barbados by Francis Alexis. The
NNP had originally included the Christian Democratic Labour
Party (CDLP) among its ranks, but the CDLP dropped out shortly
after the establishment of the NNP over what appeared to be

369

a personal dispute between Blaize and CDLP leader Winston Whyte.

The evolution of the NNP was neither easy nor smooth. The first step in the process was the April 1984 formation of the Team for National Togetherness (TNT). This initial umbrella group was to have brought the GNP, NDP, and GDM under one political banner; however, its establishment was announced publicly before the private process of negotiating party organization could get fully underway. These talks eventually bogged down over the issue of how many candidates from each of the constituent parties would be allowed to contest the parliamentary elections. Frustrated with the haggling, Brizan withdrew the NDP from the TNT in August. The GNP/GDM grouping was then renamed the Team for National Unity.

In addition to the specific dispute over candidacies, the TNT leaders also differed over broader issues of ideology and political protocol, according to some sources. These divergences seem to have pitted Blaize, the conservative elder statesman, against Brizan, the young progressive. Blaize is reported to have felt that the GNP deserved primacy within the coalition by virtue of its longer history as an established party; he is said to have demanded veto power over all proposed candidates. There may also have been disputes over specific issues, such as the presence of United States and Caribbean military forces on Grenada and the continuation of certain social programs begun under the PRG.

The seeming inability of the moderate Grenadian parties to unite was viewed with concern by the leaders of neighboring countries. Having supported military action to rid the country of a seemingly unstable Marxist-Leninist regime, these leaders did not wish to see Grenada returned to the control of Gairy, whom they viewed as the most likely beneficiary of a divided electorate. If nothing else, Gairy's return to power would have represented a public relations embarrassment of the first order. Therefore, acting in a tradition of regional consultation stretching back at least as far as the West Indies Federation of 1958–62, prime ministers J.M.G.M. "Tom" Adams of Barbados, James Mitchell of St. Vincent and the Grenadines, and John G.M. Compton of St. Lucia volunteered their services as mediators in the negotiating process. Most reports concur that the session that finally produced the NNP was held in August 1984 on Union Island in St. Vincent and the Grenadines. The neighboring prime ministers were present at the August 26 public ceremony in Grenada at which the formation of the new coalition was announced.

370

Reports of friction among the NNP membership began to circulate soon after the December 1984 elections. Factionalism within the party stemmed from the nature of its founding, the uneasiness that prevailed among the leaders of the constituent parties, and the autocratic control exercised by Blaize over party affairs. Early reports hinted at rivalry between Alexis and Brizan for the right to succeed Blaize as party leader. This notion was reinforced by the competition between the two for the post of deputy political leader, a position to which Alexis was elected at the party convention of December 1985. Subsequent events tended to draw Alexis and Brizan closer together, however. At the 1986 party convention, Blaize's associate Ben Jones replaced Alexis as deputy political leader, cementing further the dominance of Blaize's GNP faction within the NNP.

The first public demonstrations of the NNP's internal tensions were provided by the defections of two members of Parliament— Kenny Lalsingh and Phinsley St. Louis—each of whom left the party in August 1986 and formed separate political organizations. In February 1987, observers reported that Brizan, Alexis, and Tillman Thomas, the junior minister for legal affairs, had refused to sign a declaration of party unity. In April this simmering dispute boiled over when the three resigned from the government, citing their disagreement with Blaize over what had come to be known as the "retrenchment," the proposed release of 1,500–1,800 civil servants. Although they did not announce their withdrawal from the NNP at that time, Alexis and Brizan technically became part of the parliamentary opposition, reducing Blaize's majority, once fourteen to one, to nine to six.

In October 1987, the opposition coalesced under the banner of yet another political party, the National Democratic Congress (NDC). Brizan was elected as leader of the NDC, which also included Alexis, Lalsingh, Thomas, and St. Louis among its ranks. Although its level of popular support was difficult to gauge, the NDC appeared to generate some enthusiasm among those Grenadians looking for an alternative to the established political organizations headed by Blaize and Gairy.

Aside from the NNP, the only major political party in Grenada in the mid-1980s was GULP, which dated back to 1951 and was led by Gairy. Once the dominant political force on the island, Gairy and his party gradually lost the confidence of most Grenadians through corruption and repression. This erosion of public support was demonstrated by the generally positive reaction to the 1979 seizure of power by Maurice Bishop and the NJM. In the post-Bishop period, GULP clearly suffered from Gairy's enforced exile, his diminished personal popularity, and the low level of party institutionalization. GULP's disarray could be read in the party's reaction to the December 1984 elections. Immediately after the balloting, GULP appeared to represent the official parliamentary opposition to the NNP. Its one victorious member, Marcel Peters, defected after a dispute with party leader Gairy over political tactics, however. Gairy had decried the elections as fraudulent and ordered Peters to refuse his seat in the House. Peters refused, withdrew from GULP, declared his own political organization (apparently standard procedure for Grenadian politicians), and assumed the post of leader of the opposition, a position he eventually yielded to NNP defector St. Louis.

The history of GULP is the history of its leader, Eric Gairy. Gairy began his political life as a labor leader, establishing the Grenada Mental and Manual Workers Union (GMMWU) in 1950. The GMMWU was a rural workers' union that concentrated its organizing efforts within the Grenadian sugar industry. Like many young Grenadians, Gairy left the island in search of work. After a short stint as a construction worker in Trinidad and Tobago, Gairy moved on to the oil refineries of Aruba. It was there that he began his labor organizing activities, somewhat to the consternation of Dutch authorities, who reportedly deported him in 1949. After asserting his credentials as a populist leader through the vehicle of the GMMWU, Gairy successfully entered the electoral arena in 1951 under the banner of the newly formed GULP, which took 64 percent of that year's ballots (the first held under the Universal Suffrage Law of 1950). Gairy and GULP lost only two of the six general elections held from 1951 until 1979, when the party was overthrown by the NJM. The party drew heavily on the organization and resources of the GMMWU, and the membership of the two groups remained fluid throughout Gairy's years in power.

Gairy returned to Grenada in January 1984 after another involuntary exile, this one lasting almost five years. Although Gairy appeared to have retained some support among the rural population, most Grenadians seemed to have rejected him as a result of his past history of strongman rule, corruption, and harassment of political opponents.

After the electoral defeat of 1984, Gairy seemed to be making plans to broaden the appeal of GULP. In April 1985, he claimed that the party's leadership would be purged, that attempts would be made to expand its low level of support among Grenadian youth, and that all future GULP candidates for office would be drawn directly from the ranks of the party and not recruited for only one campaign. This last promise suggested an effort to institutionalize what had long been a highly personalistic political organization. GULP support appeared to be dwindling by 1987, however, as new party leaders failed to emerge, other political leaders continued to attract support among Gairy's former rural constituency, and the party restricted its activities as a result of lack of funds.

Although GULP appeared largely ineffective as a political vehicle, Gairy continued to enjoy some measure of influence on the labor front. His longtime union organization, the GMMWU, was renamed the Grenada Manual Maritime and Intellectual Workers Union (GMMIWU). Its membership base still lay among rural agricultural workers. The economic disarray left in the wake of the PRG and the void in agricultural labor organization after the demise of the Bishop regime left the GMMIWU in a good position to recruit new members and exert influence on both the government and private producers, although it, like GULP, suffered from underfunding and possible defection of its members to other organizations.

The left, consisting of the Maurice Bishop Patriotic Movement (MBPM) and the persistent remnants of the NJM, was an insignificant political force in the late 1980s. The MBPM was founded in 1984 by Kendrick Radix, an original NJM member and PRG cabinet minister who played no part in the short-lived Revolutionary Military Council. The MBPM began as the Maurice Bishop and the 19th October Martyrs Foundation, a group dedicated to raising funds for scholarships for Grenadian students (presumably for study in "progressive" or socialist countries) and to erecting a monument to Bishop and other fallen comrades. Although successful in its monument campaign, the MBPM failed to have the Point Salines International Airport named after Bishop. The transformation of the MBPM from foundation to political party occurred in August 1984; Radix claimed that only his movement could prevent Gairy's return to power. During the election campaign, he promised that an MBPM government would confiscate supposedly idle farmland that had been previously held by the PRG but had since reverted to its previous owners because of a lack of proper compensation. The movement failed to attract a popular following in the 1984 elections, however, capturing only 5 percent of the vote and no seats in Parliament.

The group still laying claim to the title of NJM represented the hard core of the organization, the remaining "Coardites" who supported the establishment of an orthodox Marxist-Leninist state but who had not involved themselves directly in the putsch of October 19, 1983. The NJM declined to participate in the elections of 1984, probably knowing that it would have drawn even less support than

Radix's MBPM (with which it continued to feud rhetorically). The continued existence of this organization despite a good deal of public antipathy was one measure of the openness of the Grenadian system.

Other small political parties continued to function in Grenada in the mid-1980s. Whyte's CDLP contested the elections but attracted only 0.26 percent of the total vote. The Grenada Federated Labour Party, an organization that first contested elections in 1957 but that subsequently lay dormant, drew only 0.02 percent of the 1984 vote.

Foreign Relations

Historically, Grenada had long manifested a pro-Western foreign policy. This is not to imply that Grenada's role in the international arena was an active one in the immediate preindependence and postindependence period. Its focus during this period was, first and foremost, a regional one, attended to in such forums as Caricom and the OECS. Beyond the horizon of regional concerns, Grenada looked to the Western powers, primarily the United States and Britain, as its political models, its economic marketplaces, and its sources of foreign aid and investment.

Foreign Relations under the People's Revolutionary Government

The advent of the People's Revolutionary Government (PRG) produced a sharp deviation in the previous norms of Grenadian policy. By the time of Bishop's overthrow and assassination in late 1983, Grenada had been converted from a relatively unassuming member of the Commonwealth to an incipient Soviet-Cuban client state with aspirations of playing a larger role on the world stage.

Almost from the inception of the PRG, Bishop moved to deemphasize traditional ties such as those with Britain and to build strong ties with the Soviet Union and its allies. Cuba was the most important of these new associations. It was evident during his lifetime that Bishop greatly admired President Fidel Castro of Cuba; after Bishop's death (and the revelations contained in some of the documents captured by United States and Caribbean forces), it became clear that he had also shared Castro's revolutionary ideology. The documents revealed that Grenadian foreign policymakers under the PRG were highly dependent upon the Cubans for advice and direction. Despite their trumpeted nationalism, the Grenadians seemed quite willing to adopt the Cuban (and, by extension, the Soviet) agenda in international arenas such as the United Nations, the Nonaligned Movement, and the Socialist International.

Grenadian relations with the Soviet Union were also strengthened during this period. Soviet specialists Jiri and Virginia Valenta
have contended that by the end of the Bishop regime, the NJM
was considered a "fraternal" party by the Communist Party of
the Soviet Union and had been referred to in terms of "new
popular-democratic statehood," a characterization that the Soviets
had applied to East European regimes in the late 1940s.

Although the Cubans provided the bulk of the economic aid from
the Council for Mutual Economic Assistance to Grenada, the
Soviets undertook to provide the requisite weaponry for a buildup
of Grenadian military capability and a general militarization of
Grenadian society. Three separate arms agreements were signed
during Bishop's tenure. After the seizure of weapons stocks by
United States-Caribbean forces in 1983, the matériel already on
the island was estimated as sufficient to equip a force of 10,000;
records subsequently revealed that not all the equipment contracted
for had yet been delivered. The presence of such an arsenal on an
island that before 1979 had maintained a police force of little more
than 100 was a matter of concern not only for the United States
but also and more particularly for the neighboring states of the
Eastern Caribbean.

In addition to establishing stronger ties with Cuba and the Soviet
Union, the PRG also established economic and diplomatic relations with Vietnam, the Democratic People's Republic of Korea
(North Korea), the German Democratic Republic (East Germany),
and Libya, among others. The Libyans were the most generous
of the island's new sources of economic aid during this period.

The events of October 1983 exposed the limitations of the PRG's
policy. The violent action taken by the Coard-Austin faction apparently took the Soviet Union, the United States, and Cuba by
surprise. Swift military action by United States and Caribbean
forces left little time for the Cubans or the PRA to fortify the island and provide additional supplies and troop reinforcements, even
if the Cubans had been willing to do so. Castro's remarks after
the intervention indicated that Cuba was not prepared to commit
significant forces to the defense of Grenada. The Soviets obviously
followed the same line of thinking, constrained as they were by
both geography and politics.

Relations with Latin American and Caribbean Countries

After taking the reins of government, Prime Minister Blaize
returned Grenadian foreign policy to its more traditional orientation, although with a distinct pro-United States flavor. A familiar
figure to most of the leaders of the OECS states, Blaize moved

375

quickly to reassure these leaders of Grenada's return to the democratic fold and to mollify the governments of other regional states
that had objected to the military intervention.

Discounting Cuba, the most negative reactions to the intervention came from Trinidad and Tobago, Guyana, and the Bahamas.
The government of Belize decried the action, but in milder terms.

The most injurious of these objections from the Grenadian viewpoint was that of Trinidad and Tobago. Close cultural, familial,
and migratory links make Grenadians sensitive to events and opinions in Trinidad and Tobago; public condemnation by the government of Prime Minister George Chambers, coupled with the
imposition of restrictions on Grenadian immigrants, puzzled and
stung most Grenadians. They were able to take some consolation,
however, in the fact that the press in Trinidad and Tobago (and,
apparently, the majority of citizens) supported the intervention and
condemned their prime minister for his opposition to it. Eventually, in 1986, persistent efforts by the Grenadians along with those
of other OECS members induced Trinidad and Tobago to drop
the visa restriction on Grenadians.

Grenada was integrated into the Regional Security System (RSS)
once the Special Service Unit (SSU) of its police force was fully
trained (see A Regional Security System, ch. 7). The military intervention of 1983 heightened the awareness among regional
governments of the need for some kind of security force that could
respond to small-scale disruptions or attempts at destabilization.
The danger had been pointed up previously by the 1979 NJM coup
in Grenada, but collective action on regional security from 1979
to 1983 had been hampered to some degree by the PRG's continued membership in regional organizations, such as Caricom and
the OECS.

Grenada's primary forum for the expression of foreign relations
concerns beyond its subregion was Caricom. The Blaize government did not play a leading role in this forum, however, preferring to lobby behind the scenes for consensus on issues of regional
concern. This approach, a logical one in view of the fact that Caricom foreign relations resolutions must be approved unanimously,
took advantage of Blaize's acceptance and connections among
regional leaders and his considerable personal persuasiveness.

Reaching somewhat beyond the limits of Caricom, the Blaize
government also engaged in some tentative economic negotiations
with the government of Puerto Rico. Governor Rafael Hernán-
dez Colón visited Grenada in April 1985. One of the principal items
on the agenda was the exploration of possible joint ventures that
would establish plants in Grenada with seed money from both

Puerto Rican-based companies and Grenadian investors. Such ventures would be designed to take advantage of tax benefits granted to investors in Puerto Rico under the United States tax code. By early 1987, these negotiations had yielded some benefit to Grenada in the form of a ''twin plant'' (a factory assembling finished products using components fashioned abroad) set up by the United States firm Johnson and Johnson to produce nurse's caps.

Relations with the United States

The government of Prime Minister Blaize, recognizing the importance of sustained United States support for Grenada, sought to identify itself closely with the United States and particularly with President Ronald Reagan's administration. After Blaize's election, he traveled frequently to Washington to lobby for sustained levels of aid, endorsed and defended United States foreign policy actions that other Third World leaders either condemned or avoided discussing (such as the United States bombing of Libya in April 1986), and hosted Reagan's brief but tumultuous visit to the island in February 1986. According to a Royal Grenada Police Force (RGPF) estimate, some 42,000 attended a rally for the United States president held in Queen's Park; if accurate, the figure represented some 47 percent of the island's population.

For its part, the Reagan administration initially sought to infuse Grenada with sufficient levels of development aid to effect the repair of all collateral damage caused by the military action of 1983, to upgrade the island's infrastructure to a point where it could compete economically with other regional states (in such areas as tourism, agriculture, and light manufacturing), and to establish improved health care and education programs. Once these goals had been accomplished to some degree, the United States plan seemed to envision economic development for Grenada through foreign investment, primarily in export-oriented enterprises and tourism.

By September 1986, postintervention United States aid to Grenada had totaled approximately US$85 million. It had become clear, however, that United States aid to Grenada would not continue at the high levels it had reached during the previous three years. A drawdown in aid was driven not only by an improving domestic situation in Grenada but also by United States budgetary constraints and the imperative of equal treatment for other Caribbean states. The reduction was reluctantly accepted by the Grenadian government; a decrease in United States economic support, however, especially a precipitous one, threatened to exert increased pressure on the Blaize government from a population whose expectations of development and increased prosperity had been raised (perhaps unrealistically) by the 1983 intervention.

In the security sphere, Grenada has been an enthusiastic participant in United States-sponsored military exercises in the Eastern Caribbean. These exercises, such as "Ocean Venture 86," have served to provide training to the SSU of the RGPF and to improve Grenadian infrastructure to a limited degree through associated civic action projects carried out by United States forces.

In the late 1980s, it appeared that the United States-Grenadian relationship would continue to be shaped and defined by the events of October 1983. For the Grenadian viewpoint on that action—variously referred to as an intervention, an invasion, or a rescue mission—one could do worse than to quote the respected Grenadian journalist Alister Hughes, who has written that

> An academic judgement in the world outside Grenada has condemned the military intervention by U.S. forces and the Caribbean Peacekeeping Force as a violation of the island's sovereignty. This view is shared in Grenada only by the small Marxist minority. The overwhelming majority see the intervention as a "rescue mission" which saved them from the anarchy which had been created and from the possible killing of thousands.

Relations with the Commonwealth and Others

Before and after the Bishop regime, Grenada identified more with the countries of the Commonwealth of Nations (see Appendix B) than with those of Latin America. The reasons for this are cultural, historical, and economic in nature. Culturally, Grenadians are still strongly influenced by British political forms and social mores. Historically, the Commonwealth countries share a common legacy of colonialism, however much that legacy may vary in its contemporary manifestations. Economically, British and other West European aid and trade mechanisms tie the Commonwealth Caribbean more into their markets than is the case for most Latin American economies. The competitive, noncomplementary nature of the agricultural export economies of the Caribbean and those of many Latin American states, particularly those of Central America, also exerts influence on their state-to-state relations.

Grenada experienced some friction in its relations with non-Caribbean Commonwealth nations after the United States-Caribbean intervention. The government of British prime minister Margaret Thatcher made no secret of its disagreement with the employment of military force in Grenada. This attitude was reflected in the position of Commonwealth secretary general Shridath Ramphal, who objected to the disbursement of Commonwealth aid funds to Grenada until all foreign military forces were withdrawn from the island. This stance, apparently accepted by most of the non-Caribbean members of the organization (New Zealand being the only such nation to support the United States-Caribbean military action), gradually gave way to a more receptive approach by most members as Grenada began to reconstruct its governmental and political system.

After rendering its initial objections, Britain became the largest Commonwealth aid donor to Grenada. Its December 1983 grant of US$1.1 million was its first to its former colony since 1978. Thereafter, it provided aid in the form of both loans and grants. This aid was expected to total more than US$7 million for the period 1985–90. British assistance proved valuable as well in such areas as police training and equipment, community development, housing, and spare parts for local industry. Britain also reassumed its position as the leading market for Grenadian exports.

The revitalization of British-Grenadian relations was symbolically confirmed by the visit of Queen Elizabeth II to the island on October 31, 1985. The Queen read the Throne Speech to open the Grenadian Parliament and was warmly received by the government and the public.

Grenadian relations with Canada since October 1983 have followed a pattern similar to those with Britain. After an initial period of friction and diplomatic disruption, relations were normalized by early 1986. Canadian aid programs (in such areas as agriculture and construction) were never formally suspended; in addition to these established programs, the Canadian government agreed in 1984 to provide aid and technical assistance toward the completion of Point Salines International Airport. Canada also assisted in the installation of a digital direct-dial telephone system.

Beyond the Commonwealth, the Blaize government acknowledged foreign aid donations from the governments of France, Venezuela, and the Republic of Korea (South Korea). In addition to providing increased economic aid, Venezuela also upgraded its diplomatic representation in Grenada from the chargé d'affaires to the ambassadorial level in 1985. Other sources of economic aid included the European Economic Community, with which Grenada is associated through the Lomé Convention (see Glossary), and, to a more limited extent, the Organization of American States.

The post-1983 governments of Grenada also took steps to downgrade their country's relations with communist countries. Relations with the Soviet Union were broken by Governor General Scoon in November 1983. Ties with North Korea were severed in January 1985. Although the Grenadians stopped short of

379

breaking relations with Cuba, these relations were downgraded and Cuban presence on the island withdrawn. The retention of downgraded relations may be attributable in part to a claim by the Cuban government, still pending in 1987, for the return of construction equipment from the Point Salines International Airport project.

The government established relations with China in October 1985. Relations with the government of Libya were broken in November 1983, in retaliation for the Libyans' strong political support for the PRG.

National Security

The Royal Grenada Police Force

After mid-1985, internal security in Grenada was the responsibility of the Royal Grenada Police Force (RGPF). Although the title of the organization is traditional, the force itself had been reconstituted and its members retrained and reequipped since the United States-Caribbean intervention of October 1983. In the immediate wake of the action by the United States military and the 350-member Caribbean Peace Force (CPF), units of these forces handled police and security duties on the island. The last of the United States military police personnel departed Grenada in June 1985; the remnants of the CPF pulled out shortly thereafter, leaving the new and inexperienced RGPF to fend for itself.

The RGPF has had a history of personal and political manipulation in Grenada. Under Gairy, the authority and professionalism of the force were undermined by the establishment of personal paramilitary units (such as the infamous "mongoose gang"), which served to intimidate Gairy's opponents and inhibit free expression of political viewpoints on the island. After Gairy's ouster in 1979, Bishop's PRG set about restructuring Grenada's security system along with its governmental, political, and economic systems. Under the PRG, the RGPF continued to exist both in name and in fact—a level of some 350 was maintained —but in practice, the RGPF yielded its responsibilities and its jurisdiction to the People's Revolutionary Army (PRA), a politicized force presumed to be loyal to Bishop and the PRG. Under the Bishop regime, the RGPF was neglected in terms of manpower, funding, training, and equipment. As was the case under the Gairy regime, the police force enjoyed neither the confidence nor the support of the Grenadian people.

In light of this repressive history, after October 1983 it became clear to both foreign and Grenadian observers that the establishment of an apolitical and professional police force was essential for the development of a representative and pluralistic system of government on the island. The most pressing need in this regard was training. For the United States, meeting this need presented a dilemma of sorts, for United States security assistance to foreign police forces had been prohibited by the United States Congress since the 1960s. Thus, some creative and cooperative programs were required.

The interim Grenadian government solved the problem by establishing an SSU, an elite eighty-member paramilitary force within the larger RGPF. Apparently both the United States and the leaders of other Caribbean nations had urged the Interim Government to form such a group. The majority of the Caribbean leaders had expressed interest in training similar forces of their own, which eventually could be integrated into a regional security system (see A Regional Security System, ch. 7). The expanded paramilitary mission of the SSU made possible the provision of United States funds through the Military Assistance Program and allowed for training of Grenadian personnel by United States Army Special Forces units.

The training of the RGPF was facilitated further by the cooperation of the British government. After the initial objections by the Thatcher government to the military intervention were smoothed over, training and assistance to the RGPF constituted one of the major British contributions toward the normalization of affairs in its former colony. Although not overwhelming in terms of numbers or expenditure, British security assistance was timely; three British police advisers were at work on the island by early 1984. Training of RGPF recruits by the British advisers was conducted on the island, mainly at Fort George. More extensive training took place off the island, at the Regional Police Training Center in Barbados (training at both sites was provided at British expense).

The total training program consisted of three phases. Phase one provided physical conditioning and basic skills for groups of Grenadian recruits during a four-week course under the supervision of United States military personnel. Phase one training also provided an opportunity for instructors to identify those recruits who would be most suitable for service in the paramilitary SSU. A fourteen-week course in basic police procedure constituted phase two for those trainees who had successfully completed the four-week session; this phase was administered by British police advisers. Most of the members of the RGPF underwent only the first two training phases. For those who qualified, phase three provided instruction in the more varied skills required for service in the SSU.

At the completion of all training phases, the RGPF counted some 600 men and women among its ranks. Included in that total was the eighty-member SSU. The domestic duties of the RGPF included airport security, immigration procedures, firefighting, and maritime interdiction (through the Grenadian Coast Guard, also a part of the RGPF). The SSU was available for peacekeeping duties in Grenada or on neighboring islands under the auspices of the RSS.

The postintervention RGPF was envisioned as an apolitical force performing purely domestic duties. The SSU, in addition to its regional obligations, was also intended to function as a domestic crowd control unit. In an effort to extend the outreach and heighten the profile of the RGPF among the population, the Interim Government of Nicholas Braithwaite expressed interest in reopening community police stations closed by the PRG. The physical disrepair of many of these stations forced the government to put this proposal on hold. Whether or not the RGPF was planning to enhance its community relations and increase its effectiveness through regular patrolling of the island was uncertain, given the traditional station-bound orientation of the force.

According to an early 1986 report in the *Grenadian Voice,* the RGPF was considering the establishment of a reserve force of volunteers who would receive police training and be prepared for mobilization under emergency conditions (presumably in case of natural disaster or generalized public unrest).

Civil and Political Unrest

Some three years after the violent events of October 1983, the potential for serious political unrest in Grenada appeared to be surprisingly low. Although various officials and members of the government had cited the potential threat to stability from disgruntled leftist elements, these pronouncements appeared to have been made primarily to rally domestic political support or to bolster requests for continued high levels of United States aid. For example, in December 1986, following the announcement of death sentences for fourteen of the eighteen defendants in the Bishop murder trial proceedings, Blaize called for the mobilization of SSUs from neighboring islands to reinforce the Grenadian SSU. The prime minister, the police commissioner, and the local media cited increased reports of gunfire around the island and a general upswing in crime and violence as justification for the appeal. The actual level of unrest seemed to be unknown, however, and the link to the trial verdict appeared to be tenuous and speculative at best.

To be sure, the dramatic actions of October 1983, generally popular though they were among the Grenadian public, did not purge the island of all dissident radical politicians or their sympathizers. The continued existence of the NJM and the establishment of the MBPM provided evidence that some Grenadians still hewed to a hard leftist political orientation. However, the lack of success by the MBPM at the ballot box in December 1984 plus the NJM's failure to contest the elections at all revealed the shallowness of popular support for these groups following years of repression under the PRG and the days of extreme violence that preceded the United States-Caribbean intervention.

Although the influence of Marxism-Leninism and its major regional proponent, Cuba, on Grenadian politics has been a fairly recent development, political violence has not been uncommon throughout the island's history. Violence carried out by his labor followers brought Gairy to prominence in 1951. The NJM coup of 1979, however, although justified by its participants as a response to Gairy's brutal repression and exploitation, was political violence of a new and different sort for Grenada. Whereas Gairy had abused the system but always maintained its forms, Bishop and his followers delivered the message that the forms themselves were objectionable. The notion that power could be wrested by force and maintained by ideologically justifiable repression is a legacy that the PRG may have left to some younger members of the Grenadian population.

Civil unrest in Grenada in the postintervention period was minimal. Reports persisted that the crime rate had risen since 1984, and RGPF statistics did indicate increases in violent crime in 1985 and 1986. The reliability of these official statistics was questionable, however, because police work in Grenada was neither painstaking nor very precise. In any case, opinion on the island appeared to reflect increasing concern over the issue of crime. Neighborhood watch organizations were being established, representatives of the private sector were promising aid to these groups as well as to the RGPF, and citizens were calling on the government to take sterner measures.

Internal security did not appear to be a serious or pressing concern for the Blaize government, despite the prime minister's periodic invocations of the leftist threat (typified by the overreaction to the Bishop murder trial verdict). Despite some problems, most of which could be attributed to the islanders' relative inexperience with a functional democratic system, the return to parliamentary democracy appeared to be proceeding apace in the late 1980s.

* * *

A number of books on Grenada have been published since 1983. Understandably, most of them focus on the military intervention and the PRG period. Two of the better products are *Revolution and*

Intervention in Grenada by Kai P. Schoenhals and Richard A. Melanson and *Grenada: Politics, Economics, and Society* by Tony Thorndike. Thorndike's is perhaps the more complete treatment, providing good historical background to a detailed study of post-1979 events. The best source for topical reporting on Grenada is the *Grenada Newsletter,* produced in St. George's.

Specific health and education data are available in the Pan American Health Organization's *Health Conditions in the Americas, 1981–1984* and *Program Budget, 1986–87,* the *World Population Profile* published by the United States Department of Commerce, and the annual report of Grenada's Ministry of Education. An understanding of Grenada's economic status may be obtained from the World Bank's *Grenada: Economic Report,* the annual *Grenada Budget Speech,* and annual reports from the Caribbean Development Bank. (For further information and complete citations, see Bibliography.)

Barbados

Official Name .... Barbados

Term for Citizens .... Barbadian(s)

Capital .... Bridgetown

Political Status .... Independent, 1966

Form of Government .... Parliamentary democracy
and constitutional monarchy

Geography
Size .... 430 sq. km.
Topography .... Rolling hills and plains
Climate .... Maritime tropical

Population
Total estimated in 1987 255,500
Annual growth rate (in percentage) in 1987 .... 0.6
Life expectancy at birth in 1983 70
Adult literacy rate (in percentage) in 1983 95
Language .... English
Ethnic groups .... Black (90 percent), mulatto (5 percent),
white (5 percent)
Religion .... Anglican (31 percent);
Church of God, Methodist, or Roman Catholic
(3 to 4 percent each); remainder other or no religion

Economy
Currency; exchange rate .... Barbadian dollar (B$);
B$2.00 = US$1.00
Gross domestic product (GDP) in 1985 .... US$1.1 billion
Per capita GDP in 1985 .... US$4,405
Distribution of GDP (in percentage) in 1985
Other services and government 66.8
Manufacturing 10.5
Tourism 9.5
Agriculture 7.2
Other 6.0

National Security
Armed forces personnel 500
Paramilitary personnel 0
Police 1,000

Barbados

Barbados has acquired the nickname "Little England" because, through the centuries, it has remained the most British of the Caribbean islands. Since wind currents made it relatively difficult to reach under sail, it was not conquered and reconquered like most of its Caribbean neighbors. British control over Barbados lasted from 1625 until independence in 1966. About fifty male settlers, including some slaves captured en route, arrived in 1627 to settle the island, which was uninhabited and had no food-bearing plants. Twelve years later, in 1639, the House of Assembly was formed, the only representative legislature in the Caribbean to remain in existence for more than three centuries. Barbadians are proud of their colonial heritage and used a statement on individual rights and privileges from the 1652 Charter of Barbados as a basis for the Constitution of 1966.

Following the introduction of sugar by a Dutchman in the early 1640s, the island was deforested, and the economy became dominated by large plantations. As the plantation economy developed, the land became consolidated in the hands of a decreasing number of white families, leading, between 1650 and 1680, to the emigration of some 30,000 landless Barbadians, who left the island for other Caribbean islands or North America. During the seventeenth and eighteenth centuries, slaves were imported from Africa by the thousands. In 1645 the black population was estimated at 5,680; by 1667 it was over 40,000. As the slave trade continued, Barbados became the most densely populated island in the Caribbean, a position that it still held in the late 1980s (see The Impact of the Conquest; The Colonial Period, ch. 1). Because labor was plentiful, few indentured servants were brought to Barbados even after emancipation in 1838.

During the eighteenth century, Barbados languished. The price of sugar fell sharply as abundant supplies were produced more cheaply in other islands. European wars and the American Revolution interfered with trade, and the British embargo on shipment of American goods to British colonies during the American Revolution also hurt Barbados severely. In the early months of the embargo, food and supplies fell so low that residents of Barbados would have faced starvation had not George III ordered special food shipments in 1778. Barbados also suffered several other calamities. Hurricanes devastated the island in 1780 and 1831. The 1780 hurricane killed over 4,000 people and destroyed most of the island's buildings and livestock; the 1831 hurricane ruined many buildings, including seven of the eleven churches on the island. In addition, a cholera epidemic killed over 20,000 people in 1854.

Throughout the nineteenth century, Barbados resisted change. Although free blacks were granted the vote in 1831 and slavery was commuted to an apprentice system in 1834, with emancipation following four years later, the ex-slaves stayed on the island and life remained essentially the same. As historian Ronald Tree has put it, the hurricane of 1831 was "followed by a hundred years of sleepy impoverishment, during which time the island was a source of constant annoyance to the Colonial Office." Barbados successfully resisted British efforts in the late eighteenth and nineteenth centuries to abolish its House of Assembly and install crown colony government (see Glossary). The British had found local assemblies to be intractable and cumbersome to manage from London. Under the system called crown colony government, which was installed in all of the Commonwealth Caribbean islands except Barbados, the British replaced these argumentative assemblies with a unicameral legislature, the majority of whose members were appointed by the governor, and in which the king theoretically represented the lower classes (see Political Traditions, ch. 1). As a result of multiple petitions, Barbados managed to retain its local House of Assembly, which functioned in addition to the governor's Legislative Council. Barbados was also successful in securing the repeal of the British sugar tax.

For almost 300 years, Barbados remained in the hands of a small, white, propertied minority who held the franchise. Reform finally came after World War I, however, as a result of ideas brought back by Clennell Wilsden Wickham of Barbados, Andrew Arthur Cipriani of Trinidad, and others who had served in the British forces abroad (see Precursors of Independence, ch. 1). Wickham returned home in 1919 fired by enthusiasm to make Barbados a more democratic place. His newspaper articles inspired Charles Duncan O'Neale to organize the Democratic League, a political party that espoused franchise reform, old-age pensions, compulsory education, scholarships, and trade union organization. The Democratic League succeeded in electing a few representatives to the House of Assembly between 1924 and 1932, but it is chiefly remembered for inspiring O'Neale's nephew, Errol Barrow, to found the Democratic Labour Party (DLP).

During the 1920s and 1930s, Barbados was confronted with a rapidly growing population, a rising cost of living, and a wage scale that was fixed at the equivalent of US$0.30 a day. Spontaneous rioting erupted throughout the Commonwealth Caribbean in the late 1930s as the region felt the effects of the worldwide depression.

In Barbados, fourteen people were killed and forty-seven wounded in protests in 1937.

The rioting spurred Grantley Adams to found the Barbados Labour Party (BLP) in 1938. (The BLP was known briefly as the Barbados Progressive League.) Adams, a lawyer who had won the Barbados Scholarship to Oxford in 1918, became the most important figure in preindependence politics. He quickly rose to prominence through his testimony before the British Moyne Commission, which was charged with investigating the causes of the regional disturbances in the late 1930s (see Labor Organizations, ch. 1). Adams argued that the main cause of the riots was economic distress. Elected to the House of Assembly in 1940, Adams became president general of the Barbados Workers Union (BWU) on its formation in 1941. Under Barbadian governor Sir Grattan Bushe, the constitution was changed to effect a semiministerial form of government, and the franchise was progressively liberalized. During the 1942 House of Assembly session, Adams led a fight for reforms that broadened the franchise by reducing the cost of qualification, increased direct taxation, established a workmen's compensation program, and protected union leaders from liability in trade disputes.

Under the terms of the Bushe reforms, Adams became leader of the government in 1946. Between 1946 and 1951, he presided over uneasy coalitions in the House of Assembly as the BLP failed to win a clear majority. In 1951, in the first election conducted under universal adult suffrage with no property qualifications, the BLP captured sixteen of the twenty-four seats. Although the BLP had finally gained a majority in the House, Adams was unable to hold the party together. The BLP and BWU, which had formerly acted in unison, pulled apart in 1954 after Adams resigned as president of the BWU, became premier (the preindependence title for prime minister), under a new ministerial system of government, and neglected to include the new BWU president, Frank Walcott, in his cabinet. Meanwhile, a new member of the House, Barrow, emerged as leader of a discontented BLP left wing, which felt that Adams was too close to the governor and not close enough to labor. Barrow had served in the Royal Air Force in World War II and subsequently studied and passed the bar in London. After returning to Barbados in 1950, he joined the BLP and was elected to the House in 1951. In 1954 Barrow left the BLP and the following year founded the DLP, which he led for the next thirty-two years. In spite of Barrow's defection, Adams led the BLP to victory in the 1956 election.

Plans for a British Caribbean federation had been drawn up in London in 1953, and elections for a federative assembly were held in 1958. The BLP also swept these elections, capturing almost all of the seats allotted to Barbados; subsequently, Adams, who had been knighted in 1952, was elected prime minister of the West Indies Federation. He was the only individual ever to hold that office because the federation dissolved in 1962, when Jamaica and Trinidad and Tobago both opted for independence (see The West Indies Federation, 1958–62, ch. 1).

Adams's devotion to the cause of federation cost the BLP dearly. H.G. Cummins, who had become premier of Barbados when Adams was elected prime minister of the West Indies Federation, was unable to hold the party together. By the late 1950s, unemployment, always a persistent problem in Barbados, exceeded 20 percent. While Adams struggled with increasing problems in the federation, Barrow supported the sugar workers in their campaign for higher wages and in turn won their support for the DLP; as a result, the DLP won the 1961 elections by a large majority. Barrow became premier and continued to lead the government until 1971. Between 1961 and 1966, the DLP government replaced the governor's Legislative Council with a Senate appointed by the governor, increased workers' benefits, instituted a program of industrialization, and expanded free education. Barrow also explored the possibility of joining another federation of the so-called Little Eight islands (Antigua and Barbuda, Barbados, Dominica, Grenada, Montserrat, St. Christopher [hereafter, St. Kitts]-Nevis-Anguilla, St. Lucia, and St. Vincent and the Grenadines); this too came to naught, however, and the DLP espoused full independence with the concurrence of the opposition parties. The DLP won the election of November 2, 1966, capturing fourteen of the twenty-four House seats. On November 30, 1966, Barbados gained independence, and Barrow became its first prime minister.

Geography

Barbados is the easternmost island of the Lesser Antilles, situated 480 kilometers north of Guyana, 160 kilometers east of St. Vincent, and 965 kilometers southeast of Puerto Rico (see fig. 1). This isolated pear-shaped island extends for 34 kilometers along a north-south axis and has a maximum breadth of 23 kilometers, giving it a total land area of 430 square kilometers (about the size of San Antonio, Texas, or half the size of New York City).

Barbados is fringed with coral reefs. The island itself is characterized by lowlands or gently sloping, terraced plains, separated by rolling hills that generally parallel the coasts. Elevations in the interior range from 180 to 240 meters above sea level. Mount Hillaby is the highest point at 340 meters above sea level. Farther south, at Christ Church Ridge, elevations range from sixty to ninety meters (see fig. 13).

Eighty-five percent of the island's surface consists of coralline limestone twenty-four to thirty meters thick; Scotland District contains outcroppings of oceanic formations at the surface, however. Sugarcane is planted on almost 80 percent of the island's limestone surface. The soils vary in fertility; erosion is a problem, with crop loss resulting from landslides, washouts, and falling rocks. Most of the small streams are in Scotland District. The rest of the island has few surface streams; nevertheless, rainwater saturates the soil to produce underground channels such as the famous Coles Cave.

Barbados lies within the tropics. Its generally pleasant maritime climate is influenced by northeast trade winds, which moderate the tropical temperature. Cool, northeasterly trade winds are prevalent during the December to June dry season. The overall annual temperature ranges from 24°C to 28°C; slightly lower temperatures prevail at higher elevations. Humidity levels are between 71 percent and 76 percent year round. Rainfall occurs primarily between July and December and varies considerably with elevation. Rainfall may average 187.5 centimeters per year in the higher central area as compared with 127.5 centimeters in the coastal zone.

Population

Barbados had an estimated population of 255,500 in 1987. Population density was 593 persons per square kilometer; slightly over one-third of the populace lived in urban areas. Annual population growth remained relatively low in the 1980s, averaging between 0.2 and 0.8 percent. In 1987 it was 0.6 percent. In spite of this success, Barbados remained the most densely populated country in the Eastern Caribbean (see Glossary).The primary reason for Barbados' small population growth was the government's ability to implement a nationwide family planning program that served to maintain a crude birth rate of 17 per 1,000 inhabitants for the 1980–86 period.

In the past, emigration played a large role in stabilizing Barbados' population. From the end of World War II until the 1970s, Barbados exported its unemployed, as did the Windward Islands. Between 1946 and 1980, its rate of population growth was diminished by one-third because of emigration to Britain. The United States replaced Britain as the primary destination of emigrants in the 1960s because of Britain's restriction on West Indian immigration.

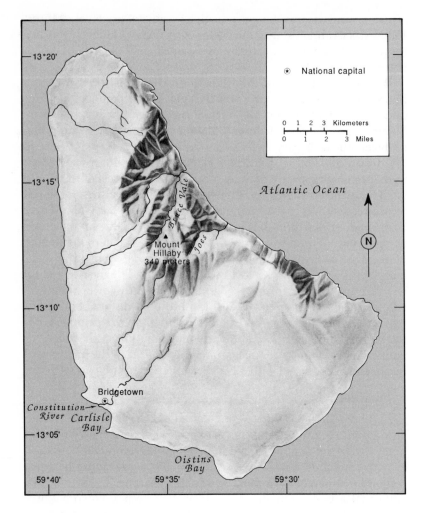

Figure 13. Barbados, 1987

In spite of continued emigration, Barbados began to experience a net inflow of workers in 1970, most coming from other Eastern Caribbean islands. By 1980 demographic figures began to stabilize because migration to Barbados had lessened, probably for economic reasons, and a relatively small natural population growth rate had been achieved. By the mid-1980s, expected real growth rates, adjusted for migration, remained below 1 percent.

Ethnically, Barbados' population was dominated by descendants of African slaves. At emancipation in the late 1830s, the size of the slave population was approximately 83,000, three times that of the entire slave population in the Windward Islands. By the 1980s, distribution of ethnic groups was typical of the Eastern Caribbean; 90 percent of the population was black, 5 percent mulatto, and 5 percent white.

Race largely defined social position in Barbados. The majority of whites still held a disproportionate amount of economic wealth in the 1980s and significantly influenced national politics through their control of business enterprises. Blacks constituted both the middle and the lower classes.

In the 1980s, there was still a displaced social subgroup of extremely poor whites in Barbados who had not been fully assimilated into society. Descendants of the white labor class that had emigrated from Britain in the early colonial period, they had quickly been replaced as an economic group by African slaves, who had been brought to the New World as an inexpensive source of labor. Known as "red legs," the subgroup lived off the sea and subsistence agriculture and eventually became entrenched social outcasts, who had little expectation of becoming members of modern society (see The Sugar Revolutions and Slavery, ch. 1).

Barbados inherited from the British a stratified society with a strong sense of class consciousness; Barbadian aspirations to reach the next rung of the social and economic ladder partially explain the industriousness of the population. Individual pride is clearly associated with economic status and has been cited as a reason for Barbados' early economic success, which surpassed that of the Windward Islands.

Religion in Barbados was also influenced by the British. The first colonizers established the Anglican Church in Barbados, where it quickly assumed a position of dominance. Alternative religions were subsequently provided by Moravian and Methodist groups. Although Anglicans were still the dominant religious group in the early 1980s, they constituted only 31 percent of the population. The Church of God and the Roman Catholic and Methodist churches each claimed to minister to between 3 and 4 percent of the population. The remainder belonged to other religions or professed no religious affiliation.

Education

Barbados had one of the oldest and most advanced education systems in the Eastern Caribbean in the late 1980s. Education dated back to 1686, when private funds were used to build the first school. Throughout the eighteenth and nineteenth centuries, education was controlled by the Anglicans, who were later joined by other religious groups. By 1962 education was free for all nationals and administered primarily by the state. This trend continued, so that by 1984 only 4 percent of the primary and secondary schools were managed by churches.

Barbados' longstanding emphasis on education was evident in the values and goals of contemporary society. Education has traditionally been associated with success and upward mobility. In 1970 Barbados officially claimed to have achieved a 99-percent literacy rate, a figure that was questioned by some observers. Despite these doubts, observers generally agreed that in the 1980s literacy in Barbados exceeded the rates of other Caribbean societies.

In 1984 Barbados had 126 primary schools, 110 of which were administered by the state. Approximately 1,350 teachers were available to instruct the 35,000 students. There were sixty-four secondary schools, five of which prepared students for technical careers. A total of 6,000 students attended secondary-school programs.

Postsecondary education consisted of seven institutions that awarded degrees or certificates. Four schools offered specific vocational training: the Barbados Institute of Management and Productivity, the Erdiston Teacher's Training College, the Tercentenary School of Nursing, and the Samuel Jackman Prescod Polytecnic.

Academic programs at the university level were conducted at the Cave Hill Campus of the University of the West Indies (UWI) and the Barbados Community College, which offered vocational and technical classes as well. The UWI also included Codrington College, a local theological seminary.

In 1979 the government created the Skills Training Programme to augment existing education programs. It was designed to fulfill the need for short but intensive training in vocational subjects and to prepare students for careers in mechanics, electronics, horticulture, masonry, plumbing, and other technical and vocational occupations.

Although the educational infrastructure was designed to meet both the nation's academic and vocational needs, observers seriously questioned Barbados' ability to provide quality instruction in fields related to tourism, agriculture, and manufacturing, the major economic undertakings in the 1980s. Few courses were actually offered in agricultural science and commerce; as a result, an inadequate number of Barbadians were being prepared to take on the responsibilities inherent in a growing economy.

The education system was also criticized for being stratified along socioeconomic lines. In general, upper-class Barbadians prepared for university studies at the best primary and secondary schools, received a disproportionate number of scholarships, and had the best records for entering the professional disciplines. On balance, however, most Barbadians felt that the education system still afforded opportunities to achieve at least limited upward mobility. The government appeared to be attempting to address specific criticisms of its educational policy; its goals for Barbadian education in the 1980s included the promotion of equal educational opportunity and enhanced technical and vocational programs in all schools. In spite of its shortcomings, the Barbadian education system remained the best in the Eastern Caribbean in the 1980s.

Health and Welfare

In the mid-1980s, Barbadian health indicators showed that the overall health status of the country had improved substantially. In addition, by 1984 the government had taken major steps toward instituting a comprehensive health care service. As a result, Barbados compared favorably with its Eastern Caribbean neighbors in quality and delivery of health services.

Barbados achieved considerable success in reducing its crude birth rate in the 1980s (see Population, this section). Mortality rates, which had been steadily improving since 1974, deteriorated slightly in 1983. The death rate for the population rose in 1983 to 7.9 deaths per 1,000 inhabitants; much of the increase was attributed to a higher infant mortality rate, which rose 15 percent to 24.5 deaths per 1,000 live births. This increase was caused largely by problems arising shortly after birth, particularly pneumonia and respiratory ailments. Life expectancy at birth in Barbados in 1983 was seventy years. Morbidity indicators in the 1980s approximated those found elsewhere in the Caribbean. Only 2.3 percent of all deaths in 1982 were attributed to infectious and parasitic diseases. Statistics from that year indicated that two-thirds of all children one year of age and younger were inoculated against diphtheria, pertussis, and tetanus and 53 percent against measles. As of mid-1987, Barbados reported fifteen cases of acquired immune deficiency syndrome.

Improved water and sewage disposal was credited with the decline of morbidity rates from 1974 to 1985. The entire population had access to potable water by 1984. In addition, the completion in 1982 of the sewage system in the capital city of Bridgetown dramatically improved the urban sanitation situation. The rest of the island depended on septic tanks for waste disposal; however, plans were underway in 1985 to extend modern sewage facilities throughout the southern and western coastal areas.

Barbados' consistently improving health conditions were the direct result of government efforts to enact a health care program. Between 1978 and 1983, Ministry of Health expenditures, including social security, represented an average of 14.5 percent of total government outlays. The government planned delivery of free health care to all Barbadians through two basic programs, the General Practitioner Service and the Barbados Drug Service. The former was designed to bring medical service to virtually all areas of the island, but it had not been fully implemented. The Barbados Drug Service began operations in 1980 and improved the delivery of prescription and over-the-counter drugs, providing increased efficiency and reduced costs.

In 1985 Barbados' health care facilities included one general hospital (Queen Elizabeth's Hospital), one psychiatric facility (the Psychiatric Hospital), six district hospitals, seven polyclinics, and four health centers. Queen Elizabeth's Hospital and the Psychiatric Hospital each contained approximately 630 beds. District hospitals offered an additional 900 beds, and private hospitals were equipped with approximately 60 beds. The polyclinics delivered basic maternal and child care, family planning, and general health education services in rural areas. The health centers offered medical care in remote locations, but they were considered poorly equipped. There were 8.8 physicians and 30 nurses per 10,000 inhabitants in 1982. The Barbados Medical School, a part of the UWI system, was located at Queen Elizabeth's Hospital.

Despite substantial improvements in Barbadian health care, some problems persisted as of the late 1980s. Continued efforts were necessary to improve health care in rural areas. New measures were also needed to deal with alcohol abuse and diseases carried by rodents and wild dogs. Most noticeable noncommunicable health problems were heart disease, diabetes, and cancer. The government sought to respond to these health problems with expanded education programs, early diagnosis, and drugs.

Economy

Barbados experienced steady economic development and diversification following World War II, outperforming in many ways all of the Windward Islands. The economy was transformed from one dependent on agriculture, primarily sugar, for one-third of its gross domestic product (GDP—see Glossary) to one considered relatively diversified with the development of tourism and manufacturing sectors. By 1980 agriculture accounted for a mere 9 percent of GDP, whereas the wholesale and retail trade had grown to 17 percent, general services to 14 percent, manufacturing to 12 percent, and government services and tourism to 11 percent each. At the same time, Barbados' standard of living had increased remarkably as the nation elevated itself from the ranks of the low-income countries to those of middle-income countries.

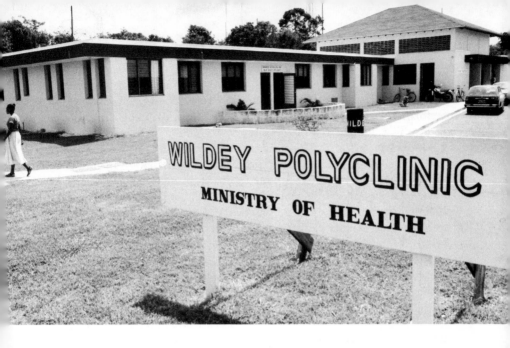

*Wildey Polyclinic, opened in 1981
Courtesy Inter-American Development Bank*

Barbados' economic success could be traced to many factors. The island had long been a model of social and political stability, which helped attract both public and private foreign investment. The government also assisted with the infrastructural development required of an expanding economy, including a sound education system.

In spite of a lengthy history of economic development, the economy floundered at times during the 1980s. In part the fluctuations were the result of the innate characteristics of a small Caribbean economy, which include a limited resource base and heavy dependence on external markets. To a large extent, however, the setbacks resulted from the worldwide recession in the 1981–83 period. In 1987, however, Barbados was still actively pursuing a policy of growth based on a diversified export market, with a prudent mixture of private and public management of economic resources.

Macroeconomic Overview

Annual economic growth in the 1960s and 1970s averaged 5 percent. The 1980s, by contrast, saw little or no real growth in the economy. In addition to being affected by the global recession in the early 1980s, the 3.5-percent growth of GDP in 1984 was offset by near zero growth in 1985 because Barbados' leading export sectors all performed poorly. In 1985 the economy expanded slightly

397

by 0.3 percent, but only because the nontrading sectors, such as mining, quarrying, utilities, construction, and government services, performed well. Otherwise, Barbados would have experienced a decline in GDP.

Among the most disturbing economic developments for the island in the 1980s was the use of protectionist policies by Trinidad and Tobago and Jamaica with respect to clothing and other goods that faced strong regional competition. The tourist sector also slumped in the early 1980s, falling victim to a strong Barbadian dollar, which greatly reduced the number of tourist visitors from Britain. Tourism lessened because of the deterioration in the exchange rate of the British pound that accompanied the strengthening of the United States dollar. The Barbadian dollar was tied to the United States dollar at a fixed exchange rate.

Preliminary statistics for 1986, however, suggested that the economy was improving dramatically, registering an annual growth rate of 5 percent. This improvement was primarily the result of enhanced performance by tourism, manufacturing, and agriculture, the three sectors generating foreign exchange earnings.

External factors also improved when the United States dollar began to depreciate in 1984. The depreciation of the United States dollar increased the foreign exchange rate of the British pound sterling in Barbados and led to a 25-percent rise in British visitors. Tourism for the first three-quarters of 1986 increased 3.2 percent; the manufacturing sector registered a 9-percent increase in production over the same period because of a recovery in chemicals and processed foods. Nonsugar agriculture also improved. The electronics industry, however, continued to decline because of strong Japanese competition, and textiles still faced regional trade restrictions.

The quick turnaround in Barbados' aggregate economic performance in 1986 graphically demonstrated its strong dependence on external markets. To a large extent, the economy's overall performance in the 1980s paralleled that of the leading export sectors; the economy, however, has been able to survive periods in which trade was sharply reduced.

The growth and diversification of the economy since World War II did not result in substantial new employment opportunities. The unemployment rate exceeded 10 percent throughout the 1980s; it averaged 18.7 percent in 1985 and 19 percent in 1986. There were three primary reasons for high unemployment. First, the decline of the agricultural sector in favor of tourism resulted in a less labor-intensive economy, causing a slow, yet inevitable, displacement of agricultural workers. Second, employment figures also reflected improved productivity across sectors. As productivity grew after World War II, fewer workers were needed even though the economy had expanded. Finally, Barbados' relatively large population also contributed to the development of an entrenched unemployment base.

In 1985 the services sector, including government workers, accounted for 35 percent of the work force. The second largest employer was restaurants and hotels, which had a combined contribution of 22.7 percent of the work force; this was followed by manufacturing (13.2 percent), agriculture and fishing (9.8 percent), and construction and quarrying (7.6 percent).

Because agriculture retained only a small percentage of the work force as the economy diversified, the manufacturing sector began to play a pivotal role in absorbing the unemployed. In the 1985–86 period, however, manufacturing experienced severe problems as a result of international competition and regional trade imbalances that directly affected employment levels. By 1986 it appeared unlikely that alternative jobs for the newly displaced manufacturing workers could be found.

Historically, Barbados has experienced periods of high inflation caused by both internal and external forces, but external causes have been responsible for the more acute inflationary periods. Domestic inflation has been fueled by government overspending financed by increasing the money supply, excess demand caused by import restrictions, and large real wage increases. Because of the open nature of the Barbadian economy and its heavy reliance on foreign markets, inflationary pressures also were exerted from abroad.

Since 1981, however, Barbados has experienced a steady decline in its inflation rate; the rate fell from a high of 14.6 percent in that year to less than 2 percent in 1986. The work force, as a whole, fared well during this period; wages rose faster than prices each year. Although wage hikes could not be justified based on productivity gains, they apparently did not have a significant impact on the general price level as evidenced by the decreasing inflation rate.

Banking and Finance

The Central Bank of Barbados (CBB) was created in 1972 to assist the government in stabilizing the economy by facilitating development and financial intermediation (see Glossary). Since 1972, Barbados has minted its own Barbadian dollar, which has been pegged to the United States dollar at a rate of B$2.00 to US$1.00.

The government created the CBB for numerous reasons, all related to gaining more control over domestic and international financial intermediation. Paramount to maintaining financial stability was Barbados' new-found control over its money supply. Unlike other Eastern Caribbean states, which were dependent on a regional financial institution for central governance of the monetary system, Barbados was capable of establishing its own monetary program to supplement fiscal policy in meeting national economic goals.

Financial priorities were also advanced by the Barbados Development Bank, which was created in 1963. It functioned as an independent corporation designed to facilitate development by encouraging domestic savings and investment and providing loans to development enterprises, cooperatives, and small businesses. It was also empowered to issue its own securities to ensure sufficient funding to meet development needs. In 1985 it reemphasized its effort to assist the small manufacturing sector, which had failed to expand significantly during the previous year.

In the mid-1980s, Barbados was also served by numerous local banks and seven foreign commercial institutions. In addition, it was the headquarters for the Caribbean Development Bank (CDB), which acted as a conduit for multilateral lending arrangements.

Role of Government

In general, the Barbadian government has taken a strong stand against government interference in the operation of the national economy. During his second term as prime minister, Barrow favored a minimal role for government in managing economic enterprises and emphasized the supportive nature of the government in promoting the development of the economy. Nevertheless, government spending has been a major tool of economic growth. The government has conducted its economic policy by employing fiscal and monetary measures and by supporting the social and productive sectors of society with public sector investment. Public sector investment, however, was also inextricably linked to outcomes of fiscal policy.

In fiscal year (FY—see Glossary) 1986, the government introduced fiscal policies aimed at enhancing the purchasing power of the private sector. Tax concessions to individuals and businesses were expected to stimulate the economy and minimize demand for wage increases, whereas increased consumption duties were designed to regulate consumer activity. Indirect taxation was to offset the loss of direct revenue from income and business tax concessions.

By late 1986, however, it was clear that the realigned tax structure would cause a large deficit. In December 1986, the CBB recorded a 118-percent increase in the national deficit compared with the previous year. The increase stemmed from the government's inability to control capital expenditures and public wage increases. Such control was a necessary precondition for the success of the new fiscal policy.

In the mid-1980s, analysts raised concerns about the potential effects of the Barbadian deficit. In spite of gains in aggregate productivity, the budget imbalance could not be corrected, and increased foreign borrowing appeared to be imminent. International concerns revolved around Barbados' ability to meet debt payments in the near future, as well as its ability to finance the public sector investment in the out years.

Although fiscal policy was a dominant economic tool of the government, monetary control played a relatively significant role when compared with operations of other Eastern Caribbean islands. The government coordinated economic policy with the CBB, rather than allowing it to develop a completely independent program. Their mutual goal was economic stability for the island, which implied controlling the money supply so that credit markets remained nonvolatile yet were sufficiently liquid to meet the demands of a developing economy.

Government influence over the economy was exercised more directly through public sector investment, which was developed and coordinated in conjunction with the five-year economic development plan. Historically, Barbados has concentrated public investment in three areas: economic infrastructure, such as roads and ports; social infrastructure, including health, education, and housing; and productive sectors, particularly agriculture and tourism. Funds for the 1986–88 period, which coincided with the last two years of the 1983 five-year economic development plan, were allocated mostly to transportation; the social sector received 26 percent of capital outlays, however, split mostly between health and education programs. Agriculture and tourism received a combined total of 30 percent of investment funds available from public sources.

Infrastructure constituted almost 36 percent of the total public sector investment for that period, which was reflected in the excellent communications and transportation networks that were available in the late 1980s. The Barbados Telephone Company operated an entirely automatic system of 75,000 telephones. Tropospheric-scatter links to Trinidad and Tobago and to St. Lucia and a satellite ground station operating with the International Telecommunications Satellite Corporation (INTELSAT) Atlantic Ocean satellite provided high-quality international service. The government-owned Caribbean Broadcasting Corporation broadcast from the capital

View of the east coast
Courtesy Barbados Board of Tourism

on 900 kilohertz and had FM service at 98.1 megahertz. Two commercial stations also broadcast from St. George's, Grenada, on 790 kilohertz and 90.7 megahertz. Evening television service was available. The *Nation* and the *Barbados Advocate* were the local daily newspapers.

Transportation infrastructure was good and comprised almost 1,500 kilometers of paved roads, a major international airport, and a deep-water port. One highway circled Barbados, and numerous other roads crisscrossed the island; buses served most towns. Grantley Adams International Airport, on the southern tip of Barbados, handled direct flights to points in North America and Western Europe. Bridgetown boasted a manmade deep-water port, which was completed in 1961 and expanded in 1978. The island had no railroads or inland water transportation.

In 1986 informed observers estimated that the next five-year plan would allocate additional capital to productive sectors (tourism, agriculture, and manufacturing) in the form of direct credit. This would take place at the expense of reduced investment in physical infrastructure. Because many of the road projects were scheduled for completion within the decade, a reallocation toward sectors that would directly assist national economic development was considered necessary to enhance the overall performance of the economy.

Foreign sources of capital, which from 1982 to 1986 had included loans or grants from development banks and government agencies, composed 40 percent of the public sector investment budget. This figure was expected to increase to 50 percent for the 1986–88 period, a situation that could further exacerbate a growing foreign debt repayment problem.

Sectoral Performance

By 1987 Barbados had a diversified economy, with numerous sectors contributing to GDP. Leading sectors of the economy in 1985, as measured by percentage of GDP, included wholesale and retail trade (20.4 percent), business and general services (16 percent), government services (14.2 percent), and tourism (9.5 percent). Contributions of productive sectors (those with tangible output) included manufacturing (10.5 percent), agriculture (7.2 percent), and construction (5.3 percent).

Barbados' primary productive sectors were agriculture, tourism, and manufacturing. Agriculture, including the fishing industry, still played an important role in the development of the economy. In the late 1980s, agricultural planners were attempting to diversify the sector. The long-term decline in sugar production was the natural result of increased production costs combined with depressed

Sugar mill
Courtesy Barbados Board of Tourism

world prices. In its stead, planners emphasized nonsugar agricultural products in order to reduce food imports and free up valuable foreign exchange for the purchase of capital goods and technology needed for economic development. Agricultural diversification, as outlined in the 1983–88 five-year development plan, also contributed marginally to reducing the unemployment rate and provided much of the society's nutritional base.

New markets in the Caribbean Community and Common Market (Caricom—see Appendix C) for fresh vegetables, flowers, and cotton allowed Barbados to increase foreign exchange earnings from agriculture. Improved output of fish, peanuts, and onions also improved its foreign exchange position by lowering agricultural imports. Figures for 1985 suggested that the 1983–88 development plan had succeeded in meeting diversification and production goals.

Agriculture, as a percentage of GDP, actually rose by 6 percent in 1985, representing increases in both sugar and nonsugar products. Sugar production rose by 20 percent in nominal terms, whereas food crops and fishing increased 11.3 percent. Unusually high growth rates occurred in cotton production, which rose by 400 percent. Food crops, however, experienced mixed production levels. These were decreases in the amounts of cabbage, carrots, peas, tomatoes, and corn produced and increases in peanuts, onions, beets, eggplant, pumpkin, broccoli, and okra.

In spite of distinct successes in agricultural diversification and production efforts, the sector had numerous problems to overcome. Sugar production remained unprofitable and required financial support through government subsidies. Analysts noted that in 1985 nonsugar agriculture had experienced production problems such as erosion, erratic rainfall patterns, and poor disease control. Marketing constraints, such as poor management, were also identified, as was inadequate coordination with external markets.

Output from the fishing industry declined by 32 percent in 1985 compared with the previous year, in spite of a marginal increase in the number of fishing vessels. This was accounted for by a combination of bad weather and imprecise reporting by fishermen to avoid paying tariffs. Government efforts to improve the fishing sector continued, however, as was evidenced by port improvements and financial assistance provided for boat purchases.

By 1985 tourism had become Barbados' primary foreign exchange earner. It accounted for 9.5 percent of GDP and was the leading sector in providing employment. Additionally, tourism had developed better economic linkages with the agricultural and industrial sectors, providing a market for locally produced foods and handicrafts. Production of fresh fruit and vegetables, fish, meat, and poultry all benefited from the tourist trade, as did handicrafts. Approximately 90 percent of all handmade goods were sold to visitors. Production of local goods sold to tourists, however, lagged behind demand, forcing Barbados to import 70 percent of all handicrafts sold to visitors in 1983.

Barbados was an early entrant into the Caribbean tourist market and enjoyed above-average earnings because of early development of its international airport. However, the change in market conditions in the 1980s eroded Barbados' dominant position, forcing it to consolidate gains rather than to continue to increase its share of the regional tourist market.

The worldwide recession of the early 1980s caused Caribbean tourism to lose ground. As the recession subsided, Barbados found itself in an increasingly competitive environment with other small island economies, particularly Grenada and St. Lucia. Both countries had emerged as significant tourist attractions, largely because of improved airport facilities.

The Barbadian government expected competition in the Caribbean tourist market to increase through the 1980s. In order to protect its share of the market, Barbados planned to address internal problems that had impeded growth of the tourist sector. Refurbishing of tourist facilities was essential if the island was to compete with the amenities available on other islands. The government also planned to develop a coordinated marketing plan to attract a greater share of United States business, as well as to dispel impressions that Barbados was expensive and less service oriented than neighboring islands. Analysts suggested that Barbados implement better management and financial controls.

Manufacturing, the third major productive sector, began to grow significantly following the creation of the government-run Barbados Industrial Development Corporation (BIDC) in 1957. The BIDC produced a long-term plan to enhance Barbados' manufacturing capability by taking advantage of low-cost labor, concessionary fiscal policies, foreign capital, a solid physical infrastructure, and political stability.

The manufacturing sector produced for both domestic and foreign markets. Primary manufactured products for domestic and external consumption included processed foods, clothing, beverages, chemical products, and tobacco, all of which required foreign capital and raw materials as primary inputs. Goods produced solely for export included handicrafts, which were produced exclusively from local raw materials, and electronic components and sportswear, which were developed through multinational enterprises and relied completely on foreign materials and capital.

Manufacturing had become a significant sector of the economy by 1985. As of this date, there were over 200 small-scale firms that contributed 10.5 percent of GDP and 13 percent of employment. In spite of this established presence, manufacturing had generally not performed up to expectations. Its contribution to economic growth and employment had not expanded significantly in the previous twenty-five years. In 1960 manufacturing accounted for 8 percent of GDP, only 2.5 percentage points below the 1985 level. The sector's contribution to employment had grown at a similarly small rate during this same period, leading some analysts to conclude that other sectors of the economy had done more for aggregate economic growth and employment than manufacturing.

Manufacturing's greatest contribution to the economy appeared to be its ability to earn foreign exchange. In 1983 electronic assembly accounted for over half of Barbados' total domestic exports. Nevertheless, heavy reliance on foreign raw materials and global competition continued to hinder the island's ability to contribute to economic growth.

In 1985 output of the manufacturing sector declined by 9.5 percent as a result of changing world market conditions. Demand for Barbados' leading export—electronic components—fell sharply as the world market became inundated with Japanese semiconductors and resistors. Furthermore, regional competition was expected to continue to restrict this sector's ability to grow so that it would probably contribute no more than 10 to 15 percent of GDP in the near future.

Barbados also began producing oil and natural gas in the 1980s; it had 3.6 million barrels of proven oil reserves and 400 million cubic meters of natural gas in 1985. Although neither oil nor gas was extracted in sufficient quantities to export, Barbados was able to produce over half of its crude oil requirements by 1984, dramatically reducing its oil import bill. Natural gas was used as a direct energy source and in the production of electricity; however, 75 percent of all natural gas was flared at the wellhead. Construction of a small liquefied petroleum gas plant was expected to be completed in late 1987; the plant would improve utilization of excess natural gas.

Foreign Trade and Balance of Payments

Barbados had expected trade to achieve its goal of export-led economic growth by the mid-1980s. By 1985, however, Barbados had experienced significant declines in all sectors that traditionally accounted for the majority of its foreign exchange earnings. The poor performance was a result of constricting regional demand for Barbadian goods and tighter trade restrictions in the Caricom market.

Barbados' foreign exchange earnings were derived from numerous goods and services. Sugar and molasses accounted for nearly 80 percent of agricultural exports in 1985 and contributed 10 percent of total merchandise exports. This sector, however, accounted for only 4 percent of total foreign exchange earnings and has continued to decline in importance since the early 1960s.

The manufacturing sector provided Barbados with 85 percent of the total value of merchandise exports and 30 percent of total foreign exchange. In 1985 electronic components represented 60 percent of total manufactured goods; secondary exports included clothing, chemicals, and rum. Tourism was the greatest foreign exchange earner in 1985; receipts totaled 38 percent of exported goods and services.

Approximately 23 percent of Barbadian exports went to other Caricom countries in 1985. Guyana and Trinidad and Tobago absorbed 68 percent of regional exports, whereas St. Lucia, Jamaica, Grenada, and St. Vincent and the Grenadines together accounted for 21 percent. The other 11 percent went to numerous other regional trading partners. Preliminary figures for 1986, however, suggested that Caricom trade would fall significantly, perhaps by as much as 20 percent. The United States purchased

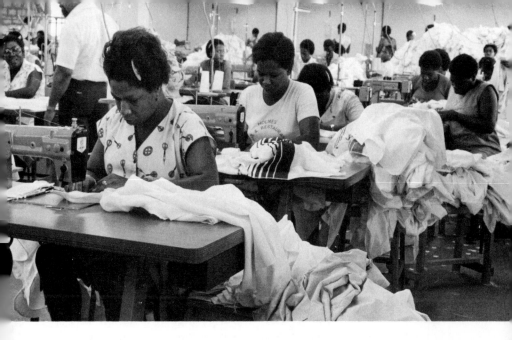

Workers making clothing at Elias Industries, Wildey
Courtesy Inter-American Development Bank

most of Barbados' electronic components and accounted for 18.4 percent of total merchandise exports. Britain and Canada constituted 5.8 percent and 1.4 percent of the Barbadian export market, respectively; the remainder was sent to numerous other countries.

Overall, exports declined 10.1 percent in 1985 because of decreased demand for all items. Electronic components, sugar, and clothing fell 10 percent, 12.2 percent, and 30.6 percent, respectively. Barbados did not expect a significant change in market conditions in the near future and was developing a market strategy that focused on extraregional economies to absorb sugar and manufactured products.

In addition to declining demand for Barbadian exports, the island's foreign exchange position was also negatively affected by currency devaluations in Trinidad and Tobago and Jamaica, as well as by large wage increases given to workers in the Barbadian tourist and manufacturing sectors. These two problems had a combined effect of lowering the country's competitive position in the region. Because of wage increases and the relatively expensive Barbadian dollar, goods and services originating in Barbados were more expensive than those of the country's primary competitors.

In 1985 Barbados' primary imports were capital goods, food and beverages, fuels and chemicals, and miscellaneous durable goods; these represented 21.7, 15.3, 10, and 5 percent, respectively, of total imports. Other consumer and intermediate goods included textiles, animal feeds, and other unspecified goods. The United States provided 41 percent of total imports and was the trading partner causing the single largest deficit. It was followed by Caricom countries, which shipped 14.7 percent of total imports; the remaining 29.2 percent came from numerous other countries. Britain and Canada supplied 9.1 percent and 5.1 percent, respectively. Trinidad and Tobago furnished 70 percent of all Caricom goods imported by Barbados, and Jamaica supplied 21 percent; the remaining 9 percent represented less significant trade relationships with other regional partners.

Barbados' balance of payments position was relatively healthy at the close of 1985, in spite of trading problems. Exports of goods and services had exceeded imports, providing a current account surplus of US$40.3 million. The surplus occurred when there was a fall in both absolute exports and imports; however, strong tourist receipts narrowed the trade deficit.

The capital account experienced heavy outlays to repay private loans, and much of this debt was essentially replaced by public borrowing. There was a capital account surplus of US$46 million in 1985. When added to the current account and adjusted for errors and omissions, the overall balance of payments was US$22.4 million.

Informed observers suggested that Barbados might experience only slight growth in the late 1980s because of declining manufacturing trade. An increase in tourist receipts and an improved competitive position were expected to help the country adjust to a decline in foreign earnings, but it appeared that increased borrowing would be needed for at least the five-year economic planning period beginning in 1988. Such borrowing would cause Barbados' 1985 debt service ratio of 8 percent of exports to double by the early 1990s. Furthermore, it was expected that a deficit in the current account in later years would cause the overall balance of payments to become negative as well. The need to purchase more intermediate goods and increase borrowing to maintain development goals, as well as greater regional competition in the tourism and manufacturing markets, was the most likely reason for this adjustment.

Government and Politics

The Governmental System

At independence in November 1966, Barbados formally adopted the Westminster parliamentary system of government, with a governor general representing the British monarch. Rights and privileges accorded to the governor in 1652 by Britain formed the basis for the Constitution of 1966, which provides for a bicameral parliamentary system headed by a prime minister and cabinet.

Under the Constitution, Parliament consists of the British monarch, represented by the governor general, the Senate, and the House of Assembly. The governor general is appointed by the monarch and serves at the monarch's pleasure. Although the governor general must act in accordance with the advice of the cabinet or one of its ministers, the governor general has considerable influence and is responsible for appointing judges, commissioners, and senators and for voting in the Senate if there is a tie. The governor general presides at all meetings of the Privy Council for Barbados, an appointed body whose duties include the right to review punishments and grant pardons.

Executive authority in Barbados rests with the governor general, the prime minister, and a cabinet of at least five ministers. The prime minister is by far the most powerful figure in the executive and within the cabinet. The prime minister chooses the cabinet ministers and may dismiss them at will. The cabinet, which is responsible to Parliament, is the principal instrument of policy and is charged with direction and control of the government, but the personality, style, and popularity of the prime minister largely determine the direction of government.

The Constitution provides for a House of Assembly of twenty-four members or as many as Parliament may prescribe. The number was increased to twenty-seven before the 1981 elections. Members are elected by universal suffrage and must be over twenty-one years of age. The leader of the majority in the House of Assembly is appointed prime minister by the governor general. The minority leader becomes leader of the opposition. The term of office is five years, but elections may be called at any time by the ruling party, and an election must be called in case of a vote of no confidence. During the first twenty years of Barbadian history, all of its governments remained in power until the five-year limit.

The Senate is a wholly appointed body. Senators must be citizens of Barbados over the age of twenty-one; twelve are appointed on the advice of the prime minister, two on the advice of the leader of the opposition, and the remaining seven at the governor general's discretion. The Senate elects its own president and deputy president and has a quorum of eight plus the presiding officer.

Bills may be introduced in either house with the exception of money bills, which must be introduced in the elected House of

Assembly. A bill becomes law after it has passed both houses and has been signed by the governor general.

Barbados' judiciary includes the Supreme Court, which consists of the High Court and the Court of Appeal. The chief justice is appointed by the governor general after consultation with the prime minister and the leader of the opposition; the other judges who make up the court are appointed on the advice of the Judicial and Legal Service Commission. Judges serve until the age of sixty-five; in case of vacancies, the governor general has the authority to appoint acting judges who serve until the appropriate consultations have been made. Appeals from decisions made by the High Court may be made to the three-judge Court of Appeal. The highest appeal is to the Judicial Committee of the Privy Council in London.

Under the Constitution, a number of public service commissions—including the Judicial and Legal Service Commission, the Public Service Commission, and the Police Commission—oversee government acts. All of the commissioners are appointed by the governor general after consultation with the prime minister and the leader of the opposition.

Political Dynamics

Since independence in 1966, responsibility for organizing the government has been almost evenly divided between the two major Barbadian parties, the DLP and BLP, which are both centrist social democratic parties with roots in the British labor movement. Although the BLP is perceived as somewhat more conservative than the DLP, there has been relatively little ideological difference. Both parties strongly support private enterprise, but both have undertaken large public works as a necessity in a country where unemployment ranges between 15 and 20 percent. In foreign policy, both the DLP and the BLP have endorsed and coordinated regional integration initiatives. Since the 1960s, party differentiation has been mainly in style and rhetoric and in the personalities of the leaders.

During the first twenty years of Barbadian independence, the DLP and BLP each ran the government for ten years. The DLP, with its founder, Barrow, as prime minister, was the majority party from 1966 to 1976 and was returned to power in 1986. The BLP was in power from 1976 to 1986 with J.M.G.M. "Tom" Adams as prime minister until his sudden death in office in 1985. After Adams's death, H. Bernard St. John became prime minister until the DLP victory in the May 1986 election. In June 1987, a year after resuming the post of prime minister, Barrow also died; thus, in the short space of twenty-six months Barbados lost the two party leaders who had run the country since 1961. Barrow was succeeded by Deputy Prime Minister Lloyd Erskine Sandiford, a member of the House since 1971 and the holder of a number of ministerial portfolios under two previous DLP governments.

Barrow, who has been called the "Architect of Independence," led the DLP from its inception in 1955 until his death in 1987. After having completed a term as premier (the preindependence title for prime minister) from 1961 to 1966, Barrow and the DLP were elected to a second five-year term on the eve of independence in November 1966. Barrow had instituted many programs in his preindependence term of 1961–66 and continued them throughout the DLP governments that lasted until 1976. Barrow's achievements included free secondary education and school meals and many capital works programs, especially public housing projects. Under his government, the Barbados economy diversified by encouraging tourism. Barbados joined the Caribbean Free Trade Association (Carifta) in 1968, continuing its efforts to achieve some regional integration, and later joined Caricom, the successor to Carifta.

During Barrow's third term (1971–76), the Barbadian economy suffered from oil price increases and the international energy crisis. Unemployment increased, and there was increasing worker dissatisfaction. In 1976 the BLP, under the leadership of Tom Adams, won the election, gaining seventeen out of twenty-four seats in the House of Assembly. Adams was the son of BLP founder Sir Grantley Adams, Barbados' most prominent preindependence leader. Tom Adams was born in 1931 and, like both his father and Barrow, had won the Barbados Scholarship (to Oxford). He had earned two degrees in England and had been active in the British Labour Party. When Adams returned to Barbados in 1962, the West Indies Federation had dissolved and the BLP was a minority party. Adams went to work as honorary secretary for the BLP and in 1966 was elected along with his father to the House of Assembly. Adams became leader of the BLP in 1971 after BLP leader St. John had been defeated in the elections. In 1976 Adams led the party to victory and was elected prime minister after a campaign focusing on the rise in unemployment, inflation, and government waste. In his first term, Adams managed to cut unemployment nearly in half, increase per capita income and growth, achieve a balance of payments surplus for three years, and expand tourism. Because of the country's economic prosperity, the BLP government was reelected for a second term in 1981, winning seventeen out of twenty-seven seats.

Adams's second term was marked by economic problems and a major crisis in Grenada. Inflation had begun to rise again in 1980, and growth slowed down from its 1979 peak of 8 percent. This trend continued, and during the early 1980s GDP declined (see Economy, this section). The economic woes caused friction at home and with Caribbean neighbors such as Trinidad and Tobago, a traditional friend. In addition, the increasing size of the military forces in Grenada and the island's failure to hold elections caused consternation and division at the 1982 Caricom conference and precipitated the organization of the Regional Security System (RSS). The situation in Grenada reached a crisis in October 1983. Adams's strong support of the United States-Caribbean intervention included sending Barbadian police officers to join the Caribbean Peace Force in Grenada and brought Adams and Barbados international attention (see Foreign Relations, this section; A Regional Security System, ch. 7). Although public opinion in Barbados supported Adams's actions, there was concern about the possible precedent set by military intervention. Adams continued to be a vigorous supporter of the RSS until his death.

Deputy Prime Minister St. John succeeded Adams as BLP prime minister in March 1985 and served in that capacity until the elections of May 1986. St. John had been a member of the BLP since 1959, a senator from 1964 to 1966 and from 1971 to 1976, and a member of the House from 1966 to 1971, and had served as deputy prime minister during both terms of the Adams government, holding a number of ministerial portfolios during that time. St. John attempted to improve the economy and mend the relationships in the Caribbean that had been strained by the economic recession and the Grenadian crisis. With an eye on the 1986 elections, St. John promised tax relief, but he was unable to create a constituency during his short time in office.

By the time of the 1986 election, unemployment in Barbados was about 19 percent. The election campaign in May 1986 was bitter and included accusations that the BLP was corrupt and racially biased in favor of whites and that it favored the middle class over the poor. The DLP promised to reduce taxes and lower the price of utilities and gasoline and also spoke of reducing participation in the RSS. The DLP was elected in a landslide, capturing all but three of the twenty-seven seats and sweeping out St. John and all but one of the BLP members elected in 1981. Barrow once again took the position of prime minister; Henry Forde, a former attorney general and minister of external affairs and the only BLP member elected in 1981 to retain his seat in the House, was named leader of the opposition.

On becoming prime minister, Barrow, in an effort to reduce unemployment, cut taxes substantially and increased public

Clapham Park
Courtesy Inter-American Development Bank

expenditures on roads and transport, creating a large fiscal deficit (see Economy, this section). Barrow continued his previous strong support for regional integration and his opposition to apartheid. During the campaign, Barrow had declared that he would reduce the Barbados Defence Force (BDF); however, Barbados remained in the RSS and took part in maneuvers with the United States and Britain.

On June 1, 1987, Barrow died of a heart attack and was succeeded by Deputy Prime Minister Sandiford. The new prime minister had been a member of the DLP since 1964. Elected to the House in 1971, he was a cabinet minister in Barrow's third administration, a senator from 1967 to 1971, and was chosen deputy prime minister in 1986. Sandiford pledged to continue the policies of Barrow.

Foreign Relations

Relations with Latin American and Caribbean Countries

Barbados played a leading role in Caribbean affairs both before and after independence. Grantley Adams was an advocate of regional federation and served as the prime minister of the short-lived West Indies Federation. As noted earlier, his successor, Barrow, labored during the immediate preindependence period to pull together the Little Eight islands. This effort did not reach the stage of formal union, however, mainly because of the protracted nature of the negotiations. By the time Britain agreed to continue grant-in-aid monies, the momentum toward federation had been lost in acrimony. Barrow marched out of the last negotiating session in April 1965, taking with him the viability of potential union. Barbados declared its independence from Britain the following year.

Barrow did not abandon his belief in Caribbean integration after the collapse of the Little Eight negotiations. Instead, he helped to shift the regional approach to the concept. As the islands moved toward independence as separate entities, the notion of political association lost much of its appeal. The attraction of economic cooperation was strong, however, given the precarious economic status of these new ministates. Recognizing this, Barrow lobbied for the establishment of Carifta as a means of promoting regional economic viability and as a way of keeping the integration movement alive. The principle of foreign policy coordination among Commonwealth Caribbean countries, as advocated by Barrow, was achieved in theory with the advent of Caricom. Barbados also advocated the creation of such other regional institutions as the UWI, the CDB, and the West Indies Shipping Corporation (WISCO—see Appendix C).

By the time the BLP returned to power in 1976 under the leadership of Tom Adams, economic integration was an ongoing process, albeit not a particularly smooth or dynamic one. Adams maintained the Barbadian commitment to this process and made some limited efforts to expand beyond Caricom and establish new economic links with Latin America. Indeed, from 1976 until 1982 Barbadian foreign policy seemed to be driven primarily by economic imperatives, such as the promotion of trade (including tourism), the attraction of capital, and the expansion of domestic industry.

By 1982, however, it was clear that Adams's thinking on regional policy had begun to focus more on security concerns and less on political and economic issues. The motivation for this change in emphasis was the establishment in Grenada of the People's Revolutionary Government (PRG). From Adams's perspective, the PRG was a regional aberration that threatened to destabilize other island governments by its example and rhetoric if not by possible active support for subversive groups. Barbados' concern over Grenada surfaced pointedly in 1982 at the third Caricom heads of government meeting in Ocho Rios, Jamaica. It was there that Adams, supported by a number of like-minded leaders, pushed for the alteration of the Caricom treaty to commit members to the maintenance of parliamentary democracy and the defense of human rights. PRG leader Bishop, the target of this effort, argued for the incorporation of economic rights, such as employment, health care, and education, under the human rights rubric; he also gave private assurances to the prime minister of Trinidad and Tobago that Grenada would hold elections, although not necessarily under the Westminster system. Adams's amendment eventually was rejected in favor of a declaration affirming Caricom's support for ideological pluralism and the right of each state to select its own pattern of development. Although it appeared at the time to be a foreign policy victory for the PRG, the conference revealed the uneasiness and divisions within the Caribbean community over the course of events in Grenada; it also furthered an attitudinal split as to how best to deal with the situation. This drift was thrown into sharp relief by the events of October 1983.

Adams was a prime mover in the events that led up to the United States-Caribbean intervention in Grenada (see Current Strategic Considerations, ch. 7). The regional relationship most seriously affected by adverse reaction to the intervention was that of Barbados and Trinidad and Tobago. The flare-up between the two was marked by charges and countercharges over the issue of whether or not Adams had informed Port-of-Spain of the operation in advance of its execution. At the height of the dispute, the Trinidad and Tobago envoy to Barbados, who contradicted Adams's claim of prior notification, was expelled. In contrast to the debate provoked in other parts of the world by the intervention, the issue of notification seemed to be the real crux of the argument between these two states; disagreement over the inherent merit of the action in Grenada appeared to be a secondary consideration for both parties. The diplomatic dispute exacerbated already existing tensions based on Trinidad and Tobago trade restrictions. This rift, although not deep or irremediable, was not healed within Adams's lifetime and was employed as a campaign issue by Barrow and the DLP in their successful return to power in 1986.

Upon his return to the country's leadership, Barrow signaled his reservations over the previous government's approach to regional security issues. Despite some rhetorical salvos against the RSS, the United States, and some more conservative regional leaders such as Dominica's Mary Eugenia Charles, Barrow took no substantive action before his death to withdraw Barbados from the existing regional agreements. It is significant to note, however, that Grenadian prime minister Herbert Blaize did not request Barbados to send forces to Grenada in December 1986 to prevent possible unrest growing out of the verdict in the Bishop murder trial (see Grenada, National Security, this ch.).

Within the wider Caribbean, Barbados continued to maintain formal and correct relations with Cuba even after the Grenada intervention. Barbados, along with Guyana, Jamaica, and Trinidad and Tobago, had defied both the United States and the Organization of American States to establish relations with Cuba in 1972 in keeping with a general commitment to ideological pluralism. The relationship between Cuba and Barbados since that time, however, had been decidedly distant, the result perhaps of the competitive nature of both countries' major export (sugar) and their incompatible political systems.

Barbadian relations with Latin American countries traditionally had been limited. Nevertheless, Barbados was one of only two Commonwealth Caribbean beneficiaries of the 1980 San José Accord between Mexico and Venezuela (Jamaica being the other), whereby the two large producers agreed to provide oil at preferential rates to a number of Caribbean Basin states. Barbados had also benefited from low-interest loans for infrastructure and housing projects through another provision of the San José Accord. As of 1986, the DLP government was reported to be seeking new export markets in Latin America, particularly in Brazil, Colombia, and Venezuela, apparently perpetuating the efforts of the BLP government.

Along with the other nations of Caricom, Barbados supported the territorial integrity of Belize in the face of a long-standing claim by Guatemala. The Barbadian foreign minister held talks with Guatemala's ambassador to Venezuela in August 1986, presumably on the subject of Belize as well as the possibility of Barbadian-Guatemalan commercial and diplomatic relations. Progress seemed to be anticipated by both sides after the 1986 assumption of power by a civilian government in Guatemala.

Relations with the United States

In the early 1980s, the Adams government's diplomatic pressure on Bishop's Grenada, its participation in the 1983 intervention, and its advocacy of a Regional Defence Force were judged by a number of observers to represent a tilt from a nonaligned policy direction to one favoring United States security interests. It was clear that Adams's advocacy of enhanced security mechanisms, which came to be known as the "Adams Doctrine," dovetailed with the main thrust of Reagan administration policy in the Caribbean Basin. However, the Adams Doctrine probably was motivated more by the then-prime minister's interpretation of previous events, e.g., the 1979 Grenadian and Nicaraguan revolutions, than by United States, i.e., Reagan administration, pressure.

Barbadian relations with the United States have always been influenced by economic factors, especially trade and tourism (see Economy, this section). The Barrow government, in a foreign policy statement issued in 1987, recognized the importance of these relations and acknowledged the contribution of the United States Agency for International Development and the Peace Corps to projects in the fields of health education, housing, and agriculture. At the same time, Barrow chided both Caribbean and United States policymakers for perpetuating excessive reliance by Caribbean countries on the United States. He expressed a preference for greater "multilateralism" in this regard, apparently a reference to the need for increased coordination of aid programs among the United States, Canada, and the European Economic Community (EEC). Consistent with his earlier positions, Barrow also argued for greater Caribbean self-reliance and improved intraregional cooperation as a hedge against dependency.

Relations with the Commonwealth and Others

Barbados utilized its membership in the Commonwealth of Nations mainly to advance its economic interests, such as the promotion

419

of tourism and the provision of aid and technical cooperation (see Appendix B). In addition, the Barbadians have also used the Commonwealth as a forum to air their long-standing condemnation of the apartheid system in South Africa and to push Britain toward a stronger stance with regard to sanctions against the South African government.

Beyond its antiapartheid stance and such related positions as support for the self-determination of Namibia and recognition of the South West Africa People's Organization, Barbados has expressed a keen interest in African affairs generally through its membership in the Commonwealth and the United Nations. The Barbadians viewed this connection as a natural one, arising from historical and cultural links as well as a convergence of economic interests. Along with many African and other Third World members, Barbados has supported the movement for a New International Economic Order and argued in favor of a code or other mechanisms for the transfer of technologies from developed to developing countries.

Barbados' primary connection with the EEC has been through the Lomé Convention (see Glossary), which is updated every five years. Barbadian negotiators were involved in the discussions that finalized Lomé III in 1985. In a show of Caricom solidarity, in 1986 Barbados protested efforts by Britain and France to block Guyana's access to funds from the CDB, to which both European nations had contributed. The British and French objected to alleged human rights abuses and electoral irregularities in Guyana, issues that Barbados had tended to overlook in the interest of Caribbean unity and support for ideological pluralism.

In keeping with this stance and its historical efforts at nonalignment, as of 1987 Barbados maintained diplomatic relations with a number of communist countries, including Albania, Czechoslovakia, Hungary, Romania, Yugoslavia, the Democratic People's Republic of Korea (North Korea), and China. These relations were not very active, although some limited technical assistance and other exchanges were undertaken with the Chinese.

National Security

The Royal Barbados Police Force

Domestic police duties in Barbados are the responsibility of the Royal Barbados Police Force (RBPF). Originally established under British colonial rule in 1835, the RBPF was one of the most professional and effective of Caribbean police forces. According to the

Constitution, appointments to the force are made by the governor general, acting in accordance with the recommendations of the Police Commission. Overall command of the RBPF is vested in the police commissioner.

According to mid-1980s press reports, the RBPF was in the process of expanding its membership from 1,000 to about 1,200. The increase, initially resisted by the BLP government, was eventually undertaken at the urging of the police commissioner and the leadership of the opposition DLP, which had attempted to score political points by portraying the BLP as unresponsive to a perceived increase in the crime rate.

The crime rate in Barbados was generally higher than that of other Eastern Caribbean states, partially as a result of its higher population density (see Population, this section). As a country with a heavy stake in the tourist trade, Barbados has been concerned as much with the foreign perception of its crime rate as with the actual statistics. The Barbadian public and government officials differed to some extent on the nature of the crime problem; the average citizen was seemingly preoccupied with crime on the streets and beaches, whereas government and police spokesmen frequently emphasized the problem of white-collar crime and the corruption that often accompanied it.

One problem on which most parties seemed to agree was that of drug abuse, which appeared to be on the increase in Barbados during the 1980s. The RBPF functioned as the exclusive antinarcotics force on the island, leaving tasks such as maritime interdiction to the coast guard. Money laundering, possibly in connection with drug trafficking, was another offense cited by officials to justify increased manpower and improved training for the RBPF. Barbados did not appear to be a major transshipment point for drug traffic to the United States, although in 1985 an RBPF spokesman expressed his belief that some shipments to Western Europe had transited the island.

One indication of heightened public concern with crime was the formation in 1986 of neighborhood watch groups in Bridgetown. The initiation of this process was announced by the attorney general, who emphasized the role of the RBPF in guiding and informing members of these groups.

Most RBPF training was conducted at the Regional Police Training Center situated near Grantley Adams International Airport. Funded and largely staffed by the British, the center conducted courses for both Barbadian and foreign students from other Commonwealth Caribbean police forces, such as those of the Cayman Islands, Grenada, Montserrat, St. Lucia, St. Vincent and the

Grenadines, the Turks and Caicos Islands, and the British Virgin Islands. More specialized training for officers was provided at police facilities in Britain.

As of 1987, the RBPF had exclusive responsibility for port security and shared airport security duties with units of the BDF.

The Barbados Defence Force

In the late 1980s, Barbados was one of only two Eastern Caribbean states to maintain a standing military force (Antigua and Barbuda was the other). The Barbados Defence Force (BDF) was established in 1978 as a force completely separate from the RBPF. It has played a leading role in the RSS. Within the RSS framework, Barbados contributed the highest percentage of the system's budget, provided BDF headquarters as the RSS base of operations (and the BDF chief of staff as RSS coordinator), and informally earmarked the BDF as the primary regional reaction force in crisis situations. This understanding may have been abandoned, however, when the BLP government was voted out of power in May 1986. Domestically, the BDF was a somewhat controversial institution insofar as its existence underscored the Barbadian (and, one might well say, the Caribbean) ambivalence toward established military organizations.

The circumstances that led then-Prime Minister Tom Adams to create the BDF were unsettling and worrisome to the government and to many Barbadians. Adams's October 1976 announcement of an aborted attempt by two United States nationals to seize power with the aid of mercenary forces (and, five days after the announcement, the explosion and crash of a Cuban airplane at Grantley Adams International Airport) exposed the vulnerability of small island governments to destabilization by outside forces (just as the 1979 overthrow of the Eric Gairy government in Grenada displayed the susceptibility of such states to takeover by domestic dissident groups). The establishment of the BDF was subsequently justified, at least in the eyes of Adams and his supporters, by its successful December 1979 intervention on Union Island in St. Vincent and the Grenadines, which quelled an uprising by militant Rastafarians (see Glossary; Regional Security Threats, 1970–81, ch. 7).

Not all Barbadians shared Adams's favorable opinion of the BDF. Barrow, as the leader of the opposition DLP, questioned the government's figures on defense spending and spoke out against what he characterized as a militarization of Barbados through the establishment of the BDF (see Controversial Security Issues, ch. 7). After his 1986 electoral victory, most observers assumed that Prime Minister Barrow would move quickly to slash the BDF's ranks and budget. However, Barrow's moves in this regard were more tentative and ambivalent than anticipated.

After his May election, Barrow publicly expressed his objections to the October 1983 intervention in Grenada, stating that he would not have allowed BDF forces to participate and would not have acquiesced to the use of Barbados as a staging area had he been prime minister at the time. He also objected to the notion of a treaty formalizing the RSS and pledged himself not to sign such a document. Barrow seemed more reassuring in a September 1986 address to BDF units, during which he denied any plans for a "wholesale retrenchment" of the force.

By December, Barrow was once again vowing to cut back BDF forces or to phase them out entirely. Barbados did not need a defense force, he stated, because the only real threat it faced emanated from the United States, a superpower. These strong words were not followed by action until March 1987, when Barrow announced a freeze in BDF recruiting, a rather conservative approach to thinning the ranks. Subsequently, the government did submit an FY 1988 budget that called for deep cuts in capital expenditure for defense. By the time of his death, it seemed clear that Barrow was intent on scaling back the size of the BDF, particularly the ground forces, and emphasizing its missions of airport security and maritime patrol and interdiction over its role as the primary reaction force within the RSS.

As conceived by Adams, the BDF was not to be tasked with domestic police duties. The prime minister believed that the assignment of internal security responsibilities to an army paved the way for domestic repression; this belief was reinforced by events in Grenada under the Bishop regime. Despite Adams's desire to distance the BDF from domestic affairs, the organization could still be considered an internal security force insofar as its primary mission was to defend the existing government against externally sponsored or assisted coup attempts. In the late 1980s, the domestic duties of BDF ground forces were limited to relief efforts in the wake of such natural disasters as hurricanes; BDF troops performed such duty not only in Barbados but also in Dominica and St. Vincent and the Grenadines.

The size of the BDF was unclear in the late 1980s; estimates ranged from 300 to 1,800, with 500 the most commonly cited figure. BDF force levels were considered confidential under the Adams government. The steady rise in defense spending from 1979 through 1986 probably indicated a steady increase in BDF personnel over that period. Because the defense budget was not made public, the breakdown of personnel versus equipment expenditures was uncertain.

The BDF included ground, naval (coast guard), and air branches. The inventories of the latter two arms were limited. The maritime responsibilities of the coast guard included interdiction of vessels engaged in smuggling and drug trafficking, search and rescue, immigration control, and protection of fishing grounds in cooperation with other regional states under the terms of the 1982 Organisation of Eastern Caribbean States (OECS—see Glossary) Memorandum of Understanding. The air branch of the BDF apparently was tasked primarily with transport duties, reflecting the BDF's important role within the RSS. The BDF was also reported to include a reserve component.

The BDF was both a recipient and a provider of training. The coast guard received the lion's share of the foreign training provided to BDF personnel. Formerly handled by Britain and the United States, this foreign training program was transferred to Canada by the Barrow government in August 1986. Barbadian trainers assisted in the instruction of paramilitary troops from other regional states.

Despite the concerns of Barrow and others, most observers in the late 1980s did not perceive the BDF to be a direct threat to democratic government. One author, Gary P. Lewis, has cited Barbados' well-established constitutional system and tradition of public accountability, as well as its relatively high level of economic development, as strong disincentives to military influence in the political arena.

*   *   *

F.A. Hoyos's *Barbados: A History from the Amerindians to Independence* and Ronald Tree's *A History of Barbados* provide a thorough account of Barbados prior to independence. Hoyos's *Builders of Barbados* and *Grantley Adams and the Social Revolution* span all of Barbadian history to the 1970s. The Barbadian journal the *Bajan* also provides useful data on recent events. Information on population, health, and education is available in a number of works, including Carleen O'Loughlin's *Economic and Political Change in the Leeward and Windward Islands,* Graham Dann's *The Quality of Life in Barbados,* Kempe Ronald Hope's *Economic Development in the Caribbean,* and the Pan American Health Organization's *Health Conditions in the Americas, 1981-1984.* Background information on the Barbadian economy is presented in the *Caribbean Economic Handbook* by Peter D. Fraser and Paul Hackett and *The Economy of*

Barbados, 1946–1980 by DeLisle Worrell; statistical data are available in the government of Barbados' annual *Barbados Economic Report* and five-year *Barbados Development Plan 1983–1988*, as well as in the annual reports by the CDB. (For further information and complete citations, see Bibliography.)

Chapter 5. The Leeward Islands

Harvesting sugarcane

LIKE THE REST OF THE INSULAR CARIBBEAN, the Leeward islands were discovered and named by the Spanish, only to have their control contested by the British and French. The term *leeward islands* is derived from the course taken by most of the sailing ships that voyaged from Britain to the Caribbean. Impelled by the trade winds, these vessels normally encountered Barbados, the island most to windward, as their first port of call. After progressing through the islands most to windward, which came to be known as the Windwards, these ships rounded off their voyages with the islands most to leeward—Montserrat, Antigua, Barbuda, St. Christopher (hereafter, St. Kitts), Nevis, Anguilla, and the Virgin Islands, among others.

Historically, the Leewards and Windwards have followed somewhat divergent paths despite their common colonial bond. The Leewards were settled earlier and were not, with the possible exception of St. Kitts, as rigorously disputed over as were the Windwards. Consequently, the period of uninterrupted British rule was longer in the Leewards. One legacy of this is the absence of French-influenced creole languages among the inhabitants of the Leewards. Despite colloquial forms of expression, English is the common tongue. In regard to religion, Roman Catholicism did not take root in the Leewards as it did in the Windwards. A number of Protestant denominations, predominantly the Anglican, Methodist, and Moravian churches, account for most of the Leewards faithful.

As a political entity, the Leewards experienced two extended periods of federation during the colonial period. The first of these, the Leeward Caribbee Islands Government, was established in 1671 and united the islands under the direction of a British governor. For a brief period in the early nineteenth century (1806–32), this grouping was divided into two separate governments. In 1871 Dominica, the British Virgin Islands, Montserrat, St. Kitts-Nevis-Anguilla, and Antigua (with Barbuda and Redonda) became the Leeward Islands Federation. Except for Dominica, which withdrew in 1940, these islands remained joined until the British dissolved the federation in 1956. Following a brief period in which they were administered as separate colonies, the former members of the Leeward Islands Federation were absorbed into the West Indies Federation in 1958 (see The West Indies Federation, 1958–62, ch. 1). The islands assumed associated statehood (see Glossary) in 1967, five years after the dissolution of the West Indies Federation. By the end of 1983, all but the dependencies (Anguilla, Montserrat, and the British Virgin Islands) had acquired full independence.

One phenomenon that binds the two island groupings together in a political and perhaps sociological and even psychological sense is the "small-island complex." Caribbean scholar Gordon K. Lewis has blamed this mind-set, which is a general feeling of inferiority suffered by the residents of small islands in relation to the residents of larger islands such as Jamaica and Trinidad and Tobago, for the failure of the West Indies Federation and other even less successful efforts at unification. Others have noted the "push and pull" effect on migration from the smaller islands to the larger islands, although these patterns are probably best examined and explained from an economic rather than a sociological-psychological point of view.

The Leewards generally have shared a similar pattern of economic development. The plantation system, characterized by production of one or possibly two major export products on land often held by absentee owners, has been another legacy of the enduring but largely static and unresponsive British control of the islands. What the system produced for Britain was sugar. Its by-products—labor strife, migration, landlessness, and poverty—were bequeathed to the workers. Thus it was that labor unions became the first vehicles for mass-based political expression in the islands. The political parties that grew out of unionism came to dominate government in the Leewards, especially after the granting of universal adult suffrage in 1951. Although the power of the labor-based parties was eventually diminished by factionalism and the rise of middle-class opposition groups (especially in St. Kitts and Nevis), their political influence has endured.

One notable political aspect of the Leewards is the high incidence of multi-island states—Antigua and Barbuda, St. Kitts-Nevis-Anguilla, and the British Virgin Islands. Such associations were encouraged by the British, who thought to enhance the economic and political viability of these small states by broadening their productive and electoral bases. The British did not sufficiently account for the small-island complex, however, and the seemingly inherent resentment it generated among the residents of the smaller islands. Thus, the grouping of unequal partners promoted unrest more than unity, particularly in the case of Anguilla. Eventually, a more positive approach to the question of multi-island federation, based on the concept of enhanced and assured autonomy for the smaller island, was achieved in Antigua and Barbuda and St. Kitts and Nevis.

Antigua and Barbuda

Official Name .... Antigua and Barbuda

Term for Citizens .... Antiguan(s) and Barbudan(s)

Capital .... St. John's

Political Status .... Independent, 1981

Form of Government .... Parliamentary democracy
and constitutional monarchy

Geography
Size .... 445 sq. km.
Topography .... Low-lying islands with
limestone formations
Climate .... Tropical, dry

Population
Total estimated in 1985 80,000
Annual growth rate (in percentage) in 1982–85 .... 1.3
Life expectancy at birth in 1985 72
Adult literacy rate (in percentage) in 1986 90
Language .... English
Ethnic groups .... Primarily black
Religion .... Anglican (75 percent); remainder other
Protestant, Roman Catholic, or Rastafarian

Economy
Currency; exchange rate .... Eastern Caribbean dollar
(EC$); EC$2.70 = US$1.00
Gross domestic product (GDP) in 1986 ... US$109 million
Per capita GDP in 1986 .... US$1,346
Distribution of GDP (in percentage) in 1984
Other services and government 44
Tourism 40
Manufacturing 8
Agriculture 8

National Security
Armed forces personnel 115
Paramilitary personnel 0
Police 350

431

Antigua and Barbuda

The islands of Antigua and Barbuda form a small nation whose strategic importance is greater than its size. Located at the outer curve of the Leeward Islands, Antigua and Barbuda are well placed for strategic defense of the Caribbean against outside forces. The natural harbors along Antigua's indented coast also offer havens for naval forces (see Current Strategic Considerations, ch. 7).

By the eighteenth century B.C., Antigua and Barbuda had been settled by their first inhabitants, the Ciboney (or Guanahuatebey) Indians. They were followed by the Arawaks, a peaceful Indian tribe that migrated from northern South America through the Caribbean islands and arrived on Antigua around A.D. 35. They began slash-and-burn cultivation of the island and introduced such crops as corn, sweet potatoes, beans, pineapples, indigo, and cotton. The Arawaks were uprooted by the Carib Indians around A.D. 1200; however, the Caribs did not settle on Antigua but used it as a base for gathering provisions (see The Pre-European Population, ch. 1).

In 1493, on his second voyage, Christopher Columbus sighted the island of Antigua and named it after Santa María de la Antigua. Early settlement, however, was discouraged by insufficient water on the island and by Carib raids. Europeans did not establish settlements on Antigua until the English claimed the island in 1632. Antigua fell into French hands in 1666 but was returned to the English the following year under the Treaty of Breda. Antigua remained under British control from 1667 until independence was granted in 1981.

From the start, Antigua was used as a colony for producing agricultural exports. The first of these were tobacco, indigo, and ginger. The island was dramatically transformed in 1674 with the establishment by Sir Christopher Codrington of the first sugar plantation. Only four years later, half of Antigua's population consisted of black slaves imported from the west coast of Africa to work on the sugar plantations. Antigua became one of the most profitable of Britain's colonies in the Caribbean (see The Sugar Revolutions and Slavery, ch. 1).

In 1685 the Codrington family leased the island of Barbuda from the English crown for the nominal price of "one fat pig per year if asked." The Codringtons used Barbuda as a source of supplies—such as timber, fish, livestock, and slaves—for their sugar plantations and other real estate on Antigua. This lease continued in the

Codrington family until 1870. Barbuda legally became part of Antigua in 1860.

Although the British Parliament enacted legislation in 1834 abolishing slavery throughout the empire, it mandated that former slaves remain on their plantations for six years (see The Post-Emancipation Societies, ch. 1). Choosing not to wait until 1840, the government on Antigua freed its slaves in August 1834. This was done more for economic than for humanitarian reasons, as the plantation owners realized that it cost less to pay emancipated laborers low wages than to provide slaves with food, shelter, and other essentials. The plantation owners continued to exploit their workers in this way into the twentieth century. The workers perceived little opportunity to change the situation, and sugar's dominance precluded other opportunities for employment on the island.

The Antiguan sugar industry was severely jolted in the 1930s, as the dramatic decline in the price of sugar that resulted from the Great Depression coincided with a severe drought that badly damaged the island's sugar crop. Social conditions on Antigua, already bad, became even worse, and the lower and working classes began to protest to the point that law and order were threatened. The Moyne Commission was established in 1938 to investigate the causes of the social unrest in Antigua and elsewhere in the Caribbean (see Labor Organizations, ch. 1). In 1940, in response to the situation, the president of the British Trades Union Congress recommended that the workers on Antigua form a trade union. Two weeks later, the Antigua Trades and Labour Union (ATLU) was created. The union soon began to win a series of victories in the struggle for workers' rights.

Despite these victories, the ATLU recognized the need to participate in the political life of the island, as the plantation owners still held all political power. Thus, in 1946, the union established a political arm, the Antigua Labour Party (ALP), and ran five parliamentary candidates who met the qualification of being property owners. All were elected; in addition, one of the five, Vere Cornwall Bird, Sr., was selected to serve on the government's Executive Council. Bird and the ATLU continued to push for constitutional reforms that would give the lower and working classes more rights. Largely because of these efforts, Antigua had full adult suffrage by 1951, unrestricted by minimum income or literacy requirements. With each general election, the union and the ALP put forth more candidates and won more seats in the Antiguan Parliament. In 1961 Bird was appointed to fill the newly created position of chief minister. Five years later, he led a delegation to

London to consider the issue of Antiguan independence. Following a constitutional conference, Antigua became an associated state (see Glossary) in February 1967, with Barbuda and the tiny island of Redonda as dependencies. Antigua was internally independent, but its foreign affairs and defense still were controlled by Britain.

During the period of associated statehood (1967–81), Antigua saw the rise of a second labor union and its affiliated political party and the beginnings of a secessionist movement in Barbuda, as well as the replacement of sugar by tourism as the dominant force in the economy. In 1978 Deputy Prime Minister Lester Bird (younger son of Vere Cornwall Bird, Sr.) and other like-minded political leaders called for full independence. Following their return to office in the 1980 general election, which was regarded as a popular mandate on independence, another constitutional conference was held in London in December 1980. An obstacle to achieving independence was the issue of Barbudan secession; this barrier was overcome when a compromise was reached that made Barbuda relatively autonomous internally. Complete independence was granted to the new nation of Antigua and Barbuda in 1981.

Geography

Antigua and Barbuda lies in the eastern arc of the Leeward Islands of the Lesser Antilles, separating the Atlantic Ocean from the Caribbean Sea (see fig. 1). Antigua is 650 kilometers southeast of Puerto Rico. Barbuda lies forty-eight kilometers due north of Antigua, and the uninhabited island of Redonda is fifty-six kilometers southwest of Antigua (see fig. 14). The largest island, Antigua, is 21 kilometers across and 281 square kilometers in area, or about two-thirds the size of New York City. Barbuda covers 161 square kilometers, while Redonda encompasses a mere 2.6 square kilometers. The capital of Antigua and Barbuda is St. John's, located at St. John's Harbour on the northwest coast of Antigua. The principal city of Barbuda is Codrington, located on Codrington Lagoon.

Antigua and Barbuda both are generally low-lying islands whose terrain has been influenced more by limestone formations than volcanic activity. The highest point on Antigua, however, is Boggy Peak, the remnant of a volcanic crater rising 399 meters. This mountain is located amid a bulge of hills of volcanic origin in the southwestern part of the island. The limestone formations in the northeast are separated from the southwestern volcanic area by a central plain of clay formations. Barbuda's highest elevation is 44.5 meters, part of the highland plateau east of Codrington. The shorelines of both islands are greatly indented, with beaches, lagoons,

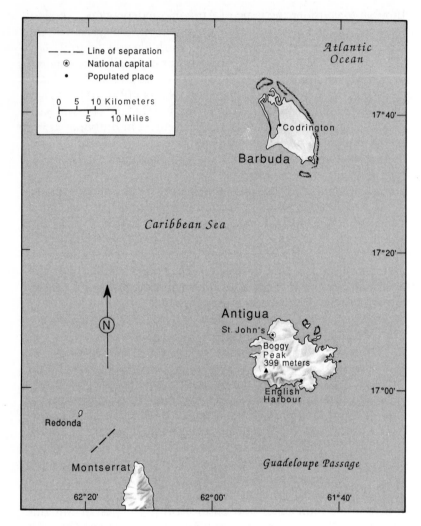

Figure 14. Antigua and Barbuda, 1987

and natural harbors. The islands are rimmed by reefs and shoals. There are few streams, as rainfall is slight. Both islands lack adequate amounts of fresh groundwater.

The islands' tropical climate is moderated by fairly constant northeast trade winds, with velocities ranging between thirty and forty-eight kilometers per hour. There is little precipitation, however, because of the islands' low elevations. Rainfall averages ninety-nine centimeters per year, but the amount varies widely from season to season. In general, the wettest period is September through November. The islands generally experience low humidity and recurrent droughts. Hurricanes strike on an average of once a year. Temperatures average 27°C, with a range from 23°C in the winter to 30°C in the summer and fall; the coolest period is December through February.

Population

In mid-1985 the population of Antigua and Barbuda was about 80,000, of which 78,500 lived on Antigua and 1,500 on Barbuda. The annual growth rate was 1.3 percent, based on a crude birth rate of 15 births per 1,000 inhabitants and a crude death rate of 5 deaths per 1,000. Infant mortality was twice that for the population as a whole, at 10 deaths per 1,000 live births. In 1981 about 34 percent of Antigua's population was classified as urban. This segment was almost completely concentrated in the capital, St. John's. Rural settlements tended to be compact villages of varying sizes, concentrated along major or secondary roadways. Nearly all of the population of Barbuda lived in the town of Codrington; the island of Redonda was uninhabited.

The people of Antigua and Barbuda were mostly black, descendants of African slaves. But the population also included some whites, descendants of British, Spanish, French, or Dutch colonists or of Portuguese, Lebanese, or Syrian immigrants. An exchange of residents had occurred between Antigua and Barbuda on the one hand and Europe and North America on the other hand as job seekers emigrated from, and retirees immigrated to, the Caribbean islands.

About 75 percent of the population belonged to the Anglican Church in the mid-1980s. The Anglican Church was acknowledged as the official church, but church and state were legally separated. The remaining 25 percent of the population included members of different Protestant denominations—Methodist, Presbyterian, and fundamentalist—as well as Roman Catholics and Rastafarians (see Glossary).

In the colonial era, Antiguan society was stratified on the basis of race. Europeans and those of European descent held the respected positions in society. They were the plantation owners and the political elites. On the other end of the spectrum were the black slaves or those of African ancestry, who lacked both political leverage and economic independence. The middle class was composed of mulattoes, who participated in commerce as merchants yet had little political clout. The abolition of slavery did little to change the class structure; nevertheless, the trade union movement and the associated transfer of political and economic power into workers' hands did much to weaken class barriers. In the late 1980s, society was divided along flexible class lines based on economic standing rather than the rigid racial criteria of the previous century.

The upper class in the late 1980s consisted mostly of foreigners but also included local investors or businessmen from the private sector. The higher positions in the party system, the civil service, the state-run enterprises, and the private sector professions were filled by the upper middle class, while the lower middle class consisted of other professionals, party functionaries, technicians, and skilled laborers. The lower class encompassed the rest of society.

Education

The education system in Antigua and Barbuda followed the British pattern and included public and private schools. Preprimary school was available for children from ages three to six. Primary education, compulsory for all children up to age twelve, was provided for five or six years. Secondary education, lasting four or five years, was offered upon the successful completion of a qualifying examination; private schools had their own qualifying examinations, while public schools used a standard test.

Postsecondary education was offered at the Antigua State College and at the local branch campus of the University of the West Indies (UWI). The Antigua State College offered a two-year program in five departments: teacher training, the advanced level in general education, commercial, engineering, and hotel and catering. Upon completion of the program, students took exams to earn certificates from external institutions, such as the UWI, Cambridge University, and the Royal Arts Society of London. Students attending the local branch campus of the UWI completed one year of studies and then continued their studies at another campus in Jamaica, Trinidad, or Barbados.

The 90-percent literacy rate indicated that the education system was reasonably successful in imparting basic skills. Despite this achievement, substantial problems remained in the late 1980s. Educational supplies and facilities were inadequate; in addition, there existed a high percentage of untrained teachers at all levels. These instructional deficiencies contributed to a national shortage of skilled labor.

In the 1980–81 school year, primary-school enrollment was 10,211 students, 78 percent of whom were in public schools. Of a total of 436 primary-school teachers, 82 percent were in the public system. Secondary schools had a total of 5,687 students and 321 teachers; 66 percent of the students and 71 percent of the teachers were in the public system. The state college consisted of 329 students; although most were from Antigua and Barbuda, some students also came from Anguilla, the Turks and Caicos Islands, and Montserrat. The two special education schools had a combined enrollment of thirty-seven students, instructed by thirteen teachers.

Health and Welfare

In the late 1980s, Antigua and Barbuda had a fairly healthy population, primarily as a result of the relatively high level of protein in the diet. Life expectancy at birth was seventy-two years. Primary causes of sickness and death, especially among children, were gastroenteritis and dysentery, both of which are caused by poor sanitary conditions and therefore are avoidable. Many parts of the islands, especially rural areas, did not have sufficient amounts of safe drinking water or adequate waste-disposal facilities. Other causes of death were heart disease, cerebrovascular disease, cancer, and influenza or pneumonia. Pertussis, yaws, and leprosy also presented health problems. Moreover, the kind of mosquito that spreads dengue and yellow fever inhabited Antigua and Barbuda. There were some cases of child malnutrition and failure to immunize children against common diseases. Diabetes and high blood pressure were common in adults. As of 1987, Antigua and Barbuda had two reported cases of acquired immune deficiency syndrome.

The main health facility, the Holberton Hospital, had a staff of full-time doctors and offered specialist services in surgery, ophthalmology, radiology, and psychiatry. A smaller hospital, with 230 beds, was located on Barbuda. Antigua also had a 160-bed mental hospital and a 40-bed leprosy hospital. In 1982 there were four health centers, supervised by district health nurses, and twenty-five multipurpose satellite health clinics. There were 30 doctors and 130 nurses and midwives; most nurses had completed a three-year training program at the Holberton Hospital. The government played an active role in providing for the social welfare of the nation's citizens. Seen as an "employer of last resort," the government occasionally purchased failing enterprises in an effort to prevent increased unemployment. The government also provided social security, medical benefits, and subsidized health care. Retired civil servants received pensions, and compensation was paid to dismissed public employees.

Economy

The economy underwent a substantial transformation in the twentieth century as tourism replaced sugar as the principal earner of foreign exchange and the primary source of employment. Like the previously dominant sugar industry, tourism was controlled

439

primarily by foreign capital. This control was in part the result of insufficient domestic capital, the local upper class having made more of its investments in commerce than in entrepreneurship. In an attempt to fill the local void, the government established state enterprises. Their specific purpose was to develop areas where foreigners were hesitant to invest, such as infrastructure or the faltering sugar industry, or to create domestic competition with foreign-owned enterprises, such as those in the tourist industry. The other major sectors of the economy, especially agriculture, were not strong enough to support the tourist industry; as a consequence, many items had to be imported.

Macroeconomic Overview

Economic growth in the early 1980s slowed after the relatively rapid expansion of the 1970s. This retardation was the result of several factors: recession in the industrial countries, trade problems within the Caribbean Community and Common Market (Caricom—see Appendix C), and a severe drought that reduced agricultural output in 1984. Increased tourism brought a slight recovery in 1985, as the gross domestic product (GDP—see Glossary) reached US$180.3 million, or US$2,273 per capita. In 1986 GDP fell again, however, to US$109 million, or US$1,346 per capita. This represented a decline of 16 percent from the 1982 GDP of US$129.5 million and a 20-percent drop from the 1982 per capita GDP of US$1,682.

Antigua and Barbuda faced a debt situation in the mid-1980s; this was partly the result of the recession of the early 1980s, which did not support the national outlays on infrastructure and other items. In 1983 the current account deficit of the central government reached 3.8 percent of GDP, with a gross external debt of 16.3 percent of GDP. By the end of 1984, debt had reached close to US$100 million. Servicing the debt cost more than US$7.4 million per year, which represented 16 percent of government revenues. Import expenses were expected to fall in the late 1980s, and tourism revenues were expected to increase, thereby helping to narrow the balance of payments gap. The central government was reducing public expenditures and state investment because of the fiscal difficulties created by the debt problem.

The Barbudan economy differed slightly from that of Antigua proper in the late 1980s because tourism was relatively less important to the smaller island's economy. Barbuda's largest source of income was remittances from relatives working in the United States or Britain. The second largest source was a subsidy from the Antiguan government, budgeted and distributed by the warden of Barbuda, the person selected to administer Barbudan economic matters. Economic activity and employment were concentrated in fishing, followed by agriculture (especially the raising of livestock) and tourism. Other sources of income included charcoal manufacturing and salt mining. Development of peanut farming and the exploitation of the island's coconut trees offered potential.

The labor force in Antigua and Barbuda consisted of 31,500 workers in 1984. In the mid-1980s, these workers were divided fairly equally among three trade unions: the ATLU, the Antigua Workers Union (AWU), and the Antigua Public Service Association. The first two were affiliated with the two main political parties, the ALP and the Progressive Labour Movement (PLM), respectively. Workers were free to choose the union to which they wanted to belong. Hence, each industry employed members of two or three labor unions. The labor union represented by the simple majority (50 percent plus one) of workers was designated to represent all of the workers in that industry during contract negotiations. Wage contracts normally were valid for three years.

Foreign nationals were allowed work permits only if there were no local applicants qualified for a specific position. Work permits generally were granted, however, for those who were involved either directly or via their companies in an investment project considered to be important to the country. Citizens of the United States, Canada, and Britain did not need visas.

Communications on Antigua were modern and adequately served all parts of the island. On Barbuda, however, communications consisted of only a few telephones, mostly in the village of Codrington. The telephone system was well maintained, fully automatic, and had over 6,700 telephones. Radio-relay links from Antigua to Saba and Guadeloupe, a submarine cable, and a ground satellite station all provided excellent international service to both islands. Antigua had three AM radio stations broadcasting on medium wave: the government-owned Antigua Broadcasting Service on 620 kilohertz, a commercial station on 1100 kilohertz, and the religious Caribbean Radio Lighthouse on 1165 kilohertz. Two shortwave stations reached points throughout the Western Hemisphere from transmitters on the island; the British Broadcasting Corporation and Deutsche Welle of the Federal Republic of Germany (West Germany) shared one transmitter, and the other relayed programs from the Voice of America. St. John's also had two small FM transmitters on 99.0 and 90.0 megahertz and television service on Channel 10. The *Workers' Voice* and the *Outlet* were the two main local newspapers. The *Herald* was a new third newspaper.

The transportation system was well developed on Antigua but practically nonexistent on Barbuda. About 240 kilometers of paved or gravel roads connected all areas of Antigua. V.C. Bird International Airport, east of St. John's, had a paved runway and handled international flights. A small, unpaved strip at the southern tip of Barbuda could accommodate only small aircraft. St. John's was the main port for the islands, but smaller vessels could also dock at English Harbour on the south side of Antigua. More than seventy-five kilometers of narrow-gauge railroad track extended south and east from St. John's. These lines, however, were used almost exclusively to transport sugarcane. Neither island had significant inland waterways.

Sectoral Performance

Sea, sun, and sand are so much a part of Antigua that they have been incorporated into the national flag. Tourism was the dominant industry in the late 1980s. It accounted directly or indirectly for 40 percent of GDP and 60 percent of employment in 1984 and was responsible for 21 percent of all foreign exchange earnings. Direct revenues from tourism were accrued by restaurants, duty-free shops, boutiques, entertainment and gambling establishments, car rental agencies, taxis, and miscellaneous other businesses. At the same time, agriculture, manufacturing, construction, public utilities, communications, trade, and banking and insurance received indirect revenues from tourism.

Despite tourism's many areas of direct or indirect contact with the domestic economy, the links in the late 1980s were weak, and many tourist dollars leaked back to the outside world. This leakage was primarily a result of the tourist industry's heavy reliance on foreign investment. Foreign investment dominated the larger resort complexes that accounted for the great majority of hotel room capacity. In many cases, the large resorts were built as self-sufficient enclaves, isolated from the rest of the island and offering all-inclusive vacations so that tourists did not need to have contact with other elements of the economy. As a consequence, much of the profit from tourism was expatriated.

The weakness of other sectors also affected links between tourism and the domestic economy. Because foreign businesses chose not to invest in areas such as agriculture and manufacturing and because local investors were also lacking, the entrepreneurial role was left to the government or else was not filled. Because of the resulting low level of productivity, the tourist industry had to import goods, such as food, that the local market could not provide. Ironically, many tourist dollars were lost in importing items purchased by the tourists. The sector most significantly affected by tourism was construction; its growth was positively related to that of investment in the tourist industry.

The nature of ownership in the tourist industry created a dilemma for the government. Since foreign-owned hotels and entertainment establishments expatriated much of tourism's financial benefits, the government encouraged national ownership of the industry. Local investors did not have sufficient capital, however, to support the large luxury resorts that were critical to employment. As a consequence, the government was forced to modify nationalistic tendencies and encourage foreign investment. Still, most of the jobs available to Antiguans and Barbudans were minimum-wage service positions; senior-level management posts in the tourist industry were held primarily by foreign nationals.

The manufacturing sector accounted for about 8 percent of GDP and 14 percent of employment in 1984. Manufacturing also represented 85 percent of total domestic exports in 1983. Despite government diversification efforts, the sector was dominated by light manufacturing. Cotton textiles and garments, distilled liquors such as rum, and pottery were the major industries in the sector; each of these was oriented toward exports. Other items manufactured in Antigua and Barbuda included paints, furniture, mattresses, metal and iron products, household appliances, electronic components, and masonry products, produced for both the local and the export (mainly Caricom) markets. The textiles and garment industry accounted for 47 percent of the manufacturing work force. The food and beverages and fabricated wood products industries accounted for 21 and 12 percent, respectively, of the sectoral work force.

Once the mainstay of the economy, agriculture has declined in importance since the collapse of the sugar industry. Agriculture generated only 7.5 percent of GDP and 12 percent of employment in 1984. Small farmers replaced the large plantation owners as the dominant producers in the agricultural sector. Production tended away from plantation crops of sugar and cotton—although sea island cotton remained an important supplier of the textile industry—and toward a varied system of fruits and vegetables to reduce food imports for the local market and tourist industry. The main crops were carrots, onions, eggplants, pumpkins, corn, cassavas, tomatoes, cabbage, cucumbers, potatoes, and yams. The livestock industry was also managed on a smaller scale and contributed to agriculture's increased relative importance in terms of GDP in the 1973–80 period. Livestock included cattle, sheep, and goats.

443

Despite the partial revival of the agricultural sector, however, several barriers to expansion remained. The most basic of these was the scarcity of fresh water, which limited irrigation. A second obstacle was the governmental land tenure system, covering 60 percent of arable land in Antigua, through which land was leased on a short-term basis. As a consequence, productive investment in the land was discouraged. Other constraints affecting agriculture included limited farm credit, deficient domestic marketing arrangements, a lack of effective agricultural information systems, and difficulties on the part of small farmers in obtaining basic agricultural services.

Role of Government

Although most economic activity was privately controlled and operated, state enterprises represented an important element in the economy in the late 1980s. Beginning with the electric power industry, the public sector expanded into agriculture, manufacturing, and tourism, as well as infrastructural services such as seaports, airports, roads, water supply, energy, and telecommunications. Productive enterprises included a cotton ginnery, an edible-oil plant, two large hotels, a commercial bank, an insurance company, the Antigua and Barbuda Development Bank, and most of the prime agricultural land.

The government's rationale for involvement in infrastructure and public utilities was that it contributed to firmer bases for further development. The purchase of failing enterprises, such as the sugar factory and the oil refinery, limited the anticipated increase in unemployment should the enterprises actually close. The government entered the tourist sector primarily to influence the employment practices of private investors. By keeping the state-owned resort open year round, the government was able to persuade the privately owned resorts to stay open as well, which alleviated unemployment in what had been the slow season. In addition, operation of the resort allowed the country to keep some of the tourist industry profits. In the manufacturing sector, the government constructed factory shells to be rented at low cost in order to attract foreign investment.

Despite achievements in some areas, such as tourism, the government's entrepreneurial efforts were relatively ineffective. Lacking an adequately trained managerial work force, the government often contracted with foreign nationals to run the state enterprises. In many cases, mismanagement grew out of the political patronage system used to fill senior public sector positions. Because the government also tended to act as the employer of last resort, it effectively gave a higher priority to reducing unemployment than to economically efficient use of labor. Despite its employment priority, the government was forced to shut down some operations, including the sugar factory and the oil refinery just mentioned, because they were serious financial liabilities.

Trade and Finance

Although Antigua and Barbuda was dependent on trade for its survival, it maintained large annual trade deficits throughout the 1980s. Manufactured goods, not including processed foods and beverages, comprised 59 percent of all exports in 1981. Food, beverages, and tobacco represented 20 percent, and other items accounted for the remaining 21 percent. Seventy percent of exports were destined for other Caricom countries, especially Trinidad and Tobago and Jamaica; the United States received 26 percent of Antiguan and Barbudan exports. Imports mainly came from the United States and included food, beverages, and tobacco (33 percent in 1981) and manufactured goods (25 percent). Other items accounted for 43 percent. Other major trading partners were Britain and Canada. In 1986 exports were estimated to equal US$51.8 million, whereas imports were US$74.1 million, for a trade deficit of US$22.3 million. This gap, although still large, was reduced from the 1982 level, when the trade deficit was US$90 million.

Like the economy in general, the finance industry in the 1980s was controlled largely by foreigners. Predominant were a small number of British and Canadian banks and insurance companies. Loans, a source of commercial and consumer credit, constituted the main link between the financial elements and the rest of the economy. The private financial institutions favored the tourist and construction industries to the detriment of other areas of the economy. Seeing this as unsatisfactory, the government established its own banks and insurance companies, including the Antigua and Barbuda Development Bank. Public institutions were a relatively insignificant part of the financial sector, however.

Antigua and Barbuda, as a member of the Organisation of Eastern Caribbean States (OECS—see Glossary), was a member of the Eastern Caribbean Central Bank. As such, it used the Eastern Caribbean dollar, which was created in July 1976 and pegged to the United States dollar at the rate of EC$2.70 equals US$1.00.

Government and Politics

The Governmental System

Antigua and Barbuda is a constitutional monarchy with a British-style parliamentary system of government. The reigning British monarch is represented in Antigua by an appointed governor general as the head of state. The government has three branches: legislative, executive, and judicial.

The bicameral Parliament consists of the seventeen-member House of Representatives, responsible for introducing legislation, and the seventeen-member Senate, which reviews and gives assent to proposed legislation. Representatives are elected by popular vote in general elections that are constitutionally mandated every five years but may be called earlier. Senators are appointed by the governor general. The major figures in Parliament and the government come from the House of Representatives. The prime minister is the leader of the party that holds the majority of seats in the House; the opposition leader is the representative, appointed by the governor general, who appears to have the greatest support of those members opposed to the majority government. The prime minister creates an executive government and advises the governor general on the appointments to thirteen of the seventeen seats in the Senate. The leader of the opposition, recognized constitutionally, is responsible for advising the governor general on the appointment of the remaining four senators to represent the opposition in the Senate. The opposition leader also consults with the governor general, in conjunction with the prime minister, on the composition of other appointed bodies and commissions. In this way, the opposition is ensured a voice in government.

The executive branch is derived from the legislative branch. As leader of the majority party of the House of Representatives, the prime minister appoints other members of Parliament to be his cabinet ministers. In late 1987, the cabinet included thirteen ministries: Ministry of Agriculture, Lands, Fisheries, and Housing; Ministry of Defense; Ministry of Economic Development, Tourism, and Energy; Ministry of Education, Culture, and Youth Affairs; Ministry of External Affairs; Ministry of Finance; Ministry of Health; Ministry of Home Affairs; Ministry of Information; Ministry of Labour; Ministry of Legal Affairs; Ministry of Public Utilities and Aviation; and Ministry of Public Works and Communications.

The judicial branch is relatively independent of the other two branches, although the magistrates are appointed by the Office of the Attorney General in the executive branch. The judiciary consists of the Magistrate's Court for minor offenses and the High Court for major offenses. To proceed beyond the High Court, a case must pass to the Eastern Caribbean States Supreme Court, whose members are appointed by the OECS. All appointments or dismissals of magistrates of the Supreme Court must meet with the unanimous approval of the heads of government in the OECS system; the prime minister of Antigua and Barbuda acts on the recommendation of the attorney general in making decisions concerning this judicial body.

The Constitution of 1981 was promulgated simultaneously with the country's formal independence from Britain. The Constitution provides a basis for possible territorial acquisitions, expands upon fundamental human rights, recognizes and guarantees the rights of opposition parties in government, and provides Barbuda with a large measure of internal self-government.

In defining the territory of Antigua and Barbuda, the Constitution includes not only the territory as recognized upon independence but also other areas that may in the future be declared by an act of Parliament to form part of the territory. This cryptic provision may have been designed to lay the basis for possible extensions of territorial waters.

The Constitution sets forth the rights of citizens, ascribing fundamental rights to each person regardless of race, place of origin, political opinions or affiliations, color, creed, or sex. It further extends these rights to persons born out of wedlock, an important provision in that legitimate and illegitimate persons did not have equal legal status under colonial rule. The Constitution includes provisions to secure life, liberty, and the protection of person, property, and privacy, as well as freedom of speech, association, and worship.

In order to quell secessionist sentiment in Barbuda, the writers of the Constitution included provisions for Barbudan internal self-government, constitutionally protecting the Barbuda Local Government Act of 1976. The elected Council for Barbuda is the organ of self-government. Acting as the local government, the council has the authority to draft resolutions covering community issues or domestic affairs; in the areas of defense and foreign affairs, however, Barbuda remains under the aegis of the national government. The council consists of nine elected members, the elected Barbudan representatives to the national Parliament, and a government-appointed councillor. To maintain a rotation of membership, council elections are held every two years.

Political Dynamics

Antigua and Barbuda's political system emerged from British political tradition and the development of trade union activism. The ATLU, established in 1940, found that its activism was not completely effective without a political voice. Seeking to gain a foothold in politics, the ATLU established a political arm, the ALP, in 1946. The ALP was structurally subordinate to the ATLU and was staffed by union personnel.

When Antigua and Barbuda achieved associated statehood in 1967, the union executives became political officials, consolidating their power. The political elites retained the political system that had developed from merging colonial politics with trade unionism, a system in which they had attained prominence. As the party gained importance, the labor union became subordinate to it.

From the start, both the ATLU and the ALP were dominated by Vere Bird, Sr., considered the "father of the country" by many because of his early efforts to promote labor unionism and independence. Although the labor union and the political party that stemmed from it were considered to be democratic, power was concentrated in the president, the general secretary, the treasurer, and the eight-member executive council elected at each annual convention. The faction led by Bird normally was able to influence the outcome of these union council elections and, subsequently, rankings within the party. Conflicts that arose within the union and the party were not resolved by compromise but by purging the opposition. Factionalism became a key characteristic of union and party dynamics.

Antigua shifted from a one-party to a two-party system after 1967. Establishment of the second party resulted from the personalistic factionalism that split the ALP and the ATLU. George Walter, leader of the dissenting faction, was dismissed from the ATLU because of his outspoken objection to the close tie between the labor union and the political party. In an attempt to regain power, Walter formed both a rival union, the AWU, and an affiliated political party, the PLM. The ATLU/ALP and the AWU/PLM became competitors for power. Although the PLM initially had factions that opposed the ALP on specific issues, the differences between the two groups were more personalistic than ideological. Both the ALP and the PLM competed intensely for the increasingly important political positions, as power became concentrated in the hands of the majority party and the attitude toward elections increasingly became "winner take all."

The two nonpersonalistic groups within the PLM were the Antigua Progressive Movement (APM) and an unnamed left-wing faction. The APM opposed the ALP on the basis of its close ties with the ATLU, believing that the labor union and the party should be completely independent. When the AWU/PLM proved to behave in the same way as the ATLU/ALP, the APM faction left the PLM in 1969 to form a purely political party, the Antigua People's Party (APP). The APP could not remain viable as an independent party, however, and soon merged with the ALP. The left-wing faction, led by Tim Hector, also left the PLM, forming the Afro-Caribbean Movement, which later became the Antigua-Caribbean Liberation Movement (ACLM). Hector had been a supporter of the Black Power movement (see Glossary) as a force in the Caribbean region (see Regional Security Threats, 1970–81, ch. 7). Despite its alleged pro-Cuban, pro-Libyan stance, the ACLM was regarded by the ALP government as a legitimate opposition party. The ACLM claimed to be a permanent voice of the opposition, never attempting to achieve a majority or to form a government, as that supposedly would compromise its principles.

In 1971 the PLM won the majority of the seats in the House of Representatives in the general election, ending the ALP's continuous dominance in national politics. During the PLM administration, however, the party instituted repressive social measures, such as limitations on freedom of the press, and ineffective economic policies that contributed to a recession. As a result, the ALP again won control of the government in the 1976 general election. Some PLM party leaders, including Walter, were tried on corruption charges stemming from their mismanagement while in office. Although Walter was released on appeal, he was barred from the 1980 elections and was replaced as PLM party leader by Robert Hall. Walter again sought a way to political power by creating the United People's Movement (UPM) with some of his supporters from the PLM.

During 1976–80, the ALP implemented policies that revitalized the economy and reopened society. These measures enabled the ALP to consolidate power at the expense of the PLM and UPM. The ALP easily won the 1980 election, campaigning on the basis of improved economic and social conditions. Using the same platform in the 1984 election, the ALP won a complete victory, capturing all seats in the House except for one taken by a pro-ALP independent from Barbuda.

As the conservative opposition parties—PLM and UPM—became defunct, a new opposition party, the United National Democratic Party (UNDP), was established by Ivor Heath in late 1984. The UNDP was formed partly in response to the growing dissatisfaction with the effective monopoly the ALP seemed to have on political power and the subsequent potential for abuse. The UNDP was composed first of remnants of the PLM and later of the UPM and envisioned itself as the voice of middle-class elements pressing for greater support of private enterprise and stronger action against corruption. Although he lacked specific goals when he established the UNDP, Heath later elaborated the issues of limited tenure for the prime minister and the security of the secret ballot. The leader of the UNDP also vowed to decentralize the government if his party were to come to power. Specifically, he proposed a system of village councils to give communities a form of local government and more control of their own affairs. In the late 1980s, only Barbuda had local self-government; the other localities fell under the authority of the Ministry of Home Affairs.

The ALP faced corruption charges in the late 1980s. The *Outlet,* the newspaper affiliated with Hector and the ACLM, accused the Bird administration of having insufficient control over casino operations, peddling passports to non-Antiguans, mismanaging foreign loans, and using Antigua and Barbuda to launder arms shipments to South Africa. The most potentially damaging scandal, however, was the 1986 corruption case involving Minister of Public Works and Communications Vere Cornwall Bird, Jr., the first son and namesake of the prime minister. The minister was accused of fraud in the negotiation and subsequent misappropriation of a French loan of US$11 million for the rehabilitation of the V.C. Bird International Airport. Sir Archibald Nedd, a retired Grenadian judge, was appointed to lead an investigation into the matter. During the course of the inquiry, the scandal spread to touch Bird, Sr., who appeared to be attempting to cover up evidence and influence the course of the investigation. Others inside the party, such as Minister of Education, Culture, and Youth Affairs Reuben Harris, provided evidence and testimony that could be seen as harmful to the case of Bird, Jr. The situation appeared to exacerbate previously existing dissension within the party and the cabinet and contributed to a crisis in ALP leadership. The previous conflict seemed to have been based on use of favoritism by Bird, Jr., in the distribution of cabinet positions and on personality clashes and power struggles within the cabinet. Sir Archibald concluded in his report that although Bird, Jr., was innocent of criminal wrongdoing, he had behaved in a manner unbecoming a minister of government. Members of the cabinet, Parliament, and opposition forces demanded that Bird, Jr., be forced to resign. Bird, Sr., however, decided to keep his son as a member of his cabinet.

Because the PLM and UPM were still weak, the only viable rival for the 1989 election seemed to be the new UNDP. In the opinion of most observers, however, its chances were slight, despite the ALP scandal, unless the new party were to widen its organizational basis beyond its original middle-class sources of support. The ACLM was not expected to win a significant number of seats in Parliament.

Foreign Relations

Strong economic and political bonds largely determined the country's foreign relations in the late 1980s. Antigua and Barbuda's primary diplomatic relations were with other Caribbean countries, the United States, Britain, and Canada; embassies were maintained in each of these countries. In other countries with which Antigua and Barbuda had diplomatic relations, no Antiguan and Barbudan ambassador was in residence, but ambassadors residing in the aforementioned countries were accredited to them as well. Firmly anticommunist, Antigua and Barbuda in 1987 was considered to be one of the most ardent supporters of the United States in the Caribbean area. Various forms of United States aid were important to Antigua and Barbuda, as was North American tourism. Of importance to the United States was the fact that Antigua occupied a strategic position and hosted a United States military presence, including air force and naval facilities. After Antigua and Barbuda gained independence, the United States consulate that had been established in 1980 was upgraded to an embassy in 1982, with a staff of eighteen.

Despite Antigua and Barbuda's bonds with both the United States and Britain, relations were tense in late 1986 as the ALP government formed the impression that the United States and Britain might favor the UNDP in the upcoming 1989 election. Realizing that the Western powers might regard Deputy Prime Minister Lester Bird, the presumed successor to his father, as too leftist, the ALP leadership accused the United States and Britain of courting Heath and promoting his party in the next elections in the hope that the UNDP would institute a more conservative government. When Heath received an official invitation to visit London, the *Herald,* the newspaper generally regarded as affiliated with Deputy Prime Minister Bird and his supporters, cited this as evidence of Britain's support of the UNDP candidate and described as inappropriate a diplomatic meeting with the leader of a party with no elected seats in the Antiguan Parliament. The *Workers' Voice,* the ATLU-supported newspaper, joined in accusing the United States of interfering in Antigua and Barbuda's internal affairs.

For his part, Deputy Prime Minister Bird criticized United States policy in the region as not sharing the national priorities held by governments in the Caribbean region. Bird also expressed reservations about the pervasive presence of United States advisers in the region, increased arms shipments from the United States to the Caribbean, and the establishment of paramilitary Special Service

Units (SSUs). Although some in his party feared a leftward turn should he gain power, Lester Bird and those with similar nationalistic views remained strongly anticommunist.

Antigua and Barbuda was a member of, among other international organizations, the Commonwealth of Nations (see Appendix B), the International Monetary Fund (IMF—see Glossary), the World Bank (see Glossary), the United Nations (UN) and several UN agencies (including the United Nations Education, Science, and Culture Organization), the OECS, the Regional Security System (RSS), Caricom, and the Organization of American States. As a member of Caricom and the Commonwealth of Nations, Antigua and Barbuda supported Eastern Caribbean integration efforts (see Postwar Federation Efforts, ch. 7).

National Security

Antiguan and Barbudan security forces consisted of the Royal Antigua and Barbuda Police Force, which was a constabulary of 350 personnel, and the Antigua and Barbuda Defence Force, which had 115 members. Although both forces reported to the deputy prime minister, they were independent of each other. The Defence Force filled the role of the SSUs established in other OECS countries; it had only a ground element, as Antigua and Barbuda had no navy or air force. The coast guard was subordinate to the Police Force.

Elements of both the Police Force and the Defence Force participated in the United States-Caribbean military intervention in Grenada in 1983 (see Current Strategic Considerations, ch. 7). Antiguan and Barbudan forces stayed in Grenada until the spring of 1985 as part of the regional peacekeeping effort. Members of Antigua and Barbuda's Defence Force returned to Grenada in late 1986 in response to a request from Grenadian prime minister Herbert Blaize. Blaize had feared the eruption of violence as the Maurice Bishop murder trial neared its end.

Antigua and Barbuda was an early supporter of the regional defense force concept. Prime Minister Bird regarded the RSS as a means of providing a counterinsurgency force in the event that revolutionary forces established themselves on Antigua and Barbuda. He felt that communist groups in the region saw the RSS as a threat and therefore were trying to discredit the system. Although some Caribbean heads of government remained opposed to the proposal, Bird continued to support the establishment of an independent, regional force and security system that could counter this perceived threat to the RSS system and, by extension, OECS member states (see A Regional Security System, ch. 7). In support of United States military aid to the region, Antigua and Barbuda received coast guard boats from the United States in the early 1980s and agreed to engage in joint coast guard patrols with Barbados, St. Kitts and Nevis, and St. Lucia. The Antigua and Barbuda Defence Force and coast guard also participated in various joint training exercises with the United States and other countries in the region. At the same time, Antigua and Barbuda agreed to permit United States facilities on Antigua to be used to train RSS personnel.

*   *   *

A very useful overview of Antigua and Barbuda at the time of independence is provided by *Antigua and Barbuda Independence,* an official publication of the government of Antigua and Barbuda edited by Ron Sanders. Paget Henry's *Peripheral Capitalism and Underdevelopment in Antigua* covers many aspects of Antiguan society and economy from a Marxist perspective. The November–December 1981 issue of the *Bulletin of Eastern Caribbean Affairs* includes several interesting articles on the Constitution, agriculture, and society. Novelle H. Richards's *The Struggle and the Conquest, Pt. II: The Locust Years* provides a helpful glimpse at interparty dynamics and political history. A closer look at Barbuda can be obtained in *Barbuda Reconnaissance* by Richard Russell and William G. McIntire; although dated in some ways, it offers useful information, especially for those interested in local geology and oceanography. (For further information and complete citations, see Bibliography.)

St. Christopher and Nevis

Official Name .... St. Christopher and Nevis

Term for Citizens .... Kittitian(s), Nevisian(s)

Capital .... Basseterre

Political Status .... Independent, 1983

Form of Government .... Parliamentary democracy
and constitutional monarchy

Geography
Size .... 269 sq. km.
Topography .... Mountainous; intermittent grasslands
and forests
Climate .... Tropical, wet

Population
Total estimated in 1986 45,000
Annual growth rate (in percentage) in 1986 .... 0.1
Life expectancy at birth in 1982 70
Adult literacy rate (in percentage) in 1986 90
Language .... English
Ethnic groups .... Black (over 90 percent);
remainder white or mulatto
Religion .... Primarily Anglican

Economy
Currency; exchange rate .... Eastern Caribbean dollar
(EC$); EC$2.70 = US$1.00
Gross domestic product (GDP) in 1985 ... US$67.3 million
Per capita GDP in 1985 .... US$1,500
Distribution of GDP (in percentage) in 1985
Government and other services 23.7
Agriculture 15.0
Manufacturing 12.8
Tourism 6.0
Other 42.5

National Security
Armed forces personnel 0
Paramilitary personnel 80
Police 220

455

St. Christopher and Nevis

St. Christopher (hereafter, St. Kitts) and Nevis share a long history of British colonization. St. Kitts has been referred to as the "mother colony of the West Indies," a reflection of its status as the first English colony in the Caribbean. Although discovered by Christopher Columbus in 1493, St. Kitts was not settled by Europeans until 1623, when a small group of Britons established themselves at Sandy Bay. As elsewhere in the Caribbean, the French were not far behind; they established settlements the following year. Nevis was colonized in 1628 by an English party dispatched from St. Kitts.

The British and French kept up an uneasy cohabitation on St. Kitts until 1713, when Britain was granted sole dominion under the Treaty of Utrecht. The only apparent cooperative venture between the two groups of settlers during this period was a series of joint military operations against the native Carib Indians that resulted in their virtual elimination from the island. Although officially sovereign, the British were unable to solidify their control over the islands and secure them against French assault until the late eighteenth century (see Historical and Cultural Setting, ch. 1). This consolidation of British rule was recognized by the Treaty of Versailles in 1783.

Under British rule, St. Kitts and, to a lesser extent, Nevis provided classic examples of the plantation system. On tracts owned by well-to-do Britons, often on an absentee basis, cash crops were raised for export by indentured laborers and, eventually, by African slaves. After brief attempts at indigo and tobacco cultivation, sugarcane was introduced to both islands by the mid-seventeenth century (see The Sugar Revolutions and Slavery, ch. 1). Sugarcane cultivation and its by-products—land scarcity, price fluctuations, seasonal employment and unemployment, and migration—went on to shape the history of St. Kitts and Nevis, although soil erosion and depletion in Nevis eventually led to the abandonment of sugarcane cultivation by the plantation owners and the establishment of peasant smallholdings.

The two islands, along with the somewhat more distant Anguilla, experienced a number of administrative configurations and changes of status during the course of colonial history. Beginning in 1671, St. Kitts and Nevis joined Antigua (with Barbuda and Redonda) and Montserrat as part of the Leeward Caribbee Islands Government under a British governor. This arrangement endured until 1806, when the Leeward Caribbees were split into two separate governmental units, with St. Kitts-Nevis-Anguilla and the British Virgin Islands comprising one of these units. The Leewards were reunited as a single administrative entity in 1871, with Dominica included in the grouping. St. Kitts-Nevis-Anguilla was established as a "presidency" within the Leeward Islands Federation in 1882, a status it kept until 1956.

The three-island grouping participated in the ill-fated West Indies Federation from 1958 to 1962 and took part in the unsuccessful negotiations of the so-called Little Eight (Antigua and Barbuda, Barbados, Dominica, Grenada, Montserrat, St. Kitts-Nevis-Anguilla, St. Lucia, and St. Vincent and the Grenadines), which broke off in 1966 when the government of Antigua and Barbuda would not agree to have its postal service absorbed into a federal framework. When these efforts failed, St. Kitts-Nevis-Anguilla, along with most of the other small Caribbean colonies, accepted the British offer of associated statehood (see Glossary), which provided for domestic self-government while Britain maintained responsibility for external affairs and defense. St. Kitts and Nevis remained an associated state until it declared full independence in 1983 (the last of the associated states to do so). By that time, Anguilla had long since declared and demonstrated its opposition to continued union with St. Kitts and had assumed dependency status (see British Dependencies: British Virgin Islands, Anguilla, and Montserrat, this ch.).

The political history of St. Kitts and Nevis is closely intertwined with its economic development (or lack of it). The issue of land is at the heart of Kittitian politics. The dominance by estate owners of this already limited natural resource and the single-minded application of that resource to one industry precluded the development of a stable peasant class. Instead, the system produced a large class of wage laborers generally resentful of foreign influence. The nature of the sugar industry itself—the production of a nonstaple and essentially nonnutritive commodity for a widely fluctuating world market—only served to deepen this hostility and to motivate Kittitian laborers to seek greater control over their working lives and their political situation.

The collapse of sugar prices brought on by the Great Depression precipitated the birth of the organized labor movement in St. Kitts and Nevis. The Workers League, organized by Robert Bradshaw in 1932, tapped the popular frustration that fueled the labor riots of 1935–36. Rechristened the St. Kitts and Nevis Trades and Labour Union in 1940, the union established a political arm, the St. Kitts and Nevis Labour Party, which put Bradshaw in the Legislative Council in 1946. The Labour Party would go on to

View of Sandy Point, St. Kitts, 1837
Courtesy Prints and Photographs Division, Library of Congress

dominate political life in the twin-island state for more than thirty years.

During its long tenure, Bradshaw's Labour government moved increasingly toward a statist approach to economic development. This tendency culminated in 1975, when the government took control of all sugarcane fields. It assumed ownership of the central sugar factory in Basseterre, the capital, the following year. By this time, opponents of the Labour government had discerned a corresponding tendency toward political rigidity and even repression, mainly through the vehicle of the St. Christopher and Nevis Defence Force. Resentment of Labour rule was particularly acute on Nevis, where citizens not only saw themselves as neglected and ignored politically but also felt that their island was being unfairly deprived of services and revenue by its larger neighbor. Nevisian disenchantment with the Labour Party proved a key factor in the party's eventual fall from power.

The decline of the Labour Party was marked by the passing of its longtime leader, Bradshaw, in 1978. He was replaced as premier (the preindependence title for prime minister) of St. Kitts and Nevis by a close associate, C. Paul Southwell. When Southwell died only one year later, the government and the party fell into a leadership crisis that strained the unity required to fend off a growing opposition. The new Labour leader, Lee Moore, apparently was unprepared to fill the void left by Bradshaw and Southwell.

By 1979, the political opposition had coalesced into two party groupings, one on St. Kitts, the other on Nevis. The Kittitian opposition party was the People's Action Movement (PAM), a middle-class organization founded in 1965 on the heels of a protest movement against a government-ordered increase in electricity rates. The PAM first participated in elections in 1966. Its platform eventually came to advocate economic diversification away from sugar and toward tourism, increased domestic food production, reduction of the voting age to eighteen, and increased autonomy for Nevis.

On Nevis, the party that came to enjoy widespread support was the Nevis Reformation Party (NRP). Established in 1970, the NRP advocated secession from St. Kitts as the only solution to the island's lack of autonomy. Campaigning almost exclusively on this issue, the party won 80 percent of the vote on Nevis in the elections of 1975, capturing both Nevisian seats in the legislature.

Labour's decline was confirmed by the elections of 1980. Although Labour outpolled the PAM on St. Kitts, taking four seats to three, the NRP again captured both seats on Nevis. This made possible the formation of a PAM/NRP coalition government in the House of Assembly (the legislative body that succeeded the colonial Legislative Council) with a bare majority of five seats to four, a development that placed the Labour Party in the unfamiliar role of parliamentary opposition. Kennedy Simmonds, a medical doctor and one of the founders of the PAM, assumed the post of premier (Simmonds had won Bradshaw's former seat in a 1979 by-election). Simeon Daniel, the leader of the NRP, was appointed minister of finance and Nevis affairs.

The change in government reduced the demand for Nevisian secession. Most Nevisians had long focused their objections to Kittitian government on the Labour Party. The PAM, advocating as it did an enhanced autonomy for Nevis, facilitated the incorporation of the NRP and its followers into national life. The PAM/NRP coalition also cleared the way for the national independence of St. Kitts and Nevis as a two-island federation. Although Simmonds and the PAM had formerly stated their opposition to full independence, they now reversed themselves, citing economic advances since the change of government and the prospect of further development through increased foreign aid after a formal separation from Britain. Accordingly, the coalition hammered out a constitution that granted Nevis considerable autonomy as well as a guaranteed right of secession (see Government and Politics, this section). A constitutional conference was held in London in December 1982, and St. Christopher and Nevis was declared an independent state on September 19, 1983.

Although Moore had participated in the constitutional conference, the Labour Party expressed strong objections to many provisions of the new Constitution, particularly those dealing with Nevis. The arrangement worked out by the PAM and NRP, it claimed, was not a true federation, since St. Kitts was not granted the same powers of local government as Nevis, i.e., there was no separate Kittitian legislature, and was not allowed the same right of secession.

Labour's objections, however, did not seem to be widely shared by the electorate. Simmonds, now the prime minister, called early elections in June 1984. In the expanded parliament, the PAM augmented its majority by capturing six seats to Labour's two. It also scored a symbolic victory by defeating Moore in his constituency and denying him the post and platform of leader of the opposition. The NRP captured all three seats in Nevis, yielding the coalition government a commanding nine to two advantage in Parliament and an apparent mandate to pursue its policies of development through diversification and an enhanced private sector.

Geography

The islands of St. Kitts and Nevis are part of the Leeward Islands group of the Lesser Antilles (see fig. 1). They are located about 113 kilometers south of Anguilla and 300 kilometers southeast of Puerto Rico. A narrow strait 3.2 kilometers wide separates the two islands. Total land area is 269 square kilometers, which makes the nation about the size of San Antonio, Texas.

Geologically, St. Kitts and Nevis are hilly or mountainous and volcanic in origin, representing adjacent peaks in a chain of partially submerged volcanic mountains. Both islands are subject to subterranean seismographic activity, which sometimes results in earthquakes. Lava deposits on the windward side of St. Kitts attest to the area's volcanic past.

St. Kitts, the larger of the two islands at 168 square kilometers, is shaped like an oval with a long neck and a small peninsula at its southeastern end (see fig. 15). The peninsula is flat and consists of salt ponds and white beaches. Towering mountains extend through the central part of the island, running from southeast to northwest. Mount Liamuiga, a dormant volcanic cone with an elevation of 1,156 meters, is the highest point on the island. Brimstone Hall, on the southwest side of the island, is 229 meters high and is composed of volcanic rock covered with a layer of limestone.

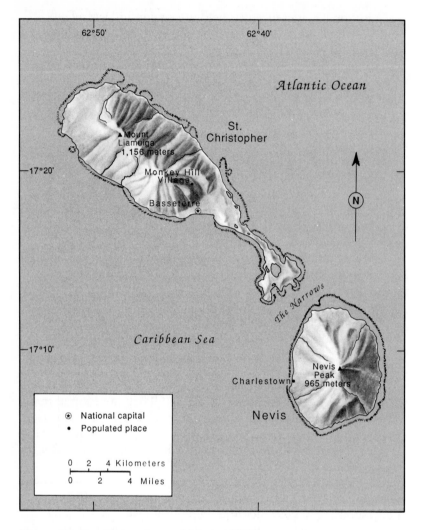

Figure 15. St. Christopher and Nevis, 1987

St. Kitts' fertile soil is well watered, has adequate drainage, and usually requires little or no irrigation. Forested areas cover 4,500 hectares of land and include both rain forests at the lower altitudes and evergreen forests above 250 meters. There are 7,700 hectares of agriculturally productive land, much of the soil consisting of a clay base. An acute erosion problem persisted into the late 1980s on certain parts of the island. Erosion was a result of a mineral deficiency caused by a lack of crop rotation, overgrazing, and inadequate intercropping.

Cone-shaped Nevis is ten kilometers wide, thirteen kilometers long, and has a total land area of ninety-three square kilometers. Nevis Peak, in the center of a chain of mountains, is the highest point on the island at 965 meters. Its rugged, heavily forested slopes rise gently from the sea. The soil on Nevis Peak is weathered; soils everywhere on Nevis are generally less fertile than those on St. Kitts and have experienced much worse erosion. Water is plentiful in the higher elevations. There is no rainy season on Nevis, but showers can be torrential. There are several hot mineral springs on the island.

Both St. Kitts and Nevis have a tropical climate tempered by the northeast trade winds; there is little daily or seasonal variation. Temperatures generally range between 18°C and 32°C and average approximately 26°C; lower temperatures prevail in the higher elevations. Humidity is generally about 70 percent. Annual precipitation varies from 100 to 300 centimeters. Neither island has the distinct rainy season characteristic of many other Caribbean islands. Winds are predominantly easterly and seldom exceed nineteen kilometers per hour except during the islands' hurricane season, which occurs from July to September.

Population

St. Kitts and Nevis had a population of about 45,000 in 1986; population density was 167 per square kilometer. Despite a crude birth rate of 26 per 1,000 inhabitants, annual population change has been about zero or slightly negative since 1970 because of continued emigration; nearly 20 percent of the population left the island each year in search of employment. Most went to Canada, Britain, or the United States and its Caribbean territories.

The long trend of labor emigration from St. Kitts and Nevis was tied to its economic and social development. Both men and women emigrated with the understanding that remittances to family members at home were expected of them for the entire time they were abroad. Some researchers have suggested that these remittances accounted for a greater percentage of disposable income than wages and salaries earned at home.

In the 1980s, more than 90 percent of Kittitians were black; most could trace their heritage to the African slave trade that was responsible for populating much of the Eastern Caribbean (see Glossary) in the seventeenth and eighteenth centuries. There was, however, a small group of white inhabitants who dominated the economy and were prominently represented in the merchant, banking, and other business professions. The remainder of the population consisted of a small group of mulattoes. Notwithstanding this apparent racial division, socioeconomic stratification on St. Kitts and Nevis was defined mostly by occupational status rather than by color.

Religious affiliation in the late 1980s was directly linked to the islands' British colonial heritage. Most citizens were at least nominal members of the Anglican Church, although exact figures were not available. The remainder of the population belonged to other Protestant denominations, including the Church of God, Methodist, and Baptist churches.

Education

Since independence in 1983, the education system of St. Kitts and Nevis has emphasized meeting the needs of a developing country, although this goal had not been fully realized by 1987. Broad policy objectives included producing trained and educated citizens capable of managing social and economic progress and unifying the populations of the two islands. At the same time, the government was dedicated to recognizing cultural, ethnic, and religious differences and providing the skills and knowledge needed to survive in an international environment known for disruptive domestic social and economic conditions.

The government's education program offered numerous alternatives. Basic academic preparation through high school was available in the mid-1980s, but public education also emphasized vocational and technical programs for students wishing to enter the work force after graduation. The government also developed "non-formal" programs to provide skills to high school dropouts and the unemployed. Development of educational facilities in the 1980s was accomplished with grants from the Organization of American States (OAS), the Caribbean Development Bank (CDB), the United States Agency for International Development (AID), and the government of Canada.

Education was coordinated at the national level by the Ministry of Education, Health, and Community Affairs. It had responsibility for the planning and administration of all public schools from primary levels through postsecondary instruction. Education was free and compulsory from ages five to fourteen. In the mid-1980s, there were more than 30 primary schools, teaching approximately 7,200 students from ages 5 through 12. There was a total of 350 teachers. In 1986 many buildings were renovated, and two new primary schools were planned, including one for Basseterre.

There were six secondary schools in St. Kitts and Nevis in the mid-1980s; four were located on the larger island. Total enrollment was about 4,200 students. There was a teaching staff of 265, which included both trained and untrained instructors. The renovation of Sandy Point and Cayon high schools in 1986 included construction of new laboratories, engineering facilities, and larger classrooms to accommodate additional vocational programs.

Postsecondary educational opportunities in St. Kitts and Nevis were available in some fields in the mid-1980s. Although there was no university on either of the islands, further study could be undertaken at the Teacher's Training College, Technical College, Nursing School, or First-Year University Education Programme. Those who completed the latter program were permitted to enroll as second-year students at the University of the West Indies (UWI).

Scholarship funds from Western Europe and Canada assisted Kittitian students attending programs at the UWI, as well as at the College of Arts, Science, and Technology in Kingston, Jamaica. Scholarships emphasized vocational disciplines such as business administration, science, and engineering.

The Ministry of Education, Health, and Community Affairs also offered informal opportunities, such as the Adult Education Programme and Community Courses workshop. The former provided academic instruction to individuals who had left the formal education system prematurely; the latter gave instruction in various vocational subjects to the general population.

In 1986 the Non-Formal Youth Skills Training Programme was instituted. Its mission was to teach high school dropouts and other unemployed youths specific skills in a short period of time to assist them with finding immediate employment. The three- to eight-week courses in garment making, automobile mechanics, leather crafts, and other skills were designed and implemented with funding from the OAS, AID, and the government of St. Kitts and Nevis.

Although improvements in the education system were still needed in the late 1980s, the government had made progress toward meeting some of the basic needs of the population. The focus on vocational training at all levels was eventually expected to reduce the high unemployment rate and improve the country's competitive position within the region by producing better trained and more highly motivated workers.

Health and Welfare

Health care services improved steadily but slowly in the 1980s. With the exception of their youth and infant populations, both islands enjoyed generally good health by Eastern Caribbean standards. High rates of malnutrition and infant mortality were the worst health problems in the mid-1980s, despite the government's intention to target youths and infants for special health care attention.

Mortality rates in St. Kitts and Nevis went virtually unchanged from 1980 to 1984. Although life expectancy at birth in 1982 was about 70 years and the crude death rate hovered between 10 and 11 per 1,000 inhabitants, neonatal (first month) and infant death rates were the highest in the Eastern Caribbean. The infant mortality rate averaged 43.5 per 1,000 live births between 1975 and 1983, and the neonatal mortality rate averaged 23.8 for the same period. The Pan American Health Organization (PAHO) noted that there had been no noticeable improvement in these statistics in the 1980s and that infant mortality rates were unlikely to change in the near future.

Morbidity patterns, although statistically less verifiable, also indicated a need to improve health care delivery to infants and young children. In the mid-1980s, gastroenteritis was highly prevalent among young children, and the general level of malnutrition in this group was among the worst of the Caribbean Community and Common Market (Caricom—see Appendix C) countries. Low birth weight, a generally accepted measure of malnutrition, was a chronic condition, affecting nearly 12 percent of total births in 1984. The incidence of low weight among children age five and younger was also high, affecting nearly 40 percent of this age-group in 1984. Combined with other medical problems associated with young children, these nutritional problems made the unusually high infant mortality rate inevitable. The development of national programs to improve the health care of expectant mothers, infants, and young children was expected to improve this situation in the future.

Although the nutritional problems of infants and young children were not solved by the mid-1980s, health services coverage, as measured by the success rate of the national inoculation programs, compared favorably with that of other Caricom countries. In 1983 nearly 90 percent of children under one year of age were given the diphtheria, pertussis, and tetanus vaccine; 93 percent were inoculated against poliomyelitis; and 69 percent were administered the tuberculosis vaccine. These levels were consistent with those of other Caricom countries, most of which were able to provide the same vaccinations to 90 to 95 percent of the targeted population.

Morbidity indicators for adults were not well documented, but available evidence suggested that diabetes, general infections, parasitic diseases, heart disease, and cancers were the most common afflictions. PAHO registered a rise in the number of hepatitis cases for 1984–85, but only one case of acquired immune deficiency syndrome was reported as of May 1986.

Environmental health indicators were up in the late 1980s. PAHO reported that nearly the entire population had access to potable water by 1983, and projects underway in 1986 included three new reservoirs in St. Kitts and well digging in Nevis. Solid waste disposal was available near Basseterre, and 96 percent of the combined population had access to sanitary waste disposal, including those serviced by pit latrines.

St. Kitts and Nevis' national health policy in the 1980s dictated that basic health services be made available to all inhabitants. This policy objective was formulated by the Health Department of the Ministry of Education, Health, and Community Affairs, which administered all public facilities, including hospitals and health centers.

In 1986 three hospitals were serving St. Kitts: the Joseph N. France General Hospital (164 beds) in Basseterre, the Pogson Hospital (28 beds) in Sandy Point, and the new Mary Charles Cottage Hospital (10 beds) in Molineax, which served the side of the island farthest from the capital. In 1986 the Pogson Hospital was renovated and expanded, and a new psychiatric wing was added to the Joseph N. France General Hospital. Nevis had one facility, the Alexandra Hospital (fifty-eight beds) in Charlestown, which was equipped for minor surgery and outpatient services.

Among St. Kitts and Nevis' specialized centers were a leprosarium and the Cardin House, a facility providing geriatric care. There were also seventeen health centers located throughout the two islands. These formed the basis for the provision of health care to the majority of the population, including the services of doctors, dentists, and nurses. Each parish was allocated at least one health center. Two or more centers were located in more heavily populated parishes. In 1984 there were about 4 doctors, 1 dentist, and 26 nurses per 10,000 inhabitants.

By the mid-1980s, the general welfare of the population was improving noticeably, largely because of government programs. Besides the water development projects on Nevis mentioned earlier, the government was instrumental in developing low-income housing projects on both islands. By 1987 the Central Housing Authority had added approximately 200 houses in new and existing neighborhoods. The government also created the Social Security Scheme in 1978 as a source of retirement benefits. The worker and employer each contributed 5 percent of the worker's salary or wages to the fund, which also represented the single largest source of public sector savings.

Economy

St. Kitts was early regarded as a logical choice for agricultural colonialism and became the launching point for seventeenth-century British expansion into the Caribbean. In many ways, St. Kitts was an ideal island for development of the colonial sugar estate; it had relatively large, fertile tracts of land, an amenable climate, and a steady pattern of rainfall. More than 300 years later, the Kittitian economy was still very dependent on sugar; but by the 1970s, government and business leaders realized that a move away from sugar was vital for continued economic growth.

Tourism and manufacturing developed slowly as economic alternatives in the 1980s, but eventually they began to challenge sugar as the primary foreign exchange earner. Because significant capital investment was a prerequisite, the transition was at first both unpredictable and uneven. Diversification within the agricultural sector, particularly toward fresh vegetables, was also a government priority. Nonsugar agriculture also experienced a similar pattern of steady but slow growth because of land restrictions and reluctance on the part of farmers to attempt smallholder farming.

Nevis, in its bid to achieve economic viability, has had less success. Historically, it lacked the richer soils and larger tracts of land available on its sister island and was consequently less suitable for cultivation of sugar. It was valued, even in colonial times, for its seclusion and beaches rather than for agriculture, a fact that may allow it to accommodate the growing international tourist market of the late twentieth century. Agriculturally, Nevis has relied heavily on the cultivation of sea island cotton as its primary export commodity. This crop, usually planted without rotation, caused a serious soil erosion problem, however, which will likely diminish the island's potential for further agricultural production for many years to come.

In the mid-1980s, the government envisioned the economic future of St. Kitts and Nevis as dependent on tourism, light manufacturing, and a scaled-down sugar industry. Although the potential seemed great, both islands were still struggling to make the necessary adjustments. The development of infrastructure and effective marketing techniques, however, may allow these three economic sectors to mature by the 1980s.

Macroeconomic Overview

Growth of the national economy in the 1980s was generally uneven because of the continued reliance on the sugar industry. Both the agriculture and the manufacturing sectors depended on sugar for large portions of their earnings, and aggregate economic performance mirrored the vagaries of the international sugar market.

Gross domestic product (GDP—see Glossary) grew, on the average, by a respectable 2.8 percent annually from 1977 to 1983. Despite significant expansion of tourism-related services, this figure would have been higher were it not for an actual decline in GDP of 2.4 percent in 1983 because of poor performance by the sugar sector. Sugar rebounded in 1984 so that aggregate economic performance rose by 3.3 percent, but GDP growth was reduced to only 1 percent in 1985, again the result of the weak performance of sugar. GDP grew in 1985 solely because of the strong performance of tourism and related construction projects.

The shift toward the service sector was evidenced by the economic figures for 1985. About 67 percent of GDP was accounted for by wholesale and retail trade, communications, and financial and government services. Agriculture and manufacturing each accounted for about 13 percent of GDP; the other economic sectors accounted for the remaining 7 percent. This trend was expected to continue into the 1990s, particularly if more tourist accommodations could be added to those already existing on the two islands.

Employment statistics in the mid-1980s, although widely regarded as unreliable, also reflected the growing importance of the tourist and manufacturing sectors. By 1982 a reported 26 percent of the work force was associated with trade, hotels, and other services, whereas 22 percent was employed by the manufacturing sector. The agricultural sector (primarily sugar) still employed one-third of the total work force, and sugar processing was still an important part of the manufacturing sector. Most of the remaining 19 percent of the labor force worked for the government, and about 5 percent were employed in the construction industry.

Despite the existence of government-run employment agencies on both islands, unemployment statistics were unavailable in the mid-1980s. Best estimates, however, placed the unemployment rate between 20 and 25 percent. This high level of unemployment has been variously attributed to the unwillingness of the labor force to attempt nonsugar agriculture and the lack of training necessary to make the transition to tourism-related services. Unemployment was not expected to decrease in the immediate future, unless the government became more successful at coordinating education and technical training with the demands of the labor market.

Inflation in the Kittitian economy was typical for a Caribbean island in the mid-1980s; it was fueled by both internal and external sources but tended to parallel world inflation because of the open nature of the domestic economy. Because St. Kitts and Nevis was so dependent on imports, the price changes of these goods often had a strong effect on the domestic inflation rate. Local inflationary pressures, such as wage increases, were also occasionally evident but generally had a minimal effect on prices in the mid-1980s.

After rising at double-digit rates in the early 1980s, inflation as measured by the consumer price index fell to 3.6 percent in 1983, 2.7 percent in 1984, and 1.8 percent in 1985. This decline reflected global trends, as well as stable prices for essential imports and minimal increases in domestic wages. Stable prices and wages were expected for the rest of the decade.

Banking and Finance

St. Kitts and Nevis had a relatively simple system of public and private financial institutions in the 1980s. As a member of the Organisation of Eastern Caribbean States (OECS—see Glossary), it had as its central monetary authority the Eastern Caribbean Central Bank (ECCB), headquartered in Basseterre. St. Kitts and Nevis also used the Eastern Caribbean dollar as its medium of economic exchange; it was pegged to the United States dollar at a rate of EC$2.70 to US$1.00 in 1987.

The two islands had six financial institutions in 1986, including both foreign and domestic concerns. Barclays Bank, the Royal Bank of Canada, and the Bank of Nova Scotia represented foreign interests, whereas domestic institutions included the St. Kitts and Nevis National Bank, the Development Bank of St. Kitts and Nevis, and the Nevis Co-operative Bank. Financial assistance was also provided by multilateral institutions, such as the CDB and the World Bank (see Glossary).

By the mid-1980s, savings levels had been deteriorating steadily since 1978. By 1981 they had become negative, forcing foreign savings to become the base for lending to both the public and the private sectors. Public sector borrowing increased in the 1980s because of the deteriorating fiscal situation caused in part by the fall in sugar tax revenues. Additionally, the private sector was saving less and purchasing more, particularly consumer durables.

Role of Government

The government played both direct and indirect roles in the national economy. Although it allowed the private sector to control most of the country's economic assets, it found itself having to assume management of the sugar industry in the 1970s, a situation that remained unchanged as of 1987. The government, however, considered its primary role as one of facilitating economic development by exercising fiscal and monetary options, managing public sector investment, and creating an attractive environment for both public and private foreign capital.

Following independence in 1983, St. Kitts and Nevis attempted to maintain a balance of revenues and expenses. By the mid-1980s, however, current expenditures and capital investment exceeded revenues. Large increases in public salaries, 45 percent in 1981 and 25 percent in 1986, were partially responsible for the growing deficit; tax receipts, however, did not realistically reflect fiscal requirements. To offset the resulting budget deficit, which reached 5 percent of GDP in 1984, the government cut capital expenditures, borrowed from domestic and foreign banks, and developed new revenue sources. Although the personal income tax was abolished in 1980, increased revenue was realized from two new taxes created in 1986, the Social Services Levy and the Employment Protection Levy. These new financial measures, in addition to import duties and utilities fees that had previously formed the basis of government revenue, allowed St. Kitts and Nevis to reverse its operational deficit and actually realize a small surplus by 1987. This was a critical development for maintaining the country's international credit rating and access to foreign loans.

Because it was a member of a regional monetary authority, St. Kitts and Nevis had a limited ability to exercise control over the economy by manipulating money supply and interest rates. The nation's primary goals of growth and stability, however, were in accordance with those of other regional economies, and balanced growth of the money supply, which was managed by the ECCB, assisted the government in financing deficits and providing funds for public sector investment. The Social Security Scheme provided local public funds for budget and public investment loans.

The government coordinated growth through a program of public sector investment, which managed foreign and domestic capital expenditures used for national development. The primary goal was to expand the country's economic base by moving away from sugar and toward tourism, manufacturing, and nonsugar agriculture. Public investment managers allocated funds to three major areas: directly productive sectors such as agriculture, industry, and tourism; economic infrastructure projects, including transportation, communications, and utilities; and social infrastructure, such as health, education, and housing. In the early 1980s, construction of economic infrastructure was emphasized to accommodate future growth in both manufacturing and tourism. Thirty percent of total expenditures were allocated to transportation. This resulted in the completion of a 250-kilometer road system, the Golden Rock International Airport, and a deep-water port in Basseterre.

Communications were also upgraded in the 1980s and were considered good on both islands. A modern telephone system consisting of more than 2,400 telephones provided excellent international service by means of radio-relay links to both Antigua and St.

Martin. St. Kitts had two AM stations: the government-owned Radio ZIZ on 555 kilohertz and the religious Radio Paradise with a powerful transmitter on 825 kilohertz. Channel 5, near Basseterre, was the principal television transmitter, and programs were rebroadcast through repeaters from the northern tip of St. Kitts on Channel 9 and Nevis on Channel 13.

Other major projects in the early 1980s included construction of new schools, diversification of agriculture, and development of a manufacturing industry. Total allocation for these areas was about 39 percent of the budget; the remaining 61 percent was split among small projects in all three major areas.

After 1984, with the completion of large portions of the supporting infrastructure, public sector investment was focused more intently on the productive sectors of the economy. Tourism received approximately 32 percent of total funds allocated through 1987; agriculture and industry followed with 12 percent and 14 percent, respectively. Economic and social infrastructure each received about 21 percent of total funding, with emphasis placed on developing new energy sources and upgrading educational facilities.

Sectoral Performance

In the late 1980s, the economic aspirations of St. Kitts and Nevis were only partially realized; a completely diversified economy had not yet been developed, and economic productivity was still highly dependent on the unreliable sugar industry. Although the number of economic sectors in 1984 seemed to indicate a growing economic base, most of the foreign and domestic earnings were still coming from sugar and related products. Key economic sectors of the economy included government services (18.3 percent of GDP), agriculture (16.6 percent), manufacturing (12.8 percent), transportation and communications (12.5 percent), wholesale and retail trade (10.9 percent), and construction (7.9 percent). Other sectors that contributed to the remaining 21 percent of GDP included banking, real estate, utilities, and other service activities.

St. Kitts and Nevis' primary productive sectors were agriculture, manufacturing, and tourism; sugar represented significant portions of both agricultural and manufacturing output. In 1984 sugar took up 90 percent of the land under cultivation, supported 30 percent of the active labor force, constituted 15 percent of GDP, and made up half of total commodity exports. Processed sugar, molasses, and other sugar derivatives also constituted much of the manufacturing output.

The national economy's dependence on sugar has been the primary impediment to further economic development because of

Dock facilities, Basseterre
Courtesy St. Christopher Tourist Bureau

the commodity's steady decline in profitability since the 1960s. On St. Kitts, sugar production began falling in 1965 and was abandoned altogether on Nevis because of rising production costs and declining prices. Long-standing quotas with Britain and the United States sustained minimal profitability a while longer, but by the mid-1970s the sugar industry could no longer operate profitably, and its operations were assumed by the government.

The government attempted to revive the sugar industry by reorganizing its functions under the National Agricultural Corporation and the St. Kitts Sugar Manufacturing Corporation, which coordinated production and marketing, respectively. These two organizations were merged in 1986 to streamline operations further; the unpredictable availability and high cost of labor, however, combined with persistently low sugar prices, required that a more efficient harvesting and processing system be developed for the industry to turn a profit. Uncontrollable factors, such as weather, would occasionally aggravate already untenable conditions.

Although the sugar industry required substantial subsidization in the 1980s, the government was unable to drop it altogether because of its pervasive influence on the national economy. Because a long-term transition was considered the only alternative, the government developed a two-pronged strategy for replacing sugar as the leading revenue producer. First, the agricultural sector was

473

to be diversified so that St. Kitts and Nevis could enter promising regional markets, such as that for cut flowers. Import substitution was also emphasized, especially the production of fruits and vegetables that were previously purchased abroad. Second, the economy was to be redirected toward tourism and manufacturing in order to take advantage of foreign exchange earning industries that were succeeding in other Caribbean economies, such as vacation resorts and electronic component assembly.

Lack of available land was a major constraint on the diversification of the agricultural sector. The government's appropriation of the sugar industry included confiscation of growers' land, much of which was to be set aside for production of alternative crops. As of 1987, however, no formal settlement had been reached, and the government had not yet obtained clear title to the property. Until land titling and redistribution problems could be solved, crop diversification was expected to remain an elusive goal.

Manufacturing played an increasingly important role in the Kittitian economy in the 1980s. An aggressive government program focusing on labor-intensive export manufactures attracted foreign firms, allowing the sector's output to reach about 13 percent of GDP in both 1984 and 1985. In the late 1980s, the government continued its energetic effort to attract foreign investment, in the hope that it would help pave the way for economic growth and absorb some of the workers laid off from the retrenching sugar industry.

Besides refined sugar products, industry included numerous kinds of firms specializing in assembly work. Garment, shoe, and electronic component assembly firms were the largest employers; smaller concerns produced processed metal, handicrafts, furniture, pottery, and boats. Although the sector as a whole was stable in the 1980s, individual industries and firms experienced variable success, some being forced to shut down shortly after production began. Nonsugar manufacturing actually experienced no growth in 1986, in spite of new factory start-ups. This was a continuing problem caused by external factors such as regional trade restrictions that often disrupted St. Kitts' export markets, especially for textiles and electronic components.

Faster growth in the industrial sector was also frustrated by internal restrictions in the 1980s. A lack of stable financing and factory space inhibited investors' interest. Government marketing strategies and the creation of the Industrial Development Corporation were expected to address these problems, as was financial assistance from the CDB.

474

Tourism grew by two-thirds from 1980 to 1984 and positively affected numerous areas of the economy, including construction, hotels, restaurants, and the wholesale and retail trade, among other services. Tourism's success was attributed to government programs that facilitated infrastructure development, hotel construction, and marketing strategies. Continuing efforts in these areas were a government priority, and tourism was expected to be the main component in the country's future economic growth.

Growth of the tourist sector was linked directly to improved accessibility. The opening of Golden Rock International Airport brought direct flights from Canada and the United States, and a large increase in the number of cruise ship calls accompanied the completion of Basseterre's deep-water port. Total ship calls jumped from six in 1979 to fifty in 1984. Although cruise ship calls declined in 1985 and 1986 because of the loss of a major carrier, the long-term expectation was for continued growth in this area of the tourist trade.

Tourist facilities were added quickly in the late 1980s to augment the small-scale accommodations that existed previously. Major resorts, such as the Royal St. Kitts Hotel and the Frigate Bay Resort, offered modern conveniences, and development of the southern peninsula would open previously uninhabited beach areas. Nevis was also planning the expansion of tourism, including the construction of new hotels and an eighteen-hole golf course.

Foreign Trade and Balance of Payments

St. Kitts and Nevis' trading patterns were well established by the 1980s, but this did not guarantee the stability of trade or the balance of payments. Although relationships with major trading partners such as the United States, Britain, and Caricom had existed for a long time, St. Kitts and Nevis' export earnings were hard to predict because of the volatility of demand for its tourist services, agricultural (sugar) products, and manufactured goods.

Raw and processed sugar products continued to lead export earnings in the 1980s, but to a lesser degree than before because of steady growth in the manufacturing and tourist sectors. Export earnings from sugar had accounted for 77 percent of the total in 1978, but they fell to 60 percent in the mid-1980s as clothing, shoes, and electronic components sold abroad in greater quantities. In spite of improved earnings from nonagricultural trade, the trade deficit continued into the 1980s. Only the growing tourist sector kept the current account deficit from being even worse.

St. Kitts and Nevis imported goods at a constant rate through the 1980s, the most significant of which were manufactured products, food, and machinery. They accounted for about 21 percent, 20 percent, and 19 percent, respectively, of total imported goods in the mid-1980s. Fuel and chemicals combined for a total of 20 percent of imports; the remaining 20 percent comprised numerous miscellaneous items. Over 55 percent of imports originated in Britain, the United States, and Puerto Rico. Trinidad and Tobago, Canada, and other countries accounted for approximately 12 percent, 6 percent, and 27 percent of imports, respectively.

Because St. Kitts and Nevis was forced to import basic necessities such as food and many manufactured products, the danger of a large current account deficit was ever present. Should sugar, light manufacturing, and tourism all perform poorly at the same time, a large deficit in the current account would be unavoidable. As of 1987, this situation had not occurred only because the tourist market had been very buoyant. Sugar output fell in the mid-1980s, while production of manufactured goods, such as garments and footwear, fluctuated with the trade restrictions characteristic of the Caricom market. This fluctuation often compounded the trade deficit.

Despite these uncertainties and the large deficit in the trade balance, St. Kitts and Nevis ran a relatively small current account deficit for 1985 of US$6.8 million. Three items helped minimize the negative trade balance: a strong positive services account composed almost entirely of tourist revenues, unrequited private remittances, and official government transfers.

The overall balance of payments for 1985 was a surplus of US$1.7 million. A capital account surplus of US$8.5 million, composed predominantly of private sector investment in tourism and communications but also bolstered by public sector loans, more than offset the current account deficit. Growing public sector loan commitments caused the World Bank to express concern over the potential for a long-term external debt obligation. But the World Bank suggested that continued growth of the tourism sector would do much to minimize St. Kitts and Nevis' debt service burden; there would be even less probability of a serious problem should sugar and manufacturing markets stabilize in the future.

Government and Politics

The Governmental System

St. Kitts and Nevis is a federal state that adheres to the forms of the British Westminster-style parliamentary system of government. The uniqueness of its 1983 Constitution derives from the

Light manufacturing, Basseterre
Courtesy St. Christopher Tourist Bureau

provisions for the autonomy of the island of Nevis with regard to certain "specified matters" and the establishment of the separate Nevis Island Assembly (legislature) to address these local concerns.

As a constitutional monarchy within the Commonwealth of Nations (see Appendix B), St. Kitts and Nevis recognizes Queen Elizabeth II or her successor as the titular head of government. The British monarch is represented by a governor general, who resides in Basseterre. Although legally responsible for the government of both islands, the governor general appoints a deputy to represent him or her on Nevis. As the highest executive authority on the islands, the governor general appoints the prime minister, the deputy prime minister, other ministers of the government, the leader of the opposition in Parliament, and members of the Public Service Commission and Police Service Commission. He may prorogue or dissolve Parliament at any time. In the judicial sphere, he has the power of pardon, "respite" (stay of execution of sentence), and remittance of all or part of the sentence of convicted criminals. As in most Commonwealth countries, however, the apparently sweeping nature of the governor general's powers is restricted by the requirement that the governor general act only in accordance with the advice of the prime minister. In St. Kitts and Nevis, the governor general is permitted to act without consultation only when the prime minister cannot be contacted because of absence or illness.

The federal government of St. Kitts and Nevis is directed by a unicameral parliament known as the National Assembly, established by the 1983 Constitution to replace the House of Assembly. After the 1984 elections, the assembly was composed of eleven elected members, or representatives, and three appointed members, or senators. Two of the senators are appointed by the governor general on the advice of the prime minister. The other is named on the advice of the leader of the opposition. Both representatives and senators serve five-year terms.

The focus of effective power in the federal government is the Cabinet of Ministers, which consists of the prime minister and other ministers drawn from the membership of the assembly (either representatives or senators). The cabinet determines the business and policies of government. According to the Constitution, the cabinet is "collectively responsible to the National Assembly," but because its members are drawn from that body, there is little likelihood of serious disagreement between the two.

Electoral districts, or constituencies, are delimited by the Constituencies Boundaries Commission. A minimum of eight constituencies on St. Kitts and three on Nevis is mandated by the Constitution. Boundaries are not established solely on the basis of population; the commission is charged to consider other factors, such as population density, fair representation for rural areas, communications differences, geographical features, and existing administrative boundaries.

The island of Nevis elects representatives both to the National Assembly and to its own Nevis Island Assembly, a separate eight-member body (five elected, three appointed) charged with regulating local affairs. The Nevis Island Assembly is subordinate to the National Assembly only with regard to external affairs and defense and in cases where similar but not identical legislation is passed by both bodies. The guidelines for legislative autonomy in Nevis are contained in the "specified matters"—areas of local administration for which the Nevisian legislature may amend or revoke provisions passed by the National Assembly. There are twenty-three specified matters, including agricultural regulations, the borrowing of monies or procurement of grants for use on Nevis, water conservation and supply, Nevisian economic planning and development, housing, utilities, and roads and highways. These restrictions on Kittitian control over internal Nevisian concerns appear to have been one of the major concessions (along with a local legislature and the right of secession) made by the PAM to the NRP in order to maintain the two-island union after independence.

Nevisian secession from the federation requires a two-thirds vote in the Nevis Island Assembly and the approval of two-thirds of the voters in a referendum. St. Kitts has no corresponding right of secession, a reminder of the separatist roots of the NRP and the desire of the smaller island to protect itself from possible exploitation by its larger neighbor.

The government of Nevis closely parallels the structure of the federal government and has a premier analogous to the prime minister, an assembly incorporating both elected and appointed members, and a body functioning as a local cabinet, the Nevis Island Administration, which includes the premier plus two or more members of the Nevis Island Assembly. Disputes between the Nevis Island Administration and the federal government must be decided by the High Court.

The High Court, which sits in Basseterre, is the final court of appeal on the islands. Appeals beyond the High Court are heard by the Court of Appeal of the Eastern Caribbean States Supreme Court. Appeals beyond that level may be taken to the Judicial Committee of the Privy Council in London, but only if they conform to certain prescribed conditions, for example, if they are issues that require constitutional interpretation or are decisions of "great general or public importance." Local magistrate's courts provide summary jurisdiction.

Political Dynamics

Politics in St. Kitts and Nevis in the 1980s was marked by a vituperative relationship between the PAM and its opposition, the Labour Party. This state of affairs derived from a history of bitter contention between the two St. Kitts-based parties and from Labour's apparent inability to adjust to the role of opposition after more than thirty years in power.

The PAM arose as an expression of middle-class opposition to the political dominance of the Labour Party. According to most observers, the reaction of the Labour government to this challenge was not a positive one. The PAM's relatively strong showing in 1966, the first year it participated in elections, apparently alerted the Labourites to the potential strength of the opposition movement. The government's initial reaction to this threat was to declare a state of emergency in June 1967, under which twenty-two PAM members were arrested. Efforts to prosecute the detainees were abandoned by the government after the first two defendants were acquitted. Both the founder of the PAM, William Herbert, and party leader Simmonds, among others, gave accounts of harass-ment, imprisonment, mistreatment, and confiscation of property at the hands of the Labour government.

For its part, the PAM also showed that it could play political hardball after it came to power in coalition with the NRP in 1980. In 1981 the government ended the practice of ''check-off'' deduc-tion of dues from the paychecks of members of the St. Kitts and Nevis Trades and Labour Union (SKNTLU), considerably com-plicating efforts by the Labour Party's union arm to raise revenues. PAM-associated unions also challenged the SKNTLU for mem-bership, particularly among dock workers. In a move that was even-tually blocked in the courts, the government attempted to shut down the headquarters of the SKNTLU (the so-called Masses House) by foreclosure through the National Bank. Ironically, this action replicated a similar effort by the Labour government in 1969, when the PAM's headquarters was purchased by the government and members were turned away by armed Defence Force personnel. Some observers felt that the PAM/NRP government took matters a step too far when it arrested Labour leader Moore in April 1987 for ''utter[ing] seditious words.'' Moore was quickly released on bond to the acclaim of a group of supporters.

After its 1980 defeat, the Labour Party appeared to apply more of its energies to criticism of the policies and actions of the PAM/NRP government than to the formulation of a coherent alternative platform. The party's 1984 manifesto called for wage increases, a 50-percent reduction in electricity rates, greater job security for workers, and the establishment of a separate govern-ment for St. Kitts comparable to that enjoyed by Nevis. This last issue echoed Labour's 1983 campaign against the independence Constitution drawn up by the PAM/NRP, a campaign that proved unsuccessful, as judged by the results of the 1984 elections. Labour leaders also leveled charges of widespread corruption among govern-ment ministers, a fairly common theme in West Indian politics. Nonetheless, these negative tactics were not coupled with any productive efforts to expand support among the sectors of the elec-torate where the Labour Party had proved weakest, namely, youth and voters on Nevis. A continued decline in SKNTLU member-ship also hampered the party's organizational efforts.

The acrimonious relations between the PAM and the Labour Party since 1980 can perhaps be best illustrated by a brief catalog-ing of the allegations each has hurled against the other through their respective party organs. Labour has charged the PAM with favoring the wealthy over the workers; with responsibility for in-creases in mental illness, drug abuse, and drug trafficking; with "undermin[ing] black self-image"; with association with international criminals; and with plans for a mass murder of Kittitians in the style of the 1978 Jonestown, Guyana, massacre. For its part, the PAM has accused the Labourites of burning sugarcane fields; of physically assaulting PAM candidates and threatening others, including the prime minister; and of employing "communist tactics" in an effort to destabilize the country and establish a one-party state.

Despite the results of the 1984 elections, the Labour Party remained a political force on St. Kitts, although in the opinion of most observers its prospects for a return to power in the 1989 election were not promising. A reassumption of power by Labour under its platform of the mid-1980s would pose a serious dilemma for the two-island federation, as it would almost certainly precipitate the secession of Nevis.

The party that would lead such a movement, the NRP, continued to dominate political life on Nevis in the late 1980s. Organized as a secessionist movement, the NRP had a poorly defined political ideology. As a coalition partner with the PAM since 1980, however, it supported the moderate policies of Simmonds and his advisers. After the 1984 elections, the NRP technically no longer held the balance of power in the National Assembly, since the PAM took six of the eleven seats contested. There were no public indications of tension between the two parties, however, and the coalition appeared secure as it looked toward another electoral test in 1989.

Foreign Relations

The Simmonds government was one of several moderate-conservative governments to come to power (or, as in the case of the Antigua Labour Party of Vere Cornwall Bird, Sr., to be reconfirmed in power) in the Eastern Caribbean around 1980. Other examples could be found in Dominica and St. Vincent and the Grenadines. These new, generally pro-United States leaders found themselves and their thinking compatible with that of then-Prime Minister J.M.G.M. "Tom" Adams of Barbados, particularly on issues of regional security. Their number eventually came to include the Grenadian government of Herbert Blaize after the postintervention elections of 1984 (see A Regional Security System, ch. 7).

The Simmonds government supported the October 1983 United States-Caribbean intervention in Grenada and dispatched a handful of police personnel to participate in the Caribbean Peace Force on the island. The intervention was generally popular among the population of St. Kitts and Nevis; some observers have suggested that

Simmonds called early elections in 1984 in order to take advantage of this support.

St. Kitts and Nevis has been an active participant in Caricom, the OECS, and the Regional Security System (RSS). The ninth meeting of the Authority of Heads of Government of the OECS (the organization's policy-making body) was held in May 1986 in St. Kitts; as rotating chairman, Simmonds headed both that meeting and the next one in Antigua in November of that year. Within the forum of Caricom, Simmonds has advocated increased cooperation to curtail drug trafficking and use within the region. Along with Dominica's Mary Eugenia Charles and Grenada's Blaize, Simmonds has raised objections to charges by leaders such as the late Errol Barrow of Barbados that the United States has attempted to militarize the Caribbean through the pretext of increased security aid and cooperation.

The Simmonds government's relations with the United States were generally smooth and productive. One exception to this concerned the United States sugar quota policy. From 16,500 tons in 1984, the quota allotted to St. Kitts and Nevis under the system of preferential purchases for foreign producers was reduced to 7,500 tons by 1987, and there was little prospect for any increase in the near future. The cut had a severe impact on the island nation's foreign exchange position because of its continuing inability to diversify its economy away from sugar production. The United States government provided some direct food aid in the form of wheat flour to St. Kitts and Nevis in an effort to ease the effect of the quota cut on the domestic economy.

Most United States economic assistance to St. Kitts and Nevis was channeled through AID and was generally intended to promote economic diversification, primarily through infrastructure-related projects. The major AID-funded project in the mid-1980s was the South East Peninsula Road, which was scheduled to progress beyond the surveying stage in late 1987. The Simmonds government hoped that this new roadway would open up the peninsula, the area of St. Kitts with the longest expanse of accessible beaches.

One rationale for the movement to full independence in 1983 was the prospect of foreign aid from sources other than Britain and the Commonwealth. Since 1983 the PAM/NRP government has pursued these new sources avidly. On a bilateral basis, aid programs were instituted with Taiwan and the Republic of Korea (South Korea). The establishment of relations with Japan and West Germany also held promise in terms of future bilateral aid. Among multilateral sources, St. Kitts and Nevis benefited from assistance from the OAS, the United Nations Children's Fund, and the European Economic Community. It also continued to participate in aid and assistance programs through the Commonwealth. The leading bilateral aid sources among the Commonwealth countries were Britain and Canada. Given the country's comparatively small area, population, and GDP, even limited foreign aid programs had the potential for significant impact, particularly in such areas as education, health, soil and forest conservation, water supply and sewerage, and job training.

As a newly independent country, St. Kitts and Nevis also qualified for loan funds from such multilateral financial institutions as the World Bank and the International Monetary Fund (IMF—see Glossary). In this regard, Simmonds was a leader in the effort by Eastern Caribbean leaders to prevent the World Bank from declaring their countries ineligible for concessionary development loans through the International Development Association (IDA) because of their high per capita incomes relative to less developed states in Africa and Latin America. The success of this effort was still in doubt in the late 1980s, as World Bank management reconfirmed in 1987 that it still intended to phase Eastern Caribbean states out of the IDA program.

National Security

The focus of security concerns on the islands has changed over the years. During the Labour administration, which ended in 1980, the possible secession of Nevis and Anguilla was considered the primary threat to security. British paratroopers had to be dispatched to Anguilla in 1969 to keep order during a period of secessionist unrest; nevertheless, Anguilla did secede that year (see British Dependencies: British Virgin Islands, Anguilla, and Montserrat, this ch.). Kittitian forces were more successful at discouraging such activity on Nevis because of its geographical proximity. According to some members of the PAM, personnel of the regular Defence Force and police were routinely employed by the Labour government to intimidate political opponents on Nevis.

After the advent of the PAM/NRP government and the movement toward independence as a two-island federation, secession became regarded as less of a threat to security. Accordingly, the regular Defence Force maintained by the Labour government was abolished in 1981. The Volunteer Defence Force was retained, but it did not appear to be active because of the lack of any serious external threat to the islands. Some former Defence Force personnel were absorbed into the Royal St. Christopher and Nevis Police Force (RSCNPF); Defence Force weaponry and other equipment were transferred to the RSCNPF. Weaponry unsuited to day-to-day police work, such as semiautomatic small arms, was adopted for use mainly by the RSCNPF's Tactical Unit and, later, the Special Service Unit (SSU).

In the late 1980s, the RSCNPF appeared to number about 300, including the 80-member SSU. The RSCNPF was headed by the commissioner of police, whose subordinates included a deputy commissioner and a superintendent of police. The appointment, discipline, and removal of police officers were regulated by the Police Service Commission, a five-member board appointed by the governor general on the advice of the prime minister. Initial recruit training was conducted at the Police Training Complex at Pond's Pasture, Basseterre. The mission of the RSCNPF was varied and included immigration and firefighting duties in addition to standard police work. The coast guard, administered by the harbor police, was organizationally integrated into the RSCNPF. The sole coast guard vessel was donated by the United States in October 1985. In addition, coast guard personnel received some training in the United States. SSU personnel received on-island instruction from a United States Army military training team. The United States was also reported to have supplied small arms, ammunition, and trucks to the SSU. Other sources of equipment donations to the RSCNPF were Britain, which provided radio equipment, and South Korea, which donated automobiles and pickup trucks.

St. Kitts and Nevis was not an original signatory to the 1982 Memorandum of Understanding that laid the groundwork for the RSS. Nonetheless, membership in the system was extended to St. Kitts and Nevis in early 1984 after it achieved full independence. As an RSS member, St. Kitts and Nevis—or, more specifically, its SSU—has participated in a number of regional military exercises with Caribbean, British, and United States forces. The Simmonds government has been a strong supporter of the RSS, particularly since the Grenada intervention (although technically that was not an RSS operation). Although the opposition Labour Party has not criticized the RSS publicly or advocated withdrawal from the system, it has tried to portray Simmonds's support as an effort to shore up his rule through the threat of military action against his opponents. The PAM has responded to these allegations by comparing Labour leader Moore and his followers to that faction of the Grenadian People's Revolutionary Government that murdered Maurice Bishop and several of his ministers on October 19, 1983, and plunged Grenada into chaos.

From the government's perspective, the most likely source of social and political unrest appeared to be agitation by the Labour

Party. PAM leaders and publications have quoted Moore as threatening the prime minister and calling for the extralegal assumption of power by his own followers. Even if true, however, these statements would appear to have been more in the nature of rhetorical excesses than genuine calls to revolution. There was no indication in the late 1980s of significant popular support in St. Kitts and Nevis for politically motivated violence against the PAM/NRP government.

Generally speaking, the society of St. Kitts and Nevis was quite open and free in terms of political and civil rights. According to the ratings assigned various countries in an article by Raymond A. Gastil in the periodical *Freedom at Issue,* published by the research and monitoring group Freedom House in New York, St. Kitts and Nevis in 1985 and 1986 was a free society with a fully competitive electoral process, freedom of the press, an impartial judiciary, and a general lack of politically motivated repression. Representatives of the PAM/NRP government have cited these ratings frequently as a riposte to charges of abuse of power leveled by the opposition.

* * *

Although there are few comprehensive sources on St. Kitts and Nevis, background information on its social development may be found in Bonham C. Richardson's *Caribbean Migrants* and Edward L. Cox's *Free Coloreds in the Slave Societies of St. Kitts and Grenada, 1763–1833.* Health, education, and population data are available in the Pan American Health Organization's *Health Conditions in the Americas 1981–1984.* Major works dealing with economic background and development include Carleen O'Loughlin's *Economic and Political Change in the Leeward and Windward Islands,* Peter D. Fraser and Paul Hackett's *Caribbean Economic Handbook,* and the World Bank's *St. Christopher and Nevis Economic Report.* Current economic data are presented in annual reports prepared by the CDB and the ECCB. Political studies on St. Kitts and Nevis are equally scarce, perhaps as a result of the nation's brief history as an independent state. The *St. Christopher and Nevis Independence Magazine, 19th September 1983* and *1986 Year in Review,* official publications, present good snapshots of the country. Current political issues and concerns on the islands are reflected in the newspapers published by the PAM (*Democrat*) and the opposition Labour Party (*Labour Spokesman*), as well as in reporting by the Caribbean News Agency and periodicals with a regional focus, such as *Latin America Regional Reports: Caribbean.* (For further information and complete citations, see Bibliography.)

British Virgin Islands

Official Name .... British Virgin Islands

Term for Citizens .... British Virgin Islander(s)

Capital .... Road Town

Political Status .... British crown colony

Form of Government .... British-appointed governor
and locally elected assembly

Geography
Size .... 153 sq. km.
Topography .... Hilly or mountainous terrain on three
of four island groups; other is a flat coral island
Climate .... Tropical, moderately wet

Population
Total estimated in 1986 12,000
Annual growth rate (in percentage) in 1982–85 .... 1.6
Life expectancy at birth in 1982 .... 70.2
Adult literacy rate (in percentage) in 1984 .... 98.3
Language .... English
Ethnic groups .... Primarily black
Religion ... Methodist (42 percent), Anglican (25 percent);
remainder other Christian denominations

Economy
Currency .... United States dollar (US$)
Gross domestic product (GDP) in 1985 ... US$84.5 million
Per capita GDP in 1985 .... US$7,260
Distribution of GDP (in percentage) in 1985
Tourism .... Approximately 50
Government and other services ...... Approximately 50

National Security
Armed forces personnel 0
Paramilitary Personnel 0
Police 100

Anguilla

Official Name .... Anguilla

Term for Citizens .... Anguillian(s)

Capital .... The Valley

Political Status .... British associated state

Form of Government .... British-appointed governor
and locally elected assembly

Geography
Size .... 91 sq. km.
Topography .... Flat coral islands
Climate .... Tropical, dry

Population
Total estimated in 1987 6,800
Annual growth rate (in percentage) in 1982–85 .... 0.7
Life expectancy at birth in 1982 .... 70.2
Adult literacy rate (in percentage) in 1984 .... 90.4
Language .... English
Ethnic groups .... Primarily black; some white
Religion ... Methodist (43 percent), Anglican (43 percent);
remainder other Christian denominations

Economy
Currency; exchange rate .... Eastern Caribbean dollar
(EC$); EC$2.70 = US$1.00
Gross domestic product (GDP) in 1983 ..... US$6 million
Per capita GDP in 1983 .... US$6,000
Distribution of GDP in 1983 .... Primarily services
and tourism

National Security
Armed forces personnel 0
Paramilitary personnel 0
Police 80

Montserrat

Official Name .... Montserrat

Term for Citizens .... Montserratian(s)

Capital .... Plymouth

Political Status .... British crown colony

Form of Government .... British-appointed governor
and locally elected assembly

Geography
Size .... 102 sq. km.
Topography .... Mountainous; narrow coastal plain
Climate .... Tropical, wet

Population
Total estimated in 1986 12,000
Annual growth rate (in percentage) in 1982–85 .... 0.6
Life expectancy at birth in 1982 .... 70.2
Adult literacy rate (in percentage) in 1981 77
Language .... English
Ethnic groups .... Primarily black; some white
Religion ... Anglican (33 percent), Methodist (25 percent);
remainder other Christian denominations

Economy
Currency; exchange rate .... Eastern Caribbean dollar
(EC$); EC$2.70 = US$1.00
Gross domestic product (GDP) in 1985 ... US$37.1 million
Per capita GDP in 1985 .... US$3,130
Distribution of GDP (in percentage) in 1985
Services 79
Manufacturing and industry 15
Agriculture 6

National Security
Armed forces personnel 0
Paramilitary personnel 0
Police 80–90

491

British Dependencies:
British Virgin Islands, Anguilla, and Montserrat

The Leeward Islands British dependencies lie east of Puerto Rico in the region where the Greater Antilles and Lesser Antilles meet. The British Virgin Islands, immediately east of their United States counterparts, consist of more than forty islands, rocks, and islets, the most important of which are Tortola (containing the capital of Road Town), Virgin Gorda, and Anegada (see fig. 16). Anguilla (pronounced "an-GWIL-a") lies some 120 kilometers east of the British Virgin Islands (see fig. 17). It is small, but its territory includes several even smaller islands. Montserrat, also a small island, lies 180 kilometers southeast of Anguilla, not far from Antigua.

Christopher Columbus discovered the Virgin Islands and Montserrat on his second voyage to the West Indies in 1493. He named the former "Las Virgines" in honor of St. Ursula, an Englishwoman who is alleged to have traveled to Germany with virgin attendants and to have been martyred there. Columbus named Montserrat after the mountain in Spain on which Ignatius Loyola established of the Society of Jesus (the Jesuits).

Whether or not Columbus also sighted Anguilla during this 1493 voyage remains uncertain. Historian Thomas Southey made the first known mention of the island in 1564, after a French expedition passed it on a voyage from Dominica to Florida. The island apparently received its present name from its long, narrow shape and serpentine shoreline. Anguilla means eel in Spanish.

In the early years of European settlement, buccaneers and pirates roamed what are now the British Virgin Islands, providing what later would be the inspiration for Robert Louis Stevenson's *Treasure Island*. These buccaneers owed allegiance to no one in particular, although a Dutch group apparently held the island of Tortola when a band of English adventurers took over in 1662. The islands were annexed by England in 1672. In 1680 a few planters moved with their families from Anguilla to Virgin Gorda, starting a steady stream of settlers. By 1717 the white population of that island totaled 317, with an additional 159 on Tortola. The early 1700s also saw the establishment of a Quaker colony, which, for a while, tried to create a separate island government under the auspices of the British crown. During the eighteenth century, extensive cultivation—mainly by slave labor imported from Africa—led to the formation of sugar, indigo, and sea island cotton plantations (see The Sugar Revolutions and Slavery, ch. 1). In 1773, upon their second petition to the crown, the planters were granted

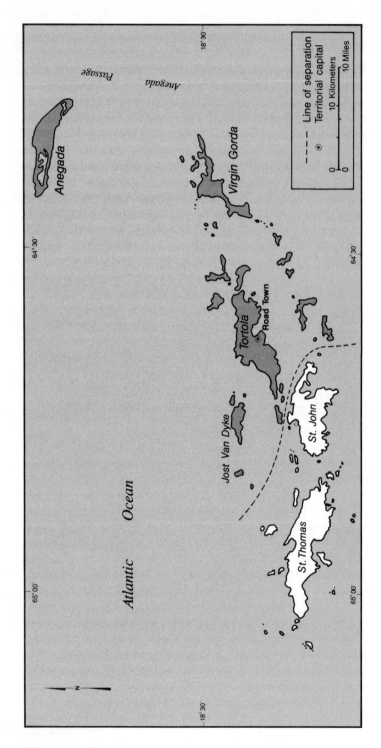

Figure 16. British Virgin Islands, 1987

civil government and constitutional courts with a completely elected twelve-member House of Assembly and a partly elected and partly appointed Legislative Council, or "Board," which met for the first time on February 1, 1774.

Anguilla was colonized by English settlers in 1650 and has remained a British colony ever since. There were, however, several raids. Carib Indians from Dominica attacked in 1656, and Irish raiders landed in 1698. A few of the Irishmen settled on the island and left descendants with Irish names. The French attacked unsuccessfully in 1745 and again in 1796.

The English first colonized Montserrat in 1632. The island fell into French hands in 1662 for a four-year period and again in 1792–93. It has remained British ever since, however. The early settlers tried to make Montserrat a prosperous plantation island. They brought African slaves to the island to cultivate sugar, limes, and vegetables, but the terrain was simply too rugged to yield these crops in great quantities. The island never became the agricultural success that the settlers envisioned.

After the British established firm control over their territories in the Leeward Islands, they combined and recombined them into various colonies and federations. In 1816, for example, St. Christopher (hereafter, St. Kitts), Nevis, and the British Virgin Islands were made into one colony with its own captain general and governor. In 1871 St. Kitts and Anguilla were made a single unit in the new Leeward Islands Federation. Soon after, Anguilla, St. Kitts, and Nevis were united into one unit of the federation and called the Presidency of St. Christopher and Nevis. The British Virgin Islands and Montserrat also were separate presidencies within the federation.

During the 1950s and 1960s, political arrangements changed rapidly. In 1956 the British government dissolved the Leeward Islands Federation, and each presidency became a separate colony. In 1958 the British established the new West Indies Federation, with St. Kitts, Nevis, and Anguilla as one unit and Montserrat another. The British Virgin Islands did not join the federation and became an individual crown colony (see Glossary), with a British "administrator" (later governor) who reported directly to the British government. When the British dissolved the West Indies Federation in 1962, Montserrat also became an individual British crown colony. Both the British Virgin Islands and Montserrat have since remained crown colonies. Under this arrangement, the British government has control not only over the islands' defense and external relations but also over the internal police force and administrative and budget matters.

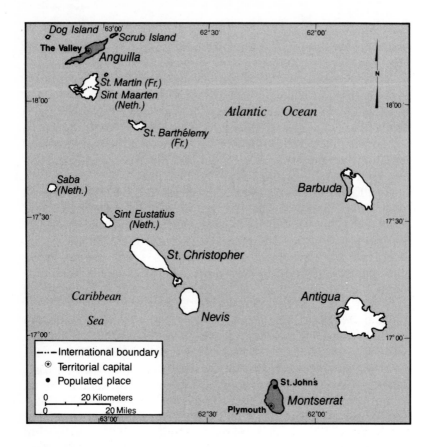

Figure 17. Anguilla and Montserrat, 1987

Anguilla's situation was even more complicated. When the West Indies Federation dissolved in 1961 and various attempts at a new federation failed, Britain formed the Windward and Leeward Islands Associated States. Under British law, associated states (see Glossary) have full internal self-government, while Britain retains control of defense and external affairs. This meant full internal self-government for the new association, including the unit of St. Kitts-Nevis-Anguilla. When St. Kitts and Nevis became an individual associated state in 1967, a further step toward self-rule, Anguillians attempted to dissociate themselves from that entity. Under the leadership of Ronald Webster, a local businessman and leader of Anguilla's only political party, the People's Progressive Party (PPP), Anguillians strongly objected to internal rule by St. Kitts. On May 30, 1967, the Anguillians evicted the St. Kitts police force and began to run their own affairs through a local council. Six weeks

496

later, Anguilla held a referendum in which all but 5 of over 1,800 voters rejected continued ties with St. Kitts and Nevis. This overwhelming sentiment may have influenced the initial low-key British response aimed at negotiating a compromise. In 1969, however, Webster led a bid to secede from the St. Kitts-Nevis-Anguilla union; the Anguillians made a "unilateral declaration of independence" under the "rebel" British flag.

Economic concerns were at the root of the 1969 secession. Anguillians claimed their island was the poor cousin of the union and received little from St. Kitts and Nevis. The Anguillians believed that colonial status meant a legal obligation on Britain's part to help with development aid.

After attempts to repair the breach between St. Kitts and Anguilla failed, St. Kitts requested that Britain land troops on Anguilla. The British did so in March 1969 and installed a British commissioner. Britain reluctantly accepted Anguilla's request for a return to colonial status.

In July 1971, the British Parliament passed the Anguilla Act, which provided that should St. Kitts-Nevis-Anguilla decide to end its associated status, Anguilla could be separated from the other islands. As independence for St. Kitts and Nevis approached, Anguilla formally separated from the state. The island became a British dependent territory in December 1980. In the late 1980s, it was still a separate dependency, an associated state administered under the terms of the British government's Anguilla Constitution Order of 1982. In accordance with this legislation, a new Constitution took effect in Anguilla on April 1, 1982. Britain also contributed considerable financial aid.

Geography

The Virgin Islands are an archipelago of more than 100 islands and cays (see Glossary) located about 95 kilometers east of Puerto Rico. The islands are politically divided into two units: the United States Virgin Islands on the west and the British Virgin Islands on the east. With a total area of 153 square kilometers, the British islands are slightly smaller than Washington, D.C., and fall into four groups: an archipelago of small islands that run southwest-northeast and end with Virgin Gorda on the east; a central group containing Tortola, the largest of the British Virgin Islands; a western group that includes the island of Jost Van Dyke and surrounding smaller cays; and Anegada, forty-eight kilometers northeast of Virgin Gorda.

With the exception of Anegada, all of the islands are hilly or mountainous and are volcanic in origin. Slopes are rugged and rise steeply from the sea. The highest point is Tortola's Mount Sage, at 543 meters. Bare outcroppings are common, and the islands have no permanent streams. Anegada, geologically distinct from the other islands, is a flat coral island composed of limestone. The soil on all the islands is poor, consisting mostly of brown loam of volcanic origin. Anegada has little soil at all.

The British Virgin Islands' climate is tropical with a pronounced rainy season from May through November. The rain falls in short, heavy showers and averages about 125 centimeters per year. Despite the moderate rainfall, porous soils and high evaporation rates allow for only xerophytic types of vegetation, that is, plants that survive in dry, hot climates. Temperatures are fairly constant, ranging from summer maximums of 31°C to winter minimums of 20°C. Trade winds are constant, blowing from the northeast in winter and from the southeast in summer. Hurricanes strike occasionally from June to November.

Anguilla, in the northern Leeward Islands, lies 240 kilometers due east of Puerto Rico and 8 kilometers from St. Martin/Sint Maarten, the nearest of the Leeward Islands to the south. Anguilla is twenty-six kilometers long and six kilometers wide, at ninety-one square kilometers about half the size of Washington, D.C. It is a flat coral island, with its highest point only sixty-five meters above sea level. Scrub Island, five square kilometers in area, lies just off Anguilla's northeast end. Dog Island, smaller than Scrub Island, lies to the northwest, as do several small cays.

Anguilla's climate is tropical, with little seasonal variation. Temperatures range from 22°C to 30°C. Rainfall is low, averaging 100 centimeters annually, with substantial variation from year to year. Hurricanes are a threat in the summer or fall. The scant rainfall and poor soil allow for only low scrub vegetation.

The small, rugged island of Montserrat is forty-three kilometers southwest of Antigua and seventy kilometers northwest of Guadeloupe. Only 11 kilometers by 18 kilometers, the pear-shaped island has an area of 102 square kilometers. Of volcanic origin, Montserrat has active sulfur vents in the mountainous south-central section. The island itself has a narrow coastal plain that rises steeply to several peaks, the highest of which, Chance Peak, reaches 915 meters. Much of central Montserrat is covered by tropical rain forest, probably the reason the island is popularly known as "the Emerald Isle."

Montserrat has a tropical climate with little seasonal variation; temperatures range from 22°C to 31°C. Rainfall is plentiful, ranging from 170 centimeters on the windward northeast slopes to 125 centimeters on the leeward southwest coastal areas. Hurricanes can strike during the summer or fall.

Population

The total population of the British Virgin Islands was estimated in 1986 to be 12,000. Annual population growth averaged 1.6 percent over the 1982–85 period. About 500 expatriates from Western Europe and North America also reportedly resided on the islands. Eighty-five percent of the total population lived on Tortola, 9 percent on Virgin Gorda, and about 3 percent each on the islands of Anegada and Jost Van Dyke. In general, the islands were underpopulated in comparison with most of the West Indies, having a population density of only 78.4 per square kilometer. Despite the relatively uncrowded conditions on the islands, the government applied very strict immigration controls against other Caribbean nationals attracted by the islands' relatively prosperous economy.

The people of the British Virgin Islands are primarily black. Life expectancy at birth among the islanders in 1982 was 70.2 years. In 1982 the birth rate was 20.3, and the infant mortality rate was 45.1 per 1,000 live births. The overall population of the British Virgin Islands was young; 34 percent were under age 15, and only 8.6 percent were over age 60.

Anguilla's population stood at 6,800 as of 1987; in addition, a small number of expatriates from North America and Western Europe lived on the island. Annual population growth averaged 0.7 percent between 1982 and 1985. About 10 percent of the population lived in the capital, The Valley, in the central part of the island. Like the British Virgin Islands, the island of Anguilla had a low population density for the Caribbean—76.9 people per square kilometer.

The people of Anguilla are mainly black, but there are some whites, descended from a party of Irishmen who landed on the island in 1698. Life expectancy at birth on Anguilla in 1982 was the same as on the British Virgin Islands (70.2). The birth rate in 1982 was 25 live births per 1,000 of the population. At the same time, the infant mortality rate was 26.7 per 1,000 live births. Approximately 28 percent of the population was under 15 years of age, and only 13 percent was over 60 years of age.

Montserrat's population in 1986 was estimated at 12,000. The population grew at an average annual rate of 0.6 percent during 1982–85. About 10 percent of the population resided in Plymouth, the capital. Montserrat's population has risen since 1970, following thirty years of emigration resulting from poor economic conditions and prospects on the island. The population density of the island in 1982 stood at 117.6 per square kilometer.

Montserrat's population is 90 percent black and mulatto, with some whites of Irish ancestry. Shortly after the initial English settlement of the island in the first half of the seventeenth century, a large group of Irishmen arrived on Montserrat. Whether they were exiled from Ireland or came voluntarily from other Caribbean islands remains unknown, but their legacy on Montserrat can be seen in a number of red-haired islanders.

Life expectancy at birth among Montserratians in 1982 was 70.2 years. The birth rate in 1982 was 22.3 live births per 1,000. The infant mortality rate on Montserrat in 1983 was 26.4 per 1,000 live births. The age distribution on Montserrat varied slightly from the pattern of the other two island groups; only 30.5 percent of the population was under 15 years of age, while close to 17 percent was over 60.

In all three territories, the predominant religion was Christianity. Approximately 42 percent of the population in the British Virgin Islands was Methodist, and 25 percent, Anglican. The remaining 33 percent of the population included Roman Catholics, Baptists, Seventh-Day Adventists, Jehovah's Witnesses, and members of the Church of God.

Anguillians belonged mostly to Anglican or Methodist congregations; each denomination claimed 43 percent of the population. Baptists, Roman Catholics, Jehovah's Witnesses, Seventh-Day Adventists, and members of Apostolic Faith and Second Bethany Gospel Hall congregations accounted for the remaining 14 percent of the population. Anguillians were highly religious, which accounted for the great opposition to casino gambling proposals in the 1980s.

Like the other two island groups, Montserrat was primarily Anglican and Methodist. Approximately 33 percent of Montserratians were Anglican, and 25 percent were Methodist. The remaining 42 percent of the population belonged to Baptist, Seventh-Day Adventist, Pentecostal, or Roman Catholic congregations.

Education

In the British Virgin Islands, education was free and compulsory to the age of fourteen. In the late 1980s, primary education was provided in twenty-five schools—sixteen government and nine private. Primary-school enrollment in 1983 was 2,093. There were four high schools with a total student population of 1,013; these provided vocational as well as general training. In 1970 only 1.7 percent of the adult population had received no schooling. This high rate of school attendance was reflected in the islanders' high literacy rate, which in 1984 stood at 98.3 percent. Few British Virgin Islanders had postsecondary schooling, however. In 1984 only 5.4 percent of the population over the age of 24 had any postsecondary education.

On both Anguilla and Montserrat, education was free and compulsory between the ages of five and fourteen. Anguilla had a primary-school enrollment of 2,068 students in 1983 and a secondary-school enrollment in 1982 of 473 students. The government operated six primary schools and one secondary school. In 1984 the literacy rate among Anguillians was 90.4 percent. Like the British Virgin Islanders, few Anguillians had a postsecondary education. In 1982 only 2.9 percent of the population over the age of 25 had had any higher education.

Montserrat's primary-school enrollment in 1981 was 1,725 students. Primary education was provided by twelve government schools, two government-aided denominational schools, and two private schools. Montserrat had a secondary school, plus two junior secondary schools for children aged twelve to fifteen who failed to pass the examination for entry into the regular secondary school. In 1981 there were 871 students enrolled in these schools. Montserrat's literacy rate was estimated at 77 percent.

Montserrat had a small technical college. The existence of the junior schools and the technical college reflected the importance the government placed on technical, vocational, and business training. Implementation of this policy, however, was hampered by a shortage of qualified instructors. The percentage of the population with higher education was low, amounting to only 2.7 percent of those over the age of 25.

The College of the Virgin Islands, located in the British Virgin Islands, was the only four-year institution of higher learning in the three territories. The University of the West Indies (UWI) had Extra-Mural Departments with resident tutors in each territory. Students could also opt to attend the UWI at its three campuses, in Mona, Jamaica; Cave Hill, Barbados; and St. Augustine, Trinidad and Tobago. Students also attended universities in Britain, Canada, the continental United States, Puerto Rico, and the United States Virgin Islands.

Health and Welfare

The general health and welfare of all three British dependencies were good and continuing to improve in the late 1980s. Each had adopted the goals of the Pan American Health Organization of good health for all by the year 2000, emphasizing preventive medical services and early maternal and child health care programs.

In the mid-1980s, mortality rates varied among the British dependencies. Montserrat had the highest death rate, 10.4 per 1,000 inhabitants, followed by Anguilla and the British Virgin Islands with 7.1 and 5.1, respectively. Interestingly, the British Virgin Islands had the highest infant mortality rate, 45.1 per 1,000 live births, followed by Anguilla and Montserrat with 26.7 and 26.4, respectively.

Programs of inoculation against diphtheria, pertussis, and tetanus had succeeded in reaching at least 90 percent of the population on all the islands; vaccinations against poliomyelitis and measles reached a minimum of 75 percent of the targeted population. Anguilla and Montserrat reached over 95 percent of their respective populations with the polio vaccine. The incidence of infectious diseases was very low for all three dependencies; none had reported any cases of acquired immune deficiency syndrome as of May 1987.

Although Britain supplied funds for health care budgets, administration and health care delivery were the responsibility of the local governments. Montserrat, the British Virgin Islands, and Anguilla allocated approximately 13 percent, 11 percent, and 10 percent, respectively, of their annual budgets to health care and related services.

Health care in the British Virgin Islands was the responsibility of the minister of social services; administrative and technical supervision rested with the chief medical officer. The national health policy mandated free health services for the entire population and was achieved through an infrastructure that included the fifty-bed Peebles Hospital in Road Town and eight district health centers. In 1984 the islands had a total of six doctors, one dentist, and sixty nurses, midwives, and assistant nurses. In addition, there were three doctors who maintained a private practice and an eight-bed hospital.

Anguilla's health system was administered by the Ministry of Health, which directed all medical facilities on the island. In 1984 there was no specified national health plan, and there was a distinct lack of trained personnel. A twenty-four-bed hospital was the primary medical facility and was supported by four district health centers and a modern dental clinic; there were five physicians on the island.

Montserrat's health services were the responsibility of the Ministry of Education, Health, and Community Services; the permanent secretary in the ministry oversaw administration and was advised on technical matters by the chief medical officer. All community health services were free with the exception of certain

The Leeward Islands

laboratory tests. Montserrat was able to provide health care to all inhabitants by 1984. Major health problems were treated at the Glendon Hospital in Plymouth, which had sixty-seven beds, and community services were provided through a network of twelve district clinics. No village was farther than about three kilometers from a district clinic.

Economy

Like most of the West Indies, the British dependencies traditionally depended on agriculture, some fishing, and a few light industries such as straw and basket work. Tortola, in the British Virgin Islands, was also the site of rum distilleries. Unemployment was high, because much of the work was seasonal. As a result, all three territories have worked hard to build up year-round tourism and attract light industries.

The gross domestic product (GDP—see Glossary) of the British Virgin Islands in 1985 was US$84.5 million, of which tourism accounted for approximately 50 percent and other services and government for approximately 50 percent. Per capita GDP in the British Virgin Islands in 1985 was estimated at US$7,260, a higher figure than that of many neighboring Caribbean states. Most of the work force was employed in the United States Virgin Islands. Tourism (26 percent), government service (20 percent), and construction (18 percent) were the principal employers of the domestic work force in the mid-1980s.

In the late 1980s, tourism was the principal economic activity in the British Virgin Islands, generating about 50 percent of the national income. The number of tourists visiting the islands increased from 70,287 in 1976 to 161,625 in 1984. The major characteristic of the islands' tourist industry was that it was based largely on yachting. Sixty-three percent of the arrivals chartered or lived on yachts. Seventy percent of the visitors came from the continental United States, 11 percent from Canada, 10 percent from Puerto Rico and the United States Virgin Islands, 7 percent from Western Europe, and 2 percent from elsewhere in the Caribbean.

Offshore financial services were also a rapidly growing part of the economy in the late 1980s. A direct result of the enactment in July 1984 of the International Business Companies Act was the incorporation of about 3,000 companies in the British Virgin Islands between July 1984 and December 1986.

Agriculture remained moderately important in the British Virgin Islands but was limited by the islands' poor soil. Farms, generally located on the larger islands, tended to be small, averaging just over seven hectares. In general, the soils of the islands were poor, and food crops were rotated with pasture. Raising cattle for export was the main agricultural industry, but some sheep and goats also were raised. Crops included sugarcane, used locally for the production of rum, and fruits and vegetables, often sold to customers in the United States Virgin Islands.

Overall, 60 percent of the total land area was in private ownership. The remainder was owned by the crown. Of the privately owned land, 75 percent belonged to native British Virgin Islanders, 18 percent to foreigners, chiefly United States citizens, and 7 percent to nonindigenous British subjects. The government used 3 percent of crown lands for its own purposes and rented 31 percent of its land to native islanders and some 7 percent to British subjects and foreigners. Fifty-nine percent of the crown lands were not in use. Nationals of other countries, including Britain, had to obtain a license to buy land.

The coastal waters of the British Virgin Islands abound in various species of fish, which provided one of the largest sources of protein in the islands and the largest export. In 1983 fish exports contributed US$216,000 to the economy. By the late 1980s, traditional sloops had given way to motorized fishing boats. Deep-sea sport fishing also had been developed and was part of the growing tourist industry in the islands.

Exports from the British Virgin Islands were negligible in comparison with imports. In 1985 exports stood at US$2.5 million and imports at US$91.4 million. Fresh fish, rum, gravel and sand, fruits, vegetables, and livestock were the primary exports. The United States Virgin Islands received about 50 percent of the exports. Other Caribbean islands accounted for most of the rest. There was negligible export trade with the United States or Britain. The islands imported building materials, automobiles, machinery, fuel, foodstuffs, manufactured goods, and chemicals, primarily from the United States (about 50 percent), the United States Virgin Islands (13 percent), and the rest of the Caribbean (27 percent). The trade deficit was made up in three ways—by remittances from British Virgin Islanders working overseas, tourist receipts, and foreign investment.

Although Anguilla was less prosperous than the British Virgin Islands, it sustained steady economic growth for the five years ending in 1986. In 1983 GDP was US$6 million and per capita GDP a respectable US$6,000. Services and tourism contributed heavily to GDP; this was reflected in the distribution of the labor force, 46.3 percent of which was in the service sector. Industry accounted for 35.2 percent of all employment, and agriculture accounted for 8.5 percent. Unemployment on Anguilla was 30 percent in 1985.

Anguilla's economic growth in the 1980s was a direct result of its improved standing as a tourist attraction. The total number of visitors rose by 16 percent from 1985 to 1986 and provided revenue for the private sector through tourist-related services and for the public sector through increased duties. In 1986 the Caribbean Development Bank (CDB) outlined new projects that would help Anguilla sustain the growth of tourism. These projects included construction of a modern, forty-four-room hospital and a new airport terminal.

Salt, a traditional export, remained Anguilla's second most important source of foreign revenue in the mid-1980s. Most of the salt was used in oil refinery operations in Trinidad. Salt production had been temporarily suspended in the late 1970s after most of the yield was destroyed by rains.

Workers' remittances from abroad also formed a large part of the island's income; 20,000 people of Anguillian ancestry lived abroad, concentrated in Slough, England, and South Amboy, New Jersey. Because there was no income tax in Anguilla, customs duties, license fees, and revenue from postage stamp sales were important sources of government income.

Domestic agriculture was a high priority on Anguilla, although the island had little arable land. Only 13 percent of Anguilla's total area was cultivable, and only a third of that was truly arable. Crops were grown primarily for domestic use. The British government has invested in irrigation and water projects, including desalination plants. Legumes, sweet potatoes, and sorghum were the main crops, mostly grown in "backyard garden-scale" plots averaging little more than one-quarter of a hectare. When rainfall was good and crop surpluses resulted, the territory exported small amounts of vegetables and fruits to neighboring islands.

Anguillians raised cattle, goats, sheep, and pigs for domestic use and for export. The island also exported lobsters, although overfishing had depleted the once valuable lobster beds. In 1983 Anguilla exported fish and shellfish valued at US$49,000.

Exports from Anguilla in 1981 had a total value of US$5.4 million. Most of Anguilla's exports were to other Caribbean islands; little was destined for either the United States or Britain. Import statistics were not available, but the United States accounted for a large proportion of Anguilla's imports.

The per capita GDP of Montserrat was far lower than that of the other two island groups, standing at only US$3,130 in 1985. GDP was US$37.1 million in 1985, of which 79 percent was generated by services, 15 percent by manufacturing and industry, and 6 percent by agriculture. Tourism alone generated about 25 percent of Montserrat's GDP. Because of tourism's significance, large amounts of the available foreign aid, mostly from Britain, were used on such projects as the improvement of airport and dock facilities.

Like the labor forces of Anguilla and the British Virgin Islands, the Montserratian work force was concentrated primarily in services. Sixty-four percent of the labor force was employed in the service sector, 25.7 percent in industry, and 10 percent in agriculture in 1983. Thirty-five percent of the island's women were active in the labor force in 1982. Unemployment was estimated at 5.3 percent in 1985.

Thirty-five percent of the island's annual income came from remittances by overseas citizens; between 1959 and 1962, one-third of the population left for Britain. Expatriates living on the island contributed 25 percent of GDP. The government has attracted foreign light manufacturing (mainly of plastic bags, textiles, and electronic appliances), which accounted for 90 percent of the total value of exports in 1984. The sea island cotton industry was also important. In addition, more than twenty offshore banks (see Glossary) had been established. These were subject to strict government controls.

Barely 18 percent of Montserrat's total area is suitable for crops and pasture. Soils are poor, and scant rainfall and periodic droughts frequently limit yields. As on Anguilla, the British government invested in irrigation and water projects. Montserrat's farmers grew limes, bananas, vegetables, and some cotton. When rainfall was good and crop surpluses resulted, Montserrat also exported small amounts of vegetables and fruits to neighboring islands. In general, however, agriculture was declining on Montserrat; the island's Ministry of Agriculture estimated that only twenty farmers were consistent producers. Montserrat also raised livestock for domestic use and export. Seafood, mostly fish, also was exported.

Like Anguilla and the British Virgin Islands, Montserrat imported far more than it exported. In 1985 exports were valued at only US$2.8 million, while imports amounted to US$18.3 million. Most of Montserrat's imports came from the United States (33 percent) and the European Economic Community (32 percent). Exports went mainly to other Caribbean islands (59 percent) and to Western Europe (18 percent).

In the mid-1980s, communication and transportation networks in the British Virgin Islands were among the least developed in the Commonwealth Caribbean. The islands had about 3,000 telephones; interisland service was poor, although a submarine cable provided somewhat more reliable international connections. One

AM radio station on 780 kilohertz and a television transmitter using Channel 5 provided limited service on Tortola. The *Island Sun,* published weekly, was the British Virgin Islands' only local newspaper. There were just over 100 kilometers of surfaced roads, but they were generally narrow and in poor condition. Virgin Gorda and Road Town on Tortola had the only two paved airfields. Regularly scheduled flights linked Road Town with San Juan, Puerto Rico, and St. Thomas in the United States Virgin Islands. The port at Road Town could handle large ships. The islands had no railroads or inland waterways.

The communication and transportation systems on Anguilla were small but modern and met the needs of the island's population. The island had 890 fully automatic telephones with international service available. The government-owned Radio Anguilla broadcast on 1505 kilohertz; Caribbean Beacon, a religious organization, had strong transmitters on 690 and 1610 kilohertz and a small FM station on 100.1 megahertz. There were no television transmitters or local newspapers. About sixty kilometers of all-weather roads reached all areas of the island. Regularly scheduled flights from neighboring islands landed at Wallblake Airport on the south coast. Road Bay, on the north-central side of the island, was the principal port. The island had no rail or inland water facilities.

Communications on Montserrat were excellent. A subsidiary of Cable and Wireless, a British telecommunications firm, had just over 3,000 telephones with good islandwide and international service. The number of broadcast facilities, considering the size of the island, was quite high. Radio Montserrat, owned by the government, broadcast on 880 kilohertz. The commercial Radio Antilles had two FM transmitters on 99.9 and 104.0 megahertz, a station on 740 kilohertz that relayed Radio Canada programs in the evening, and a powerful transmitter on 930 kilohertz with programming in English and French that could be heard throughout the Eastern Caribbean (see Glossary). Deutsche Welle, the official shortwave service of West Germany, operated a relay on Montserrat for programming to the Western Hemisphere. The television station on Channel 7 could be received throughout the island as well as on Antigua and St. Kitts. No local newspapers were published.

Development of Montserrat's transportation infrastructure was hindered by the mountainous terrain. A 200-kilometer paved road ran along the west, north, and east coasts; 80 kilometers of gravel roads linked smaller villages. Plymouth was the island's principal port. The only airfield was about ten kilometers from Plymouth; it had regularly scheduled flights to neighboring islands. There were no railroads or navigable inland waterways.

The British Virgin Islands and Anguilla supplied electricity at the United States standard of 120 volts, whereas Montserrat used the European standard of 220 volts. Currencies in the territories varied. Although the British Virgin Islands was part of the British pound sterling system, the only currency in actual use was the United States dollar, a situation related to the territory's proximity to Puerto Rico and the United States Virgin Islands. Both Anguilla and Montserrat used the British-sponsored Eastern Caribbean dollar, although United States dollars circulated freely on Anguilla. The Eastern Caribbean dollar was pegged to the United States dollar at a rate of EC$2.70 to US$1.00 in 1987.

Government and Politics

The Governmental System

In the late 1980s, all three territories remained British dependencies. British officials were responsible for defense and foreign relations, and local elected officials were responsible for most internal affairs except security. As mentioned, the British Virgin Islands and Montserrat were crown colonies, and Anguilla was an associated state. Because of their links to Britain, all three territories were part of the Commonwealth of Nations (see Appendix B).

A new constitution was introduced in the British Virgin Islands in April 1967. An amended Constitution took effect on June 1, 1977, giving local citizens more extensive self-government. Under its terms, the British-appointed governor is responsible for defense and internal security, external affairs, terms and conditions of service of public officers, and administration of the courts. The governor also possesses reserved legislative powers over matters affecting his or her special responsibilities. There is an Executive Council, with the governor as chairman, one ex officio member (the attorney general), a chief minister (the leader of the elected members of the Legislative Council) who has responsibility for finance, and three other ministers (appointed by the governor on the advice of the chief minister). The Executive Council makes administrative decisions and oversees public agencies. Finally, there is a Legislative Council, consisting of a speaker (chosen from outside the council), one ex officio member (the attorney general), and nine members elected from single-member districts. The Legislative Council makes laws and ordinances. The voting age is eighteen. Elections are held at least once every five years.

Anguilla is administered under the Anguilla Constitution Order of 1982 and the Constitution, which took effect on April 1, 1982. Government arrangements are similar to those in the British

Virgin Islands. The British monarch is represented locally by a governor, who presides over the Executive Council and the House of Assembly. The governor is responsible for defense, external affairs, internal security (including the police), the public service, the judiciary, and the audit. On matters of internal security (including the police), the public service, and the appointment of an acting governor, however, the governor is required to consult the chief minister before making major decisions. The Executive Council consists of the chief minister and not more than three other ministers (appointed by the governor from the elected members of the House of Assembly) and two ex officio members (the attorney general and the permanent secretary for finance). The House of Assembly is elected for five years by universal adult suffrage and consists of seven elected members, two ex officio members (the attorney general and the permanent secretary for finance), and two other members who are nominated by the governor after consultation with the chief minister. There is provision for a speaker.

Montserrat's Constitution took effect on January 1, 1960. The territory is governed by a British-appointed governor and has its own Executive Council and Legislative Council. As in the other two territories, the governor is responsible for defense, external affairs, and internal security. The Executive Council consists of the governor as president, the chief minister and three other ministers, the attorney general, and the secretary for finance. The Legislative Council consists of a speaker chosen outside the council, seven elected members, two official members, and two appointed members.

The Eastern Caribbean States Supreme Court is the principal judicial body for all three territories. Appeals can be made to the Judicial Committee of the Privy Council in London.

Political Dynamics

The British Virgin Islands had a highly stable two-party system in the late 1980s. One observer has called the territory a haven of political tranquillity with little apparent interest in political activity, virtually immune to the political, social, and economic pressures that beset the region.

H. Lavity Stoutt, leader of the Virgin Islands Party (VIP), became the islands' first chief minister in April 1967. In a 1975 election, Stoutt's party and the rival United Party (UP) each won three of the seven elective seats on the Legislative Council. Willard Wheatley, then an independent, won the last seat and held the balance of power. He served as chief minister, with Stoutt as deputy chief minister.

In the first election held under the new Constitution (of June 1, 1977), in November 1979, independent candidates won five of the nine (increased from seven) elective seats, and the VIP won the other four. Stoutt became chief minister. In the November 1983 election, the VIP and the UP, the latter then headed by Wheatley, each gained four seats. The one successful independent candidate, Cyril Romney, became chief minister and formed a coalition government with the UP. In September 1986, Stoutt again became chief minister as the VIP captured a majority in the Legislative Council elections.

These transfers of power did not result in great changes in policy. There was real reluctance among the populace to discuss independence or constitutional change. Most citizens apparently preferred continued affiliation with Britain.

Since Anguilla's 1969 secession from St. Kitts and Nevis, politics on the island has been a contest between Ronald Webster, who led the secession, and his political rivals. In the mid-1980s, the territory's two major parties—the Anguilla Democratic Party (ADP) and the rival Anguilla National Alliance (ANA)—had no real policy differences. Both supported continued affiliation with Britain.

In the March 1976 House of Assembly elections, Webster, then head of the PPP, won and was appointed chief minister. In February 1977, Webster lost a motion of confidence, and Emile Gumbs replaced him as chief minister and as leader of the PPP (renamed the Anguilla National Alliance in 1980). Webster returned to power at the head of the recently formed Anguilla United Party in a May 1980 general election. In 1981, after political friction within the House of Assembly, Webster formed yet another party, the Anguilla People's Party (APP), and won that June's election. An early general election was held in March 1984, which resulted in the ANA's capturing of four of the seven House of Assembly seats. Evidently, Webster's plan to cut dependency on Britain by reducing British aid and increasing internal taxes had proved highly unpopular.

Gumbs became chief minister after the 1984 election and, under great popular pressure, abandoned Webster's tax plan. He then emphasized a policy of revitalizing the island's economy through tourism and foreign investment. Webster resigned from the leadership of the APP, since renamed the Anguilla Democratic Party (ADP). New party leader Victor Black vowed to resist any attempt by Webster to regain control of the ADP.

Although the majority of the population expressed no desire for independence, in 1985 the new government did request and was granted wider powers for the Executive Council. It also asked Britain for more aid and investment.

510

Anguillians have traditionally had high economic expectations and until the mid-1980s strongly favored economic development. At that point, doubts arose over three issues. One was the uncontrolled growth of foreign-owned villas, which caused soaring beachside real estate prices. Anguilla responded with strict height and size regulations and new restrictions on expatriate land sales. Second, debate raged over whether or not to allow casino operations. One minister resigned over the proposal, and it appeared that casino development would not proceed in deeply religious Anguilla. Finally, the island increased offshore financial activity, only to find fee income low and both the British Treasury and the United States Internal Revenue Service concerned about suspect operations, particularly the "laundering" of money from drug trafficking.

In September 1984, a United Nations (UN) decolonization mission made one of its periodic visits to assess island attitudes toward possible independence. Summarizing current sentiments on Anguilla, the mission noted general dissatisfaction with economic conditions and the limits of self-rule under the existing Constitution. Nevertheless, the report concluded: "While independence remains an ultimate aim for Anguilla, there was a genuine apprehension among the people of the territory that independence without a substantial measure of economic viability might, in fact, place Anguilla in a new situation of external dependence on one land or another."

In the 1970s and 1980s, Montserratian politics were dominated by Austin Bramble, leader of the Progressive Democratic Party (PDP), and John Osborne, head of the People's Liberation Movement (PLM). Bramble served as chief minister for eight years beginning in 1970. In November 1978, however, he was replaced by Osborne as the PLM captured all seven elective seats in the Legislative Council. Osborne's control of the chief minister's post was ratified on two subsequent occasions. The PLM won five seats in the February 1983 election and four in the August 1987 election. The latter ballot marked the first electoral effort of the National Democratic Party (NDP). The NDP, which was headed by Bertrand Osborne, won two seats on the Legislative Council.

Although personality issues appeared to dominate Montserratian politics, some policy distinctions among the parties could be identified. The PLM supported independence, a position rejected by both the PDP and the NDP. In the 1970s and early 1980s, the only party advocating independence was the United National Front, a small movement headed by George Irish, leader of the Montserrat Allied Workers Union. In 1984, however, John Osborne startled Montserratians by suddenly calling for independence. Osborne's

511

proposal was rooted in his anger over the British veto of Montserrat's participation in the Caribbean Peace Force dispatched to Grenada. Although intervention in Grenada was popular with most citizens on Montserrat, independence was not. As a consequence, Osborne promised that no decision on independence would be made until a referendum was held.

The PLM, PDP, and NDP also differed on economic development strategies. In the early 1980s, the government unveiled a multimillion-dollar casino and hotel development plan for the northern side of the island. The plan was strongly criticized by the PLM's opponents, who argued unsuccessfully that the measure should be put to a referendum. The situation became quite complicated in 1984 when two different Miami-based development companies each claimed that they had been granted rights to the casino and hotel project. In a strange twist, Bramble and his brother were arrested by the Palm Beach, Florida, police on burglary charges, while allegedly seeking a videotaped deposition on the matter made by a government official. In mid-1987 the PDP and the NDP were accusing the government of mismanaging the development project and the overall economy.

Foreign Relations

Britain continued to handle the external affairs of all three territories. Relations with neighboring islands were generally good, although Anguilla remained wary of St. Kitts and Nevis.

The three territories belonged to various international and regional associations. The British Virgin Islands belonged to the Commonwealth of Nations and the CDB and was an associate member of the Organisation of Eastern Caribbean States (OECS—see Glossary). Anguilla also was a member of the Commonwealth, the Caribbean Association of Industry and Commerce, the Eastern Caribbean Central Bank (ECCB), and the Civil Aviation Authority. Some other islands had objected to Anguilla's joining the ECCB, alleging that the free market in United States dollars that existed on Anguilla was a major contributor to foreign exchange leakage from the region using the Eastern Caribbean dollar, the common currency used by OECS members as well as Anguilla and Monteserrat. Anguilla's attempt in 1984 to join the OECS was rejected. Montserrat belonged to the ECCB, as well as the Commonwealth, the International Conference of Free Trade Unions, the Caribbean Association of Industry and Commerce, the Caribbean Community and Common Market (Caricom—see Appendix C), the UN Economic Council for Latin America, and the CDB. It was also a full member of the OECS.

National Security

Police forces in the three territories were small and under British control. The British Virgin Islands Police Force consisted of a chief of police, ninety-six police officers, and three civilian officers. Most of the police were native British Virgin Islanders. The headquarters was in Road Town on Tortola. In addition to the usual crime prevention and law enforcement activities associated with a police force, the police in the British Virgin Islands were responsible for firefighting. They also operated one marine patrol craft and two launches for use in enforcing the three-nautical-mile territorial limit of the islands, for fishery protection, and for anti-smuggling and antidrug operations.

The Anguilla Police Force was formed in 1972 to replace a detachment of the London Metropolitan Police that had served on the island since 1969, when the island seceded from the St. Kitts-Nevis-Anguilla union. In the 1980s, the force was headed by a chief of police, who reported to the minister of home affairs. There were eighty police officers, as well as special officers who could be deputized as necessary. The force's formal duties included national security, and, as such, it operated two ships for fishery protection and antismuggling operations. Most officers were native Anguillians, but some were recruited in St. Vincent and the Grenadines. Headquarters was in The Valley. The British operated the criminal justice system.

The Royal Montserrat Police Force had eighty to ninety members commanded by a chief of police. As in Anguilla, the Montserratian force was responsible for enforcing the territorial waters limit and for fishery protection. On Monserrat, these duties were the specific responsibility of the Marine Police, which had the use of one marine patrol craft.

No insurgencies or mass-based antigovernment groups existed in these three territories in the late 1980s. Strikes occasionally occurred over wages and related issues, but political strikes appeared nonexistent. Since the British government retained responsibility for defense, British Army units would undoubtedly be brought in to handle any serious domestic unrest.

Britain maintained no army or naval units in the dependencies. The closest British Army forces were in Belize. Although Montserrat and the British Virgin Islands were members of the OECS as of 1987, neither had joined the Regional Security System (RSS). Montserrat also refrained from participating in OECS voting in late October 1983 to support the United States-Caribbean intervention in Grenada (the British Virgin Islands was not yet a member

of the OECS). Futhermore, paramilitary forces from these territories were unlikely to participate in any proposed regional post-
Grenada defense and security arrangements, since Britain had
opposed such involvement by its dependent territories. Nevertheless, the British Virgin Islands were in the area patrolled by the
United States Coast Guard forces based in the United States Virgin
Islands (see Current Strategic Considerations, ch. 7).

*   *   *

In 1987 there were few works that focused solely on the British
Virgin Islands, Anguilla, or Montserrat. The most useful sources
of information on these islands can be found in a series of yearbooks and in compendium discussions of all the Caribbean islands.
The Caribbean Handbook, edited by Jeremy Taylor, is one of the most
comprehensive discussions of all of the Caribbean islands. Included
in each country's profile are sections on history, commerce, finance,
government, and general business regulations. *The Europa Year Book*
provides current data and background, and the *Latin America and
Caribbean Review* (published yearly), edited by Richard Green, is
an excellent source on economic and political events of the past
year. Current events can be followed through the monthly British
newsletter, *Latin American Monitor: Caribbean.* Useful business information can be found in the *Business Traveller's Handbook,* edited
by Jane Walker. Two works by residents of the islands also are
worth noting. Colville Petty's *Anguilla: Where There's a Will There's
a Way* presents an Anguillian view of the break with St. Kitts and
Nevis. H.A. Fergus's *Montserrat: Emerald Isle of the Caribbean* describes
day-to-day life on Montserrat. (For further information and complete citations, see Bibliography.)

Chapter 6. The Northern Islands

Spanish caravel bound for the New World

THE NORTHERN ISLANDS is a term of convenience used in this study to refer to the independent Commonwealth of the Bahamas and two British dependent territories, the Cayman Islands and the Turks and Caicos Islands. All three are located in the northern Caribbean Basin. Both the Bahamas and the Turks and Caicos Islands form part of the Bahamas archipelago, which extends 80 kilometers southeast of Florida to approximately 150 kilometers north of Haiti and the Dominican Republic. The Cayman Islands lie approximately 150 kilometers south of Cuba and 290 kilometers northwest of Jamaica.

All three island groupings share a similar historical development. Christopher Columbus most likely made his first landfall in the New World on a Bahamian island, although exactly where has been debated for years. He discovered the Cayman Islands on his third voyage in 1503. Although Ponce de Leon is said to have discovered the Turks and Caicos in 1512, some historians still speculate that Columbus landed on one of these islands during his first voyage in 1492. In mid-1987 preparations were underway for the celebration of the quincentenary of the discovery of the New World; replicas of Columbus's ships were being constructed in Spain to recreate the historic transatlantic voyage in 1992. The ships were scheduled to drop anchor in the Bahamas on October 12 of that year, focusing world attention on the small Caribbean nation.

The islands shared common political linkages at various times in the nineteenth and twentieth centuries. The Turks and Caicos formed part of the Bahamas in the first half of the nineteenth century. By the second half of the nineteenth century, both the Turks and Caicos and the Caymans were Jamaican dependencies and remained so until Jamaican independence in 1962. At that time, both sets of islands became separate British colonies, a status that they retained as of the late 1980s. The Bahamas, which became a British colony in the mid-seventeenth century, attained independence as a sovereign nation in 1973. In the late 1980s, all three island groupings maintained membership in the British Commonwealth of Nations (see Appendix B).

The Bahamas dwarfs both the Caymans and the Turks and Caicos in area, population, and gross domestic product (GDP—see Glossary). Despite differences, these three societies shared several common social and economic characteristics in the late 1980s. The populations of all three groupings had a strong African heritage.

Tourism and financial services were major elements of the domestic economies in all three island groupings. The Bahamian and Caymanian economies were particularly developed in these two sectors, resulting in relatively high per capita income for the region and for the developing world in general. The economy of the Turks and Caicos lacked the necessary infrastructure to exploit these activities fully; however, it was steadily establishing important tourist and financial service sectors in the mid-1980s with the help of British investments.

Finally, all three island groupings were affected in the 1980s by drug trafficking. Both the Bahamas and the Turks and Caicos became transit points for traffickers from South America; in addition, both societies experienced severe social and political crises resulting from drug-related corruption. Traffickers were also believed to have laundered funds in Caymanian banks. This major international problem was being addressed throughout the area under pressure and with assistance from the United States.

The Bahamas

Official Name .... Commonwealth of the Bahamas

Term for Citizens .... Bahamian(s)

Capital .... Nassau

Political Status .... Independent, 1973

Form of Government .... Parliamentary democracy
and constitutional monarchy

Geography
Size .... 13,934 sq. km.
Topography .... Flat, low-lying islands
Climate .... Semitropical

Population
Total estimated in 1986 235,000
Annual growth rate (in percentage) in 1973–83 .... 2.1
Life expectancy at birth in 1984 69
Adult literacy rate (in percentage) in 1984 93
Language .... English; some Haitian creole
Ethnic groups ...... Black (85 percent), white (15 percent)
Religion .... Primarily Anglican, Baptist,
or Roman Catholic

Economy
Currency; exchange rate .... Bahamian dollar (B$);
B$1.00 = US$1.00
Gross domestic product (GDP) in 1985 .... US$1.8 billion
Per capita GDP in 1985 .... US$7,822
Distribution of GDP (in percentage) in 1985
Tourism 70
Industry 10
Banking and finance 7
Other services 8
Agriculture 5

National Security
Armed forces personnel 531
Paramilitary personnel 0
Police 1,447

The Bahamas

The Bahamas stands out among the Commonwealth Caribbean nations because of its relative wealth and prosperity, political stability, and close proximity to the United States. The Bahamas also bears the distinction of being the first of the Caribbean islands discovered by Columbus in 1492 on his first transatlantic voyage in search of a new route to India. Several islands in the Bahamas have been named as Columbus's first landing site in the Caribbean, but until very recently, Watling Island was the most widely accepted location; in 1926 it was renamed San Salvador, the name bestowed by Columbus himself. In 1986, however, after an extensive five-year investigation, a National Geographic Society team announced that Samana Cay, a small isolated island in the far eastern Bahamas, was the most probable location of Columbus's first landfall.

Upon his arrival, Columbus encountered natives known as Lucayans, related to the Arawak Indians (see The Pre-European Population, ch. 1). Within a quarter of a century, however, the Lucayans had been decimated, the result of diseases brought by the Europeans and of having been forced to work in the mines of Hispaniola (the island containing present-day Haiti and the Dominican Republic). For the next century, the Bahamas was a forgotten colony. Attention was focused instead on the mineral wealth of the other Caribbean islands.

The first permanent settlement was not established until 1649, when Puritans from the English colony of Bermuda founded Eleuthera, which in Greek means "place of freedom." The colonists, known as Eleutheran Adventurers, set out to establish a colony where they could practice their religion freely, as in the colonies settled by the Pilgrims in New England. In 1666 other English settlers established a colony on New Providence and founded Charlestown, which was renamed Nassau near the end of the seventeenth century. Throughout the seventeenth century, the islands served as a favorite base for pirates, but after the era of piracy came to a close in 1718, commerce was restored to the settlement.

British loyalists and their slaves arrived from the mainland colonies in the wake of the British defeat in the American Revolution. In the 1780s, the population of New Providence tripled, and the first substantial settlement was made on Great Abaco Island. Cotton plantations were established as the southern life of the North American mainland colonies was reproduced in the Bahamas. However, the Abolition of Slavery Act of 1833 and the termination of post-abolition apprenticeships and indentured servanthood in 1838 marked the end of slavery in the Bahamas (see The Post-Emancipation Societies, ch. 1). The Bahamian economy prospered during the United States Civil War, as Nassau served as an important base for blockade-running by the Confederate States. The war's end, however, set in motion an economic tailspin that lasted for the next half-century. Little economic development occurred other than in the areas of sponging, pineapple cultivation, and tourism.

The passage of the Volstead Act (Prohibition Act) by the United States in 1919 was a bonanza for the Bahamas. The islands served as a base for United States prohibition runners, and the port of Nassau became congested once again. The introduction of commercial aircraft in the 1930s enabled the Bahamas tourism sector to develop as a mainstay of the nation's economy. The development of tourism helped mitigate the combined impact of the United States repeal of prohibition in 1933 and a marine disease in 1938 that devastated the sponging industry. During World War II, the Bahamas prospered as Britain established two air force bases on the islands; the Royal Air Force set up a bomber base to ferry new airplanes to European combat zones and to operate a training school for flight and antisubmarine operations in the Caribbean.

After World War II, the Bahamas developed economically and politically. The nation began to exploit its tourism sector more fully; by the end of the 1940s, tourism had become the principal business. In the 1960s, the nation also developed into an international finance center because of taxation and foreign capital movement legislation in the United States and Western Europe. In 1987 tourism and banking remained the two most important economic sectors in the Bahamas.

The Bahamas also underwent a major political transformation in the postwar era. The first political parties and trade union federations were founded in the 1950s. In 1964, after more than two centuries of British colonial rule, constitutional changes were negotiated at a conference in London; a new constitution replaced the nation's old representative government with a premier (the preindependence title for prime minister) and a cabinet. In 1967 a bicameral legislature was established, and the first independent government was elected. Full internal self-government was achieved with the signing of the 1969 constitution; and the name of the colony was officially changed to the Commonwealth of the Bahamas. A final constitutional conference was held in 1972, paving the way for national independence. On July 10, 1973, the new independence Constitution was presented to Prime Minister Lynden O.

Pindling by Prince Charles on behalf of Queen Elizabeth II; with that, the Bahamas became a sovereign independent nation.

Geography

The Bahamas is an archipelago of approximately 700 flat, low-lying islands in the western Atlantic Ocean (see fig. 1). It extends from eighty kilometers east of Florida to eighty kilometers northeast of Cuba. In addition to the United States and Cuba, neighbors of the Bahamas include Haiti and the Turks and Caicos Islands; both are located to the southeast of the Bahamas. The Tropic of Cancer runs through the middle of the archipelago, passing across the lower part of Great Exuma Island and the upper part of Long Island. Although the total land area of the archipelago is 13,934 square kilometers, slightly larger than New Jersey and Connecticut combined, the islands are sprawled over an area of approximately 259,000 square kilometers (see fig. 18; table 6, Appendix A).

The islands are surface projections of two oceanic banks, the Little Bahama Bank and the Great Bahama Bank. The highest point is only sixty-three meters above sea level on Cat Island; the island of New Providence, where the capital city of Nassau is located, reaches a maximum elevation of only thirty-seven meters. The land on the Bahamas has a foundation of fossil coral, but much of the rock is oolitic limestone; the stone is derived from the disintegration of coral reefs and seashells. The land is primarily either rocky or mangrove swamp. Low scrub covers much of the surface area. Timber is found in abundance on four of the northern islands: Grand Bahama, Great Abaco, New Providence, and Andros. On some of the southern islands, low-growing tropical hardwood flourishes. Although some soil is very fertile, it is also very thin. Only a few freshwater lakes and just one river, located on Andros Island, are found in the Bahamas.

The climate of the archipelago is semitropical and has two seasons, summer and winter. During the summer, which extends from May through November, the climate is dominated by warm, moist tropical air masses moving north through the Caribbean. Midsummer temperatures range from 21°C to 34°C with a relative humidity of 60 to 100 percent. In winter months, extending from December through April, the climate is affected by the movement of cold polar masses from North America. Temperatures during the winter months range from 15°C to 24°C.

Yearly rainfall averages 132 centimeters and is usually concentrated in the May–June and September–October periods. Rainfall often occurs in short-lived, fairly intense showers accompanied by strong gusty winds, which are then followed by clear skies.

Winds are predominantly easterly throughout the year but tend to become northeasterly from October to April and southeasterly from May to September. These winds seldom exceed twenty-four kilometers per hour except during hurricane season. Although the hurricane season officially lasts from June to November, most hurricanes in the Bahamas occur between July and October; as of late 1987, the last one to strike was Hurricane David in September 1979. Damage was estimated at US$1.8 million and mainly affected agricultural products. The most intense twentieth-century hurricane to strike the Bahamas was in 1929; winds of up to 225 kilometers per hour were recorded. Many lives were lost, and there was extensive damage to buildings, homes, and boats.

Population

According to the 1980 census, the Bahamas had a population of 209,505. Unofficial estimates in mid-1986 placed the population at 235,000. Census data indicated that 64.6 percent of the population lived on the main island of New Providence and another 15.8 percent on Grand Bahama. The remaining inhabitants were spread out among the numerous outlying islands known as the Family Islands or Outer Islands. Between 1973 and 1983, the average annual population growth rate in the Bahamas was 2.1 percent; however, this rate masked wide variations across the islands. New Providence and Grand Bahama showed major increases of 32.8 percent and 27.6 percent, respectively; modest increases were also experienced in Great Abaco Island (12.6 percent) and in Eleuthera, Harbour Island, and Spanish Wells as a group (11.6 percent).

Nevertheless, a majority of the islands actually experienced a decline in their populations. Prominent losses were recorded in Acklins Island (34.2 percent), Ragged Island (29.8 percent), and Crooked Island (25 percent). Census figures confirmed not only a sizable interisland migration pattern to New Providence and Grand Bahama but also an intraisland migration from the older city areas to the suburban areas. The latter trend was particularly evident in New Providence.

Ethnically, some 85 percent of the population was black. Most were descendants of slaves imported directly from North Africa or brought by British loyalists who escaped from the North American colonies at the conclusion of the American Revolution. Approximately 15 percent of the population was white, mainly originating from early British and North American settlers, especially from the Carolinas, New York, and Virginia. Included in the 15 percent was a small Greek community, the descendants of Greeks who came to the Bahamas as sponge fishermen.

A growing number of illegal Haitian immigrants were also found in the Bahamas; according to the United States Department of State's *Country Reports on Human Rights Practices for 1985,* this number was estimated at 20,000 to 40,000. The Haitians primarily filled employment vacancies at the bottom of the Bahamian economy; many were gardeners, domestics, and farm laborers. Although English was the official language of the country, some creole was spoken among these Haitian immigrants. A September 1985 treaty signed between the Bahamas and Haiti legalized the status of undocumented Haitians who had arrived prior to 1981; others were to be repatriated in an orderly and humane manner. In 1986 more than 2,000 were repatriated under the treaty, but the legalization process of Haitians eligible for citizenship had not yet begun.

The Bahamas was predominantly a Christian country. In the late 1980s, the principal denominations were Anglican, Baptist, and Roman Catholic. In addition to the Anglican and Baptist churches, the Protestant presence included Christian Scientist, Church of God, Lutheran, Methodist, Plymouth Brethren, Presbyterian, Seventh-Day Adventist, and Jehovah's Witnesses congregations; many of the smaller sects adhered to an evangelical perspective. Small Greek Orthodox and Jewish communities also were present in the Bahamas. Many of the country's independent schools were affiliated with churches and included Anglican, Methodist, and Roman Catholic institutions.

Education

Education in the Bahamas was mandatory between the ages of five and fourteen. In early 1987, the Ministry of Education was responsible for 226 schools, 83.2 percent of which were run by the government and 16.8 percent of which were independent. New Providence claimed 38 government schools and 13 independent schools; the Family Islands and Grand Bahama had 150 government schools and 25 independent schools. Schools were classified into three major categories: primary schools for children ages five to ten; secondary schools for ages eleven to seventeen; and all-age schools. In general, schools in the Family Islands were for all ages because of long distances to residences; in New Providence and Grand Bahama, students were most often separated by age. In 1985 the Bahamas reported a school population of 60,355, approximately 77 percent of whom attended government-run schools and 23 percent, private schools. Education was free in government schools. Many independent secondary schools were referred to as colleges.

Since the 1960s, the government has made a substantial effort to improve the country's education system. Government expenditures on education rose from 10.7 percent of total government expenditures in 1955 to a high of 25 percent in 1974 but declined to 17.4 percent in 1984. The ratios of students to staff improved steadily from thirty-four to one in 1976 to twenty-one to one in 1983. The literacy rate in 1984 was estimated at 93 percent. Primary-school enrollment increased from 78 percent in 1970 to 99 percent in 1983.

Despite these significant achievements, educational problems remained. The *Country Reports on Human Rights Practices for 1985* indicated that there was "a weakening of education in the public school system as a result of shortages of teachers, equipment, and supplies as well as the physical deterioration of many schools." The Ministry of Education itself admitted that the results of national tests taken by students in 1985 demonstrated "serious deficiencies" throughout the education system. In the mid-1980s, the government increased emphasis on technical and vocational training.

The College of the Bahamas opened its doors in 1974; the government-owned institution offered a two- or three-year program leading to an associate degree in one of six academic divisions. In the spring of 1986, the college reported an enrollment of 1,834. The college offered programs in conjunction with the University of Miami. In addition, since the 1960s the Bahamas also had been associated directly with the University of the West Indies (UWI), which, with its three campuses in Barbados, Jamaica, and Trinidad and Tobago, served much of the English-speaking Caribbean. The UWI also had a hotel and tourism management program in the Bahamas. In addition to these local and regional colleges, many Bahamians attended institutions of higher learning in the United States, Canada, and Britain.

Health and Welfare

The Bahamas in general had a healthy population in the mid-1980s. Substantial progress had been made in the country's health care over the previous two decades, as indicated by several life expectancy indicators. By 1984 the crude death rate had declined to a low of 5.1 per 1,000 inhabitants, and life expectancy at birth was estimated at 69 years. The infant mortality rate in 1985 was measured at a low 27.5 per 1,000 live births. Specific health-related data revealed a 9.5-percent increase in the number of hospital beds from 1974 to 1983; the ratio of population to hospital beds also improved from 260 to 1 to 234 to 1 over the same period. From 1970 to 1983, the ratios of population to doctors and nurses

One-room schoolhouse,
Great Guana Cay,
Great Abaco Island
Courtesy John F. Hornbeck

Community telephone,
Great Guana Cay,
Great Abaco Island
Courtesy Ethel S. Hornbeck

improved from 1,630 to 1 to 1,018 to 1 and from 260 to 1 to 234 to 1, respectively.

The Ministry of Health was responsible for setting national health policies and for implementing health programs. A tiered network of private and public health facilities made up the national health sector; referral linkages existed among the different facilities. The country's three government-run hospitals were the Princess Margaret Hospital in Nassau, a 484-bed general hospital; the Sandilands Rehabilitation Centre on New Providence, consisting of a 158-bed geriatric facility and a 259-bed psychiatric facility; and the Rand Memorial Hospital on Grand Bahama, a 74-bed general hospital. In addition, Rassin Hospital, in Nassau, was a privately run general hospital with twenty-six beds. In the Family Islands, primary health care was delivered through a network of public health centers and clinics staffed by physicians, dentists, community nurses, midwives, and health aides. In 1984 the Family Islands' nineteen health districts contained twelve health centers, thirty-four main clinics, and forty-six satellite clinics staffed by nineteen physicians, three dentists, and eighty-three nurses. Patients in the Family Islands requiring additional medical assistance were flown to Princess Margaret Hospital. Most Bahamian doctors and dentists received their degrees from schools in Britain, Canada, or the United States.

In 1982 the major causes of death in the Bahamas were, in descending order of incidence: cancer, heart disease, accidents and violence, bronchitis, emphysema and asthma, cerebrovascular diseases, and diseases originating in the perinatal period. A comprehensive system of inoculation was responsible for the nonoccurrence of many infectious and parasitic diseases, including typhoid, poliomyelitis, diphtheria, pertussis, and tetanus. Some cases of tuberculosis, hepatitis, and malaria were reported among Haitian refugees living in close quarters, but no major outbreaks had occurred in the general population. According to a 1986 World Bank (see Glossary) report, no major malnutrition problems were recorded. The report also indicated that the country had begun to experience diseases normally associated with developed countries, such as diabetes and hypertension. The Ministry of Health reported fifty-six cases of acquired immune deficiency syndrome in 1985 and thirty-four cases in the first half of 1986.

Most of the islands had potable drinking water from underground wells. Access to piped water was highly uneven. Estimates in 1976 indicated that all urban residents, but only 13 percent of the rural population, had access to such a service. New Providence experienced particular difficulty in satisfying its fresh water needs.

It supplemented its ten underground well fields with distilled sea water and received fresh water shipped from nearby Andros Island. Nearly 20 percent of New Providence's fresh water in 1983 was barged in from Andros Island. Septic tanks and drainage pits required waste water removal in some lowland areas.

In the late 1980s, the country faced a growing housing shortage. A 1986 World Bank study noted that ''new housing production over the past decade has been below required levels, creating a backlog of housing demand, particularly for the lower income groups.'' The report also noted that considerable rehabilitation on existing dwellings was needed. Forty percent of all housing was in average to poor condition, and two out of three households did not have water piped into the dwelling. The government became increasingly involved in housing via this rehabilitation effort, new construction of urban public housing, private construction incentive grants, and construction loans.

In 1974 the government introduced the country's first national social insurance program; the system provided benefits to qualified contributors for retirement, disability, sickness, maternity, funeral expenses, industrial benefits, and survivor's assistance. Noncontributory assistance was available for old-age pensions, survivor's benefits, and disability. Total contributions rose steadily from a low of US$700,000 in 1975 to an estimated US$11.3 million in 1982. Most of these benefits were paid out for noncontributory old-age pensions.

Economy

In the mid-1980s, the Bahamas was classified as an upper middle-income developing country and ranked among the wealthiest nations in the Caribbean region. Tourism was the nation's primary economic activity. In 1986 the World Bank reported that tourism directly and indirectly accounted for approximately 50 percent of employment. Tourism's share of the gross domestic product (GDP—see Glossary) was estimated at 70 percent by the United States Department of Commerce.

In order to lessen the economy's dependency on tourism, the government has followed a policy of diversification since the 1970s, emphasizing development in the industrial and agricultural sectors. Success, however, has been limited. The nation experienced setbacks in the early 1980s with the closing of steel and cement plants and oil refineries. Because industries locating in the Bahamas tended to be capital intensive, the industrial sector's share of the labor force was estimated at just 6 percent in 1979. Industry's share of GDP was estimated at about 10 percent in the mid-1980s.

The agricultural sector (including fishing) also employed only about 6 percent of the labor force in the early 1980s. Despite various programs to boost production, the World Bank estimated that agriculture in the Bahamas accounted for less than 5 percent of GDP in 1986. The nation's banking and finance sector experienced significant growth in the 1970s and 1980s. This sector contributed approximately 7 percent to GDP in the mid-1980s but employed only about 3,000 Bahamians.

The overall performance of the economy during the past several decades has been positive. In the 1960s, the country recorded robust economic growth; growth rates averaged 9 percent annually as direct foreign investment spurred the development of tourism. Economic performance in the 1970s was not as successful. The international economic recession caused a reduction in investment, especially after the 1973 and 1979 oil price shocks. Bahamian independence in 1973 also caused a certain amount of uncertainty, contributing further to reduced foreign investment. Toward the end of the decade, however, economic performance improved, led by growth in tourism; investment soon followed suit, resulting in a boom in the construction sector and an increase in employment levels.

The economy continued to perform well in the early and mid-1980s. Real GDP growth in the 1980–84 period averaged 3 percent. The only notable setback occurred in 1981, when recession in the United States resulted in a decline in stopover visitors (hotel occupants rather than cruise ship or day visitors) and the manufacturing sector was hurt by the closing of several plants; real GDP for that year fell by 9 percent. Tourism recovered quickly, however. In 1982 about 1.7 million foreign tourists visited the Bahamas, and by 1986 that figure had grown to 3 million. GDP was US$1.8 billion in 1985, and per capita GDP was estimated at US$7,822.

The nation was not without economic problems. Growth and development were not uniform throughout the country. Most development occurred in New Providence and Grand Bahama, causing significant migration from the Family Islands to these two urban centers. This migration strained the infrastructure and social sectors of New Providence and Grand Bahama. The government also was faced with the heavy burden of spreading facilities and services throughout the Family Islands. A second problem of the Bahamian economy was its dependence on a single sector, tourism; that sector's well-being was in turn affected by the economy in the United States, the source of most tourists. To reduce this dependency, the government actively pursued a policy of diversification.

Finally, the country was afflicted with the problem of structural unemployment; in 1986 unemployment levels were estimated in the 17- to 22-percent range. Industrial development tended to be capital intensive because of a high wage structure and a scarcity of technically skilled labor.

Tourism

As already indicated, tourism has been the motor of the Bahamian economy for the past several decades; the nation's geography, including its climate, natural beauty, and proximity to the United States, have made it a prime tourist spot. Tourism is the major determinant of the well-being of the Bahamian economy and has maintained steady growth since World War II. The government has successfully implemented policies to increase private confidence and investment in the sector. It has transformed tourism into a year-round industry, overcoming the seasonal fluctuation of demand by aggressively promoting specialized summer tourist attractions. In 1986 the World Bank estimated that the Bahamas accounted for 20 percent of stopover visitors in the Caribbean region as well as having a large share of cruise ship passenger arrivals.

The Bahamas achieved record high levels of foreign visitors in 1985 and 1986 with 2.6 and 3 million visitors, respectively. The statistical breakdown of foreign arrivals in 1985 included 52 percent stopover visitors, 43 percent cruise ship arrivals, and 5 percent day visitors. Total tourist expenditures in 1985 amounted to US$870 million. Most of the expenditures were attributed to stopover visitors, who accounted for 92 percent of the total in 1984; by contrast, cruise ship passengers accounted for just 6.6 percent of total visitor expenditures in that year.

The major tourist centers were New Providence (Nassau, Cable Beach, and Paradise Island) and Grand Bahama (Freeport). Fifty-eight percent of stopover visitors in 1984 went to New Providence, 25 percent to Grand Bahama, and 17 percent to the Family Islands. Most of the tourist growth in the mid-1980s occurred in New Providence. Grand Bahama experienced a steady decline in tourist arrivals, reaching a five-year low in 1984, whereas the Family Islands had a steady flow of tourists. The average length of stay for stopover visitors had declined substantially from 7.14 days in 1980 to 6.46 days in 1984, reflecting the trend toward short package vacations of three to four days.

The government was actively involved in the tourist sector in the mid-1980s. The government-owned Hotel Corporation of the Bahamas, established in 1974, had seven major hotels (four in Nassau and three in Freeport). All were managed by international hotel management companies. The Hotel Corporation also owned a golf course, a marina, and four casinos (two in New Providence and two in Grand Bahama). In 1983 the corporation completed work on a new 700-room hotel at Cable Beach with a convention center and a casino.

The Ministry of Tourism marketed and monitored tourist services; a World Bank study labeled it one of the most effective tourist ministries in the world. In addition to its headquarters in the Bahamas, the ministry also operated offices in nine cities in the United States, three in Canada, and three in Western Europe. Bahamasair, the national airline, provided the only scheduled interisland air service. Competing with several airlines in the North American market, Bahamasair managed to control over 25 percent of North American routes to the Bahamas.

Since its development after World War II, the tourist industry has been dependent on the North American market. In the early 1980s, this dependency increased further. Between 1980 and 1984, Canada's and Western Europe's percentage share of the market decreased. The major factor in the increased United States share of tourist trade was the strong value of the United States dollar, to which the Bahamian dollar was pegged. Bahamian vacations for Canadians and West Europeans became all the more expensive. This dependency on the United States for tourist receipts made the Bahamian economy quite vulnerable to downturns in the United States economy. A 1986 World Bank study indicated the strong relationship between the performance of the tourism sector and the performance of the United States economy. A decline in the strength of the United States dollar has boosted the Canadian and West European share of the market, but continued benefits along these lines depend on the capability of the Ministry of Tourism to tap those markets effectively. To this end, the ministry maintained offices in Canada and Western Europe.

In late 1986, the government's plans for improvements in the tourist sector included programs to improve marketing and infrastructure and to work toward balanced growth of tourism to the Family Islands. A multimillion-dollar marketing campaign was planned, followed by the launching of a national magazine campaign across North America. Major tourist infrastructure programs included improvements to Nassau International Airport and Nassau Harbour and upgrading of docks and airports in key Family Islands. The government also planned to bring more cruise ships to the Family Islands to tap the potential of these underutilized tourist spots.

View of downtown Nassau and Nassau Harbour
Courtesy Mark P. Sullivan

Banking and Finance

The second most important Bahamian economic activity in the late 1980s was banking and finance. The nation's proximity to Miami and its location in the same time zone as New York City enhanced these activities. A large number of trust and finance companies and investment firms were established in the 1950s, following the imposition of restrictive finance laws in many industrialized countries. Enactment of regulations in the Bahamas in 1965, however, provided for the licensing and supervision of the banking industry, cutting back drastically the number of financial institutions. Steady growth took place after 1967, the only setback occurring in the mid-1970s following the formation of the Central Bank of the Bahamas. The new Central Bank increased its monitoring of the industry.

By the end of 1985, there were 374 banking and trust institutions registered in the Bahamas. Of these, 270 were permitted to deal with the public; 96 were restricted to dealing with or on behalf of certain people or companies; and 8 held nonactive licenses. Of these 270 public financial institutions, 134 were Eurocurrency (see Glossary) branches of banks in Western Europe, Hong Kong, the United States, or South America; 84 were subsidiaries of finance institutions based outside the Bahamas; 33 were Bahamas-based banks or trust companies; 10 were officially designated to deal in

535

gold and in Bahamian and foreign currencies; and only 9 were trust companies designated to act as custodians and dealers in foreign securities.

The proliferation of financial institutions encouraged the development of ancillary services such as accounting, computing, and law. It also required the installation of an advanced telecommunications system, a development that benefited other economic sectors as well.

Several factors combined to make the Bahamas a significant center of finance in the late 1980s. First, the country had tax-haven status: no taxes on income, profits, capital gains, or inheritance. Second, the Bahamas offered liberal legal provisions for the registration and licensing of financial institutions and bank secrecy laws. Third, the Bahamas benefited from its stable political climate. Finally, it offered investors the convenience of geographic proximity to the United States. In January 1985, the financial sector was strengthened by the adoption of a code of conduct that gave the Central Bank a more supervisory role over the banking system. The main purpose of the code was to prevent money laundering. Large cash transactions were prohibited, unless they were made by well-established customers. Lawyers and accountants could no longer sign over accounts of offshore customers without approval of the Central Bank.

Following the example of the banking and finance sector, other offshore activities also gained importance in the mid-1980s. Although liberal legislation for ship registration was passed in 1976, the Bahamas did not attract a major shipping industry until the 1980s. By December 1985, a total of 370 ships were registered, representing 5 million gross tons; in 1987 the Bahamas was the third largest flag-of-convenience nation behind Liberia and Panama. An even younger Bahamian industry was offshore insurance and reinsurance. Legislation was passed in 1983 to remove all taxes on premiums and restrictions on investments for this activity.

Industrial Sector

In the late 1980s, the Bahamian industrial sector consisted of several large-scale activities (chemicals, pharmaceuticals, and oil) and a variety of small-scale industries (food processing, paints, purified water, rum and other alcoholic beverages, salt, and soft drinks). The large-scale activities were located on Grand Bahama, whereas small-scale industries were concentrated in both Grand Bahama and New Providence. The industrial sector experienced setbacks in the early 1980s, when declining demand caused steel and cement plants to close. In mid-1985 the Bahamas Oil Refining Company (BORCO), the fourth largest refinery in the world, shut down its refining operations in response to the oil glut on the world market. BORCO continued its oil transshipment operations, however, importing large quantities of oil from the Middle East and Africa for transshipment and for domestic use. In the Bahamas, oil exploration by several international companies began in the early 1980s; marine geologists believed vast deposits of oil and natural gas might be found.

Chemical and pharmaceutical plants fared well in the early 1980s. Exports of chemical products increased by over 100 percent in the 1980–84 period. Several large chemical and pharmaceutical industries were located on Grand Bahama. Light industrial activities experienced slight growth in the early 1980s. Salt was mined on Great Inagua, and small amounts of aragonite sand were mined near the Bimini Islands for export. The rum industry grew. Bacardi operated a major distillery in New Providence. In 1986 construction began on a brewery sponsored by a consortium made up of Bacardi, Guinness, and Heineken to produce a new beer with a Bahamian name.

Since the 1950s, the government had consistently encouraged efforts to diversify the economy. Industrial incentive legislation, however, dated back to the 1950s, when the Hawksbill Creek Agreement allowed the Grand Bahama Port Authority to develop industry on that island. In 1970 the Industries Encouragement Act provided incentives for manufacturers of approved products. Incentives included the duty-free importation of machinery and raw materials and tax exemptions. In 1971 the Agriculture Manufacturers Act provided similar incentives for that industry. In 1981 the Bahamas Agricultural and Industrial Corporation was established as a central agency for potential investors seeking advice and assistance. Finally, in 1984 legislation created a free-trade zone in New Providence similar to the one in Grand Bahama established by the Hawksbill Creek Agreement.

Aside from a weak external market for oil products, the industrial sector faced several other difficulties. The Bahamas had a very limited market size. Wage rates tended to be high, and skilled workers were lacking. Capital-intensive industries developed despite the government's desire to locate labor-intensive industries there, especially in New Providence. This development underscored the growing problem of structural unemployment. A 1986 report by the Inter-American Development Bank (IDB) indicated that a major task for the government would be to provide 3,000 to 3,500 jobs annually in the late 1980s and early 1990s for graduating youths.

Agricultural Sector

In the late 1980s, the agricultural sector consisted mainly of small farms producing poultry, fruit, and vegetables for the local market and exporting some citrus fruits and seasonal vegetables. Government policy focused on reducing food imports, expanding and diversifying agricultural exports, and increasing linkages between the agricultural sector and tourism. The government emphasized the promotion of foreign investment, including joint ventures, and the development of farming among young Bahamians. Investments in research and extension and marketing facilities led to continued growth in winter vegetables and fruit and poultry products. The BAIC promoted employment creation through joint ventures offering access to modern marketing, management, technology, and venture capital, all in short supply in the Bahamas. Inherent problems in developing the agricultural sector, however, were the scarcity and expense of local labor.

A considerable capacity existed for expansion of the agricultural sector. In 1986 the World Bank estimated that only 10 percent (16,200 hectares) of cultivable land was being farmed. Potential products included citrus crops for export, edible oils, peanuts, avocados, cut flowers, and hot peppers. Agricultural production statistics made clear the need to tap this poorly utilized economic sector. In 1985 the IDB estimated that Bahamian farmers produced just 20 percent of the food consumed on the islands, requiring the importation of millions of dollars worth of food annually; the food import bill for that year amounted to about US$200 million. According to international agencies, the nation's food bill could be met by developing suitable land on Great Abaco Island, Andros Island, and Grand Bahama.

Considerable potential also existed in the small fisheries sector. The first commercial harvest of shrimp occurred in 1984, but this barely scratched the surface of fisheries potential. In 1985 crawfish were the most valuable domestic export, with exports valued at US$18.6 million. The nation's fishing fleet was expanding, and shallow water fisheries were being developed.

Economic Policy and Management

Although government policy was overtly capitalist, state ownership was significant in the economy. In addition to the central government, the public sector also consisted of the National Insurance Board, which was responsible for administering the country's social insurance program, and six nonfinancial corporations:

four in public utilities (Bahamas Electricity Corporation, Bahamas Water and Sewer Corporation, Bahamas Telecommunications Corporation, and the Broadcasting Corporation of the Bahamas) and two tourism-related firms (Bahamasair and the Hotel Corporation of the Bahamas). According to the World Bank, these public corporations performed well in the early 1980s; significant financial improvements occurred in 1983 and 1984 and were responsible in part for improvement of the overall financial position of the public sector. In particular, the electricity and hotel corporations registered operating balance surpluses by 1984 after several years of large capital expenditures.

Central government revenue increased steadily in the first half of the 1980s, from US$261 million in 1980 to US$350.3 million in 1984; estimates for revenue in 1985 and 1986 were US$424 and US$458 million, respectively. Expenditures also increased during the same period, from US$258.9 million in 1980 to an estimated US$458 million in 1986. During most of the period, the government recorded a fiscal deficit on its public accounts; a low of US$81.2 million was recorded in 1983 and was primarily the result of capital expenditures in the hotel sector of the tourist industry. In 1984 capital expenditures decreased and brought the fiscal deficit down to US$15.9 million. Projections for 1985 and 1986 were for small surpluses in the public accounts (see table 7, Appendix A).

The income tax structure in the late 1980s was relatively inelastic because the Bahamas had no personal or corporate income taxes. Revenue was tied to indirect taxation on international trade, in the form of import, export, and stamp duties, and to direct taxes on tourist items, such as hotel rooms and casino gambling. Other direct taxes included a property tax, a motor vehicle tax, and a stamp tax. International trade taxes contributed the most to revenues, accounting for 70 percent of all tax revenues and 55 percent of total government revenues in 1984. In the first half of the 1980s, total tax revenue constituted up to 80 percent of total government revenues.

Nontax revenue included administrative fees and charges, income from government property, interest and dividends, and reimbursements. The largest of these were administrative fees and charges, which almost doubled in 1980; in 1984 they accounted for 40 percent of all nontax revenue and almost 9 percent of total revenue. Also in 1984, property revenue increased when the government signed a ten-year US$100 million agreement with the United States to lease submarine testing facilities on Andros Island. In the first half of the 1980s, nontax revenue generally accounted for approximately 20 to 27 percent of total revenue.

In the early 1980s, over 40 percent of government expenditures went to wages and salaries for public employees. Increases in capital expenditures in the 1981–83 period were responsible for much of the growth in total expenditures. In 1984, however, capital expenditures declined after completion of a major hotel, convention, and casino project. Much of the increase for this year went to current costs, principally salary increases. In the 1985 and 1986 budgets, the emphasis was on education, health, and police services.

A significant portion of total government outlays in the mid-1980s was devoted to servicing the public debt. Debt servicing accounted for 18 percent of total expenditures in 1984; it was projected to reach 25 percent in 1985 before dropping to 23 percent in 1986. Ironically, the debt problem was a direct result of the high per capita income in the Bahamas. Income levels precluded the nation from obtaining soft loans from international financial institutions, including the World Bank; as a consequence, the government was forced to rely on Bahamian banks for credit.

Outstanding public sector external debt increased by almost US$130 million in 1981–82 as a result of two loans that financed projects for the hotel corporation. The total external debt of the public sector reached a high of US$237.9 million in 1983 but had dropped to US$209.3 million by late 1984. The decline was brought about by the completion of the hotel project and also by the significant principal repayments made by the public corporations, most notably the electricity corporation, which repaid US$15 million of principal ahead of schedule. Traditionally, the external debt service ratio of the public sector has been low, fluctuating between 3 and 6 percent of exports of goods and services and 8 and 10 percent of government revenues. These figures remained unchanged despite the large loans in 1981 and 1982. They were unlikely to increase because the government had concluded a 1986 refinancing package with a commercial bank syndicate to lengthen the amortization schedule of the original hotel corporation loan.

The country's central financial institution was the Central Bank of the Bahamas. Established in 1974, it was charged with safeguarding the value of the Bahamian dollar, regulating credit and note issue, administering exchange control regulations, managing bank and trust legislation, and compiling financial statistics. The government's adoption of a code of conduct for the banking and finance industry in 1985 increased the Central Bank's supervisory role over that industry. The Central Bank adhered to a policy of strict discipline to create monetary stability and a strong balance of payments.

540

The Central Bank of the Bahamas, Nassau
Courtesy Mark P. Sullivan

The Bahamian dollar has been kept at par with the United States dollar since 1973. The Central Bank maintained an informal policy on interest rates, generally keeping local rates in line with movements in the United States. In April 1986 the Central Bank lowered its discount rate to 7.5 percent; commercial banks followed and cut their prime lending rate to 9 percent. Although the Central Bank had encouraged commercial·banks to lend to productive sectors of the economy rather than to consumers, banks were reluctant to adhere to that recommendation. Indeed, the percentage of private sector loans devoted to personal consumer use increased from 42.4 percent in 1977 to 61 percent in 1984.

In the mid-1980s, the Bahamas generally enjoyed a favorable balance of payments position. Large negative trade balances were counteracted by large inflows in the net services account. Despite these large inflows, however, the current account ran a deficit from 1981 through 1985. The net capital account registered surpluses in 1981–82 but went into deficit after 1983–85 in response to a reduction in public sector inflows following the completion of the hotel corporation's hotel and casino project. Net international reserves continually registered surpluses in the early 1980s; in 1984 especially, net reserves improved substantially to US$38 million and were expected to register a US$31 million surplus in 1985 (see table 8, Appendix A).

541

In the 1980s, the country's major nonpetroleum exports were pharmaceuticals, chemicals, rum, crawfish, salt, and aragonite. Major imports, including oil for domestic consumption, were foodstuffs, tobacco, beverages, machinery and transport equipment, automobiles, and finished manufactured goods, including furniture, clothing, footwear, toys, and jewelry. The United States was the most important trading partner in both exports and imports.

Transportation infrastructure on the islands was good. There were 3,350 kilometers of roads, of which 1,350 kilometers were paved and 1,250 were gravel. New Providence and Grand Bahama were the islands with the most extensive road systems, but good roads also were found on Cat Island, Long Island, Eleuthera, and on sections of Andros Island, Great Abaco Island, and Great Exuma Island. In 1985 there were 67,848 motor vehicles registered, 70 percent of which were concentrated in New Providence. Of the total number of vehicles, approximately 77 percent were private automobiles. The urban centers of Nassau and Freeport did not have major public transportation systems, relying instead on a plentiful supply of metered taxis; New Providence had a system of small minibuses known as jitneys. No railroads or inland waterway systems existed on the islands. Interisland transportation was served by charter, commercial, and private aircraft. The country had forty-nine government-run or private airfields, including two international airports (Nassau and Freeport) and one airfield run by the United States Air Force (Grand Bahama); nineteen of the airfields served as official ports of entry. Interisland travel was also covered by private boats and by a government mailboat system; approximately twenty mailboats departed Nassau for the Family Islands each week. The country had twenty-three ports, including the main harbors at Nassau and Freeport.

For a developing nation, the Bahamas possessed advanced telecommunications and international communications systems. An automatic telephone system provided service to 62,000 telephones. Both Nassau and Freeport had twenty-four-hour international telephone and telegraph service, whereas the Family Islands were generally served by only daytime service. The system was aided by a tropospheric scatter link station in Nassau and a Bahamas-Florida submarine cable that provided excellent reception and eliminated problems of atmospheric interference. Radio and television broadcasting was operated by the Broadcasting Corporation of the Bahamas. It ran three radio stations; ZNS-1 and ZNS-2 operated from Nassau, and ZNS-3 operated in Freeport to serve the northern islands. One color television station, ZNS-13, operated out of Nassau. It opened officially in 1977 and served an area within a 209-kilometer radius of Nassau.

Government and Politics

The Governmental System

In the late 1980s, the Bahamas had a democratic system based on the British Westminster parliamentary model of government. The 1973 Constitution proclaims the Bahamas a sovereign democratic state; sets requirements for citizenship; guarantees fundamental human rights; establishes the executive, legislative, and judicial branches of government; and creates three civil service commissions: the Public Service Commission, the Judicial and Legal Commission, and the Police Service Commission. Although an independent member of the Commonwealth of Nations since 1973, the Bahamas retains the British monarch as its chief of state, represented in the Bahamas by an appointed governor general (see Appendix B).

Chapter III (Articles 15–28) of the Constitution details the protection of fundamental rights and freedoms in the Bahamas, including the right to life, liberty, security, and protection of the law; freedom of conscience, expression, assembly, and association; and protection of the privacy of the home and other property from deprivation without compensation. Moreover, the Constitution provides for protection of these rights and freedoms without discrimination based on race, national origin, political opinion, color, creed, or sex. These provisions were not just theoretical considerations but were actually carried out in practice, according to the Department of State's *Country Reports on Human Rights Practices for 1986.*

Constitutional amendments require a combination of an act of Parliament and popular referendum. Entrenched constitutional provisions, such as those relating to the establishment of the civil service or the qualifications for members of Parliament, require a two-thirds majority in both houses and passage by a popular referendum. Specially entrenched provisions, such as those relating to citizenship, fundamental rights, and the establishment and powers of Parliament, the cabinet, and the judiciary, require a three-fourths majority in both houses and passage by referendum.

Parliament consists of a bicameral legislature made up of the sixteen-member Senate and the forty-nine-member House of Assembly. Parliament also technically includes the British monarch represented by the governor general, but that individual serves no real function in the daily parliamentary process. Under the

Constitution, Parliament may make laws for the peace and good government of the Bahamas. Laws are generally enacted by Parliament in the following manner. A bill is introduced in the House of Assembly, read three times, debated, and, if passed, becomes an act. The act is read three times in the Senate and then sent to the governor general. The governor general signs the act, which upon being published in the official journal of the government becomes a law. Bills may officially be introduced in either house of Parliament, except for money bills, which may only be introduced in the House of Assembly, and may be passed with or without amendment, subject to the agreement of both houses.

The House of Assembly elects one member from each of forty-three constituencies or single-member districts for terms not to exceed five years. The House of Assembly performs all major legislative functions. The leader of the majority party in the House is appointed prime minister by the governor general, and the leader of the major opposition party is designated as leader of the opposition. The House of Assembly elects a speaker and a deputy speaker to preside over the House.

The number of constituencies is established in Article 68 of the Constitution, but Article 70 mandates a procedural review of these constituencies at least every five years. The Constituencies Commission reviews the number and boundaries of the constituencies, taking into account the number of voters, the needs of sparsely populated areas, and the ability of elected members to maintain contact with voters from a wide geographic area. The Constituencies Commission consists of the speaker of the House of Assembly, a justice of the Supreme Court, and three members of the House of Assembly—two from the majority party and one from the opposition. The 1973 Constitution first established thirty-eight constituencies. That number was increased to forty-three in time for the 1982 elections and to forty-nine for the 1987 elections.

The Senate is appointed by the governor general. Nine members are chosen on the advice of the prime minister, four on the recommendation of the leader of the opposition, and the remaining three on the advice of the prime minister after consultation with the leader of the opposition. The Senate has limited functions in the parliamentary process. It elects a president and a vice president to preside over its proceedings.

The executive authority of government officially rests with the British monarch, represented by the governor general. The general direction and control of government, however, are vested in a cabinet, led by the prime minister, who serves as the chief executive of the government. The cabinet also consists of at least eight other ministers, including the attorney general, who are drawn from the membership of Parliament. In late 1987, the cabinet consisted of the Office of the Attorney General and the heads of eleven ministries: agriculture, trade, and industry; education; employment and immigration; finance; foreign affairs; health; housing and national insurance; tourism; transport and local government; works and utilities; and youth, sports, and community affairs. The minister of finance must be a member of the House of Assembly. If the attorney general is appointed from the Senate, no more than two other ministers may be drawn from the ranks of the Senate; if the attorney general is from the House of Assembly, however, three ministers may be chosen from the Senate. A number of parliamentary secretaries are also appointed from the membership of Parliament to assist the ministers. Permanent secretaries also serve in the ministries; they are appointed by the Public Service Commission to these highest civil service positions. Institutionally, the cabinet collectively is responsible to Parliament. The prime minister is responsible for keeping the governor general informed of the general conduct of the government.

The judiciary of the Bahamas is independent of executive control. It consists of the Court of Appeal at the highest level, followed by the Supreme Court, magistrate's courts, and Family Islands commissioners, who often act as magistrates. The Court of Appeal consists of a president and two other justices. If needed, a final appeal may be made to the Judicial Committee of the Privy Council in London. Bahamian law is based on English common law, but a large body of Bahamian statute law also exists.

Local government in the Family Islands falls administratively under the Department of Local Government of the cabinet's Ministry of Transport and Local Government. The Family Islands are divided into nineteen districts administered by twenty-three commissioners appointed by the government and supervised from Nassau. Several of the larger islands with relatively greater populations are split up into several districts (see table 9, Appendix A). In addition to the commissioners, elected House of Assembly members often deal with local matters, thereby filling the void created by the absence of an elected local government.

Political Dynamics

The history of Bahamian independence is not only the story of a colony breaking away from its mother country. It is also the account of how a political party and nationalist movement, the Progressive Liberal Party (PLP), achieved the peaceful transfer of political power from a white elite—the local allies of the colonial power—to an independent black government.

For decades prior to the achievement of internal self-government, the Bahamas' political and economic systems were dominated by a small elite referred to as the "Bay Street Boys," so named because most of their businesses and economic activities were concentrated along Bay Street in Nassau. The postwar era, however, brought about significant changes in the nation's political system and genuine political participation by the masses. In 1953 the first Bahamian political party, the PLP, was formed by blacks discontented with the policies of the governing elite; the PLP's popular success forced the elite in 1958 to form a party of its own, the United Bahamian Party (UBP).

Two events in the 1950s helped propel the PLP into a position of political strength. First, in 1956 an antidiscrimination resolution passed the House of Assembly and kindled political awareness among the black population. The PLP benefited from this awareness and became the party of black Bahamian pride. The second significant event, the 1958 general strike led by Randol Fawkes of the Bahamas Federation of Labour, strengthened the PLP's image as a champion of the working masses. Although the PLP was not directly involved in the strike at first, its leaders observed the strike's success and sought to be identified as the political party associated closely with it. The nineteen-day work stoppage focused world attention on the Bahamas and caused the British Colonial Office to give increased attention to Bahamian affairs. The strike also provided the impetus for electoral reform; the British added four legislative seats to New Providence.

Despite a vigorous campaign, the PLP lost badly to the UBP in the 1962 general election; the party attributed its overwhelming defeat to unfair electoral boundaries. Despite the PLP defeat, however, the UBP could not impede the process of political change in the Bahamas. Steps toward internal self-government proceeded under the UBP as party leader Sir Roland Symonette became the country's first premier (the preindependence title for prime minister) in 1964.

During the next several years of UBP rule, the PLP waged a media and propaganda campaign to focus attention on the alleged unfairness of electoral boundaries. A dramatic act of defiance occurred in 1965 when Lynden O. Pindling, then the official leader of the opposition, protested by throwing the speaker's mace out of a window when the House of Assembly was in session. The PLP proceeded to boycott the House for almost nine months. This action caused a split in the PLP as three House members broke off to form the National Democratic Party. In 1966 the remaining members of the PLP returned to the House, however, in

Rawson Square,
Bay Street, Nassau
Courtesy Mark P. Sullivan

Government House, Nassau
Courtesy Mark P. Sullivan

anticipation of upcoming elections; by 1967 new boundaries had been drawn. The PLP attacked the distribution of constituencies as well as the lack of limits on electoral expenses. Although race was an important issue in the elections, disclosures of UBP corruption and conflicts of interest concerning consultant fees and gambling at Freeport also became major campaign themes. The PLP won eighteen seats and was able to form a government with the help of the Labour Party formed by union leader Fawkes in the early 1960s. Pindling became premier of the nation's first independent black government; jubilant supporters labeled him ''Black Moses'' Pindling.

The PLP moved quickly to consolidate its political power base by calling for general elections in 1968. The election, which took place in an environment of intense racial polarization, resulted in an overwhelming PLP triumph as the party captured twenty-eight of the thirty-eight seats in the House of Assembly. In 1969 further constitutional changes followed a conference in London; full internal self-government was achieved, and Pindling became prime minister.

Although the PLP was riding high, the problem of internal party unrest continued. In 1970 eight PLP members of the House of Assembly were suspended from the party for acting ''contrary to the interests of the party.'' This faction went on to form a new party known as the Free Progressive Liberal Party, severely slashing the PLP's majority in the House of Assembly. In 1971 opposition groups united under the banner of a new party, the Free National Movement (FNM); its membership consisted of the Free Progressive Liberal Party, the remnants of the UBP, and the small NDP.

Despite a united opposition in the 1972 general elections, the PLP achieved a commanding parliamentary majority, winning twenty-eight seats compared with the FNM's ten. The PLP's tabling of the independence issue in 1972 caused a split in the already weak opposition. Several long-standing UBP members who opposed independence resigned from the FNM, leaving the party weak and divided. The FNM party was weakened further as independence arrived in 1973. In 1976 five FNM House members resigned and formed the Bahamian Democratic Party (BDP).

General elections in 1977 consisted of competition among the PLP, the FNM, the new BDP, and a small party known as the Vanguard Nationalist and Socialist Party (Vanguard Party), which had been formed in 1971 by some members of the PLP's youth organization. The PLP once again scored a resounding victory, winning thirty House seats compared with six for the BDP and two for the FNM; the Vanguard Party received only fifty-five votes in five contested races. By 1979 the major opposition parties had merged once again into a reconstituted FNM. The House was increased to forty-three seats for the 1982 general elections; the election itself was a contest among the PLP, the FNM, and the Vanguard Party. Once again the PLP emerged victorious with 32 seats to the FNM's 11 seats; the Vanguard Party, contesting 18 seats and receiving just 173 votes, did not win any representation.

The PLP's continued popularity and electoral successes since its first victory in 1967 were explained by several factors. Under Pindling's leadership, major public works and government-sponsored housing programs improved material conditions for the majority of Bahamians. In addition, PLP victories reflected socio-political stability and therefore stimulated private enterprise. In fact, improved material conditions under PLP rule were most probably brought about by the increased economic opportunities for all Bahamians. PLP popularity was also reinforced by several royal visits in the 1970s and 1980s. Prime Minister Pindling himself, the father of Bahamian independence and a charismatic leader, was an important factor in PLP success. Finally, the PLP benefited from the weakness of the opposition. In the late 1980s, the FNM had no experience in office, nor did it espouse an ideology or program attractive enough to draw voters away from the PLP, which remained the party identified with black majority rule and the attainment of Bahamian nationhood.

In 1987 the PLP and the FNM remained the two major political parties, represented respectively by Prime Minister Pindling and Kendal Isaacs, the leader of the opposition in the House. Both parties were moderate pro-Western parties committed to democracy and free enterprise. The racial factor had ceased to be an issue in Bahamian politics, as both political parties had a black majority. A few white Bahamians held high-level civil service and political positions. Women participated in all levels of government and politics; in 1987 several women served as permanent secretaries of the executive government, one as a member of the House, and four as members of the Senate.

The nation's political culture in the 1980s was characterized by a strong tradition of freedom of speech and freedom of the press. Three privately owned daily newspapers, two published in Nassau and one in Freeport, were printed. The newspapers frequently carried reports of parliamentary and public debate. In addition, several newsweeklies, some of which were published by political parties, were available. Although the press was free and privately run, radio and television stations were run solely by the government and were accused of restricting access for the opposition. The government and the PLP received favorable treatment from the broadcasting corporation to the detriment of the FNM and even PLP dissidents. In an attempt to overcome this broadcasting barrier, in late 1986, the FNM broadcast a fiery speech by Isaacs from a privately owned radio station in Florida.

The June 1987 general elections took place against a backdrop of government corruption vis-à-vis the transit of illegal drugs, related socioeconomic problems of rising crime and increased drug addiction, and redrawing of electoral boundaries. Prime Minister Pindling's government was hit by a major drug scandal soon after his 1982 electoral triumph. A 1983 report on United States television alleged that the prime minister was involved in the drug trade. Pindling responded by establishing a Royal Commission of Inquiry to investigate the charge. In its December 1984 finding, the commission contended that the drug trade permeated Bahamian society. Several ministers and senior government officials were implicated, as well as the Police Force and the Customs Department and Immigration Department. Although the report did not offer any evidence of direct involvement by Pindling, it did note that the prime minister had spent eight times more money than he had earned over a seven-year period.

The scandal caused a major shake-up in the PLP government. In October 1984, finance minister and PLP deputy leader Arthur Hanna resigned in protest of Pindling's handling of the situation. Two ministers who opposed Pindling's actions were dismissed by the prime minister as he defended his political position, and two others resigned because of investigations of their involvement in the drug trade. Although Pindling was untouched by evidence, his political position was weakened by the seriousness of the charges involved. Nevertheless, the prime minister refused to call early elections and decided to weather the political storm.

The drug transit issue also was intimately related to many of the nation's socioeconomic problems, including a rising crime rate and a substantial increase in drug addiction. These problems had also been fueled by a high unemployment rate, particularly among the nation's youth. In 1986 the Bahamas National Task Force Against Drugs reported that the domestic drug trade had assumed epidemic proportions; the ready availability of cocaine had resulted in high addiction levels.

In the mid-1980s, several private programs attempted to address the problem. Following the report of the Royal Commission of Inquiry, the government became increasingly involved in combating drug addiction. Legislation in 1986 introduced stiff penalties for drug traffickers. In late 1986, the government's Drug Abuse Rehabilitation Program received funds from the United Nations Fund for Drug Abuse Control to increase activities in the prevention and treatment of drug abuse. The government also increased spending for the Royal Bahamas Defence Force (RBDF), most of which was directed to antidrug operations.

In 1986 the Constituencies Commission's procedural review of electoral constituencies for the House of Assembly prompted significant political debate. The commission proposed adding six seats to the forty-three-member House; five seats would be added for New Providence and one for Grand Bahama. The opposition FNM objected to the addition of so many seats for New Providence, when only 1,500 voters had been added to the electoral register since the 1982 general elections. They also alleged that this was a deliberate scheme to slow electoral registration in Grand Bahama, an FNM stronghold. For the 1982 elections, 11,803 voters were registered in Grand Bahama, whereas only 8,696 were registered for the 1987 elections; according to an FNM member of Parliament, the number of voters would have been considerably higher if the registration process had not been slowed. Criticism was also made of the high representation given to Andros Island when compared with Great Abaco Island and Eleuthera. In 1982 Andros Island had three constituencies with voter registrations of 3,542, as compared with Great Abaco Island's two constituencies with voter registrations of 3,213 and Eleuthera's three constituencies with voter registrations of 5,100. The Constituencies Commission for 1987 proposed no changes in these electorates despite the increase of Great Abaco Island's voters to 3,608 and the decrease of Andros Island's voters to 3,368, along with Eleuthera's continued 5,100 voters. Opposition leaders also criticized the addition of electoral constituencies in general because it indicated an unwillingness to delegate power to local government; adding constituencies to the House of Assembly continued the system whereby members represented both national and local interests.

Observers had generally agreed that the 1987 election would be the closest in Bahamian history; indeed, many believed that Isaacs would lead the FNM to victory. However, the PLP scored a stunning triumph, capturing 54 percent of the votes and 31 of the 49 House seats. The FNM gained fifteen seats, and two went to independent candidates. The winner of the remaining seat was undetermined as of late June 1987. In an electoral postmortem, Isaacs indicated that public concern over corruption was apparently not as significant as he had thought. Equally important, however, was Pindling's skillful appeal to nationalistic sentiments during the campaign. Responding to United States government criticisms of the Bahamian drug problem, the prime minister charged that his country had become the scapegoat for the inability of the United States to control drugs. In one rally, Pindling turned the tables on the United States by accusing the Central Intelligence Agency and Drug Enforcement Administration of running drugs through the Bahamas. Pindling also gained political mileage through his public expressions of outrage over the decision of a subcommittee of the United States Senate Foreign Relations committee to send a delegation to monitor the election. In the wake of the PLP's electoral success, many expected in mid-1987 to see the political rehabilitation of at least some of the cabinet members who had resigned over their alleged involvement in the drug trade.

Foreign Relations

Although it is a small developing nation, the Bahamas has managed to involve itself in a wide range of international affairs. It became a member of the United Nations (UN) in 1973. In the late 1980s, the Bahamas belonged to a number of international organizations, including the World Bank, the General Agreement on Tariffs and Trade (de facto), the International Monetary Fund (IMF—see Glossary), the International Civil Aviation Organization, the World Health Organization, and the World Meteorological Organization. The Bahamas also belonged to several other intergovernmental organizations, such as the Pan American Health Organization, as well as to several regional development banks, including the European Investment Bank, the IDB, and the Caribbean Development Bank. It was a signatory of the Treaty for the Prohibition of Nuclear Weapons in Latin America (Tlatelolco Treaty) and a member of the Nonaligned Movement. Regionally, the Bahamas was a member of the Organization of American States (OAS) and the Caribbean Community and Common Market (Caricom—see Appendix C).

In the first few years following independence, the Bahamas identified closely with United States interests. By the early 1980s, however, it was evident that the Bahamas was moving toward greater involvement in regional and international affairs and was not necessarily seeking to satisfy the United States. It joined the OAS in 1982 and Caricom in 1983 after a lengthy period of close cooperation with the latter organization. In 1984 it hosted Caricom's seventh Heads of Government Conference. The Bahamas opposed the 1983 United States-Caribbean intervention in Grenada, labeling it a "premature overreaction," and declared that there should be no intervention in the affairs of other states.

Town of Great Guana Cay, Great Abaco Island
Courtesy John F. Hornbeck

Since independence, the Bahamas has been a member of the Commonwealth of Nations (see Appendix B), the organization bringing together nations and dependent territories presently or previously under British sovereignty. In 1985 the Bahamas hosted a Meeting of Heads of Government of the Commonwealth; Queen Elizabeth II paid an official visit to the Bahamas at that time. As a former British colony, the Bahamas also was one of the African, Caribbean, or Pacific countries affiliated with the European Economic Community under the Lomé Convention (see Glossary).

Although the Bahamas had diplomatic relations with over forty nations throughout the world, it maintained diplomatic missions in only four countries: Canada, Britain, Haiti, and the United States. High commissioners served as official representatives to Canada and Britain, whereas a chargé d'affaires was assigned to Haiti. Bahamian officials in the United States included an ambassador in Washington and consuls general in both Miami and New York. The Bahamas also maintained a permanent mission to the UN in New York with a resident ambassador.

Just five nations maintained diplomatic or consular missions in the Bahamas. The United States and Haiti each had embassies, the Dominican Republic and The Gambia had consulates, and Brazil maintained a vice consulate. The Gambia maintained a

553

consulate as a result of close relations with the Bahamas in the Commonwealth and because a majority of Bahamians were of West African origin. Additionally, twenty-five nonresident ambassadors and thirteen nonresident high commissioners (ambassador-level representatives of Commonwealth nations) were accredited to the Bahamas. The Honorary Consul Corps provided representatives from twenty-five countries; these officials assisted foreign nationals in emergencies. The corps consisted of, in descending order of rank, consuls, honorary consuls, consular agents, and commercial representatives.

Traditionally, the most important factor influencing Bahamian foreign relations has been the nation's geography, especially its proximity to the United States, Cuba, and Haiti. Of these three neighbors, the United States has been the most important. Throughout Bahamian history, the United States has played a significant role in the nation's economy.

In the late 1980s, the United States and the Bahamas were parties to over thirty treaties and agreements covering aviation, consuls, customs, defense, extradition, investment guarantees, postal matters, property, shipping, social security, taxation, telecommunications, trademarks, visas, and weather stations. The United States also operated naval and air facilities in the Bahamas. The United States Navy's Atlantic Underseas Test and Evaluation Center, located on Andros Island, was involved in underwater research and submarine testing. On Grand Bahama, the United States Air Force operated an auxiliary airfield that assisted the United States National Aeronautics and Space Administration in tracking test flights from Cape Canaveral. In April 1984, the Bahamas signed an agreement whereby the United States would pay US$100 million over a 10-year period for the use of these sites. In addition to an embassy in Nassau, the United States also maintained preclearance units at the nation's two international airports at Freeport and Nassau. The units were composed of employees of the Customs Service, the Department of Agriculture's Plant and Animal Inspection Service, and the Immigration and Naturalization Service and were designed to help United States travelers complete their customs and immigration formalities before entering the United States.

In March 1985, the Bahamas was designated a beneficiary of the Caribbean Basin Initiative (CBI—see Appendix D). As a result of the structure of the Bahamian economy, however, the CBI had virtually no impact on the Bahamian economy. The Bahamas was unable to participate in the special tax provision involving deductions for business people because it had not entered into a tax information exchange agreement with the United States. In a December 1986 speech to Parliament, Prime Minister Pindling asserted that limited trade concessions meant little in an environment of slow global economic expansion, declining commodity prices, and rising protectionism.

Beginning in 1980, the Bahamas and the United States agreed to intensify efforts to hinder the illegal flow of drugs, and they coordinated a drug interdiction program (see Current Strategic Considerations, ch. 7). The United States Anti-Drug Abuse Act of 1986 authorized the establishment of the United States-Bahamas Drug Interdiction Force and the construction of a joint United States Coast Guard-Bahamas drug interdiction docking facility. The law authorized expenditures for helicopters and improved communications detection equipment. The Bahamas-United States Mutual Legal Assistance Treaty, designed to hinder drug traffickers from money laundering, was expected to be signed in late 1987.

Although the United States had more drug interdiction agreements with the Bahamas than with any other country, United States officials in the late 1980s at times questioned Pindling's commitment to the narcotics control effort. In 1987 the Bahamian government took umbrage at various statements on this issue by United States officials, regarding them as unacceptable intrusions in the islands' domestic politics. The Pindling government responded by engaging in such actions as temporarily suspending the airport parking privileges of the United States ambassador. It remained to be seen whether Pindling would engage in more substantive retaliation in the wake of his impressive electoral triumph in June 1987.

The country's proximity to Haiti has made it a haven for economic refugees from that nation. The number of illegal Haitian immigrants has increased steadily over the last several decades, as have accompanying social and economic problems. Haitian immigrants began to trickle into the Bahamas in 1948; by the late 1950s, that trickle was described by government officials as a flood. Roundups and deportations began at that time and reached an annual high of 2,899 deportees in 1963, when the government resolved to clear out the illegals. Following the election of a black independent government in 1967, a change in official policy was expected; a leading PLP figure indicated that expulsion was out of the question because so many Haitian illegals were raising families. The new government, however, initiated a repatriation program similar to that in 1963 and deported 2,589 Haitians in 1967.

Illegal Haitian immigrants kept arriving despite the regular roundups and detentions and the implementation of a new "Bahamas for Bahamians" policy that was intended to phase out the employment of expatriates. According to the 1973 Constitution, those born in the Bahamas to noncitizen parents may register for citizenship only at age eighteen or within twelve months of that birthday, provided that no dual citizenship is involved. (Before independence every person born in the Bahamas was able to claim Bahamian citizenship.) Despite these restrictions, by early 1980 the illegal Haitian immigration had reached enormous proportions, with an estimated 25,000 in a country having fewer than 210,000 people.

The situation developed into a major political issue as the expense of health care and other services for these illegals increased along with Bahamian unemployment. In September 1985, some alleviation was noted when the governments of the Bahamas and Haiti signed a treaty whereby Haitians who arrived prior to 1981 would be legalized. A two-month voluntary repatriation period was established, after which deportation would be carried out in an orderly and humane manner. As of early 1987, however, an estimated 20,000 to 40,000 Haitians still resided in the country. None had been accorded legal status under the terms of the treaty. About 2,000 had been repatriated, but many of those detained for deportation were quartered in less than humane facilities. In 1986 it was estimated that over 300 Haitians had returned voluntarily. Both the United States Department of State and human rights groups in the Bahamas have expressed concern over the treatment of illegal Haitians.

For years, Bahamian relations with Cuba were strained by disagreement over territorial fishing rights. The disagreement came to a head in May 1980, when Cuban military aircraft sank a Bahamian patrol vessel, the *Flamingo,* after it had apprehended two Cuban fishing boats; four Bahamian marines were killed during the event (see Regional Security Threats, 1970–81, ch. 7). The Bahamas demanded an unconditional apology and full reparations. Cuba agreed to the Bahamian demand and paid US$5 million to replace the patrol vessel and US$400,000 to the families of the four marines. The two nations continued diplomatic relations despite the incident. In May 1986 a new nonresident Cuban ambassador presented his credentials to the government and encouraged the development of Bahamian-Cuban diplomatic, commercial, and cultural relations. Cuba was the only communist nation with which the Bahamas maintained diplomatic relations.

Although Bahamian relations with Britain in the late 1980s were most often overshadowed by its relations with its giant neighbor to the north, important links persisted. Over 300 years of British colonial rule left many relations still intact. Membership in the

Commonwealth increased Bahamian contact with former British colonies around the globe. Important linkages also existed in legal institutions, such as the right of Bahamians to final, judicial appeal to the Judicial Committee of the Privy Council in London. British cultural influence on the Bahamas was also strong. Finally, although trade between the two nations was relatively small compared with trade with the United States, it was still significant. In 1984 Bahamian domestic exports to Britain were 7.2 percent of the total figure; imports from Britain accounted for approximately 7.7 percent of the Bahamian total.

National Security

In the late 1980s, Bahamian security concerns focused on three areas: the use of Bahamian waters and territory as a transit point for the illegal transshipment of drugs; illegal immigration; and the poaching of Bahamian fishing resources. Since 1980 the Royal Bahamas Defence Force (RBDF) has been the primary force in combating these threats to national security. In 1986 the RBDF was a 531-member force headed by a commander and headquartered at a base at Coral Harbour on New Providence.

Government expenditures for the RBDF were US$9.1 million in 1984, approximately 2.5 percent of total government expenditures; estimates for 1985 and 1986 spending were in the same range. In late 1986, the force commissioned three new thirty-three-meter craft, which greatly increased its effectiveness. The high-speed boats were fitted with modern electronic surveillance and navigational equipment to combat illegal immigration, poaching, and smuggling. The RBDF also was equipped with one thirty-one-meter patrol craft, five eighteen-meter craft, and several high-speed boats for shallow water patrols in the Family Islands. In 1986 a new dry dock was planned at Coral Harbour to allow the RBDF to carry out its own maintenance and repairs. The force also had a small air wing; in late 1986 plans called for a compound to be established at Nassau International Airport. Basic training for marines took place at Coral Harbour, whereas officers were trained at the Royal Naval College in Dartmouth, England. Both marines and officers were sent on special training courses to Canada, Britain, and the United States.

Since 1980 the United States has assisted the Bahamas in combating the transit of illegal drugs. In 1986 a joint interdiction force was established. A joint docking facility was planned, and the United States Congress provided four EC–2 carrier-based radar aircraft to track drug airplanes passing through the Bahamas.

Internal security was provided by the Royal Bahamas Police Force. The Police Force, headed by a commissioner, had a strength of 1,447 in 1983, 75 percent of whom were concentrated in New Providence. At the end of 1981, thirty-one police stations served the Family Islands (excluding Grand Bahama). In the early 1980s, police stations in New Providence, Grand Bahama, Great Abaco Island (Marsh Harbour), Andros Island (Nicolls Town), the Bimini Islands (Alice Town), and Eleuthera (Governor's Harbour and Rock Sound) provided twenty-four-hour service, whereas other Family Islands stations provided service for approximately ten to sixteen hours a day.

Although both the defense and the police forces were generally well regarded by the population, both had been beset by some drug-related corruption. A Royal Commission of Inquiry in 1984 concluded that corruption existed in the upper and lower levels of the Police Force as well as in the Immigration Department and Customs Department. Another problem in the Police Force in the 1980s was police brutality, especially in the course of arrests or in obtaining confessions. The Department of State's *Country Reports on Human Rights Practices for 1986* stated that police brutality remained a problem; in 1986 both United States and Bahamian detainees reported abuses.

In 1984 expenditures for the Police Force amounted to US$25.9 million, 7 percent of total government expenditures; estimates for expenditures in 1985 and 1986 were for absolute increases of approximately US$4 million for each year. The Police College provided training for all recruits and refresher courses for officers, police reservists, beach wardens, and local constables. Recruits were given a twenty-week basic course, which included physical training, self-defense, firearms use, and first aid. The Fire Services Division consisted of regular fire brigades in New Providence and Grand Bahama and voluntary fire brigades in the Family Islands. The Criminal Investigation Department was responsible for investigating major crime throughout the Bahamas.

In 1987 a planned reorganization of the Police Force was expected to focus on general administration, the local and overseas training of officers, and criminal investigation procedures. Several additional police stations also were planned, and new recruitment was expected to increase the strength of the force. Improvements in transportation were expected, as concern continued over transportation conditions for police in the Family Islands.

Bahamian prisons were operated by the Prisons Department of the Ministry of National Security. In 1983 the department housed 806 prisoners: 100 female prisoners and 706 male prisoners, including 82 first offenders, 224 regular prisoners, 200 in medium security, and 200 illegal immigrants. In the late 1980s, prisons were reported to be overcrowded and unsanitary. In September 1986, the Supreme Court noted that prison conditions constituted a "highly unpleasant environment" and urged improvement. Much of the overcrowding was caused by the detainment of Haitians for immigration violations; they were routinely denied bail on the basis that they would flee before prosecution. In 1986 Bahamian human rights activists condemned the inhumane and degrading facilities at Fox Hill Prison, the main prison on New Providence; according to reports, 300 Haitians had been crowded in the prison for two and one-half years awaiting deportation. The Department of State's *Country Reports on Human Rights Practices for 1986* noted that Nassau's downtown jail was crowded and dirty and that food was barely adequate. The report also stated that the central lockup facility at Freeport was unsanitary.

* * *

The best general guide to the Bahamas is the *Bahamas Handbook and Businessman's Annual,* which provides a comprehensive description of most aspects of Bahamian society, including demographic, economic, and political details. Some of the best studies of Bahamian history include Paul Albury's *The Story of the Bahamas,* Michael Craton's *A History of the Bahamas,* and Doris Johnson's *The Quiet Revolution in the Bahamas.* Craton's work also includes a concise chapter on the Pindling era. The most comprehensive study, however, of contemporary Bahamian politics is provided by Colin A. Hughes in *Race and Politics in the Bahamas.* The best study of the nation's economy is provided by the World Bank in *The Bahamas: Economic Report,* published in 1986. Other current sources of economic data are reports by the United Nations Economic Commission for Latin America and the Caribbean, the Inter-American Development Bank, and the United States Department of Commerce. The best source for demographic data is the government of the Bahamas, which has published several population studies. The Department of Statistics of the Bahamas also publishes accurate, informative statistics in a variety of recurring reports. (For further information and complete citations, see Bibliography.)

Cayman Islands

Official Name .... Cayman Islands

Term for Citizens .... Caymanian(s)

Capital .... George Town

Political Status .... British crown colony

Form of Government .... British-appointed governor and locally elected assembly

Geography
Size .... 260 sq. km.
Topography .... Low-lying limestone and coral islands
Climate .... Tropical

Population
Total estimated in 1985 20,000
Annual growth rate (in percentage) in 1985 .... 3.5
Life expectancy at birth in 1984 70
Adult literacy rate (in percentage) in 1986 .... 97.5
Language .... English
Ethnic groups ..... Black (25 percent), white (20 percent), mulatto (55 percent)
Religion .... Primarily Protestant

Economy
Currency; exchange rate .... Cayman Islands dollar (CI$); CI$0.84 = US$1.00
Gross domestic product (GDP) in 1985 .. US$254.5 million
Per capita GDP in 1985 .... US$12,789
Distribution of GDP .... Not available

National Security
Armed forces personnel 0
Paramilitary personnel 0
Police 170

Turks and Caicos Islands

Official Name .... Turks and Caicos Islands

Term for Citizens .... No standard term

Capital .... Cockburn Town

Political Status .... British crown colony

Form of Government .... British-appointed governor
and locally elected assembly

Geography
Size .... 430 sq. km.
Topography .... Low-lying coral islands
Climate .... Tropical

Population
Total estimated in 1985 8,600
Annual growth rate (in percentage) in 1985 .... 3.3
Life expectancy at birth in 1985 .... 70.2
Adult literacy rate (in percentage) in 1985 .... 86.7
Language .... English
Ethnic groups .... Black (90 percent);
remainder white or mulatto
Religion .... Primarily Protestant

Economy
Currency .... United States dollar (US$)
Gross domestic product (GDP) in 1984 .... US$26 million
Per capita GDP in 1984 .... US$3,478
Distribution of GDP .... Not available

National Security
Armed forces personnel 0
Paramilitary personnel 0
Police 90

British Dependencies:
The Cayman Islands and the Turks and Caicos Islands

The Cayman Islands and the Turks and Caicos Islands are two British dependencies in the northern part of the Caribbean. The Cayman Islands consist of three islands: Grand Cayman, Little Cayman, and Cayman Brac. The capital is George Town, on Grand Cayman. The Turks and Caicos Islands consist of some forty islands forming the southeastern end of the Bahamas archipelago. The capital is Cockburn Town, on Grand Turk Island. English is the official language of both territories.

Christopher Columbus sighted the Caymans during his 1503 voyage, naming them "Las Tortugas" because of the large number of turtles he found there. By 1530 the islands were known as the Caymanus, a name that may have derived from confusion between the iguana, which is found on the islands, and the alligator (*cayman* in Spanish). Ponce de Leon is generally believed to have discovered the Turks and Caicos in 1512, but some scholars still speculate that Columbus may have landed on one of the islands, probably East Caicos or Grand Turk Island, on his great voyage in 1492.

No serious effort was made to settle either group of islands in the first decades after European discovery. Ships of various nations stopped at the Caymans to get food, mainly turtles. Both groups of islands became haunts for pirates, particularly the Turks and Caicos. From there, raiders attacked Spanish galleons sailing from Cuba, Hispaniola (the island containing present-day Haiti and the Dominican Republic), and Central America en route to Europe. The earliest European settlers in both territories were a mixture of buccaneers, shipwrecked sailors, and debtors.

Spain held early control over the Caymans, but the islands were ceded by Spain to the English crown in 1670 under the terms of the Treaty of Madrid. The first British settlement took place in 1734 after the first land grant. After 1734 most of the colonists came from Jamaica, and the Caymans became a dependency of Jamaica. The islands of Cayman Brac and Little Cayman were settled in 1833 by several families from Grand Cayman, but no administrative connection existed until a justice of the peace arrived on Cayman Brac in 1877. Sailing ships continued to visit the islands into the nineteenth century, but later steamships stopped rarely. Life in the Caymans was generally quiet until the middle of the twentieth century.

The Turks and Caicos, located closer to colonial territories held by various European powers, had a more colorful early history.

The first permanent settlers were salt collectors from Bermuda who arrived on Grand Turk Island in 1678. They successfully defended their settlement against a Bahamian annexation attempt in 1700, a Spanish invasion in 1710, and a French invasion in 1763. The French succeeded with their second attempt, in 1764, and exiled the Bermudians to Haiti. By the beginning of the nineteenth century, however, the British had regained control and made the Turks and Caicos part of the Bahamas. In 1848 the islands separated from the Bahamas and briefly had their own president and council until Jamaica annexed them in 1874 and made them a Jamaican dependency.

Both the Caymans and the Turks and Caicos remained formal Jamaican dependencies until 1959, and the governor of Jamaica held responsibility for them until Jamaican independence in 1962. At that point, both territories became separate British dependencies. The Caymans created a separate constitution in 1959, and a British administrator was appointed for the Caymans in 1962 (the title was changed to governor in 1971). The 1959 Constitution was revised in 1972. The Turks and Caicos received their own governor in 1972 and established a new constitution in 1976.

In the late 1980s, the Cayman Islands were politically stable and highly prosperous by Caribbean standards. Tourism and offshore banking (see Glossary) and financial services, the latter made possible by the islands' tax-haven status, were the two main industries.

Although not as prosperous as the Cayman Islands, the Turks and Caicos Islands also relied on tourism and offshore financial services as mainstays of their economy. Economic similarities between the two British dependencies, however, did not carry over to the political sphere; politics in the Turks and Caicos was much more contentious. In 1985 these islands were rocked by a major drug scandal, when the chief minister, the minister of commerce and development, and another member of the Legislative Council were arrested in Miami in a "sting" operation run by the United States Drug Enforcement Administration (DEA). The operation was carried out with the full knowledge and consent of the British governor on the Turks and Caicos and the British government in London. The governor has taken a strong stand against drug smuggling and alleged corruption, a position that has helped restore the confidence of foreign investors.

Geography

The Cayman Islands are located in the Caribbean Sea south of Cuba, from which they are separated at the closest point by about 240 kilometers (see fig. 19). The three islands are an outcropping of the Cayman Ridge, a submarine mountain range that extends west from the Sierra Maestra mountain range in Cuba. Grand Cayman is the largest of the islands with a total area of 195 square kilometers. Cayman Brac, 142 kilometers northeast of Grand Cayman, is only 20 kilometers long by 2 kilometers wide. Little Cayman, eight kilometers west of Cayman Brac, is sixteen kilometers by two kilometers in size. The total land area of the three islands is 260 square kilometers, or approximately that of Austin, Texas.

All three islands are low lying and are composed of limestone and consolidated coral. A seventeen-meter hill at the northwest tip of Grand Cayman is its highest point. The highest point on Little Cayman is only twelve meters in elevation. Cayman Brac is distinguished by a forty-three-meter limestone cliff that rises from the sea on its eastern tip. Vegetation is largely scrub with mangrove swamps covering about a third of all the islands' area.

The climate is tropical, tempered by the northeasterly trade winds. Temperatures are fairly constant, ranging from summer maximums of 30°C to winter minimums of 20°C. The rainy season extends from mid-May through October; the remaining months are relatively dry. Hurricanes pose a threat from midsummer until November, although no hurricane has struck the islands directly since 1932.

Located 920 kilometers southeast of Miami and about 50 kilometers southeast of the Bahamian island of Mayaguana, the Turks and Caicos are a group of 8 major islands and more than 40 small islets and cays (see Glossary). The islands are made up of two groups separated by the thirty-five-kilometer-wide Turks Island Passage: the westernmost Caicos Islands, including six of the major islands, and the easternmost Turks Islands with the remaining two major islands (see fig. 20). The islands have a total land area of 430 square kilometers, about the size of San José, California.

Geologically, the islands are a part of the Bahamas archipelago, which rises above a shallow submarine platform. All are low lying, with the highest point barely fifteen meters above sea level. Soils are poor, shallow, and infertile. Low scrub covers most of the islands, although several of the larger Caicos Islands have stands of pine. Mangrove swamps fringe coastal areas. No streams are found on the islands, but a few have brackish ponds.

The climate is tropical with distinct wet and dry seasons. Annual precipitation varies from 100 to 150 centimeters. Rain falls in heavy brief showers, almost entirely in the period from May to October. Temperatures average 27°C in summer and 21°C in winter. Maximums and minimums seldom exceed 32°C or 16°C.

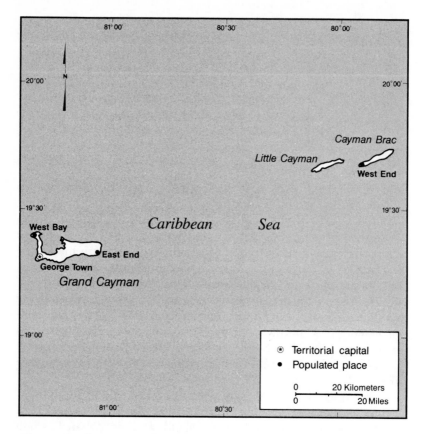

Figure 19. Cayman Islands, 1987

In summer, trade winds blow from the southeast, whereas in winter the northeast trades predominate. Hurricanes occasionally affect the islands in late summer or fall.

Population

The total estimated population of the Cayman Islands in 1985 was 20,000, growing at an annual rate of 3.5 percent. Ninety percent of the population lived on Grand Cayman; most of the remainder lived on Cayman Brac. Little Cayman had very few inhabitants, but the construction of tourist facilities there was increasingly attracting workers and other residents. Immigrant workers comprised about a third of the total population on the islands and held 20 percent of the jobs.

The population density per square kilometer in 1985 was moderate at 75.8. In 1984 the average life expectancy at birth stood at seventy years. In 1984 the birth rate was moderately high by world standards at 21.4 per 1,000; infant mortality stood at 5.9 per 1,000 live births. Twenty-nine percent of the population was under the age of fifteen. The people of the Cayman Islands had varying ethnic backgrounds: 25 percent were black; 20 percent, white; and 55 percent, mulatto.

The Turks and Caicos had a 1985 population of approximately 8,600, growing at an annual rate of 3.3 percent. The population continued to fluctuate, however, because of a high birth rate and the constant movement of young men in search of work between the Turks and Caicos and the Bahamas. Blacks made up 90 percent of the total; the remainder were mulatto or white.

Although the Turks and Caicos were still relatively undeveloped in the mid-1980s, some illegal immigrant workers, mostly from Haiti and the Dominican Republic, arrived in the islands to perform low-wage hotel jobs spurned by local citizens. Although their labor contributed to the tourism industry, in 1985 the illegals became such a burden on the islands' already-overstretched funds for health and welfare that the government made its first forced deportation of Haitians.

Population density in the Turks and Caicos Islands remained very low, at sixteen persons per square kilometer. In 1982 the birth rate was a moderately high 25.5 per 1,000; infant mortality stood at 24 per 1,000 live births. In 1985 the average life expectancy at birth was 70.2 years.

The people of both territories were predominantly Protestant. In the mid-1980s, 35 percent of the Caymanians were Presbyterian; 25 percent belonged to the Church of God; and 40 percent belonged to other Christian churches. Approximately 42 percent of the citizens of the Turks and Caicos Islands were Baptist; 19 percent, Methodist; 17 percent, Anglican; and 22 percent, members of other Christian churches.

Education

Education in the Cayman Islands and the Turks and Caicos Islands was compulsory for children between the ages of five and sixteen and free of charge in government schools. The Cayman Islands had nine government-run primary schools, three state secondary schools, and six church-sponsored schools at both levels. The Turks and Caicos had fourteen government primary schools, three private primary schools, and three public secondary schools. Years of inadequate funding left the Turks and Caicos Islands with poor schools, making later job training a necessity. Although some fishermen in these islands were retrained as construction workers and others found jobs in the hotels, more retraining was essential. The territory had a chronic shortage of skilled workers.

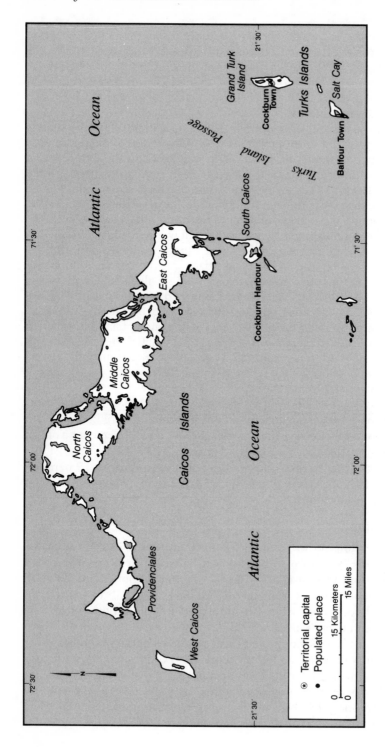

Figure 20. Turks and Caicos Islands, 1987

There were two senior education institutions on the Cayman Islands: the Cayman International College and the Cayman Law School. In addition, the Cayman government contributed to the University of the West Indies (UWI). Both the Cayman Islands and the Turks and Caicos Islands offered a number of government scholarships for students who wished to attend the UWI or colleges or universities in Britain, Canada, or the United States.

Literacy for Caymanians above the age of 15 stood at 97.5 percent in 1986. In 1986 the ratio of elementary school students to teachers was a relatively low 14.3 to 1. The elementary school enrollment that year was 2,077, with an additional 2,265 students in secondary schools. Only 2.9 percent of the population over age 25 had postsecondary education.

Literacy for Turks and Caicos citizens over age 15 was 86.7 percent in 1985. The 1985 ratio of elementary school students to teachers was 20.8 to 1. In 1985 approximately 1,540 students attended elementary schools, and 707 attended secondary schools. Although overall literacy was lower than in the Cayman Islands, a higher percentage of the population over 25 years of age—4.9 percent—had postsecondary education.

Health and Welfare

In the 1980s, health care in the Cayman Islands compared favorably with the situation found elsewhere in the Commonwealth Caribbean. Mirroring a pattern seen in developed societies, the major causes of death were noncommunicable diseases, especially those of the circulatory system. Ninety percent of children were immunized against diphtheria, pertussis, tetanus, and poliomyelitis as of 1984. Increased attention was given to environmental health issues in the wake of the economic growth that occurred in the late 1970s. Grand Cayman had a privately operated desalination plant that provided high-quality water. Little Cayman and Cayman Brac employed a cistern and groundwater supply combination. Despite the generally positive picture, health officials were concerned with a growing substance abuse problem, inadequate mental health care, and an absence of nursing homes. As of December 1986, the Cayman Islands had reported one case of acquired immune deficiency syndrome (AIDS).

Inpatient and outpatient services were available at two government-administered hospitals on Grand Cayman and Cayman Brac; these institutions contained a total of sixty-six beds in 1984. Maternal and child care, immunizations, and routine nursing care were also available through six district clinics. The islands had 16 physicians in 1984, approximately 1 for every 800 citizens. Some of the doctors were government medical officers provided by the British. The islands also had fifty-five nurses and eleven midwives.

The government provided some social services, but most islanders depended on the churches and other voluntary community groups for assistance. State pensions did not exist in the mid-1980s.

As in the Cayman Islands, noncommunicable diseases were the major causes of death in the Turks and Caicos Islands. Despite this similarity, health conditions were generally poorer in the Turks and Caicos. The Turks and Caicos had a relatively high level of leprosy, estimated at 5 cases per 1,000 population in the early 1980s. The territory was also concerned with the spread of malaria by Haitian workers and increased drug addiction. In 1984 about 60 percent of children under one year of age were immunized against diphtheria, pertussis, tetanus, and poliomyelitis. The Turks and Caicos lacked a public piped water system; as a result, the vast majority of the population relied on rainwater roof catchments and storage cisterns. This had contributed to an enormous mosquito population and sporadic *Aëdes aegypti* infestations. As of December 1986, there were two reported cases of AIDS.

The Turks and Caicos had a thirty-bed general hospital on Grand Turk Island and twelve primary care health clinics scattered throughout the territory. There was 1 doctor for roughly every 2,000 citizens. As in the Cayman Islands, the British government provided medical officers. The Turks and Caicos had twelve nurses and eleven midwives. Most social services were provided by the churches.

Economy

In the mid-1980s, the Cayman Islands were one of the most prosperous areas in the Caribbean. The gross domestic product (GDP—see Glossary) in 1985 was approximately US$254.5 million, with a per capita GDP of US$12,789. Approximately 75 percent of all workers were employed in the service sector. Industry accounted for an additional 23 percent of workers; the remaining 2 percent were in agriculture. Forty-two percent of adult women were in the work force in 1979. As with most Caribbean islands, imports to the Cayman Islands greatly exceeded exports. In 1983 imports totaled US$140.4 million, while exports totaled only US$2.4 million. Major trading partners were the United States, Trinidad and Tobago, Britain, and the Netherlands Antilles.

Until 1970, fishing generated most of the Cayman Islands' income. In the 1960s, however, the islands began systematically to nurture two industries—offshore financial services and tourism.

Two of the numerous banks located in the Cayman Islands
Courtesy Warren Yeager

The territory passed new banking laws and made extensive invest-ments in infrastructure, including roads, airports, and wells and desalination plants for water supplies. By the late 1980s, the is-lands had become the Caribbean's leading tax haven. Citizens, per-manent foreign residents, and corporations paid no income, property, inheritance, or capital gains taxes. In 1985 approximately 19,000 companies were registered in the islands, including 498 banks and trust companies and 369 insurance companies. Revenues from company registration fees, trust and insurance licenses, and stamp duties brought in almost US$18 million during 1983. About the same amount was collected in import duties, and total revenue exceeded government expenditures by almost US$2 million. Banks on the islands handled an estimated US$1 billion a day in Euro-currency (see Glossary) deals. External assets of banks licensed in the Cayman Islands totaled US$127 billion at the end of 1982.

The Cayman Islands also has succeeded in building its tourist industry. Infrastructure for tourism has been developed substan-tially, and new hotels and condominiums have been built on all three islands. Tourist arrivals soared 300 percent between 1973 and 1984, largely because of more cruise ship arrivals. In 1986 more than 382,000 tourists visited the islands, including 216,000 cruise ship passengers. In 1985 tourism contributed US$75 million to the economy and employed one-fourth of the work force.

Despite the relative prosperity of the Cayman Islands, problems remained. The tourism boom had inflated land prices to such an extent that young islanders found it difficult to build homes. Agricul-ture was almost nonexistent in the Caymans because of low rain-fall and poor soils. Over 90 percent of the islands' food was imported, a major part of the Caymans' import bill. However, de-velopment efforts had made the islands self-sufficient in eggs and bananas, and beef, oranges, and tomatoes also were produced.

Serious questions also had been raised about the offshore bank-ing industry. In the early 1980s, United States officials became con-cerned that Cayman banks were becoming havens for illegally obtained drug monies. The United States Department of Justice estimated that between 20 and 40 percent of the US$76 billion generated annually by illegal narcotics trafficking in the United States and the Caribbean was laundered through offshore banks in the Caribbean, where criminals were shielded from investiga-tors by secrecy laws. The United States government therefore put pressure on Britain and the Cayman Islands to modify bank secrecy regulations to allow the United States attorney general access to Cayman bank and business records. On August 27, 1984, the two countries and the Cayman Islands signed a pact requiring the islands' administrators to obtain requested records within fourteen days of receiving a certification that the records were needed for an investigation of a drug-related offense.

The Cayman Islands had a modern communication system in the 1980s. The British firm Cable and Wireless operated an entirely automatic system of over 9,000 telephones. A small ground satellite station and submarine cables provided international links to the United States and Panama. Four radio stations on Grand Cayman served the island, broadcasting on 1205 and 1555 kilohertz and on 101.1 and 105.3 megahertz. The *Cayman Compass* and the *Sun* were both published five times a week.

Transportation among the islands was relatively good. In 1984 the territory had 252 vessels over 100 gross tons; the large number reflected the islands' sizable charter boat business. George Town was a major port. Populated sites on all three islands were linked by 160 kilometers of all-weather roads. Municipal buses ran between George Town and West Bay on Grand Cayman. Owen Roberts International Airport outside George Town and an airfield at the western end of Cayman Brac had paved runways to accommodate international flights. There were no railroads or inland waterways.

In the late 1980s, the Turks and Caicos economy was considerably less prosperous than that of the Cayman Islands. The GDP in 1984 was approximately US$26 million, with a per capita GDP of US$3,478. Services employed 61.8 percent of the work force, industry 23.3 percent, and agriculture 14.9 percent. Thirty-three percent of adult women were in the work force in 1979. Imports exceeded exports by over US$18 million in 1982. Major trading partners were the United States and Britain.

Historically, economic development in the Turks and Caicos had been limited by weak infrastructure. The highway system on the islands was underdeveloped in the 1980s. South Caicos and Grand Turk Island had a total of 24 kilometers of paved roads; the other islands had a total of about 100 kilometers of gravel roads. However, the completion in 1983 of a British-financed airport on Providenciales was an important stimulus to the rapidly growing tourism industry. Within a year, a major international hotel chain had begun operations on the islands; the chain opened 100 additional rooms in 1985 as tourist demand exceeded expectations. In 1986 arrivals of stopover visitors to the Turks and Caicos increased by 22 percent over the previous year, one of the highest growth rates in the Caribbean. Two additional hotels were expected to be constructed in 1987. Large ships could be accommodated on South Caicos, Salt Cay, Grand Turk Island, and Providenciales. In addition to Providenciales, Grand Turk Island had an airfield with a runway capable of handling international flights.

As in the Cayman Islands, offshore financial services were an important component of the Turks and Caicos economy in the 1980s. More than 4,000 companies registered in the islands in the mid-1980s to take advantage of the absence of company and income taxes and exchange controls. In 1986, however, the industry stagnated in response to increased competition from other Caribbean islands and investor concerns regarding the political situation in the Turks and Caicos.

Fishing had also become an important industry by the mid-1980s; lobster, conch, conch shells, and fish were the territory's principal exports. Exports of fish to the United States, the main customer, totaled US$3 million in 1983. Despite its importance, the industry was plagued by serious technological and marketing problems; overfishing was also a major concern. Almost all foodstuffs other than fish were imported by the Turks and Caicos. Low rainfall, poor soils, and the inadequacy of irrigation systems confined agriculture to small amounts of subsistence farming.

The Turks and Caicos government experienced chronic budget deficits in the 1980s; as a consequence, operating subsidies and development aid from Britain were essential. The 1983 closure of the last United States military base on the islands—a navy facility on Grand Turk Island—led to a loss in rent equal to 10 percent of total government revenues. In an effort to reduce expenditures, the government initiated a privatization policy in 1985; within two years, much of the debt-ridden electricity department had been transferred to private control. Because of the government's action, the deficit was reduced from US$4.3 million in 1984 to US$2.2 million for the fiscal year (FY—see Glossary) ending March 1987.

In the 1980s, domestic communications in the Turks and Caicos were only fair; international communications were of better quality. Although the islands had 1,400 telephones, service was often erratic and was limited to Grand Turk Island, North Caicos, South Caicos, and Providenciales. Two submarine cables and a small ground satellite station provided modern international links. Broadcasting was limited to one AM radio station on Grand Turk Island on 1460 kilohertz. The *Turks and Caicos News* was published weekly.

Government and Politics

The Governmental System

In the late 1980s, both territories were still British crown colonies. Each had a British governor and a ministerial form of government consisting of an Executive Council (cabinet) and a

View of the north shore,
Grand Cayman
Courtesy Warren Yeager

Legislative Assembly (in the Cayman Islands) or a Legislative Council (in the Turks and Caicos Islands).

Under the Caymans' Constitution, the British governor is responsible for defense and internal security, external affairs, and public service. On all other matters, the governor must either accept the recommendations of the Executive Council or receive approval for his veto from the British secretary of state for foreign and Commonwealth affairs. The Executive Council, which is responsible for the daily administration of the affairs in the Caymans, consists of the financial secretary, the attorney general, the administrative secretary (all appointed by the governor), and four other members elected by the Legislative Assembly from their own number. The governor presides as chairman of the Executive Council. The unicameral Legislative Assembly, consisting of twelve elected members and three ex officio members appointed by the governor, is entrusted with making laws.

The governmental system in the Turks and Caicos was similar. Under the August 1976 Constitution, the governor retains responsibility for external affairs, internal security, defense, and certain other matters. The Executive Council consists of three ex officio members appointed by the governor—the financial secretary, the chief secretary, and the attorney general—as well as a chief minister elected by the Legislative Council and three other ministers appointed by the governor from the elected members of the Legislative

Council. The governor presides over the Executive Council. The bicameral Legislative Council consists of a speaker, the three ex officio members of the Executive Council, and eleven members elected by residents age eighteen and over.

Political Dynamics

In the late 1980s, Caymanian politics was relatively calm. The Caymans had no officially recognized political parties; elections for the twelve elective seats in the Legislative Assembly were contested by "teams" of candidates, as well as by independents. The teams showed no differences in policy or ideology. All candidates traditionally pledged to work for continued economic success and for continued dependent status. In the November 1980 elections, the Unity Team, led by Jim Bodden, won eight of the twelve seats. The Dignity Team, headed by Benson Ebanks, won two seats, and two went to independents. The Dignity Team later fell apart when one of its two legislators joined the Unity Team.

Elections were held again in November 1984 against a backdrop of dissatisfaction with Bodden's Unity Team. Many voters felt it was time for a change; public disquiet had grown over the rapid rise in the immigrant work force. Criticism was voiced that Bodden and his government should have moved more quickly to preserve the good name of the colony and its financial services when the United States alleged that Caymanian banks had been used to launder illegal drug monies. Independents captured nine seats in the election, but the other three remained in the hands of the Dignity Team; Ebanks became chief minister. Despite the change in leadership, continued economic prosperity helped to maintain political stability in the territory.

Cayman Islands residents have expressed the strong wish to remain British dependents; this position was voiced twice to United Nations groups, in 1977 and again in 1981. The finance secretary commented that "venturing into independence" was not a viable route to prosperity for small countries and that the British link inspired investor confidence. Moreover, support for Britain was shown in 1982 when the Cayman Islands sent a US$1 million donation to the Falklands Fund from private and public sources.

Politics in the Turks and Caicos Islands differed from the situation in the Cayman Islands in three notable ways. First, the Turks and Caicos had two defined political parties. Second, independence was a salient issue and a determinant in party identification. Finally, the political landscape in the 1980s had been shaped by government corruption.

The first elections in the Turks and Caicos under the revised 1976 Constitution took place that year and were won by the pro-independence People's Democratic Movement (PDM). Independence appealed to many in the Turks and Caicos, who were influenced by the Jamaican independence process in the early 1960s. In early 1980, Britain agreed that if the governing PDM won elections later that same year, the islands would receive independence and a payment of around US$21.6 million. However, the PDM chief minister, J.A.G.S. McCartney, was killed in an accident that May. Lacking his strong leadership, the PDM lost the November 1980 election to the Progressive National Party (PNP), which supported continued dependent status. At the next general election, in May 1984, the PNP, led by Chief Minister Norman Saunders, won eight of the eleven elective seats. During that campaign neither party raised the issue of independence, largely because citizens had become aware of the value of regular British financial aid. Both parties were committed to free enterprise and to the development of the Turks and Caicos through tourism and offshore financial services.

The PNP's 1984 election victory could be explained in part by growing economic prosperity over the preceding four years. Government revenues had risen; more banks had established offices in the islands; the airport on Providenciales had been finished; and tourism had expanded dramatically.

In 1985 the Turks and Caicos were rocked by a major drug scandal. In March, Chief Minister Saunders, Minister of Commerce and Development Stafford Missick, and another PNP member were arrested in Miami by DEA agents, in cooperation with the islands' own governor and police force. During the trial, the prosecution showed a videotape of Saunders receiving US$20,000 from a DEA undercover agent. The DEA said that Saunders took the money in return for promises to protect drug shipments from Colombia as they passed through his native island of South Caicos on their way to the United States.

Saunders and Missick were found guilty of drug conspiracy charges by a Miami court on July 21, 1985, although Saunders was acquitted of the more serious charge of conspiring to import cocaine into the United States. Missick was convicted of the additional charge of cocaine importation. Saunders and Missick were subsequently sentenced to prison terms of eight and ten years, respectively; each was fined US$50,000.

Although precise data on citizen attitudes were not available, many islanders resented the fact that Saunders was arrested in a United States "sting" operation carried out with the knowledge and consent of the British governor and the British government; they contended that Saunders had been set up. Some of these islanders also thought that the popular Saunders, the national tennis champion as well as the chief minister, should have been brought to trial at home. In spite of these feelings, however, the islands remained calm after the arrests. Most people were primarily concerned about the effect that any adverse publicity would have on the territory's fragile economy.

With three of its legislators in jail, the PNP still held a majority of five to three in the Legislative Council. The PNP selected the former minister of public works and utilities, seventy-two-year-old Nathaniel "Bops" Francis, to be the new chief minister. Ariel Misick received the key appointment of minister of commerce and development. The reorganized government's top priority was to maintain investor confidence and proceed with planned development projects. The new government also took pains to tell both London and Washington that it condemned drug trafficking in the islands.

Political turmoil in the Turks and Caicos did not end with the Saunders conviction. In July 1986, the British took the unusual step of imposing direct British rule on the territory, following publication of the report of a Royal Commission of Inquiry into arson, corruption, and related matters. That report severely criticized both the Turks and Caicos government and the opposition for alleged malpractice and criminality. The report also made recommendations for constitutional reform.

Although Governor Christopher Turner announced the decision of direct British rule on July 25, 1986, Chief Minister Francis had actually resigned just before the announcement after reading press accounts that London was prepared to use British troops available in Belize in the event of local hostility to the order. Perhaps because of the possibility of British military action, the islands remained calm after the announcement. As part of the July 25 decision, Governor Turner created an advisory council of four prominent residents to assist him during the two years a constitutional commission reviewed possible changes in the islands' governmental structure. That constitutional commission began its work in November 1986 under the leadership of Sir Roy Marshall, a former vice chancellor of the UWI.

In mid-1987 officials from the Turks and Caicos visited Ottawa and offered the Canadian government the opportunity to annex the islands. According to the Turks and Caicos representatives, polls indicated that 90 percent of the residents of the islands favored some form of special relationship with Canada. From the

World War I monument, George Town, Grand Cayman
Courtesy Warren Yeager

perspective of the Turks and Caicos, the principal attraction of annexation undoubtedly was economic; its citizens wanted a North American standard of living that the islands could not meet. Indeed, one observer had questioned whether a territory of only 8,600 people, scattered over 8 islands with no agricultural resources, an infant tourist industry, and only a limited pool of skilled labor, could really succeed as a viable economic entity.

The prospect of annexation was also attractive to many Canadians who were frustrated with the unfavorable exchange rate encountered during vacations to the United States or to Caribbean nations whose currencies were pegged to the United States dollar. Canadian prime minister Brian Mulroney referred the annexation proposal to a special parliamentary committee for examination. Nonetheless, it appeared unlikely that the Canadian government would quickly adopt such a proposal; in 1986 the Canadian External Affairs Department recommended against a similar annexation attempt, fearing the possibility of racial tension between white Canadians and black islanders.

Foreign Relations

The British government retained control over all foreign policy and defense matters for these dependent territories. The two territories participated in the Commonwealth of Nations (see Appendix

B) and, because of their ties to Britain, were considered states associated with the European Economic Community, a status that greatly facilitated trade with the rest of Western Europe. No British Army or British Navy forces were based in the two territories. Military security was provided by British forces stationed in Belize. In addition to the Commonwealth of Nations, both the Cayman Islands and the Turks and Caicos Islands belonged to the Caribbean Development Bank.

National Security

Neither the Cayman Islands nor the Turks and Caicos Islands had armed forces—either under local or under British control. Each territory did, however, have a small local police force that was under British control.

The Royal Cayman Islands Police Force (RCIP), with limited resources, was considered one of the best in the Caribbean. The police totaled 170, of whom 161 were stationed on Grand Cayman and the remainder on Cayman Brac. They were supported by volunteer special constables. The RCIP had three main departments: General Duties Department, Criminal Investigation Department, and Traffic Department. The Criminal Investigation Department included the Special Branch, the Commercial Crime Branch, the Drug Squad, and the Crime Intelligence Section. The Maritime Section, with three boats at Grand Cayman and one at Cayman Brac, performed coastal patrol duties. British instructors provided police training. The islands had only one prison, with a maximum capacity of twenty inmates. Major offenders were sometimes transferred to prisons on Jamaica.

The crime rate in the Cayman Islands was low. Efforts against drug trafficking were moderately successful, with 140 drug arrests in 1982. The RCIP Drug Squad received technical assistance from the United States DEA.

The Royal Turks and Caicos Islands Police Force had ninety members under a chief of police. Most were stationed on Grand Turk Island, with other police stations on Providenciales and South Caicos. The police handled coastal patrol duties. Training was provided at a center on Grand Turk Island. Like the RCIP, the Royal Turks and Caicos Islands Police Force operated under British control.

No insurgencies or related activities were reported in either the Cayman Islands or the Turks and Caicos Islands in 1987.

* * *

Literature specific to these two groups of islands is limited. The most useful sources of information are a series of yearbooks and compendium discussions of the Caribbean islands. Richard Green's *Latin America and Caribbean Review* (published yearly) is an excellent source of information on economic and political events of the past year. Current events can be followed through the monthly British newsletter the *Latin American Monitor: Caribbean*. Useful business information can be found in Jane Walker's *Business Traveller's Handbook*. (For further information and complete citations, see Bibliography.)

Chapter 7. Strategic and Regional Security Perspectives

St. Ann's Fort, Barbados, built by the British in the early eighteenth century

STRATEGIC AND REGIONAL security issues pertaining to the Commonwealth Caribbean insular subregion need to be considered, to a certain extent, within the wider context of the Caribbean Basin region. This geopolitical concept encompasses all of the Caribbean island polities, as well as the rimland countries of the United States, Mexico, Belize, Guatemala, Honduras, Nicaragua, Costa Rica, Panama, Colombia, Venezuela, and Guyana.

Of the Latin American rimland countries, only Venezuela, which exports petroleum to the United States through the Caribbean and has 2,816 kilometers of Caribbean coastline, has played an economic and diplomatic role of any significance to the Commonwealth Caribbean since the late 1970s. Venezuela's influence was most noticeable in the late 1970s and early 1980s. In general, however, aside from its longstanding territorial dispute with Guyana, Venezuela did not play an important security role in the Commonwealth Caribbean as of late 1987. For this reason, it is not discussed in this chapter. The only non-Commonwealth countries in the Caribbean Basin discussed here in a geopolitical context are the United States and Cuba, whose strategic or other interests have influenced the security of the English-speaking islands. The strategic interests of two extrahemispheric powers—Britain and the Soviet Union—also are examined for the same reason.

The strategic aspects of the Commonwealth Caribbean islands largely account for United States, Soviet, and Cuban interest in this subregion, as well as in the Caribbean Basin area in general. The transition to independence of the Commonwealth Caribbean islands during the period from the early 1960s to the early 1980s was accompanied by a gradual withdrawal of Britain's security and defense responsibilities. This situation created a strategic vacuum in the subregion and made the islands more vulnerable to external subversion. Since the 1960s, Cuba and the Soviet Union, in growing competition with the United States, have attempted to fill this vacuum, albeit in an incremental way in order to avoid provoking a United States response.

As German submarines demonstrated during World War II, the geography of the Caribbean Sea region is ideal for interdiction of the vital sea-lanes on which much American and world trade depend. Efforts by the United States to reinforce and resupply European allies in time of war also would be dependent on these Caribbean lifelines. Cuba and the Soviet Union have developed the military capabilities to interdict shipping on the Caribbean sea-lanes and control vital ''choke points'' among the numerous passages and straits in the region, as well as the Panama Canal. The Soviet Union and Cuba nearly gained a foothold in Grenada in the early 1980s, but the landing on the island of combined United States-Caribbean forces on October 25, 1983, dealt their strategic plans for the Eastern Caribbean (see Glossary) a major setback. The swift military action by the United States, which contrasted markedly with Britain's hesitation, enhanced United States influence in the Commonwealth Caribbean and appeared to confirm regional perceptions that the United States was assuming responsibilities once held by the British.

For the Commonwealth Caribbean islands, regional security issues are of much greater concern than strategic affairs. The English-speaking islands of the Eastern Caribbean became increasingly interested in a regional security arrangement following the 1979 coup in Grenada by Maurice Bishop's New Jewel Movement (NJM), a self-described pro-Cuban Marxist-Leninist party, and several incidents involving mercenary or other subversive activities in the region. In October 1982, five Eastern Caribbean states—Barbados, Antigua and Barbuda, Dominica, St. Lucia, and St. Vincent and the Grenadines—signed a memorandum of understanding creating a Regional Security System (RSS). Nevertheless, in the late 1980s the English-speaking Caribbean remained a highly vulnerable area guarded mainly by police. This subregion continued to have one of the highest concentrations of pro-Western democratic governments in the world, and it looked primarily to the United States, not Britain, for economic, military, and other security assistance.

The Strategic Setting

The proximity of the region to the United States and the many key passages (choke points) and vital sea-lanes running through the Lesser Antilles and Bahamian archipelago and through the Greater Antilles make the Commonwealth Caribbean a strategically significant part of the world and thus an arena of international power competition. Until a revolution brought Fidel Castro to power in Cuba in 1959, the hegemony of the United States in the Caribbean had been unchallenged since the late nineteenth century. In October 1962, the Soviet Union challenged that hegemony and threatened the United States by attempting to install ballistic missiles in Cuba. Although the United States forced the Soviet Union to withdraw its missiles, during the 1970s and 1980s the Soviets developed the island into a Soviet base and the Cuban military into one of the most powerful in Latin America. Furthermore, Soviet naval deployments to the Caribbean, which had been nonexistent until 1969, became an annual or semiannual event.

Bounded by the Bahamas in the north and Barbados in the east, the Caribbean is one vast natural chain commanding the trade routes running between the Atlantic and Pacific and from north to south (see fig. 21). Controlling both ends of this natural barrier would be a clear strategic advantage. There are thirteen key sea-lanes in the Caribbean, eleven of which lie between the smaller islands and are deep enough to be used by any ship afloat. The relatively narrow passages in the Caribbean constitute choke points through which merchant or naval shipping must pass in transiting to and from North America's Gulf ports and the Atlantic Ocean. Should these passages come under hostile control, sea traffic could be seriously impeded or blocked.

In the Gulf of Mexico and Caribbean Sea, a navigable area of more than 2,156,500 square kilometers, the 13 principal high-density sea-lanes pass through 4 major choke points—the Yucatán Channel, Windward Passage, Old Bahamas Channel, and Straits of Florida—all of which are vulnerable to Cuban interdiction. The Straits of Florida, Mona Passage, Windward Passage, and Yucatán Channel are the main gateways for vessels entering or leaving the Caribbean, and the Straits of Florida provide the only open-sea connection for the Gulf of Mexico. Tankers entering the Caribbean from the Persian Gulf and West Africa mainly use three passages: Galleons Passage, Old Bahamas Channel, and Providence Channel. There are a number of lesser passages as well.

Once the United States became the dominant power in the Caribbean, it began taking the region for granted as its "backyard" or the "American Mediterranean." Consequently, the United States often underestimated the region and rarely accorded it priority in its foreign and security policies. After the Grenada intervention in late October 1983, the United States began significantly increasing assistance to RSS member states to improve regional security capabilities, as well as to improve their capabilities for narcotics interdiction and search-and-rescue operations. This aid consisted of training and the provision of coast guard vessels and light infantry equipment. Although capable of dealing with regional security threats such as a mercenary attack or a rebellion, the RSS in the late 1980s was no defense against possible future military aggression by Cuba.

Britain's only significant military presence in the Western Hemisphere was its sizable force in the Falkland/Malvinas Islands and its 1,800-member force in Belize, including Royal Air Force

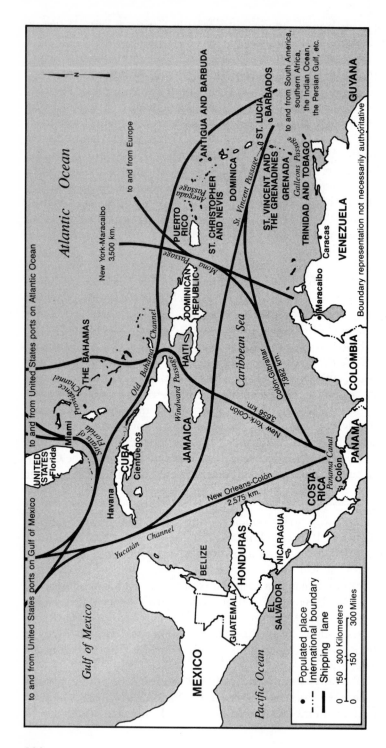

Figure 21. Caribbean Sea-Lanes

units. As head of the Commonwealth of Nations, however, Britain was still one of the most important influences in the English-speaking Caribbean (see Appendix B). Although no longer responsible for the defense and security of most Commonwealth members in the region, Britain continued to maintain a Royal Navy ship in the area and to provide advisers and financing for RSS coast guard shore facilities, as well as police training for 200 Caribbean nationals a year at British military and security establishments.

Britain showed its flag in the region on January 19, 1987, by dispatching 10 Royal Navy warships carrying 4,000 sailors for 3 months of Caribbean exercises. The forces were scheduled to engage mostly in antisubmarine warfare operations and North Atlantic Treaty Organization (NATO) war games. Britain's defense chief, Admiral Sir John Fieldhouse, paid a two-day visit to the Bahamas that February for "routine talks on matters of mutual interest."

In contrast to Britain, France maintained a permanent and relatively powerful military presence in the region in its departments of Guadeloupe, Martinique, and French Guiana. Nevertheless, France traditionally had not interfered in the affairs of its English-speaking neighbors in the Eastern Caribbean.

Historical Background

Colonial Rivalry

Until the end of the nineteenth century, the United States had to compete at various times with Spanish, British, French, and Dutch power in the Caribbean. The region assumed strategic significance as early as the seventeenth century when Spain's rivals began colonization attempts. During this period, France and England took advantage of numerous opportunities in the Eastern Caribbean. Spain had established garrison outposts on many of the Caribbean islands in order to guard its trade route to Mexico and Panama. As Spain's military power declined beginning in the mid-seventeenth century, however, its Caribbean sea-lanes became more vulnerable. The Dutch seized Curaçao to use as a base for harassing Spain's shipping, and England captured Jamaica from Spain. In addition, the eighteenth-century power struggle in Europe was projected into the Caribbean, where the Netherlands was the first to be forced out. With the onset of the American Revolution, the Americans began building a navy to secure the "back door" of the new nation, thereby dashing French dreams of Caribbean domination.

591

The fierce colonial rivalry in the region required the permanent stationing of British naval and military forces on the commercially important Caribbean islands of Barbados, St. Lucia, and Jamaica, as well as Bermuda in the Atlantic. In 1798 the British established a volunteer defense force known as the West India Regiment. Although primarily responsible for defending and maintaining order in Britain's West Indian colonies, the British-trained and British-commanded regiment also fought for Britain in the American Revolution, the War of 1812, and various campaigns in West Africa.

The Treaty of Vienna in 1815 ensured British command of the Caribbean for most of the nineteenth century. Britain never missed an opportunity to use its naval strength in the Caribbean until the signing in 1850 of the Clayton-Bulwer Treaty, in which Britain and the United States declared that they would not unilaterally seek to exercise dominion over any part of Central America, excluding British Honduras (present-day Belize).

United States Preeminence

President James Buchanan first enunciated the perceived need for the United States to play a police role in the Caribbean as a way of ensuring the safety of foreign nationals and of enforcing the Monroe Doctrine by keeping European powers from intervening in the area. Congress, however, denied him authority to use military forces for that purpose. Nevertheless, before the end of the century, Britain had permanently ended its traditional competition with the United States in the Caribbean in order to attend to priorities in Asia and Africa. By the 1890s, American expansionists had rejuvenated the Monroe Doctrine, and the American public regarded the Caribbean as America's "backyard." Captain Alfred Thayer Mahan, one of the leading expansionists of the day, argued for a navy strong enough to completely control the region, which he described as a "cluster of island fortresses," and the approaches to the Panama Canal (then under construction).

Victory in the Spanish-American War of 1898–99 gave the United States a commanding position not only in the Pacific but also in the Caribbean. Thereafter, the United States began to develop a sphere of influence in the Caribbean by establishing a preponderant naval and military presence. As a consequence of its annexation of Puerto Rico and creation of a Cuban protectorate, the United States not only gained sites for naval bases but also acquired control of the major sea approaches to the future Panama Canal. President Theodore Roosevelt and Secretary of War Elihu Root often expressed the view that their policy was directed not toward acquisition of territory but toward discouragement of European encroachments in the strategically vital Caribbean area.

During the first half of the twentieth century, the military presence of the United States in the Caribbean was fortified diplomatically, financially, and commercially. American influence in the region prevailed by the 1920s. Furthermore, numerous interventions in the Caribbean and Central America by United States military forces during the first quarter of the century served to maintain the status quo, preempt European involvement, safeguard the Panama Canal and its approaches, and generally protect perceived American interests. These interventions earned the United States an unenviable reputation among the smaller Hispanic countries of the Caribbean Basin. The United States refrained, however, from intervening in the affairs of Britain's Caribbean colonies.

World War II

At the outbreak of World War II, the United States assumed Britain's defense responsibilities in the Caribbean. In September 1940, the two countries agreed to the Lend-Lease Agreement (also called the Bases-for-Destroyers Agreement). It involved the loan of forty out-of-date American destroyers in return for leasing, rent free for ninety-nine years, British naval and air bases on five British West Indian islands—the Bahamas, Jamaica, Antigua, St. Lucia, and Trinidad and Tobago—as well as British Guiana, Bermuda, and Newfoundland. The Lend-Lease Agreement was signed formally in London on March 27, 1941. Under its terms, the United States established eleven military bases in the area (and in Bermuda) and quickly transformed five British colonies in the West Indies into outposts of Caribbean defense for use against German submarine warfare. After President Franklin D. Roosevelt designated the Caribbean as a coastal frontier, the Eastern Caribbean became the forward edge of American defense strategy during the war. American strategists at that time referred to the West Indies as "the bulwark that we watch."

The strategic significance of the Caribbean became evident during the war. More than 50 percent of the supplies sent to Europe and Africa from the United States were shipped from ports in the Gulf of Mexico. One year after the Pearl Harbor attack, the United States Caribbean Defense Command reached a total of 119,000 personnel, half of them stationed in Panama to protect the canal from Japanese attack. Although the expected Japanese attack did not come, the Germans inflicted massive damage on shipping in the Caribbean in 1942. German submarines even slipped into the region's small harbors to shell shore targets and to sink cargo ships

593

at anchor. By the end of the year, U-boats operating in the Caribbean had sunk 336 ships, at least half of which were oil tankers, with a total weight of 1.5 million tons.

The Postwar Strategic Vacuum

After the war, the Commonwealth Caribbean temporarily reverted to the British sphere of influence and looked to Britain for defense and security needs. Although the Caribbean colonies held no strategic importance for Britain after World War II, the British remained interested in the region, owing to moral, constitutional, and economic obligations. Continuing a course it had started during the war, Britain gave its Caribbean colonies increasingly more self-government but retained an unlimited obligation for their defense against external aggression. The United States demonstrated its reduced strategic interests in the English-speaking Caribbean by closing most of its bases on the islands by the mid-1950s. Nevertheless, Barbados and the Turks and Caicos Islands were added to the 1941 Lend-Lease Agreement in November 1956.

As the Cold War intensified in the 1950s, the United States and Britain became increasingly concerned about the threat of communism in their respective spheres of interest in Latin America and the English-speaking Caribbean. For example, Britain, at American urging, sent troops to British Guiana (present-day Guyana) in 1953 to prevent a perceived communist takeover threat posed by Cheddi Jagan's People's Progressive Party. Except for British Guiana, however, the Commonwealth Caribbean remained on the periphery of America's Cold War concerns during the 1950s. America's preoccupations in the Western Hemisphere were centered mainly on events in Hispanic countries, such as the military coup in Guatemala in 1954, and the new situation created by the fall of long-time pro-American dictators in Colombia in 1957, Venezuela in 1958, Cuba in 1959, and the Dominican Republic in 1961.

Fidel Castro's seizure of power in Cuba in 1959 and the increasingly evident pro-Soviet orientation of his regime prompted the United States to devote increased attention and resources to its interests in the English-speaking Caribbean. Thus, the United States signed military agreements with Jamaica and Antigua in 1961. The pact with Jamaica gave the United States basing rights, including the right to operate a loran station on the island. The accord with Antigua allowed the United States to open a naval base on the island for use in oceanographic research and submarine surveillance, as well as an air force base for electronic tracking. The United States also retained a small naval base in Barbados and an electronic tracking facility on St. Lucia. In Trinidad and Tobago, however, the late Prime Minister Eric Williams negotiated the withdrawal of the American military presence. The naval base in the Chaguaramas Bay area was closed in 1967, and the Omega navigational aid station was removed in 1980 (see The Road to Independence, ch. 3).

By 1962, when Jamaica and Trinidad and Tobago became independent, it had become increasingly evident that security and defense responsibilities for the Commonwealth Caribbean were beginning to shift from Britain to the United States. For example, Britain requested and received American assistance in 1962, when British military forces were again sent to British Guiana during a period of racial and labor union violence confronting the government of Prime Minister Jagan.

From the 1950s to the 1970s, the United States closely monitored internal political developments in the Commonwealth Caribbean. American cultural and economic influences became increasingly important in the English-speaking Caribbean in the 1950s and 1960s. American economic influence in the region, deriving particularly from heavy investments in oil in Trinidad and Tobago and bauxite (see Glossary) in Jamaica, worked to the American advantage until the 1970s, when the West Indians became more sensitive about their economic dependence on the United States and Western Europe.

Current Strategic Considerations

Britain's Withdrawal

At probably no time during the last three centuries were Britain's strategic interests in the Caribbean less significant than in the late 1980s. Once its former Caribbean colonies began to achieve independence in 1962, Britain's policy had been to withdraw from individual security, but not economic, commitments to the Commonwealth Caribbean. In early 1987, only five British island dependencies remained: Anguilla, British Virgin Islands, Cayman Islands, Montserrat, and Turks and Caicos Islands. These are the smallest Commonwealth Caribbean islands, and none plays a significant role in regional politics. British interests in the Caribbean had been reduced mainly to trade, investment, and limited economic and security assistance.

According to one analyst of the British Caribbean, in the early 1980s the conservative government of Prime Minister Margaret Thatcher fully supported the geopolitical view of the Caribbean held by the United States administration of President Ronald

Reagan. As early as 1980, the Thatcher government described Cuba as "a destabilizing force in the area" and accused the Castro regime of exporting subversion. Britain joined the United States in pressuring Prime Minister Bishop's government to hold free and fair elections and to release political prisoners.

Despite Britain's cooperation, the Thatcher government, according to an American official, complained about lack of prior consultation in the decision to intervene on Grenada, which became essentially a United States-Commonwealth Caribbean operation. Partly as a result, the Thatcher government declined to endorse the joint United States-Caribbean military action in Grenada in late October 1983. Jamaican prime minister Edward Seaga noted that the English-speaking Caribbean felt "a certain amount of bitterness" at British opposition to the Grenada intervention, and that London could no longer assume "some right of prior consultation in matters that affect us here." Nevertheless, the visit to Grenada by Queen Elizabeth II on October 31, 1985, helped to ameliorate regional resentment against perceived British indifference and to revive British prestige in the region.

Its greatly reduced presence notwithstanding, Britain remained a significant political and economic power in the region in the late 1980s by virtue of its continued status as head of the Commonwealth of Nations. In this capacity, the British still had certain political and security ties to their independent former colonies. For example, the English-speaking islands continued to rely exclusively on the Westminster model of parliamentary democracy, and Britain continued its tradition of providing police training. Apart from the United States, Britain also was still the principal trading partner of the Commonwealth Caribbean.

The Increased Role of the United States

Traditional Interests

Traditionally, the United States has attempted to establish and maintain a peaceful, secure, stable, and friendly southern flank. It has sought to prevent hostile foreign powers from establishing military bases and facilities, engaging in destabilizing balance of power struggles, or supporting subversive activities in the Caribbean region; guarantee the United States access to strategic raw materials, trade, investment opportunities, and transportation routes; protect American territories (Puerto Rico and the United States Virgin Islands) and military installations; and promote economic development in the region.

Referring in 1984 to American interests specific to the Commonwealth Caribbean, Vaughan A. Lewis, director of the Organisation of Eastern Caribbean States (OECS—see Glossary), noted five separate but related concerns: security, communications (e.g., sea-lanes and shipping), natural resources, immigration, and narcotics trafficking. The latter two were relatively new concerns. By the early 1980s, the Caribbean Basin area had become a major transit route for narcotics smuggled into the United States from South America, and was also the largest source of legal and illegal immigrants in the United States, according to the Department of State.

Despite its important strategic interests in the Caribbean, the United States was reluctant to fill the security vacuum created when Britain began pulling out of the region at the end of the 1970s. There were diplomatic, political, and economic reasons for the United States not to move too quickly. It did not want to appear to be pushing Britain out of its traditional sphere of influence. Moreover, the United States recognized that the people in the English-speaking Caribbean, although seeking a measure of independence from Britain, remained identified politically and culturally with the British.

Heightened Security Concerns, 1979–83

Several developments in 1979 generated a more active American interest in the Caribbean Basin region and contributed to a reassessment of the strategic equation by the administration of President Jimmy Carter. These included Bishop's seizure of power in Grenada, the Nicaraguan revolution, the presence of a Soviet combat brigade in Cuba, the Cuban deployment of troops to Ethiopia to counter a Somali invasion of that Marxist country, and the Soviet invasion of Afghanistan, a move that heightened American concerns over Soviet expansionist intentions.

The Soviet combat brigade issue in particular prompted the Carter administration to establish the Caribbean Contingency Joint Task Force (CCJTF) at Key West, Florida, on October 1, 1979. The CCJTF was equipped with a squadron of A-4 attack bombers and a radar-jamming navy electronics warfare squadron. The sending of a 1,500-member United States Marines task force to stage a beach landing at Guantanamo Bay, Cuba, that year also dramatized the new emphasis by the United States on regional security and defense. In addition, United States naval vessels began showing the flag throughout the Caribbean. The increased visibility of the United States in the region, however, was not uniformly welcomed by the island nations. The left-of-center governments of Jamaica, Guyana, Grenada, and St. Lucia criticized President

Carter's decision to increase the United States military presence in the Caribbean on the grounds that it could "escalate tension and threaten the peace and stability of the region." They also rejected "any perception of the Caribbean region as a sphere of influence for any great power."

The Carter administration's security concerns deepened in the spring of 1980 when Bishop said that Cuban and Soviet aircraft would be allowed landing rights in Grenada. During the first nine months of 1980, United States Navy ships paid more than two dozen port calls in the Eastern Caribbean. Although the United States had granted recognition to the Bishop regime after it came to power, the Carter administration suspended all official contact with the government as a result of Grenada's reliance on Cuban forces, military advisers, and other aid.

The Reagan administration continued the policy of shunning Grenada, citing a security threat to the United States from the 3,048-meter-long airstrip being built by Cubans at Point Salines. The United States claimed that the airfield could be used for military purposes. United States concerns heightened in the early 1980s as the result of a renewal of Cuban subversion in the Caribbean Basin region; the growing insurgency in El Salvador; the Soviet-assisted military buildups in Cuba, Nicaragua, and Grenada; and the flight of refugees from Cuba, Haiti, and other Caribbean islands, as well as from Central America. As Grenada's ties with Cuba and the Soviet Union expanded in the early 1980s, the United States gave more priority to security contingency planning in the Eastern Caribbean. In one of the largest naval exercises by the United States since World War II, United States forces engaged in Operation "Ocean Venture" on the Puerto Rican island of Vieques between August and October 1981. That November the United States Department of Defense upgraded its regional defense network to command status by consolidating the two-year-old CCJTF at Key West, Florida, with the Antilles Defense Command in Puerto Rico. The resulting command, called the United States Forces Caribbean Command, was created on December 1, 1981, as one of three NATO Atlantic commands. Its area of responsibility covered "waters and islands of the Caribbean, Gulf of Mexico, and parts of the Pacific bordering Central and South America." The new command included naval and air forces, as well as army and marine units. Until then the United States Southern Command headquarters in the Panama Canal area had the United States Army's only major forward-based forces in the region. The primary United States naval facility at Roosevelt Roads, Puerto Rico, had neither ships nor aircraft permanently assigned.

*New Jewel Movement photograph of
the Point Salines airfield under construction in Grenada
Courtesy United States Department of Defense*

Five English-speaking island nations in the Eastern Caribbean—Antigua and Barbuda, Barbados, Dominica, St. Lucia, and St. Vincent and the Grenadines—established their own basis for regional security cooperation by signing on October 29, 1982, in Bridgetown, Barbados, the Memorandum of Understanding (see A Regional Security System, this ch.). In March 1983, shortly after the RSS was adopted formally, veteran prime minister Vere Cornwall Bird, Sr., of Antigua and Barbuda described the nascent regional defense and security system as "insurance against the violent overthrow of democratically elected governments," such as took place on Grenada in 1979. "We cannot afford to have another Cuba or another Grenada," he declared. That month President Reagan, displaying aerial reconnaissance photographs, underscored the threat of "another Cuba" in Grenada by announcing that the island was building, with Cuban assistance, an airfield, a naval base, a munitions storage area, barracks, and Soviet-style training areas.

In October 1983, the political situation in Grenada deteriorated suddenly, and the Commonwealth Caribbean perceived itself as facing an ominous threat to its security and constitutional system of government. On October 13, 1983, a harder line and more militant pro-Soviet NJM faction led by Deputy Prime Minister

Bernard Coard ousted Prime Minister Bishop in an armed coup and placed him under house arrest. Coard proclaimed himself prime minister and installed the ruling sixteen-officer Revolutionary Military Council (RMC). Some observers attributed the coup in part to Bishop's attempts during the final months of his rule to distance his government from Cuba and the Soviet Union. On October 19, People's Revolutionary Army (PRA) troops executed Bishop and three of his closest deputies and killed scores of civilians. The next day, General Hudson Austin, the PRA commander, proclaimed himself head of the new RMC. The coup, the assassinations, and the other carnage outraged Commonwealth Caribbean leaders.

Intervention in Grenada

Alarmed at the radical turn that Grenada appeared to be taking, the RSS member islands and Jamaica asked the United States to intervene. Before acting on the informal OECS request, Reagan sent a special ambassadorial emissary to consult with the OECS and other regional leaders. The emissary met in Barbados on October 23 with the prime ministers of Dominica, Barbados, and Jamaica—Mary Eugenia Charles, J.M.G.M. "Tom" Adams, and Edward Seaga, respectively—who all strongly reiterated their appeal for American assistance. Subsequently, Grenada's governor general, Paul Scoon, despite being under house arrest, made a confidential appeal for action by OECS members and other regional states to restore order on the island. Scoon, a native Grenadian, represented Queen Elizabeth II, Grenada's titular head of state (see Grenada, Government and Politics, ch. 4). On October 24, the OECS requested United States participation—together with Jamaica, Barbados, and four OECS members (Antigua and Barbuda, Dominica, St. Lucia, and St. Vincent and the Grenadines)— in a military action against the Coard-Austin regime. Seaga, who played the leading role among Caribbean leaders, later revealed that the formal request was made after the United States had promised "immediate action." OECS director Lewis later stated, however, that the decision to seek United States troops was made only after OECS nations realized they lacked the forces to take control of Grenada.

Final preparations for Operation "Urgent Fury" began on October 24, when United States forces landed at staging sites on Barbados. Early the next morning, combined United States-Caribbean forces consisting of 1,900 United States Marines and United States Army rangers and 300 soldiers and policemen from 6 Commonwealth Caribbean islands landed on Grenada at several locations, including the Point Salines airstrip, then under construction by Cubans. The United States military later announced that more than 6,000 United States troops had participated in the invasion. None of the members of the Caribbean force took part in any fighting. They guarded Grenadian prisoners and Cuban internees and later accompanied United States troops on security patrols of St. George's and other areas. The combined forces established authority within a few days after overcoming limited initial resistance by PRA troops and fiercer resistance by 784 Cubans, of whom 24 were killed in action and 59 wounded. Within two weeks, the Cubans, seventeen Libyans, fifteen North Koreans, forty-nine Soviets, ten East Germans, and three Bulgarians had returned to their countries. By December 15, all United States combat forces had withdrawn, leaving only training, police, medical, and support elements.

In explaining its participation in the Grenada operation, the United States government cited, in addition to the aforementioned OECS appeals, the need to ensure the safety of the roughly 1,000 United States students on the island, whose lives it claimed were endangered by the breakdown of law and order and a "shoot-on-sight" curfew. The Reagan administration also expressed concern that the students might be used as hostages. A total of 599 United States citizens were evacuated safely, at their request; those who were interviewed expressed great relief at being out of Grenada.

The Department of State also set forth the legal aspects of the Reagan administration's position by stressing the right of the United States under international law to protect the safety of its citizens, the right of the OECS nations to take collective action against a threat of external aggression, and the right of the United States to take action in response to requests from the OECS and the governor general of Grenada. Critics accused the Reagan administration of violating United Nations (UN) and Organization of American States (OAS) prohibitions on intervention and the use of force. United States military intervention constituted, in their view, a gross violation of Grenada's territorial integrity and political sovereignty. Supporters of the administration's position pointed out, however, that Article 22 of the OAS Charter specifically allows members with regional security treaties to take collective action in response to threats to peace and security and that Article 52 of the UN Charter similarly recognizes the right of regional security organizations to take collective action.

The applicability of the right to intervene to protect United States citizens may have been weakened somewhat by an obscure provision of international law stipulating that such interventions must be limited strictly to protecting the foreign national from injury.

Whether or not the ouster of the unrecognized RMC regime exceeded that restriction was unclear. Furthermore, some commentators argued that the Soviet and Cuban presence in Grenada did not constitute "external aggression" because it was requested by the (unelected) regime.

Geopolitical and strategic concerns, although not specifically cited, also clearly weighed in the decision of the United States government to act. Without making a public issue of the Bishop regime's Marxist-Leninist system of government, the Reagan administration became increasingly concerned over the deepening of Grenada's political ties to the Soviet Union and Cuba. Of particular concern to United States policymakers was the potential use of the island as a Soviet-Cuban base for intervention in nearby governments, interdiction of vital sea-lanes, reconnaissance by long-range aircraft, and transport of troops and supplies from Cuba to Africa and from Eastern Europe and Libya to Central America.

United States strategic affairs analysts have noted that, had Grenada become a Soviet-Cuban base, maritime and air traffic along the coast of Venezuela and westward toward the Panama Canal could have been controlled from the island. The Galleons Passage, one of the main deep-water oil-tanker passages into the region, passes Grenada's southern coast. The Caribbean's southeastern approaches offer a naval force the opportunity to dominate the sea-lanes running from the Strait of Hormuz to the North Atlantic oil-shipping routes. Moreover, much of the Caribbean's production and refining capability is within tactical air range of Grenada, which lies fewer than 483 kilometers from the oil fields of Trinidad and Tobago and eastern Venezuela. Within a 925-kilometer radius of Grenada—the range of Cuba's MiG-23 fighter-bombers—are the oil fields, refineries, tanker ports, and sea-lanes that have supplied a large share of the petroleum imported by the United States.

In support of its claim that Grenada might have served as a Soviet-Cuban base of operations in the region, the Reagan administration noted the presence in Grenada in October 1983 of the well-armed and militarily trained Cubans, mostly construction workers but also some Cuban troops from the Revolutionary Armed Forces and the Ministry of Interior; fortifications, including the battalion-sized military camp built by the Cubans at Calivigny; warehouses filled with weapons and munitions; the nearly finished 3,048-meter Point Salines runway; personnel from Eastern Europe, Africa, and East Asia; and captured documents, which included five secret military agreements: three with the Soviet Union, one with the People's Democratic Republic of Korea (North Korea), and one with

Cuba. Some leading specialists on Soviet and Cuban policies in Latin America believe that the voluminous secret files discovered in Grenada after the invasion amply document the NJM's attempts at Marxism-Leninism and its extensive political, ideological, and military ties with the Soviet Union and Cuba.

Another, uncited, reason for the involvement of the United States clearly was concern over the potential use of the island as a staging area for regional subversion. Reagan had stated earlier in 1983 that Grenada was "a Soviet-Cuban colony being readied for use as a major military bastion to export terror." Although Grenada had not yet begun exporting revolution to the region, captured Grenada documents provided ample evidence of these subversive intentions, as discussed in meetings between Grenadian leaders and their high-level Soviet counterparts. For example, one document read as follows: "Our revolution has to be viewed as a worldwide process with its original roots in the Great October Revolution. For Grenada to assume a position of increasingly greater importance, we have to be seen as influencing at least regional events. We have to establish ourselves as the authority on events in at least the English-speaking Caribbean, and be a sponsor of revolutionary activity."

As the first military intervention by the United States in the English-speaking Caribbean, the Grenada action marked what may be seen as the final act in the displacement of Britain by the United States as the region's principal power. In a speech to the Royal Commonwealth Society in London in November 1983, then-Barbadian prime minister Adams declared, "In hemispheric terms, 1983 is bound to be seen as the watershed year in which the influence of the United States . . . came observably to replace that of Great Britain in the old British colonies."

The United States Presence in the Region

Both Britain and the United States had diplomatic representation in the region in the late 1980s. Britain maintained ties to its former Caribbean colonies through West Indian diplomatic representation in London and the Meeting of Heads of Government of the Commonwealth, as well as through the British High Commission in Barbados, the High Commission representatives on each OECS island, and representatives or ambassadors to the Bahamas, Jamaica, and Trinidad and Tobago. The post-1983 diplomatic representation of the United States in the Commonwealth Caribbean islands included embassies located in the Bahamas, Jamaica, Barbados, Grenada, and Trinidad and Tobago. This representation remained largely unchanged from the early 1980s, with the exception of the opening of a United States embassy in Grenada in 1984. The United States ambassador to Barbados was simultaneously accredited to five OECS countries: Antigua and Barbuda, Dominica, St. Lucia, St. Christopher (hereafter, St. Kitts) and Nevis, and St. Vincent and the Grenadines. Only Jamaica and Barbados had a resident American military attaché; the United States defense attaché in Venezuela was accredited to Trinidad and Tobago.

Unlike Britain, the United States also maintained a military presence in the Commonwealth Caribbean islands in the late 1980s, although it was limited to small naval and air bases in Antigua and Barbuda and the Bahamas. Under a new basing agreement signed in April 1984, the United States agreed to pay the Bahamas US$100 million over a 10-year period for the use of 3 navy and air force sites. In the late 1980s, the United States Navy's Atlantic Underseas Test and Evaluation Center in the Bahamas and the United States Virgin Islands was still considered to be of critical importance to developing American antisubmarine warfare capabilities. American naval analysts have pointed out that the archipelago island geography of the Caribbean complicates monitoring of enemy submarines in the region by serving as a barrier against detection by the passive sound surveillance underwater system (sosus). Nevertheless, new technology reportedly made sosus-monitoring stations on certain islands dispensable. The American naval facility in Barbados, which included a sosus listening post, was removed in 1978 and relocated to Antigua. In the early 1980s, the United States considered closing its small naval facility on Antigua, including the United States Oceanographic Research Center there; but after the Grenada operation, plans were developed to convert the base into a training facility.

From the 1960s until the early 1980s, the United States Air Force and United States Navy also had maintained small bases on Grand Turk Island. In 1982 the air force decided to leave the island because its facility there was no longer cost effective or necessary. In 1983 the naval base was closed. For economic reasons the Turks and Caicos government strongly urged continuation of the United States facilities; in 1986 the government again indicated that it would like Washington to reestablish a military presence on the island.

United States Strategic Interests

Since the Manifest Destiny era of the mid-nineteenth century and the interventionist period of the early twentieth century, the United States has shown a strong interest in controlling maritime choke points in the Caribbean. The Caribbean region's proximity to the mainland makes it especially important to the defense of the United States. American strategic affairs analysts generally seem to agree that if any of the Caribbean rimlands or islands were to serve as a military base of the Soviet Union, Cuba, or another enemy power, United States and regional security would be endangered and the tasks of continental defense, American importation of strategic minerals and petroleum, and resupply of NATO forces in a global conflict would be further complicated. Moreover, the Reagan administration and proponents of its worldview have argued that the unchallenged peacetime expansion of military power into the Caribbean by the Soviet-Cuban-Nicaraguan triad could undermine the position of the United States in the Western Hemisphere politically and psychologically and undercut American credibility elsewhere in the world. Academic critics of these security views have tended to minimize or discount altogether the significance of additional Soviet-Cuban bases being established in the Caribbean Basin, arguing in part that the United States would take appropriate military action against them in the event of a major war.

The Caribbean region is the strategic link between the North Atlantic and South Atlantic for navies operating in the two oceans. The United States-NATO ''swing strategy'' is dependent on the security of the Caribbean sea-lanes. Global United States military strategy relies on moving United States-based forces across the Atlantic in the event of a crisis in Europe or elsewhere.

In addition to moving troops, as much as 60 percent of the supplies needed to replenish NATO forces, including petroleum, oil, and lubricants (POL), would be shipped from United States ports in the Gulf of Mexico or would pass through the Panama Canal. Fifty percent of these supplies would transit the Straits of Florida, in easy striking distance of Cuban torpedo boats and airplanes. In the event of a NATO-Warsaw Pact conflict, most refined petroleum products required for the Allied war effort would come from United States refining facilities along the Gulf coast and major refining centers along the island chain encircling the Caribbean Sea and the coasts of South America.

United States trade is also dependent on the security of the Caribbean. All thirteen sea-lanes in the Caribbean are included in the thirty-one sea-lanes in the world designated ''essential'' by the United States government. A lifeline of seaborne commerce and communication, the Caribbean is an area of convergence of major interoceanic trade routes and a logistical and supply route for the United States. Ships plying these trade routes move bulk commodities and general cargo between the main production and consumption areas in Western Europe, southern Asia, Africa, the Middle East, and the Western Hemisphere. According to the United States Department of Transportation, 1986 data indicate that somewhat more than half of the cargo flowing into the Caribbean originated in the United States, roughly a quarter in Western Europe, and most of the remainder in Asia.

The aggregate strategic and economic significance of the Caribbean to the vital interests of the United States may equal or exceed that of the Persian Gulf. In the mid-1980s, roughly 50 percent of United States exports and 65 to 75 percent of combined oil and strategic minerals imports were handled in the Gulf of Mexico ports of Houston, Galveston, Beaumont, New Orleans, and Mobile and passed through the Panama Canal or the Gulf of Mexico. The Caribbean sea-lanes, including the Panama Canal, also carried over 70 percent of United States imports of strategic minerals in the mid-1980s. Virtually all of the United States defense industry's vital supplies of manganese and chromium followed the South Atlantic sea-lanes from the Cape of Good Hope to United States ports.

The strategic importance of the Caribbean sea-lanes to the United States and Western Europe began to increase in the mid-1980s as strategic minerals became scarcer and imports from South Africa were jeopardized by the growing conflict over that country's apartheid policy. Should the Suez Canal be blocked during wartime, traffic probably would increase because more Europe-bound ships would have to take Caribbean routes. Both Western Europe and Japan were highly dependent on the Caribbean sea-lanes for trade. No less than one-half of Western Europe's imported petroleum passed through the Caribbean in 1986. About 25 percent of Western Europe's foodstuffs, as well as important minerals such as uranium, manganese, chromium, platinum, and vanadium, followed this route.

The development of Latin American and Caribbean nations as major producers of primary minerals for industrialized states increased their importance to the United States in the 1980s. The Caribbean Basin is an important source of many American raw material imports, especially strategic minerals such as antinomy, barite, bismuth, flourite, graphite, gypsum, mercury, rhenium, selenium, silver, sulfur, and zinc. Jamaica has been a principal Caribbean supplier of bauxite and alumina (see Glossary) to the United States.

In the late 1980s, the United States also was importing POL products from several Caribbean Basin countries, primarily

Venezuela but also from the Commonwealth Caribbean, mainly Trinidad and Tobago and the Bahamas. In 1986 Trinidad and Tobago accounted for 50 percent of United States imports of these products from the region (about a 17-percent increase over 1982 imports from that nation), and the Bahamas accounted for 17 percent (about a 3-percent decrease from 1982 imports). Moreover, in the late 1980s, a little over 10 percent of United States imported petroleum, including its oil imports from Venezuela, was refined in Caribbean ports, such as those in the Bahamas and Trinidad and Tobago. Before being shipped to the United States, much of the imported oil not refined in Caribbean ports was transferred from supertankers to smaller vessels at deep-water Caribbean harbors. The Commonwealth Caribbean's three transshipment sites were located next to refineries at South Riding Point, Bahamas; Cul de Sac Bay, St. Lucia; and off Grand Cayman.

Interdiction of Narcotics Trafficking

The extensive use of Commonwealth Caribbean islands as transit points for the smuggling of narcotics into the United States by foreign traffickers in the 1980s became of increasing concern not only to the United States government but also to island governments faced with the associated problems of growing corruption and youth drug addiction. By the mid-1980s, Commonwealth Caribbean countries such as the Bahamas and Jamaica were shifting rapidly from primarily transit countries to transit-consumer countries, according to the United States Department of State's Bureau of International Narcotics Matters.

In the late 1980s, Jamaica was the only Commonwealth Caribbean nation producing significant amounts of narcotics for clandestine export to the United States. In 1980 it overtook Mexico as the second largest supplier, after Colombia, of marijuana to the United States and maintained that position for much of the decade. During that period, Jamaica accounted for an estimated 13 to 15 percent of the marijuana smuggled into the United States mainland, according to the Department of State. Commonwealth Caribbean islands, including Jamaica, also were used heavily as a transit point for drug trafficking between South America and North America. The Eastern Caribbean archipelago has served as a shipment route for cocaine smuggled from Colombia and Bolivia to the New York City area.

The Bahamas had served historically as a conduit for contraband smuggled into and out of the United States. After 1976 the archipelago became an important drug-trafficking zone for

Colombian marijuana and other Latin American narcotics. Situated close to Florida and other states in the southeastern United States, it became a transit zone for drugs produced in Colombia and Jamaica and transported to the United States by boat or private aircraft. According to February 1987 press reports, Norman's Cay, a small island about sixty kilometers southeast of Nassau, had served as the main transshipment point for the Medellín Cartel of Colombian cocaine smugglers since the late 1970s. Having about 700 islands scattered over 259,000 square kilometers of ocean, the 1,207-kilometer-long Bahamian archipelago is ideal for drug smugglers. According to the United States Drug Enforcement Administration, ships bearing tons of marijuana, often accompanied by cargoes of cocaine, entered the southern Bahamas after passing through the Windward Passage and transited either the Caicos, Mayaguana, or Crooked Island Passage. They also entered from the east through the Northeast Providence Channel, after navigating the Mona Passage or taking a longer route on the eastern flank of the Caribbean.

The logistics of drug interdiction in the Caribbean are extremely difficult. In addition to the Bahamas islands, there are more than 300 other islands and several thousand cays (see Glossary). The Caribbean landmass includes 13,576 kilometers of coastline, 32 major ports, and over 400 airfields, not counting clandestine strips; it is spread across a region that measures about 2,640,000 square kilometers. Nevertheless, United States law enforcement agencies and Caribbean governments, particularly those of the Bahamas and Jamaica, have cooperated actively in combating drug trafficking during the 1980s. After the Grenada operation in October 1983, the United States began to seek the cooperation of Commonwealth Caribbean islands to interdict narcotics trafficking. All of the United States military aid to the Bahamas, Jamaica, and Trinidad and Tobago for fiscal year (FY—see Glossary) 1986, budgeted at US$8.375 million, was intended for fighting drug traffickers. Jamaica alone received US$8.275 million of that amount. At an RSS Council of Ministers meeting in Castries, St. Lucia, in October 1986, the Eastern Caribbean states agreed in principle to take joint action against drug trafficking by establishing a regional coast guard surveillance program. They also agreed to conduct joint drug interdiction exercises aimed at occupying certain sea-lanes used by narcotics traffickers.

The Soviet Presence

United States hegemony in the Caribbean in the twentieth century had remained until the Cuban revolution in 1959, an event that made the Soviet Union recognize the vulnerability of America's "backyard." By 1962 the Soviet Union had established a military outpost in Cuba and later that year began to emplace strategic missiles on the island. Although forced to withdraw the missiles as a result of the Cuban missile crisis in October 1962, the Soviets retained a combat brigade there. The Soviet Union also began to devise a more sophisticated strategy designed to exploit the new opportunities opened up by the Cuban revolution, but without risking another direct military confrontation with the United States. The main objectives of the new Soviet strategy in the Caribbean region, as assessed by American analysts, were to erode American influence further, expand Soviet influence and power, establish Soviet proxies, expand Soviet military and intelligence facilities and capabilities, make the United States withdraw from other parts of the world in an effort to consolidate defense of its vulnerable southern flank, and complicate American defense planning by increasing the sea-denial capabilities of the Soviet Union and its proxies.

In the early 1960s, the Soviet Union reportedly also began preparing for future naval activity in the Caribbean region by using its oceanographic research fleet to survey the area around Cuba and the Mona, Windward, and Anegada passages. The resulting data facilitated the Soviet attempt to develop surface and underwater weapons, surveillance systems, antisubmarine warfare, mine warfare, and amphibious landing data. Meanwhile, Soviet merchant vessels opened the Caribbean to Soviet maritime power. Seventy-eight Soviet merchant vessels were reported sighted in 1963; by 1968 the number had increased to 247 ships.

Prior to Castro's seizure of power, Soviet naval warships rarely visited the Western Hemisphere. They first entered the Caribbean region in July 1969 but caused little concern in the United States because world attention at the time was focused on the Apollo 11 moon landing. The Soviet military presence in the Western Hemisphere became more pronounced during the 1970s. The completion of the Soviet submarine base at Cienfuegos on Cuba's southern coast in 1970 (under the guise of a sugar terminal) allowed submarines of the Soviet Union and later Cuba to begin operating in Caribbean waters. In the spring of 1970, the Caribbean played an important role in the Soviet Union's first global naval exercise, Okean-70. In addition, the first Soviet Tu-95 Bear D reconnaissance and antisubmarine aircraft landed in Cuba that April. Since 1975 these aircraft have operated out of the San Antonio de los Baños airfield and, beginning in September 1982, along the eastern coast of the United States and in the Caribbean. In 1983 Tu-142 Bear F aircraft began using the same airfield, marking another gradual improvement in Soviet antisubmarine warfare capability in the region. During the 1969-86 period, twenty-six Soviet task forces were deployed to the Caribbean, and almost all of them visited Cuban ports, usually Havana and Cienfuegos. The early deployments included port visits to Jamaica and Barbados.

According to the United States Department of Defense, the Soviet naval deployments are used to show the flag in the Caribbean and occasionally in the Gulf of Mexico and to exercise with Cuban navy and air force units. The Soviets have deployed a wide range of ships and submarines, including guided missile cruisers, guided missile frigates, destroyers, and nuclear-powered cruise missile and attack submarines.

The Soviet Union traditionally has viewed the Caribbean as America's "strategic rear," according to American academic and military specialists on Soviet naval strategy. Cuba has served Soviet interests not only by promoting activities inimical to American and Commonwealth Caribbean interests, such as narcotics smuggling, regional subversion, support for radical regimes, and military intervention in Africa, but also by developing into a potential military threat in the event of war. Soviet strategy in the Caribbean region has called for gaining control, directly or indirectly, over the four major choke points in the region's sea-lanes, as well as developing the capability to interdict the major maritime routes transiting the area.

The German U-boat threat in the Caribbean during World War II clearly demonstrated the vulnerability of the Caribbean sea-lanes to interdiction and of the refineries to attack. The Nazi submarines wreaked havoc on shipping even though they were few in number, never totaling more than a dozen, and operated in the area without benefit of friendly regional ports or air cover. Moreover, during the war the United States could avail itself fully of Cuba as a naval base and source of supply. By contrast, in the event of a general war in the late 1980s, Soviet and Cuban submarines operating from Cuba would have advantages that the Germans lacked. The Soviet nuclear submarine base in Cienfuegos would make the island a potential base for submarine warfare in the Caribbean. Furthermore, since the 1970s the Soviets have tracked the movement of United States warships from the Soviet signals intelligence collection facility in Lourdes, Cuba. Given these advantages, American naval analysts believe that in the event of a major war Soviet and Cuban submarines might succeed in cutting off the four main choke points in the Caribbean, interdicting American shipping heading eastward from the Persian Gulf to the western coast of the United States, and attacking the United States mainland.

The Soviet choke-point strategy may help to explain why the Soviets apparently coveted Grenada, a small island with no significant resources. In 1983, when Maurice Bishop was still in power in Grenada, United States government military strategists feared that use of the island in conjunction with bases in Cuba and Nicaragua would enable the Soviet Union to project tactical power over the entire Caribbean Basin. According to this scenario, in the event of a major war Soviet-controlled air and naval forces operating from all three of these countries would have an ideal capability for sabotaging the United States-NATO "swing strategy" through harassment of the NATO supply lines. According to American naval analysts, Soviet strategy projected that Cuba- and Nicaragua-based Soviet forces would engage in persistent harassment and sea-denial operations in an effort to close the four major choke points in the Caribbean sea-lanes.

The Cuban Presence

In an effort to break out of its isolation and expand its influence in the Western Hemisphere, Cuba began a diplomatic and propaganda offensive in the early 1970s that included the Commonwealth Caribbean. Despite their concerns over Cuban subversive activities, as well as growing Soviet-Cuban ties and Cuba's intervention in Angola, the four newly independent Commonwealth Caribbean states—Barbados, Guyana, Jamaica, and Trinidad and Tobago—defied both the United States and the OAS and established relations with Cuba in December 1972. Cuba subsequently established technical and commercial exchanges with Guyana and even closer ties with the Michael Manley government in Jamaica. Cuba's relations with the Manley government helped provide the Castro regime with the diplomatic support that it sought in Third World forums. The Manley and Castro governments became increasingly active in the Nonaligned Movement and were outspoken on Third World issues; both signed numerous agreements during the decade. Cuba also opened diplomatic ties with the Bahamas in 1976 but failed to make any further diplomatic advances in the Commonwealth Caribbean until Maurice Bishop seized power in Grenada in 1979.

Cuba's political offensive made use of Cuban cultural exports and "solidarity brigades" of teachers, doctors, engineers, and advisers to local political groups. Unable to serve as a development model, however, Cuba provided only revolutionary legitimacy and the means for seizing power. By the late 1970s, the Commonwealth Caribbean islands, particularly Jamaica, were clearly a principal focus of Cuban subversive efforts in the region (see Regional Security Threats, 1970–81, this ch.).

In addition to being concerned by Cuba's subversive activities in the Caribbean region and its close ties with Jamaica in the 1970s, the United States became increasingly concerned by Cuba's growing military capabilities. American military analysts noted that these capabilities posed potential threats not only to the Commonwealth Caribbean islands but also to the Caribbean sea-lanes. Furthermore, Cuba developed a growing capability in the 1980s to carry out amphibious operations against the Eastern Caribbean ministates. The Cuban navy's acquisition in 1982 of two Polnocny-class amphibious landing ships from the Soviet Union, in addition to its smaller amphibious craft, gave Cuba the capability to place an initial assault force of about 1,000 soldiers, with either tanks or artillery support, on nearby island nations. In its 1986 *Handbook on the Cuban Armed Forces,* the United States Defense Intelligence Agency estimated that the Cuban air force and civil air fleet could land a force of 15,000 to 25,000 combat soldiers anywhere in the Caribbean Basin region within 2 to 3 weeks and have important elements in place within a few hours. Cuban merchant marine and fishing vessels also could transport personnel to any country in the Caribbean. The former has engaged in extensive training exercises for that very purpose. The United States is the only regional power with the means to repel such attacks.

Writing about choke-point warfare and interdiction in the Gulf of Mexico and the Caribbean in 1887, Mahan stated that strategy was a study of positions and that positions should be considered for both their military and their commercial value. After a study of the passages, islands, and harbors of Cuba, he concluded that the island not only was an exemplary haven for submarines and torpedo boats but also held the key to the entire Caribbean Basin. By the mid-1980s, Cuba had the military capabilities to interdict vital sea-lanes in the Caribbean and Gulf of Mexico and to control key passages. Cuba's strategic location between the Yucatán Channel and the Straits of Florida places the island in an excellent blocking position.

With extensive funds, equipment, and advice provided by the Soviet Union between 1978 and 1982, Cuba has built a modern air force, navy, and army with offensive interdiction capabilities. The Cuban air force's inventory of over 200 Soviet jet fighter-bombers and interceptors in the mid-1980s far surpassed the other air forces in the Caribbean Basin region. Nevertheless, Cuba's three squadrons of MiG-23s, with their 520-nautical-mile (964-kilometer) range, were capable of striking only three Commonwealth Caribbean members—Jamaica, the Bahamas, and the Turks and Caicos Islands—as well as Hispaniola (the island containing Haiti and the Dominican Republic) and part of the Florida peninsula. The fact that all of the Eastern Caribbean islands and Venezuela are outside this range may help to explain why the 3,048-meter Point Salines runway in Grenada would have been of strategic value to the Cubans and Soviets.

The Cuban navy also posed a significant potential threat to sea-lanes in the Caribbean and Gulf of Mexico. As a result of the acquisition of two Koni-class submarine warfare frigates in the early 1980s, the Cuban navy developed an ocean antiship capability for the first time. Cuba demonstrated its ability to project an offensive operation into the Caribbean in a May 1983 exercise. The Cuban antiship capability also included three Foxtrot-class diesel submarines and two highly capable kinds of missile patrol boats: Styx missile-equipped Osa-I- and Osa-II-class torpedo hydrofoils. These warships enabled the navy to conduct operations throughout the Caribbean and Gulf of Mexico and, to a limited degree, in the Atlantic. The Cuban navy probably would use its Foxtrot-class submarines and missile attack boats as the primary means of disrupting the sea-lanes. These craft would be supported both by the Koni-class frigates and by the land-based aircraft of the Cuban air force. The navy's interdiction efforts could be augmented by vessels of the merchant and fishing fleets, which could deploy sea mines in the sea-lanes. The use of Cuba to support Soviet naval units was demonstrated in early October 1986 when a Cuban ship went to the rescue of a Soviet Yankee-class nuclear submarine that caught fire in the Atlantic and sank before it could be towed to Cuba.

The Regional Security Setting

Throughout the period of British rule from the early nineteenth century until the move to independence in the 1950s and 1960s, the Commonwealth Caribbean islands relied on British protection. After independence, however, the islands to some extent went their separate ways and were preoccupied by their own national interests and security and defense concerns. In the late 1980s, these islands were still a largely undefended region; only Antigua and Barbuda, the Bahamas, Barbados, Jamaica, and Trinidad and Tobago maintained defense forces, ranging in size from about 100 to 2,100 members (see table 10, Appendix A).

Despite their relative unimportance in terms of territorial size, population, and gross domestic product (GDP—see Glossary), the English-speaking Caribbean islands were a factor in the inter-American system in the 1980s owing in large part to the strength of their voting bloc (a solid one-third of the OAS members). Because of this regional identity, scholars have recognized the English-speaking islands as constituting a subsystem of the Latin American system. One specialist on Commonwealth Caribbean affairs has observed that West Indian collective security issues can be understood only within the general dynamics of West Indian politics rather than OAS-based collective security arrangements, such as the Inter-American Treaty of Reciprocal Assistance (Rio Treaty). This is attributed to the lack of solidarity sentiments between the West Indies and the inter-American system.

Regional attitudes hardened as a result of two events that took place in the early 1980s. One was the war between Argentina and Britain in 1982 over the Falkland/Malvinas Islands. With the exception of Grenada, the Commonwealth Caribbean islands sided with Britain in the war. The other was the joint United States-Caribbean operation against Grenada in 1983, an action that was condemned unanimously by Hispanic Latin America.

Because there is no consistent regional consensus on security and other issues, however, the English-speaking island subsystem cannot be treated as a monolithic bloc. For example, four Commonwealth Caribbean states—Trinidad and Tobago, the Bahamas, Belize, and Guyana—opposed taking joint military action with the United States in Grenada in October 1983. Furthermore, unlike most of the Commonwealth Caribbean, both the Bahamas and Trinidad and Tobago are signatories of the Rio Treaty, the former since November 24, 1982, and the latter since June 12, 1967.

The 1979 coup in Grenada was the first violent, nonconstitutional overthrow of an elected government in the history of the Commonwealth Caribbean. The potential military and subversive threat to the region posed by the Grenada situation spurred regional efforts to establish an RSS in the Eastern Caribbean with United States, British, and some Canadian assistance. Although these efforts did little to facilitate the combined United States-Caribbean military operation in Grenada in October 1983, they have developed significantly since then. An examination of regional security issues in the context of postwar regional integration efforts helps to explain how the RSS developed in the Eastern Caribbean.

Postwar Federation Efforts

Britain's experiments in federation in its West Indian colonies had long been frustrated by regional insularity and parochialism.

Fort Picton, Tobago
Courtesy Trinidad and Tobago Tourist Board

Regional cooperation increased during World War II, however, owing to the threat of a common outside enemy. The Anglo-American Caribbean Commission, established in 1942, played an important role in further regional integration efforts. The Second West India Conference in 1946 also was considered a landmark in international and regional cooperation because it provided the dependent territories their first opportunity to participate in a multilateral meeting aimed at forging joint policies with Britain and the United States.

Because of decolonization plans, Britain placed renewed emphasis on political and economic federation in the postwar era (see Political Independence, ch. 1). Its resources drained by the war, Britain began promoting self-government within the Commonwealth in general, a long process that involved gradually granting the West Indian islands autonomy and then independence. The formulas of federation and associated statehood (see Glossary) were ways of solving the British problem of establishing a system that maintained regional order after independence. Nevertheless, the small size of the British West Indian islands and their populations, their lack of resources, and their dependence on outside markets made the decolonization process especially difficult.

Although the leading West Indians, particularly Jamaica's Norman W. Manley and Trinidad and Tobago's Eric Williams, favored federation as the best means to implement decolonization, the efforts at federation in the late 1950s and early 1960s failed (see The West Indies Federation, 1958–62, ch.1). The West Indies Federation, the first major change toward greater self-rule in the region, lasted only from 1958 to 1962. With its headquarters located in Port-of-Spain, Trinidad and Tobago, the federation united Jamaica, Barbados, Trinidad and Tobago, and the British colonies in the Leeward and Windward islands. The New West India Regiment, a British-trained and British-armed unit, was reconstituted to serve as the defense force for the short-lived federation. The latter collapsed, however, within months after Jamaica, concerned that the costs of membership outweighed the benefits, withdrew following a national referendum on the issue in September 1961. Jamaica and Trinidad and Tobago instead decided to become independent in 1962; the former acquired two battalions of the dissolved regiment, and the latter, one battalion.

Because of the failure of federation, a concept that the United States had favored, American policy toward the region lost what little direction it had. The fact that Jamaica and Trinidad and Tobago assumed independence without problem may have constrained further movement toward regional federation. In the mid-1960s, another attempt was made to join the remaining so-called Little Eight islands (Antigua and Barbuda, Barbados, Dominica, Grenada, Montserrat, St. Kitts-Nevis-Anguilla, St. Lucia, and St. Vincent and the Grenadines) into the Federation of the Eastern Caribbean, with Barbados playing the leading role in the organization's Regional Council. Financial requirements of federation quickly frightened off Barbados and Antigua and Barbuda, however. When Barbados became independent in 1966, the federation disintegrated. Nevertheless, a general framework for regional security collaboration was established. The formation of economic associations during the 1960s, including the Caribbean Free Trade Association (Carifta) in 1965, also helped to reinforce West Indian identity as a subregion.

During their emergence as independent states, the islands of the Eastern Caribbean largely ignored security-related issues, according to Gary P. Lewis. In 1966 the former Regional Council was superseded by the West Indies States Association (WISA), a stopgap administrative arrangement that gave the Windward and Leeward islands limited autonomy. Six of the seven WISA members— Antigua and Barbuda, Dominica, Grenada, St. Kitts-Nevis-Anguilla, St. Lucia, and St. Vincent and the Grenadines—assumed full responsibility for their own internal self-government and security, while the seventh, Montserrat, remained a crown colony (see

Glossary). Britain retained responsibility for defense and foreign affairs for its associated states.

In 1967, after Britain informed WISA members that defense and security assistance to the region would be provided only in response to an "external threat," efforts to establish a regional security force in the Eastern Caribbean were given new impetus. Nevertheless, Britain continued to provide some police training and advice. With the WISA Council of Ministers serving as a means for coordinating joint action, regional leaders agreed on the need for military or paramilitary forces to control outbreaks of violence or other subversive activities.

In the ensuing debate, some regional leaders decided on the need for security forces, while others argued that the individual islands were incapable of supporting either security forces or standing armies. Some questioned the need for military forces in view of the British defense guarantee and the likelihood that local forces could do little to prevent aggression by an extraregional power. Jamaica and Trinidad and Tobago recognized, however, the need for security forces to patrol their territorial waters and carry out search-and-rescue operations and other security-related duties. Therefore, both countries established national forces in the mid-1960s by incorporating former members of the New West India Regiment (see The Public Security Forces, ch. 2; National Security, ch. 3).

The small islands of the Eastern Caribbean, being more vulnerable than Jamaica and Trinidad and Tobago, favored the creation of a regional military force. An early indication of the difficulty of such an undertaking was the islands' failure in 1967 to coordinate a regional force to prevent the unilateral secession from St. Kitts-Nevis-Anguilla of the tiny island of Anguilla, which sought to reestablish its colonial ties to Britain. British paratroopers were landed on the coral island to restore order and British control in 1969 (see British Dependencies: British Virgin Islands, Anguilla, and Montserrat, ch. 5).

The formation of WISA led to greater economic and international coordination among the Eastern Caribbean states. In 1968 Carifta's membership was widened to include WISA members. That year, four of the smaller Eastern Caribbean territories— Dominica, Grenada, Montserrat, and St. Lucia—formed the Eastern Caribbean Common Market, which was later joined by Antigua and Barbuda (1981), St. Kitts and Nevis (1980), and St. Vincent and the Grenadines (1979). Little progress was made, however, toward creating a regionally integrated unit, so in 1973 the Carifta members agreed to replace their ineffective organization with the Caribbean Community and Common Market

(Caricom—see Appendix C). (The Bahamas joined Caricom in 1983). In addition to furthering economic cooperation, Caricom was intended to coordinate foreign policy among its member states.

Regional Security Threats, 1970–81

The relative stability characterizing the Westminster-style democracies of the Commonwealth Caribbean began to crumble in the late 1960s and early 1970s when Jamaica and Trinidad and Tobago were shaken by political violence. Until they began achieving independence, the Commonwealth Caribbean islands had been relatively immune from subversion because of the efficient protection provided by British security and defense guarantees. The Black Power movement (see Glossary) was behind much of the social disorder, although criminal violence also rose to unprecedented levels. Black Power activists almost succeeded in overthrowing Prime Minister Williams in Trinidad and Tobago in 1970, but government troops finally suppressed the revolt with the assistance of a planeload of arms and ammunition purchased from the United States and Venezuela (see Political Dynamics, ch. 3). Another small Marxist group continued to carry out terrorist attacks on the island for a few years.

The leaders of most of the Marxist-Leninist-oriented opposition groups in the region were known to have had close contact with Cuba. Barbados and Trinidad and Tobago were particularly concerned about Cuban involvement in the indigenous Black Power movement. Virtually all of the Commonwealth Caribbean islands had at least one small extremist group that was an occasional security threat.

Eastern Caribbean security concerns were heightened in the 1976–78 period as a result of a major terrorist attack and two abortive mercenary actions in Barbados. A Cubana Airlines DC–8 airplane exploded shortly after it took off from Grantley Adams International Airport in Barbados on October 6, 1976; all seventy-three passengers and five crew members were killed in the incident, a bombing attributed to Caracas-based anti-Cuban terrorists. Only 5 days earlier, then-Prime Minister Tom Adams had announced that 2 United States citizens had plotted to overthrow his government with the assistance of a 260-member mercenary force. In December 1978, Barbados thwarted a coup plot by an expatriate arms dealer and a mercenary force.

Revolutionary activities in Grenada in early 1979 stunned Commonwealth Caribbean capitals, as well as London and Washington. For the first time in the history of the Commonwealth Caribbean, an elected government was overthrown in an armed

618

coup. Grenada had been ruled for most of the decade by an autocratic-leaning prime minister, Eric Matthew Gairy, whose increasingly unpopular Grenada United Labour Party government was widely regarded as corrupt, incompetent, and an embarrassment to the region. On March 13, 1979, a group of supporters of Grenada's main parliamentary opposition party, Maurice Bishop's NJM, overthrew the Gairy regime in an armed coup while the prime minister was in the United States. Meeting in Barbados on March 14 and 15, 1979, the concerned leaders of six Eastern Caribbean countries discussed security implications of the coup. At a meeting held in Antigua and Barbuda five days later, leaders of Antigua and Barbuda, Dominica, Montserrat, St. Kitts and Nevis, St. Lucia, and St. Vincent and the Grenadines decided to examine the feasibility of establishing a regional defense force empowered to intervene in future rebellions "by armed and trained revolutionaries" against any of the governments concerned. Despite the initial alarm, the region established diplomatic relations with the de facto People's Revolutionary Government (PRG) because Gairy was widely disliked and ridiculed while Bishop was known regionally and liked and because of "a West Indian regional identity and sense of solidarity." Regional leaders also took note of Bishop's assurances that free and fair elections would be held.

The new Bishop government soon gave the region cause for concern. Within two weeks of opening diplomatic relations with Cuba on March 16, 1979, Cuban arms shipments and advisers began arriving on the island. The PRG regime replaced the entire professional police force and army with the political People's Revolutionary Army (PRA), arrested many political opponents, and suspended the Grenadian Constitution. By mid-April 1979, the PRA, with Cuban weapons and training assistance, had grown to a 2,000-member force, including the People's Revolutionary Militia (PRM), outstripping the combined forces of Grenada's OECS neighbors. (The PRA and PRM later became part of the People's Revolutionary Armed Forces—PRAF.)

On April 30, 1979, Barbadian prime minister Adams met with Trinidad and Tobago's prime minister Williams and issued a memorandum of understanding that noted the "growing complexity of the security problems of the Caribbean region," which they identified as "terrorism, piracy, the use of mercenaries, and the introduction into the region of techniques of subversion." Only a week later, on May 5, the government of Antigua and Barbuda claimed that it had foiled a Cuban-backed coup plot organized by the Antiqua-Caribbean Liberation Movement in collaboration with Kendrick Radix, then-attorney general of the new PRG government in Grenada. The Bishop regime's reneging on its promise to hold free and fair elections and its increasingly close ties to the Soviet Union and Cuba added to the growing regional anxiety.

The Carter administration responded to the Caribbean developments in 1979 by sending a special envoy on an emergency tour of the English-speaking islands. That October, the envoy held the third in a series of meetings in London to plan joint United States-British responses to Caribbean economic and security problems, including a proposed multinational seaborne patrol force in the Eastern Caribbean. The susceptibility of the Commonwealth Caribbean islands to a seaborne attack had been demonstrated by various incidents in which mercenaries were involved. Britain, already sensitive to charges that it had abandoned its former colonies, sent a naval team to the region to make recommendations for a joint coast guard facility in Barbados, St. Vincent and the Grenadines, and St. Lucia. In early 1979, Britain agreed to provide coast guard training and support for Barbados and St. Vincent and the Grenadines to "knit together" the smaller island forces.

The United States began a small International Military Education and Training program, primarily coast guard training, in Barbados in 1979. The United States also began providing coast guard vessels and some coast guard assistance to the region after the governments of Antigua and Barbuda, Barbados, St. Kitts and Nevis, and St. Lucia agreed to engage in joint coast guard patrols. This informal security arrangement helped to establish the basis for a future regional security system.

A precedent for regional security cooperation was set in early September 1979, after militant Rastafarians (see Glossary) led by Lennox Charles seized Union Island in St. Vincent and the Grenadines. R. Milton Cato of the center-right St. Vincent Labour Party, who had taken office as prime minister two days earlier, requested military assistance from neighboring Barbados. The Barbados Labour Party (BLP) government of Prime Minister Adams responded by sending detachments of the Barbados Defence Force (BDF) to St. Vincent on December 16. While the BDF troops guarded Kingstown, Vincentian security forces were able to capture the insurgents (see St. Vincent and the Grenadines, National Security, ch. 4).

Cuban activities in the Commonwealth Caribbean region in 1979–80 also were a source of increased regional security concerns. One incident that made Cuba look belligerent to its northern Commonwealth Caribbean neighbor, the Bahamas, and may have served as an act of regional intimidation took place on May 10, 1980. On that date, the Royal Bahamas Defence Force patrol boat

Flamingo took two Cuban fishing boats in tow on charges of poaching in Bahamian territorial waters south of Ragged Island. Before the clearly marked Bahamian patrol boat could return to home port, Cuban MiGs strafed and sank it, killing four crewmen and wounding three others. The next day Cuban MiGs engaged in prolonged buzzing of Ragged Island in the Bahamas. Moreover, Cuban troops were transported by helicopter to the same island in pursuit of the surviving crew members of the sunken patrol vessel. In a statement issued on May 12, Cuba claimed that the MiGs were responding to a reported act of piracy. Bahamian prime minister Lynden O. Pindling, calling the attack "an atrocious act of aggression," said his government was "particularly appalled by the inhumane act of firing on defenseless men struggling in the water" and claimed that the MiGs also had made "simulated rocket runs" over Bahamian territory at treetop level. The Bahamian government threatened to take Cuba before the UN Security Council for aggression, but Cuba apologized formally on May 29 and agreed to pay compensation (see The Bahamas, Foreign Relations, ch. 6).

Cuban military and political relations with Grenada and Cuba's growing subversive activities in Jamaica also contributed to a marked deterioration in Cuba's relations with the Commonwealth Caribbean islands. Cuba suffered serious political setbacks in the region in 1980 as a result of the dramatic shift in the regional climate caused by the electoral victories of Ronald Reagan in the United States and Edward Seaga in Jamaica, the latter representing the conservative Jamaica Labour Party (JLP). Leftist pro-Cuban candidates lost elections in Antigua and Barbuda, St. Vincent and the Grenadines, Dominica, and St. Kitts and Nevis. On taking office as prime minister in 1981, Seaga expelled Cuban ambassador Armando Ulises Estrada, a known Cuban intelligence agent, because of his role in coordinating the smuggling of arms and ammunition into Jamaica through a Cuban front corporation. By early 1981, Cuba was without any allies in the Caribbean other than Grenada. Cuban activities in the Commonwealth Caribbean suffered an additional setback when the Seaga government broke relations with Cuba on October 29, 1981, after the Castro regime ignored Jamaican warnings to withdraw all of its intelligence operatives from Jamaica.

The continued vulnerability of the democratic governments in the Eastern Caribbean was demonstrated again in March 1981, when an armed mercenary group of North American white supremacists and neo-Nazis attempted a coup in Dominica. The mercenaries wanted to replace Mary Eugenia Charles's Dominican Freedom Party government with the pro-South African

621

administration of former Prime Minister Patrick John (see Dominica, Government and Politics; Dominica, National Security, ch. 4). The island government was able to thwart the plot, however, without calling for assistance from the BDF. The Charles government subsequently adopted stringent security laws: the Prevention of Terrorism Act and the State Security Act.

A Regional Security System

The cumulative effect of the various incidents since 1978 and Cuba's activities in the English-speaking Caribbean prompted the WISA to reassess the former practice of providing minimal security and defense. On July 4, 1981, members agreed to replace the WISA, which had proven to be an extremely ineffective decision-making body, with the OECS, headquartered in Castries, St. Lucia. The OECS was designed to strengthen Eastern Caribbean ties and address issues of more specific concern to its seven members, particularly those relating to economic integration and coordination of foreign policy and defense and security matters. As a former WISA member, Montserrat, although still a British dependency, was also admitted into the OECS.

Article 8 of the OECS treaty established the basis for future regional security cooperation by charging the ministerial-level Defence and Security Committee of the OECS with ''responsibility for coordinating the efforts of Member States for collective defence and the maintenance of peace and security against external aggression.'' It also made the OECS responsible for developing ''close ties among the Member States of the Organization in matters of external defence and security, including measures to combat the activities of mercenaries, operating with or without the support of internal or national elements.'' In effect, the OECS treaty served as a regional security arrangement of the OECS countries, none of which had ratified the Rio Treaty. Exercising its prerogative, St. Kitts and Nevis chose not to participate in the defense and foreign policy provisions of the treaty.

Barbados was conspicuously absent from the OECS membership, not being a WISA member, but it was no less concerned about its security posture. One researcher at the College of the Virgin Islands (United States territory) illustrates Barbados' evolving attitudes toward security and defense by contrasting the positions of Adams and his BLP, as contained in their 1976 and 1981 party platforms. The earlier platform stated that the party would not commit the country to any defense pacts and would limit the defense forces to the minimum needed to maintain law and order. The 1981 position, in contrast, emphasized the need for a limited defense force capable of protecting the country against "potential marauders, terrorists, and mercenaries."

For Dominica's prime minister Charles, the creation of the OECS constituted only a first step toward establishment of regional security cooperation in the area of defense and security. In December 1981, Charles emphasized the need for joint training of security personnel in order to develop a defense system to prevent recurrences of attempted coups, such as the one that took place in Roseau, Dominica, on December 19. The prime minister saw such acts as having a destabilizing effect in the region. Charles's concerns were heard in Washington, which increased United States security assistance to the Eastern Caribbean in FY 1983. United States military aid to Dominica rose from US$12,000 in 1981 (it had been nothing in previous decades) to US$317,000 in 1983. United States military assistance to Barbados increased from US$61,000 in 1981 to US$170,000 in 1982. St. Vincent and the Grenadines received US$300,000 in military assistance from the United States in 1982, compared with nothing in previous decades.

On October 29, 1982, Barbados and four OECS countries—Antigua and Barbuda, Dominica, St. Lucia, and St. Vincent and the Grenadines—took an important step toward establishing an RSS by signing, in Bridgetown, Barbados, the Memorandum of Understanding. The move was prompted by growing concern among island leaders about the Grenadian regime's intentions. The three remaining OECS members—Grenada, Montserrat, and St. Kitts and Nevis—did not sign. Under the RSS, a member state whose security was threatened or who needed other kinds of emergency assistance could call on other member states. According to the Memorandum of Understanding, members were obliged "to prepare contingency plans and assist one another on request in national emergencies . . . and threats to national security." RSS members could choose not to participate in any RSS operation or training exercise because they were not party to a binding treaty, but rather an informal memorandum. Threats to national security covered by the memorandum included armed insurgencies, mercenary actions, army mutinies, armed seizure of facilities by insurgents, and armed secession attempts by smaller islands. The security arrangement also provided for cooperation in areas such as natural disasters, pollution control, maritime policing duties, smuggling prevention, search-and-rescue operations, immigration, customs and excise control, and fisheries protection.

The accord established the structural basis for the RSS, including arrangements for joint training and cost sharing. Barbados, as the largest participant, assumed 49 percent, or US$240,000, of

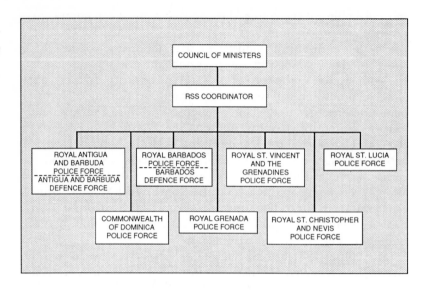

Figure 22. Organization of the Regional Security System (RSS), 1987

the cost of supporting the RSS apparatus, and the other islands paid 51 percent, based on an assessment of US$35,000 each. The RSS plan called for creation of an eighty-member paramilitary Special Service Unit (SSU) on each island. In a crisis, the SSUs would be coordinated by an RSS operations room at BDF headquarters at St. Ann's Fort in Bridgetown, Barbados, headed by the RSS coordinator, a Barbadian (see fig. 22). BDF chief of staff Brigadier Rudyard Lewis was elected to serve as the first RSS coordinator. The coordinator reported to the Council of Ministers, which was composed of those government officials entrusted with security in each member country. In a meeting held on February 19, 1983, in Castries, St. Lucia, the heads of government of St. Lucia, Barbados, Dominica, Antigua and Barbuda, and St. Vincent and the Grenadines finalized arrangements for the RSS.

Despite the formation of the RSS, the English-speaking islands of the Eastern Caribbean did not follow the United States political and economic boycott of Grenada. They remained convinced that Washington's concern had more to do with strategic competition with the Soviet Union than with the problems of greater concern to the ministates in the region: economic and social problems and efforts to increase Caribbean economic cooperation. The estimated US$23 million that Grenada received in foreign aid in 1982, mostly from Soviet bloc countries, did not go unnoticed by the Commonwealth Caribbean islands. Nevertheless, security issues became of overriding concern in the region as a result of the crisis in Grenada in October 1983.

Meeting in Barbados on October 21, the Defence and Security Committee of the OECS requested assistance from Barbados and Jamaica and nominated Dominican prime minister Charles to formally notify Britain and the United States of the OECS decision to take joint action to restore order in Grenada. The request for United States intervention reportedly was made orally to United States diplomats in Barbados that evening. In its formal request for United States assistance, made in writing on October 23, the OECS cited the consequent unprecedented threat to the peace and security of the region created by the vacuum of authority in Grenada and violations of human rights, including killings. The OECS request also noted the likely imminent introduction of military forces and supplies to consolidate the position of the government, the potential use of the island as a staging area for aggression against its neighbors, and the unnecessary expansion of the Grenadian army's capabilities.

In an emergency session held in Trinidad and Tobago on October 23, the Caricom heads of government were unable to reach a consensus on the proposals for joint action. They agreed only to impose sanctions on Grenada, including suspension of its Caricom membership. Trinidad and Tobago's prime minister George Chambers, the Caricom chairman, and Guyana's prime minister Forbes Burnham led the opposition to invading the island; they were supported by the Bahamas and Belize. Chambers reportedly was subsequently excluded from final planning for the military action, which was conducted by the nine other Caricom member states, including Jamaica, that favored the operation. The OECS actively supported the joint United States-Caribbean operation of October 25, 1983, although three OECS members—Grenada, St. Kitts and Nevis, and Montserrat—did not participate in the voting (see Current Strategic Considerations, this ch.). An OECS statement noted that "the extensive military buildup on Grenada over the past few years has created a situation of disproportionate military strength between Grenada and other OECS countries."

In keeping with their prior positions, the Bahamas, Guyana, and Trinidad and Tobago publicly condemned the intervention. Chambers's stance was not shared by the Trinidadian press, however, which portrayed him as out of touch with other Caribbean nations. A poll published in the *Trinidad and Tobago Express* on October 30, 1983, also showed 61 percent of Trinidadians and Tobagonians supporting the invasion and United States involvement and 56 percent in favor of committing Trinidadian troops to the assault.

After the Grenada operation, the United States, Britain, and neighboring states such as Barbados began assisting the island to rebuild its security forces. The 350-member, multinational Caribbean Peace Force (CPF) maintained security on the island for the rest of the year, and United States combat forces departed Grenada on December 14, 1983. Following the departure of the combat forces, British and Barbadian police and United States Green Beret advisers regrouped and retrained the 270 personnel left in the Grenada police force and incorporated them into a new force. Barbados contributed by instructing some of the Grenadian recruits at the Regional Police Training Center in Barbados. The United States military team supplemented the British and Barbadian police training by forming an eighty-member Grenadian SSU and providing it with basic light infantry training and equipment.

At the specific request of the OECS, the United States also began increasing its military training assistance to the RSS member states. In February and March 1984, eight-member United States Green Beret teams trained eighty SSU personnel on each of the RSS islands, including newly independent St. Kitts and Nevis. The latter was admitted into the RSS at a meeting of the RSS Council of Ministers in Bridgetown on February 7, 1984. United States efforts also went into developing and equipping a coast guard force for the region.

When the RSS Council of Ministers met again in Bridgetown on March 17, 1984, the leaders of the 6 RSS islands adopted a plan for creating a mobile, 200-member task force and a coordination agreement among the various island coast guard services. The heads of government in the region discussed regional security again at a meeting held on November 23, 1984. CPF forces withdrew from Grenada on September 22, 1985.

On November 30, 1984, United States, Canadian, and British representatives met with officials from the RSS member states in Bridgetown, Barbados, to discuss financial and material support for the RSS. They also reportedly discussed the establishment of a Barbados-based central command and training structure, as well as the provision for suitable logistical support. Under the proposed structure, each nation would have an SSU consisting of police or defense forces capable of acting on their own or in a regional capacity.

Testifying before the United States Congress during hearings on the foreign assistance budget for the Eastern Caribbean in early 1985, officials from the Department of State and the Department

Caribbean Peace Force soldiers in Grenada
Courtesy United States Department of Defense

of Defense stressed the fragile economies of the islands and the absence of foreign threats to regional security. Accordingly, the 1986 United States budgetary request, as in the past, balanced military and economic assistance on a ratio of one to four. United States military assistance for the region in FY 1986 was set at US$10 million, the same as for FY 1985. The FY 1986 United States military aid package was primarily for logistical support for patrol boats and communications equipment, with an additional US$400,000 for military education and training for the SSUs. Having acquired coast guard boats from the United States in the mid-1980s, Dominica, Antigua and Barbuda, St. Lucia, and Grenada were among the five Eastern Caribbean nations to carry out joint maneuvers with six United States Navy vessels in November 1984. The joint naval exercises involved search-and-rescue operations and other coast guard functions. Grenada was admitted into the RSS at a meeting of Eastern Caribbean leaders held in Kingston, Jamaica, on February 26, 1985.

The RSS regional security concept was put into practice in a five-day exercise by United States, British, and RSS forces in September 1985. Called Operation "Exotic Palm," it was the first regional military exercise to be held in the Eastern Caribbean. Operation Exotic Palm involved 200 Caribbean troops from 7 West Indian nations, including Jamaica, and 300 United States troops,

627

as well as a United States Navy destroyer and a British frigate and support ship. Under the scenario, thirty to fifty insurgents seized an airport in St. Lucia, whereupon RSS forces retook the field and flushed the fleeing rebels out of a forested area. Despite heavy rains during the first two days, the US$1 million exercise was considered a success. Trinidad and Tobago did not participate but sent observers. St. Vincent and the Grenadines was the only RSS member to decline any involvement; it did so because of the opposition of its prime minister, James F. "Son" Mitchell, to the regional military roles of the RSS and the United States.

St. Lucia's prime minister, John G.M. Compton, proposed extending the RSS to include the other islands within the thirteen-nation Caricom. Neither of the two principal West Indian nations lying just outside the RSS region—Jamaica and Trinidad and Tobago—was interested in joining, however, in part because of fears that they would be expected to assume most of the financial burden. In an October 20, 1985, news conference, Jamaican prime minister Seaga pledged his country's willingness to provide technical training and other assistance for the RSS forces, but he reaffirmed his government's unwillingness to join any such regional grouping.

Despite its stance on RSS membership, Jamaica participated—along with forces of the United States, Britain, and all RSS members except Barbados—in an exercise called "Ocean Venture 86," held in April and May 1986. The maneuvers—involving 700 members of the United States Green Berets, Marines, and 101st Air Assault Battalion units, and 160 RSS personnel—included landings on Grenada and the Puerto Rican island of Vieques.

Convening in Castries, St. Lucia, in October 1986, the RSS Council of Ministers decided, in its first meeting in twenty months, not to adopt a treaty making the RSS a formal organization but to continue operating the system under the 1982 Memorandum of Understanding. Dominica's prime minister Charles argued unsuccessfully that a formal RSS treaty would permit some kind of official agreement with France and Venezuela. For two weeks later that month, joint exercises called "Upward Key 86" were conducted on and off the coast of Barbuda. The maneuvers involved 240 troops from the United States, Antigua and Barbuda, and St. Kitts and Nevis in a series of land, sea, and air operations.

Their stated objections to the RDF proposal and the military features of the RSS notwithstanding, prime ministers Errol Barrow of Barbados and Mitchell of St. Vincent and the Grenadines retained their island nations' RSS memberships. Barbados went its own way on the issue of United States coast guard training by signing a coast guard training agreement with Canada on August 29, 1986. Barrow affirmed in September 1986 that Barbados was willing to continue hosting the RSS headquarters and to participate in United States and British training of RSS forces. Both Barrow and Mitchell also were on record as staunchly supporting the RSS's coast guard role in narcotics interdiction, search and rescue, and other law enforcement activities. Barrow pledged that Barbados would continue to regard the RSS as a means of furthering regional cooperation in the areas of narcotics and contraband control, maritime training, and fisheries protection. St. Vincent and the Grenadines, for its part, was one of only two RSS-member countries not in arrears with RSS payments in late 1986 (the other being St. Kitts and Nevis).

Operation "Camile," the first exercise to include units from all RSS members, was held in early May 1987. RSS troops, as well as forces from Jamaica, Britain, and the United States, participated in the maneuvers. The exercise emphasized civil defense, disaster relief, and coast guard functions, rather than military operations, and included a rehearsal of evacuation of civilians endangered by a volcanic eruption.

By mid-1987 the RSS member states undoubtedly were better prepared to cope with security problems as a result of the modest security measures implemented by the Eastern Caribbean islands with outside assistance, the RSS training exercises, and greater regional security cooperation. Nevertheless, the English-speaking island nations remained a largely undefended concentration of island democracies that were still highly vulnerable to subversion and attacks by terrorists or mercenaries, as well as to social violence. Four years after the October 1983 intervention in Grenada, declining economic prospects and rapidly increasing population growth had raised social tensions throughout the English-speaking Caribbean, potentially making the subregion vulnerable to a new generation of radicals. Without outside assistance, they were also defenseless against any possible future military aggression by an extraregional power. The Soviet Union, Cuba, and Libya did not abandon their interests in the subregion after their debacle in Grenada.

In addition, beginning in the summer of 1984, Libyan agents appeared to be playing an active role among dissidents on the English-speaking Caribbean islands. According to the United States Department of State and the Department of Defense, the loss of the Libyan People's Bureau in Grenada in October 1983 forced Tripoli to attempt to establish subversive centers in other diplomatic posts in the region, including an "Islamic Teaching Center" in Barbados. The State Department also claimed in August 1986 that Libya was providing covert funding to radical groups in at least seven Caribbean countries, including Antigua and Barbuda, Dominica, and St. Lucia, and urging leftist leaders in the region to use violent means to achieve power.

Controversial Security Issues

After the signing of the RSS Memorandum of Understanding in 1982, some opposition groups in the Eastern Caribbean charged that the security plan was a United States idea, designed to keep conservative, pro-United States governments in power. These groups, and particularly Barbados' Democratic Labour Party (DLP), criticized the alleged secretiveness of their governments' participation in the RSS and in developing the SSUs. Conservative leaders, such as Dominica's Charles, countered that the RSS idea was developed by Caribbean leaders and that there was nothing secret about Dominica's RSS activities, which usually involved coast guard assistance, or its SSU, which carried out normal police duties when not training or exercising as a unit.

In addition to the regional debate over the pros and cons of the RSS itself, two related security issues were controversial in the 1980s: a proposal to establish a Regional Defence Force (RDF) and charges of "militarization" of the Eastern Caribbean. The plan to establish a regional force had been canceled in the late 1960s as a result of disagreements over the location of the proposed force and its leadership, in which country ultimate authority over it should reside, and logistical problems and financial constraints. The idea of establishing an RDF was again considered by the Eastern Caribbean islands in 1976, as well as shortly after the Grenada coup in 1979, but was shelved on both occasions owing to practical and political obstacles. During 1980 serious talks got underway on establishing a 120-member regional defense force "to deal with any internal armed threat to an elected government."

Barbadian prime minister Adams revived the RDF proposal in 1982 when the RSS was formed, but it was rejected as too costly. Undeterred, he again brought up the idea at the RSS meeting held in Castries, St. Lucia, in February 1983. By formally introducing his so-called "Adams Doctrine" in a speech to the annual conference of his governing BLP on January 21, 1984, Adams emerged as the principal proponent for establishing an RDF in the region. He recommended one regional army, consisting of 1,000 to 1,800 troops, instead of a number of national armies, because a combined force would provide an additional safeguard against insurrections, mercenaries, and military revolts.

An RDF would have been unprecedented for a region that had been guarded mainly by police since the islands began to become independent from Britain in the early 1960s. Despite their considerable strategic importance, none of the Eastern Caribbean islands had maintained more than a token military force. Only Barbados and Antigua and Barbuda still had defense forces in the late 1980s. The Barbados Defence Force (BDF), formerly the long-standing Barbados Regiment, was created by the BLP government in 1979. Comprising army, marine, and air divisions, the BDF was reported in 1986 to have from 300 to 1,800 troops (the latter figure was announced by Prime Minister Barrow himself). Most knowledgeable observers generally agreed, however, that the BDF had about 500 members. The 115-member Antigua and Barbuda Defence Force lacked the training, equipment, and organization of the BDF.

The other English-speaking islands in the Eastern Caribbean also were guarded mainly by police. Dominica's prime minister Charles disbanded the Dominican Defence Force in April 1981 after at least five key officers were implicated in a failed coup attempt involving United States and Canadian mercenaries. In 1979 the same force had intervened in a crowd-control incident and opened fire, killing two persons. The resulting constitutional crisis led to the collapse of the government of then-prime minister Patrick John (see Dominica, Government and Politics, ch. 4). St. Kitts and Nevis also abolished its fourteen-year-old defense force in 1981, owing to its costliness and ineffectiveness, and converted its soldiers into policemen and firemen. It retained only its Volunteer Defence Force and the Royal St. Christopher and Nevis Police Force.

The RDF proposal would have expanded the 1982 RSS agreement to include a regional ground force element. Adams explained that the RDF proposal called for "the abandonment of individual defence forces and the incorporation of the existing forces into a regional force which would have a unified command under general political direction." According to St. Lucian prime minister Compton, the RDF would move into any island "which showed signs of invasion from internal subversion or outside intruders."

The RSS Council of Ministers, meeting in Bridgetown on February 7, 1984, studied a report on the implications of establishing an RDF. These leaders also raised the RDF question the next day in a meeting with visiting United States secretary of state George P. Shultz, with whom Prime Minister Adams held a private meeting. By that time, the RDF proposal envisioned an 1,800-member force costing US$100 million over 5 years (a figure that included purchases of helicopters and coast guard vessels).

In a meeting at BDF headquarters in Bridgetown on March 17, 1984, the leaders of the six RSS island nations resumed discussion of the proposal to establish an RDF instead of national armies. By October, however, they had scaled down plans for a Barbados-based RDF, primarily owing to the cost factor but also in response to charges of militarization of the region. Some critics were concerned that an RDF would divert scarce funds from badly needed economic development projects. Mitchell, who took office as prime minister of St. Vincent and the Grenadines in a landslide victory in July 1984, announced that his New Democratic Party (NDP) was opposed to heavy spending on arms and armies in the region because of concerns about "militarization."

A five-year plan proposed at the RSS meeting held on November 23, 1984, called for expanding the multilateral RDF into a permanent Caribbean Defence Force. With headquarters in Barbados and garrisons in Grenada and Antigua and Barbuda, it would have consisted of about 1,800 personnel, including 700 combat infantry troops and some 1,100 members of coast guard and air support elements. Implementation of the initiative, however, would have been dependent on increases in United States security assistance and exemption from a technical United States legislative restriction prohibiting the provision of foreign police training. When regional military leaders estimated the cost of the proposed RDF at US$60 million over five years, Washington rapidly cooled on the idea.

When Adams died from a heart attack in March 1985, the RDF plan lost its main advocate. After Barrow took office as prime minister in Barbados in May 1986, he joined ranks with Prime Minister Mitchell of St. Vincent and the Grenadines and succeeded in blocking the RDF proposal. Opposition to the RDF idea among some island leaders also was a factor in its demise. Nevertheless, Antigua and Barbuda's prime minister Vere Cornwall Bird, Sr., still advocated the establishment of an independent, regional collective defense and security system in order to counter what he perceived to be a communist threat aimed at destabilizing the OECS member states.

The efforts by the English-speaking islands of the Eastern Caribbean to establish an RDF and an RSS, with both British and United States military assistance, were characterized by critics as tantamount to militarizing the region. Some academics contended that the region had become militarized. Even OECS director Vaughan Lewis expressed reservations about the possible political consequences of establishing SSUs on the islands. "The reinforcement of local security systems," he explained, "leads to an upsetting of the balance between the various socio-political sectors . . . . The modernization process suggests to the military a sense of their own particular status as the only virtuous sector—as the guardians of the system . . . . This sets the basis for the coup and counter-coup system.''

In 1986 the two most outspoken proponents of the militarization charge were prime ministers Barrow and Mitchell of Barbados and St. Vincent and the Grenadines, respectively. At his first news conference on June 2, 1986, Barrow told reporters that he held reservations on the RSS similar to those held by Mitchell, including the suspicion that the RSS idea had United States origins. Although both leaders kept their nations in the RSS, they declined to allow their RSS forces to participate in at least two RSS exercises in 1985 and 1986. Barrow and Mitchell also stressed the need for training the police forces of the RSS member countries in internal security measures, instead of providing military-style training for defense and paramilitary forces.

In a letter dated September 2, 1986, and addressed to the prime ministers of the other RSS member states, Barrow stated his government's ''strong reservations over the use of our resources for militaristic purposes or for unjustifiable usurpation of the sovereignty of our country by alien influences.'' At the same time, Barrow announced that Barbados would not agree to upgrade the RSS Memorandum of Understanding to the status of a treaty but would continue using it as the basis for security cooperation between Barbados and the Eastern Caribbean. Other regional leaders, principally prime ministers Charles of Dominica and Bird of Antigua and Barbuda, strongly defended the RSS and rejected the militarization argument. Barrow's death from a heart attack in early June 1987 removed the leading critic of the alleged militarization of the subregion.

By 1987 the charges of militarization seemed to have been overstated. Unlike in Bishop's Grenada, the Eastern Caribbean appeared to lack the usual indicators of militarization, such as the formation of people's militias, military involvement in government, military buildups, or significant shares of GDP being devoted to the military sector. Spending increases for police and security forces appeared to be directed toward antidrug operations. Whereas the proportion of expenditures on the military in Trinidad and Tobago, Jamaica, and Guyana more than doubled during the 1972–79 period, none of these governments were considered to have particularly close relations with the United States.

The one-to-four ratio of United States military and economic assistance to the Eastern Caribbean in FY 1986 did not suggest a United States effort to militarize the subregion either. Although police force elements acquired paramilitary capabilities with United States assistance, these SSUs were limited to about eighty members each. Moreover, the largest defense force in the subregion, the BDF, had only about 500 members. In some circumstances, however, there appeared to be a potential for SSUs to be misused as a political instrument in support of or against a governing party. The holding of RSS military exercises with United States forces also was a new development for the subregion.

*   *   *

Yereth Kahn Knowles's doctoral dissertation, *Beyond the Caribbean States,* offers a scholarly account of post-World War II efforts to form federations and a regional security system. Useful information on the RSS is also contained in the following journal articles: Bernard Diederich's "The End of West Indian Innocence: Arming the Police"; Gary P. Lewis's "Prospects for a Regional Security System in the Eastern Caribbean"; and Graham Norton's "Defending the Eastern Caribbean." Relevant discussions of the militarization issue are Dion E. Phillips's "The Increasing Emphasis on Security and Defense in the Eastern Caribbean" and David A. Simmons's "Militarization of the Caribbean: Concerns for National and Regional Security."

Especially useful journal articles on strategic affairs include Edward A. Padelford's "Caribbean Security and U.S. Political-Military Presence"; Vaughan A. Lewis's "The US and the Caribbean: Issues of Economics and Security"; and George Black's "Mare Nostrum: U.S. Security Policy in the English-Speaking Caribbean." Books with insightful discussions of the strategic setting include those by Harold Mitchell, Lester D. Langley, John Bartlow Martin, Robert Agro-Melina and John Cronin, Thomas D. Anderson, and Robert J. Hanks. (For further information and complete citations, see Bibliography.)

Appendix A

Table 1. Metric Conversion Coefficients and Factors

When you know	Multiply by	To find
Millimeters	0.04	inches
Centimeters	0.39	inches
Meters	3.3	feet
Kilometers	0.62	miles
Hectares (10,000 m²)	2.47	acres
Square kilometers	0.39	square miles
Cubic meters	35.3	cubic feet
Liters	0.26	gallons
Kilograms	2.2	pounds
Metric tons	0.98	long tons
....	1.1	short tons
....	2,204	pounds
Degrees Celsius	9	degrees Fahrenheit
(Centigrade)	divide by 5 and add 32	

Table 2. Jamaica. Value of the Jamaican Dollar Compared with the United States Dollar, Selected Years, 1971–87*

Date	Value per United States Dollar	Date	Value per United States Dollar
December 1971	J$0.77	January 1984	J$3.55
January 1973	J$0.91	September 1984	J$4.00
January 1978	J$1.05	December 1984	J$4.85
May 1978	J$1.55	March 1985	J$5.50
May 1979	J$1.78	October 1985	J$6.40
November 1983	J$3.15	June 1987	J$5.50

* Includes only basic or official rates, not parallel, Caribbean Community and Common Market, or special rates. Jamaican dollar became pegged to United States dollar in 1973.

Source: Based on information from Bank of Jamaica, *Statistical Digest,* Kingston, Jamaica, December 1985, Appendix 1.

Table 3. Jamaica. Bauxite and Alumina Production and Exports, 1980–85 (in thousands of tons)

	1980	1981	1982	1983	1984	1985
Production						
Bauxite	12,053	11,682	8,378	7,683	8,937	5,675
Alumina	2,456	2,556	1,758	1,851	1,749	1,513
Exports						
Bauxite						
Crude	6,060	5,294	4,079	3,009	4,559	2,325
Locally processed ...	5,918	6,312	4,223	4,674	4,176	3,914
Total Bauxite	11,978	11,606	8,302	7,683	8,735	6,239
Alumina	2,395	2,549	1,755	1,907	1,713	1,622

Source: Based on information from Jamaica, National Planning Agency, *Economic and Social Survey of Jamaica, 1985,* Kingston, Jamaica, 1986, 8.3–8.4.

Table 4. Jamaica. Balance of Payments, 1981–85
(in millions of United States dollars)

	1981	1982	1983	1984	1985 [1]
Merchandise					
Exports (f.o.b.) [2]	974.0	768.5	685.7	702.4	568.5
Imports (c.i.f.) [3]	1,296.7	1,204.4	1,124.2	1,183.2	1,143.7
Merchandise balance	− 322.7	− 435.9	− 438.5	− 480.8	− 575.2
Services					
Exports					
Foreign travel	n.a.	336.2	399.3	406.6	406.8
Investment income	n.a.	97.1	63.8	18.8	48.6
Other	n.a.	187.9	176.3	199.5	184.1
Total exports	n.a.	621.2	639.4	624.9	639.5
Imports					
Foreign travel	n.a.	30.1	25.0	21.3	20.0
Investment income	n.a.	280.6	248.9	320.6	359.4
Other	n.a.	247.4	247.0	275.6	240.2
Total imports	n.a.	558.1	520.9	617.5	619.6
Services balance	− 138.4	63.1	118.5	7.4	19.9
Balance of goods and services ..	− 461.1	− 372.8	− 320.0	− 473.4	− 555.3
Net transfers					
Receipts	123.3	134.5	94.7	181.6	201.0
Payments	1.0	15.9	6.8	61.0	60.8
Net transfers balance	122.3	118.6	87.9	120.6	140.2
Current account balance	− 338.8	− 254.2	− 232.1	− 352.8	− 415.1
Net capital movements					
Official	240.2	446.0	321.0	362.9	249.0
Private	− 3.9	25.7	− 255.1	215.6	84.3
Net capital movements balance	236.3	471.7	65.9	578.5	333.3
Current and capital transactions	− 102.5	217.5	− 166.2	225.7	− 81.8
Changes in reserves [4]	90.5	− 83.3	289.1	− 225.7	81.8

n.a.—not available.
[1] Provisional.
[2] Free on board.
[3] Cost, insurance, and freight.
[4] Minus sign signifies increase in reserves.

Table 5. *Trinidad and Tobago. Petroleum Production, 1981–85*

	Unit	1981	1982	1983	1984	1985
Crude oil production	thousands of cubic meters	10,988	10,274	9,275	9,841	10,232
Oil exports	– do –	5,978	5,275	4,768	5,170	5,912
Locally refined oil	– do –	3,933	5,043	4,321	4,475	4,599
Refined imported crude oil	– do –	6,138	3,719	n.a.	n.a.	n.a.
Asphalt production	thousands of tons	23.2	29.7	38.2	31.1	21.4
Asphalt exports	– do –	17.5	19.4	24.0	23.8	20.2
Natural gas production	millions of cubic meters					
Fuel..............	– do –	2,865	3,921	3,102	2,552	2,966
Processed	– do –	346	687	920	1,105	1,163
Other	– do –	1,057	959	1,122	1,716	1,766
Vented and losses	– do –	1,682	1,350	1,175	1,856	1,678
Total natural gas production	– do –	5,950	6,917	6,319	7,229	7,573

n.a.—not applicable.

Source: Based on information from Central Bank of Trinidad and Tobago, *Annual Report, 1985*, Port-of-Spain, Trinidad and Tobago, 1986, 71, Table 1.9.

Table 6. The Bahamas. Population, Land Area, and Population Density of the Major Islands, 1980

Island(s)	Population [1]	Area (in square kilometers)	Population Density (per square kilometer)
Acklins	616	389	1.6
Andros	8,397	5,957	1.4
Berry	509	31	16.4
Bimini	1,432	23	62.3
Cat	2,143	389	5.5
Crooked	517	238	2.2
Eleuthera, Harbour, and Spanish Wells	10,600	518	20.5
Grand Bahama	33,102	1,373	24.1
Great Abaco and Little Abaco ...	7,324	1,681	4.4
Great Exuma	3,672	290	12.7
Great Inagua and Little Inagua ..	939	1,671	0.6
Long	3,358	448	7.5
Long Cay	33	23	1.4
Mayaguana	476	285	1.7
New Providence	135,437	207	654.3
Ragged	146	23	6.3
San Salvador and Rum Cay	804	241	3.3
TOTAL	209,505	13,787[2]	15.2[3]

[1] Population statistics refer to results of the 1980 census; by 1986 the Bahamas had an estimated population of 235,000.
[2] Total land area of the Bahamas is 13,934 square kilometers.
[3] Based on 1986 estimated population of 235,000, the population density was 16.8 in that year.

Source: Based on information from *Bahamas Handbook and Businessman's Annual, 1987,* Nassau, The Bahamas, 1986, 327–28; and Bahamas, Ministry of Education, *Atlas of the Commonwealth of the Bahamas,* Kingston, Jamaica, 1985, 5.

Table 7. *The Bahamas. Government Revenues and Expenditures, 1980–86*
(in millions of Bahamian dollars) [1]

	1980	1981	1982	1983	1984	1985 [2]	1986 [2]
Revenues							
Tax Revenues	204.0	211.7	219.2	253.4	273.9	342.0	369.0
Non-tax revenues	57.0	81.4	76.4	60.6	76.4	81.0	89.2
Total revenues	261.0	293.1	295.6	314.0	350.3	423.0	458.2
Expenditures							
Current							
Wages and salaries	114.0	134.4	146.4	166.7	n.a.	n.a.	n.a.
Goods and services	57.0	68.3	64.8	72.1	n.a.	n.a.	n.a.
Interest payments	22.1	24.2	35.9	40.2	n.a.	n.a.	n.a.
Subsidies and transfers ..	16.9	18.9	25.9	28.7	n.a.	n.a.	n.a.
Commercial services	9.6	10.2	10.6	10.9	n.a.	n.a.	n.a.
Total current	219.6	256.0	283.6	318.6	n.a.	n.a.	n.a.
Capital							
Formation	25.1	29.2	30.4	19.1	n.a.	n.a.	n.a.
Transfers	11.7	12.7	10.0	3.5	n.a.	n.a.	n.a.
Loans and advances	2.1	53.9	43.0	53.9	n.a.	n.a.	n.a.
Purchase of assets and loss from sale of assets ...	0.4	n.a.	n.a.	0.1	n.a.	n.a.	n.a.
Total capital	39.3	95.8	83.4	76.6	n.a.	n.a.	n.a.
Total expenditures ...	258.9	351.8	367.0	395.2	366.2	421.8	458.0
Fiscal deficit or surplus (net financing requirement) ..	2.1	−58.7	−71.4	−81.2	−15.9	1.2	0.2

n.a.—not available.
[1] The Bahamian dollar has been kept at par with the United States dollar since 1973.
[2] Preliminary.

Source: Based on information from World Bank, *The Bahamas: Economic Report*, Washington, 1986, 93–96; and *Bahamas Handbook and Businessman's Annual, 1987*, Nassau, The Bahamas, 1986, 336–37.

Table 8. The Bahamas. Balance of Payments, 1981–85
(in millions of Bahamian dollars) [1]

	1981	1982	1983	1984	1985 [2]
Current account					
Merchandise (f.o.b.) [3]					
Exports	177	201	225	263	296
Imports	790	699	803	856	891
Merchandise balance	− 613	− 498	− 578	− 593	− 595
Net Services	563	441	549	546	538
Transfers	− 3	4	7	2	7
Current account balance	− 53	− 53	− 22	− 45	− 50
Capital account (net)	163	46	− 5	− 32	− 6
Change in reserves [4]	− 5	− 11	− 8	− 38	− 31

[1] The Bahamian dollar has been kept at par with the United States dollar since 1973.
[2] Preliminary.
[3] Free on board.
[4] Minus sign signifies increase in reserves.

Source: Based on information from Inter-American Development Bank, *Economic and Social Progress in Latin America: 1986 Report,* Washington, 1987, 196.

Table 9. The Bahamas. Administrative Districts of the
Family Islands, 1987

Island(s)	District (Seat) *
Acklins and Crooked	Acklins and Crooked Islands (Colonel Hill)
Andros	Nicolls Town Andros Town Kemps Bay
Bimini and Berry	Bimini and Berry Islands (Alice Town)
Cat	Cat Island (New Bight)
Eleuthera	Governor's Harbour Rock Sound
Grand Bahama	Eight Mile Rock High Rock
Great Abaco and Little Abaco	Cooper's Town Marsh Harbour Sandy Point
Great Exuma and Ragged	Great Exuma and Ragged Islands (George Town)
Great Inagua and Little Inagua	Great Inagua (Matthew Town)
Harbour	Harbour Island (Dunmore Town)
Long	Long Island (Clarence Town)
Mayaguana	Mayaguana (Abraham's Bay)
San Salvador	San Salvador (Cockburn Town)

* When not indicated in parentheses, the district seat is located in the town for which the district is named.

Table 10. *Police, Paramilitary, and Defense Forces of the Commonwealth Caribbean Islands, 1987*

Country or Dependency	Force(s)	Size
Anguilla	Anguilla Police Force	80
Antigua and Barbuda	Royal Antigua and Barbuda Police Force	350
	Antigua and Barbuda Defence Force	115
The Bahamas	Royal Bahamas Police Force	1,447
	Royal Bahamas Defence Force	531
Barbados	Royal Barbados Police Force	1,200
	Barbados Defence Force	500
British Virgin Islands	Royal British Virgin Islands Police Force	100
Cayman Islands	Royal Cayman Islands Police Force	170
Dominica	Commonwealth of Dominica Police Force (includes 80-member Special Service Unit [SSU])	390
Grenada	Royal Grenada Police Force (includes 80-member SSU)	600
Jamaica	Jamaica Constabulary Force	5,601
	Jamaica Defence Force	1,780
Montserrat	Royal Montserrat Police Force	80–90
St. Christopher (St. Kitts) and Nevis	Royal St. Christopher and Nevis Police Force (includes 80-member SSU)	300
St. Lucia	Royal St. Lucia Police Force (includes 80-member SSU)	350
St. Vincent and the Grenadines	Royal St. Vincent and the Grenadines Police Force (includes 80-member SSU)	570
Trinidad and Tobago	Trinidad and Tobago Police Service	3,000
	Trinidad and Tobago Defence Force	2,130
Turks and Caicos Islands	Royal Turks and Caicos Islands Police Force	90

Appendix B

The Commonwealth of Nations

THE COMMONWEALTH OF NATIONS, more commonly known simply as the Commonwealth, is a voluntary association of independent sovereign states, including Britain and former British territories. Any former British territory may seek Commonwealth membership, which is granted by unanimous consent of the members. The Commonwealth also includes associated states (see Glossary) of Britain, crown colonies (see Glossary) of Britain, and dependencies of Australia and New Zealand (see table A, this appendix).

Table A. Members of the Commonwealth of Nations, 1987

Independent Members

Antigua and Barbuda
Australia
The Bahamas
Bangladesh
Barbados
Belize
Botswana
Britain
Brunei
Canada
Cyprus
Dominica
Fiji
The Gambia
Ghana
Grenada
Guyana
India
Jamaica
Kenya
Kiribati
Lesotho

Malawi
Malaysia
Maldives
Malta
Mauritius
Nauru
New Zealand
Nigeria
Papua New Guinea
St. Christopher and Nevis
St. Lucia
St. Vincent and the
   Grenadines
Seychelles
Sierra Leone
Singapore
Solomon Islands
Sri Lanka
Swaziland
Tanzania
Tonga
Trinidad and Tobago

Table A. —Continued

Tuvalu	Western Somoa
Uganda	Zambia
Vanuatu	Zimbabwe

Dependencies and Associated States of Britain

Anguilla	Falkland Islands
Bermuda	Gibraltar
British Antarctic Territory	Hong Kong
British Indian Ocean	Isle of Man
Territory	Montserrat
British Virgin Islands	Pitcairn Islands
Cayman Islands	St. Helena
Channel Islands	Turks and Caicos Islands

Dependencies of Australia

Australian Antarctic Territory	Cocos (Keeling) Islands
Coral Sea Islands Territory	Heard and McDonald Islands
Christmas Island	Norfolk Island

Dependencies of New Zealand

Cook Islands	Ross Dependency
Niue	Tokelau

Source: Based on information from "The Commonwealth," in *The Europa Year Book 1987,*
1, London, 1987, 114.

In member nations in which the British monarch serves as the head of state, she or he is represented by an appointed governor general, who is independent of the British government. In other Commonwealth nations, the monarch is represented by a high commissioner who has the status of an ambassador. Member states meet regularly to discuss issues, coordinate mutual economic and technical assistance, and formulate proposals regarding international economic affairs.

History

The Commonwealth of Nations is a twentieth-century creation, but its origins go back to events in 1867. In that year the British Parliament passed the British North American Act, creating the self-governing Dominion of Canada. Canada was the first British colony to gain self-government, and from that time on Britain began to redefine its relationship with its colonies. Australia became a dominion in 1900, New Zealand in 1907, and the Union of South Africa in 1910.

Canada, Australia, New Zealand, and the Union of South Africa dispatched troops to aid in the British war effort in World War I. They also participated in the postwar peace conference and in the creation of the League of Nations. Such actions led Britain to acknowledge these countries more as equals than as former colonies.

In 1926 the Imperial Conference of Commonwealth members adopted the Balfour Formula on the status of the dominions. The conference defined the dominions and Britain as "autonomous communities within the Empire, equal in status, in no way subordinate to one another in any aspect of their domestic or external affairs, though united by a common allegiance to the Crown, and freely associated as members of the British Commonwealth of Nations." The formula continued, "Every self-governing member of the Empire is now the master of its destiny. In fact, if not always in form, it is subject to no compulsion whatsoever."

The British government codified these basic principles of equal status and free association in 1931 in the Statute of Westminster, which has been characterized as the "Magna Carta of the Commonwealth." The statute also recognized the full legislative autonomy of the dominions and offered all former colonies the right to secede from the Commonwealth.

The Ottawa Imperial Conference of 1932 added an economic dimension to the Commonwealth by creating the Commonwealth Preference, a system of preferential tariffs that applied to trade between Britain and the other Commonwealth members. Under this system, Britain imported goods from other Commonwealth countries without imposing any tariffs. Commonwealth members were encouraged to negotiate similar trade agreements with one another. For the next decade and a half the Commonwealth in essence functioned as an economic bloc vis-à-vis the rest of the world. However, following World War II, as world and British trade policies were liberalized, the bloc gradually disintegrated. The Commonwealth Preference was finally terminated in 1977 as a condition of Britain's entrance into the European Economic Community (EEC). Nevertheless, Commonwealth nations have been linked to the EEC through the Lomé Convention (see Glossary), which offers former colonies of EEC members in Africa, the Pacific, and the Caribbean preferential access to EEC markets and economic assistance. The Lomé Convention is updated every five years.

A new Commonwealth gradually emerged after World War II, reflecting the progress of decolonization and the needs of new members. In the process, the Commonwealth became both more decentralized and more concerned with economic and social needs. In 1947 Britain granted complete independence to India and Pakistan, and in 1948 Ceylon (present-day Sri Lanka) and Burma gained independence. Burma did not join the Commonwealth, but the other three became independent Commonwealth members. In deference to India, a self-declared republic, the Commonwealth dropped the requirement of formal allegiance to the crown. In 1949 the Irish Republic seceded, although the citizens of the republic continue to enjoy the rights and privileges of British subjects. In 1961 South Africa left the Commonwealth because its racial policies differed from the values of all other Commonwealth members.

During the 1960s and 1970s, a large number of British colonies achieved independence and joined the expanded Commonwealth, including most former colonies in sub-Saharan Africa, the Caribbean, and the Pacific. Some former British colonies did not join, however. Pakistan left in 1972, after Britain and other members recognized Bangladesh, formerly East Pakistan. (However, in mid-1987 Pakistan petitioned to rejoin the Commonwealth, and action on the request was regarded as likely to occur at the next Meeting of Heads of Government of the Commonwealth.)

Principles

Although the Statute of Westminster affirms the principles of free association and equal status, the contemporary Commonwealth has no written charter or formal treaty. Instead, its governing features are found in a few basic procedures, its periodic declarations of principle, and an organization designed for consultations and mutual assistance. This framework is both flexible and adaptable and is a major reason why the Commonwealth has survived major changes in membership and member interests.

Two central procedures govern the Commonwealth—its process of making decisions by consensus and its biennial Meeting of Heads of Government of the Commonwealth. The latter are held in odd-numbered years and in different cities and regions within the Commonwealth. In alternate years senior officials hold policy-review meetings. Finance ministers meet annually, and other meetings are held as appropriate.

Over time, the Commonwealth has become more oriented toward its less-developed members. Major declarations of principle reflect this trend. The Declaration of Commonwealth Principles, adopted at the 1971 Singapore meeting, affirmed the members' belief ''in the liberty of the individual, in equal rights for all citizens regardless of race, color, creed or political belief, and in their inalienable right to participate by means of free and democratic processes in framing the society in which they live.'' The declaration also opposed all forms of colonial domination and racial oppression.

The 1977 meeting in Gleneagles, Scotland, issued the Agreement on Apartheid in Sport, reaffirming opposition to apartheid but allowing each member to decide whether or not to participate in sporting events with South Africa. The 1979 conference in Lusaka, Zambia, issued both an important framework for a peaceful settlement of Southern Rhodesia's transition to an independent Zimbabwe under black majority rule and a strong Commonwealth declaration condemning racism. Members also adopted the 1981 Melborne Declaration on relations between the developed and developing nations; the 1983 New Delhi Statement on Economic Action; and the 1983 Goa Declaration on International Security.

The October 1985 meeting in Nassau, the Bahamas, passed resolutions calling for cooperation in fighting international terrorism and drug trafficking, bans on nuclear testing, and the use of chemical weapons. As part of the Commonwealth's continuing condemnation of South Africa's racial policies, it also established the Commonwealth Group of Eminent Persons (Comgep). Comgep was tasked to encourage dialogue to end apartheid in South Africa.

Despite a broad consensus among members condemning apartheid, issues concerning South Africa have led to the most serious divisions within the Commonwealth. In 1982 the Commonwealth Games Federation held its first extraordinary meeting to discuss a tour of New Zealand by South African rugby teams. In 1986 over half of the member states pulled their teams out of the Commonwealth Games, held that year in Britain, in protest over South African participation. Conspicuously absent were the predominantly black Caribbean and African states.

Organization and Activities

The central organization for consultation and cooperation is the Commonwealth Secretariat, established in 1965. The Secretariat, located in London, is headed by a secretary general, elected by the heads of government for a five-year term. The Secretariat organizes conferences and meetings, coordinates a broad range of activities, and disseminates information. Since World War II member heads of state have attended the biennial Meetings of Heads of Government of the Commonwealth. Also, meetings are held periodically on specific matters concerning foreign affairs, defense, finance, and international debt. For example, the national finance ministers routinely meet immediately before the annual meetings of the World Bank (see Glossary) and the International Monetary Fund (IMF—see Glossary) to discuss international monetary and economic issues. The Secretariat's departments deal with administration, economic affairs, education, export market development, finance, food production and rural development, information, international affairs, legal matters, medical affairs, personnel, and youth.

Two permanent directorates are within the Secretariat, the Commonwealth Fund for Technical Cooperation (CFTC) and the Industrial Development Unit. The CFTC was established in April 1971 to provide technical assistance for economic and social development in Commonwealth developing countries. The fund is financed by all Commonwealth nations on a voluntary basis; the CFTC's governing body includes representatives of all its contributors. The Industrial Development Unit promotes the establishment and modernization of industries in member countries.

The Commonwealth Secretariat is funded by member payments, determined individually on the basis of per capita income. Britain pays 30 percent of the Secretariat's budget.

In addition to the Secretariat, a number of Commonwealth components are noteworthy. Government and private funds are sent to less-developed members through the Commonwealth Development Corporation. Specialized organizations include the Commonwealth Agricultural Bureau, the Institute of Commonwealth Studies, the Association of Commonwealth Universities, and various Commonwealth groups for communications, health, the law, the professions, and science and technology. The Commonwealth Games Federation, based in London, has held games every four years since 1930. The Commonwealth also maintains close links with other international organizations, including the United Nations (UN). In October 1976 the UN General Assembly granted the Commonwealth official observer status.

Regional Groupings

Aside from its general departments and specialized organizations, the Commonwealth also has four "regional groupings." One is the Colombo Plan, founded in 1951 and headquartered in Colombo, Sri Lanka; it is designed to promote economic and social development in Asia and the Pacific. Economic assistance is provided to Commonwealth and non-Commonwealth countries in the region by Australia, Britain, Canada, Japan, and the United States. A related program, the Conference of Heads of Government of Asian and Pacific Commonwealth Member States, began in 1978 and exists to encourage cooperation for regional development.

The other two regional groupings deal with the Caribbean: the Caribbean Community and Common Market (Caricom—see Appendix C) and the Organisation of Eastern Caribbean States (OECS—see Glossary), an associate institution of Caricom. Encompassing Antigua and Barbuda, Dominica, Grenada, Montserrat, St. Christopher and Nevis, St. Lucia, and St. Vincent and the Grenadines, as well as the British Virgin Islands as an associate member, the OECS aims at coordinating member states' foreign policy and relations with international institutions. It also has responsibility for the Eastern Caribbean Currency Authority; the Eastern Caribbean Common Market, established in 1968 and later an associate institution of the Caricom; and the Eastern Caribbean States Supreme Court.

*   *   *

Information on the history and development of the Commonwealth of Nations can be found in numerous sources. Giuseppe Schiavone's *International Organizations* and Alan J. Day's *Treaties and Alliances of the World* are excellent sources of information. H. Duncan Hall's *Commonwealth: A History of the British Commonwealth of Nations* is particularly useful for historical background. Guy Arnold's *Economic Co-operation in the Commonwealth* provides useful insights into attempts at economic coordination among member states. (For further information and complete citations, see Bibliography.)

Appendix C

The Caribbean Community and Common Market

IN THE LATE 1980s, the members of the Caribbean Community and Common Market (Caricom) consisted of Antigua and Barbuda, the Bahamas, Barbados, Belize, Dominica, Grenada, Guyana, Jamaica, Montserrat, St. Christopher (hereafter, St. Kitts) and Nevis, St. Lucia, St. Vincent and the Grenadines, and Trinidad and Tobago. The members faced problems typical of many developing societies: high birth rates, unemployment and an unskilled labor force, inadequate infrastructure, balance of payments constraints, and insufficient domestic savings to achieve development goals. In addition, Caricom members lacked diversified economies and were incapable of producing most capital goods and some basic consumer goods necessary for productive expansion. The Caricom members, therefore, were forced to rely heavily on imports of essential goods. As a result, development goals were subordinated because of the need to raise foreign exchange to pay for the imports.

Since 1981 the ability of Caricom members to raise the needed capital via export expansion has been severely limited by the lack of export diversification and the reliance on primary products and tourism services, which are extremely vulnerable to changing forces of demand, supply, and price in the international political economy. In the late 1980s, intraregional cooperation was urgently needed to create an atmosphere conducive to overcoming the handicaps of small market size, economic fragmentation, and external dependence.

Caricom's goal of regional integration was designed to serve as a catalyst for sustained growth in the short or medium term by allowing for market expansion, harmonization of production strategies, and development of economies of scale. Integration was also expected to promote industrial growth by eliminating excess capacity in the manufacturing sector and to stimulate investment in new sectors of the expanded market. The long-term hope was for balanced growth, minimal unemployment, a higher standard of living, and optimal use of available human and natural resources.

Background and Objectives

Following the example of the European Economic Community (EEC), many nations have organized themselves into regional integration organizations, such as Latin America's Central American

Common Market, the Latin America Integration Association, and the Andean Pact. The Commonwealth Caribbean made a serious move toward establishing a unit of integration by creating the West Indies Federation in 1958. The federation, formed under the auspices of the British, was doomed from the start by nationalistic tendencies and the lack of taxation privileges, and it failed when Jamaica and Trinidad and Tobago attained independence and withdrew in 1962. Nevertheless, a few institutions, such as the University of the West Indies (UWI) and the Regional Shipping Council, were established under the short-lived federation and continue today. After the demise of the West Indies Federation, economist W. Arthur Lewis attempted to organize a smaller organization among the so-called Little Eight islands (Antigua and Barbuda, Barbados, Dominica, Grenada, Montserrat, St. Kitts-Nevis-Anguilla, St. Lucia, and St. Vincent and the Grenadines); however, his efforts yielded little success.

The first call for a regional Caribbean community was made in a January 1962 speech by Eric Williams, former prime minister and first head of state of independent Trinidad and Tobago. However, it was not until the late 1960s that advocates of a new federation focused their attention on the issue of regional integration. In July 1965, Antigua and Barbuda, Barbados, and Guyana signed the Treaty of Dickenson Bay, which established the Caribbean Free Trade Association (Carifta). Under the terms of the 1968 Treaty of St. John's, Carifta was widened to include Anguilla, Dominica, Grenada, Jamaica, St. Kitts and Nevis, St. Lucia, Montserrat, St. Vincent and the Grenadines, and Trinidad and Tobago. Although a free-trade area was established, Carifta did not provide for the free movement of labor and capital or the coordination of agricultural, industrial, defense, and foreign policies. Thus, over the next five years, little progress was made toward creating a regionally integrated unit. In 1970 the prospect of Britain's joining the EEC alerted the islands to their vulnerability to any disruption in their preferential trading ties with Britain. In the same year, economists at the UWI issued a report contending that the creation of a free-trade area alone was not sufficient to procure full gains from regional integration. These events led to the development of the present Caricom structure.

In 1973 the Carifta members signed the Treaty of Chaguaramas, replacing the ineffective Carifta structure with Caricom. Caricom has three essential components: economic integration based on a regional common market; functional cooperation in such areas as culture, education, health, labor relations, tourism, and transportation; and coordination of foreign and defense policies.

Although the regional common market is an integral part of the broader based community arrangements, it has a completely separate identity juridically. Thus, it was possible for the Bahamas to become a member of the community in 1983 without joining the Common Market. In 1981 the Eastern Caribbean (see Glossary) islands of Antigua and Barbuda, Dominica, Grenada, Montserrat, St. Kitts and Nevis, St. Lucia, and St. Vincent and the Grenadines established an associate entity, the Organisation of Eastern Caribbean States (OECS—see Glossary), which replaced the West Indies States Association (WISA) as the islands' administrative body. The OECS coordinates development strategies among its members and provides for cooperation in economic, foreign policy, and defense matters. The OECS was created after studies indicated that most of the benefits derived from integration were flowing to the larger islands (especially Jamaica and Trinidad and Tobago) at the expense of the smaller.

Institutional Structure

The institutional structure of Caricom consists of the Heads of Government Conference, the Common Market Council of Ministers, the Caribbean Community Secretariat, and other special bodies (see fig. A, this appendix). Unlike in the EEC, each member has a right of veto. Decision making in Caricom, although centralized at some levels, is quite decentralized at others.

The Heads of Government Conference is the supreme decision making body. Each member of Caricom has one vote, and a unanimous vote is required to legislate decisions or to make policy recommendations. The conference determines the policies to be pursued by Caricom's related institutions. This conference also is responsible for concluding all treaties, making financial disbursements, and maintaining relations with other international organizations.

The Common Market Council of Ministers is the second principal body of Caricom and the principal body of the regional Common Market. The Common Market Council consists of one ministerial representative from each member. Decisions are made by unanimous vote, with minor exceptions. The council resolves problems and makes proposals to the Heads of Government Conference to achieve efficient development and operation of the Common Market.

The Caribbean Community Secretariat is Caricom's principal administrative component. The Secretariat operates to serve the interests of the region rather than those of each government. Although the Secretariat has no decision making power, its

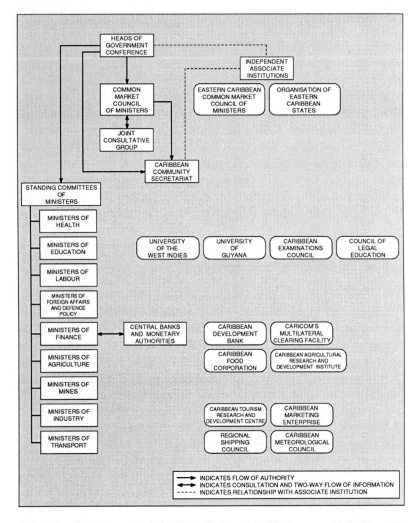

Source: Based on information from Sidney E. Chernick, *The Commonwealth Caribbean: The Integration Experience,* Baltimore, 1978, 11.

Figure A. Institutional Organization of the Caribbean Community and Common Market, 1987

discussions, studies, and projects have made it a dynamic element in the integration process.

Other offices responsible for specific sectoral aspects of regional integration are the nine Standing Committees of Ministers (health, education, labor, foreign affairs and defense policy, finance, agriculture, mines, industry, and transport). In addition, independent associate institutions include the Caribbean Development Bank (CDB), the Caribbean Examinations Council, the Council of Legal Education, the University of Guyana, the UWI, the Caribbean Meteorological Council, the Caribbean Food Corporation, the Regional Shipping Council, and the Caribbean Marketing Enterprise. Finally, the Joint Consultative Group, comprising business, consumer, and trade groups, meets to review the integration process and ensure interest group participation in Caricom activities.

Market Integration Mechanisms

Caricom seeks to achieve economic integration through market forces. The Common Market was established to promote intraregional trade. It achieves this through trade liberalization by removing duties, licensing arrangements, quotas, and other tariff and nontariff barriers to trade; the Rules of Origin; the Common External Tariff (CET) and the Common Protective Policy (CPP); and trade arrangements such as the Agricultural Marketing Protocol and the Oils and Fats Agreement.

The Common Market contains a number of important mechanisms for liberalizing trade. These include eliminating extraregional export duties, removing quantitative restrictions on regional exports, permitting free transit for products of members, and eliminating quantitative restrictions on imported goods. Article 28 of the Treaty of Chaguaramas permits the application of quantitative restrictions if the member has severe balance of payments problems. However, because of the invocation of this clause in 1977 by both Guyana and Jamaica and the continuing economic problems confronting the Caricom members, removal of this provision was being considered in 1987.

The Rules of Origin establish the conditions of eligibility of regional products so that they may be considered of Common Market origin and thus qualified for preferential treatment. In 1986 a new set of Rules of Origin was adopted to increase the use of regional products and promote employment, investment, and savings of foreign exchange. Given the scarcity of products within Caricom in the late 1980s, observers believed that achieving high levels of regional value-added worth even with the new Rules of Origin would be difficult.

The Treaty of Chaguaramas mandates gradually implementing the CET and CPP. The CET stimulates production by imposing low tariffs on capital goods and industrial raw materials and higher tariffs on finished products. The CPP standardizes quantitative restrictions to protect specific regional industrial sectors. Together, the CET and CPP, coupled with intraregional trade liberalization, were expected to stimulate reciprocal investment and trade among members. In reality, these had not been achieved by the late 1980s because of problems in implementing the CPP and excluding goods from the CET.

The final market integration mechanism aims at providing guaranteed markets and prices for Caricom exports to overcome the volatile trade in primary commodities. The Agricultural Marketing Protocol and the Oils and Fats Agreement regulate intraregional trade via certain buy-and-sell accords at fixed prices resulting from shortages or surpluses within Caricom. Caricom also has the Guaranteed Market Scheme, whereby in certain circumstances Jamaica, Barbados, and Trinidad and Tobago will purchase fixed quantities of agricultural products from the other members.

Mechanisms of Cooperation in Marketing and Production

Joint regional action in production and marketing activities is viewed by Caricom as a means of coordinating and controlling each member's output to avoid injury to other members or to the entire region. Coordinating policies is also intended to encourage specialization and complementary production. One important mechanism in this regard is regional industrial programming aimed at promoting specialization and economic diversification and avoiding duplication of investment. Although regional industrial programming was first considered in 1973, concrete actions did not begin until 1985 with the completion of the first phase of regional industrial programming. Of the thirty-five projects originally considered, only twenty-three have been identified as feasible. Only sixteen had been implemented by 1986. The most cited example of industrial cooperation and integration was a regional alumina (see Glossary) refinery that was to use bauxite (see Glossary) from Jamaica and Guyana and oil from Trinidad and Tobago. Although the project was thoroughly discussed during the 1970s, it remained doubtful in the late 1980s that such a project would ever be realized. In addition, related agricultural programs offered joint efforts to provide extension, marketing, and research and development services to reduce unit costs, increase quality and yield, and slash imports of basic foodstuffs.

The Regional Food and Nutrition Strategy is the main instrument for Caricom's agricultural development. The strategy establishes a framework and identifies priorities for a regional approach to agricultural self-sufficiency. The Caribbean Food Corporation, founded in 1976, is the main mechanism for planning and implementing the strategy's objectives. Also, the Caribbean Food and Nutrition Institute was established by Caricom at the UWI in Mona, Jamaica.

Transportation is indispensable for effective trade, export promotion, and other integration objectives. Cooperation in maritime transportation is envisioned through the West Indies Shipping Corporation (WISCO), which was established in 1961 and restructured in 1975. WISCO theoretically provides services to all Caricom nations. In early 1987, however, Belize, Dominica, and St. Vincent and the Grenadines withdrew from WISCO, claiming they had received few benefits from the service. In the late 1980s, air transportation remained inadequate because of the lack of coordination among the existing airlines. Standardizing air transport by coordinating and planning routes and fares, as well as mergers, was necessary to improve service and reduce costs.

Tourism is important to the region by providing foreign exchange, increasing employment, encouraging the production of tourist-oriented products and services, and stimulating the construction of basic infrastructure. Some regional cooperation in tourism has been carried out by the Caribbean Tourism Association, the Caribbean Tourism Research and Development Centre (located in Barbados), and the Hotel Training School at the UWI in the Bahamas. Nevertheless, in the late 1980s further cooperation was needed to link the tourism sector to the rest of the economy and to establish regional tourism enterprises.

Mechanisms of Financial Cooperation

Financial cooperation tries to fulfill the objectives of economic integration by facilitating payments for intraregional trade and by mobilizing investment funds to productive sectors of the economy. The principal vehicle for financial cooperation is the Caricom Multilateral Clearing Facility (CMCF). It was established in 1977 by the central banks and other financial entities of Caricom's members. The facility's objectives are to reduce the use of foreign exchange and expedite intraregional payments through credit and other financial arrangements. Other related mechanisms include harmonizing exchange rates by pegging the six existing currencies to the United States dollar and by issuing regional traveler's checks through the Central Bank of Trinidad and Tobago. Finally, the CDB contributes to the equitable development of the region by providing low-interest loans for projects and related integration plans.

659

Functional Cooperation

The Treaty of Chaguaramas also envisioned coordinating efforts in many noneconomic areas. The Caricom structure has formalized and expanded this kind of cooperation to include meteorological services and hurricane insurance; health and nutrition services; technical assistance; public utilities; education and job training; broadcasts, printed media, and information; culture and language; social security, labor, and industrial relations; science and technology; and harmonizing the laws and legal systems within Caricom. This cooperation has been successful in improving services to the members (especially the smaller ones) and lowering costs of activities through joint ventures. The regional university and health and nutrition systems are examples of successful functional cooperation.

Coordination of Defense and Foreign Policies

The Heads of Government Conference and the Standing Committee of Ministers of Foreign Affairs and Defence Policy are responsible for coordinating the defense and foreign policies of members to increase their international bargaining power. Caricom has been able to present a regional foreign policy position in defense of the principles of regional security and nonintervention; support of the territorial integrity of Guyana and Belize in their border disputes; and various negotiations for the Lomé Convention (see Glossary), by which many Third World nations have gained preferential access to EEC markets and economic assistance.

A Brief Evaluation of the Integration Effort

One method of evaluating Caricom's integration efforts is to look at three of its principal goals: defense and foreign policy coordination, functional cooperation, and economic and trade cooperation. In the late 1980s, some positive results had been achieved in defense and foreign policy coordination. Caribbean expressions of solidarity on issues of regional security and territorial integrity focused international attention on the region and strengthened Caricom's bargaining position in negotiations with regional and extraregional nations and in international forums. Ultimately, however, parochial concerns have always overshadowed regional interests. The ideological pluralism of the region and the often drastic changes in government orientation have hurt the coordination process through bilateralism and polarization of interests.

Functional cooperation had improved by the late 1980s, as reflected in the successful regional air transport, education, and health systems. However, Caricom had not expanded beyond these programs to develop common cultural and political linkages.

Although a Caribbean parliament could potentially be an important force, in the late 1980s none appeared likely to materialize. Many observers argued that Caricom had spread itself too thin and should concentrate on solving problems rather than expanding.

Economic and trade cooperation had also improved. Examples of such improvements are Caricom's collective ability to mobilize large volumes of external capital, to gain greater access to third-country markets, to facilitate significant financial transfers to its members (especially to those not producing or refining oil), and to achieve a fair degree of access to internal markets. Nevertheless, two outstanding shortcomings remained: the failure to achieve significant benefits from the complementary use of the region's human and natural resources and the inability to formulate a common policy vis-à-vis foreign investment. Both of these issues have immense significance for the long-term development objectives of greater self-reliance and reduced external dependence.

Although the increase in intraregional trade in the 1973-81 period consisted largely of manufactured consumer products not previously traded, such an increase indicated neither diversification nor specialization of production as envisioned by Caricom's designers. On the contrary, duplication of production was evident. When coupled with the foreign exchange crisis and the weak extraregional trade performance since 1981, the nations have been forced to borrow from abroad; this has caused increased foreign debt and reduced imports of consumer goods, which comprise much intraregional trade. The Caribbean Community Secretariat reported that the decline in intraregional trade was approximately 33 percent in 1986, following declines of 3.3 percent in 1985, 10.9 percent in 1984, and 12.2 percent in 1983. Finally, many observers have noted the polarized development patterns and disproportionate gains from Caricom's integration mechanisms. Nevertheless, this polarization may not be an inherent fault of Caricom, but rather the result of a political economy that many argue continues to be biased toward the more developed nations. Thus, simple changes in trade patterns could not modify the situation without substantial structural change.

Since its inception, Caricom has experienced continuous crises. These have occurred to such a degree that many observers have come to regard the situation as a natural condition associated with developing nations, especially in light of external debt and trade constriction. However, in 1987 a group of Caribbean experts expressed cautious optimism because the institutional framework of the community remained intact, intraregional dialogue was maintained, and trade and functional cooperation continued to show resilience.

Events Affecting the Community in the 1980s

A purposeful and cooperative spirit characterized Caricom's seventh summit conference, which was held in Guyana in July 1986. The highlights of this conference included establishing a regional Export Credit Facility (ECF) by July 1987 and implementing the regional industrial programming by late 1986.

In a declaration published at the end of the summit, Caricom leaders decided to implement the articles dealing with external trade, industrial policy, and joint development of resources. The creation of the ECF (ratified in May 1987) was aimed at providing pre- and post-shipment credit for Caricom manufacturers exporting goods both inside and outside Caricom, excluding such traditional products as bananas, bauxite, oil, and sugar. The industrial policy was intended to encourage regional joint ventures and investment initiatives geared toward improving the production structure of the Caricom members.

Approximately 25 percent of the funding for the ECF—around US$75 million—will be subscribed by the Caricom nations. The remainder will be raised through loans from the CDB, the World Bank (see Glossary), and other sources. Colombia has offered to provide technical assistance and will help to coordinate the ECF program. At the seventh summit conference, talks continued on reactivating the CMCF, whose activities were suspended in 1983 after reaching its credit ceiling via emergency loans to Jamaica and Guyana. Related to this, Barbados and Guyana discussed a US$100 million joint venture in lumber production and marketing that should help Guyana finance its debt to the CMCF. (In 1987 Jamaica was several years in arrears on its debt to the CMCF.)

Much of the discussion at the seventh summit conference focused on the 1984 Nassau Agreement. This agreement, aimed at reducing trade barriers and harmonizing external tariffs, recommended the use of the CET, not quantitative restrictions, to protect industrial development. The agreement also advocated removing price controls, developing incentives for industrial production, and improving training programs for displaced workers. A proposal for creating a common monetary unit was rejected on the grounds that the frequent fluctuation in Caricom's exchange rates would undermine such efforts. Nevertheless, summit participants decided that the members should consult Caricom's financial institutions if planning devaluations or pegging exchange rates.

In addition to the collective decisions reached at this summit, certain bilateral accords and negotiations were announced. One principal accord involved air transport between Jamaica and Trinidad and Tobago. Air Jamaica was granted landing rights in Port-of-Spain (with intermediate locations), whereas Trinidad and Tobago's carrier, British West Indian Airways, was authorized to service Kingston with intermediate stops. Barbados and Trinidad and Tobago announced talks aimed at a similar accord.

* * *

In the years since Caricom was established in 1973, a considerable amount of material has been published on the structure, positive and negative aspects, and future of the organization. The Inter-American Development Bank's *Ten Years of Caricom* and *Economic and Social Progress in Latin America* and the Caribbean Community Secretariat's yearly publication, *Report to the Secretary General of Caricom,* are recommended. A concise overview of Caricom may be found in Eduardo Margain's *Development Challenges and Cooperation in the Commonwealth Caribbean;* detailed essays on Caricom and the Commonwealth Caribbean may be found in Anthony Payne and Paul Sutton's *Dependency under Challenge.* (For further information and complete citations, see Bibliography.)

Appendix D

Caribbean Basin Initiative

THE CARIBBEAN BASIN INITIATIVE (CBI), first proposed in 1982, is a broad United States foreign policy program designed to promote economic development and political stability. The CBI is not limited to the Commonwealth Caribbean nations but extends to the entire Caribbean Basin, also including selected countries of Central America, northern South America, and the non-English-speaking Caribbean (see table A, this appendix). The CBI consists of trade, economic assistance, and investment incentive measures to generate economic growth in the region through increased private sector activity.

Table A. Potential Beneficiaries of the Caribbean Basin Initiative, 1986

Anguilla	Guyana
Antigua and Barbuda	Haiti
Aruba	Honduras
The Bahamas	Jamaica
Barbados	Montserrat
Belize	Netherlands Antilles
British Virgin Islands	Nicaragua
Cayman Islands	Panama
Costa Rica	St. Christopher and Nevis
Dominica	St. Lucia
Dominican Republic	St. Vincent and the Grenadines
El Salvador	Suriname
Grenada	Trinidad and Tobago
Guatemala	Turks and Caicos Islands

Source: Based on information from United States, International Trade Commission, *Annual Report on the Impact of the Caribbean Basin Economic Recovery Act on U.S. Industries and Consumers: First Report, 1984–85,* Washington, September 1986, 1–8.

The most significant aspect of the program is the Caribbean Basin Economic Recovery Act (CBERA) of 1983. The CBERA provides Caribbean Basin countries with duty-free access to the United States market for most categories of exported products until September 30, 1995. It also includes special tax provisions for the tourist sector, as well as measures to support the economic development of Puerto Rico and the United States Virgin Islands. In addition to the CBERA, other CBI measures include increased United States economic assistance, a wide range of government and private sector investment promotion programs, support from multilateral development institutions and their donor nations, and Caribbean Basin country self-help efforts.

Background

The CBI resulted from a series of 1981 meetings involving United States, Canadian, and Caribbean Basin officials. In a July 1981 meeting in Nassau, the United States special trade representative and the United States secretary of state met with the foreign ministers of Canada, Mexico, and Venezuela. Each agreed to support a multilateral action program for the region, within which each country and dependent territory would develop its own programs. Multilateral and bilateral meetings were held between the members of the so-called Nassau group and representatives of the Caribbean Basin countries.

The CBI package announced by President Ronald Reagan in a February 1982 address before the Organization of American States (OAS) consisted of foreign assistance, a free trade arrangement, and tax incentives for United States investors. The foreign aid portion of the CBI, which proposed an additional US$350 million for the Caribbean region for fiscal year (FY—see Glossary) 1982, was passed by the 97th Congress and became law in September 1982 (Public Law 97-257). (Two-thirds of this total was slated for Central America, with the remainder earmarked for the Caribbean.) The trade portion, contained in the CBERA, was passed by the 98th Congress in July 1983 and signed into law in August 1983 (Public Law 98-67). The CBERA also contained a tax benefit allowing United States citizens and companies to make deductions for expenses from conventions and business meetings held in CBI countries. The investment tax incentive portion of the package was left out of the legislation's final version. Also, a number of products were excluded from the eligibility list of duty-free exports.

Highlights of the Caribbean Basin Economic Recovery Act

Duty-Free Treatment

Section 211 of the CBERA gives the president the authority to grant duty-free treatment to eligible countries and dependent territories for eligible products, and Section 212 outlines the criteria for eligibility. The president may not designate a communist country or a country that fails to meet certain criteria regarding the expropriation of United States property; does not take adequate steps to prevent narcotics from entering the United States; fails to recognize arbitral awards to United States citizens; provides preferential treatment to the products of another developed country, adversely affecting trade with the United States; engages in the broadcast of United States copyrighted material without the owner's consent; or fails to enter into an extradition treaty with the United States.

In addition, the president is required to take into account eleven discretionary criteria. The criteria focus on the degree to which the potential beneficiary is prepared to provide equitable and reasonable access to its markets and basic commodity resources; follows the accepted rules of international trade; uses export subsidies or imposes export performance requirements or local content requirements that distort international trade; and undertakes self-help measures to promote its own economic development.

Twenty-eight countries or dependencies of the Caribbean, Central America, and northern South America are considered potential beneficiaries. By 1986 twenty-two of these had been designated for the duty-free provisions of the CBI, the exceptions being Guyana, Nicaragua, Suriname, Anguilla, the Cayman Islands, and the Turks and Caicos Islands, none of which applied for designation.

Section 213 sets forth the criteria for determining which articles may enter the United States free of customs duty. To qualify, a product must be grown, produced, or manufactured in one or more of the beneficiary countries. If produced from components from a non-CBI country, the product's direct processing costs must total at least 35 percent of the product's final cost. United States component parts may account for only 15 of these percentage points, the remaining 20 percent coming from non-CBI countries. Specific articles are excluded, including textiles and apparel subject to textile agreements, canned tuna, petroleum and petroleum products, footwear, work gloves, luggage, handbags, flat leather goods such as wallets, leather apparel, and watches and watch parts if any components originate in a communist country. Duty-free sugar exports are limited either by absolute quotas or by "competitive need" limits contained in the Generalized System of Preferences (GSP); these restrictions are intended to ensure that duty-free sugar imports will not impede the United States price support system for domestically produced sugar.

Section 214 outlines special measures for Puerto Rico and the United States Virgin Islands to ensure healthy economic development.

These measures increase the permissible foreign content for United States insular possessions from 50 to 70 percent and treat the products of all insular possessions as favorably as products from CBI beneficiary countries.

Tax Provisions

Section 221 amends the United States Internal Revenue Code by transferring all taxes collected on rum imports from the Caribbean to the treasuries of Puerto Rico and the United States Virgin Islands. Section 222 also amends the Internal Revenue Code by allowing deductions for business expenses when attending conventions, seminars, or other meetings in a CBI beneficiary country or dependent territory provided that the country or dependent territory enters into a tax information exchange agreement (TIEA) with the United States. By the end of 1987, just three of the twenty-eight potential CBI beneficiaries—Barbados, Grenada, and Jamaica—were qualified for the convention tax deduction benefit.

Other Measures and Programs Related to the Caribbean Basin Initiative

Economic Aid

In the first half of the 1980s, United States economic aid to the CBI region increased substantially. From FY 1982 to FY 1985, economic assistance nearly tripled to US$1.8 billion. (However, as was the case with the supplemental allocation for FY 1982, the majority of assistance for FY 1985 went to Central America; less than 20 percent was destined for the Caribbean.) Approximately three-fourths of the total package was funneled into the Economic Support Fund (ESF) program. Although the ESF enables governments to meet immediate expenditures, it also allows them to delay potentially necessary fiscal reforms. Since FY 1987, absolute levels of economic assistance to the region have been declining because of United States efforts to reduce its government's budget deficit.

Investment Incentives and Promotion Programs

United States efforts in the CBI region also included measures to increase the level of private investment. In 1984 United States legislation created new sales export companies, known as Foreign Sales Corporations (FSCs), which were designed to generate government revenue for the host country and add to its international business infrastructure. FSCs provide United States firms with income tax exemptions and low operating costs; in exchange, FSCs must be incorporated outside the United States in insular territories or in countries that have concluded TIEAs with the United States. By 1987 Barbados, Grenada, and Jamaica had concluded effective TIEAs and were therefore eligible for FSCs. New legislation in 1986 also made countries with effective TIEAs eligible for investments with funds generated in Puerto Rico (via Section 936 of the Internal Revenue Code).

The United States also concluded bilateral investment treaties with two CBI countries, Haiti and Panama, and held discussions about negotiating such a treaty with most other nations in the region. The Department of Commerce, the Department of State, and the Office of the United States Trade Representative have primary responsibility for implementing promotion programs for investment in CBI countries. In 1984 the Department of Commerce established the CBI Center to provide support services for companies interested in developing businesses in the region. In March 1987, the Office of the United States Trade Representative appointed a CBI ombudsman to serve in Washington as a problem solver for firms participating in the initiative. In addition, the Overseas Private Investment Corporation, a United States government entity charged with insuring foreign investments of American firms, dedicated approximately half its portfolio in the early 1980s to the Caribbean Basin.

Textile Initiative

In early 1986, President Reagan strengthened the CBI by introducing a new program to promote investment in the textile industries of CBI countries. The program guaranteed access to the United States market for certain textile and apparel imports. In addition, higher levels of access were provided for textiles manufactured from material originating in the United States. As of mid-1987, bilateral textile agreements had been signed with the Dominican Republic, Haiti, Trinidad and Tobago, and Jamaica.

Complementary Trade Preference Programs

Several other United States trade preference programs apply worldwide, rather than just to the Caribbean area. The GSP permits approximately 2,800 products to be imported duty free into the United States from developing nations around the world. All of the potential beneficiary countries under the CBERA are eligible for benefits of the GSP, which in 1984 was extended until 1993. A second trade preference program covers two items of the Tariff Schedules of the United States (TSUS) that provide for reduced duties for products of United States origin that are assembled or processed in other countries. Finally, the TSUS also allows special duty rates for certain products of countries that have been designated least developed developing countries (LDDCs) of the GSP. To date, the only CBI country that is eligible for special treatment as an LDDC is Haiti.

Multilateral Support

Other countries of the Caribbean Basin (Colombia, Mexico, and Venezuela) have instituted development programs in the region, as have Britain, Canada, the European Economic Community (EEC), the Federal Republic of Germany (West Germany), France, the Netherlands, and Japan. Mexico and Venezuela established the Joint Oil Facility in 1980 to provide concessionary oil rates to ten countries of the Caribbean Basin; the agreement was a milestone in cooperation among developing nations. Colombia has offered special trade credits and technical assistance programs to several governments in the region.

In 1986 Canada announced plans to implement an economic and trade development assistance program for the Commonwealth Caribbean. The program, known as Caribcan, provided for duty-free access to the Canadian market of 99.8 percent of current Commonwealth Caribbean imports. Excluded from the program were textiles, clothing, footwear, luggage and handbags, leather garments, lubricating oils, and methanol. The EEC's most important program is the Lomé Convention (see Glossary), which covers numerous African, Caribbean, and Pacific countries, including twelve CBI beneficiaries. The Lomé Convention is updated every five years. Lomé III, which took effect in March 1985, offers duty-free access to the EEC as well as economic aid and investment incentives. Work of multilateral institutions such as the Inter-American Development Bank, the International Monetary Fund (IMF—see Glossary), and the World Bank (see Glossary) also complements the CBI program, as do the programs of consultative groups such as the Caribbean Group for Cooperation in Economic Development.

Impact

Assessing the effectiveness of a 12-year trade program that began in 1983 is difficult. Initial reports indicated that the overall trade performance for the CBI region was disappointing; CBI exports to the United States in 1985 were 24 percent lower than in 1983. The decline was a result of weak markets, mainly in oil, but also in bauxite (see Glossary), alumina (see Glossary), and sugar. Final 1986 figures were expected to show further declines because of a

United States decision to lower its sugar import quota; the OAS estimated that the decrease would cost Caribbean producers US$250 million.

Despite the overall decline in exports, the United States Department of Commerce pointed out that from 1983 to 1985 there was a 14-percent increase in nontraditional exports, such as apparel, electronics, vegetables, seafood, and wooden furniture. Furthermore, if oil-producing countries of the region are excluded, exports to the United States increased in most areas of the region. Exports from Central America, the Central Caribbean, and the Eastern Caribbean (see Glossary) increased by 13.4, 15.9, and 19.0 percent, respectively. All of the oil-producing exporting countries of the region, however, experienced substantial declines in total exports to the United States. In 1981 United States imports from these countries amounted to US$6 billion, but by 1985 that figure had dropped to US$2.7 billion.

The direct investment benefits of the CBI have not been substantial. New United States investment in the region amounted to approximately US$208 million during the first eighteen months of the CBI, generating roughly 35,000 new jobs. However, this new investment amounted to less than 2 percent of the total United States direct investment in the region and thus represented only a slight improvement. In addition, income derived from direct investment actually declined, bringing down the former relatively high rate of return for businesses in the region. The direct investment figures did not include the planned divestitures of major companies in Jamaica (Reynolds Metals), Costa Rica (United Brands), and the Netherlands Antilles (Exxon). The few new projects included data processing, electronics, manufacturing, and hotel development.

In its September 1986 report on the first two years of CBERA operation, the United States International Trade Commission (ITC) emphasized the percentage increases in exports destined for the United States from non-oil-refining CBI countries. An average increase of 14.8 percent was noted in exports from these Central American and Caribbean CBI nations. Nevertheless, the report observed that these increases compared unfavorably with the 33.8-percent growth rate of American imports worldwide. The ITC report concluded that the impact of the CBERA on United States industries and consumers had been minimal. The report also noted the problems involved with export-oriented economic development in the Caribbean region. According to the ITC, growth in Caribbean exports is likely to be slow because producers in the region face a number of constraints, including high transportation costs, inadequate infrastructure, and a lack of experience and access to marketing channels in the United States. Subsequent ITC reports will be published annually, as mandated by law, until the expiration of the CBERA in 1995.

The reactions of CBI countries and dependent territories to the CBI have been mixed. Although several, most notably Costa Rica, have praised the CBI, many of the smaller ones have expressed concerns over the CBI's shortcomings. In August 1985, the prime ministers of eleven Caribbean states informed President Reagan of their concern about increased United States protectionism. They also pointed out that the CBI excludes products that are important for foreign exchange earnings and employment potential, most notably textiles, footwear, and leather products. At the 1986 Caribbean Community and Common Market (Caricom—see Appendix C) summit meeting in Guyana, Caribbean leaders indicated further reservations about the CBI. They reported that aid levels to Caricom nations had stagnated since the increases of 1983 and also pointed out that smaller countries of the Eastern Caribbean lacked the necessary infrastructure to take advantage of CBI benefits. Several suggestions to improve the CBI came out of the summit meeting, including an increased United States sugar quota, a 10-percent tax credit for United States investors in the region, and an increase in development aid, particularly for infrastructure projects, through regional development institutions, such as the Caribbean Development Bank.

* * *

Since the CBI was first proposed in 1982, much material has been published on the principles, benefits, and shortcomings of the program. Notable United States government publications include the Department of Commerce's annual guidebook on the CBI; the Department of State's *Background on the Caribbean Basin Initiative* (1982); the United States International Trade Commission's *Annual Report on the Impact of the Caribbean Basin Economic Recovery Act on U.S. Industries and Consumers,* first published in 1986; and Elliot Abrams's "CBI and the U.S. National Interest." An extensive review of the CBI was also presented in the published hearings of the Subcommittee on Oversight of the House of Representatives' Committee on Ways and Means, held in February 1986. Journal articles providing background on the CBI include "Sinking in the Caribbean Basin" by Robert Pastor, "The Reagan Caribbean Basin Initiative, Pro and Con," published in the *Congressional Digest,* and Nicholas Raymond's "Caribbean Basin Initiative Revisited." (For further information and complete citations, see Bibliography.)

Bibliography

Chapter 1

Ahye, Molly. *Cradle of Caribbean Dance.* Port-of-Spain, Trinidad and Tobago: Heritage Cultures, 1983.

Alegria, Ricardo. "Etnografía Taina y los Conquistadores," *Revista del Museo de Antropología, Historia y Arte de la Universidad de Puerto Rico,* 1, No. 1, July–December 1979, 5–15.

Augier, F.R., et al. *The Making of the West Indies.* London: Longmans, 1960.

Baedeker's Caribbean, Including Bermuda, 1987. Englewood Cliffs, New Jersey: Prentice-Hall, 1986.

Barry, Tom, Beth Wood, and Deb Preusch. *The Other Side of Paradise: Foreign Control in the Caribbean.* New York: Grove Press, 1984.

Basdeo, Sahadeo. "Walter Citrine and the British Caribbean Workers Movement During the Moyne Commission Hearing, 1938–1939." Pages 259–73 in Blanca Silvestrini (ed.), *Politics, Society, and Culture in the Caribbean.* San Juan: University of Puerto Rico, 1983.

Beckford, George L. *Persistent Poverty: Underdevelopment in Plantation Economies of the Third World.* New York: Oxford University Press, 1972.

Bessil-Watson, Lisa. *Handbook of Churches in the Caribbean.* Bridgetown, Barbados: Cedar Press, 1982.

Blanshard, Paul. *Democracy and Empire in the Caribbean.* New York: Macmillan, 1947.

Braithwaite, Edward. *The Development of Creole Society in Jamaica, 1770–1820.* New York: Oxford University Press, 1971.

Brana-Shute, Rosemary. *A Bibliography of Caribbean Migration and Caribbean Immigrant Communities.* Gainesville: Center for Latin American Studies, University of Florida, 1983.

Brereton, Bridget. *A History of Modern Trinidad, 1783–1962.* London: Heinemann, 1981.

_____. *Race Relations in Colonial Trinidad, 1870–1900.* Cambridge: Cambridge University Press, 1979.

Bridenbaugh, Carl, and Roberta Bridenbaugh. *No Peace Beyond the Line: The English in the Caribbean, 1624–1690.* New York: Oxford University Press, 1972.

Brizan, George I. *Grenada, Island of Conflict: From Amerindians to People's Revolution, 1498–1979.* (Third World Studies.) London: Zed Books, 1984.

Bryce-Laporte, Roy, et al. *Return Migration and Remittances: Developing a Caribbean Prospective.* Washington: Smithsonian Institution, 1982.

Buckley, Roger. *Slaves in Red Coats: The British West India Regiments, 1795-1815.* New Haven: Yale University Press, 1979.

Bullbrook, J.A. *On the Excavation of a Shell Mound at Palo Seco, Trinidad.* New Haven: Yale University Press, 1953.

Caldecott, Alfred. *The Church in the West Indies.* (New ed.) London: Cass, 1970. Originally published in 1898.

Campbell, Carl. "The Opposition to Crown Colony Government in Trinidad Before and After Emancipation, 1813-46." Page 67 in Barry W. Higman (ed.), *Trade, Government, and Society in Caribbean History, 1700-1920.* Kingston, Jamaica: Heinemann, 1983.

Campbell, Mavis C. *The Dynamics of Change in a Slave Society: A Sociopolitical History of the Free Coloreds of Jamaica, 1800-1865.* Cranbury, New Jersey: Associated University Presses, 1976.

The Caribbean: Survival, Struggle, and Sovereignty. Washington: EPICA Task Force, 1985.

Chernick, Sidney E. *The Commonwealth Caribbean: The Integration Experience.* Baltimore: Johns Hopkins University Press, 1978.

Clarke, Edith. *My Mother Who Fathered Me: A Study of the Family in Three Selected Communities in Jamaica.* London: Allen and Unwin, 1957.

Cohen, David W., and Jack P. Greene (eds.). *Neither Slave Nor Free: The Freedmen of African Descent in the Slave Societies of the New World.* Baltimore: Johns Hopkins University Press, 1972.

Collier, Simon, Harold Blakemore, and Thomas E. Skidmore (eds.). *The Cambridge Encyclopedia of Latin America and the Caribbean.* Cambridge: Cambridge University Press, 1985.

Conniff, Michael L. *Black Labor on a White Canal: Panama, 1904-1981.* Pittsburgh: University of Pittsburgh Press, 1985.

Cox, Edward L. *Free Coloreds in the Slave Societies of St. Kitts and Grenada, 1763-1833.* Knoxville: University of Tennessee Press, 1984.

Crahan, Margaret E., and Franklin W. Knight (eds.). *Africa and the Caribbean: The Legacies of a Link.* Baltimore: Johns Hopkins University Press, 1979.

Craton, Michael. *A History of the Bahamas.* (3d ed.) Waterloo, Canada: San Salvador Press, 1986.

_____. *Searching for the Invisible Man.* Cambridge: Harvard University Press, 1978.

_____. *Testing the Chains: Resistance to Slavery in the British West Indies.* Ithaca: Cornell University Press, 1982.

Craton, Michael, and James Walvin. *A Jamaican Plantation: The History of Worthy Park, 1670-1970.* London: Allen, 1970.

Crosby, Alfred W., Jr. *The Columbian Exchange: Biological and Cultural Consequences of 1492.* Westport, Connecticut: Greenwood Press, 1972.

Curtin, Philip. *The Atlantic Slave Trade: A Census.* Madison: University of Wisconsin Press, 1969.

_____. *Two Jamaicas: The Role of Ideas in a Tropical Colony, 1830–1865.* Cambridge: Harvard University Press, 1955. Reissued, New York: Atheneum, 1970.

Davis, David Brion. *The Problem of Slavery in the Age of Revolution.* Ithaca: Cornell University Press, 1976.

_____. *The Problem of Slavery in Western Culture.* Ithaca: Cornell University Press, 1966.

Davis, Stephen, and Peter Simon. *Reggae Bloodlines: In Search of the Music and Culture of Jamaica.* (rev. ed.) New York: Anchor Books, 1979.

Delson, Roberta M. (ed.). *Readings in Caribbean History and Economics.* New York: Gordon and Breach, 1981.

Denevan, William M. (ed.). *The Native Population of the Americas in 1492.* Madison: University of Wisconsin Press, 1976.

Drescher, Seymour. *Econocide: British Slavery in the Era of Abolition.* Pittsburgh: University of Pittsburgh Press, 1977.

Dunn, Richard S. *Sugar and Slaves: The Rise of the Planter Class in the English West Indies, 1624–1713.* Chapel Hill: University of North Carolina Press, 1972.

Eaton, George E. *Alexander Bustamante and Modern Jamaica.* Kingston, Jamaica: Kingston, 1975.

Elliott, J.H. *Imperial Spain, 1469–1716.* London: Macmillan, 1963.

Floyd, Troy S. *The Columbus Dynasty in the Caribbean, 1492–1526.* Albuquerque: University of New Mexico Press, 1973.

Fortune, Stephen. *Merchants and Jews: The Struggle for British West Indian Commerce, 1650–1750.* Gainesville: University of Florida Press, 1984.

Garcia, A. *History of the West Indies.* London: George C. Harrap, 1965.

Gaspar, Barry. *Bondmen and Rebels: A Study of Master-Slave Relations in Antigua.* Baltimore: Johns Hopkins University Press, 1985.

Gibson, Charles. *Spain in America.* New York: Harper and Row, 1966.

The Gleaner Geography and History of Jamaica. Kingston, Jamaica: Gleaner, 1973.

Gordon, Shirley C. *Reports and Repercussions in West Indian Education, 1835–1933.* London: Ginn, 1963.

Goslinga, Cornelis C. *The Dutch in the Caribbean and on the Wild Coast, 1580–1680.* Gainesville: University of Florida Press, 1971.

Goveia, Elsa. *Slave Society in the British Leeward Islands at the End of the Eighteenth Century.* New Haven: Yale University Press, 1965.

Granzotto, Gianni. *Christopher Columbus. The Dream and the Obsession: A Biography.* New York: Doubleday, 1985.

Green, William A. *British Slave Emancipation: The Sugar Colonies and the Great Experiment, 1830–1865.* Oxford: Clarendon Press, 1976.

Greene, J.E. *Race and Politics in Guyana.* Mona, Jamaica: Institute of Social and Economic Research, University of the West Indies, 1974.

Hagelbert, G.B. *The Caribbean Sugar Industries: Constraints and Opportunities.* New Haven: Antilles Research Program, 1974.

Hall, Douglas. *Free Jamaica, 1838–1865: An Economic History.* New Haven: Yale University Press, 1959. Reprinted, London: 1976.

Hamshere, Cyril. *The British in the Caribbean.* Cambridge: Harvard University Press, 1972.

Handler, Jerome S. *The Unappropriated People: Freedmen in the Slave Society of Barbados.* Baltimore: Johns Hopkins University Press, 1974.

Haraksingh, Kusha. "Labor, Technology, and the Sugar Estates in Trinidad, 1879–1914." Pages 133–46 in Bill Albert and Adrian Graves (eds.), *Crisis and Change in the International Sugar Economy, 1860–1914.* Edinburgh: ISC Press, 1984.

Haynes, Cleviston. "Sugar and the Barbadian Economy, 1946–1980." Pages 81–105 in DeLisle Worrell (ed.), *The Economy of Barbados, 1946–1980.* Bridgetown, Barbados: Central Bank of Barbados, 1982.

Henige, David. "On the Contact Population of Hispaniola: History as Higher Mathematics," *Hispanic American Historical Review,* 58, No. 2, May 1978, 217–37.

Henriques, Fernand. *Children of Caliban: Miscegenation.* London: Secker and Warburg, 1974.

Henry, Paget, and Carl Stone (eds.). *The Newer Caribbean: Decolonization, Democracy, and Development.* (Inter-American Politics series, 4.) Philadelphia: Institute for the Study of Human Issues, 1983.

Heuman, Gad J. *Between Black and White: Race, Politics, and the Free Coloreds in Jamaica, 1792–1865.* Westport, Connecticut: Greenwood Press, 1981.

Higman, Barry W. *Slave Population and Economy in Jamaica, 1807–1834.* Cambridge: Cambridge University Press, 1976.

_____. *Slave Populations of the British Caribbean, 1807–1834.* Baltimore: Johns Hopkins University Press, 1984.

Higman, Barry W. (ed.). *Trade, Government, and Society in Caribbean History, 1700–1920.* Kingston, Jamaica: Heinemann, 1983.

Hill, Errol. *The Trinidad Carnival: Mandate for a National Theatre.* Austin: University of Texas Press, 1972.

Hoetink, H. *Caribbean Race Relations: A Study of Two Variants.* London: Oxford University Press, 1967.

Inter-American Development Bank. *Economic and Social Progress in Latin America: 1986 Report.* Washington: 1987.

Jacobs, H.P. *Sixty Years of Change, 1806–1866 (Progress and Reaction in Kingston and the Countryside).* Kingston, Jamaica: Planning Institute of Jamaica, 1973.

Jacobs, W. Richard, and Ian Jacobs. *Grenada: Route to Revolution.* Havana: Casa de las Americas, 1979.

Jamaica. Department of Statistics. *Pocketbook of Statistics: Jamaica, 1983.* Kingston, Jamaica: 1984.

Jones, Joseph, and Johanna Jones. *Authors and Areas of the West Indies.* Austin: Steck-Vaughn, 1970.

Karch, Cecilia A. "The Role of the Barbados Mutual Life Assurance Society During the International Sugar Crisis of the Late 19th Century." Pages 95–130 in K.O. Laurence (ed.), *A Selection of Papers Presented at the Twelfth Conference of the Association of Caribbean Historians* (1980). Bridgetown, Barbados: Government Printing Department, n.d.

Kiple, Kenneth. *The Caribbean Slave: A Biological History.* Cambridge: Cambridge University Press, 1984.

Klein, Herbert. *African Slavery in Latin America and the Caribbean.* New York: Oxford University Press, 1986.

Knight, Franklin W. *The African Dimension of Latin American Societies.* New York: Macmillan, 1974.

———. *The Caribbean: The Genesis of a Fragmented Nationalism.* New York: Oxford University Press, 1978.

———. "Jamaican Migrants and the Cuban Sugar Industry, 1900–1934." Pages 94–114 in Manuel Moreno Fraginals, Frank Moya Pons, and Stanley Engerman (eds.), *Between Slavery and Free Labor: The Spanish-Speaking Caribbean in the Nineteenth Century.* Baltimore: Johns Hopkins University Press, 1985.

Knowles, W. *Trade Union Development and Industrial Relations in the British West Indies.* Berkeley and Los Angeles: University of California Press, 1959.

Langley, Lester D. *Struggle for the American Mediterranean: United States-European Rivalry in the Gulf Caribbean, 1776–1904.* Athens: University of Georgia Press, 1976.

———. *The United States and the Caribbean in the Twentieth Century.* Athens: University of Georgia Press, 1982.

Laurence, K.O. *Immigration into the West Indies in the 19th Century.* London: Ginn, 1971.

Lewis, David. *Reform and Revolution in Grenada, 1950–1981.* Havana: Casa de las Americas, 1984.

Lewis, Gordon K. *The Growth of the Modern West Indies.* New York: Monthly Review Press, 1968.

———. *Main Currents in Caribbean Thought.* Baltimore: Johns Hopkins University Press, 1983.

Lewis, W. Arthur. *Labour in the West Indies: The Birth of a Workers Movement.* (New ed.) London: New Beacon Books, 1977.

Lindsay, Louis. *The Myth of Independence: Middle Class Politics and Non-Mobilization in Jamaica.* Mona, Jamaica: Institute of Social and Economic Research, University of the West Indies, 1975.

Lockhart, James, and Stuart B. Schwartz. *Early Latin America: A History of Colonial Spanish America and Brazil.* Cambridge: Cambridge University Press, 1983.

Lovejoy, Paul E. "The Volume of the Atlantic Slave Trade: A Synthesis," *Journal of African History,* 22, No. 4, 1982, 473–501.

Loven, Sven. *Origins of the Tainan Culture.* Göteborg, Sweden: Elanders, 1935.

Lynch, John. *Spain under the Hapsburgs.* (2 vols.) New York: Oxford University Press, 1964.

McNeill, William H. *The Rise of the West.* Chicago: University of Chicago Press, 1963.

Mandle, Jay R. *Patterns of Caribbean Development: An Interpretative Essay on Economic Change.* New York: Gordon and Breach, 1982.

———. *The Plantation Economy: Population and Economic Change in Guyana, 1838–1860.* Philadelphia: Temple University Press, 1973.

Manley, Norman Washington. *Norman Washington Manley and the New Jamaica: Selected Speeches and Writings, 1938–1968.* (Ed., Rex M. Nettleford.) Kingston, Jamaica: Longmans Caribbean, 1971.

Marshall, Woodville K. "Vox Populi: The St. Vincent Riots and Disturbances of 1862." Pages 85–116 in Barry W. Higman (ed.), *Trade, Government, and Society in Caribbean History, 1700–1920.* Kingston, Jamaica: Heinemann, 1983.

Meinig, D.W. *The Shaping of America: A Geographical Perspective on 500 Years of History, 1: Atlantic America, 1492–1800.* New Haven: Yale University Press, 1986.

Millette, James. *The Genesis of Crown Colony Government: Trinidad, 1783–1810.* Curepe, Trinidad and Tobago: Moko Enterprises, 1970.

Mintz, Sidney W. *Caribbean Transformations.* Baltimore: Johns Hopkins University Press, 1974.

———. *Sweetness and Power: The Place of Sugar in Modern History.* New York: Viking Press, 1985.

Mintz, Sidney W., and S. Price (eds.). *Caribbean Contours.* Baltimore: Johns Hopkins University Press, 1985.

Moore, Richard B. *Caribs, "Cannibals," and Human Relations.* New York: Pathway, 1972.

Mordecai, John. *The West Indies: The Federal Negotiations.* London: Allen and Unwin, 1968.

Morison, Samuel E. *Admiral of the Ocean Sea: A Life of Christopher Columbus.* (2 vols.) Boston: Northeastern University Press, 1983.

Mortimer, Delores, and Roy Bryce-Laporte (eds.). *Female Immigrants to the United States: Caribbean, Latin American, and African Experiences.* Washington: Smithsonian Institution, 1981.

Munroe, Trevor. *The Politics of Constitutional Decolonization: Jamaica, 1944-62.* Mona, Jamaica: Institute of Social and Economic Research, University of the West Indies, 1972.

Nettleford, Rex M. *Identity, Race, and Protest in Jamaica.* New York: Morrow, 1972.

————. *Manley and the Politics of Jamaica: Towards an Analysis of Political Change in Jamaica, 1938-1968.* Mona, Jamaica: Institute of Social and Economic Research, University of the West Indies, 1971.

O'Shaughnessy, Hugh. *Grenada: Revolution, Invasion, and Aftermath.* London: Sphere Books, 1984.

Palmer, Colin A. *Human Cargoes: The British Slave Trade to Latin America.* Urbana: University of Illinois Press, 1981.

Palmer, Ransford W. *Caribbean Dependence on the United States Economy.* New York: Praeger, 1979.

————. *Problems of Development in Beautiful Countries: Perspectives on the Caribbean.* Lanham, Maryland: North-South, 1984.

Parry, John H. *The Age of Reconnaissance.* New York: Macmillan, 1963.

Parry, John H., and Philip M. Sherlock. *A Short History of the West Indies.* New York: Macmillan, 1971.

Parry, John H., Philip M. Sherlock, and Anthony P. Maingot. *A Short History of the West Indies.* (4th ed.) New York: St. Martin's Press, 1987.

Pastor, Robert A. (ed.). *Migration and Development in the Caribbean: The Unexplored Connection.* (Westview Special Studies on Latin America and the Caribbean.) Boulder: Westview Press, 1985.

Payne, Anthony. *The International Crisis in the Caribbean.* Baltimore: Johns Hopkins University Press, 1984.

Payne, Anthony, and Paul Sutton (eds.). *Dependency under Challenge: The Political Economy of the Commonwealth Caribbean.* London: Butler and Tanner, 1984.

Penrose, Boies. *Travel and Discovery in the Renaissance, 1420-1620.* Cambridge: Harvard University Press, 1952.

Puckrein, Gary A. *Little England: Plantation Society and Anglo-Barbadian Politics, 1627–1700.* New York: New York University Press, 1984.

Ragatz, L. *The Fall of the Planter Class in the British Caribbean, 1763–1833.* (New ed.) New York: Octagon Books, 1971.

Ramchand, Kenneth. *The West Indian Novel and Its Background.* London: Faber and Faber, 1970.

Raynal, Abbe. *Philosophical and Political History of the Settlements and Trade of the Europeans in the East and West Indies.* (6 vols.) New York: Negro Universities Press, 1969.

Richardson, Bonham C. *Caribbean Migrants: Environment and Human Survival in St. Kitts and Nevis.* Knoxville: University of Tennessee Press, 1983.

———. *Panama Money in Barbados, 1900–1920.* Knoxville: University of Tennessee Press, 1985.

Rodney, Walter. *A History of the Guyanese Working People, 1881–1905.* Baltimore: Johns Hopkins University Press, 1981.

Ryan, Selwyn. *Race and Nationalism in Trinidad and Tobago.* Toronto: University of Toronto Press, 1972.

Samaroo, Brinsley. "The Trinidad Labor Party and the Moyne Commission, 1938." Pages 259–73 in Blanca Silvestrini (ed.), *Politics, Society, and Culture in the Caribbean.* San Juan: University of Puerto Rico, 1983.

Sauer, Carl. *The Early Spanish Main.* Berkeley and Los Angeles: University of California Press, 1966.

Schuler, Monica. *"Alas, Alas, Kongo": A Social History of Indentured African Immigration into Jamaica, 1841–1865.* Baltimore: Johns Hopkins University Press, 1980.

Semmel, Bernard. *Democracy Versus Empire: The Jamaica Riots of 1865 and the Governor Eyre Controversy.* New York: Doubleday, 1969.

Sewell, William G. *Ordeal of Free Labor in the British West Indies.* New York: Harper and Brothers, 1862.

Sheppard, Jill. *The "Redlegs" of Barbados: Their Origins and History.* (The Caribbean—Historical and Cultural Perspectives series.) Millwood, New York: KTO Press, 1977.

Singham, Archie W. *The Hero and the Crowd in a Colonial Polity.* New Haven: Yale University Press, 1968.

Stephens, E.H., and John D. Stephens. *Democratic Socialism in Jamaica.* Princeton: Princeton University Press, 1986.

Steward, Julian, and Louis Faron. *Native Peoples of South America.* New York: McGraw-Hill, 1959.

Stone, Carl. *Class, Race, and Political Behaviour in Urban Jamaica.* Mona, Jamaica: Institute of Social and Economic Research, University of the West Indies, 1973.

————. *Democracy and Clientelism in Jamaica*. New Brunswick, New Jersey: Transaction Books, 1980.

————. *Power in the Caribbean Basin: A Comparative Study of Political Economy*. Philadelphia: Institute for the Study of Human Issues, 1986.

Thomas, Clive Y. *Plantations, Peasants, and State*. Los Angeles: Center for Afro-American Studies, University of California, 1984.

Watson, Karl. *The Civilised Island: Barbados. A Social History, 1750–1816*. Bridgetown, Barbados: Graphic Printers, 1979.

West, Robert C., and John P. Augelli (eds.). *Middle America: Its Lands and Peoples*. (2d ed.) Englewood Cliffs, New Jersey: Prentice-Hall, 1976.

Willey, Gordon. *The Entry of Man into the West Indies*. New Haven: Yale University Press, 1960.

Willey, Gordon (ed.). *Prehistoric Settlement Patterns in the New World*. New York: Wenner-Gren, 1956.

Williams, Eric. *Capitalism and Slavery*. (New ed.) New York: Russell and Russell, 1961.

————. *From Columbus to Castro: The History of the Caribbean, 1492–1969*. New York: Harper and Row, 1970.

————. *Inward Hunger: The Education of a Prime Minister*. Chicago: University of Chicago Press, 1969.

Wood, Donald. *Trinidad in Transition*. Oxford: Oxford University Press, 1968.

The World Almanac and Book of Facts, 1987. New York: Newspaper Enterprise Association, 1986.

Chapter 2

Americas Watch. *Human Rights in Jamaica*. (An Americas Watch Report.) New York: 1986.

Amnesty International. *Jamaica: The Death Penalty*. London: 1984.

Andrade, John. *World Police and Paramilitary Forces*. New York: Stockton Press, 1985.

Ashby, Timothy. "The U.S. Message for Jamaica's Seaga: It's Time to Keep Your Promise," *Backgrounder*, September 2, 1986, 12.

Ayub, Mahmood Ali. *Made in Jamaica: The Development of the Manufacturing Sector*. (World Bank Staff Occasional Papers, No. 31.) Baltimore: Johns Hopkins University Press, 1981.

Bacon, Peter R. *Flora and Fauna of the Caribbean*. Port-of-Spain, Trinidad and Tobago: Key Caribbean, 1978.

Bank of Jamaica. *Statistical Digest*. Kingston, Jamaica: December 1985.

Barry, Tom, Beth Wood, and Deb Preusch. *The Other Side of Paradise: Foreign Control in the Caribbean.* New York: Grove Press, 1984.

Bastin, Ronald. "Contradictory Aspects of Tourism in the Caribbean." Mona, Jamaica: Institute of Social and Economic Research, University of the West Indies, 1982.

Bell, Wendell. "Independent Jamaica Enters World Politics: Foreign Policy in a New State," *Political Science Quarterly,* 92, Winter 1977–78, 683–703.

Bernal, Richard L. "The Vicious Circle of Foreign Indebtedness: The Case of Jamaica." Pages 111–28 in Antonio Jorge, Jorge Salazar-Carrillo, and Frank Diaz-Pou (eds.), *External Debt and Development Strategy in Latin America.* New York: Pergamon Press, 1985.

Black, Clinton V. *The Story of Jamaica: From Prehistory to the Present.* London: Collins, 1965.

Bolling, H. Christine. *Jamaica: Factors Affecting Its Capacity to Import Food.* (Department of Agriculture, Foreign Agriculture Economic Reports, 176.) Washington: GPO, 1983.

Bonner, Arthur. "Michael Manley's Race with Time," *Nation,* 224, January 22, 1977, 30–34.

Brooks, John (ed.). *The 1986 South American Handbook.* Bath, United Kingdom: Trade and Travel, 1985.

Caribbean/Central American Action. *1986 Caribbean and Central America Databook.* Washington: 1985.

Carr, Peter R. "Health Systems Development in the English-Speaking Caribbean: Toward the Twenty-First Century," *Bulletin of the Pan American Health Organization,* 19, No. 4, 1985, 368–83.

Cobb, Charles E., Jr. "Jamaica: Hard Times, High Hopes," *National Geographic,* 167, No. 1, January 1985, 114–40.

The Diagram Group. *Atlas of Central America and the Caribbean.* New York: Macmillan, 1985.

Dorst, Jean. *South America and Central America: A Natural History.* London: Hamish Hamilton, 1967.

Duncan, Cameron. "The IMF and Jamaica." Washington: Department of Economics, The American University, 1986.

Edie, Carlene J. "Domestic Politics and External Relations in Jamaica under Michael Manley, 1972–1980," *Studies in Comparative International Development,* 21, Spring 1986, 71–94.

English, Adrian J. *Armed Forces of Latin America.* London: Jane's, 1984.

Evans, F.C. *A First Geography of Jamaica.* Cambridge: Cambridge University Press, 1984.

Forbes, John D. *Jamaica: Managing Political and Economic Change.* (AEI Special Analyses.) Washington: American Enterprise Institute, 1985.

Girvan, Norman. *Foreign Capital and Underdevelopment in Jamaica.* Mona, Jamaica: Institute of Social and Economic Research, University of the West Indies, 1971.

Hellinger, Steve, and Doug Hellinger. *Supporting Central American and Caribbean Development: A Critique of the Caribbean Basin Initiative and an Alternative Regional Assistance Plan.* Washington: Development Group for Alternative Policies, 1982.

Hurwitz, Samuel J. *Jamaica: A Historical Portrait.* New York: Praeger, 1971.

Inter-American Development Bank. *Economic and Social Progress in Latin America: 1986 Report.* Washington: 1987.

International Institute for Strategic Studies. *The Military Balance, 1986–1987.* London: 1986.

International Monetary Fund. *International Financial Statistics.* Washington: 1987.

Jalloul, Janet. "Jamaica Educational Survey." Washington: Department of Education, The American University, 1985.

Jamaica. Department of Statistics. *Population Census, 1982: Preliminary Report.* Kingston, Jamaica: 1983.

―――. *Statistical Yearbook of Jamaica, 1980.* Kingston, Jamaica, 1981.

Jamaica. Jamaica National Investment Promotion. *Industrial Minerals: Industry Profile.* Kingston, Jamaica: n.d.

―――. *JNIP Annual Report, 1984.* Kingston, Jamaica: 1985.

Jamaica. Ministry of Health. *A Statement on National Population Policy.* Kingston, Jamaica: 1981.

Jamaica. National Planning Agency. *Agro-21 Master Plan: Making Agriculture Jamaica's Business.* Kingston, Jamaica: 1982.

―――. *Economic and Social Survey of Jamaica, 1980.* Kingston, Jamaica: 1981.

―――. *Economic and Social Survey of Jamaica, 1981.* Kingston, Jamaica: 1982.

―――. *Economic and Social Survey of Jamaica, 1982.* Kingston, Jamaica: 1983.

―――. *Economic and Social Survey of Jamaica, 1983.* Kingston, Jamaica: 1984.

―――. *Economic and Social Survey of Jamaica, 1984.* Kingston, Jamaica: 1985.

―――. *Economic and Social Survey of Jamaica, 1985.* Kingston, Jamaica: 1986.

―――. *Economic and Social Survey of Jamaica, 1986.* Kingston, Jamaica: 1987.

Jamaica. Planning Institute of Jamaica. *Statistical Yearbook of Jamaica, 1980.* Kingston, Jamaica: 1981.

Jamaica. Statistical Institute of Jamaica. *Census of Agriculture, 1978–1979,* I and II. Kingston, Jamaica: 1985.

―――. *Demographic Statistics, 1983.* Kingston, Jamaica: 1984.

―――. *Household Expenditure Survey, 1984,* I. Kingston, Jamaica: 1987.

"Jamaica Readies Debt Swap," *Business Latin America,* April 9, 1987, 111.

James, Preston. *Latin America.* New York: Odyssey Press, 1969.

Jefferson, Owen. *The Post-War Economic Development of Jamaica.* Mona, Jamaica: Institute of Social and Economic Research, University of the West Indies, 1972.

Kaufman, Michael. *Jamaica under Manley: Dilemmas of Socialism and Democracy.* Westport, Connecticut: Lawrence Hill, 1985.

Koslofsky, Joanne. "Going Foreign: Causes of Jamaican Migration," *NACLA Report on the Americas,* 15, No. 1, January–February 1981, 2–24.

Kurian, George Thomas. *The New Book of World Rankings.* New York: Facts on File, 1979.

Lack, David. *Island Biology.* London: Blackwell Scientific, 1976.

Latin America Bureau. *The Poverty Brokers: The IMF in Latin America.* London: 1983.

Lewis, Gordon K. *The Growth of the Modern West Indies.* New York: Monthly Review Press, 1968.

Lewis, John P., and Valeriana Kallab (eds.). *U. S. Foreign Policy and the Third World—Agenda, 1983.* New York: Praeger, 1983.

Lewis, W. Arthur. *Labour in the West Indies: The Birth of a Workers Movement.* (New ed.) London: New Beacon Books, 1977.

Looney, Robert E. *The Jamaican Economy in the 1980s: Economic Decline and Structural Adjustment.* Boulder: Westview Press, 1987.

McFarlane, C.P. *Facts on Jamaica: Physiography.* Kingston, Jamaica: Department of Statistics, 1973.

Martin, Atherton, Steve Hellinger, and Daniel Soloman. *Prospects and Realities: The CBI Revisited.* Washington: Development Group for Alternative Policies, 1985.

Massing, Michael. "The Jamaican Experiment," *Atlantic Monthly,* 252, September 1983, 37–51.

Mitchell, Harold. *Europe in the Caribbean: The Policies of Great Britain, France, and the Netherlands Towards Their West Indian Territories.* New York: Cooper Square, 1973.

Morgan, Janet. "Blueprint Island: A Survey of Jamaica," *Economist* [London], 286, February 12, 1983, 1–18.

Nurkse, Lawrence. "Los Sindicatos en el Caribe Anglófono," *Nueva Sociedad* [Caracas], 88, November–December 1986, 57–68.

O'Shaughnessy, Hugh. "Behind the Violence in Jamaica: Political and Economic Pressures on the Manley Government," *Round Table: The Commonwealth Journal of International Affairs* [London], No. 264, October 1976, 379–87.

Oxfam. *Debt and Poverty: A Case Study of Jamaica.* London: 1985.

Pan American Health Organization. "AIDS Surveillance in the Americas: Report Through 31 December 1985," *Epidemiological Bulletin*, 7, No. 2, 1986, 7–8.

Pastor, Robert A. (ed.). *Migration and Development in the Caribbean: The Unexplored Connection.* (Westview Special Studies on Latin America and the Caribbean.) Boston: Westview Press, 1985.

Payne, Anthony. "From Michael with Love: The Nature of Socialism in Jamaica," *Journal of Commonwealth and Comparative Politics* [London], 14, No. 1, March 1976, 82–100.

_____. "Jamaica and Cuba 1959–86: A Caribbean Pas de Deux," *Round Table: The Commonwealth Journal of International Affairs* [London], No. 302, 1987, 184–98.

_____. "Jamaica: The 'Democratic Socialist' Experiment of Michael Manley." Pages 18–42 in Anthony Payne and Paul Sutton (eds.), *Dependency under Challenge: The Political Economy of the Commonwealth Caribbean.* London: Butler and Tanner, 1984.

Population Reference Bureau. *1987 World Population.* Washington: April 1986.

Seyler, Daniel J. "The Politics of Development: The Case of Jamaica and the Caribbean Basin Initiative." Washington: School of International Service, The American University, 1986.

Sharpley, Jennifer. "Jamaica, 1972–80." Pages 115–63 in Tony Killick (ed.), *The IMF and Stabilization: Developing Country Experiences.* New York: St. Martin's Press, 1984.

Stephens, Evelyne Huber, and John D. Stephens. "Bauxite and Democratic Socialism in Jamaica." Pages 33–66 in Peter Evans, Dietrich Rueschemeyer, and Evelyne Huber Stephens (eds.), *States Versus Markets in the World System.* Beverly Hills: Sage, 1985.

_____. "The Transition to Mass Parties and Ideological Politics: The Jamaican Experience since 1972," *Comparative Political Studies*, 19, No. 4, January 1987, 443–83.

Stone, Carl. "Class and the Institutionalisation of Two-Party Politics in Jamaica," *Journal of Commonwealth and Comparative Politics* [London], 14, No. 2, July 1976, 177–96.

_____. *Democracy and Clientelism in Jamaica.* New Brunswick, New Jersey: Transaction Books, 1980.

_____. "Democracy and Socialism in Jamaica, 1962–79," *Journal of Commonwealth and Comparative Politics* [London], 19, No. 2, July 1981, 115–33.

_____. "Jamaica in Crisis: From Socialist to Capitalist Management," *International Journal*, 40, Spring 1985, 282–311.

_____. "The Jamaican Reaction: Grenada and the Political Stalemate," *Caribbean Review*, 12, No. 4, Fall 1983, 31–32.

_____. "Jamaica's 1980 Elections: What Manley Did Do; What Seaga Need Do," *Caribbean Review*, 10, No. 2, Spring 1981, 5–7.

_____. "The 1976 Parliamentary Election in Jamaica," *Journal of Commonwealth and Comparative Politics* [London], 15, No. 3, November 1977, 250–65.

_____. "Running Out of Options in Jamaica: Seaga and Manley Compared," *Caribbean Review*, 15, No. 3, Winter 1987, 10–12.

_____. "Seaga Is in Trouble: Polling the Jamaican Polity in Mid-Term," *Caribbean Review*, 11, No. 4, Fall 1982, 5–7.

Taylor, Jeremy (ed.). *The Caribbean Handbook, 1986.* St. John's, Antigua and Barbuda: FT Caribbean, 1986.

Tollefson, Scott D. "Jamaica: The Limits of a Showcase Policy," *SAIS Review*, 5, No. 2, Summer–Fall 1985, 189–204.

United Nations. *World Health Statistics Annual, 1983.* New York: 1984.

_____. *World Population Prospects, 1982.* New York: 1983.

United Nations. Food and Agriculture Organization. *1984 Fertilizer Yearbook*, 34. Rome: 1985.

_____. *1986 Country Tables.* Rome: 1986.

United States. Agency for International Development. *Country Development Strategy Statement: Jamaica FY 1986.* Washington: GPO, 1984.

United States. Central Intelligence Agency. *The World Factbook, 1985.* Washington: GPO, 1985.

_____. *The World Factbook, 1987.* Washington: GPO, 1987.

United States. Congress. 98th, 2d Session. Senate. Committee on Foreign Relations. *Extradition Treaty with Jamaica.* Washington: GPO, 1984.

United States. Department of Commerce. *Caribbean Basin Business Bulletin*, 2, No. 6, Washington: 1985.

_____. *1987 CBI Guidebook.* Washington: GPO, 1986.

United States. Department of Commerce. Bureau of the Census. *World Population, 1983.* Washington: GPO, 1983.

United States. Department of Commerce. International Trade Administration. *Foreign Economic Trends and Their Implications for the United States: Jamaica.* Washington: GPO, 1986.

United States. Department of State. *Country Reports on Human Rights Practices for 1986.* (Report submitted to United States Congress, 100th, 1st Session, Senate, Committee on Foreign Relations, and House of Representatives, Committee on Foreign Affairs.) Washington: GPO, February 1987.

United States. Department of State. Bureau of Public Affairs. *Background Notes: Jamaica.* Washington: January 1987.

United States. Department of the Interior. Bureau of Mines. *Mineral Facts and Problems.* (Bulletin 675.) Washington: GPO, 1985.

United States. General Accounting Office. *Caribbean Basin Initiative: Need for More Reliable Data on Business Activity Resulting from the Initiative.* Washington: GPO, 1986.

Volsky, George. "Jamaican Drug Gangs Thriving in U.S. Cities." *New York Times,* July 19, 1987, 3.

Waters, Anita M. *Race, Class, and Political Symbols: Rastafari and Reggae in Jamaican Politics.* New Brunswick, New Jersey: Transaction Books, 1985.

"Why Jamaica's Economy May Run Aground," *Business Week,* October 18, 1982, 162.

Whyte, Millicent. *A Short History of Education in Jamaica.* (Caribbean Education series.) London: Hodder and Stoughton, 1983.

Williams, Eric. *From Columbus to Castro: The History of the Caribbean, 1492-1969.* New York: Harper and Row, 1970.

World Bank. *World Debt Tables, 1986-1987.* Washington: 1987.

_____. *World Development Report, 1985.* New York: Oxford University Press, 1985.

_____. *World Development Report, 1987.* New York: Oxford University Press, 1987.

Zach, Paul (ed.). *Jamaica.* Hong Kong: ABA Productions, 1983.

(Various issues of the following publications were also used in the preparation of this chapter: *Daily Gleaner* [Kingston, Jamaica], 1984-87; *Development Dialogue,* 1980-82; *Financial Times* [London], 1987; *JNIP News* [Kingston, Jamaica], 1986-87; *New World Quarterly* [Kingston, Jamaica], 1967-68; *Quarterly Economic Report* [Kingston, Jamaica], 1986-87; *Social and Economic Studies* [Mona, Jamaica], 1982-83; and *Social Science Medicine,* 1983-84.)

Chapter 3

American Telephone and Telegraph Company. *The World's Telephones.* Morris Plains, New Jersey: 1983.

Andrade, John. *World Police and Paramilitary Forces.* New York: Stockton Press, 1985.

Anthony, Michael. *Glimpses of Trinidad and Tobago.* Port-of-Spain, Trinidad and Tobago: Columbus, 1974.

Ashley, Paul. "The Commonwealth Caribbean and the Contemporary World Order: The Cases of Jamaica and Trinidad." Pages 159-76 in Paget Henry and Carl Stone (eds.), *The*

Newer Caribbean: Decolonization, Democracy, and Development. (Inter-American Politics series, 4.) Philadelphia: Institute for the Study of Human Issues, 1983.

Barry, Tom, Beth Wood, and Deb Preusch. *The Other Side of Paradise: Foreign Control in the Caribbean.* New York: Grove Press, 1984.

Boodhoo, Ken I. "The Multinational Corporation, External Control, and the Problem of Development: The Case of Trinidad and Tobago." Pages 62–70 in Richard Millett and W. Marvin Will (eds.), *The Restless Caribbean: Changing Patterns of International Relations.* New York: Praeger, 1979.

Boodhoo, Ken I. (ed.). *Eric Williams: The Man and the Leader.* Lanham, Maryland: University Press of America, 1986.

Bourne, Peter G. *Fidel: A Biography of Fidel Castro.* New York: Dodd, Mead, 1986.

Brereton, Bridget. *A History of Modern Trinidad, 1783–1962.* London: Heinemann, 1981.

Caribbean Development Bank. *Annual Report, 1986.* Wildey, Barbados: Letchworth Press, 1987.

Central Bank of Trinidad and Tobago. *Annual Report, 1985.* Port-of-Spain, Trinidad and Tobago: 1986.

Deosaran, Ramesh. *Eric Williams: The Man, His Ideas, and His Politics.* Port-of-Spain, Trinidad and Tobago: Signum, 1981.

The Diagram Group. *Atlas of Central America and the Caribbean.* New York: Macmillan, 1985.

Economist Intelligence Unit. *Quarterly Economic Review of Trinidad and Tobago, Guyana, Barbados, Windward and Leeward Islands: Annual Supplement, 1985.* London: Economist, 1986.

English, Adrian J. *Armed Forces of Latin America.* London: Jane's, 1984.

Fraser, Peter D., and Paul Hackett (eds.). *Caribbean Economic Handbook.* London: Euromonitor, 1985.

Frost, Jens (ed.). *World Radio TV Handbook, 1986.* Hvidore, Denmark: Glenn Heffernon, 1986.

Green, Richard (ed.). *Latin America and Caribbean Review, 1985.* Saffron Walden, Essex, United Kingdom: World of Information, 1984.

Harewood, Jack. *Caribbean Demography Workbook.* St. Augustine, Trinidad and Tobago: University of the West Indies, 1976.

———. *Female Fertility and Family Planning in Trinidad and Tobago.* Kingston, Jamaica: University of the West Indies, 1978.

———. *The Population of Trinidad and Tobago.* Paris: 1975.

Hope, Kempe Ronald. *Economic Development in the Caribbean.* New York: Praeger, 1986.

————. "The Emigration of High-Level Manpower from Developing to Developed Countries (with Reference to Trinidad and Tobago)," *International Migration* [Geneva], 14, No. 3, 1976, 209–18.

Ince, Basil A. "Coping with Oil Wealth: The Case of Trinidad and Tobago and the Commonwealth Caribbean." Pages 111–34 in R.M. Ritter and David H. Pollack (eds.), *Latin American Perspectives for the 1980s.* New York: Praeger, 1983.

Inter-American Development Bank. *Economic and Social Progress in Latin America: 1984 Report.* Washington: 1985.

————. *Economic and Social Progress in Latin America: 1985 Report.* Washington: 1986.

————. *Economic and Social Progress in Latin America: 1986 Report.* Washington: 1987.

International Institute for Strategic Studies. *The Military Balance, 1986–1987.* London: 1986.

International Monetary Fund. *Direction of Trade Statistics.* Washington: 1986.

————. *International Financial Statistics.* Washington: 1987.

Jamaica. Planning Institute of Jamaica. *Quarterly Economic Report* [Kingston, Jamaica], 2, No. 3, 1985.

La Guerre, John Gaffar. "General Elections of 1981 in Trinidad and Tobago," *Journal of Commonwealth and Comparative Politics* [London], 21, No. 2, July 1983, 134–57.

Lewis, Gordon K. *The Growth of the Modern West Indies.* New York: Monthly Review Press, 1968.

Lewis, John P., and Valeriana Kallab (eds.). *U.S. Foreign Policy and the Third World—Agenda, 1983.* New York: Praeger, 1983.

MacDonald, Scott B. "The Future of Foreign Aid in the Caribbean after Grenada: Finlandization and Confrontation in the Eastern Tier," *Inter-American Economic Affairs,* 38, Spring 1985, 59–74.

————. *Trinidad and Tobago: Democracy and Development in the Caribbean.* New York: Praeger, 1986.

McLin, Jon. *Social and Economic Effects of Petroleum Development in Non-OPEC Developing Countries: Synthesis Report.* Geneva: International Labour Organisation, 1986.

Mahabir, Winston. *In and Out of Politics.* Port-of-Spain, Trinidad and Tobago: Imprint Caribbean, 1978.

Malik, Yogendra K. *East Indians in Trinidad.* London: Oxford University Press, 1971.

Malloch, Theodore R. "Trinidad and Tobago." Page 126 in Richard F. Staar (ed.), *Yearbook on International Communist Affairs.* Stanford, California: Hoover Institution Press, 1983.

Mandle, Jay R. *Patterns of Caribbean Development: An Interpretative Essay on Economic Change.* New York: Gordon and Breach, 1982.

Millett, Richard, and W. Marvin Will (eds.). *The Restless Caribbean: Changing Patterns of International Relations.* New York: Praeger, 1979.

Millette, James. *The Politics of Succession: A Topical Analysis of the Political Situation in Trinidad and Tobago.* Curepe, Trinidad and Tobago: Moko Enterprises, 1970.

Nogueira, Uziel. "The Energy Sector of Trinidad and Tobago." Washington: Inter-American Development Bank, 1987.

Nurkse, Lawrence. "Los Sindicatos en el Caribe Anglófono," *Nueva Sociedad* [Caracas], 88, November–December 1986, 57–68.

Ottley, Carlton Robert. *A Historical Account of the Trinidad and Tobago Police Force from the Earliest Times.* Port-of-Spain, Trinidad and Tobago: Privately published, 1964.

Oxaal, Ivor. *Black Intellectuals and the Dilemmas of Race and Class in Trinidad.* Cambridge, Massachusetts: Shenkman, 1982.

_____. "The Intellectual Background to the Democratic Revolution." Pages 20–48 in Wendell Bell (ed.), *The Democratic Revolution in the West Indies.* Cambridge, Massachusetts: Shenkman, 1967.

Painter, David S. "Collective Security and the Inter-American System," *Historical Issues,* No. 9511, November 1986, 1–3.

Palmer, Ransford W. *Problems of Development in Beautiful Countries: Perspectives on the Caribbean.* Lanham, Maryland: North-South, 1984.

Pan American Health Organization. *Health Conditions in the Americas, 1981–1984.* Washington: 1985.

_____. *Program Budget, 1986–87.* Washington: 1985.

Parris, Carl D. "Resource Ownership and the Prospects for Democracy: The Case of Trinidad and Tobago." Pages 313–26 in Paget Henry and Carl Stone (eds.), *The Newer Caribbean: Decolonization, Democracy, and Development.* (Inter-American Politics series, 4.) Philadelphia: Institute for the Study of Human Issues, 1983.

Pollard, H.J. "The Erosion of Agriculture in an Oil Economy: The Case of Export Crop Production in Trinidad," *World Development* [London], 13, No. 7, 1985, 819–35.

Power, Kevin P. *Caribbean Basin Trade and Investment Guide.* Washington: Washington International Press, 1984.

Robinson, A.N.R. *Budget Speech, 1987.* Port-of-Spain, Trinidad and Tobago: Government Printery, 1987.

_____. *The Mechanics of Independence: Patterns of Political and Economic Transformation of Trinidad and Tobago.* Cambridge: MIT Press, 1971.

Royal Bank of Trinidad and Tobago. "An Economic Profile." Port-of-Spain, Trinidad and Tobago: 1983.

Ryan, Selwyn. *The Politics of Succession: A Study of Parties and Politics in Trinidad and Tobago.* St. Augustine, Trinidad and Tobago: University of the West Indies, 1978.

———. "Tobago's Quest for Autonomy: From Colony to War to . . .," *Caribbean Review,* 14, No. 2, Spring 1985, 7–9.

Ryan, Selwyn, Eddie Greene, and Jack Harewood. *The Confused Electorate: A Study of Political Attitudes and Opinions in Trinidad and Tobago.* St. Augustine, Trinidad and Tobago: University of the West Indies, 1979.

Sandoval, José Miguel. "State Capitalism in a Petroleum-Based Economy: The Case of Trinidad and Tobago." Pages 247–68 in Fitzroy Ambursley and Robin Cohen (eds.), *Crisis in the Caribbean.* New York: Monthly Review Press, 1983.

Smith, Michael G. "Trinidad." Pages 89–97 in Michael G. Smith (ed.), *Culture, Race, and Class in the Commonwealth Caribbean.* Kingston, Jamaica: University of the West Indies, 1984.

Sutton, Paul. "Black Power in Trinidad and Tobago: The Crisis of 1970," *Journal of Commonwealth and Comparative Politics* [London], 21, No. 2, 1983, 116–31.

———. "Trinidad and Tobago: Oil Capitalism and the 'Presidential Power' of Eric Williams." Pages 42–76 in Anthony Payne and Paul Sutton (eds.), *Dependency under Challenge: The Political Economy of the Commonwealth Caribbean.* London: Butler and Tanner, 1984.

Taylor, Jeremy (ed.). *The Caribbean Handbook, 1986.* St. John's, Antigua and Barbuda: FT Caribbean, 1986.

Trinidad and Tobago. Embassy to the United States. *Economic Profile on Trinidad and Tobago for Foreign Investors.* Washington: August 1983.

Trinidad and Tobago. Ministry of Finance and Planning. *Estimates of Expenditures for the Year 1986.* Port-of-Spain, Trinidad and Tobago: Government Printery, 1986.

Trinidad and Tobago. Ministry of Finance and Planning. Central Statistical Office. *Annual Statistical Digest, 1984.* Port-of-Spain, Trinidad and Tobago: 1985.

———. *Financial Statistics, 1983.* Port-of-Spain, Trinidad and Tobago: 1984.

———. *Labour Force.* Port-of-Spain, Trinidad and Tobago: 1986.

———. *National Income of Trinidad and Tobago, 1966–1985.* Port-of-Spain, Trinidad and Tobago: 1987.

———. *Overseas Trade Report, 1985.* Port-of-Spain, Trinidad and Tobago: 1986.

————. *Population and Vital Statistics, Report 1982–83.* Port-of-Spain, Trinidad and Tobago: 1987.

————. *Report on Education Statistics, 1982–83.* Port-of-Spain, Trinidad and Tobago: 1986.

————. *Review of the Economy, 1985.* Port-of-Spain, Trinidad and Tobago: 1986.

————. *Review of the Economy, 1986.* Port-of-Spain, Trinidad and Tobago: 1987.

United Nations. Food and Agriculture Organization. *1985 FAO Production Yearbook.* Rome: 1986.

————. *1986 Country Tables.* Rome: 1986.

————. *Yearbook of Fishery Statistics, 1984.* Rome: 1986.

United States. Agency for International Development. Office of Foreign Disaster Assistance. *Countries of the Caribbean Community: A Regional Profile.* Washington: 1983.

United States. Central Intelligence Agency. *The World Factbook, 1987.* Washington: GPO, 1987.

United States. Congress. 100th, 1st Session. House of Representatives. Committee on Appropriations. *Foreign Assistance and Related Programs: Appropriations for 1988.* Washington: GPO, 1987.

United States. Department of Commerce. *1987 CBI Guidebook.* Washington: GPO, 1986.

United States. Department of Energy. *The Petroleum Resources of Venezuela and Trinidad and Tobago.* (Foreign Energy Supply Assessment series, DOE/E1A–0398.) Washington: GPO, 1983.

Williams, Eric. *From Columbus to Castro: The History of the Caribbean, 1492–1969.* New York: Harper and Row, 1970.

————. *Inward Hunger: The Education of a Prime Minister.* Chicago: University of Chicago Press, 1969.

Woodcock, Henry I. *A History of Tobago.* London: Frank Cass, 1971.

World Bank. *World Debt Tables, 1986–1987.* Washington: 1987.

————. *World Development Report, 1984.* New York: Oxford University Press, 1984.

————. *World Development Report, 1987.* New York: Oxford University Press, 1987.

Young, Alma H., and Dion E. Phillips (eds.). *Militarization in the Non-Hispanic Caribbean.* Boulder: Lynne Rienner, 1986.

(Various issues of the following publications were also used in the preparation of this chapter: *Caribbean Insight* [London], 1986–87; Foreign Broadcast Information Service, *Daily Report: Latin America,* 1983–87; Joint Publications Research Service, *Latin America Report,* 1986–87; *Latin American Monitor* [London], 1984–85; *Latin American Weekly Report* [London], 1986–87; *Latin America Regional Reports: Caribbean* [London], 1981–87; *Social and Economic Studies*

[Mona, Jamaica], 1982–83; *Trinidad and Tobago Express* [Port-of-Spain, Trinidad and Tobago], 1981–87; and *Trinidad Guardian* [Port-of-Spain, Trinidad and Tobago], 1986–87.)

Chapter 4
Dominica

Atwood, Thomas. *History of the Island of Dominica.* London: Cass, 1971.

Barry, Tom, Beth Wood, and Deb Preusch. *The Other Side of Paradise: Foreign Control in the Caribbean.* New York: Grove Press, 1984.

Beckford, George L. *Persistent Poverty: Underdevelopment in Plantation Economies of the Third World.* New York: Oxford University Press, 1972.

Birnbaum, Stephen (ed.). *Birnbaum's Caribbean, Bermuda, and the Bahamas, 1986.* Boston: Houghton Mifflin, 1985.

Boromé, Joseph. "How Crown Colony Government Came to Dominica by 1898." Pages 120–50 in *Aspects of Dominican History.* Roseau, Dominica: Government Printing Division, 1972.

Brooks, John (ed.). *The 1987 South American Handbook.* (63d ed.) Bath, United Kingdom: Trade and Travel, 1986.

Caribbean Development Bank. *Annual Report, 1986.* Wildey, Barbados: Letchworth Press, 1987.

The Development Group for Alternative Policies. *Supporting Central American and Caribbean Development: A Critique of the Caribbean Basin Initiative and an Alternative Regional Assistance Plan.* Washington: 1983.

The Diagram Group. *Atlas of Central America and the Caribbean.* New York: Macmillan, 1985.

Dolman, Anthony J. *Islands in the Shade: The Performance and Prospects of Small Island Developing Countries.* The Hague: Institute of Social Studies Advisory Service, 1984.

Dominica. Ministry of Finance. Statistical Division. *Annual Overseas Trade Report (1985).* Roseau, Dominica: 1986.

_____. *Statistical Digest, No. 6 (1985).* Roseau, Dominica: 1986.

Eyre, Alan. *A New Geography of the Caribbean.* (5th ed.) London: George Philip and Son, 1979.

Frost, Jens (ed.). *World Radio TV Handbook, 1986.* Hvidore, Denmark: Glenn Heffernon, 1986.

Girvan, Norman. *Working Paper, No. 7: Aspects of the Political Economy of Race in the Caribbean and in the Americas.* Mona, Jamaica: Institute of Social and Economic Research, University of the West Indies, 1975.

Gomes, P.I. (ed.). *Rural Development in the Caribbean.* New York: St. Martin's Press, 1985.

Honychurch, Lennox. *The Dominica Story: A History of the Island.* Roseau, Dominica: Dominica Institute, 1984.

Larson, Edwin E., and Peter W. Birkeland. *Putnam's Geology.* (4th ed.) New York: Oxford University Press, 1982.

Lewis, Vaughan A. (ed.). *Size, Self-Determination, and International Relations: The Caribbean.* Mona, Jamaica: Institute of Social and Economic Research, University of the West Indies, 1976.

Macmillan Education. *Macmillan Caribbean Certificate Atlas.* London: 1979.

Pan American Health Organization. *Health Conditions in the Americas, 1981–1984.* Washington: 1985.

_____. *Program Budget, 1986–87.* Washington: 1985.

_____. "Status of AIDS in the Americas," *Epidemiological Bulletin,* 7, Nos. 5–6, December 1986, 1.

Paxton, John (ed.). *The Statesman's Year-Book: Statistical and Historical Annual of the State of the World for the Year 1986–1987.* New York: St. Martin's Press, 1986.

Phillips, Dion E. "The Increasing Emphasis on Security and Defense in the Eastern Caribbean." Pages 42–64 in Alma H. Young and Dion E. Phillips (eds.), *Militarization in the Non-Hispanic Caribbean.* Boulder: Lynne Rienner, 1986.

Putnam, William Clement. *Putnam's Geology.* New York: Oxford University Press, 1978.

Rickards, Colin (ed.). *Caribbean Year Book, 1979–80.* Toronto: Caribook, 1980.

Schoenhals, Kai P., and Richard A. Melanson (eds.). *Revolution and Intervention in Grenada: The New Jewel Movement, the United States, and the Caribbean.* (Westview Special Studies on Latin America and the Caribbean.) Boulder: Westview Press, 1985.

Shillingford, John D. *The Major Agricultural Land Types in Dominica.* Ithaca: Department of Agricultural Economics, Cornell University, 1972.

Speed, Robert C., et al. (eds.). *Lesser Antilles Arc and Adjacent Terrains.* (Regional Atlas series.) Woods Hole, Massachusetts: Marine Science International, 1984.

Taylor, Jeremy (ed.). *The Caribbean Handbook, 1986.* St. John's, Antigua and Barbuda: FT Caribbean, 1986.

United States. Agency for International Development. Office of Foreign Disaster Assistance. *Countries of the Caribbean Community: A Regional Profile.* Washington: 1983.

United States. Central Intelligence Agency. *The World Factbook, 1986.* Washington: GPO, 1986.

United States. Department of State. Bureau of Public Affairs. *Atlas of the Caribbean Basin*. (2d ed.) Washington: GPO, 1984.

West, Robert C., and John P. Augelli (eds.). *Middle America: Its Lands and Peoples*. (2d ed.) Englewood Cliffs, New Jersey: Prentice-Hall, 1976.

Wood, Peter. *Caribbean Isles (A Ready Reference Guide to the Caribbean)*. New York: Time-Life Books, 1975.

World Bank. *Dominica: Priorities and Prospects for Development*. Washington: 1985.

(Various issues of the following publications were also used in the preparation of this section: Foreign Broadcast Information Service, *Daily Report: Latin America*, 1983–87; Joint Publications Research Service, *Latin America Report*, 1983–87; and *Latin American Weekly Report* [London], 1985–87.)

St. Lucia

Alleyne, Mervin C. "Language and Society in St. Lucia." Pages 198–212 in David Lowenthal and Lambros Comitas (eds.), *Consequences of Class and Color: West Indian Perspectives*. Garden City, New York: Anchor Books, 1973.

Anderson, Thomas D. *Geopolitics of the Caribbean: Ministates in a Wider World*. (Politics in Latin America: A Hoover Institution series.) New York: Praeger, 1984.

Bair, Frank E. (ed.). *Countries of the World and Their Leaders Yearbook, 1986*. Detroit: Gale Research, 1985.

Banks, Arthur S. (ed.). *Political Handbook of the World, 1984–1985*. Binghamton, New York: CSA, 1985.

Beshoff, Pamela. "Foreign Policy Co-operation and Regional Integration in the Caribbean," *Millennium: A Journal of International Studies* [London], 15, No. 1, 1986, 91–107.

Birnbaum, Stephen (ed.). *Birnbaum's Caribbean, Bermuda, and the Bahamas, 1986*. Boston: Houghton Mifflin, 1985.

Brooks, John (ed.). *The 1987 South American Handbook*. (63d ed.) Bath, United Kingdom: Trade and Travel, 1986.

Caribbean/Central American Action. *1986 Caribbean and Central America Databook*. Washington: 1985.

Caribbean Development Bank. *Annual Report, 1985*. Wildey, Barbados: Letchworth Press, 1986.

Compton, John G.M. *Budget Address, 1985*. Castries, St. Lucia: Government of St. Lucia, 1985.

_____. *Budget Address, 1986*. Castries, St. Lucia: Government of St. Lucia, 1986.

695

The Diagram Group. *Atlas of Central America and the Caribbean.* New York: Macmillan, 1985.

Easter, B.H. *St. Lucia and the French Revolution.* Castries, St. Lucia: Voice, 1969.

Eastern Caribbean Central Bank. *Report and Statement of Accounts.* Basseterre, St. Christopher and Nevis: 1985.

Economist Intelligence Unit. *Quarterly Economic Review of Trinidad and Tobago, Guyana, Barbados, Windward and Leeward Islands: Annual Supplement, 1985.* London: Economist, 1986.

Fraser, Peter D., and Paul Hackett (eds.). *Caribbean Economic Handbook.* London: Euromonitor, 1985.

Frost, Jens (ed.). *World Radio TV Handbook, 1986.* Hvidore, Denmark: Glenn Heffernon, 1986.

Goodwin, Clayton (ed.). *The Caribbean Handbook, 1984–85.* St. John's, Antigua and Barbuda: FT International, 1984.

Green, Richard (ed.). *Latin America and Caribbean Review, 1986.* Saffron Walden, Essex, United Kingdom: World of Information, 1985.

Hunte, George. *The West Indian Islands.* New York: Viking Press, 1972.

Institute of Social and Economic Research. University of the West Indies. *Project Report to the Government of St. Lucia.* Mona, Jamaica: 1982.

Jesse, Charles, and B.H. Easter. *A Short History of the Town and District of Vieux Fort, St. Lucia.* Castries, St. Lucia: St. Lucia Archaeological and Historical Society, 1971.

Lewis, Gary P. "Prospects for a Regional Security System in the Eastern Caribbean," *Millennium: A Journal of International Studies* [London], 15, No. 1, 1986, 73–90.

Niddrie, David L. "The Caribbean." Pages 77–132 in Harold Blakemore and Clifford T. Smith (eds.), *Latin America: Geographical Perspectives.* New York: Methuen, 1983.

O'Loughlin, Carleen. *Economic and Political Change in the Leeward and Windward Islands.* New Haven: Yale University Press, 1968.

Pan American Health Organization. *Health Conditions in the Americas, 1981–1984.* Washington: 1985.

————. *Program Budget, 1986–87.* Washington: 1985.

————. "Status of AIDS in the Americas," *Epidemiological Bulletin,* 7, Nos. 5–6, December 1986, 7–8.

Parry, John H., and Philip M. Sherlock. *A Short History of the West Indies.* New York: Macmillan, 1971.

Power, Kevin P. *Caribbean Basin Trade and Investment Guide.* Washington: Washington International Press, 1984.

Resource Center. *Focus on the Eastern Caribbean: Bananas, Bucks, and Boots.* Albuquerque: 1984.

"Saint Lucia." Pages 2331–36 in *The Europa Yearbook, 1987,* II. London: Europa, 1987.

Sherlock, Philip M. *West Indian Nations: A New History.* New York: St. Martin's Press, 1972.

St. Clair, Daniel W. (ed.). *St. Lucia Yearbook, 1981.* Castries, St. Lucia: Voice, 1981.

St. Lucia. *The Saint Lucia Constitution Order, 1978.* London: Her Majesty's Stationery Office, 1978.

St. Lucia. Ministry of Health. *Progress Report on Health Conditions: Quadrennium 1982–85.* Castries, St. Lucia: Government of St. Lucia, 1986.

St. Lucia. St. Lucia National Development Corporation. *Advertising Supplement to the Wall Street Journal.* Castries, St. Lucia: Government of St. Lucia, April 9, 1986.

Stone, Carl. *Power in the Caribbean Basin: A Comparative Study of Political Economy.* Philadelphia: Institute for the Study of Human Issues, 1986.

United States. Agency for International Development. *Regional Non-Formal Skills Training Project: Project Evaluation Summary.* Washington: 1984.

———. *Social and Institutional Profiles for St. Lucia, Dominica, Antigua and Barbuda, St. Kitts-Nevis.* Washington: 1983.

United States. Agency for International Development. Office of Foreign Disaster Assistance. *Countries of the Caribbean Community: A Regional Profile.* Washington: February 1983.

United States. Central Intelligence Agency. *The World Factbook, 1986.* Washington: GPO, 1986.

United States. Department of Commerce. International Trade Administration. *Foreign Economic Trends and Their Implications for the United States: St. Lucia.* Washington: GPO, 1986.

United States. Department of State. Bureau of Public Affairs. *Background Notes: St. Lucia.* Washington: 1984.

West, Robert C., and John P. Augelli (eds.). *Middle America: Its Lands and Peoples.* (2d ed.) Englewood Cliffs, New Jersey: Prentice-Hall, 1976.

World Bank. *St. Lucia: Economic Performance and Prospects.* Washington: 1985.

———. *The World Bank Atlas, 1986.* Washington: 1986.

(Various issues of the following publications were also used in the preparation of this section: Foreign Broadcast Information Service, *Daily Report: Latin America,* 1987; Joint Publications Research Service, *Latin America Report,* 1987; and *Latin American Weekly Report* [London], 1987.)

St. Vincent and the Grenadines

Andrade, John. *World Police and Paramilitary Forces*. New York: Stockton Press, 1985.

Banks, Arthur S. (ed.). *Political Handbook of the World, 1984–1985*. Binghamton, New York: CSA, 1985.

Birnbaum, Stephen (ed.). *Birnbaum's Caribbean, Bermuda, and the Bahamas, 1986*. Boston: Houghton Mifflin, 1985.

Blaustein, Albert P., and Gisbert H. Flanz (eds.). *Constitutions of the Countries of the World*. Dobbs Ferry, New York: Oceana, 1984.

Brana-Shute, Gary. "An Eastern Caribbean Centrist," *Caribbean Review*, 14, No. 4, Fall 1985, 27–29.

Brana-Shute, Gary, and Rosemary Brana-Shute. "The Unemployed of the Eastern Caribbean: Attitudes and Aspirations." (Research paper.) Gainesville, Florida: December 1980.

Brooks, John (ed.). *The 1986 South American Handbook*. Bath, United Kingdom: Trade and Travel, 1985.

Butland, Gilbert J. *Latin America*. New York: John Wiley and Sons, 1972.

Caribbean/Central American Action. *1987 Caribbean and Central America Databook*. Washington: 1986.

Caribbean Development Bank. *Annual Report, 1986*. Wildey, Barbados: Letchworth Press, 1987.

Carr, Peter R. "Health Systems Development in the English-Speaking Caribbean: Toward the Twenty-First Century," *Bulletin of the Pan American Health Organization*, 19, No. 4, 1985, 368–83.

Chernick, Sidney E. *The Commonwealth Caribbean: The Integration Experience*. Baltimore: Johns Hopkins University Press, 1978.

The Diagram Group. *Atlas of Central America and the Caribbean*. New York: Macmillan, 1985.

Diederich, Bernard. "The End of West Indian Innocence: Arming the Police," *Caribbean Review*, 13, No. 2, Spring 1984, 10–12.

Dorst, Jean. *South America and Central America: A Natural History*. London: Hamish Hamilton, 1967.

Economist Intelligence Unit. *Quarterly Economic Review of Trinidad and Tobago, Guyana, Barbados, Windward and Leeward Islands: Annual Supplement, 1985*. London: Economist, 1986.

Ellis, Patricia. "Non-Formal Education, Women, and Development in the English-Speaking Caribbean," *Bulletin of Eastern Caribbean Affairs* [Cave Hill, Barbados], 11, No. 2, May–June 1985, 23–33.

Emmanuel, Patrick. "Elections and Parties in the Eastern Caribbean," *Caribbean Review*, 10, Spring 1981, 14–16.

Eyre, Alan. *A New Geography of the Caribbean.* (5th ed.) London: George Philip and Son, 1979.

Green, Richard (ed.). *Latin America and Caribbean Review, 1986.* Saffron Walden, Essex, United Kingdom: World of Information, 1985.

Grieb, Kenneth J. *Research Guide to Central America and the Caribbean.* Madison: University of Wisconsin Press, 1985.

Halbury's Laws of England. (4th ed., vol. 6.) London: Butterworths, 1974.

International Development Association. *Report and Recommendation of the President of the International Development Association to the Executive Directors on a Proposed Credit of SDR 4.8 Million to the Eastern Caribbean States Fourth Caribbean Development Bank Regional Vocational and Technical Education Project.* (Report No. P–4420–CRG.) Washington: April 2, 1987.

Jane's Fighting Ships, 1984–85. (Ed., John Moore.) London: Jane's, 1985.

Laine, Kingsley. "An Overview of the Vincentian Economy," *Bulletin of Eastern Caribbean Affairs* [Cave Hill, Barbados], November–December 1979, 13.

Levy, Anthony Lancelot (ed.). *Personalities Caribbean.* Kingston, Jamaica: Personalities, 1983.

Lewis, Gary P. "Prospects for a Regional Security System in the Eastern Caribbean," *Millennium: A Journal of International Studies* [London], 15, No. 1, 1986, 73–90.

Millett, Richard, and W. Marvin Will (eds.). *The Restless Caribbean: Changing Patterns of International Relations.* New York: Praeger, 1979.

Niddrie, David L. "The Caribbean." Pages 77–132 in Harold Blakemore and Clifford T. Smith (eds.), *Latin America: Geographical Perspectives.* New York: Methuen, 1983.

Pan American Health Organization. *Health Conditions in the Americas, 1981–1984.* Washington: 1985.

————. "Status of AIDS in the Americas," *Epidemiological Bulletin,* 7, Nos. 5–6, December 1986, 1.

Paxton, John (ed.). *The Statesman's Year-Book: Statistical and Historical Annual of the States of the World for the Year 1986–1987.* New York: St. Martin's Press, 1986.

Population Reference Bureau. *1987 World Population.* Washington: April 1986.

"Saint Vincent and the Grenadines." Pages 2337–42 in *The Europa Yearbook 1987,* II. London: Europa, 1987.

Sim, Richard, and James Anderson. *The Caribbean Strategic Vacuum.* (Conflict Studies, 121.) London: Institute for the Study of Conflict, August 1980.

United Nations. Fund for Population Activities. *The English-Speaking Caribbean.* New York: 1978.

United States. Agency for International Development. Office of Foreign Disaster Assistance. *Countries of the Caribbean Community: A Regional Profile.* Washington: February 1983.

United States. Central Intelligence Agency. *The World Factbook, 1987.* Washington: GPO, 1987.

United States. Congress. 97th, 2d Session. House of Representatives. Committee on Foreign Affairs. *Eastern Caribbean: Report of a Staff Study Mission to the Dominican Republic, Antigua, Dominica, Barbados, and St. Vincent, January 5-19, 1982.* Washington: GPO, May 1982.

United States. Department of State. *Country Reports on Human Rights Practices for 1986: St. Vincent and the Grenadines.* (Report submitted to United States Congress, 100th, 1st Session, Senate, Committee on Foreign Relations, and House of Representatives, Committee on Foreign Affairs.) Washington: GPO, February 1987.

United States. Department of State. Bureau of Public Affairs. *Atlas of the Caribbean Basin.* (2d ed.) Washington: GPO, 1984.

"Weekly Arms Transfer Tables," *Defense and Foreign Affairs,* August 25-31, 1986, 8.

West, Robert C., and John P. Augelli (eds.). *Middle America: Its Lands and Peoples.* (2d ed.) Englewood Cliffs, New Jersey: Prentice-Hall, 1976.

World Bank. *St. Vincent and the Grenadines: Economic Situation and Selected Development Issues.* Washington: 1985.

A Year Book of the Commonwealth, 1982. London: Her Majesty's Stationery Office, 1982.

Young, Alma H., and Dion E. Phillips (eds.). *Militarization in the Non-Hispanic Caribbean.* Boulder: Lynne Rienner, 1986.

(Various issues of the following publications also were used in the preparation of this section: *Caribbean and West Indies Chronicle* [London], 1984; *Caribbean Insight* [London], 1986-87; *Caribbean Monthly Bulletin* [Río Piedras, Puerto Rico], 1983-84; *Caribbean Review,* 1981-85; Foreign Broadcast Information Service, *Daily Report: Latin America,* 1986-87; *Keesing's Contemporary Archives* (changed to *Keesing's Record of World Events* in January 1987) [London], 1969, 1980-87; *Latin American Monitor: Caribbean* [London], 1984-87; *Latin America Regional Reports: Caribbean* [London], 1983; *New York Times,* 1980, 1984; *Trinidad Guardian* [Port-of-Spain, Trinidad and Tobago], 1986-87; and *Vincentian* [Kingstown, St. Vincent and the Grenadines], 1987.)

Grenada

Archer, Ewart. "Gairyism, Revolution and Reorganisation: Three Decades of Turbulence in Grenada," *Journal of Commonwealth and Comparative Politics* [London], 23, No. 2, July 1985, 91-111.

Beshoff, Pamela. "Foreign Policy Co-operation and Regional Integration in the Caribbean," *Millennium: A Journal of International Studies* [London], 15, No. 1, Spring 1986, 91-107.

Birnbaum, Stephen (ed.). *Birnbaum's Caribbean, Bermuda, and the Bahamas, 1986.* Boston: Houghton Mifflin, 1985.

Blaize, Herbert A. *Grenada Budget Speech.* St. George's, Grenada: Government Printer, February 20, 1987.

Boodhoo, Ken I. "Violence and Militarization in the Eastern Caribbean: Grenada." Pages 65-89 in Alma H. Young and Dion E. Phillips (eds.), *Militarization in the Non-Hispanic Caribbean.* Boulder: Lynne Rienner, 1986.

Britain. Directorate of Overseas Surveys. *Grenada: Island of Spice.* (4th ed.) London: Government of the United Kingdom, 1985.

Brooks, John (ed.). *The 1987 South American Handbook.* (63d ed.) Bath, United Kingdom: Trade and Travel, 1986.

Caribbean Development Bank. *Annual Report, 1985.* Wildey, Barbados: Letchworth Press, 1985.

Carr, Peter R. "Health Systems Development in the English-Speaking Caribbean: Toward the Twenty-First Century," *Bulletin of the Pan American Health Organization,* 19, No. 4, 1985, 368-83.

Cobb, Charles E., Jr., and David A. Harvey. "Marking Time in Grenada," *National Geographic,* 166, No. 5, November 1984, 688-710.

"The Commonwealth Parliamentary Association," *Round Table: The Commonwealth Journal of International Affairs* [London], No. 300, October 1986, 310-12.

Davidson, Scott. *Grenada: A Study in Politics and the Limits of International Law.* Aldershot, United Kingdom: Avebury, 1987.

The Diagram Group. *Atlas of Central America and the Caribbean.* New York: Macmillan, 1985.

Diederich, Bernard. "The End of West Indian Innocence: Arming the Police," *Caribbean Review,* 13, No. 2, Spring 1984, 10-12.

Dominique, Francois (ed.). *Grenada: Intervention, Invasion, Rescue Mission?* n. pl.: F. Dominique, 1984.

Duncan, W. Raymond. "Grenada." Pages 90-94 in Richard F. Staar (ed.), *Yearbook on International Communist Affairs, 1983.* Stanford, California: Hoover Institution Press, 1983.

Duvas, Raymund P. *A History of the Island of Grenada, 1498-1796.* St. George's, Grenada: Carenage Press, 1974.

Economist Intelligence Unit. *Quarterly Economic Review of Trinidad and Tobago, Guyana, Barbados, Windward and Leeward Islands: Annual Supplement, 1985.* London: Economist, 1986.

Emmanuel, Patrick A.M. "Revolutionary Theory and Political Reality in the Eastern Caribbean," *Journal of Inter-American Studies and World Affairs,* 25, No. 2, May 1983, 193–227.

Eyre, Alan. *A New Geography of the Caribbean.* (5th ed.) London: George Philip and Son, 1979.

Fenton, Robert E. "Caribbean Coast Guard: A Regional Approach," *Naval War College Review,* 37, March–April 1984, 26–40.

Frost, Jens (ed.). *World Radio TV Handbook, 1986.* Hvidore, Denmark: Glenn Heffernon, 1986.

Gonzalez, Edward. "The Cuban and Soviet Challenge in the Caribbean Basin," *Orbis,* 29, Spring 1985, 73–94.

Gottemoeller, Rose E. *Transforming Clients into Surrogates: The Soviet Experience.* Santa Monica: Rand, 1985.

Green, Richard (ed.). *Latin America and Caribbean Review, 1986.* Saffron Walden, Essex, United Kingdom: World of Information, 1985.

Grenada. *The Grenada Constitution Order, 1973.* St. George's, Grenada: Government Printer, 1974.

Grenada. Ministry of Education. *Report for 1980.* St. George's, Grenada: 1980.

Harewood, Jack. "Population Growth in Grenada in the Twentieth Century," *Social and Economic Studies* [Kingston, Jamaica], 15, No. 2, June 1966, 61–84.

"Independence for Grenada—Myth or Reality?" (Paper presented at Conference on the Implications of Independence for Grenada, St. Augustine, Trinidad and Tobago.) St. Augustine, Trinidad and Tobago: Institute of International Relations, Univeristy of the West Indies, 1974.

Institute of Caribbean Studies. Caribbean Monthly Bulletin. *Documents on the Invasion of Grenada.* Río Piedras, Puerto Rico: University of Puerto Rico, 1984.

Kay, Francis. *This Is Grenada.* Privately published, 1966.

Ledeen, Michael A. "Marxist Follies," *Harper's,* 268, No. 1605, February 1984, 24–27.

Ledeen, Michael A., and Herbert Romerstein. *Grenada Documents: An Overview and Selection.* Washington: GPO, 1984.

Lewis, Gary P. "Prospects for a Regional Security System in the Eastern Caribbean," *Millennium: A Journal of International Studies* [London], 15, No. 1, Spring 1986, 73–90.

Lewis, John F., and Bernard M. Gunn. "Aspects of Island Arc Evolution and Magnetism in the Caribbean: Geochemistry of

Some West Indian Plutonic and Volcanic Rocks." Pages 171–77 in Cecily Petzall (ed.), *Transactions: Caribbean Geological Conference.* Caracas: 1972.

Lewis, Vaughan. "Foreign Relations of the English-Speaking Caribbean." Pages 67–73 in Library of Congress, Congressional Research Service (ed.), *The English-Speaking Caribbean: Current Conditions and Implications for U.S. Policy.* Washington: GPO, 1985.

MacDonald, Scott B. "The Future of Foreign Aid in the Caribbean after Grenada: Finlandization and Confrontation in the Eastern Tier," *Inter-American Economic Affairs,* 38, Spring 1985, 59–74.

McKenzie, Alan B. *Creole-Leninism: Grenada, A Case Study.* Monterey, California: Naval Postgraduate School, December 1984.

Macmillan Education. *Macmillan Caribbean Certificate Atlas.* London: 1979.

Maingot, Anthony P. "Politics Caribbean Style," *Caribbean Review,* 14, No. 2, Spring 1985, 5–6.

Mallin, Jay, Sr. "U.S., Britain Building Grenadian Security Force," *Washington Times,* December 7, 1984, 5.

Menon, P.K. "The Organization of Eastern Caribbean States— An Important Milestone in Sub-Regional Integration," *Inter-American Law Review,* 17, Winter 1986, 297–311.

Millette, Robert, and Mahin Gosine. *The Grenada Revolution: Why It Failed.* New York: Africana Research, 1985.

Mitchell, Harold. *Caribbean Patterns.* Edinburgh: Chambers, 1972.

Naipaul, V.S. "An Island Betrayed," *Harper's,* 268, No. 1606, March 1984, 61–72.

Norton, Graham. "Defending the Eastern Caribbean," *World Today* [London], 40, June 1984, 254–60.

O'Loughlin, Carleen. *Economic and Political Change in the Leeward and Windward Islands.* New Haven: Yale University Press, 1968.

Palmer, Ransford W. *Caribbean Dependence on the United States Economy.* New York: Praeger, 1979.

Pan American Health Organization. *Health Conditions in the Americas, 1981–1984.* Washington: 1985.

_____. *Program Budget, 1986–87.* Washington: 1985.

Pastor, Robert A. "Does the United States Push Revolutions to Cuba? The Case of Grenada," *Journal of Inter-American Studies and World Affairs,* 28, No. 1, Spring 1986, 1–34.

Pryor, Frederic L. *Revolutionary Grenada: A Study in Political Economy.* New York: Praeger, 1986.

Ryan, Selwyn. "The Grenada Questions: A Revolutionary Balance Sheet," *Caribbean Review,* 13, No. 3, Summer 1984, 6–9.

Schoenhals, Kai P., and Richard A. Melanson (eds.). *Revolution and Intervention in Grenada: The New Jewel Movement, the United States, and the Caribbean.* (Westview Special Studies on Latin America and the Caribbean.) Boulder: Westview Press, 1985.

Schwartz, Stephen. "Caliban's Children: Reflections on Grenada," *Journal of Contemporary Studies,* 7, Fall 1984, 49–57.

Segal, Aaron. "Background to Grenada: When the Social Scientists Invaded," *Caribbean Review,* 12, No. 4, Fall 1983, 40–44.

_____. "Caribbean Realities," *Current History,* 84, No. 500, March 1985, 127–29.

Singham, A.W. *The Hero and the Crowd in a Colonial Polity.* New Haven: Yale University Press, 1968.

Smith, Michael G. *The Plural Society in the British West Indies.* Berkeley and Los Angeles: University of California Press, 1965.

Speed, Robert C., et al. (eds.). *Lesser Antilles Arc and Adjacent Terrains.* (Regional Atlas series.) Woods Hole, Massachusetts: Marine Science International, 1984.

St. Clair-Daniel, W. "Caribbean Concepts of Parliament," *Parliamentarian* [London], 66, October 1985, 211–13.

Thorndike, Tony. *Grenada: Politics, Economics, and Society.* Boulder: Lynne Rienner, 1985.

United States. Agency for International Development. *Summary Highlights of the A.I.D. Program in Grenada.* Washington: 1986.

United States. Agency for International Development. Office of Foreign Disaster Assistance. *Countries of the Caribbean Community: A Regional Profile.* Washington: February 1983.

United States. Central Intelligence Agency. *The World Factbook, 1986.* Washington: GPO, 1986.

United States. Congress. 98th, 1st Session. House of Representatives. Committee on Foreign Affairs. Subcommittee on International Security and Scientific Affairs and on Western Hemisphere Affairs. *U.S. Military Actions in Grenada: Implications for U.S. Policy in the Eastern Caribbean.* Washington: GPO, 1984.

United States. Congress. 98th, 2d Session. House of Representatives. Committee on Armed Services. *Report of the Delegation to Eastern Caribbean and South American Countries.* (Committee Print, No. 16.) Washington: GPO, February 1984.

United States. Congress. 99th, 1st Session. House of Representatives. Committee on Foreign Affairs. Subcommittee on Western Hemisphere Affairs. *U.S. Policy on Latin America, 1985.* Washington: GPO, January 29, 1985.

United States. Department of Commerce. Bureau of the Census. *World Population Profile, 1985.* Washington: GPO, October 1986.

United States. Department of Commerce. International Trade Administration. *Foreign Economic Trends and Their Implications for the United States: Grenada.* Washington: GPO, 1986.

United States. Department of State. Bureau of Public Affairs. *Atlas of the Caribbean Basin.* (2d ed.) Washington: GPO, 1984.

_____. *Background Notes: Grenada.* Washington: July 1985.

United States. Department of State. Foreign Affairs Information Management Center. *Grenada Post Report.* Washington: GPO, 1985.

Valenta, Jiri, and Virginia Valenta. "Leninism in Grenada," *Problems of Communism,* 33, July–August 1984, 1–23.

Walker, Andrew. "Security of the Eastern Caribbean," *Jane's Defence Weekly* [London], 7, No. 2, January 17, 1987, 61.

West, Robert C., and John P. Augelli (eds.). *Middle America: Its Lands and Peoples.* (2d ed.) Englewood Cliffs, New Jersey: Prentice-Hall, 1976.

World Bank. *Eastern Caribbean States: Fourth Caribbean Development Bank Regional, Vocational and Technical Education Project.* (P–4430–CR6.) Washington: April 2, 1987.

_____. *Grenada Economic Report.* Washington: World Bank, 1985.

(Various issues of the following publications were also used in the preparation of this section: *Caribbean and West Indies Chronicle* [London], 1986–87; *Caribbean Contact* [Bridgetown, Barbados], 1986; *Caribbean Insight* [London], 1985–86; *Caribbean Monthly Bulletin* [Río Piedras, Puerto Rico], 1984; Foreign Broadcast Information Service, *Daily Report: Latin America,* 1983–87; *Grenada Informer* [St. George's, Grenada], 1986; *Grenada Newsletter* [St. George's, Grenada], 1984–86; *Grenadian Voice* [St. George's, Grenada], 1986; Joint Publications Research Service, *Latin America Report,* 1986–87; *Keesing's Contemporary Archives* [London], 1986; *Latin American Weekly Report* [London], 1986; and *Latin America Regional Reports: Caribbean* [London], 1986–87.)

Barbados

Anderson, Thomas D. *Geopolitics of the Caribbean: Ministates in a Wider World.* (Politics in Latin America: A Hoover Institution series.) New York: Praeger, 1984.

Andrade, John. *World Police and Paramilitary Forces.* New York: Stockton Press, 1985.

Barbados. Barbados Government Information Service. *Facts on Barbados.* St. Michael, Barbados: Barbados Government Printing Department, 1985.

Barbados. Barbados Industrial Development Corporation. *The Manufacturers' Handbook.* Bridgetown, Barbados: 1983.

Barbados. Barbados Statistical Bulletin Service. *Overseas Trade,* 4, No. 8, 1986.

Barbados. Ministry of Finance and Planning. *Barbados Development Plan, 1983-1988.* Bridgetown, Barbados: 1983.

_____. *Barbados Economic Report, 1985.* Bridgetown, Barbados: 1986.

_____. *Barbados Economic Report, 1986.* Bridgetown, Barbados: 1987.

Beshoff, Pamela. "Foreign Policy Co-operation and Regional Integration in the Caribbean," *Millennium: A Journal of International Studies* [London], 15, No. 1, Spring 1986, 91-107.

Birnbaum, Stephen (ed.). *Birnbaum's Caribbean, Bermuda, and the Bahamas, 1986.* Boston: Houghton Mifflin, 1985.

Blackman, C.N., and W.A. Cox. "Factors in the Development of a Migration Policy for the Caribbean." Pages 12-27 in Central Bank of Barbados (ed.), *Economic Review.* Bridgetown, Barbados: 1986.

Brizan, George I. *Grenada, Island of Conflict: From Amerindians to People's Revolution, 1498-1979.* (Third World Studies.) London: Zed Books, 1984.

Brooks, John (ed.). *The 1987 South American Handbook.* (63d ed.) Bath, United Kingdom: Trade and Travel, 1986.

Bryan, Anthony T. "Cuba's Impact in the Caribbean," *International Journal* [Toronto], 40, No. 2, Spring 1985, 331-47.

Campbell, P.F. *An Outline of Barbados History.* Bridgetown, Barbados: Caribbean Graphics, 1974.

Caribbean Development Bank. *Annual Report, 1985.* Wildey, Barbados: Letchworth Press, 1986.

Conway, Dennis. *Caribbean Migrants: Opportunistic and Individualistic Sojourners.* (Universities Field Staff International, UFSI Reports. No. 24.) Indianapolis: 1986.

Dann, Graham. *The Quality of Life in Barbados.* London: Macmillan, 1984.

The Diagram Group. *Atlas of Central America and the Caribbean.* New York: Macmillan, 1985.

Economist Intelligence Unit. *Quarterly Economic Review of Trinidad and Tobago, Guyana, Barbados, Windward and Leeward Islands: Annual Supplement, 1985.* London: Economist, 1986.

Faria, Norman. "A Message for Washington," *South* [London], October 1986, 59.

Fraser, Peter D., and Paul Hackett (eds.). *Caribbean Economic Handbook.* London: Euromonitor, 1985.

Frost, Jens (ed.). *World Radio TV Handbook, 1986.* Hvidore, Denmark: Glenn Heffernon, 1986.

Gomes, P.I. *Barbados: The Post Independence Period, 1966–1971.* St. Augustine, Trinidad and Tobago: University of the West Indies, 1978.

Gooding, E.G.B. *Wayside Trees and Shrubs of Barbados.* London: Macmillan Education, 1973.

Hope, Kempe Ronald. *Economic Development in the Caribbean.* New York: Praeger, 1986.

Hoyos, F.A. *Barbados: A History from the Amerindians to Independence.* London: Macmillan Education, 1976.

————. *Barbados: Our Island Home.* London: Macmillan Education, 1979.

————. *Builders of Barbados.* London: Macmillan Caribbean, 1972.

————. *Grantley Adams and the Social Revolution.* London: Macmillan Education, 1974.

Inter-American Development Bank. *Economic and Social Progress in Latin America: 1986 Report.* Washington: 1987.

International Monetary Fund. *International Financial Statistics.* Washington: 1987.

Lewis, Gary P. "Prospects for a Regional Security System in the Eastern Caribbean," *Millennium: A Journal of International Studies* [London], 15, No. 1, Spring 1986, 73–90.

Lewis, Gordon K. *The Growth of the Modern West Indies.* New York: Monthly Review Press, 1968.

Lewis, Vaughan A. "The Commonwealth Caribbean." Pages 110–30 in Christopher Clapham (ed.), *Foreign Policy Making in Developing States.* Westmead, Farnborough, Hampshire, United Kingdom: Saxon House, 1977.

Long, Frank. "Industrialization and the Role of Industrial Development Corporations in a Caribbean Economy: A Study of Barbados, 1960–80," *Inter-American Economic Affairs,* 37, No. 3, Winter 1983, 33–56.

Lynch, Louis. *The Barbados Book.* New York: Coward, McCann, and Geoghegan, 1973.

Lynn, Bruce G. *Barbados: A Smiling Island.* Hollywood, Florida: Dukane Press, 1970.

MacDonald, Scott B. "The Future of Foreign Aid in the Caribbean after Grenada: Finlandization and Confrontation in the Eastern Tier," *Inter-American Economic Affairs,* 38, Spring 1985, 59–74.

Mack, Raymond W. "Race, Class, and Power in Barbados." Pages 140–64 in Wendell Bell (ed.), *The Democratic Revolution in the West Indies.* Cambridge, Massachusetts: Schenkman, 1967.

Maingot, Anthony P. "American Foreign Policy in the Caribbean: Continuities, Changes, and Contingencies," *International Journal* [Toronto], 40, No. 2, Spring 1985, 312–30.

Mitchell, Harold. *Caribbean Patterns.* Edinburgh: Chambers, 1972.

Mottley, Elton Elombe, and Roderick Broome. *People, Parties, and Politics.* Bridgetown, Barbados: Ashanti Books, 1976.

Norton, Graham. "Defending the Eastern Caribbean," *World Today* [London], 40, June 1984, 254–60.

O'Loughlin, Carleen. *Economic and Political Change in the Leeward and Windward Islands.* New Haven: Yale University Press, 1968.

Palmer, Ransford W. *Caribbean Dependence on the United States Economy.* New York: Praeger, 1979.

Pan American Health Organization. *Health Conditions in the Americas, 1981–1984.* Washington: 1985.

_____. *Program Budget, 1986–87.* Washington: 1985.

_____. "Status of AIDS in the Americas," *Epidemiological Bulletin*, 7, Nos. 5–6, December 1986, 1.

Paxton, John (ed.). *The Statesman's Year-Book: Statistical and Historical Annual of the State of the World for the Year 1986–1987.* New York: St. Martin's Press, 1986.

Payne, Anthony. "Whither Caricom? The Performance and Prospects of Caribbean Integration in the 1980s," *International Journal* [Toronto], 40, No. 2, Spring 1985, 207–28.

Polanyi-Levitt, Karl. "The Origins and Implications of the Caribbean Basin Initiative: Mortgaging Sovereignty?" *International Journal* [Toronto], 40, No. 2, Spring 1985, 229–81.

Sheppard, Jill. *The "Redlegs" of Barbados: Their Origins and History.* (The Caribbean—Historical and Cultural Perspectives series.) Millwood, New York: KTO Press, 1977.

Simmons, David A. "Militarization of the Caribbean: Concerns for National and Regional Security," *International Journal* [Toronto], 40, No. 2, Spring 1985, 348–76.

Simmons, Peter. "'Red Legs': Class and Color Contradictions in Barbados," *Studies in Comparative International Development,* 11, No. 1, Spring 1976, 3–24.

Tree, Ronald. *A History of Barbados.* London: Granada, 1972.

United States. Agency for International Development. Bureau of Science and Technology. *Draft Environmental Profile on Barbados.* Washington: May 1982.

United States. Central Intelligence Agency. *The World Factbook, 1986.* Washington: GPO, 1986.

United States. Department of Commerce. International Trade Administration. *Foreign Economic Trends and Their Implications for the United States: Barbados.* Washington: GPO, 1986.

United States. Department of State. Foreign Affairs Information Management Center. *Barbados Post Report.* Washington: 1983.

Watson, Hillbourne. "A Note on the 1986 General Election in Barbados," *Caribbean Studies Newsletter,* 13, No. 2, Summer 1986, 5–6.

Watts, David. *Man's Influence on the Vegetation of Barbados, 1627 to 1800.* London: Hull, 1966.

West, Robert C., and John P. Augelli (eds.). *Middle America: Its Lands and Peoples.* (2d ed.) Englewood Cliffs, New Jersey: Prentice-Hall, 1976.

Worrell, DeLisle (ed.). *The Economy of Barbados, 1946–1980.* Bridgetown, Barbados: Central Bank of Barbados, 1982.

(Various issues of the following publications were also used in the preparation of this section: *Bajan* [Bridgetown, Barbados], 1985–86; *Barbados Advocate* [Bridgetown, Barbados], 1985–87; *Bulletin* [Bridgetown, Barbados], 1976–79; *Caribbean Insight* [London], 1986; *Daily Gleaner* [Kingston, Jamaica], 1986; Foreign Broadcast Information Service, *Daily Report: Latin America,* 1983–87; Joint Publications Research Service, *Latin America Report,* 1983–87; *Keesing's Contemporary Archives* [London], 1971–86; *Latin American Monitor: Caribbean* [London], 1987; *Nation* [Bridgetown, Barbados], 1987; and *Voice* [Bridgetown, Barbados], 1987.)

Chapter 5

Antigua and Barbuda

Antigua and Barbuda. Ministry of Economic Development and Tourism. *Investing in Antigua and Barbuda.* St. John's, Antigua and Barbuda: 1986.

Antigua and Barbuda. Ministry of Education and Culture. *Report on the Education Division, 1979–1981.* St. John's, Antigua and Barbuda: n.d.

Antigua: Report for the Years 1963 and 1964. London: Her Majesty's Stationery Office, 1966.

Birnbaum, Stephen (ed.). *Birnbaum's Caribbean, Bermuda, and the Bahamas, 1986.* Boston: Houghton Mifflin, 1985.

Caribbean Development Bank. *Regional Forestry Sector Study: Country Report—Antigua and Barbuda.* Wildey, Barbados: 1983.

Challenger, Brian. "The Antiguan Economy: 1967–1981," *Bulletin of Eastern Caribbean Affairs* [Cave Hill, Barbados], 7, No. 5, November–December 1981, 12–18.

Davis, Gregson. *Antigua Black: Portrait of an Island People.* San Francisco: Scrimshaw Press, 1973.

Green, Richard (ed.). *Latin America and Caribbean Review, 1985.* Saffron Walden, Essex, United Kingdom: World of Information, 1984.

Henry, Paget. *Peripheral Capitalism and Underdevelopment in Antigua.* New Brunswick, New Jersey: Transaction Books, 1985.

_____. "State-Class Relations in Antigua," *Bulletin of Eastern Caribbean Affairs* [Cave Hill, Barbados], 7, No. 5, November–December 1981, 7–11.

Power, Kevin P. *Caribbean Basin Trade and Investment Guide.* Washington: Washington International Press, 1984.

Prime, Timothy S. *Economic Impact of Tourism in Antigua.* Christ Church, Antigua and Barbuda: Caribbean Tourism Research and Development Centre, 1981.

Putney, Allen D. *Survey of Conservation Priorities in the Lesser Antilles: Final Report.* St. Croix, United States Virgin Islands: Eastern Caribbean Natural Area Management Program, 1982.

Richards, Novelle H. *The Struggle and the Conquest, Pt. II: The Locust Years.* St. John's, Antigua and Barbuda: West Indies Workers Voice Printery, 1981.

Richards, Vincent A. "The Role of Agriculture in the Economic Development of Antigua and Barbuda," *Bulletin of Eastern Caribbean Affairs* [Cave Hill, Barbados], 7, No. 5, November–December 1981, 19–23.

Russell, Richard, and William G. McIntire. *Barbuda Reconnaissance.* Baton Rouge: Louisiana State University Press, 1966.

Sanders, Ron (ed.). *Antigua and Barbuda Independence.* St. John's, Antigua and Barbuda: Department of Information, Ministry of Foreign Affairs, Economic Development, Tourism, and Energy, 1982.

Schweser, Helen, and Agnes A. Blaize. *The Development of a Health Education Department in a Less Developed Caribbean Country.* Washington: People-to-People Health Foundation, Project HOPE, 1976.

Simon, Justin. "The Antiguan and Barbudan Independent Constitution, 1981: A Westminster Model with a Difference," *Bulletin of Eastern Caribbean Affairs* [Cave Hill, Barbados], 7, No. 5, November–December 1981, 1–6.

United States. Agency for International Development. Office of Foreign Disaster Assistance. *Countries of the Caribbean Community: A Regional Profile.* Washington: February 1983.

United States. Central Intelligence Agency. *The World Factbook, 1986.* Washington: GPO, 1986.

United States. Department of State. Bureau of Public Affairs. *Background Notes: Antigua and Barbuda.* Washington: 1985.

World Bank. *Antigua and Barbuda: Economic Report.* Washington: 1985.

(Various issues of the following publications were also used in the preparation of this section: *Daily Gleaner* [Kingston, Jamaica], 1987; Foreign Broadcast Information Service, *Daily Report: Latin America,* 1986–87; and Joint Publications Research Service, *Latin America Report,* 1986–87.)

St. Christopher and Nevis

Alexis, Francis. "British Intervention in St. Kitts," *New York University Journal of International Law and Politics,* 16, Spring 1984, 581–600.

Andrade, John. *World Police and Paramilitary Forces.* New York: Stockton Press, 1985.

Birnbaum, Stephen (ed.). *Birnbaum's Caribbean, Bermuda, and the Bahamas, 1986.* Boston: Houghton Mifflin, 1985.

Blaustein, Albert P., and Gisbert H. Flanz (eds.). *Constitutions of the Countries of the World.* Dobbs Ferry, New York: Oceana, 1984.

Caribbean/Central American Action. *Investing in St. Kitts and Nevis.* Washington: 1986.

Caribbean Development Bank. *Annual Report, 1986.* Wildey, Barbados: Letchworth Press, 1987.

Carr, Peter R. "Health Systems Development in the English-Speaking Caribbean: Toward the Twenty-First Century," *Bulletin of the Pan American Health Organization,* 19, No. 4, 1985, 368–83.

Cox, Edward L. *Free Coloreds in the Slave Societies of St. Kitts and Grenada, 1763–1833.* Knoxville: University of Tennessee Press, 1984.

The Diagram Group. *Atlas of Central America and the Caribbean.* New York: Macmillan, 1985.

Eastern Caribbean Central Bank. *Report and Statement of Accounts.* Basseterre, St. Christopher and Nevis: 1985.

Emmanuel, Patrick A.M. "Comment on Proposals for an Independence Constitution for St. Kitts and Nevis," *Bulletin of Eastern Caribbean Affairs* [Cave Hill, Barbados], 8, No. 1, March–April 1982, 50–52.

Finkel, Herman J. "Patterns of Land Tenure in the Leeward and Windward Islands and Their Relevance to Problems of Agricultural Development in the West Indies." Pages 291–304 in Michael M. Horowitz (ed.), *Peoples and Cultures of the Caribbean.* Garden City, New York: Natural History Press, 1971.

Fraser, Peter D., and Paul Hackett (eds.). *Caribbean Economic Handbook*. London: Euromonitor, 1985.

Gastil, Raymond D. "The Comparative Survey of Freedom," *Freedom at Issue*, No. 88, January–February 1986, 7–17.

Gladwin, Ellis. *Living in the Changing Caribbean*. New York: Macmillan, 1970.

Green, Richard (ed.). *Latin America and Caribbean Review, 1985.* Saffron Walden, Essex, United Kingdom : World of Information, 1984.

Hendrickson, Embert J. "The Eastern Caribbean's Newest States: No Left Turn," *World Today* [London], 37, November 1981, 441–47.

Hunte, George. *The West Indian Islands*. New York: Viking Press, 1972.

Ince, Basil A., et al. *Issues in Caribbean International Relations*. Lanham, Maryland: University Press of America, 1983.

"An Independent St. Christopher and Nevis Becomes the Forty-Eighth Member," *Commonwealth Law Bulletin* [London], 9, No. 4, October 1983, 1491–97.

Lewis, Gordon K. *The Growth of the Modern West Indies*. New York: Monthly Review Press, 1968.

Lewis, W. Arthur. "The Agony of the Eight." Pages 215–35 in David Lowenthal and Lambros Comitas (eds.), *The Aftermath of Sovereignty: West Indian Perspectives*. Garden City, New York: Anchor Books, 1973.

Midgett, Douglas. "An Analysis of the 1984 General Elections in St. Kitts-Nevis," *Bulletin of Eastern Caribbean Affairs* [Cave Hill, Barbados], 10, No. 1, March–April 1984, 18–27.

Mitchell, Harold. *Caribbean Patterns*. Edinburgh: Chambers, 1972.

O'Loughlin, Carleen. *Economic and Political Change in the Leeward and Windward Islands*. New Haven: Yale University Press, 1968.

Pan American Health Organization. *Health Conditions in the Americas, 1981–1984*. Washington: 1985.

Phillips, Dion E. "The Increasing Emphasis on Security and Defense in the Eastern Caribbean." Pages 42–64 in Alma H. Young and Dion E. Phillips (eds.), *Militarization in the Non-Hispanic Caribbean*. Boulder: Lynne Rienner, 1986.

Richardson, Arthur G. "Reform Education in St. Kitts and Nevis," *Bulletin of Eastern Caribbean Affairs* [Cave Hill, Barbados], 10, No. 1, March–April 1984, 20–24.

Richardson, Bonham C. *Caribbean Migrants: Environment and Human Survival on St. Kitts and Nevis*. Knoxville: University of Tennessee Press, 1983.

Sherlock, Philip. *The Land and People of the West Indies*. Philadelphia: J.B. Lippincott, 1967.

St. Christopher and Nevis. *Estimates for the Year 1983.* Basseterre, St. Christopher and Nevis: 1983.

_____. *1986 Year in Review.* Basseterre, St. Christopher and Nevis: 1986.

_____. *St. Christopher and Nevis Independence Magazine, 19th September 1983.* North Miami, Florida: Gimmick Advertising, 1983.

St. Christopher and Nevis. Department of Labour and Tourism. *St. Christopher and Nevis Annual Report of the Department of Labour for the Year 1984.* Basseterre, St. Christopher and Nevis: 1984.

St. Christopher and Nevis. Ministry of Agriculture. *St. Kitts Fact Sheet on Agriculture.* Basseterre, St. Christopher and Nevis: 1984.

St. Christopher and Nevis. Ministry of Education, Health, and Social Affairs. *St. Kitts—Nevis Educational Statistics, 1980–81.* Basseterre, St. Christopher and Nevis: 1981.

St. Christopher-Nevis-Anguilla. *Annual Report on the Royal St. Christopher-Nevis-Anguilla Police Force for the Year 1967.* Basseterre, St. Christopher and Nevis: Police Force, 1968.

Sutton, Paul (ed.). *Dual Legacies in the Contemporary Caribbean: Continuing Aspects of British and French Dominion.* Totowa, New Jersey: Frank Cass, 1986.

United Nations. Economic Commission for Latin America and the Caribbean. *Economic Activity in Caribbean Countries, 1982.* New York: 1983.

_____. *Economic Survey of Latin America and the Caribbean, II: The Caribbean Economies.* New York: July 1986.

United States. Agency for International Development. Office of Foreign Disaster Assistance. *Countries of the Caribbean Community: A Regional Profile.* Washington: February 1983.

United States. Congress. 98th, 2d Session. House of Representatives. Committee on Armed Services. *Report of the Delegation to Eastern Caribbean and South American Countries.* (Committee Print, No. 16.) Washington: GPO, February 1984.

World Bank. *St. Christopher and Nevis Economic Report.* Washington: 1985.

(Various issues of the following publications were also used in the preparation of this section: *Democrat* [Basseterre, St. Christopher and Nevis], 1987; Joint Publications Research Service, *Latin America Report,* 1983–86; *Labour Spokesman* [Basseterre, St. Christopher and Nevis], 1987; *Latin American Monitor* [London], 1987; *Latin American Weekly Report* [London], 1985; and *Latin America Regional Reports: Caribbean* [London], 1987.)

British Dependencies: British Virgin Islands, Anguilla, and Montserrat

Andrade, John. *World Police and Paramilitary Forces.* New York: Stockton Press, 1985.

Anguilla Census of Population, 1984. London: Overseas Development Administration, 1985.

Annual Report of the Royal British Virgin Islands Police Force, 1983. Road Town, British Virgin Islands: 1984.

Baedeker's Caribbean, Including Bermuda, 1987. Englewood Cliffs, New Jersey: Prentice-Hall, 1986.

Banks, Arthur S. (ed.). *Political Handbook of the World, 1984–1985.* Binghamton, New York: CSA, 1985.

Birnbaum, Stephen (ed.). *Birnbaum's Caribbean, Bermuda, and the Bahamas, 1986.* Boston: Houghton Mifflin, 1985.

_____. *Birnbaum's Caribbean, Bermuda, and the Bahamas, 1987.* Boston: Houghton Mifflin, 1986.

Britain. Colonial Office. *British Virgin Islands, 1975.* London: Her Majesty's Stationery Office, 1975.

"British Dependent Territories: Anguilla, British Virgin Islands, Montserrat." Pages 2918–20 in *The Europa Year Book 1987,* II. London: Europa, 1987.

British Virgin Islands: Report for the Year 1974. London: Her Majesty's Stationery Office, 1975.

British Virgin Islands. Statistical Division. *Trade Report for the British Virgin Islands, 1981.* Road Town, British Virgin Islands: 1982.

Brooks, John (ed.). *The 1987 South American Handbook.* (63d ed.) Bath, United Kingdom: Trade and Travel, 1986.

Caribbean Development Bank. *Annual Report, 1986.* Wildey, Barbados: Letchworth Press, 1986.

The Diagram Group. *Atlas of Central America and the Caribbean.* New York: Macmillan, 1985.

Dun and Bradstreet International. *Dun and Bradstreet International Market Guide for Latin America, January 1986.* New York: 1986.

Economist Intelligence Unit. *Quarterly Economic Review of Trinidad and Tobago, Guyana, Barbados, Windward and Leeward Islands.* London: Economist, 1986.

Fergus, H.A. *Montserrat: Emerald Isle of the Caribbean.* London: Macmillan Caribbean, 1983.

Fraser, Peter D., and Paul Hackett (eds.). *Caribbean Economic Handbook.* London: Euromonitor, 1985.

Green, Richard (ed.). *Latin America and Caribbean Review, 1986.* Saffron Walden, Essex, United Kingdom: World of Information, 1985.

Bibliography

Harrigan, N., and P. Varlack. *British Virgin Islands: A Chronology.* London: n. pub., 1971.

Inter-American Development Bank. *Economic and Social Progress in Latin America: 1986 Report.* Washington: 1987.

Jane's Fighting Ships, 1984-85. (Ed., John Moore.) London: Jane's, 1985.

Montserrat. Statistical Office. *Ninth Statistical Digest, 1984.* Plymouth, Montserrat: 1985.

Pan American Health Organization. *Health Conditions in the Americas, 1981-1984.* Washington: 1985.

_____. *Program Budget, 1986-87.* Washington: 1985.

_____. "Status of AIDS in the Americas," *Epidemiological Bulletin,* 7, Nos. 5-6, December 1986, 1.

Paxton, John (ed.). *The Statesman's Year-Book: Statistical and Historical Annual of the State of the World for the Year 1986-1987.* New York: St. Martin's Press, 1986.

Petty, Colville. *Anguilla: Where There's a Will There's a Way.* The Valley, Anguilla: C.L. Petty, 1984.

Population Reference Bureau. *1987 World Population.* Washington: 1986.

Rickards, Colin (ed.). *Caribbean Year Book, 1979-80.* Toronto: Caribook, 1980.

Taylor, Jeremy (ed.). *The Caribbean Handbook, 1986.* St. John's, Antigua and Barbuda: FT Caribbean, 1986.

Third World Guide, 1986-87. New York: Grove Press, 1986.

United States. Central Intelligence Agency. *The World Factbook, 1986.* Washington: GPO, 1986.

Walker, Jane (ed.). *Business Traveller's Handbook: A Guide to Latin America.* New York: Facts on File, 1981.

West, Robert C., and John P. Augelli (eds.). *Middle America: Its Lands and Peoples.* (2d ed.) Englewood Cliffs, New Jersey: Prentice-Hall, 1976.

Woodfield, Cyril A. (ed.). *British Virgin Islands: The Welcome Tourist Guide.* Road Town, British Virgin Islands: Island Publishing Services, 1983.

(Various issues of the following publications were also used in the preparation of this section: *Caribbean and West Indies Chronicle* [London], 1984-86; *Daily Gleaner* [Kingston, Jamaica], 1987; Foreign Broadcast Information Service, *Daily Report: Latin America,* 1986-87; Joint Publications Research Service, *Latin America Report,* 1986-87; *Keesing's Contemporary Archives* (changed to *Keesing's Record of World Events* in January 1987) [London], 1984-87; and *Latin American Monitor: Caribbean* [London], 1984-87.)

Chapter 6
The Bahamas

Albury, Paul. *The Story of the Bahamas.* New York: St. Martin's Press, 1975.

The Bahamas. *Report of the Commission of Inquiry Appointed to Inquire into the Illegal Use of the Bahamas for the Transshipment of Dangerous Drugs Destined for the United States of America, November 1983–December 1984.* Nassau, The Bahamas: 1984.

The Bahamas. Cabinet Office. *Independence for the Commonwealth of the Bahamas.* Nassau, The Bahamas: 1972.

The Bahamas. Department of Statistics. *Census of Population and Housing, 1980: Preliminary Review.* Nassau, The Bahamas: 1981.

———. *Demographic Aspects of the Bahamian Population, 1901–1974.* Nassau, The Bahamas: 1976.

———. *National Accounts of the Bahamas, 1973–1979.* Nassau, The Bahamas: 1979.

———. *Report of the 1980 Census of Housing.* Nassau, The Bahamas: 1984.

———. *Social Statistics Report.* Nassau, The Bahamas: 1982.

———. *Some Aspects of Fertility in New Providence.* Nassau, The Bahamas: 1981.

———. *Staff Papers.* Nassau, The Bahamas: 1983.

———. *Statistical Abstract, 1983.* Nassau, The Bahamas: 1984.

———. *Vital Statistics Report, 1983.* Nassau, The Bahamas: 1985.

The Bahamas. Ministry of Education. *Atlas of the Commonwealth of the Bahamas.* (rev. ed.) Kingston, Jamaica: Kingston, 1985.

The Bahamas. Ministry of Education and Culture. *Archives Exhibition: Junkanoo.* Nassau, The Bahamas: 1978.

———. *Constitutional Development of the Bahamas.* Nassau, The Bahamas: 1979.

The Bahamas. Public Records Office. Archives Section. *A Selection of Historic Buildings of the Bahamas.* Nassau, The Bahamas: 1975.

The Bahamas. Royal Bahamas Police Force. *Annual Report for the Year 1981.* Nassau, The Bahamas: 1981.

"Bahamas: A Paradise for Tourists and Bankers," *Courier* [Brussels], No. 88, November–December 1984, 23–26.

Bahamas Business Guide. Nassau, The Bahamas: Commonwealth, 1982.

Bahamas Handbook and Businessman's Annual, 1985. Nassau, The Bahamas: Etienne Dupuch, Jr., 1984.

Bahamas Handbook and Businessman's Annual, 1987. Nassau, The Bahamas: Etienne Dupuch, Jr., 1986.

Banks, Arthur S. (ed.). *Political Handbook of the World, 1984–1985.* Binghamton, New York: CSA, 1985.

Barratt, P.J.H. *Grand Bahama.* Harrisburg, Pennsylvania: Stackpole Books, 1972.

Benchley, Peter. "The Bahamas: 'Boom Times and Buccaneering'," *National Geographic,* 162, No. 3, September 1982, 364–95.

Blackburne, Kenneth. "Changing Patterns of Caribbean International Relations: Britain and the British Caribbean." Pages 204–18 in Richard Millett and W. Marvin Will (eds.), *The Restless Caribbean: Changing Patterns of International Relations.* New York: Praeger, 1979.

Blaustein, Albert P., and Gisbert H. Flanz (eds.). *Constitutions of the Countries of the World.* Dobbs Ferry, New York: Oceana, 1984.

Boultbee, Paul G. *Bahamian Reference Collection: Bibliography.* (2d ed.) Nassau, The Bahamas: College of the Bahamas, 1981.

Brooks, John (ed.). *The 1987 South American Handbook.* Bath, United Kingdom: Trade and Travel, 1986.

Craton, Michael. *A History of the Bahamas.* (3d ed.) Waterloo, Canada: San Salvador Press, 1986.

Fraser, Peter D., and Paul Hackett (eds.). *Caribbean Economic Handbook.* London: Euromonitor, 1985.

Halkitis, Michael. *The Climate of the Bahamas.* Nassau, The Bahamas: Bahamas Geographical Association, 1980.

Hannau, Hans W. *The Bahama Islands.* New York: Doubleday, 1974.

Holm, John A., and Alison Watt Shilling. *Dictionary of Bahamian English.* Cold Spring, New York: Lexik House, 1982.

Hughes, Colin A. *Race and Politics in the Bahamas.* New York: St. Martin's Press, 1981.

Hunte, George. *The Bahamas.* London: B.T. Batsford, 1975.

Inter-American Development Bank. *Economic and Social Progress in Latin America: 1986 Report.* Washington: 1987.

International Monetary Fund. *Balance of Payments Statistics,* 37, No. 9, September 1986, 4–50.

Johnson, Doris. *The Quiet Revolution in the Bahamas.* Nassau, The Bahamas: Family Islands Press, 1972.

Judge, Joseph. "Where Columbus Found the New World," *National Geographic,* 170, No. 5, November 1986, 566–99.

Kurian, George Thomas. *Encyclopedia of the Third World.* (rev. ed.) New York: Facts on File, 1982.

Lawes, Dianne Nicholson. *Bahamas, 1984.* New York: Fisher Travel Guides, 1984.

Marshall, Dawn I. *"The Haitian Problem": Illegal Migration to the Bahamas.* Mona, Jamaica: Institute of Social and Economic Research, University of the West Indies, 1979.

Padelford, Edward A. "Caribbean Security and U.S. Political-Military Presence," *Strategic Review,* Fall 1986, 54–62.

Pan American Health Organization. *Health Conditions in the Americas, 1981–1984.* Washington: 1985.

Paxton, John (ed.). *The Statesman's Year-Book: Statistical and Historical Annual of the State of the World for the Year 1986–1987.* New York: St. Martin's Press, 1986.

Power, Kevin P. *Caribbean Basin Trade and Investment Guide.* Washington: Washington International Press, 1984.

Rees, John. "The Bahamas Now Looks to Kendall Isaacs," *Review of the News,* May 19, 1982, 39–48.

Symonette, Michael A. *The New Bahamians.* Nassau, The Bahamas: Bahamas International, 1982.

Thompson, Anthony A. *An Economic History of the Bahamas.* Nassau, The Bahamas: Commonwealth, 1979.

United Nations. Economic Commission for Latin America and the Caribbean. *Economic Survey of Latin America and the Caribbean, 1983.* Santiago, Chile: 1985.

United States. Central Intelligence Agency. *The World Factbook, 1986.* Washington: GPO, 1986.

United States. Congress. 98th, 1st Session. House of Representatives. Committee on Foreign Affairs. *U.S. Narcotics Interdiction Programs in the Bahamas.* (Hearings September 28, October 19, and November 2, 1983.) Washington: GPO, 1984.

United States. Congress. 99th, 1st Session. House of Representatives. Committee on Ways and Means. *Designation of the Bahamas as a Beneficiary Country under the Caribbean Basin Economic Recovery Act.* (House Document 99–40.) Washington: GPO, 1985.

United States. Department of Commerce. International Trade Administration. *Foreign Economic Trends and Their Implications for the United States: The Bahamas.* Washington: GPO, March 1986.

———. *Investment in Foreign Countries, IV. Western Hemisphere (Excluding Canada).* Washington: GPO, August 1985.

United States. Department of State. *Country Reports on Human Rights Practices for 1984.* (Report submitted to United States Congress, 99th, 1st Session, Senate, Committee on Foreign Relations, and House of Representatives, Committee on Foreign Affairs.) Washington: GPO, February 1985.

———. *Country Reports on Human Rights Practices for 1985.* (Report submitted to United States Congress, 99th, 2d Session, Senate, Committee on Foreign Relations, and House of Representatives, Committee on Foreign Affairs.) Washington: GPO, February 1986.

————. *Country Reports on Human Rights Practices for 1986.* (Report submitted to United States Congress, 100th, 1st Session, Senate, Committee on Foreign Relations, and House of Representatives, Committee on Foreign Affairs.) Washington: GPO, February 1987.

United States. Department of State. Bureau of Public Affairs. *Background Notes: The Bahamas.* Washington: GPO, December 1984.

United States. Department of State. Foreign Affairs Information Management Center. *Bahamas Post Report.* Washington: GPO, August 1985.

Unites States. Department of State. Office of the Legal Adviser. *Treaties in Force.* Washington: GPO, 1985.

World Bank. *The Bahamas: Economic Report.* Washington: 1986.

————. *The World Bank Atlas, 1986.* Washington: 1986.

(Various issues of the following publications were also used in the preparation of this section: *Christian Science Monitor,* 1986–87; *Country Report: Jamaica, Belize, Bahamas, Bermuda* [London], 1984–87; Foreign Broadcast Information Service, *Daily Report: Latin America,* 1985–87; Joint Publications Research Service, *Latin America Report,* 1985–87; *Latin America and Caribbean Review* [Saffron Walden, Essex, United Kingdom], 1985–87; *New York Times,* 1985–87; *Quarterly Economic Review of Jamaica, Belize, Bahamas, Bermuda* [London], 1984–87; *Tribune* [Nassau, The Bahamas], 1985–87; and *Washington Post,* 1986–87.)

British Dependencies: The Cayman Islands and the Turks and Caicos Islands

Andrade, John. *World Police and Paramilitary Forces.* New York: Stockton Press, 1985.

Baedeker's Caribbean, Including Bermuda, 1987. Englewood Cliffs: Prentice-Hall, 1986.

Banks, Arthur S. (ed.). *Political Handbook of the World, 1985–1986.* Binghamton, New York: CSA, 1986.

Birnbaum, Stephen (ed.). *Birnbaum's Caribbean, Bermuda, and the Bahamas, 1986.* Boston: Houghton Mifflin, 1985.

————. *Birnbaum's Caribbean, Bermuda, and the Bahamas, 1987.* Boston: Houghton Mifflin, 1986.

"British Dependent Territories: Cayman Islands, Turks and Caicos Islands." Pages 2929–31 in *The Europa Year Book, 1987,* II. London: Europa, 1986.

Brooks, John (ed.). *The 1987 South American Handbook.* (63d ed.) Bath, United Kingdom: Trade and Travel, 1986.

Caribbean Development Bank. *Annual Report, 1986.* Wildey, Barbados: Letchworth Press, 1987.

Cayman Islands. *Cayman Islands Annual Report, 1981.* George Town, Cayman Islands: 1982.

_____. *Cayman Islands Annual Report, 1983.* George Town, Cayman Islands: 1984.

_____. *Cayman Islands Annual Report, 1984.* George Town, Cayman Islands: 1985.

_____. *Statistical Abstract of the Cayman Islands, 1983.* George Town, Cayman Islands: Cayman Islands Statistical Unit, 1984.

The Diagram Group. *Atlas of Central America and the Caribbean.* New York: Macmillan, 1985.

Fraser, Peter D., and Paul Hackett (eds.). *Caribbean Economic Handbook.* London: Euromonitor, 1985.

Green, Richard (ed.). *Latin America and Caribbean Review, 1986.* Saffron Walden, Essex, United Kingdom: World of Information, 1985.

Hamaludin, Mohamed (ed.). *Cayman Islands Handbook and Businessman's Guide 1982–1983.* George Town, Cayman Islands: Northwestern, 1982.

Inter-American Development Bank. *Economic and Social Progress in Latin America: 1986 Report.* Washington: 1987.

Kennedy, Denis (ed.). *The Atlas of Central America and the Caribbean.* New York: Macmillan Education, 1985.

Paxton, John (ed.). *The Statesman's Year-Book: Statistical and Historical Annual of the State of the World for the Year 1986–1987.* New York: St. Martin's Press, 1986.

Population Reference Bureau. *1987 World Population.* Washington: 1986.

Rickards, Colin (ed.). *Caribbean Year Book, 1979–80.* Toronto: Caribook, 1980.

"Stern Warning to PNP from Misick," *Caribbean Insight* [London], 9, No. 6, June 1986, 12–13.

Third World Guide, 1986–1987. New York: Grove Press, 1986.

United States. Central Intelligence Agency. *The World Factbook, 1986.* Washington: GPO, 1986.

Walker, Jane (ed.). *Business Traveller's Handbook: A Guide to Latin America.* New York: Facts on File, 1981.

"Warning to Other Islands in Turks and Caicos Dismissals," *Caribbean Insight* [London], 9, No. 8, August 1986, 1.

West, Robert C., and John P. Augelli (eds.). *Middle America: Its Lands and Peoples.* (2d ed.) Englewood Cliffs, New Jersey: Prentice-Hall, 1976.

(Various issues of the following publications were also used in the preparation of this section: *Caribbean and West Indies Chronicle* [London], 1985–87; *Cayman Horizons* [George Town, Cayman Islands], 1986–87; *Keesing's Contemporary Archives* (changed to *Keesing's Record of World Events* in January 1987) [London], 1984–87; *Latin American Monitor: Caribbean* [London], 1985–87; and *Washington Post,* 1986–87.)

Chapter 7

Agro-Melina, Robert Joseph, and John Francis Cronin. *The U.S.S.R.'s Courting of Latin America: Soviet Forward Policy and Strategy in the Southern Western Hemisphere.* (Studies in International Affairs and Critical Trends, No. 1.) n. pl.: Horizon (published for the Institute for Analysis of Critical Trends, Laguna Beach, California), 1984.

Anderson, Thomas D. *Geopolitics of the Caribbean: Ministates in a Wider World.* (Politics in Latin America: A Hoover Institution series.) New York: Praeger, 1984.

Andrade, John. *World Police and Paramilitary Forces.* New York: Stockton Press, 1985.

Andre, David J. "Gathering Storm in the Eastern Caribbean," *Military Review,* July 1981, 2–14.

Arthur, Stanley. *Grenada and East Caribbean Security.* (Conflict Studies, No. 177.) London: Institute for the Study of Conflict, 1985.

Ashby, Timothy. *The Bear in the Back Yard.* Lexington, Massachusetts: Lexington Books, 1987.

Beshoff, Pamela. "Foreign Policy Co-operation and Regional Integration in the Caribbean," *Millennium: A Journal of International Studies* [London], 15, No. 1, Spring 1986, 91–107.

Black, George. "Mare Nostrum: U.S. Security Policy in the English-Speaking Caribbean," *NACLA Report on the Americas,* 19, July–August 1985, 13–48.

Blechman, Barry M., and Stephanie E. Levinson. "Soviet Submarine Visits to Cuba," *United States Naval Institute Proceedings,* September 1975, 31–39.

Callcott, Wilfrid Hardy. *The Caribbean Policy of the United States, 1890–1920.* New York: Octagon Books, 1966.

Center for Strategic and International Studies. *Russia in the Caribbean.* (Special Report Series, No. 13, Pt. 1.) Washington: 1973.

Diederich, Bernard. "The End of West Indian Innocence: Arming the Police," *Caribbean Review*, 13, No. 2, Spring 1984, 10–12.

Dismukes, Bradford, and Abram N. Shulsky. "Submarine Deployments to Cuba." Pages 353–54 in Bradford Dismukes (ed.), *Soviet Naval Diplomacy*. New York: Pergamon Press, 1979.

Duncan, W. Raymond. "Caribbean Leftism," *Problems of Communism*, May–June 1978, 33–57.

Dunn, Peter M., and Bruce W. Watson (eds.). *American Intervention in Grenada: The Implications of Operation "Urgent Fury."* (Westview Special Studies in Military Affairs.) Boulder: Westview Press, 1985.

Erismand, H. Michael, and John D. Martz (eds.). *Colossus Challenge: The Struggle for Caribbean Influence*. Boulder: Westview Press, 1982.

Fenton, Robert E. "Caribbean Coast Guard: A Regional Approach," *Naval War College Review*, 37, March–April 1984, 26–40.

Gershman, Carl. "Soviet Power in Central America and the Caribbean: The Growing Threat to American Security," *AEI Foreign Policy and Defense Review*, 5, No. 1, 1984, 37–46.

Gordon, Marvin F. "The Geopolitics of the Caribbean Basin," *Military Review*, August 1986, 16–27.

Gouré, Leon, and Morris Rothenberg. *Soviet Penetration of Latin America*. (Monographs in International Affairs.) Miami: University of Miami, 1975.

Greene, J.E. "Contemporary Politics in the English-Speaking Caribbean." Pages 83–96 in Angel Calderón Cruz (ed.), *Contemporary Caribbean Issues*. Río Piedras, Puerto Rico: Caribbean Studies Institute, University of Puerto Rico, 1979.

Hanks, Robert J. *The Unnoticed Challenge: Soviet Maritime Strategy and the Global Choke Points*. (Institute for Foreign Policy Analysis in association with the Fletcher School of Law and Diplomacy.) Washington: Corporate Press, 1980.

Ince, Basil A. "The Commonwealth Caribbean in International Politics." Pages 97–117 in Angel Calderón Cruz (ed.), *Contemporary Caribbean Issues*. Río Piedras, Puerto Rico: Caribbean Studies Institute, University of Puerto Rico, 1979.

International Institute for Strategic Studies. *The Military Balance, 1986–1987*. London: 1986.

International Security Council. "The Soviet Challenge in Central America and the Caribbean," *CAUSA International*, 1985.

Jones, Ronald E. "Cuba and the English-Speaking Caribbean." Pages 131–45 in Cole Blasier and Carmelo Mesa-Lago (eds.), *Cuba in the World*. Pittsburgh: University of Pittsburgh Press, 1979.

Karnes, Thomas L. "The United States and the Caribbean Basin in Historical Perspective." Pages 65–90 in Donald E. Schulz and Douglas H. Graham (eds.), *Revolution and Counterrevolution in Central America and the Caribbean.* Boulder: Westview Press, 1984.

Knowles, Yereth Kahn. *Beyond the Caribbean States: A History of Regional Cooperation in the Commonwealth Caribbean.* Río Piedras, Puerto Rico: Caribbean Studies Institute and Study Center for Latin America, University of Puerto Rico, 1972.

Laing, Edward A. "Independence and Islands: The Decolonization of the British Caribbean," *Journal of International Law and Politics* [London], 12, Fall 1979, 281–312.

Langley, Lester D. *The United States and the Caribbean in the Twentieth Century.* Athens: University of Georgia Press, 1982.

Leiken, Robert S. *Soviet Strategy in Latin America.* (Washington Papers, 10, No. 93.) New York: Praeger, with Center for Strategic and International Studies, Georgetown University, 1982.

Lewis, Gary P. "Prospects for a Regional Security System in the Eastern Caribbean," *Millennium: A Journal of International Studies* [London], 15, No. 1, 1986, 73–90.

Lewis, Vaughan A. "The US and the Caribbean: Issues of Economics and Security," *Caribbean Review,* 11, Spring 1982, 6–9.

Maingot, Anthony P. "Cuba and the Commonwealth Caribbean: Playing the Cuban Card." Pages 19–41 in Barry B. Levine (ed.), *The New Cuban Presence in the Caribbean.* Boulder: Westview Press, 1983.

_____. "Integrating the Non-Hispanic Caribbean States into the Inter-American Defense System—the Lessons of Grenada." (Paper presented at National Defense University's Symposium on Inter-American Security Policy, November 13, 1986.) Washington: 1986.

Maira, Luis. "Caribbean State Systems and Middle-Status Powers: The Cases of Mexico, Venezuela, and Cuba." Pages 177–204 in Paget Henry and Carl Stone (eds.), *The Newer Caribbean: Decolonization, Democracy, and Development.* (Inter-American Politics series, 4.) Philadelphia: Institute for the Study of Human Issues, 1983.

Manyoni, Joseph R. "Emergence of Black Power." Pages 101–15 in Robert Moss (ed.), *The Stability of the Caribbean.* London: Institute for the Study of Conflict, 1973.

Martin, John Bartlow. *U.S. Policy in the Caribbean.* (A Twentieth Century Fund Essay.) Boulder: Westview Press, 1978.

Menon, P.K. "The Organization of Eastern Caribbean States—An Important Milestone in Sub-Regional Integration," *Inter-American Law Review,* 17, Winter 1986, 297–311.

723

Mitchell, Harold. *Europe in the Caribbean: The Policies of Great Britain, France, and the Netherlands Toward Their West Indian Territories.* New York: Cooper Square, 1973.

Moorer, Thomas H., and Georges A. Fauriol. *Caribbean Basin Security.* (Washington Papers, 104.) New York: Praeger, with Center for Strategic and International Studies, Georgetown University, 1984.

Norton, Francis Wright. "Caribbean Naval Activity." Pages 208–15 in Bruce W. Watson (ed.), *The Soviet Navy: Strengths and Liabilities.* Boulder: Westview Press, 1986.

Norton, Graham. "Defending the Eastern Caribbean," *World Today* [London], June 1984, 254–60.

O'Rourke, Ronald. "U.S. Strategic Sealift: Sustaining the Land Battle," *Naval Forces,* 7, No. 3, 1986, 31–36.

Padelford, Edward A. "Caribbean Security and U.S. Political-Military Presence," *Strategic Review,* Fall 1986, 54–62.

Pastor, Robert A. (ed.). *Migration and Development in the Caribbean: The Unexplored Connection.* (Westview Special Studies on Latin America and the Caribbean.) Boulder: Westview Press, 1985.

Payne, Anthony. *The International Crisis in the Caribbean.* Baltimore: Johns Hopkins University Press, 1984.

Phillips, Dion E. "The Increasing Emphasis on Security and Defense in the Eastern Caribbean." Pages 42–64 in Alma H. Young and Dion E. Phillips (eds.), *Militarization in the Non-Hispanic Caribbean.* Boulder: Lynne Rienner, 1986.

Plischke, Elmer. *Microstates in World Affairs: Policy Problems and Options.* (AEI Studies in Foreign Policy.) Washington: American Enterprise Institute, 1977.

Quester, George H. "Trouble in the Islands: Defending the Micro-States," *International Security,* 8, No. 2, Fall 1983, 160–75.

Ronfeldt, David. *Geopolitics, Security, and U.S. Strategy in the Caribbean Basin.* (Project Air Force report prepared for United States Air Force.) Santa Monica: Rand, November 1983.

Sanchez, Nestor D. "Regional Security: United States Security Interests and Concerns in Latin America," *California Western International Law Journal,* 12, Summer 1982, 434–46.

Schoenhals, Kai P., and Richard A. Melanson (eds.). *Revolution and Intervention in Grenada: The New Jewel Movement, the United States, and the Caribbean.* (Westview Special Studies on Latin America and the Caribbean.) Boulder: Westview Press, 1985.

Seidenman, Paul. "Caribbean: The Urgency Grows," *National Defense,* December 1982, 20–25.

Sim, Richard, and James Anderson. *The Caribbean Strategic Vacuum.* (Conflict Studies, 121.) London: Institute for the Study of Conflict, August 1980.

Simmons, David A. "Militarization of the Caribbean: Concerns for National and Regional Security," *International Journal* [Toronto], 40, No. 2, Spring 1985, 348–76.

Stoiko, Michael, and George Luedeke, Jr. "Advancing South with Advanced Vehicles," *United States Naval Institute Proceedings,* 112, No. 2, February 1986, 81–88.

Theberge, James D. *Russia in the Caribbean.* Washington: Center for Strategic and International Studies, Georgetown University, 1973.

_____. *The Soviet Presence in Latin America.* New York: Crane, Russak, 1974.

Theberge, James D. (ed.). *Soviet Seapower in the Caribbean: Political and Strategic Implications.* (Praeger Special Studies.) New York: Praeger, 1972.

Tiryakian, Josefina Cintron. "The Military and Security Dimensions of U.S. Caribbean Policy." Pages 48–71 in H. Michael Erisman (ed.), *The Caribbean Challenge: U.S. Policy in a Volatile Region.* Boulder: Westview Press, 1984.

United States. Congress. 96th, 1st Session. House of Representatives. Committee on Foreign Affairs. Subcommittee on Inter-American Affairs. *Economic and Political Future of the Caribbean.* (Hearings.) Washington: GPO, 1979.

United States. Congress. 98th, 1st Session. House of Representatives. Committee on Foreign Affairs. *U.S. Narcotics Interdiction Programs in the Bahamas.* (Hearings September 28, October 19, and November 2, 1983.) Washington: GPO, 1984.

United States. Congress. 98th, 2d Session. House of Representatives. Committee on Armed Services. *Report of the Delegation to Eastern Caribbean and South American Countries.* (Committee Print, No. 16.) Washington: GPO, February 1984.

United States. Congress. 99th, 1st Session. House of Representatives. Committee on Foreign Affairs. *The English-Speaking Caribbean: Current Conditions and Implications for U.S. Policy.* Washington: GPO, 1985.

United States. Defense Intelligence Agency. *Handbook of the Cuban Armed Forces.* (Defense Research Reference series.) Washington: May 1986.

United States. Department of State. Bureau of International Narcotics Matters. *International Narcotics Strategy Report, 1985.* Washington: February 1, 1985.

United States. Department of State and Department of Defense. *Grenada: A Preliminary Report.* Washington: December 16, 1983.

_____. *The Soviet-Cuban Connection in Central America and the Caribbean.* Washington: March 1985.

Valenta, Jiri. "Soviet Strategy in the Caribbean Basin," *United States Naval Institute Proceedings,* 108, No. 5, May 1982, 169-81.

Volsky, George. "The Eastern Caribbean." Pages 131-42 in Robert Wesson (ed.), *Communism in Central America and the Caribbean.* Stanford University: Hoover Institution Press, 1982.

Wagner, Jacqueline A. Braveboy. "Changes in the Regional Foreign Policies of the English-Speaking Caribbean." Pages 223-38 in Elizabeth G. Ferris and Jennie K. Lincoln (eds.), *Latin American Foreign Policies: Global and Regional Dimensions.* Boulder: Westview Press, 1981.

Watson, Bruce W. *Red Navy at Sea.* Boulder: Westview Press, 1982.

Appendixes

Abrams, Elliot. "CBI and the U.S. National Interest," *Department of State Bulletin,* April 1986, 84-89.

Arnold, Guy. *Economic Co-operation in the Commonwealth.* Oxford: Pergamon Press, 1967.

Banks, Arthur S. (ed.). *Political Handbook of the World, 1985-86.* Binghamton, New York: CSA, 1986.

Blake, Byron, and Kenneth Hall. "The Caribbean Community: Administrative and Institutional Aspects," *Journal of Common Market Studies* [London], 16, No. 3, March 1978, 211-28.

"Caribbean Community and Common Market—CARICOM." Pages 108-09 in *The Europa Year Book, 1987,* I. London: Europa, 1987.

Caribbean Community Secretariat. *Report of the Secretary General of the Caribbean Community, 1985.* Georgetown, Guyana: 1986.

"Caribbean Leaders Back New Moves for Economic Integration," *Caribbean Insight* [London], 9, No. 7, July 1986, 1-2.

Chernick, Sidney E. *The Commonwealth Caribbean: The Integration Experience.* Baltimore: Johns Hopkins University Press, 1978.

"The Commonwealth." Pages 114-20 in *The Europa Year Book, 1987,* I. London: Europa, 1987.

Day, Alan J. (ed.). *Treaties and Alliances of the World.* (3d ed.) Detroit: Gale Research, 1981.

"Glimmer of Hope for CARICOM Trade," *Caribbean Insight* [London], 10, No. 7, March 1987, 1.

Gonzalez, Anthony P. "Future of Caricom: Collective Self-Reliance in Decline?" *Caribbean Review,* 13, No. 4, Fall 1984, 8-11.

Hall, H. Duncan. *Commonwealth: A History of the British Commonwealth of Nations.* London: Van Nostrand Reinhold, 1971.

Inter-American Development Bank. *Economic and Social Progress in Latin America: Economic Integration, 1984.* Washington: 1984.

————. *Ten Years of Caricom.* Georgetown, Guyana: 1983.

"In the Caribbean," *Washington Post,* November 3, 1986, A14.

Margain, Eduardo. *Development Challenges and Co-operation in the Commonwealth Caribbean.* Washington: Inter-American Development Bank, 1983.

Overseas Development Council. "The Caribbean Basin Initiative: Update," *Policy Focus,* No. 3, 1985, 1–8.

Palmer, Ransford W. *Problems of Development in Beautiful Countries: Perspectives on the Caribbean.* Lanham, Maryland: North-South, 1984.

Pastor, Robert. "Sinking in the Caribbean Basin," *Foreign Affairs,* 60, No. 5, Summer 1982, 1038–58.

Payne, Anthony. "Whither Caricom? The Performance and Prospects of Caribbean Integration in the 1980s," *International Journal* [Toronto], 40, No. 2, Spring 1985, 207–28.

Payne, Anthony, and Paul Sutton (eds.). *Dependency under Challenge: The Political Economy of the Commonwealth Caribbean.* London: Butler and Tanner, 1984.

Powers, Kevin P. *Caribbean Basin Trade and Investment Guide.* Washington: Washington International Press, 1984.

Ramsaran, Ramesh. "Caricom: The Integration Process in Crisis?" *Journal of World Trade Law,* 12, 1978, 208–17.

Raymond, Nicholas. "Caribbean Basin Revisited," *Editorial Research Reports,* 1, No. 5, February 1985, 83–100.

"The Reagan Caribbean Basin Initiative, Pro and Con," *Congressional Digest,* 62, No. 3, March 1983, 69–96.

Sanford, Jonathan, and Lawrence Silverman. *Caribbean Basin Initiative, 1983.* (Library of Congress, Congressional Research Service, Major Issues System, MB83222.) Washington: February 1984.

Schiavone, Giuseppe (ed.). *International Organizations: A Dictionary and Directory.* Chicago: St. James Press, 1983.

Stokes, Bruce. "Reagan's Caribbean Basin Initiative on Track, but Success Still in Doubt," *National Journal,* 17, January 26, 1985, 205–10.

Taylor, Jeffrey H. "Efforts Toward Economic Integration: CARICOM as a Case Study." (Master's thesis.) Washington: George Washington University, 1985.

United States. Congress. 98th, 1st Session. House of Representatives. Committee on Ways and Means. *Caribbean Basin Economic Recovery.* Washington: GPO, 1983.

————. Congress. 99th, 2d Session. House of Representatives. Committee on Ways and Means. Subcommittee on Oversight. *Review of the Impact and Effectiveness of the Caribbean Basin Initiative.* (Hearings.) Washington: GPO, 1986.

United States. Department of Commerce. International Trade Administration. *Caribbean Basin Initiative: 1986 Guidebook.* Washington: 1986.

United States. Department of State. *Background on the Caribbean Basin Initiative.* (Special Report, No. 97.) Washington: March 1982.

————. *GIST: Caribbean Basin Initiative.* Washington: March 1987.

United States. International Trade Commission. *Annual Report on the Impact of the Caribbean Basin Economic Recovery Act on U.S. Industries and Consumers: First Report, 1984–85.* Washington: September 1986.

Wylie, Scott. "CBI: One Year Later," *Business America,* January 7, 1985, 2–4.

Zegaris, Bruce. "The Caribbean Basin Initiative," *Tax Notes,* 28, August 26, 1985, 1021–25.

Glossary

alumina—The derivative of the metal ore bauxite (*q.v.*), used to make aluminum.

associated state(hood)—A system of British colonial administration under which a colony has full internal self-government while Britain retains control over defense and foreign affairs. Associated states are governed by a British-appointed governor and a locally elected assembly. An associated state has more control over internal affairs than does a crown colony (*q.v.*); thus, associated statehood is one step closer to self-government. In late 1987, Anguilla was the only remaining associated state in the Commonwealth Caribbean.

bauxite—An earthy metal ore mined for its derivative, alumina (*q.v.*), used in the manufacturing of aluminum.

Black Power movement—A political and cultural black consciousness movement that began in the United States in the late 1960s and later spread throughout the Caribbean, causing widespread strikes and protests in the early 1970s.

cay—A low island or reef of sand or coral. In the Bahamas it may refer to a low sandy outlet or to an island. The customary spelling in the United States, *key,* is not used in the Caribbean.

crown colony (government)—A system of British colonial administration under which Britain retains control over defense, foreign affairs, internal security, and various administrative and budget matters. Crown colonies are governed internally by a British-appointed governor and a locally elected assembly. In late 1987, the British crown colonies in the Caribbean consisted of the British Virgin Islands, the Cayman Islands, Montserrat, and the Turks and Caicos Islands. Prior to the Morant Bay Rebellion in Jamaica in 1865, crown colony government was limited to Trinidad and St. Lucia. Over the next thirty-five years, however, Britain abolished the old representative assemblies that had flourished on many of the islands, and the colonies were governed directly by the Colonial Office in Britain and by a British-appointed governor on each island who was assisted by a local council, most of whose members were appointed by the governor. As the nineteenth century progressed, however, an increasing number of officials were locally elected rather than appointed. This so-called system of modified crown colony rule began in Jamaica and was emulated in other West Indian colonies in the 1920s and 1930s.

Following the report of the Moyne Commission in 1940, the crown colony system was further modified to make local councils even more representative and to give local officials more administrative responsibility. Nevertheless, defense, foreign affairs, and internal security remained the prerogatives of the crown.

Eastern Caribbean—A term used to describe the islands east of Puerto Rico and north of Trinidad and Tobago. The Eastern Caribbean includes both independent nations and British, French, Dutch, and United States dependencies.

economies of scale—Decreases in the unit cost of production associated with increasing output.

807 program—Refers to items 806.3 and 807 of the Tariff Schedules of the United States that allow the duty-free entry of goods whose final product contains a certain portion of raw material or labor value added in the United States and the Caribbean Basin.

enclave industry—Foreign-owned firms that manufacture products exclusively for export. These businesses usually are labor-intensive, light assembly operations. Host nations provide investors with a range of benefits that typically include subsidized factory spaces in industrial parks near ports or airports; exemptions from import duties for raw materials, equipment, and machinery used in manufacturing; and suspensions of capital gains, income, and real property tax requirements for several years.

Eurocurrency—A country's currency on deposit outside the country. Most Eurocurrency claims are Eurodollars, which are dollar claims on banks located outside the United States. The Eurocurrency market is a wholesale market.

export-led growth—An economic development strategy that emphasizes export promotion as the engine of economic growth. Proponents of this strategy emphasize the correlation between growth in exports and growth in the aggregate economy.

financial intermediation—The process of taking in money (borrowing) so that it can be made available to individuals or institutions in the form of loans or investment.

fiscal year (FY)—The fiscal year varies throughout the Commonwealth Caribbean. For example, in Anguilla, the Bahamas, Grenada, Trinidad and Tobago, and the Turks and Caicos Islands the fiscal year corresponds to the calendar year, whereas in Antigua and Barbuda, Barbados, the British Virgin Islands, the Cayman Islands, Jamaica, and Montserrat the fiscal year covers the period April 1–March 31, and in Dominica the fiscal year runs from July 1 to June 30. In this volume, however, fiscal year, when used, refers to the United States fiscal year, which runs from October 1 to September 30.

Gross domestic product (GDP)—A measure of the total value of goods and services produced by the domestic economy during a given period, usually one year. Obtained by adding the value contributed by each sector of the economy in the form of profits, compensation to employees, and depreciation (consumption of capital). Only domestic production is included, not income arising from investments and possessions owned abroad, hence the use of the word *domestic* to distinguish GDP from gross national product (*q.v.*).

gross national product (GNP)—The total market value of all final goods and services produced by an economy during a year. Obtained by adding the gross domestic product (*q.v.*) and the income received from abroad by residents less payments remitted abroad to nonresidents.

import substitution industrialization—An economic development strategy that emphasizes the growth of domestic industries, often by import protection using tariff and nontariff measures. Proponents favor the export of industrial goods over primary products.

International Monetary Fund (IMF)—Established along with the World Bank (*q.v.*) in 1945, the IMF is a specialized agency affiliated with the United Nations that takes responsibility for stabilizing international exchange rates and payments. The main business of the IMF is the provision of loans to its members when they experience balance-of-payments difficulties. These loans often carry conditions that require substantial internal economic adjustments by the recipients.

Lomé Convention—A series of agreements between the European Economic Community (EEC) and a group of African, Caribbean, and Pacific (ACP) states, mainly former European colonies, providing duty-free or preferential access to the EEC market for almost all ACP exports. The Stabilization of Export Earnings (Stabex) scheme, a mechanism set up by the Lomé Convention, provides compensation for ACP export earnings lost through fluctuations in the world prices of agricultural commodities. The Lomé Convention also provides for limited EEC development aid and investment funds to be disbursed to ACP recipients through the European Development Fund and the European Investment Bank. The Lomé Convention is updated very five years. Lomé I took effect on April 1, 1976; Lomé II, on January 1, 1981; and Lomé III, on March 1, 1985.

Offshore banking—Term applied to banking transactions conducted between participants located outside the country. Such transactions increased rapidly worldwide after the mid-1960s because of the growth and liquidity of Eurocurrency (*q.v.*) markets.

Organisation of Eastern Caribbean States (OECS)—A regional body founded in 1981 by the seven former members of the West Indies States Association (WISA), which had been created in 1966. Original members were Antigua and Barbuda, Dominica, Grenada, Montserrat, St. Christopher and Nevis, St. Lucia, and St. Vincent and the Grenadines. The British Virgin Islands later became an associate member. Headquartered in Castries, St. Lucia, the OECS is designed to coordinate economic, foreign policy, and defense matters among its members and to facilitate their relations with various international organizations. The OECS is an associate institution of the Caribbean Community and Common Market (Caricom—see Appendix C) and oversees cooperation of its members in several Eastern Caribbean institutions: the Eastern Caribbean Currency Authority, the Eastern Caribbean Common Market, the Eastern Caribbean Central Bank, and the Eastern Caribbean States Supreme Court. The primary administrative organs of the OECS are the Authority of Heads of Government (the supreme policy-making body), the Foreign Affairs Committee, the Defence and Security Committee, and the Economic Affairs Committee. After the 1983 coup in Grenada, the OECS members jointly requested United States military intervention on that island. Four OECS members (Antigua and Barbuda, Dominica, St. Lucia, and St. Vincent and the Grenadines) joined with Barbados in October 1982 in signing the Memorandum of Understanding Relating to Security and Military Cooperation, which formed the basis for the creation of the Regional Security System (RSS).

Paris Club—A Paris-based organization that represents commercial banks in the rescheduling of national debts.

Rastafarian(ism)—An Afro-Christian revivalist cult formed in Jamaica in the early 1920s. The so-called Rastafarian Brethren emphasized rejection of both Jamaican and European culture in favor of eventual repatriation to Africa. Identifying Africa with Ethiopia, Rastafarians viewed the former emperor Haile Selassie of Ethiopia as God incarnate. As hope of returning to Africa dwindled, Rastafarianism became more of a religious than a political movement. Rastafarians developed a system of beliefs compatible with their poverty and aloofness from society and similar to mystical experiences found in other protest religions. Rastas (as they are known in common parlance) have come to symbolize the movement away from white domination and toward a heightened black identity and pride. Rasta thought, reggae music, dance, and literature have been popularized throughout West Indian culture.

structural adjustment program—A sectoral economic program designed to restructure an economy to be more responsive to market mechanisms. Often required of countries receiving assistance from the International Monetary Fund (*q.v.*).

value-added tax—An incremental tax applied to the value added at each stage of the processing of a raw material or the production and distribution of a commodity. It is calculated as the difference between the product value at a given state and the cost of all materials and services purchased as inputs. The value-added tax is a form of indirect taxation, and its impact on the ultimate consumer is the same as that of a sales tax.

World Bank—The informal name used to designate a group of three affiliated international institutions: the International Bank for Reconstruction and Development (IBRD), the International Development Association (IDA), and the International Finance Corporation (IFC). The IBRD, established in 1945, has the primary purpose of providing loans to developing countries for productive projects. The IDA, a legally separate loan fund administered by the staff of the IBRD, was set up in 1960 to furnish credits to the poorest developing countries on much easier terms than those of conventional IBRD loans. The IFC, founded in 1956, supplements the activities of the IBRD through loans and assistance designed specifically to encourage the growth of productive private enterprises in less developed countries. The president and certain senior officers of the IBRD hold the same positions in the IFC. The three institutions are owned by the governments of the countries that subscribe their capital. To participate in the World Bank group, member states must first belong to the International Monetary Fund (*q.v.*).

Index

Abolition of Slavery Act (1833–34), 21, 266, 434, 521–22
Abyssinia, 12
Acklins Island, 526
ACLM. *See* Antigua-Caribbean Liberation Movement (ACLM)
acquired immune deficiency syndrome (AIDS): Anguilla, 502; Antigua and Barbuda, 439; the Bahamas, 530; Barbados, 395; British Virgin Islands, 502; Cayman Islands, 571; Dominica, 274; Grenada, 354; Jamaica, 68; Montserrat, 502; St. Christopher and Nevis, 466; St. Lucia, 299; St. Vincent and the Grenadines, 327; Trinidad and Tobago, 183; Turks and Caicos Islands, 572
Adams, Grantley, 30, 389, 390, 413, 416
Adams, J.M.G.M. "Tom," 370; death of, xxi, 632; and defense force, 422, 423; and intervention in Grenada, 600, 603; as prime minister, 412, 413–14, 417–18; and regional security, 342, 481, 618, 620, 630, 631, 632
Adams Doctrine, 419, 630
Addis Ababa, 139
afranchis (free black inhabitants), 264
Africa, 11, 223, 483; cultural influence of, 41–42, 293; former colonies in, 124, 647; and Jamaica, 139; and Lomé Convention, 670; slave ships from, 49
African languages, 297
African slaves, 16, 22, 61, 177, 264, 270, 297, 321, 325, 352, 392, 437, 463, 495, 526
African states: protest against South Africa, 649
Afro-Caribbean religions, 34
Agreement on Apartheid in Sport, 649
Agricultural Marketing Protocol, 658
agriculture, 6; Anguilla, 505; Antigua and Barbuda, 440, 442, 443–44; the Bahamas, 532, 538; Barbados, 396, 398, 401, 404, 405, 406, 408; British Virgin Islands, 503–4; Cayman Islands, 572; colonial period, 16; Dominica, 258, 270, 279–80; Grenada, 258, 345, 356, 357, 362, 363–64;

Jamaica, xxvii, 69, 72–73, 74, 77, 81, 102–10; Montserrat, 506; regional cooperation, 656–57; St. Christopher and Nevis, 462, 468, 469, 471, 472, 473–74; St. Lucia, 188, 258, 300–2, 305–6; St. Vincent and the Grenadines, 258, 332–33, 334; Trinidad and Tobago, 186, 190, 191–92, 193, 197, 220–28; Turks and Caicos Islands, 575
Agro-21, 109, 110
AID. *See* United States Agency for International Development
AIDS. *See* acquired immune deficiency syndrome
air force: the Bahamas, 557; Barbados, 424; Jamaica, 144–45, 146; Trinidad and Tobago, 250, 251
airlines and airports: Anguilla, 507; Antigua and Barbuda, 440, 442; the Bahamas, 534, 542, 554, 557; Barbados, 404, 663; British Virgin Islands, 507; Cayman Islands, 575; Dominica, 279, 287; Grenada, 357, 360, 362, 373, 379; Jamaica, 100–101, 156, 663; Montserrat, 507; regional integration, 659; St. Christopher and Nevis, 475; St. Lucia, 304, 306; St. Vincent and the Grenadines, 329, 334; Trinidad and Tobago, 215, 216, 217–18, 242, 251, 252, 663; Turks and Caicos Islands, 575, 576, 579
Albania, 420
Albemarle, duke of, 49
Alcan, 77
Alcoa, 77
Alexis, Francis, 369, 371
Algeria, 139
Algiers, 140
Alice Town, 558
Allied Forces, 190
alumina. *See* bauxite and alumina
Amerada Hess Company, 306, 309
"American Mediterranean," 589
American Revolution, 143, 387, 521, 591, 592
Americans: arrested for drug offenses, 156; and coup attempt, 422; mercenaries, 289, 631

739

Index

Published Country Studies

(Area Handbook Series)

550-65	Afghanistan	550-153	Ghana
550-98	Albania	550-87	Greece
550-44	Algeria	550-78	Guatemala
550-59	Angola	550-174	Guinea
550-73	Argentina	550-82	Guyana
550-169	Australia	550-151	Honduras
550-176	Austria	550-165	Hungary
550-175	Bangladesh	550-21	India
550-170	Belgium	550-154	Indian Ocean
550-66	Bolivia	550-39	Indonesia
550-20	Brazil	550-68	Iran
550-168	Bulgaria	550-31	Iraq
550-61	Burma	550-25	Israel
550-37	Burundi/Rwanda	550-182	Italy
550-50	Cambodia	550-30	Japan
550-166	Cameroon	550-34	Jordan
550-159	Chad	550-56	Kenya
550-77	Chile	550-81	Korea, North
550-60	China	550-41	Korea, South
550-26	Colombia	550-58	Laos
550-33	Commonwealth Caribbean, Islands of the	550-24	Lebanon
550-91	Congo	550-38	Liberia
550-90	Costa Rica	550-85	Libya
550-69	Côte d'Ivoire (Ivory Coast)	550-172	Malawi
550-152	Cuba	550-45	Malaysia
550-22	Cyprus	550-161	Mauritania
550-158	Czechoslovakia	550-79	Mexico
550-36	Dominican Republic/Haiti	550-76	Mongolia
550-52	Ecuador	550-49	Morocco
550-43	Egypt	550-64	Mozambique
550-150	El Salvador	550-88	Nicaragua
550-28	Ethiopia	550-157	Nigeria
550-167	Finland	550-94	Oceania
550-155	Germany, East	550-48	Pakistan
550-173	Germany, Fed. Rep. of	550-46	Panama

550-156	Paraguay	550-89	Tunisia
550-185	Persian Gulf States	550-80	Turkey
550-42	Peru	550-74	Uganda
550-72	Philippines	550-97	Uruguay
550-162	Poland	550-71	Venezuela
550-181	Portugal	550-32	Vietnam
550-160	Romania	550-183	Yemens, The
550-51	Saudi Arabia	550-99	Yugloslavia
550-70	Senegal	550-67	Zaire
550-180	Sierra Leone	550-75	Zambia
550-184	Singapore	550-171	Zimbabwe
550-86	Somalia		
550-93	South Africa		
550-95	Soviet Union		
550-179	Spain		
500-96	Sri Lanka		
550-27	Sudan		
550-47	Syria		
550-62	Tanzania		
550-53	Thailand